PE

SELF _____ ERNMENT IN

TRANSITIONAL SOCIETIES

Judicial councils and other judicial self-government bodies have become a worldwide phenomenon. Democracies are increasingly turning to them to insulate the judiciary from the daily politics, to enhance independence and ensure judicial accountability. This book investigates the different forms of accountability and the taxonomy of mechanisms of control to determine a best practice methodology. The author expertly provides a meticulous analysis, using over 800 case studies from the Czech and Slovak disciplinary courts from 1993 to 2010 and creates a systematic framework that can be applied to future cases.

David Kosař is currently Head of the Department of Constitutional Law and Political Science at Masaryk University Faculty of Law. He clerked for a Justice and then the Vice-President of the Supreme Administrative Court, and for a Justice of the Constitutional Court of the Czech Republic.

COMPARATIVE CONSTITUTIONAL LAW AND POLICY

Series Editors

Tom Ginsburg, *University of Chicago*
Zachary Elkins, *University of Texas at Austin*
Ran Hirschl, *University of Toronto*

Comparative constitutional law is an intellectually vibrant field that encompasses an increasingly broad array of approaches and methodologies. This series collects analytically innovative and empirically grounded work from scholars of comparative constitutionalism across academic disciplines. Books in the series include theoretically informed studies of single constitutional jurisdictions, comparative studies of constitutional law and institutions, and edited collections of original essays that respond to challenging theoretical and empirical questions in the field.

Books in the Series

Perils of Judicial Self-Government in Transitional Societies: Holding the Least Accountable Branch to Account
David Kosař

Engaging Social Rights
Brian Ray

Making We the People
Chaihark Hahm and Sung Ho Kim

Radical Deprivation on Trial
Cesar Rodríguez-Garavito and Diana Rodríguez-Franco

Unstable Constitutionalism
Edited by Mark Tushnet and Madhav Khosla

Magna Carta and Its Modern Legacy
Edited by Robert Hazell and James Melton

International Courts and the Performance of International Agreements: A General Theory with Evidence from the European Union
Clifford Carrubba and Matthew Gabel

Reputation and Judicial Tactics: A Theory of National and International Courts
Shai Dothan

Constitutions and Religious Freedom
Frank Cross

Constitutionalism in Asia in the Early Twenty-First Century
Edited by Albert Chen

Social Difference and Constitutionalism in Pan-Asia
Edited by Susan H. Williams

Constitutions in Authoritarian Regimes
Edited by Tom Ginsburg and Alberto Simpser

Presidential Legislation in India: The Law and Practice of Ordinances
Shubhankar Dam

Social and Political Foundations of Constitutions
Edited by Denis J. Galligan and Mila Versteeg

Consequential Courts: Judicial Roles in Global Perspective
Edited by Diana Kapiszewski, Gordon Silverstein and Robert A. Kagan

Comparative Constitutional Design
Edited by Tom Ginsburg

PERILS OF JUDICIAL SELF-GOVERNMENT IN TRANSITIONAL SOCIETIES

Holding the Least Accountable Branch to Account

DAVID KOSAŘ

CAMBRIDGE
UNIVERSITY PRESS

CAMBRIDGE
UNIVERSITY PRESS

University Printing House, Cambridge CB2 8BS, United Kingdom

One Liberty Plaza, 20th Floor, New York, NY 10006, USA

477 Williamstown Road, Port Melbourne, VIC 3207, Australia

4843/24, 2nd Floor, Ansari Road, Daryaganj, Delhi - 110002, India

79 Anson Road, #06-04/06, Singapore 079906

Cambridge University Press is part of the University of Cambridge.

It furthers the University's mission by disseminating knowledge in the pursuit of education, learning and research at the highest international levels of excellence.

www.cambridge.org
Information on this title: www.cambridge.org/9781107531048

© David Kosař 2016

This publication is in copyright. Subject to statutory exception and to the provisions of relevant collective licensing agreements, no reproduction of any part may take place without the written permission of Cambridge University Press.

First published 2016
First paperback edition 2017

A catalogue record for this publication is available from the British Library

Library of Congress Cataloging in Publication data
Names: Kosař, David, 1979– author.
Title: Perils of judicial self-government in transitional societies : holding the least accountable branch to account / David Kosař, 1979–
Description: New York : Cambridge University Press, 2016. |
Series: Comparative constitutional law and policy
Identifiers: LCCN 2015030771 | ISBN 9781107112124 (hardback)
Subjects: LCSH: Judicial independence. | Judicial power. |
Political questions and judicial power. | Transitional justice.
Classification: LCC K3367.K67 2016 | DDC 347/.012–dc23
LC record available at http://lccn.loc.gov/2015030771

ISBN 978-1-107-11212-4 Hardback
ISBN 978-1-107-53104-8 Paperback

Cambridge University Press has no responsibility for the persistence or accuracy of URLs for external or third-party internet websites referred to in this publication, and does not guarantee that any content on such websites is, or will remain, accurate or appropriate.

For Pavla

CONTENTS

ACKNOWLEDGMENTS

Far more people than I could mention here have helped me to get the manuscript to its present shape, having provided comments and criticisms on its previous drafts, presented at various occasions and some of them published in forms of articles. Instead of risking forgetting someone, I would like to personally thank the three "trios" without whom I would not have been able to "get the job done" at all.

First, I thank the "CEU trio" of judges/academics whom I happened to meet at the CEU, Aharon Barak, András Sajó, and the late Roger Errera, for triggering my interest in judicial accountability and shaping my early thoughts on this topic. Second, I am indebted to the "Czech trio," Michal Bobek, Jan Komárek, and Zdeněk Kühn, for having always been on my side and for commenting on various parts of this work as well as the final draft. Their feedback and support cannot be overemphasized. Third, I am immensely grateful to the "New York trio," Stephen Holmes, Tom Ginsburg, and Ran Hirschl, for their ongoing mentorship, encouragement, and trust. Most of all, they believed in the project long before it materialized into a full-length book. Stephen Holmes was a patient mentor who guided me throughout the entire process of writing. Tom Ginsburg and Ran Hirschl provided me with helpful suggestions and also showed me what it means to be an academic. In addition to these three "trios," I would like to thank Robert Zbíral and Hubert Smekal, two most promising Czech political scientists, and two anonymous reviewers for reading the entire manuscript and for their thoughtful suggestions.

The European Commission provided me a generous grant (Marie Curie Actions – Support for training and career development of researcher [CIG], Grant Agreement No.: PCIG10-GA-2011–303933) to conduct the two case studies on the Czech Republic and Slovakia and present their results at conferences on both sides of the Atlantic. I am also grateful to the NYU Summer Writing Program for funding my two-month stay at the NYU Global Research Center in Berlin in summer 2012, to the French Embassy in Prague for supporting my research at the Aix-Marseille

Université in September 2013, to the Max Planck Institute for Comparative Public Law and International Law for allowing me to access its fantastic library and to discuss the key chapters of this book in summer 2014, and to the Jan Hus Foundation for allowing me to "buy time" to finish this manuscript. However, I owe the greatest debt of gratitude to Pavla for her infinite understanding and constant support.

CAVEATS

The empirical part of this book (Chapters 4–7) studies the years between 1993 and 2010. The subsequent developments in the Czech Republic and Slovakia are mentioned only if they illuminate the main findings of this book. The remaining parts of this book reflect the state of the art as of June 30, 2014. The subsequent developments are discussed only selectively.

Usual caveats apply. All opinions expressed in this book are personal to the author and should not be attributed to any institution he was or has been working with during the writing of this book. Any mistake, of course, remains author's own.

~

Introduction

While one might still believe that the judicial power is "the least dangerous branch" of government,[1] it is no longer accepted that the judiciary
wields only limited power. The evidence is clear. The power of courts has
increased worldwide at an unprecedented pace in the last few decades.
Judges often clash with the executive and interfere with the agendas of
parliaments. As a result, virtually all developed legal cultures now accept
that judges are *not* like umpires whose job is just "to call balls and strikes,"
to paraphrase the Chief Justice of the United States Supreme Court, John
Roberts,[2] that they sometimes resort to judicial law-making and that they
from time to time get involved in politics.

In addition to the normative issues about the role of judges in democratic society, there has always been a more mundane side of the coin.
There is no doubt that judges are expected to be exemplary citizens.
However, they may take bribes, accept problematic gifts from attorneys or
foundations, attempt to evade taxes, commit perjury, or engage in other
fraudulent and deceptive conduct. They may also commit reprehensible
acts in their private lives. They can beat their wives, drive a car under the
influence of alcohol or drugs, or take part in sadomasochistic practices.

These examples of judicial misconduct lead to the conclusion that
judges should be held accountable. This is not a novel demand. All states
acknowledged this need a long time ago and allowed for the disciplining of
judges, via either impeachment or a specific procedure before disciplinary
courts. Many countries devised additional mechanisms such as retention
reviews, judicial performance evaluations, or complaint agencies. Civil

---

[1] The Federalist No. 78, 464 (Alexander Hamilton) (Clinton Rossiter ed., 2003). See also
Alexander Bickel, *The Least Dangerous Branch* (Bobs-Merrill 1962).
[2] The precise statements made by Chief Justice Roberts are as follows: "Judges are like umpires.
Umpires don't make the rules, they apply them" and "[m]y job is to call balls and strikes and
not to pitch or bat" (*Confirmation Hearing on the Nomination of John G. Roberts, Jr. to be
Chief Justice of the United States Before the S. Comm. on the Judiciary*, 109th Cong. 55 (2005)
[statement of John G. Roberts, Jr., Nominee to be Chief Justice of the United States]).

law countries hold their judges to account also by other means such as denying their promotion to a higher court or to the position of a chamber president.

However, judicial accountability inevitably clashes with judicial independence, a cornerstone of the rule of law. All democratic countries thus have to find the right equilibrium between these two principles. Even established democracies cannot escape this conundrum. But this clash of judicial accountability and judicial independence is particularly challenging for countries that are in the process of transition to democracy.

The postcommunist Central and Eastern Europe (CEE) serves as a prime example of how difficult the balancing of these two values may be. In a sense, the transitional justice setting functions as a magnifying glass for the ubiquitous underlying tensions. When the communist regimes in the CEE collapsed in the late 1980s, each state in that region was faced with the tasks of depoliticizing[3] the judiciary and restoring judicial independence. However, it was an uphill struggle for postcommunist political elites to reform their judiciaries as they faced many obstacles. First, the judiciary was kept on a short leash during the communist era. The so-called state administration of courts, which consisted of a rigorous oversight of courts by *prokuratura*, the Communist Party's tight control of regular retentions of judges and the careful selection of court presidents, who were handpicked by the officials of the Communist Party, made clear that the judiciary remained subservient.[4] Democratic politicians had to dismantle all of these pernicious mechanisms. In addition, the status of judges was very low in communist society. Judges earned less than miners or even bus drivers[5] and thus the best law school graduates opted for private practice or administrative jobs.[6] In fact, law as such was a rather marginal discipline during the communist era and did not attract the brightest

---

[3] By depoliticizing I mean reducing the level of political control exercised by the governing political party. It is important to emphasize the historical context, namely that this effort reacted to the omnipotent Communist Parties in the region.

[4] *See* John Hazard, *Communists and Their Law* (University of Chicago Press 1969); Attila Rácz, *Courts and Tribunals: A Comparative Study* (Akadémia Kiadó 1980), 41–100; or René David and John Brierley, *Major Legal Systems in the World Today* (3rd ed., Stevens 1985) 155–306. For a more recent exposition of this problem, *see* Zdeněk Kühn, *The Judiciary in Central and Eastern Europe: Mechanical Jurisprudence in Transformation?* (Brill 2011), in particular 52–62.

[5] Kühn 2011, above note 4, at 53.

[6] See Alan Uzelac, "Survival of the Third Legal Tradition?" (2010) 49 *South Carolina Law Review* 377, 385–387.

people, who preferred better paid and less politicized vocations.[7] Not surprisingly, the reputation and morale of the judiciary were low.

The postcommunist elites thus had to change not only the institutional setup of the judiciary but also the mindset and performance of judges.[8] The situation got even worse once the revolutionary moment passed. An already limited pool of available candidates for the position of a judge shrank further.[9] Communist hard-liners on the bench often retired voluntarily while top law graduates opted to enter booming private practice, and there was only a small number of "outsiders" such as lawyers from dissident movement or emigrants who could fill the resulting vacancies.[10] Therefore, most CEE countries had to rebuild their judiciaries with essentially the same personnel as before at the higher levels of the judicial hierarchy and with young and inexperienced graduates at its lower echelons.[11]

This "default configuration" of the CEE judiciaries in the early 1990s posed a significant challenge to judicial reforms in that region. Any reform in the CEE had to overcome personal continuity within the judiciary and facilitate not only the institutional but also the mental transition of the judiciary.[12] The "institutional transition" part of the equation required the restoration of judicial independence and the reform of the system of court administration. The "mental transition" part of the equation created, among other things, the need to avoid existing authoritarian

---

[7] For further details of this phenomenon, see ibid., at 52–55.

[8] See Michal Bobek, "The Fortress of Judicial Independence and the Mental Transitions of the Central European Judiciaries" (2008) 14 European Public Law 99.

[9] For a more specific account of this phenomenon, see Chapters 5 (on the Czech Republic) and 6 (on Slovakia).

[10] East Germany was an exception as there were plenty of available "outsiders" in West Germany, who could fill the abandoned posts within the judiciary on the territory of the former German Democratic Republic after the reunification of Germany. This fact also explains why the purges within the judiciary after the fall of the communist regime in East Germany were more thorough than in other CEE countries. For further details, see Erhard Blankenburg, "The Purge of Lawyers after the Breakdown of the East German Communist Regime" (1995) 20 Law & Social Inquiry 223; or Inga Markovits, "Children of a Lesser God: GDR Lawyers in Post-Socialist Germany" (1996) 94 Michigan Law Review 2270, 2271–2272.

[11] There are exceptions to this rule – East Germany and Poland. On East Germany, see note 10. Poland is an exception since most judges of the Polish Supreme Court (not of the lower courts) were removed from office after the fall of the communist regime. On purging the Supreme Court in Poland, see, for example, Lech Garlicki, "Politics and Political Independence of the Judiciary" in András Sajó and L. R. Bentch (eds.), Judicial Integrity (Brill Academic Publishers 2004) 125, 137–138; or Wojciech Sadurski, Rights before Courts: A Study of Constitutional Courts in Postcommunist States of Central and Eastern Europe (Springer 2005), 43.

[12] See also Bobek 2008, above note 8, at 107–111.

and hierarchical patterns within the judiciary, enhance professionalism of judges, increase their performance, eradicate corruption, and change their perception of judicial duties. Put differently, the CEE countries needed to find a new balance between judicial independence and judicial accountability.

The million-dollar question was how to achieve these opposing goals and find a proper equilibrium between them. Most policy makers did their best, and each CEE country eventually adopted its own set of measures in the first wave of judicial reforms immediately after the fall of communism (the so-called transition wave). In the 1990s, new actors emerged on the scene – the European Union and the Council of Europe – and pushed for the second wave of judicial reforms (the so-called pre-accession wave).[13] Their organs, supported by nongovernmental organizations (NGOs) and professional organizations of judges, came up with a universal solution. They enticed the CEE legislatures to create an independent body, the judicial council,[14] and transfer most powers affecting the judiciary from the Ministry of Justice to that newly established body.

Most CEE countries took advice from the European institutions and eventually adopted the judicial council model of court administration. Hungary[15] and Slovakia[16] established independent judicial councils with

[13] For the distinction between the "transition wave" and the "pre-accession wave" of judicial reforms in the CEE, see Daniela Piana, "The Power Knocks at the Courts' Back Door – Two Waves of Postcommunist Judicial Reforms" (2009) 42 *Comparative Political Studies* 816.

[14] Judicial councils can be roughly defined as intermediary bodies between the political branches and the judiciary that have advisory or decision-making powers mainly in the appointment, promotion, and discipline of judges. However, the European Union and the Council of Europe advocated a particular model of judicial council, which I identify in Section III of this chapter.

[15] For further details, see Károly Bárd, "Judicial Independence in the Accession Countries of Central and Eastern Europe and the Baltics" in András Sajó and Lorri Rutt Bentch (eds.), *Judicial Integrity* (Martinus Nijhoff 2004) 265; Zoltán Fleck, "Judicial Independence and Its Environment in Hungary" in Jiří Přibáň, Pauline Roberts, and James Young (eds.), *Systems of Justice in Transition: Central European Experiences since 1989* (Ashgate 2003); Béla Pokol, "Judicial Power and Democratization in Eastern Europe" in *Proceedings of the Conference Europeanisation and Democratisation: The Southern European Experience and the Perspective for the New Member States of the Enlarged Europe* (2005) 165; or Zoltán Fleck, "Judicial Independence in Hungary" in Anja Seibert-Fohr (ed.), *Judicial Independence in Transition* (Springer 2012) 793.

[16] For further details, see Ján Svák, "Slovenská skúsenosť s optimalizáciou modelu správy súdnictva" in Jan Kysela (ed.) *Hledání optimálního modelu správy soudnictví pro Českou republiku* (2008) 54; and David Kosař, "Transitional Justice and Judicial Accountability: Lessons from the Czech Republic and Slovakia" (2010) (unpublished manuscript, available at http://ssrn.com/abstract=1689260).

wide powers in 1997 and 2002, respectively. Slovenia set up its judicial council in 1997, Estonia and Lithuania did so in 2002, and Latvia joined the club in 2010. Poland, Romania, and Bulgaria witnessed a slightly different development as all three countries laid down the foundations of their judicial councils immediately after the democratic revolution, but most of them later reconfigured them in order to meet the requirements of the "Euro-template."[17] Poland adopted a moderate judicial council as early as in 1989 and constitutionalized it in 1997.[18] Romania established its judicial council in 1989 and revamped it according to pan-European standards in 2003–2004.[19] Bulgaria set up its judicial council with the enactment of the constitution of the Republic of Bulgaria in 1991 and expanded its powers in 2002.[20] In contrast, the Czech Republic retained the old Ministry of Justice model with a central role for the executive branch and became the "black sheep" among the CEE countries.[21]

To sum up, all but one country in the CEE eventually opted for the judicial council model of court administration.[22] The institutional design and political ideas underlining the judicial council model are thus clear. What is much less clear is by whom and how judges in the CEE were actually held to account in the postcommunist era and whether the judicial council model affected the use of mechanisms of judicial accountability. This is so because of several factors.

---

[17] For more details on this template, see Chapter 3.

[18] For further details, see Adam Bodnar and Lukasz Bojarski, "Judicial Independence in Poland" in Anja Seibert-Fohr (ed.), *Judicial Independence in Transition* (Springer 2012) 667.

[19] For further details, see Bogdan Iancu, "Constitutionalism in Perpetual Transition: The Case of Romania" in Bogdan Iancu (ed.), *The Law/Politics Distinction in Contemporary Public Law Adjudication* (2009) 187, 196–198; Cristina Parau, "The Drive for Judicial Supremacy" in Anja Seibert-Fohr (ed.), *Judicial Independence in Transition* (Springer 2012) 619; Ramona Coman and Cristina Dallara, "Judicial Independence in Romania" in Anja Seibert-Fohr (ed.), *Judicial Independence in Transition* (Springer 2012), 835; or Cristina Parau, "The Dormancy of Parliaments: The Invisible Cause of Judiciary Empowerment in Central and Eastern Europe" (2013) 49 *Representation – Journal of Representative Democracy* 267, 272.

[20] For further details, see Maria Popova, "Why the Bulgarian Judiciary Does Not Prosecute Corruption?" (2012) 59 *Problems of Post Communism* 35; or Thierry Delpeuch and Margarita Vassileva, "Lessons from the Bulgarian Judicial Reforms: Practical Ways to Exert Political Influence on a Formally Very Independent Judiciary" in Leny E. de Groot-van Leeuwen and Wannes Rombouts (eds.), *Separation of Powers in Theory and Practice: An International Perspective* (Wolf Legal Publishers 2010) 49.

[21] For explanation of this resistance in the Czech Republic, see Chapter 5.

[22] Many scholars have been perplexed about why the parliaments gave up their power so easily. See, for example, Parau 2013, above note 19.

First, most literature on courts in the CEE focuses primarily on the judicial independence side of the coin[23] and tends to address judicial accountability rather shortly. Piana's monograph on "Judicial Accountabilities in New Europe,"[24] which looks at judicial accountabilities[25] in five postcommunist countries (Bulgaria, the Czech Republic, Hungary, Poland, and Romania), is the most notable exception.[26] Piana provides several valuable insights about courts in the CEE. However, she provides an incomplete picture about the Czech judiciary, because, as I will explain in Chapter 5, she fails to fully acknowledge the real role and powers of court presidents in the Czech judicial system.

Second, the CEE judiciaries are known for their lack of transparency and thus it is very difficult to conduct an empirical study of most aspects of judicial accountability. Even the European Commission with its enormous resources, unmatched by those of any academic institution, managed to collect only limited empirical data about the CEE judiciaries during the Accession Process. Third, when we zero in on a narrower issue of the impact of judicial councils in the CEE, we can see that the policy documents on judicial councils produced by the European Union and the Council of Europe rarely mention judicial accountability,[27] despite the fact that scholars pointed out that judicial councils might sometimes enhance judicial accountability rather than judicial independence.[28] Hence, there is a gap in the literature, both on accountability of judges in the CEE and on the impact of the judicial councils on the use of accountability mechanisms.

[23] See, for example, Bobek 2008, above note 8; Frank Emmert, "The Independence of Judges – A Concept Often Misunderstood in Central and Eastern Europe" (2001) 3 *European Journal of Law Reform* 405; Daniel Ryan Koslosky, "Toward an Interpretive Model of Judicial Independence: A Case Study of Eastern Europe" (2009) 31 *University of Pennsylvania Journal of International Law* 203; Maria Popova, "Political Competition as an Obstacle to Judicial Independence: Evidence From Russia and Ukraine" (2010) 43 *Comparative Political Studies* 1202; Anja Seibert-Fohr (ed.), *Judicial Independence in Transition* (Springer 2012); or Markus Zimmer, "Judicial Independence in Central and East Europe: The Institutional Context" (2006) 14 *Tulsa Journal of Comparative and International Law* 53.

[24] Daniela Piana, *Judicial Accountabilities in New Europe: From Rule of Law to Quality of Justice* (Ashgate 2010).

[25] Piana distinguishes five types of accountability (legal, managerial, institutional, societal, and professional) and thus she speaks of "accountabilities" in plural.

[26] For other works, see Bobek 2008, above note 8; or chapters on the CEE countries in Seibert-Fohr 2012, above note 23.

[27] See CCJE, Opinion no.10 (2007), Part VI; or Budapest Resolution, para. 10.

[28] Nuno Garoupa and Tom Ginsburg, "Guarding the Guardians: Judicial Councils and Judicial Independence" (2009) 57 *American Journal of Comparative Law* 103, 110.

This brings me to the explanation of why I chose the Czech Republic and Slovakia for my case studies. Both these two countries had to find a new balance between judicial independence and judicial accountability after the fall of the Czechoslovak communist regime, and thus it is particularly important to analyze how Czech and Slovak judges are held to account. Two deliberate choices define the scope of this book. First, I study accountability as a mechanism and thus I focus on whether there are relations that can be called accountability mechanisms, how these mechanisms function, and what their effects are.[29] Second, I consider judges central to the functioning of the judicial branch and hence I narrow my analysis to accountability mechanisms applicable to individual judges. In sum, I study three core accountability issues:

(1) Who holds judges to account? Is it primarily the Minister of Justice, as the standard literature suggests, or someone else?
(2) How much are judges held to account? That is, how frequently (quantitative aspect) and how severely (qualitative aspect)?
(3) Do any judicial accountability perversions such as judicial accountability avoidance, simulating judicial accountability, output excesses of judicial accountability, and selective accountability emerge?

However, these two case studies promise more. They allow me to study not only patterns of judicial accountability in new democracies, but also the impact of different models of court administration on judicial accountability, because the comparison of these two countries is the closest we can get to a natural experiment. Czechs and Slovaks shared, almost uninterruptedly,[30] a common institutional structure from the independence of Czechoslovakia in 1918 until its dissolution in 1992. Their countries also have the same essential features: a communist past, a civil law system, a career model of the judiciary, a centralized model of constitutional review, and membership of the European Union and the Council of Europe. The natural experiment produced by the dissolution of Czechoslovakia in 1993 and the comparison of its two former federal states, characterized by identical (not just similar) "background conditions," is exceptionally

---

[29] For my definition of judicial accountability, see Chapter 1.
[30] The only exception is the period between 1939 and 1945, when the Third Reich occupied the Czech provinces and the so-called Slovak State (*Slovenský Štát*) was created on the territory of Slovakia. For further details about this period and its impact on the Slovak nation, see Nadya Nedelsky, "The Wartime Slovak State: A Case Study in the Relationship between Ethnic Nationalism and Authoritarian Patterns of Governance" (2001) 7 *Nations and Nationalism* 215.

useful when trying to hold constant certain crucial independent variables (the length of previous democratic experience, authoritarian break, and the year of political transformation).[31] Moreover, both countries retained the Ministry of Justice model of court administration immediately after the dissolution of Czechoslovakia. The Big Bang came in 2003, when the Judicial Council of the Slovak Republic (hereinafter "JCSR") started to operate in Slovakia.[32] Therefore, Czech and Slovak judiciaries are matched on all important variables, but since 2003 they have varied on one independent variable – the model of court administration. In other words, these two case studies provide a nearly ideal ground for identifying the consequences of the judicial self-government.

The core of this book is thus a paired comparison that is built on the "most similar cases" logic[33] – it compares the judicial council model in Slovakia with the Ministry of Justice model in the Czech Republic. More specifically, this book explores the use of mechanisms of judicial accountability in the Czech Republic and Slovakia between 1993 and 2010.[34] Two critical junctures delineate my case studies. The first took place in 1993, when Czechoslovakia split into two separate states, the Czech Republic and Slovakia. Both countries initially kept the Ministry of Justice model with a central role for the executive branch.[35] The second critical juncture occurred in 2003, when the JCSR started to operate in Slovakia, whereas the Czech Republic kept the Ministry of Justice model of court administration. This book exploits this opportunity and examines the impact of the JCSR on the use of mechanisms of judicial accountability.

For methodological clarity, it is helpful to break down the "Does the Judicial Council Euro-model of court administration increase accountability of individual judges?" question into two separate questions dealing

---

[31] For a similar argument, see Fernando Casal Bértoa, "Parties, Regime and Cleavages: Explaining Party System Institutionalization in East Central Europe" (2012) 28 *East European Politics* 452, 456.

[32] As I will explain subsequently, the JCSR was de jure established by the 2001 Constitutional Amendment, but it became fully operational only in 2003.

[33] On the "most similar cases" logic in comparative constitutional law, see Ran Hirschl, "The Question of Case Selection in Comparative Constitutional Law" (2005) 53 *American Journal of Comparative Law* 125, 133–139.

[34] The closing date (2010) results from a pragmatic consideration of the feasibility of the empirical study. It would simply be too difficult to cope with the most recent data. For instance, some disciplinary motions against judges have been pending before courts for years and other data (such as the amounts of salary bonuses in Slovakia) are not often immediately available.

[35] The features of this model will be presented in more detail in Chapter 3.

with the quantitative and qualitative aspects. Drawing on a systematic analysis of these two jurisdictions, I thus address four major questions:

(1) Does the Judicial Council Euro-model of court administration alter the allocation of power among actors who may hold judges to account? That is, does it empower regular judges, as suggested by advocates of judicial councils? Or does it empower someone else?

(2) Does the Judicial Council Euro-model decrease the frequency of uses of mechanisms of judicial accountability (quantitative aspect), or does it actually increase the usage and consequences of available mechanisms of judicial accountability?

(3) Does the Judicial Council Euro-model decrease the seriousness of its consequences (qualitative aspect), that is reduce the imposed sanctions and granted rewards, or vice versa?

(4) What is the impact of the Judicial Council Euro-model on judicial accountability perversions such as judicial accountability avoidance, simulating judicial accountability, output excesses of judicial accountability, and selective accountability? Does it reduce them? Or does it allow these perversions of judicial accountability to flourish?

In short, this book not only studies how judges are held to account but also puts the claims about judicial councils and their consequences regarding judicial accountability to the test.

I. The Puzzle

Holding judges to account in the Czech Republic and Slovakia presents several puzzles. The most intriguing one is that those Slovak judges who initially opposed the judicial council model took over the judicial council eventually. Štefan Harabin, the President of the Slovak Supreme Court in 1998–2003, was in fact the most vocal critic of the JCSR during the parliamentary debates in 2000–2001 and in the first years of its operation. He was not responsible for putting the model on. Yet he soon adjusted to the new model, managed to capture the JCSR in 2009, and started to use the mechanisms of judicial accountability at his disposal as a tool of power.

Nor was the JCSR created for the fear of future electoral loss by the ruling party who installed Harabin to the presidency of the Slovak Supreme Court in 1998. The Movement for Democratic Slovakia (HZDS), the party that ruled Slovakia since 1992 until 1998 and that elected Harabin to the position of the president of the Supreme Court, actually went into opposition few months after Harabin's installment. HZDS neither proposed nor voted for[36] the judicial council model of court administration. It was the new centrist coalition, which opposed Harabin,[37] and passed the constitutional amendment in 2001[38] that erected the JCSR.

The creation of the JCSR thus cannot be explained by the hegemony preservation thesis[39] or the insurance theory.[40] It was not a skillfully executed plan of the pre-JCSR political or judicial elites adopted in order to preserve their powers. To the contrary, the beneficiary of the judicial council model was neither its author nor its proponent, but its major critic. The Slovak case study thus shows that the world of unintended consequences is strong and that developments in Slovakia cannot be explained by standard strategic theories.

The Slovak case study likewise does not fit in the "two-wave-theory" of judicial reforms in the CEE. The standard "two-wave-theory" of judicial suggests that there exist two types of judicial reforms in the CEE, the "transition wave" that took place immediately after the democratic revolution (i.e., between 1989 and 1997) and the "pre-accession" wave that covered reforms adopted during the pre-accession period (i.e., between 1998 and 2006), and argues that those actors who emerged as winners from the first wave of reforms (the Ministry of Justice or the judicial council) were better placed in the second wave and exploited the opportunities provided by the European Union to entrench existing domestic allocations of power.[41] In other words, these winners used their leverage from the "transition wave" to increase their own powers or at least to prevent the transferal of significant powers to other organ. This should, according to the "two-wave-theory," explain why there was little institutional innovation and policy change in the pre-accession period and why the influence of the European Union did not lead to common norms and values.

However, Slovak judicial reforms took the entirely opposite path. The Ministry of Justice who emerged as a winner from the "transition wave" reforms not only did not manage to maintain or improve its position

---

[36] In fact, all MPs from HZDS voted against the 2001 Constitutional Amendment in the National Council of the Slovak Republic (the legislature) on February 23, 2001. See Chapter 6, Section II.B.

[37] In fact, it attempted to impeach Harabin in 2000. For further details, see Chapter 6.

[38] The final vote on the Constitutional Bill on February 23, 2001 was ninety MPs for, fifty-seven MPs against, one MP abstained (two MPs were missing).

[39] See Ran Hirschl, *Towards Juristocracy: the Origins and Consequences of the New Constitutionalism* (Harvard University Press 2004).

[40] See Tom Ginsburg, *Judicial Review in New Democracies: Constitutional Courts in Asian Cases* (CUP 2003).

[41] See Piana 2009, above note 13; or Piana 2010, above note 24, at 162–165.

during the pre-accession period, but actually lost most of its powers that were transferred to the JCSR in 2001. Contrary to the predictions of the "two-wave-theory" of judicial reforms, the winner from the "transition wave" became a loser in the "pre-accession" period.

The Czech case study challenges the other three theories explaining the rise of judicial self-government in the CEE – the external incentives (accession conditionality) theory, the transnational networks theory, and the dormancy of parliaments. The accession conditionality theory does not work for the Czech Republic, because it rejected the judicial council model altogether and still became a member of the European Union without any troubles at all.[42] The transnational "epistemic communities" of judges, scholars, and legal experts also did not manage, despite their significant efforts, to bring the judicial council into being in the Czech Republic. Instead, the Czech legislature prevailed over their preferences and templates. The Czech case study does not support even the last promising theory explaining the rise of judicial self-government in the CEE – the dormancy of national Parliaments. According to this theory, almost never during the several series of judiciary institutional redesigns since 1989 have parliaments in the CEE offered serious resistance to their own correlative disempowerment.[43] However, the Czech parliament vetoed creation of a judicial council in 2000 and there has been no serious attempt to revive this idea since then.[44] As Parau has rightly pointed out, why the Czech MPs resisted the judicial council template while all other CEE parliaments did not is thus another puzzle that needs further investigation.[45]

To make things even more complicated, the Czech case study shows, contrary to general wisdom, that judicial self-government may flourish even under the Ministry of Justice model of court administration. More specifically, court presidents gradually took most mechanisms of judicial

---

[42] For further details, see Chapter 5.

[43] See Parau 2013, above note 19. Note that Parau's theory is broader and apart from explaining the creation of judicial councils in the CEE, it also attempts to explain a creation of majority-magistrate Constitutional Court (CC) with final authority over the meaning of the Constitution and a specialist Training Academy monopolizing the education of magistrates. For the latter two institutions, it works well.

[44] For further details, see Chapter 5.

[45] Parau 2013, above note 19, at 273. See also Piana 2009, above note 13; Michal Bobek, "The Administration of Courts in the Czech Republic – In Search of a Constitutional Balance" (2010) 16 *European Public Law* 251; or Zdeněk Kühn, "Judicial Administration Reforms in Central-Eastern Europe: Lessons to be Learned" in Anja Seibert-Fohr (ed.) *Judicial Independence in Transition* (Springer 2012). This issue will be revisited in Chapter 5, Section II.A.

accountability away from the political actors and firmly entrenched their position. In other words, the Czech judicial governance, despite being without a judicial council, seems to be much closer to judicial governance in countries with a judicial council than one would expect after reading the relevant Czech laws. Hence, how was it possible for court presidents to become the most powerful players despite operating in the Ministry of Justice model is also puzzling.

The present book explains these puzzles by looking beyond the Ministry of Justice and judicial councils templates. In fact, these two models can be only facades that do not explain the architecture of the Czech and Slovak judiciaries. In order to understand, how these two judiciaries really work and how they developed after the fall of communist regime, it is important to dig deeper. One must also look at the small-scale mechanisms such as case assignment techniques, various types of promotion of judges, or salary bonuses, and provide an empirically grounded account of how these mechanisms operate in practice. Based on the longitudinal empirical analysis of holding judges to account in two postcommunist judiciaries, this book shows that everything is more complicated than it seems. Judicial legacies of the past do play a critical role and tiny details, usually disregarded by the literature on judicial governance, often have decisive impact.

At this point it is necessary to stress that what scholars trained in the United States or the United Kingdom know about their judiciaries will not help them in assessing civil law systems. Despite increasing convergence between common law and civil law jurisdictions, the significant differences remain and each system employs different accountability techniques.[46] In the United States judges are chosen for what they had accomplished in other legal professions before they became judges and the prospects of their promotion is low, while in civil law countries they are trained within the judiciary to become judges and gradually climb up the ladder within the judicial hierarchy. This difference has important repercussions. As common law countries recruit judges in the later stage of their careers and know well whom they pick they do not need many accountability mechanisms after judges are appointed. In contrast, civil law countries appoint their judges at the early age and thus need more accountability mechanisms to induce judges to not deviate too much from generally recognized standards.

---

[46] This phenomenon is revisited in Chapter 2.

Most importantly, civil law judicial systems provide far more carrots for judges[47] than their common law counterparts. Apart from promotion to a higher court, judges can be promoted to a position of a chamber president, become permanent members of the grand chamber, be seconded to higher courts, or become court presidents. Promotion is thus not an exception but a rule in civil law systems. Besides these types of promotion the civil law systems often also allow for several accountability mechanisms that are completely unknown to the common law world, such as the temporary assignment of judges to the ministries or salary bonuses for judges. In other words, the standard common law account that "[a judge] gets a fixed salary, period"[48] simply does not work for civil law judiciaries. Moreover, the emphasis in the civil law systems is on mechanisms internal to the judiciary, as befits countries whose judges make careers in hierarchical institutions. The use and abuse of mechanisms of judicial accountability in civil law systems is thus more difficult to police as it takes place behind the closed doors. This "in-house" accounting in turn reduces the oversight of the judiciary by politicians and the media.[49]

The postcommunist civil law systems are even more special. In the postcommunist countries, disciplinary motions against judges can be arbitrary. Unlike in the established democracies, disciplinary motions are sometimes initiated against independent judges and not against corrupt or subservient judges. Likewise, judges can be reassigned to other panels requiring different specialization not because of their expertise, for efficiency reasons, or on the grounds of necessity, but as a form of retaliation. Similarly cases are sometimes distributed among judges in order to please "loyal" judges and punish the critics. Finally, salary bonuses do not have to necessarily reflect performance of judges and might be arbitrary. It is with this mindset that one must approach and judge holding judges to account in CEE.

By providing two contextualized ethnographies of postcommunist judiciaries, this book thus contributes not only to the literature on internationally directed judicial reforms, legal change after communism, and transitional justice, but also to accountability studies, the literature on courts in the civil law countries, and to scholarship on monitoring top

---

[47] For further details, see Chapter 2.
[48] See Richard A. Posner, "What Do Judges and Justices Maximize? (The Same Thing Everybody Else Does)" (1993) 3 *Supreme Court Economic Review* 1, 5.
[49] This issue is revisited in Chapter 8, Section V.

bureaucrats. Moreover, while this book focuses primarily on accountability of judges, it also tells us a lot about judicial independence.

II. The Approach

This book differs from the traditional treatment of the relationship between judicial independence and judicial accountability as it places the notion of judicial accountability at the center of the inquiry. While judicial independence is widely studied from a comparative, institutional as well as a positive-political-theory point of view,[50] judicial accountability has received far less attention.[51] This is particularly true for civil law judiciaries that have so far successfully resisted robust debate on the accountability of their members. This book attempts to fill this gap in the literature.

The book is also novel in other respects. First, it intentionally moves beyond a typical emphasis on executive–judiciary relations and significantly broadens the number of "accounting agents" under consideration. Most importantly, it zeroes in on court presidents whose role has been underestimated. Second, it focuses primarily on how mechanisms of judicial accountability operate in practice. It does not stop at what the law says about those mechanisms (de jure judicial accountability) and instead looks at how judges are actually held to account (de facto judicial

---

[50] See, for example, Stephen B. Burbank and Barry Friedman (eds.), *Judicial Independence at the Crossroads: An Interdisciplinary Approach* (Sage 2002); Tom S. Clark, *The Limits of Judicial Independence* (CUP 2010); Adam Dodek and Lorne Sossin (eds.), *Judicial Independence in Context* (Irwin Law 2010); John Ferejohn, "Independent Judges, Dependent Judiciary: Explaining Judicial Independence" (1999) 72 *Southern California Law Review*. 353; Peter H Russell and David O'Brien (eds.), *Judicial Independence in the Age of Democracy: Critical Perspectives from around the World* (University of Virginia Press 2001); Randall Peerenboom (ed.), *Judicial Independence in China: Lessons for Global Rule of Law Promotion* (CUP 2009); J. Mark Ramseyer, "The Puzzling (In)Dependence of Courts: A Comparative Approach" (1994) 23 *The Journal of Legal Studies* 721; Shimon Shetreet, *Judicial Independence: The Contemporary Debate* (Springer 1985); Shimon Shetreet and Christopher Forsyth, *The Culture of Judicial Independence* (Brill 2011); Georg Vanberg, "Establishing and Maintaining Judicial Independence" in Keith E. Whittington, et al. (eds.), *The Oxford Handbook of Law and Politics* 99 (OUP 2008); or Seibert-Fohr 2012, above note 23.

[51] But see Guy Canivet, Mads Andenas, and Duncan Fairgrieve (eds.), *Independence, Accountability, and the Judiciary* (British Institute of International and Comparative Law 2006); Hakeem Yusuf, *Transitional justice, Judicial Accountability and the Rule of Law* (Routledge 2010); Piana 2010, above note 24; G. Alan Tarr, *Without Fear or Favor: Judicial Independence and Judicial Accountability in the States* (Stanford University Press 2012); or Shimon Shetreet and Sophie Turenne, *Judges on Trial: Independence and Accountability of the English Judiciary* (2nd ed., CUP 2013).

accountability). Here I agree with John Ferejohn who has argued that "it seems impossible to engage in meaningful normative discourse – to criticize practices or give advice – without some conception of how political institutions either do or could be made to work."[52]

Third and most importantly, it studies mechanisms of judicial accountability empirically. This is challenging, given the fact that civil law courts are less transparent than their common law counterparts. Nevertheless, I believe that any comparison of institutions must meet two requirements. It must be "symmetrical," which means that it is a mistake "to take a cynical or pessimistic view of some institutions and an unjustifiably rosy view of others."[53] In addition, a sound institutional analysis must also be "evenhandedly empirical," that is "realistic about the capacities of all relevant actors."[54] For this book these two requirements mean that it is a mistake to take a cynical or pessimistic view of the Ministry of Justice model of court administration and an unjustifiably rosy view of the judicial council model. Only symmetrical and empirical analysis can answer the question of how each of these models has worked in the CEE and what was their impact on judicial accountability.

The book itself consists of three parts and is structured so that the general framework can be applied to other case studies in future. The first part, which consists of Chapters 1, 2, and 3, is theoretical and analytical. This part lays down a general systematic framework to study judicial accountability. It analyses the concept, identifies mechanisms of judicial accountability, and shows how different models of court administration may affect the use of these mechanisms. To emphasize the generality of the theoretical arguments developed in this part and to make it easier to "transport" them to other contexts, this theoretical part is as far as possible divorced from the particulars of the Czech Republic and Slovakia.[55] The second part, which consists of Chapters 4, 5, 6, and 7, is largely empirical and focuses exclusively on the Czech Republic and Slovakia. It provides

---

[52] John Ferejohn, "Law, Legislation, and Positive Political Theory" in Jeffrey S. Banks and Eric Alan Hanushek (eds.), *Modern Political Economy: Old Topics, New Directions* 192 (CUP 1995).

[53] Adrian Vermeule, *Judging under Uncertainty: An Institutional Theory of Legal Interpretation* (Harvard University Press 2006) 17. Here I rely heavily on Jan Komárek, "Institutional Dimension of Constitutional Pluralism" in Matej Avbelj and Jan Komárek (eds.), *Constitutional Pluralism in the European Union and Beyond* 231 (Hart 2012).

[54] Ibid., at 18.

[55] In structuring my book I drew inspiration from Georg Vanberg, *The Politics of Constitutional Review in Germany* (CUP 2005).

a small-N longitudinal analysis of the use of mechanisms of judicial accountability in the Czech Republic and Slovakia from 1993 to 2010 and assesses how mechanisms of judicial accountability worked in these two countries. Based on this analysis, I distill which changes in Slovakia were indeed *caused* by the Judicial Council Euro-model. The third part, Chapter 8, looks beyond the Czech Republic and Slovakia and addresses broader implications of the results of my two case studies. A more detailed description of each chapter follows in Section IV.

III.   Overview of the Argument

The main argument put forth in this book is that the Judicial Council of the Slovak Republic, based on the judicial council "Euro-model," enhanced judicial accountability, empowered judicial leadership (viz., court presidents), and increased the frequency of accountability perversions. The three parts of this argument are closely intertwined. The analysis of the effects of the JCSR in Slovakia revealed a clear pattern: the introduction of the strong judicial council model (the Judicial Council Euro-model) of court administration into a bureaucratic judiciary in the medium-term empowered judicial leadership, namely court presidents, who then used their newly accrued powers to punish their critics and reward their allies within the judiciary in order to preserve their privileges and influence. This, in turn, led to the rise of accountability perversions, the most danger-ous of which is selective accountability. I refer to this theory as the "judi-cial leadership theory" (JLT) of judicial councils.

To make my argument more credible, I look for alternative explanations for the events in Slovakia after the introduction of the JCSR, including, among other things, the failure within the judiciary to deal with the past after the fall of the communist regime, the level of division of the judiciary, the level of corruption within the judiciary, and the specifics of the Slovak legal culture. Nevertheless, I conclude that these factors cannot alone suf-ficiently explain the actions within the Slovak judiciary after 2003, when the JCSR started to fully operate. Here the Czech case study comes to the fore. Based on the most similar cases logic of my case studies I ruled out all but two alternative explanations. These two are the level of division within the judiciary and the level of corruption among judges, both of which were arguably higher in Slovakia at the moment when the JCSR was imple-mented. The precise impact of these two factors must be tested on another pair of case studies, but they, in my opinion, did not cause but merely con-tributed to the events that happened after 2003.

I also address the objections relying on the specific trajectory of Slovak politics and the role of the controversial President of the Slovak Supreme Court, Štefan Harabin. Regarding the former, I show that both the Czech and the Slovak political regimes are bipolar and yield very similar scores regarding parliamentary fragmentation, party system closure, and electoral volatility.[56] The differences among the two states, namely more complex cleavages in Slovakia and a higher level of party system institutionalization and higher polarization in the Czech Republic, are not significant enough to explain the changes after the introduction of the JCSR. Regarding the latter, a comparison of the "pre-JCSR" and "post-JCSR" periods in Slovakia, in both of which Harabin held the position of Chief Justice, reveals that Harabin could never accomplish with the allegedly old-fashioned Ministry of Justice model what he accomplished with the Judicial Council Euro-model. It was the JCSR that gave him power over all Slovak judges.

Some definitions are necessary to make sense of my argument. By "judicial accountability" I mean a negative or positive consequence that an individual judge expects to face from one or more principals (from the executive and/or the legislature and/or the court presidents and/or other actors) in the event that his behavior and/or decisions deviate too much from a generally recognized standard.[57] This book thus studies only those institutional mechanisms that are ex post, that may entail consequences, and that target individual judges. This definition is also free from strong[58] normative elements. It does not use judicial accountability in the sense of a virtue and does not formulate a set of substantive standards for good governance. Instead, it focuses on whether there are relations that can be called accountability mechanisms, how these mechanisms function, and what their effects are.[59] By "Judicial Council Euro-model" I mean a peculiar model of judicial council that meets five basic criteria, namely entrenching that body in the Constitution, ensuring that judges have at least parity in that body, vesting the real decision-making power with that body, transferring most "personal competences" regarding a career in the

---

[56] Fernando Casal Bértoa, "Post-Communist Politics: On the Divergence (and/or Convergence) of East and West Government and Opposition" (2013) 48 *Government and Opposition* 398, 402–413 and 417.

[57] For a more detailed exposition of my definition of judicial accountability, see Chapter 1.

[58] However, I agree that any concept of judicial accountability contains an irreducible normative core. For further details, see Chapter 1.

[59] For my definition of judicial accountability, see Chapter 1.

judiciary to that body, and selecting the Chief Justice or its equivalent as the chairman of the judicial council.[60]

By proposing the JLT of judicial councils, I am essentially making an institutionalist argument. However, in making this argument I do not imply that the Czech and Slovak judiciaries functioned in a social and cultural vacuum.[61] In the final chapter, I make clear that many patterns in the Czech and Slovak judiciaries developed in the communist era and some of them even earlier. Hence, there is a reasonable historical explanation for the current strong role of court presidents and Supreme Court Justices that dates back to the Czechoslovak state.

Yet this book offers more than assessment of the impact of a judicial council on judicial accountability in one country. It uses the Czech and Slovak case studies to test and generate the hypotheses regarding the use of mechanisms of judicial accountability in both established and new democracies. Moreover, it also challenges the standard view of the effects of judicial councils and raises several questions as to their suitability for countries that are in the process of transition to democracy.

The main theoretical contribution of my two longitudinal case studies is to identify actors who actually held Czech and Slovak judges to account and how they did it. The patterns of the use of mechanisms of judicial accountability after the fall of the communist rule are not, however, unique to the Czech Republic and Slovakia. In the final chapter of this book, I present evidence from secondary sources that similar patterns emerged in other transitional societies in the CEE and outside Europe. Many of these countries established strong judicial councils, a study of which allows other scholars to test my judicial leadership theory. Some of them did not. Nevertheless, both for those countries with a judicial council and those without, four general lessons can be drawn.

The first is that the milder treatment of internal in contrast to external accountability is misleading as the internal pressure can be at least as dangerous as the external one. This means that we should keep a close eye on the powers within the judiciary and on court presidents in particular. Second, there has recently been too much emphasis on the independence of the judiciary, both in scholarly literature and in policy documents, whereas the independence of individual judges has been rather neglected.

---

[60] For a more detailed exposition of the Judicial Council Euro-model, see Chapter 3.
[61] For a similar approach, see Lisa Hilbink, *Judges beyond Politics in Democracy and Dictatorship: Lessons from Chile* (CUP 2007) 7. Where I differ from Hilbink is that I do not intend to make a historical argument in this book.

It is high time to swing the pendulum back. We should also accept that the independence of the judiciary and the independence of individual judges are two different things and that enhancing the former does not automatically improve the latter. The Slovak case study provides ample evidence that the autonomous model of the judiciary advocated by the European Union and the Council of Europe may lead to "the system of dependent judges within independent judiciary."

Third, holding judges to account during the transitional period is highly peculiar. The specifics of judiciaries in transition, institutional legacies from the past such as strong powers of court presidents and Supreme Court justices, personal continuity within the judiciary, a temporary shortage of judges, overemphasis on judicial independence, increased incentives for corruption, and the limited transparency, each on its own, affect the functioning of mechanisms of judicial accountability in those countries. Ignoring any of these specific features may have long-lasting deleterious effects. Finally, despite my preference for a definition that treats judicial accountability as a mechanism, it is crucial for every society to develop its own conception of judicial accountability-as-a-virtue. Here established democracies have an advantage as they have more developed sense among academics, lawyers, and judges themselves of the qualities that make for a good judge. I refer to these excellences appropriate to the role of a judge as "judicial virtues."[62] In contrast, transitional societies lag behind in this respect, and as long as they do not find at least a basic consensus on judicial virtues and create their own "expectations context of accountability," no reforms or institutions will do the job. One can transplant models of court administration or revise existing mechanisms of judicial accountability, but no one can transplant judicial virtues.

IV.   Plan of the Book

Chapter 1 defines the notion of judicial accountability. It discusses and explains why I focus on the institutional relationship between judges and forums which can hold them to account (accountability as a mechanism) rather than on the propriety of the behavior of judges (accountability as a virtue). Subsequently, it deals with each element of the concept of

---

[62] My concept of judicial virtues builds on the "virtue jurisprudence," which is a normative and explanatory theory of law that utilizes resources of virtue epistemology, virtue ethics, and virtue politics to answer the central questions of legal theory, including the theories of judging. See, for example, Lawrence Solum, "Virtue Jurisprudence: A Virtue-Centred Theory of Judging" (2003) 34 *Metaphilosophy* 178.

judicial accountability in more detail. Then it introduces the distinction between de jure and de facto accountability and argues that de facto judicial accountability matters more. Finally, it identifies several accountability perversions that are worthy of empirical investigation. This chapter is a necessary building block for the following chapter on mechanisms of judicial accountability as it provides criteria for identifying those mechanisms. Without a precise definition of judicial accountability, a selection of these mechanisms would inevitably be subjective and thus either overbroad or underinclusive. This chapter thus allows the book to stand on firm analytical grounds and to avoid using the term "judicial accountability" amorphously or as a mere "buzz word" for all that is positive in the judiciary.[63]

Chapter 2 identifies mechanisms of judicial accountability and contingent circumstances of holding judges to account. First, this chapter briefly discusses what judges maximize. The core of this chapter then provides taxonomy of mechanisms that fall within the ambit of the definition of judicial accountability adopted in the previous chapter. This part of Chapter 2 defines what is "in." However, there are also mechanisms that may influence the functioning of mechanisms of judicial accountability, even though they do not count as such. These "contingent circumstances" of judicial accountability include (1) ex post mechanisms that affect court officials, judges in general, entire courts, or the judiciary as a branch of government rather than individual judges, (2) screening mechanisms, (3) transparency mechanisms, (4) quasi-appellate mechanisms, and (5) criminal mechanisms and genuinely pathological mechanisms of judicial accountability. I address these five groups of mechanisms that are "out" in order to see the contours of mechanisms of judicial accountability more clearly. Finally, this chapter explains the differences in holding judges to account between recognition (common law) jurisdictions and career (civil law) jurisdictions.

Chapter 3 proposes that the model of court administration affects the use of mechanisms of judicial accountability. It briefly describes the historical development of court administration in Europe and the rise of judicial councils worldwide. Subsequently, I identify the Judicial Council Euro-model, which has been widely advocated by the European Union and the Council of Europe and eventually implemented by most countries in

---

[63] This is a common problem of available literature on judicial accountability. See David Kosař, "The Least Accountable Branch (Review Essay)" (2013) 11 *International Journal of Constitutional Law* 234 (where I argue that if we want to make progress in studying judicial accountability, each author must pay more attention to the concept of judicial accountability and adopt a clear definition of that concept).

the CEE. Then, I define the specific features of the Euro-model that explain what distinguishes it from its alternatives. Finally, I address the potential impact of the Judicial Council Euro-model on judicial accountability and set the stage for the case studies.

Chapter 4 is a prequel to case studies on the Czech Republic and Slovakia. It first defines the scope of the empirical analysis and explains the research design of the case studies. Then it describes the methodology and data collection. Finally, this chapter addresses potential inaccuracies of the empirical analysis that must be taken into account when interpreting its results.

Chapter 5 studies the use of mechanisms of judicial accountability in the Czech Republic from 1993 until 2010. The aim of this chapter is to show what mechanisms were used during this period, which actors controlled those mechanisms, and how exactly Czech judges were held to account. However, this chapter also serves a higher purpose in this book, because it is instrumental for understanding the impact of the introduction of the judicial council in Slovakia in 2002. In order to see the difference between the judicial council model and the Ministry of Justice model of court administration more clearly, the analysis of mechanisms of judicial accountability is divided into two phases: 1993–2002 (when the Ministry of Justice model operated in both countries) and 2003–2010 (when Slovakia used the new Judicial Council Euro-model and the Czech Republic kept the old Ministry of Justice model). The first part of this chapter addresses four general factors: Czech politics between 1993 and 2010, consequences of the division of Czechoslovakia, the impact of the EU accession process, and dealing with the past within the Czech judiciary. Subsequently, this part identifies key figures in the Czech judiciary. The second part explains how the Czech Ministry of Justice model of court administration operated between 1993 and 2010. The third part shows how Czech judges were held to account under the Ministry of Justice model between 1993 and 2002, whereas the fourth part assesses the use of mechanisms of judicial accountability under the same model between 2003 and 2010. The fifth part then briefly summarizes the findings of this chapter.

Chapter 6 focuses on the use of mechanisms of judicial accountability in Slovakia from 1993 until 2010. The aim of this chapter is again to show what mechanisms were used during that period, which actors controlled those mechanisms, and how exactly Slovak judges were held to account. This chapter follows the structure of the previous chapter on the Czech Republic. The first part addresses the same four general issues – Slovak politics between 1993 and 2010, consequences of the split of Czechoslovakia, the impact of the EU accession process, and dealing with the past within the Slovak judiciary – and identifies key actors in the Slovak judiciary. The second part discusses how the Slovak Ministry of Justice model and the Judicial Council of the Slovak Republic came into being, addresses major changes to these models adopted between 1993 and 2010, and explains the political vectors behind them. The following two parts contain the core findings of this book. The third part reports how Slovak judges were held to account under the Ministry of Justice model (1993–2002). The fourth part analyzes the use of mechanisms of judicial accountability under the Judicial Council Euro-model (2003–2010). The last part briefly summarizes the findings of this chapter.

Chapter 7 evaluates the results from the previous two chapters. I compare how Czech and Slovak judges were held to account in both periods – between 1993 and 2002 (when both countries retained the Ministry of Justice model) and between 2003 and 2010 (when Slovakia switched to the Judicial Council Euro-model, while the Czech Republic still used the Ministry of Justice model). These two cross-country comparisons, when combined with intracountry comparisons in Chapters 5 and 6, allow me to assess the impact of the Judicial Council of the Slovak Republic in Slovakia. More specifically, the Czech case study is used as a control for the findings in Slovakia in order to differentiate the causal effects of the JCSR from a mere correlation. Finally, I identify and discuss alternative explanations for the changes within the Slovak judiciary that took place between 2003 and 2010.

Chapter 8 discusses broader implications of the results of the Czech and Slovak case studies. It argues that court presidents are the invisible masters of the CEE judiciaries and proposes a judicial leadership theory of judicial councils. Then it demonstrates that the Judicial Council Euro-model increases the autonomy of the judiciary, but this move does not necessarily improve the independence of individual judges. Subsequently it examines specifics of the use of mechanisms of judicial accountability in transitional societies. Next, it explains why the fire alarms did not work in Slovakia and how this affects the way politicians should monitor judges. Finally, it revisits the relationship between judicial accountability as a virtue and as a mechanism, which I introduced in Chapter 1. I eventually conclude that these two concepts are closely related and the main problem of judiciaries in transitional societies is that they have less developed conceptions of accountability-as-a-virtue, which in turn negatively affects the use of existing mechanisms of judicial accountability.

PART ONE

Judicial Accountability: Theoretical Framework

1

The Concept of Judicial Accountability

Judicial accountability presents us with a puzzle. Judges are supposed to be neutral arbiters of disputes that cannot be solved by agreement of the parties to the dispute. On the other hand, judges are still humans with their own interests, own background, and own biases. Therefore, one cannot automatically accept that all judges are "good guys," that they always "get it right" or that they are "morally better" than other actors. It is also increasingly accepted that judges do not always merely interpret laws and they sometimes resort to judicial law-making.[1]

Hence, there is a need to hold judges to account. However, this need raises many difficult issues which will be discussed by way of specific examples. The first is the recent suspension of a well-known Spanish judge Baltasar Garzón. Garzón, an investigative judge[2] of the *Audiencia Nacional*, was indicted on three counts. As to the first count, the disciplinary prosecutor alleged that Garzón had archived a case against a director of Bank Santander in return for payments that allowed him to deliver lectures in New York in 2005 and 2006. The second count alleged that Garzón had issued an order that permitted eavesdropping on conversations between prison inmates and their counsel in a high-profile corruption case, the so-called "Gürtel inquiry," even though such an order in corruption cases[3] does not have a legal basis in Spanish law.

---

[1] I am aware that the role of judges and judging differs from one country to another. See e.g., Symposium Roundtable "An Exchange with Jeremy Waldron" published in *International Journal of Constitutional Law* (Volume 7, Issue 1, 2009). See also Jan Komárek, 'Judicial Lawmaking and Precedent in Supreme Courts: The European Court of Justice Compared to the US Supreme Court and the French Cour de Cassation' (2008–2009) 11 Cambridge Yearbook of European Legal Studies 399; and Georg Vanberg, The Politics of Constitutional Review in Germany (CUP 2005) 12.

[2] Note that Garzón was not a judge in a narrow sense, who takes part in deliberation. He was a "Juez de Instrucción" (investigative judge) which means that he conducted the investigation and the evidence gathering, but did not decide on the cases.

[3] Spanish law expressly permits such orders only for terrorism cases.

These two counts accused Garzón of committing serious disciplinary offences. However, it was the third count which was the most controversial and which attracted the greatest attention worldwide. It did so because it touched upon the hot political issue that divides the Spanish nation – the (lack of) dealing with the past after the fall of General Franco's regime – and was thus perceived by many as politically motivated.[4] In April 2010, Garzón was indicted for abusing his judicial authority by opening an inquiry into alleged crimes against humanity committed by the Franquist government during the Spanish Civil War (1936–1939) and the years of Franco's authoritarian regime which followed. The indictment alleged that Garzón had exceeded his jurisdiction, because the 1977 General Amnesty Act barred any investigations relating to politically motivated criminal offences that occurred before 1976. The Spanish Supreme Court eventually found Garzón guilty on only one charge, the allowing of illegal wiretapping in the so-called Gürtel inquiry,[5] but suspended him from judicial office for eleven years,[6] which effectively meant the end of his judicial career in Spain. The Garzón case thus shows how a disciplinary motion can effectively finish a judge's career and limit his discretion in deciding cases.

Another controversial example of holding a judge to account for his decision is the fate of Judge Orlet in Germany in the mid-1990s.[7] Judge Rainer Orlet presided over the trial of Günter Deckert, a far-right activist who publicly vilified Jews for their claims about the Holocaust. A criminal court in Mannheim presided over by Orlet eventually found Deckert guilty of inciting racial hatred, but gave him a relatively mild sentence, because the judges found him to be an "upright citizen" and "a good family man." The

---

[4] For a chronicle of the investigation and reaction to it in Spain, see *Un Juez Ante La Justicia* [*A Judge Before the Court*], El Pais (Spec. Issue) (Spain), available at www.elpais.com/especial/caso-garzon/. See also Paloma Aguilar, "Judiciary Involvement in Authoritarian Repression and Transitional Justice: The Spanish Case in Comparative Perspective" (2013) 7 *International Journal of Transitional Justice* 245, 263.

[5] Judgment of the Spanish Supreme Court, February 9, 2012, STS 79/2012.

[6] The charge alleging that he was indicted because he decided cases relating to companies with which he purportedly had a relationship or had received funds from while he was on leave from the bench ("Bank Santander" case) was abandoned, because it exceeded the statute of limitations (Decision of the Spanish Supreme Court, February 13, 2012, ATS 729/2012). Finally, the Spanish Supreme Court did not find against Garzón in the remaining case and acquitted him of abusing his powers in investigating the Franco era crimes (see Judgment of the Spanish Supreme Court, February 27, 2012, No. 101/2012).

[7] In describing the Judge Orlet case I rely heavily on Donald Kommers. See Donald P. Kommers, The Constitutional Jurisprudence of the Federal Republic of Germany (2nd ed., Duke University Press 1997) 132–133.

judgment[8] was written by Orlet himself. Commentators agreed that, apart from the aforesaid problematic comments, it was a competent judgment.

Nevertheless, those comments sparked outrage and Orlet faced strong pressure to resign. This pressure came not only from political actors, the public and lay judges, but also from his colleagues on the bench. At the federal level, the legislature reacted with the so-called Auschwitz Lie statute that explicitly bans denial of the Holocaust. At the state level, representatives of the Baden-Württemberg parliament called for Orlet's impeachment, even though his conduct was not an impeachable offence under the state constitution. In addition to pressure from politicians, the media and the public subjected Orlet to a continual barrage of vilification and ridicule, his colleagues issued a press release dissociating themselves from any problematic connotations of Orlet's opinion, and he himself was reassigned to another panel of the Mannheim court.

Meanwhile, Orlet took temporary sick leave from his official duties. His sudden "illness" was suspicious, but the Mannheim court insisted that it had nothing to do with the Deckert opinion. When Orlet returned to the court, he faced not only renewed threats of impeachment, but also rebellion from lay judges who refused to sit with him. The "judge bashing" ended only with Orlet's early retirement. It is generally accepted that it was a forced retirement resulting from both external and internal pressure. This Orlet case thus tells us that judge can be held to account by various actors at the same time and can be ousted from the office even without initiating a formal disciplinary motion.

Further mechanisms of judicial accountability can be found in both developed and transitional states. Many states of the United States stipulate the retention election procedure that allows periodic review of judges' performance. The recent *Caperton* case[9] even inspired John Grisham to write a novel on this topic.[10] The U.S. Senate may also impeach federal judges. Even though this procedure has been used only sparingly, in 1804 the Federalists attempted to impeach an Associate Justice of the Supreme Court of the United States Samuel Chase. In Germany, maverick judges can be denied promotion.[11] In Japan, the General Secretariat of

---

[8] Decision of the Mannheim Regional Court (*Landgericht*) of June 22, 1994, published in *Neue Juristische Wochenshrift* 249 (1994).

[9] *Caperton v. A. T. Massey Coal Co.* 129 S. Ct. 2252 (2009).

[10] *See* Pamela Karlan, "Electing Judges, Judging Elections, and the Lessons of Caperton" (2009) 123 Harvard Law Review 80, 80, note 2.

[11] See Stephen Ross Levitt, "The Life and Times of a Local Court Judge in Berlin" (2009) 10 *German Law Journal* 169, 197–198.

the Supreme Court relocates judges who rule against the national government on sensitive issues to rural areas and other undesirable locations.[12] In the Czech Republic, President Václav Klaus dismissed the Chief Justice of the Supreme Court initially without providing any justification and later claiming that the Chief Justice was a poor manager.[13] In Slovakia, the Supreme Court President distributed the salary bonuses spanning from zero to ten thousands of euro to reward loyal judges and punish his critics.[14] Even nonmonetary benefits can be used to hold judges to account effectively. For instance, in Russia and Ukraine court presidents can delay or deny subsidized housing to which judges are entitled, decide on judges' vacation packages, and provide the access to day care for their children.[15]

These examples illustrate the scope of this book and show that judges can be held to account by various mechanisms and by various actors, including those within the judiciary. While it is important to note that an extreme form of judicial accountability can be found in authoritarian and totalitarian regimes, where political forces have the ability to purge the judiciary almost without limit, the examples from developed states serve to demonstrate that judges are held to account everywhere and may pursue various aims. Hence, the need to hold judges to account is not specific to developing democracies. It arises under all regimes.

Some of the abovementioned examples of "accounting" are controversial and one may plausibly argue that the "accounting" in some of these cases went too far. However, judges are human, with their own interests, own backgrounds, and own biases. They also have their weaknesses. They can be corrupt[16] or may use public funds for personal gain.[17]

---

[12] See, for example, J. Mark Ramseyer and Eric Rasmusen, *Measuring Judicial Independence: The Political Economy of Judging in Japan* (University of Chicago Press 2003), 41–47; or David Law, "The Anatomy of a Conservative Court: Judicial Review in Japan" (2009) 87 *Texas Law Review* 1545, 1560–1562.

[13] For more details, see Chapter 5; or Michal Bobek, "The Administration of Courts in the Czech Republic – In Search of a Constitutional Balance" (2010) 16 *European Public Law* 251, 263–265.

[14] See Chapter 6.

[15] See, for example, Peter H. Solomon, "The Accountability of Judges in Post Communist States: From Bureaucratic to Professional Accountability" in Anja Seibert-Fohr (ed.), *Judicial Independence in Transition* (Springer 2012) 909–935, at 912; or Maria Popova, *Politicized Justice in Emerging Democracies: A Study of Courts in Russia and Ukraine* (CUP 2012), in particular at 139–145.

[16] See, for example, Transparency International, *Global Corruption Report: Corruption in Judicial Systems* (CUP 2007).

[17] See, for example, Raphael Minder, "Spain's Chief Justice Quits Over Claims of Misusing Public Money" *The New York Times* (New York, June 21, 2012); or Joe Cochrane, "Top

They may have an alcohol problem that affects their performance on the bench or may become drug addicts.[18] They may just be lazy or incompetent. They can take part in reprehensible conduct such as sadomasochistic practices[19] or go astray in many other ways. Last but not least, several authors have pointed out that judges often collaborated with totalitarian or authoritarian regimes and supported those regimes in pursuing their agendas.[20]

Hence, a lack of judicial accountability may also be problematic. Two examples of such accountability gap, both of which are the result of disciplinary proceedings against judges, come from the Czech Republic. In the first case, the Supreme Court held that a judge (then-judge of the Supreme Court itself) who repeatedly plagiarized complete articles of other scholars was not removed or otherwise penalized.[21] In the second case, a judge who overslept, missed a scheduled hearing, and then faked the transcript of that hearing was subjected to a mere salary reduction.[22] In these two cases one may persuasively argue that the "accounting" did not go far enough.

In sum, judicial accountability can be either "overinclusive" or "underinclusive," but it is nevertheless present in all countries.[23] The main issue, therefore, is not whether judges are held to account but rather how often, by what means, for what, and by whom. The aim of this chapter is to define the concept of judicial accountability and to provide an analytical framework for identifying mechanisms of judicial accountability and for categorizing these mechanisms along various dimensions.

Indonesian Judge Held in Corruption Case" *The New York Times* (New York, October 3, 2013).

[18] See, for example, Rogelio Pérez-Perdomo, "Independence and Accountability" in Rudolf V. Van Puymbroeck (ed.), *Comprehensive Legal and Judicial Development: Towards an Agenda for a Just and Equitable Society in the 21st Century* (World Bank Publications 2001) 207.

[19] See, for example, K.A. and A.D. v. Belgium, App. nos. 42758/98 and 45558/99, European Court of Human Rights.

[20] See, for example, David Dyzenhaus, *Judging the Judges, Judging Ourselves: Truth, Reconciliation and the Apartheid Legal Order* (Hart Publishing 2003); Lisa Hilbink, *Judges beyond Politics in Democracy and Dictatorship: Lessons from Chile* (CUP 2007); or Hakeem Yusuf, *Transitional Justice, Judicial Accountability and the Rule of Law* (Routledge 2010).

[21] Decision of the Supreme Court of the Czech Republic of October 30, 2008, case no. 1 Skno 10/2008.

[22] Decision of the Supreme Court of the Czech Republic of March 5, 2008, case no. 1 Skno 9/2007.

[23] Geyh shows that even U.S. federal judges are, contrary to general wisdom, subject to several mechanisms of judicial accountability. See Charles Gardner Geyh, "Informal Methods of Judicial Discipline" (1993–1994) 142 *University of Pennsylvania Law Review* 243.

I.   Unpacking the Notion of Accountability

We live in an age of accountability. The term "public accountability" became fashionable in the 1990s and since then the search for accountability has permeated the public sphere.[24] The judiciary was initially shielded from calls for public accountability (at least in Europe), but it did not escape the scrutiny for long, and the term "accountability" has been increasingly invoked also with regard to judges. Accountability can be investigated on a number of different dimensions – as a phrase or a slogan, as an idea, or as a concept.[25] Here I will focus predominantly on the concept of accountability.

Scholars and policy-makers invoke this concept in various contexts and in combination with various adjectives. One may, thus, hear about legal and political accountability;[26] about political, legal, administrative, professional, and social accountability;[27] about financial, moral, legal, and constitutional accountability;[28] about corporate, hierarchical, collective, and individual accountability;[29] and about vertical, diagonal, and horizontal accountability.[30] These classifications are endlessly variable and reflect the fact that different authors mean different thing when they speak about accountability.[31]

The only point on which those authors converge is that accountability is closely related to power. Voltaire has stated it quite eloquently: "With great power comes great responsibility."[32] More recently, Comte-Sponville

[24] See, for example, Andreas Schedler and others (eds.), *The Self-Restraining State: Power and Accountability in New Democracies* (Lynne Rienner Publishers 1999); Richard Mulgan, *Holding Power to Account: Accountability in Modern Democracies* (Palgrave Macmillan 2003); or Mark Bovens, "Analysing and Assessing Accountability: Conceptual Framework" (2007) 13 *European Law Journal* 447.

[25] Similar complexities arise with the study of topics such as "democracy" and "representation": see, for example, the observations in John Dunn, *Democracy: A History* (Atlantic Monthly Press 2005) 13–21; or Hanna Fenichel Pitkin, *The Concept of Representation* (University of California Press 1967) 1.

[26] John Ferejohn, "Accountability in a Global Context" IILJ Working Paper 5/2007, 4–7 www.iilj.org/publications/2007-5Ferejohn.asp.

[27] Bovens 2007, above note 24, at 455–457.

[28] Andreas Schedler, "Conceptualizing Accountability" in Andreas Schedler and others (eds.), *The Self-Restraining State: Power and Accountability in New Democracies* (Lynne Rienner Publishers 1999) 13, 22.

[29] Bovens 2007, above note 24, at 458–459.

[30] Ibid., at 460.

[31] On types of accountability, see Mulgan, above note 24, at 30–35.

[32] Jean Voltaire, Adrien Quentin Beuchot, and Pierre Auguste Migerm, *Œuvres de Voltaire, Volume 48* (Paris: Lefèvre, 1832).

notes, "to be accountable is to be able and obliged to answer for one's action. It is therefore to assume one's own power, even in failure, and to accept the consequences."[33] David Dyzenhaus makes this connection even more explicit, when he claims that "[a]ccountability, as it is commonly used, is a term of art developed in a political science literature about ways of exercising controls of the *exercise of power.*"[34] Thus, it is possible to conclude that power and accountability go hand in hand[35] and that consequently "there is no power without [accountability], and the stronger the former, the greater the latter."[36]

In a logical extension of this argument, there is no need to hold agents to account if they do not have any meaningful power. In the context of the judiciary, for instance, this means that "a court without constraint would be practically immaterial if it lacked all power, because it had no jurisdiction or because its rulings were ignored."[37] If the courts lack significant powers, there is less pressure to hold judges to account. The reasons for this tolerance are obvious, since "accounting agents" can tolerate judges' independence in relatively harmless areas of law.[38] Similarly, when a totalitarian regime exercises complete control over the judiciary (for instance

---

[33] André Comte-Sponville, *Dictionnaire philosophique* (PUF 2001) 624 (quoted in Guy Canivet, "The Responsibility of Judges in France" in Guy Canivet, Mads Andenas and Duncan Fairgrieve (eds.), *Independence, Accountability, and the Judiciary* (British Institute of International and Comparative Law 2006) 30. See also Schedler, above note 28, at 13.

[34] David Dyzenhaus, "Accountability and the Concept of (Global) Administrative Law" in *Global Administrative Law* (Acta Juridica, 2009) 3, 25 (emphasis added).

[35] In this aspect, judicial accountability diverges from judicial independence since judicial independence is neither sufficient nor necessary for power (Lewis Kornhauser, "Is Judicial Independence a Useful Concept?" in Stephen B. Burbank and Barry Friedman (eds.) *Judicial Independence at the Crossroads: An Interdisciplinary Approach* (SAGE Publications 2002) 47.

[36] Canivet, above note 33, at 30.

[37] Frank Cross, "Judicial Independence" in Keith E. Whittington and others (eds.), *The Oxford Handbook of Law and Politics* (USA, OUP 2008), 561 (citing Kornhauser, above note 35, at 57).

[38] Franco's Spain and Pinochet's Chile are often cited as examples of authoritarian regimes where ordinary judges enjoyed a relatively high level of independence but had so little power that their independence was trivial. Both Franco and Pinochet tolerated the independence of *ordinary* judges since they created a parallel system of *special* courts and channeled politically sensitive cases to the latter. See José J. Toharia, "Judicial Independence in an Authoritarian Regime: The Case of Contemporary Spain" (1975) 9 *Law & Society Review* 475; Christopher M. Larkins, "Judicial Independence and Democratization: A Theoretical and Conceptual Analysis" (1996) 44 *The American Journal of Comparative Law* 612; and Lisa Hilbink, "Agents of Anti-Politics: Courts in Pinochet's Chile" in Tom Ginsburg and Tamir Moustafa (eds.), *Rule by Law: The Politics of Courts in Authoritarian Regimes* (CUP 2008).

by controlling selection of judges who are elected for a short term and may be dismissed without stating reasons), there is no need for accountability since judges do not have any discretion in their application of the law.[39]

But the link between accountability and power is insufficient for the purposes of defining the term "accountability." Hence, it is necessary to revisit the basic question: what is meant by accountability?[40] John Ferejohn argues that "to say that one agent (A), is accountable to another agent (B) is to say that A has a kind of duty (moral or legal) to B and that B has means to enforce it."[41] Conversely, B has certain rights or powers over A, such as the right to demand an account of why A took or failed to take certain actions, the authority to compel A to act in some particular way or the capacity to penalize or reward A.[42] Rephrasing this in principal–agent model vocabulary, "[t]he rights of the principal to hold the agent to account are expressed … as the set of reward/punishment schemes that [he] is able to impose on the agent."[43]

Whether we accept the principal–agent model or not,[44] Ferejohn's definition is a good starting point for discussing the notion of accountability since it indicates three critical issues that need to be addressed by any

---

[39] I leave aside the question whether such complete control of the judiciary is possible at all. For the sake of argument, I will now presume that it is. On the distinction between "control" and "accountability," see Bovens 2007, above note 24, at 453–454; and Mulgan, above note 24, at 8–9 and 18–20.

[40] I will skip dictionary definitions, the historical roots of this term and a change in its meaning over time. For a brief analysis of these aspects, see Bovens 2007, above note 24, 449–450.

[41] Ferejohn 2007, above note 26, at 2–3.

[42] Ibid., at 2–3.

[43] Ibid., at 3.

[44] The application of the principal–agent theory to the judiciary, without any caveats, is considered controversial, because due to the importance of judicial independence the relationship between judges and those who hold them to account is much looser and at the same time more complex than in strictly hierarchical institutions. Several authors thus suggest that a variant of this theory – principal–trustee theory – offers a more useful approach to accountability in this context; see Dimitrios Kyritsis, "Representation and Waldron's objection to judicial review" (2006) 26 *Oxford Journal of Legal Studies* 733; Alec Stone Sweet, "Constitutional Courts and Parliamentary Democracy" in Mark Thatcher and Alec Stone Sweet (eds.), *The Politics of Delegation* (Routledge 2003) 77; András Sajó, Courts as Representatives (lecture), November 18, 2012, available at www.fljs.org; or Karen J. Alter, "Agents or Trustees? International Courts in Their Political Context" (2008) 14 *European Journal of International Relations* 33. However, I consider the agent–trustee distinction as too sharply drawn (see Richard Bellamy, "The Democratic Qualities of Courts: A Critical Analysis of Three Arguments" (2013) 49 *Representation* 333, 342–344; or Richard Bellamy and Cristina Parau, "Introduction: Democracy, Courts and the Dilemmas of Representation" (2013) 49 *Representation* 255, 256–261) and thus I stick to the standard principal–agent framework.

definition, namely (1) is the term "accountability" reserved solely for ex post mechanisms or for both ex ante and ex post mechanisms? (2) must accountability mechanisms entail consequences for the actor who is held accountable?[45] and (3) does accountability encompass only sanctions or both sanctions and rewards? If the answer to all three questions is yes, then the definition is one of accountability in the narrowest sense. Conversely, if the answer to all three questions is no, what results is accountability in the broadest sense.

The first important debate is concerned with whether the term "accountability" should be reserved solely for ex post measures or whether it also encompasses mechanisms of purely ex ante nature. Ex post mechanisms include, among other things, removal from office, disciplinary motions, withdrawal of budget, and other monetary sanctions, while screening mechanisms such as the election and appointment of agents are typical mechanisms of ex ante nature.

Several authors suggest that the term "accountability" includes both ex ante and ex post controls.[46] These supporters of "broad accountability" invoke a variety of arguments to sustain their assertion. The first is that to limit accountability to retrospective mechanisms distorts the overall picture of a given agency since the ex ante and ex post dimensions are closely intertwined.[47] Some authors go further and suggest that ex ante and ex post accountability operate in an inverse relationship – the more ex ante accountability is in place, the less ex post accountability is needed.[48] Second, the line between retrospective accounting and proactive measures can be very thin since even those measures (such as elections) that are generally perceived as being retrospective in nature are often used as forward-looking mechanisms.[49] Third, principals need information in order to control their agents and so information-inducing mechanisms

---

[45] In other words, must the principal be able to impose sanctions or grant rewards? The alternative answer is that accountability does not necessarily entail a power of the principal to impose sanctions. This means that if a particular mechanism obliges an agent "merely" to produce certain information or/and justify its conduct to a principal (*without a* power of the principal to sanction the agent), it is still an accountability mechanism.

[46] For a recent example, see Alan Paterson, *Lawyers and the Public Good: Democracy in Action?* (CUP 2011) 137–141.

[47] See, for example, Schedler, above note 28, at 13.

[48] See ibid.

[49] See, for example, James Fearon who claims that the punitive character of elections is exaggerated (James D. Fearon, "Electoral Accountability and the Control of Politicians: Selecting Good Types versus Sanctioning Poor Performance" in Adam Przeworski and others (eds.), *Democracy, accountability, and representation* (CUP 1999)).

are an essential component of accountability.[50] To put it bluntly, the argument is that if a principal does not have sufficient information, there is no ex post accountability. Fourth, a restrictive definition of accountability fails to acknowledge the fact that both ex ante and ex post mechanisms are a source of legitimacy for a given organization.[51] Finally, the supporters of "broad accountability" lament that a narrow definition excludes all mechanisms of participation in institution-building and all procedural rules.[52]

Despite these arguments, justifications for the use of "narrow accountability," which confines the definition to the after-the-fact controls, are more convincing.[53] First and foremost, a narrower definition makes it possible to distinguish accountability from other concepts such as responsibility, control, responsiveness, and transparency.[54] Such a definition also emphasizes the difference between mere *calling* to account and *holding* to account and makes it clear that only the latter is genuine "accounting."[55] In addition, one may argue that an analytical concept that is free from the controversial evaluative connotations is more desirable.[56] Last but not least, a narrow definition of judicial accountability is more consistent with the historical and etymological roots of the term "accountability."[57] As Philp has argued, ex ante measures are merely "the contingent circumstances or additional requirements that might influence whether a certain form of accountability will bring about a certain set of results."[58]

It is clear that if a narrow definition of accountability is adopted, then, among other things, several important mechanisms such as the appointment of officials are left out. In the context of judicial accountability, a narrow definition of accountability excludes the selection of judges, the

---

[50]   See, for example, Schedler, above note 28, at 13.
[51]   Alan Paterson, "The Scottish Judicial Appointments Board: New Wine in Old Bottles?" in Kate Malleson and Peter H. Russell (eds.), *Appointing Judges in an Age of Judicial Power: Critical Perspectives from around the World* (University of Toronto Press 2006) 17.
[52]   Dyzenhaus 2009, above note 34, at 25–26.
[53]   See, for example, Bovens 2007, above note 24, at 452–454; or Mulgan, above note 24, at 19–20. For a similar claim in the context of judicial accountability, see Stefan Voigt, "The Economic Effects of Judicial Accountability: Cross-country Evidence" (2008) 25 *European Journal of Law and Economics* 95, 97–98.
[54]   See Mulgan, above note 24, at 7–20.
[55]   See ibid., at 9.
[56]   Some authors even claim that "broad accountability" is an essentially contested and contestable concept. See Bovens 2007, above note 24, at 450 (referring to Walter B. Gallie, "Essentially Contested Concepts" in Max Black (ed.), *The Importance of Language* (Prentice-Hall 1962), 121–146).
[57]   See Bovens 2007, above note 24, at 448–449.
[58]   Mark Philp, "Delimiting Democratic Accountability" (2009) 57 *Political Studies* 28, 32.

publication of judgments, or judicial training. However, judicial accountability is a narrower concept than judicial governance.[59] Nor is its aim to explore everything that may influence judicial decision-making and judicial behavior. Similarly, the intention is not to study "judicial governance," but only to focus on its subset, that is on mechanisms of judicial accountability. In other words, the ambition is not to provide a full picture of the judiciary in a given country which, I concede, creates limitations on the analysis.[60]

The second issue is whether accountability mechanisms must entail a power vested in the principal to impose sanctions. Schedler, for instance, claims that "even if [a sanction is] missing we may still legitimately speak of acts of accountability,"[61] whereas Bovens concurs with Fearon,[62] Mulgan,[63] and Strom[64] that "the possibility of sanctions of some kind is a constitutive element of narrow accountability and that it should be included in the definition."[65] But their disagreement is only apparent, since their answers depend heavily on what they mean by the term "sanction."[66] If we divorce the word "sanction" from its formal and legal connotation and adopt a broad definition of it that also covers informal sanctions such as public disapproval or loss of prestige, we may conclude that the possibility of sanctions is a constitutive element of accountability.

Finally, principals may also *reward* agents instead of sanctioning them. This is perhaps the least controversial issue since there is no reason to exclude mechanisms involving positive consequences from the definition of accountability. In fact, it is generally acknowledged that both "sticks" and "carrots" are successful in achieving the desired goal. As Bentham once said, the two great "engines" of human behavior are punishment and reward.[67] Carrots and sticks are also closely interrelated as the denial

---

[59] *Contra* Daniela Piana, *Judicial Accountabilities in New Europe: From Rule of Law to Quality of Justice* (Ashgate 2010) 31.

[60] For this reason I will address these "contingent circumstances" in the Czech and Slovak case studies in Part Two of this book.

[61] Schedler, above note 28, at 17.

[62] Fearon, above note 49, at 55.

[63] Mulgan, above note 24, at 9–11.

[64] Kaare Strom, "Delegation and accountability in parliamentary democracies" (2000) 37 *European Journal of Political Research* 261.

[65] Bovens 2007, above note 24, at 451.

[66] Compare Schedler who does not consider a sanction to be a constitutive element of accountability but defines "sanction" narrowly (Schedler, above note 28, at 16) with Bovens who claims that the possibility of sanctions should be included in the definition of accountability but defines "sanction" very broadly (Bovens 2007, above note 24, at 452).

[67] Jeremy Bentham, *An Introduction to the Principles of Morals and Legislation* (first published 1781, OUP 1996), Ch. XVI, 201. This famous idiom was coined by Baron de Montesquieu.

of a carrot, such as denial of promotion,[68] can also be viewed as a stick. Furthermore, many mechanisms may operate as both rewards and punishments. For instance, if judges' salaries depend on individual productivity,[69] such a system "punishes" unproductive judges and "rewards" their colleagues who have high productivity. Therefore, my definition of accountability includes both mechanisms that entail sanctions and those that may result in rewards.

II.   Specifics of Judicial Accountability

Until recently, judges have managed to escape the reach of "public accountability mantra" since they have always been perceived primarily as "accounting agents" rather than as "accountable agents."[70] The long-standing American obsession with the countermajoritarian difficulty is rather an exception to the rule. However, the landscape changed rapidly at the end of the twentieth century due to the unprecedented growth of judicial power globally.[71] Due to this trend, it is increasingly difficult, whether in consolidated democracies or in states which are in the process of transition to democracy, to claim that judges do not need to be held to account.

Before defining the precise contours of judicial accountability, it is important to make a few general remarks on several unique aspects of it. First, one of the main techniques of accountability – removal from office – is generally not available in the context of judicial accountability. Richard Posner put it bluntly

> A [U.S.] federal judge can be lazy, lack judicial temperament, mistreat his staff, berate without reason the lawyers who appear before him, be reprimanded for ethical lapses, verge on or even slide into senility, be continually reversed for elementary legal mistakes, hold under advisement for years cases that could be decided perfectly well in days or weeks, leak confidential information to the press, pursue a nakedly political agenda,

---

See Charles de Secondat Montesquieu, *The Spirit of the Laws*, Vol. 11 (first published 1748, CUP 1989) chapter 6.

[68] On the denial of promotion within civil law judiciaries, see Chapter 2, Section II.B.

[69] See the Spanish system of remunerating judges that related judges' salaries to individual productivity (Francesco Contini and Richard Mohr, "Reconciling Independence and Accountability in Judicial Systems" (2007) 3 *Utrecht Law Review* 26, 36–37).

[70] See, for example, Siri Gloppen and others, *Courts and Power in Latin America and Africa* (Palgrave Macmillan 2010).

[71] This trend will be addressed in more detail in Section IV of this chapter.

and misbehave in other ways that might get even a tenured civil servant or university professor fired; he will retain his office.[72]

Posner's account must, of course, be accompanied by several caveats. Certain jurisdictions (such as the United States on the state level, Japan,[73] Andorra, Switzerland, Latvia, Moldova, Georgia and for some positions also in the United Kingdom)[74] appoint or at least allow the appointment of judges for a limited term after which those judges have to seek reappointment or face other retention procedures.[75] Several European civil law countries that apply a career model of the judiciary require new judges to undergo a "testing period" at the beginning of their career before they can be appointed for life.[76] Some states (such as the United States, Germany, and South Africa) stipulate impeachment procedures for judges. Finally, the codes of disciplinary procedure in most states provide for the removal of a judge as a sanction of last resort.

Thus, in general, only a few countries allow judges to be appointed for a limited term (and, if so, then this procedure is limited only to particular layers within the judicial system);[77] the use of initial "testing periods" of new judges is on the decline in civil law jurisdictions; impeachment proceedings are initiated very rarely if at all; and the sanction of removal is considered only in a small proportion of disciplinary motions against judges. Furthermore, even under the presumption that these measures can be applied, most of them cannot be applied immediately. Instead, they are available only at certain points in time (the longer the limited term, the less accountability) or only once (at the end of the "testing period"), or they require a significant amount of time and resources (impeachment and disciplinary motions). Therefore, the quest for judicial accountability

[72] Richard A. Posner, "What Do Judges and Justices Maximize? (The Same Thing Everybody Else Does)" (1993) 3 *Supreme Court Economic Review* 1, 4–5. Posner also claims that there are few carrots available for judges apart from the pension, but this insight does not apply to civil law judiciaries; see Chapter 2.

[73] See Art. 79 para. 2 and Art. 80 para. 1 of the Constitution of Japan (Kenpo); or David Law, "The Anatomy of a Conservative Court: Judicial Review in Japan" (2009) 87 *Texas Law Review* 1545, 1589. For further details, see Chapter 2.

[74] For further details on the European countries, see the 2012 CEPEJ Report, 274–275.

[75] Note that if a judge does not want to serve for a second term, the accountability issue does not arise. This is typical in situations when a judge is appointed "temporarily" with a specific task such as reducing the excessive case load at a given court.

[76] In 2012, the concept of "judges on probation," when judges are requested to work for a testing period before their appointment for life, was available in eighteen European countries and the probation period varied from one to five years; see the 2012 CEPEJ Report, 274–275.

[77] For instance, federal judges in the United States are appointed for life.

is dominated by the search for a substitute for the key accountability mechanism in other contexts – the sanction of removal. So as not to be misunderstood, this chapter does not argue that the abovementioned sanctions, even if rarely used, play no role at all (be it psychological, sociological, or legitimizing) in a judicial context.[78] The argument, rather, is that their role is very limited.

Second and linked with this, a specific feature of the accountability of judges concerns the "legalization" of judicial accountability. This means that the political accountability of judges which allows wider discretion was eroded and later replaced by legal accountability which relies strictly on legal standards.[79] This shift from political to legal accountability in the context of judicial accountability was observed by Mauro Cappelletti as early as in the 1980s.[80] Since then the "legalization" of judicial accountability has gradually progressed.[81]

Third, any attempt to find judges accountable faces another hurdle: the expertise on judging is concentrated within the guild itself – that is within the judiciary. Even in countries where judges do not enjoy as a high reputation as in the United States and the United Kingdom and thus a position as a judge does not attract the top candidates, it is very difficult to best judges on the art of judging and the knowledge of law in general. This problem is exacerbated even more when judges unite – a rather common phenomenon when someone attempts to improve judicial accountability. The fact that the agents (judges) know their own business better than the principals (citizens and politicians) is a common problem of the principal–agent theory. Agency theorists refer to this form of agency loss as "information asymmetry."[82] In the context of the judiciary, the information asymmetry is very high.

---

[78] In fact, judges confirm that these sanctions play a role. See, for example, Martina Künnecke, "The Accountability and Independence of Judges: German Perspectives" in Guy Canivet, Mads Andenas, and Duncan Fairgrieve (eds.), *Independence, Accountability, and the Judiciary* (British Institute of International and Comparative Law 2006) 217, 228 (on Germany). See also J. Mark Ramseyer, "The Puzzling (In)Dependence of Courts: A Comparative Approach" (1994) 23 *The Journal of Legal Studies* 721, 724 (note 14) (on Japan).

[79] This distinction between political and legal accountability is also to a certain extent arbitrary and requires several caveats. This issue will be discussed in more detail in Section III.E.

[80] See Mauro Cappelletti, "Who Watches the Watchmen? A Comparative Study of Judicial Responsibility" (1983) 31 *American Journal of Comparative Law* 1.

[81] Even though, we must distinguish between sticks and carrots. The former has undergone significant "legalization," whereas the latter still retains a strong political component.

[82] See Ken Binmore, *Game Theory: A Very Short Introduction* (OUP 2007) 102–103; Patrick Dumont and Frédéric Varone, "Delegation and Accountability in Parliamentary

At a later point, accountability for judicial decisions will be distinguished from accountability for a judge's behavior. For now it suffices to say that the information asymmetry is higher regarding the former and lower regarding the latter.[83] Despite these differences between decisional and behavioral accountability, asymmetry of knowledge has three general implications in the context of the judiciary.

The first implication is that neither the general public nor politicians can hold judges to account in a meaningful way if they rely solely on their own knowledge. This means that judges and their actions "must be held to account by the small group of people who have the time and the training to follow their work closely."[84] As a result, it is necessary to broaden the number of principals and, more specifically, to include more knowledgeable accounting agents. These "knowledgeable accounting agents" can be located both outside and inside the judiciary. Academics and practicing lawyers are examples of the former category[85] and court presidents, senior judges, and other judicial officers[86] are an example of the latter. Put differently, citizens and politicians need whistle-blowers to draw their attention to the fact that there is something wrong within the judiciary.[87]

The second problem that the asymmetry of knowledge poses is that even top courts issue hundreds (in common law countries) or thousands (in most

Democracies: Smallness, Proximity and Shortcuts" in Dietmar Braun and Fabrizio Gilardi (eds.), *Delegation in Contemporary Democracies* (Routledge 2006); Nuno Garoupa and Tom Ginsburg, "The Comparative Law and Economics of Judicial Councils" (2009) 27 *Berkeley Journal of International Law* 53, 57; or Eric A. Posner, "Agency Models in Law and Economics" in Eric A. Posner (ed.), *Chicago Lectures in Law and Economics* (Foundation Press 2000).

[83] For a nonlawyer it is much easier to assess whether a judge behaved inappropriately (ethical issues) than whether he applied the law correctly (issues of legal craftsmanship).

[84] Paul Beaumont, "The European Court of Justice. By Hjalte Rasmussen" (short review)' (*European Law Books*) <www.europeanlawbooks.org/reviews/detail.asp?id=103> [accessed August 1, 2013].

[85] *Cf.* Posner who claims that judges in the United States do not take academic criticism seriously (Richard A. Posner, *How Judges Think* (Harvard University Press 2008) 204–205).

[86] Under "other judicial officers" I mean advocates general (*avocats général*), government commissioners (*commissaires du gouvernement*), public rapporteurs (*rapporteurs public*), and similar positions. See Vlad Perju, "Reason and Authority in the European Court of Justice" (2009) 49 *Virginia Journal of International Law* 307, 339–341; Mitchel de S. O. L'E Lasser, *Judicial Deliberations: A Comparative Analysis of Judicial Transparency and Legitimacy* (OUP 2004) 47–60 and 113–140; or Luc Huybrechts, "A Commentary on Lasser's Analysis from the Belgian Court of Cassation's Perspective" in ibid., 189 and 192–194.

[87] Stephen Holmes, "Judicial Independence as Ambiguous Reality and Insidious Illusion" in Ronald Dworkin (ed.), *From Liberal Values to Democratic Transition: Essays in Honor of János Kis* (Central European University Press 2004) 9.

civil law countries) of judgments on the merits per year.[88] Again, there must be someone who will do the prescreening and draw principals' attention to the most important cases. Similarly, mechanisms must be in place for identifying the worst or the repeated[89] behavioral excesses of judges, since it is otherwise impossible to control hundreds or thousands of judges effectively.[90] Principals thus need a mix of hierarchical (second-party) and third-party supervision as well as whistle-blowers within the judiciary.[91]

Finally, the third implication is that input from the international community is limited since each legal system is unique and context specific.[92] No "outsider" (e.g., foreign "judicial reform specialist") can effectively criticize the functioning of the judiciary without insider information. This means that "accounting agents" of the judiciary must rely almost exclusively on "domestic" whistle-blowers.

III.   The Concept of Judicial Accountability

Having identified the specifics of judicial accountability, it is possible to proceed to define the contours of the concept of judicial accountability. The question "what is meant by judicial accountability" can best be answered if this complex question is divided into six small subquestions. These six subquestions read as follows: (1) who is a "judge"? (i.e., who is accountable?) (2) to whom are judges accountable? (3) for what are judges accountable? (4) through what processes are judges accountable? (5) by what standards is a judge's accountability judged? and finally (6) with what effects are judges accountable?[93] These questions will be addressed one by one.

---

[88]   If we go down the ladder of the judicial hierarchy, differences in number of cases between the common law and the civil law courts diminish since common law trial courts also decide thousands of cases.

[89]   That again calls for greater participation of the Bar as advocates are the only group that appears before the courts on a regular basis.

[90]   Some authors argue that the size of the agency is a separate variable in the principal–agent framework (Dumont and Varone, above note 82, at 52–76).

[91]   For a concise summary of these three techniques of monitoring the bureaucracies, see Tom Ginsburg, "Comparative Administrative Procedure: Evidence from Northeast Asia" (2002) 13 *Constitutional Political Economy* 247, 248–250; or Matthew D. McCubbins, Roger G. Noll, and Barry R. Weingast, "Political Control of the Bureaucracy" in P. Newman (ed.) *The New Palgrave Dictionary of Law and Economics* (Palgrave Macmillan 1998) 50, 53–55.

[92]   In the majority of countries, the language barrier arises as well.

[93]   In defining these questions, I build heavily on Jerry Mashaw, "Accountability and Institutional Design: Some Thoughts on the Grammar of Governance" in Michael W. Dowdle (ed.), *Public Accountability: Designs, Dilemmas and Experiences* (CUP 2006) 118.

A.   Who Is Accountable?

Regarding the question of *who* is accountable, most authors differentiate between the collective accountability of the judiciary and individual accountability of judges.[94] Piana goes even further and implicitly defines three levels of actors: the judiciary (meta-level), a particular court (meso-level), and individual judges (micro-level).[95] To make things even more complicated, the adjective "judicial" may in fact have more meanings. It may refer to (1) an individual judge; (2) a panel of judges; (3) a particular court; (4) the judiciary as a branch of government; or (5) the "functioning of the system of justice."

The boundaries between these meanings are often blurred, and most accountability measures affect more than one of these five dimensions of the "judicial" element of judicial accountability. A budget cut imposed on a particular court affects individual judges sitting in that court since a slow computer, no access to the Internet, and the lack of supporting administrative staff significantly influence the judge's performance and may, in the long run, create a foundation for disciplinary motion.

Even those measures that are considered "purely individual," such as disciplinary motions, the appointment of judicial officials, or the promotion of judges, have significant spill-over effects. The appointment or promotion of a poor judge will clearly influence the performance of the entire court. The selection of a poor president of the court can cause even greater harm. Similarly, a successful disciplinary motion against an individual judge will shed bad light not only on a given court and its president but also on the judiciary as a whole. And if successful disciplinary motions occur on a large scale, they may even hamper the functioning of the system of justice.

Nevertheless, the core function of judges is "judging," and this function is exercised by human beings and not by an abstract entity. Courts do

---

[94] See, for example, Andrew Le Sueur, "Developing Mechanisms for Judicial Accountability" in Guy Canivet, Mads Andenas, and Duncan Fairgrieve (eds.), *Independence, Accountability, and the Judiciary* (British Institute of International and Comparative Law 2006) 55–56; Sophie Boyron, "The Independence of the Judiciary: A Question of Identity" in ibid., 77, 93 and 96–98; or Yusuf, above note 20, at 15.

[95] See, for example, Piana 2010, above note 59, at 182 and 184. *See also* Diana Woodhouse, "Judicial Independence and Accountability within the United Kingdom's New Constitutional Settlement" in Guy Canivet, Mads Andenas, and Duncan Fairgrieve (eds.), *Independence, Accountability, and the Judiciary* (British Institute of International and Comparative Law 2006) 121, 129 (who distinguishes between accountability of individual judges, accountability of courts as institutions, and accountability of the judiciary).

not decide cases. The judiciary does not decide cases. Judges decide cases. Therefore, the judiciary is a "they," not an "it."[96] To be sure, measures aimed at entire courts, at all judges, or at the judiciary as a branch of government may influence individual judges, but only indirectly. Any accountability measure has a greater potential to be effective if it targets individual judges. For instance, it is hard to believe that a five percent decrease in the salaries of *all* judges due to an economic crisis[97] significantly influences individual judges in their decision making or behavior. The effects of such a decrease are rather marginal. But compare this across-the-board salary reduction with a five percent reduction in the salary of an individual judge.[98] The impact will be far more dramatic as the latter measure allows favoring some judges and "punishing" the other. As will be shown, this selective accountability is particularly dangerous.[99] Moreover, many accountability measures such as disciplining, retention, promotion, or impeachment are primarily individual, even though they may have spill-over effects on the other dimensions of judicial accountability. Therefore, what matters most is what affects individual judges. As the old proverb says "near is my shirt, but nearer is my skin." That is why my definition of judicial accountability focuses on mechanisms that target individual judges.

But even if we agree on the level of the "judicial" we want to study, the answer to the accountability-of-whom question is still far from clear. I will use the English and French judiciary to demonstrate this claim. As several commentators rightly emphasize, there are different categories of judges in England as well as in France to whom different rules apply. In France, one may distinguish between *magistrats du siège* (judges who decide cases) and *magistrats du parquet* (the investigative judges in criminal cases) or between private law judges and administrative judges.[100] Similarly, in the

---

[96] Adrian Vermeule, "The Judiciary Is a They, Not an It: Interpretive Theory and the Fallacy Of Division" (2009) 14 *Journal of Contemporary Legal Issues* 549.

[97] Due to the recent financial crisis in Europe, several countries – for instance Ireland and Estonia – reduced salaries of judges by a referendum or by a statute. See the Twenty-Ninth Amendment of the Constitution of Ireland (Judges' Remuneration) Bill 2011 (No. 44 of 2011), which relaxes the previous prohibition on the reduction of the salaries of Irish judges. On reduction of the salaries of Estonian judges, see Timo Ligi, "Judicial Independence in Estonia" in Anja Seibert-Fohr (ed.), *Judicial Independence in Transition* (Springer 2012) 739–791, at 766–767.

[98] Volatile salaries of individual judges were allowed for instance in Spain, where the remuneration of judges related judges' salaries to individual productivity (see Contini and Mohr, above note 69, at 36–37) and in Slovakia (see Chapter 6).

[99] See Section VI of this chapter.

[100] Boyron, above note 94, at 77, 93. See also Thierry Renoux, "Juges et magistrats" in Thierry Renoux (ed.), *La Justice en France* (La documentation française 2013).

United Kingdom, one must differentiate between judges of the High Court and upward and circuit judges, district judges, and even judges of various administrative tribunals. This insight is particularly important for comparative studies on judicial accountability. As Sophie Boyron persuasively argues, "the whole of the French judiciary should not be compared with the British higher judiciary (a mistake often made)."[101] Instead, one must either compare the French career judiciary (i.e., professional judges in both the administrative and private law courts) to all English professional judges (i.e., circuit judges, recorders, district judges, high court judges, Lord Justices of Appeal and Law Lords) or limit oneself to the English higher judiciary which in the French system would find its equivalent in *la haute magistrature*.[102]

Caution must be exercised in drawing conclusions from studying judicial accountability also in other jurisdictions. In fact, many European countries have a dual ordinary judiciary: the criminal and civil courts on the one hand and administrative courts on the other.[103] In addition, many countries have established specialized constitutional courts, which remain outside the structure of the ordinary judiciary, and operate according to specific rules that apply exclusively to constitutional justices.[104] If we cross the Atlantic, we must keep in mind that the accountability of U.S. federal judges differs from that of state judges, and even within the U.S. federal judiciary one must distinguish between the so-called Article III judges (judges of district courts and circuit courts and Justices of the Supreme Court of the United States), who are subject to very few mechanisms of judicial accountability, and other federal judges (such as magistrate judges, bankruptcy judges, or administrative judges), who are usually appointed for specified terms of office and face additional forms of accountability.[105]

In this book I deliberately focus on the accountability of full-time professional judges of the ordinary courts. This means that the book ignores, among others, judges of constitutional courts, judges of military courts

[101] Boyron, above note 94, at 77, 96.
[102] Ibid. By *la haute magistrature* in France, Boyron means in particular members of the *Cour de Cassation*, the *Conseil d'État*, and the first presidents of the court of appeal.
[103] See, for example, John Bell, "Reflections on Continental European Supreme Courts" in Guy Canivet, Mads Andenas, and Duncan Fairgrieve (eds.), *Independence, Accountability, and the Judiciary* (British Institute of International and Comparative Law 2006) 253.
[104] See ibid., and Künnecke 2006, above note 78, 222–225. For a recent take on the constitutional courts in Europe, *see* Victor Ferreres Comella, *Constitutional Courts and Democratic Values: A European Perspective* (Yale University Press 2009).
[105] *See* Edwin L. Felter, "Accountability in the Administrative Law Judiciary: The Right and the Wrong Kind" (2008) 86 *Denver University Law Review* 157.

and other specialized courts, ad hoc judges, part-time judges, judicial officers such as general advocates, as well as mediators, law clerks, prosecutors, jurors, and other lay-people sitting on judicial panels.[106] Therefore,
only full-time professional judges of the ordinary courts will be referred to
as "judges" from now on, unless specified otherwise.

B.   Accountability to Whom?

The question "to whom are judges accountable?" is central to judicial
accountability. Until recently, most commentators have focused predominantly on accountability to the executive branch. This is not surprising
since the executive branch has historically played the most significant role
in holding judges to account, and since its interference has been considered to be the most dangerous. However, reducing the accountability of
judges solely to the executive–judiciary relationship is an oversimplifica-
tion of the complex notion of judicial accountability.[107] Furthermore, such
reduction risks confusing judicial accountability with the notion of separation of powers.[108]

Judges can be accountable to many principals: (1) the executive; (2) the
legislature; (3) to various actors within the judiciary such as the court
presidents, senior judges, and judicial unions; and (4) other actors stay-
ing outside the three branches such as the Bar, the Ombudsman, or the
people. Each of these principals has its own mechanisms for holding
judges to account. Some of these mechanisms are specific to a particular
principal (e.g., only the legislature may use impeachment), some can be
employed by all principals (e.g., complaints against judges), and some can
be designed in various ways in order to encompass one or more accounting agents (e.g., disciplinary motions can be initiated, inter alia, by court
presidents, the Minister of Justice, the Government, the head of state, the
legislature, or by the Ombudsman).

Historically, accountability to the executive has attracted the most
attention. Thus, a plethora of publications addresses this relationship, even though predominantly from the point of view of judicial

---

[106] National laws often define judges more broadly. For instance, the term "magistrates" refers
to both judges and prosecutors in Italy and France. Similarly, various judicial officers such
as advocates general also tend to be considered as members of the judicial corps in many
countries (e.g., in Belgium, France, Portugal, and in the Netherlands).

[107] See, for example, Cross, above note 37, at 558–561; or Bovens 2007, above note 24, at
454–462.

[108] See Kornhauser, above note 35, at 47.

independence. Various additional rationales have been invoked to define accountability to the executive. The most prominent are the separation of powers rationale and the protection of individual or minority rights. Despite these challenges, accountability to the executive is prevalent in all judicial systems. If judges fail to be at least minimally sensitive to the interests of powerful political actors, they will sooner or later provoke a backlash from these actors and may eventually lose.[109] The experience of the first post-Soviet Russian Constitutional Court, which aggressively confronted President Yeltsin, provides a poignant example.[110] The first "switch in time that saved nine" of Associate Justice Owen Roberts in *West Coast Hotel Co. v. Parish*[111] in the wake of President Roosevelt's "court-packing plan," as well as the second "switch in time that saved nine" of Chief Justice Roberts that saved Obamacare,[112] attests to the fact that U.S. judges care about the views of the executive too. The question is thus not whether the judiciary is or should be accountable to the executive, but rather to what extent the judiciary is accountable to the executive in a given country.

Accountability to the legislature has been widely studied only in the United States, but even here scholars have focused primarily on a narrow set of mechanisms[113] such as impeachment and retention

---

[109] See, for example, Georg Vanberg, "Establishing and Maintaining Judicial Independence" in Keith E. Whittington and others (eds.), *The Oxford Handbook of Law and Politics* (USA, OUP 2008) 115.

[110] See Alexei Trochev, *Judging Russia: Constitutional Court in Russian Politics, 1990–2006* (CUP 2008) 93–117 and 289–292; or Herman Schwartz, *The Struggle for Constitutional Justice in Post-Communist Europe* (University of Chicago Press 2000) 162.

[111] 300 U.S. 379 (1937). The jurisprudential shift by Associate Justice Owen Roberts in *West Coast Hotel Co.* has been generally interpreted as a strategic political move to protect the integrity of the Supreme Court of the United States and induce President Franklin Roosevelt to abandon his "court-packing plan," which would have expanded the size of the Supreme Court bench from nine to fifteen justices.

[112] See *National Federation of Independent Business v. Sebelius*, 567 U.S. _ (2012), where the Supreme Court of the United States, in an opinion written by Chief Justice Roberts, upheld the individual mandate to buy health insurance as a constitutional exercise of the taxing power of Congress by 5:4 vote and thus saved the key piece of President Obama's federal health care reform (which is commonly called "Obamacare"). Immediately following the judgment of the Supreme Court of the United States, commentators started to speculate that the joint dissent was the original majority opinion and that Chief Justice Roberts changed his vote between March and the publication of the judgment. A few months later, the incumbent Obama won his second term as the President of the United States. That is why the second "switch in time that saved nine."

[113] Note that the issue of appointments as U.S. federal judges has no doubt generated the most voluminous scholarship. However, my definition of judicial accountability does not include the appointment of judges and thus I do not mention this literature here.

mechanisms.[114] However, Parliaments may play an even greater role in other judicial systems. They may either directly appoint or promote judges (at least to the higher echelons of the judiciary); they may appoint representatives to judicial councils or judicial appointment commissions; they may directly or indirectly appoint and dismiss court officials; they may have powers to impeach judges or vote to dismiss them from the bench (with the use of retention or reelection systems); and they may decide on judges' salaries and set budgets for the courts.

Furthermore, Parliaments have the legislative power to lay down statutory rules on virtually any aspect of the judicial system. These rules may stipulate, among other things, limited terms of office for judges or court officials, compulsory judicial training, rules on the reassignment of judges and on the temporary assignment of judges to nonjudicial posts,[115] rules on the publication of judgments, definitions of disciplinary offences, judicial performance evaluations and their criteria, mechanisms for handling complaints against judges, or the scope of the civil and criminal liability of judges.

It may be argued that personal composition of the executive and the legislature often overlap, that the powers of these two branches are often blurred,[116] and that the Parliament can be taken over by the executive. These concerns are further increased in parliamentary systems where the government is generated by the parliament itself after elections take place. While these issues should not be underestimated, it is nevertheless preferable to treat the two "more political branches" separately. First, Parliamentary systems[117] have mechanisms of their own (such as supermajority requirements, constructive votes of no confidence, "two-headed"

---

[114] See, for example, Brandice Canes-Wrone, Tom S. Clark, and Jee-Kwang Park, "Judicial Independence and Retention Elections" (2012) 28 *Journal of Law, Economics, & Organization* 211.

[115] This "traveling among branches" is a common phenomenon in civil law systems (see, e.g., Giuseppe Di Federico, "Independence and Accountability of the Judiciary in Italy: The Experience of a Former Transitional Country in a Comparative Perspective" in András Sajó (eds.), *Judicial Integrity* (Brill Academic Publishers 2004) 193–195. It would prevent many problems in civil law countries if they adopted the view that the move from the judiciary to the more political branches is a "one-way path."

[116] For instance, according to the French Constitution of 1958, the executive branch exercises certain legislative functions.

[117] Furthermore, the parliamentary systems with proportional voting systems almost never produce "absolute winners" (a party that wins majority of *all* seats in the Parliament) and thus election winners (the party with the highest number of votes) are forced to build coalitions, which speak with one voice only on a limited number of issues. Bicameralism produces further obstacle to the unification of the executive and legislative powers.

executive"[118] etc.) that prevent too much overlap between the executive and the legislature. Second, Parliaments have at their disposal mechanisms of judicial accountability which are not available to the executive (such as impeachment). In sum, in most democratic societies, the executive and the legislature are sufficiently distinct entities.[119]

As for accountability to other actors, it varies from one country to another. In some countries judges are held to account directly to the people. More specifically, lay people can, among other things, decide on retention elections, sit on appointment or promotion commissions, on disciplinary panels and in judicial councils, or submit complaints against judges. Besides the people, there are various other actors that may be involved in accounting of judges. These actors include litigants, the Bar, legal scholars, the General Prosecutor, or the Ombudsman. Each of these principals is specific and has different means for holding judges to account at its disposal. Members of the Bar and legal scholars may sit on merit commissions or judicial councils that decide on promotion of judges and their views are usually taken seriously by judges. The General Prosecutor may be vested with the power to file disciplinary motions against judges. Litigants can lodge complaints if they are dissatisfied with the performance of judges, even though their complaints are often perceived as self-serving. In sum, the role of these principals varies from one legal culture to another.

In contrast to that to the previous principals, the accountability of judges to their colleagues on the bench is a phenomenon that is generally overlooked.[120] Most studies simplify the internal constraints imposed on judges and limit them to the appellate process. However, there are other means, and potentially more intensive ones, by which court presidents, senior judges, or judicial unions can hold other judges to account. Historically, this form of internal judicial accountability has been particularly important in civil law countries that adhere to "hierarchical" judicial systems.[121]

---

[118] By the "two-headed" executive I mean systems, where the Prime Minister and the President share the executive powers and can more or less effectively counterbalance each other.

[119] This conclusion, of course, does not apply to authoritarian regimes.

[120] Cf. Art. 2 of the Universal Charter of the Judge adopted by IAJ on November17, 1999: "... The judge, as holder of judicial office, must be able to exercise judicial powers free from social, economic and political pressure, and *independently from other judges and the administration of the judiciary*" (emphasis added).

[121] See Javier Couso, "Judicial Independence in Latin America: The Lessons of History in the Search for an Always Elusive Ideal" in Tom Ginsburg and Robert A. Kagan (eds.), *Institutions & Public Law: Comparative Approaches* (Peter Lang Publishing 2005) 207; or Künnecke 2006, above note 78, at 226. On the distinction between hierarchical ideal of authority in civil law countries and the coordinate ideal of authority in common law countries, see Chapter 2, Section IV.

While the powers of these principals within the judiciary vary from one country to another, they often possess strong tools for holding judges of their courts to account. The most intensive mechanisms of accountability are in the hands of court presidents. These measures may include case assignment, taking decisions on the specialization of judges within a given court,[122] the assignment of law clerks, the power to initiate disciplinary motions, significant say in promoting judges, the power to divide bonus payments among judges, the power to decide on nonmonetary benefits such as subsidized housing, working conditions, material support and "leave of absence" (for reasons of judicial training abroad or the temporary assignment of a judge outside the judiciary), and the power to decide on the scope and manner of judicial training. Court presidents are particularly strong in postcommunist countries. In Mediterranean judiciaries, where judges had enough time to gel and identify common interests, senior judges or judicial unions play a similar role. For instance, in Italy the so-called *correnti*, political factions within the National Association of Magistrates, have a major say within the judiciary.[123] Similarly, in France professional organizations control the *commissions d'avancément* (promotion commissions) that can easily deny promotion to judges who refused to join them.[124]

Thus, all "accounting agents" may significantly influence the judiciary. Obviously, the accountability of judges to these "accounting agents" is far more complex than the foregoing sketch shows, since the above to some extent downplays the accountability relationships among "accounting agents." Some of these relationships have already been mentioned. For instance, in parliamentary systems the executive is accountable to the legislature, which is itself accountable to the voters. Similarly, court officials are accountable to their appointing body, the composition of which may vary significantly since court officials may be appointed by the Parliament, by the Executive (be it the President, the Government in the narrow sense,

---

[122] By decisions on judges' specialization I mean a situation when the court consists of several chambers, each of which has a specific case load and the court president can decide in which chamber a particular judge will sit.

[123] See Carlo Guarnieri and Patrizia Pederzoli, *The Power of Judges: A Comparative Study of Courts and Democracy* (OUP 2002), 54; or Carlo Guarnieri, "Judicial Independence in Europe: Threat or Resource for Democracy?" (2013) 49 *Representation* 347, 348.

[124] I am grateful for this insight to Thierry Renoux. For further details regarding the *commissions d'avancément*, see Antoine Garapon and Harold Epineuse, "Judicial Independence in France" in Anja Seibert-Fohr (ed.), *Judicial Independence in Transition* (Springer 2012) 273–305, at 285–286.

the Prime Minister or the Minister of Justice), by judges themselves, by a specialized body (such as a judicial council or a judicial appointment commission), or even through a process that involves two or more of these actors. In fact, the forms of this relationship, the lines of accountability, and their specific content seem endlessly variable.[125]

In the most extreme situation, court presidents can even operate as "transmission belts" for the executive, which results in the "accountability nesting" problem.[126] However, even in China, Russia, and Ukraine, where the Communist Party or the Presidential administration exercises the greatest pressure on court presidents, the latter managed to carve out some room of maneuver.[127] A potential overlap between "accounting agents" poses another problem. Members of the executive can hold seats in the legislature. Judges can be temporarily assigned to the executive. All of these accounting agents (members of the executive, the legislature, the people, court presidents, and other principals) may also have their private disputes, and thus all of them may appear before the court as litigants. Nevertheless, these overlaps exist only on the margins and each agent has its own core mechanisms for holding judges to account. The unstable boundaries between the four "accounting agents" and some degree of accountability nesting thus do not undermine the argument that each of these "accounting agents" is sufficiently distinct from the others.

C.   Accountability for What?

A separate definitional question is "accountability *for what*?" Even the most fervent supporters of judicial independence do not suggest that judges should enjoy total independence. As Judge Kozinski aptly noted, judicial independence does not mean that U.S. judges can "[get] on the bench dressed like Ronald McDonald [or] ... write all ... opinions in law French."[128] More generally, it is claimed that "independence is desirable ... because it frees judges from *inappropriate* considerations,"[129] that "judicial

---

[125] Ferejohn 2007, above note 26, at 4 (note 3).
[126] This issue is discussed in more detail in Chapter 2, Section III.A, and Chapter 8, Section I.
[127] See ibid.
[128] Alex Kozinski, "The Many Faces of Judicial Independence" (1998) 14 *Georgia State University Law Review* 861, 862.
[129] Vanberg 2008, above note 109, at 101 (emphasis added). See also Kornhauser, above note 35, at 48–50.

independence should be limited to the independence to act *"judicially,"*[130] or that judges should not go "too far."[131]

Leaving aside the controversial questions concerning the meaning of "inappropriate," "acting judicially," and "going too far," a plausible conclusion is that the authors of these statements pay attention primarily to decisional accountability. However, to hold judges to account for the content of their decisions is only part, though a very important part, of accountability. In fact, Kozinski's comment makes it clear that judges should be accountable not only for their decisions, but also for their behavior on the bench. This idea can be extrapolated even further to encompass within the bracket of "behavioral accountability" the extrajudicial activities of judges. There is no doubt that judges are expected to be exemplary citizens.[132] Accordingly, alcohol or drug abusers, perpetrators of violence, plagiarists, people with ties to the mafia, and corruptible individuals should not sit on the bench.[133] Hence, the extrajudicial activities of judges inevitably fall within the ambit of the "judicial role."

Since behavioral accountability affects decisional accountability and vice versa, it is appropriate to focus on both decisional and behavioral accountability.[134] This chapter uses the term "decisional accountability" to describe the concept of holding judges answerable for their judicial decisions. Answerability for judicial decisions should be considered broadly so as to encompass not only the substantive content of a decision but also its form, layout, and comprehensibility.[135] "Behavioral accountability" includes holding judges answerable for their conduct on the bench as well as for their extrajudicial behavior.

---

[130] Kornhauser, above note 35, at 561.

[131] E. W. Thomas, *The Judicial Process: Realism, Pragmatism, Practical Reasoning and Principles* (CUP 2005) 84.

[132] Pérez-Perdomo, above note 18, at 212.

[133] See above notes 16–20.

[134] On the decisional/behavioral (sometimes referred to as substantive/procedural) distinction of judicial accountability, see David Brody, "The Use of Judicial Performance Evaluation to Enhance Judicial Accountability, Judicial Independence, and Public Trust" (2008) 86 *Denver University Law Review* 115, 123–124; and Voigt, above note 53, at 97.

[135] It is telling that many judges in the CEE consider the pressure to avoid Latin terms, to divide the text of the ruling into numbered paragraph, or to state facts in chronological order an attack on their judicial independence. For further examples of distorting judicial independence see Frank Emmert, "The Independence of Judges – A Concept Often Misunderstood in Central and Eastern Europe" (2001) 3 *European Journal of Law Reform* 405.

Some authors add a third category of accountability that primarily covers the selection and tenure of judges and use the term "institutional accountability"[136] or "political accountability"[137] to refer to these processes. However, this third category is misleading since it mixes *ex ante* with ex post mechanisms and confuses the "for what" with the "to whom" dimensions of judicial accountability.[138]

First, my definition of judicial accountability covers only ex post mechanisms. Thus, screening mechanisms such as judicial elections and the appointment of judges, and other mechanisms of ex ante nature, such as the requirement to publish all judgments, are outside the scope of this book. I do not dispute that these mechanisms may contribute to achieving the same aims as ex post mechanisms – that is, to ensure that judges behave properly and that they implement proper decision-making processes.[139] On the contrary, some of these mechanisms, such as requiring that judicial decisions be published, may be necessary for holding judges to account. They could even be called "preconditions for judicial accountability" or, as Philp has argued, "the contingent circumstances or additional requirements that might influence whether a certain form of accountability will bring about a certain set of results."[140] However, as there is no "accounting" involved in these mechanisms of ex ante nature,[141] they do not count as mechanisms of judicial accountability.[142] These mechanisms should rather be included under the umbrella of other concepts such as transparency, forward-looking controls, or responsiveness.

On the other hand, not all mechanisms of "institutional accountability" are necessarily ex ante in nature. For instance, case assignment and reassignment of judges across panels (if not strictly random) are clearly ex post measures. However, these two mechanisms are already covered by

---

[136] Mads Andenas and Duncan Fairgrieve, "Judicial Independence and Accountability: National Traditions and Standards" in Guy Canivet, Mads Andenas, and Duncan Fairgrieve (eds.), *Independence, Accountability, and the Judiciary* (British Institute of International and Comparative Law 2006) 23–24.

[137] Wendell L. Griffen, "Judicial Accountability and Discipline" (1998) 61 *Law and Contemporary Problems* 75, 75.

[138] Furthermore, this book uses the term "political accountability" to refer to one of the standards of accountability (see Section III.E).

[139] Even though two people may disagree what "proper" means in this context.

[140] Philp, above note 58, at 32.

[141] See discussion in Section II.

[142] For a more detailed discussion of which mechanisms count as mechanisms of judicial accountability and which do not, see Chapter 2.

the notions of "decisional accountability" and "behavioral accountability." Therefore, the term "institutional accountability" does not add any value in this context.

Second, the view that accountability mechanisms must necessarily be limited only to mechanisms by which the other two political branches hold judges to account is also fallacious. There are many mechanisms that can be used by principals other than politicians. For instance, in many countries, case assignment and various types of promotion[143] are controlled by court presidents. Once again, the term "institutional accountability" does not have any additional value. Instead, it spreads confusion. Therefore, both "institutional accountability" and "political accountability" are inappropriate terms in the context of the accountability-for-what question.

D.   Through What Processes?

The three remaining questions – "through what processes?", "by what standards?", and "with what effect?" – are closely interrelated. They can easily be put under one umbrella and treated as a single question: "How are judges held to account?". However, for analytical reasons, it is useful to keep these three dimensions of judicial accountability separate. "Processes," in this context, mean various mechanisms of judicial accountability, while "effects" mean the effects of these mechanisms and "standards" mean the standards applied by them.

As mentioned earlier with reference to processes, accountability mechanisms must meet two fundamental criteria. They must be ex post in nature and they must result in a sanction or a reward.[144] These two criteria limit the number of mechanisms of judicial accountability. However, even though the present definition of accountability is relatively narrow, a plethora of mechanisms fall within the ambit of this definition. These mechanisms include, inter alia, impeachment, retention, disciplinary motions, complaints, promotion, judicial performance evaluations, case assignment, and volatile salaries.[145] A separate chapter (Chapter 3) is devoted to mechanisms of judicial accountability and thus it is appropriate to turn immediately to the fifth question.

---

[143] Apart from permanent promotion to a higher court, judges can be also seconded, promoted to the position of a chamber president, or appointed to the Grand Chamber. For further details, see Chapter 2.

[144] I also made clear that the sanction can be either negative or positive.

[145] See Chapter 2.

E. By What Standards?

"Standards of judicial accountability" also vary from one mechanism to another. Broadly speaking, there are two types of standards: (1) political standards; and (2) legal standards.[146] Thus, it is necessary to distinguish between political and legal accountability. Ferejohn defines "political accountability" as a situation when "A [e.g., a judge] is politically accountable to B [to judge's principal] if B can take some direct action that can help or harm B."[147] According to Ferejohn, "political accountability is fundamentally arbitrary in the sense that it is up to the 'principal' to base decisions on reasons, or to refuse to do so."[148] Therefore, the principal can act with or without a cause.

As to legal accountability, Ferejohn claims that "A [e.g., a judge] is *legally* accountable to B [the judge's principal] if B is able to *get a court* to impose sanctions on A for failing to execute his duties to B."[149] This means that "the agent is required to take or refrain from taking certain actions and must defend her actions in a legal forum."[150] The main difference between political and legal accountability is that "legal accountability is not arbitrary but is based on reasons, reasons connecting behavior to the relevant law binding the agent."[151] Thus, under legal accountability the agents are rewarded or punished for reasons provided by law, whereas under political accountability there is a zone of discretion for what the agents can be rewarded or punished "arbitrarily."

However, these two accountability standards are what Max Weber called "ideal types."[152] They are "exaggerated or one-sided descriptions of what is obviously a richer and more complex reality, but whose very unreality aids us to disentangling the various elements that existing practices and institutions invariably contain."[153] Just like political accountability, legal accountability can be arbitrary and is sometimes even less predictable than political accountability. Conversely, political accountability is

---

[146] I adopt definitions of political and legal accountability from John Ferejohn; see Ferejohn 2007, above note 26, at 3. However, I am aware that other authors adopt different definitions of these two terms: see, for example, Mulgan, above note 24, above note 32–33.

[147] Ferejohn 2007, above note 26, at 3.

[148] Ibid., at 5 (emphasis in the original).

[149] Ibid., at 3 (emphasis added).

[150] Ibid., at 5.

[151] Ibid., at 5–6.

[152] Max Weber, *The Methodology of the Social Sciences* (Edward Shils and Henry A. Finch trs, Free Press 1949) 90.

[153] Anthony T. Kronman, *Max Weber* (Stanford University Press 1983) 7.

not entirely arbitrary. Political accountability merely applies different criteria, employs different reasoning, and speaks to a different audience. In the real world, principals can rarely hold agents to account without cause and political accountability can never be exercised "arbitrarily" in the pure sense of this word. Therefore, we should be careful not to see legal accountability in too rosy colors or to take an a priori pessimistic view of political accountability.

It has also been observed that a specific feature of judicial accountability is the significant degree to which judicial accountability has been "legalized." However, two caveats must be added to this claim. First, despite the general trend toward the "legalization" of judicial accountability, the extent and pace of that "legalization" differs across states. "Legalization" of judicial accountability is far from complete in any country. This leads us to the second caveat – it is impossible to eradicate political accountability altogether. For instance, there is always an element of discretion in promoting judges to a higher court. The only way to curb the discretion of the promoting body (be it the legislature, the Minister of Justice, the President with the Senate, or the judicial council) is to prohibit promotions altogether or to adopt a system that relies strictly on the criterion of seniority. However, the former solution is incompatible with the career model of the judiciary[154] and the second is highly problematic as it does not motivate judges to excel.[155]

F.   With What Effect?

The effects of judicial accountability mechanisms are mechanism-specific. Some mechanisms may lead to the loss of judicial office (e.g., retention, impeachment, or disciplinary motions), some mechanisms primarily affect the case load and the salary of judges (e.g., promotion) and some may "merely" have the result of damaging a judge's reputation (e.g., judicial performance evaluations).

Some mechanisms, such as case assignment or volatile salaries, are double-edged swords as they can be used either to reward or to sanction

---

[154] Note that several commentators observed that promotion is also increasingly more common within the judiciary in the United Kingdom; see, for example, Boyron, above note 94, at 77, 97; and Lord Mance, "External Institutional Control over Judges" in Guy Canivet, Mads Andenas, and Duncan Fairgrieve (eds.), *Independence, Accountability, and the Judiciary* (British Institute of International and Comparative Law 2006) 269.

[155] For further details regarding promotion of judges, see Chapter 2.

judges. Principals[156] can use case assignment as a "carrot" by assigning interesting and novel cases to "favored" judges. They can use case assignment as a "stick" by assigning mundane and repetitive cases to "recalcitrant" judges. Similarly, a principal can "help" his "favored" judges by assigning to them only cases within their area of expertise. Interestingly, in civil law countries principals can also please their "favored" judges by assigning them easy cases and punish "recalcitrant" judges by assigning difficult cases.[157] All of these techniques were utilized either in the Czech Republic or Slovakia.[158]

The whole debate about case assignment may sound strange to a common law jurist for two reasons. First, common law systems do not recognize the German-style right to a legal judge.[159] The power of the court president to distribute cases among panels or among judges within a particular panel is considered legitimate. This is in stark contrast with the practice in most countries in Continental Europe that require the assembly of the judicial panel that is to decide a particular dispute in advance *and* on objective criteria. If one of these two criteria is not met, it is a violation of the right to a legal judge (*gesetzlicher Richter*).[160] The difference is evidenced in the so-called *Pinochet* cases decided by the Appellate Committee of the UK House of Lords. In November 1998, The House of Lords, by three votes to two, refused Augusto Pinochet immunity from prosecution on the theory that he was a former head of state.[161] However,

---

[156] There is a huge variety among the models of case assignment. However, the court presidents play the decisive role in most civil law countries. See Philip M. Langbroek and Marco Fabri, *The Right Judge for Each Case: A Study of Case Assignment and Impartiality in Six European Judiciaries* (Intersentia 2007).

[157] I intentionally use the term "difficult cases" instead of the term "hard cases" in order to avoid any connotation with Dworkin's definition of "hard cases." By "difficult cases" I mean not only cases that require moral reasoning or the application of principles, but also cases that require a complex assessment of the facts, have a foreign law element or require the reading of a huge number of supplementary documents. In sum, "difficult cases" are time-consuming cases.

[158] See Chapters 5 and 6.

[159] Note that the meaning of the principle of the "legal judge" (sometimes also referred to as the principle of the "natural judge") varies from one country to another (see, e.g., International Commission of Jurists, *International Principles on the Independence and Accountability of Judges, Lawyers and Prosecutors*, 2nd ed., Geneva, 2007, 7–11). This concept thus may set different requirements, the most stringent set of which is applicable in Germany (see Langbroek and Fabri, above note 156).

[160] For a more detailed discussion of the right to a legal judge, see Chapter II, Section II.C.

[161] *R v Bartle and the Commissioner of Police for the Metropolis and Others, Ex Parte Pinochet.* [1998] UKHL 41; [2000] 1 AC 61; [1998] 4 All ER 897; [1998] 3 WLR 1456 (November 25, 1998).

once it was revealed that one of the judges taking part in the November judgment had links with Amnesty International, the House of Lords decided to set the November judgment aside[162] and the case was reconsidered by a different five-judge panel.[163] The House of Lords never provided an explanation for why all five judges were replaced and on what criteria the new judges were selected. However, the most shocking aspect of this case for a civil law jurist is not that this happened, but that House of Lords' move was not questioned by scholars and the media. In civil law countries, the House of Lords' actions would be considered a flagrant violation of the right to a legal judge.

Second, a common law jurist is familiar with filtering mechanisms, such as leave to appeal or writs a certiorari, which are used to reduce the case load of courts operating at the higher echelons of the judicial system. These mechanisms ensure that very few "easy cases" reach the higher courts. In contrast, the ordinary courts in civil law countries, including the supreme courts, generally do not have such mechanisms at their disposal. This means that a typical civil law judge, including the judges of top courts, must decide hundreds of cases per year. Thus, a civil law judge appreciates receiving easy cases (broadly defined), which enable him to minimize his docket,[164] allow him to spend more time on difficult cases (broadly defined), or increase his leisure time.[165]

In sum, the "effect" can be either that of a carrot or that of a stick. Both carrots and sticks may be monetary, material as well as immaterial. Carrots may take the form of pay rises, increased pensions, the assignment of interesting cases, or simply an increase in prestige. Sticks can take the form of dismissal, temporary reduction of salary, relocation to lower courts, reprimand, or a loss of reputation.[166] The effects of each mechanism of judicial accountability are discussed in more detail in Chapter 2.

---

[162] *Re Pinochet* [1999] UKHL 52 (January 15, 1999).

[163] *In re Pinochet* [1999] UKHL 1; [2000] 1 AC 119; [1999] 1 All ER 577; [1999] 2 WLR 272 (January 15, 1999).

[164] In fact, it seems to be a common strategy of both civil law and common law judges to minimize their workload while maximizing their reputation and chances of elevation to a higher court. See Stephen J. Choi and others, "What Do Federal District Judges Want? An Analysis of Publications, Citations and Reversals" (2012) 28 *Journal of Law, Economics, & Organization* 518.

[165] See Posner, R. A. 1993, above note 72.

[166] See Mary L. Volcansek and others, *Judicial Misconduct: A Cross-National Comparison* (University Press of Florida 1996).

G. Definition of Judicial Accountability

After answering the abovementioned six questions, it is possible to adopt a working definition of judicial accountability that reads as follows: "judicial accountability is a negative or positive consequence that an individual judge expects to face from one or more principals (from the executive and/ or from the legislature and/or from court presidents and/or from other actors) in the event that his behavior and/or decisions deviate too much from a generally recognized standard."[167]

This definition treats judicial accountability as none of a "catch-all," a "buzz-word," or a necessarily "good" thing. Judicial accountability is not a "catch-all" for everything that affects decision making or the behavior of judges as it does not cover every aspect of judicial governance. It is not a "buzz-word" for everything good in the judiciary since there are other positive values and institutional mechanisms apart from judicial accountability. Finally, it is not necessarily good since virtually any mechanism of judicial accountability is susceptible to abuse.

This definition also makes it clear that I am studying judicial accountability as a mechanism rather than as a virtue.[168] I see judicial accountability as an institutional relationship in which a judge can be held to account by a forum and I focus on whether there are such relations at all, whether these can be called accountability mechanisms, how these mechanisms function, and what their effects are. Hence, I use judicial accountability primarily in a narrow descriptive sense.[169] In contrast, I do not use judicial accountability as a normative concept. I do not formulate a set of substantive standards for good judging and proper judicial behavior, and I do not assess whether judges comply with these standards.[170]

For that reason, my definition encompasses a broad array of mechanisms, including those, such as retention elections of judges, which can in some countries be considered unconstitutional.[171] The rationale behind

---

[167] This definition relies heavily on the analysis of Stefan Voigt in Voigt, above note 53, at 97.
[168] On these two concepts of accountability, see Mark Bovens, "Two Concepts of Accountability: Accountability as a Virtue and as a Mechanism" (2010) 33 *West European Politics* 946.
[169] On accountability as a mechanism, see ibid. at 950–954.
[170] On accountability as a virtue, see ibid. at 948–950.
[171] Many civil law countries consider this mechanism to be incompatible with judicial independence and, hence, unconstitutional. This is particularly so in postcommunist countries, which witnessed the abuse of retention of judges during the communist era; on this point see Concurring Opinion of Judge Garlicki joined by Judge Pellonpää in *Gurov v. Moldova*, App. no. 36455/02, European Court of Human Rights, July 11, 2006, § 3 in fine.

this inclusive position is that if one excludes certain mechanisms which are considered controversial or even unconstitutional in some countries, the result would be to convey an implicit message about who should hold judges to account, how, and for what. Too narrow an approach that excludes controversial mechanisms would in my opinion obscure how mechanisms of judicial accountability actually work. Therefore, my general approach is that I do not take a position on whether or not a certain mechanism is desirable and on the extent to which it can be or has been misused.[172]

I believe that this is the correct way to proceed, as most authors tend to infuse their lists of mechanisms of judicial accountability with their normative biases. For instance, Stefan Voigt distinguishes between judicial dependency and judicial accountability and claims that "[t]he most important difference between the two concepts is that an accountable judge will have to incur extra costs if she disregards or violates the law whereas a dependent judge will have to incur extra costs although she meticulously follows the letter of the law."[173] According to Voigt, mechanisms that lead to judicial dependency are "bad" and thus do not count as mechanisms of judicial accountability. In other words, he implicitly puts forward the argument that only those mechanisms that do not have negative effects on judges should be considered mechanisms of judicial accountability. Unfortunately, this position is untenable, unless one explains who decides *what* the letter of law is and what set of rules judges should follow.

Nevertheless, I agree that any concept of judicial accountability contains an irreducible normative element. Hence I exclude certain mechanisms even if they meet all three requirements – that they are of ex post nature, may entail consequences, and target individual judges. But in contrast to Voigt, I define this normative core more narrowly, and thus I leave out only those mechanisms that are *generally* considered criminal or pathological. These genuinely criminal or pathological mechanisms include, for instance, bribes, death threats aimed at judges, or infamous "telephone justice."[174] All other mechanisms that at least in some democratic countries are considered acceptable fall within the ambit of my definition of judicial accountability.[175]

---

[172] The only exception is the category of criminal mechanisms and genuinely pathological mechanisms which I discuss in Chapter 2.

[173] Voigt, above note 53, at 97–98.

[174] These criminal and pathological mechanisms are discussed in Chapter 2.

[175] Mechanisms of judicial accountability are discussed in more detail in Chapter 2.

IV.   Why Judicial Accountability Matters?

There are two answers to this question. A pragmatic one concerns a worldwide trend – growth in the power of courts. An unprecedented increase in the power of judges and the judicialization of politics are hallmarks of our times.[176] Judges are no longer considered *la bouche de la loi* ("the mouthpiece of the law").[177] They also engage in judicial law-making and we know that they enjoy significant discretion. Some authors go even further and claim that judges are not necessarily subservient to the law and tradition, but that they instead maximize income and leisure just like everyone else.[178] Hence, many commentators believe that the formula "the stronger the power of a given institution, the greater the need for its accountability" applies to courts as well and that adopting mechanisms that would hold judges to account is now more necessary than ever before.

This does not mean that the judiciary was powerless until the 1980s. Montesquieu's notion of the "judge as a mouthpiece" was always exaggerated and often served as a shield for the judiciary.[179] It was rather a perception created by judges themselves to deny the fact that they enjoy significant discretion and sometimes "make the law." But this "agency slack" has recently been broken even in civil law countries whose judges denied the existence of law-making powers more ferociously than their common law counterparts.[180]

True, one may hesitate, as many scholars and judges on both sides of the Atlantic do,[181] to accept Posner's claim that judges act as "occasional

---

[176] See, for example, Cappelletti, above note 80; Alec Stone Sweet, *Governing with Judges: Constitutional Politics in Europe* (OUP 2000); Guarnieri and Pederzoli, above note 123; or Ran Hirschl, *Towards Juristocracy: The Origins and Consequences of the New Constitutionalism* (Harvard University Press 2004).

[177] This famous idiom was coined by Baron de Montesquieu. See Montesquieu, above note 67, Chapter 6.

[178] See Posner, R. A. 1993, above note 72. For a more recent analysis of this issue, see Choi and others, above note 164.

[179] *Cf.* Karel Schönfeld, "Rex, Lex et Judex: Montesquieu and la bouche de la loi revisited" (2008) 4 *European Constitutional Law Review* 274 (who claims that the *bouche de la loi* passage itself has been misinterpreted). See also Philippe Raynaud, "La loi et la jurisprudence, des lumières à la révolution française" (1985) 30 Archives de philosophie du droit 61.

[180] But see the discussion below which makes it clear that this depiction of civil law judges is exaggerated.

[181] It is a common failure to claim that in the United States the claim that "judges make law, plain and simple" is *traditionally* accepted (see, e.g., Lasser, above note 86, at 303). Judicial law-making is controversial in the United States too. See Brian Z. Tamanaha, *Beyond the Formalist-Realist Divide: The Role of Politics in Judging* (Princeton University Press 2010); or Jeffrey Sutton, "A Review of Richard A. Posner, How Judges Think (2008)" (2010) 108 *Michigan Law Review* 859. See also Jan Komárek, "Questioning Judicial Deliberations" (2009) 29 *Oxford Journal of Legal Studies* 805, 824 (who explicitly criticizes Lasser for over-simplification of this issue).

legislators."[182] These scholars[183] and judges[184] deny that "hard cases" and the indeterminacy or underdeterminacy of the sources of the law entail that judges should "make the law" in the sense that this phrase has when it is applied to legislatures. Instead, they distinguish between judicial *legislating* and judicial *law-making* and sometimes also between the acts of "making law" for an *individual* case and producing *general* norms.[185]

On the other hand, the outdated view that judges and scholars in Continental Europe deny judges' law-making power should also be rejected. In most European countries it is increasingly accepted that judges "make the law" and are sometimes involved in politics.[186] Prominent German,[187] Swiss,[188] and French[189] scholars attest to this view. Komárek

[182] Posner, R. A. 2008, above note 85, Chapter 3 (and in particular at 81).

[183] See Tamanaha's and Komárek's contributions cited in note 181. See also John Gardner, "Some Types of Law" in Douglas E. Edlin (ed.), *Common Law Theory* (2007) 51.

[184] For instance, Justice Scalia held that "[judges] make [law] ... *as judges make it*, which is to say *as though* they were 'finding' it – discerning what the law *is*, rather than decreeing what it is today *changed to*, or what it will *tomorrow be*" (*James B. Beam Distilling Co. v. Georgia* 501 US 529, 549 (1991) (Scalia concurring)(emphasis in the original)). Recall also the "balls and strikes" talk of Chief Justice Roberts mentioned in the introduction. More recently, another successful nominee to the U.S. Supreme Court Sonia Sotomayor was criticized for her speech in 2005 where she said that "Court of Appeals is where policy is *made*" (see Charlie Savage, "A Judge's View of Judging Is on the Record" *New York Times* (New York, May 15, 2009) (emphasis added)). For explicit criticism of Posner's position, see Sutton, above note 181 (especially note 11 that provides further references).

[185] For an overview of this debate, see Jan Komárek, "Reasoning with Previous Decisions: Beyond the Doctrine of Precedent" (2013) 61 *American Journal of Comparative Law* 149.

[186] Post-communist states (most of them now members of the EU) are cited as an example of the exception to this rule. See Zdeněk Kühn, "Worlds Apart: Western and Central European Judicial Culture at the Onset of the European Enlargement" (2004) 52 *American Journal of Comparative Law* 531, 558–562.

[187] German legal scholars distinguish the "mere" interpretation of the law [*Auslegung*] and the further development of the law [*Rechtsfortbildung*]. More specifically, Carl Larenz distinguishes between the following three categories: (1) interpretation [*Auslegung*]; (2) further development of the law within the statute [*gesetzesimmanente Rechtsfortbildung*]; and (3) further development of the law beyond the statute but within the legal system [*Rechtsfortbildung über den Plan des Gesetzes hinaus* or *gesetzübersteigende Rechtsfortbildung*] (Carl Larenz and Claus-Wilhelm Canaris, *Methodenlehre der Rechtswissenschaft* (3rd ed., Springer 1995) 133–262). I am thankful to Michal Bobek for this clarification.

[188] See, for example, Hugo Uyterhoeven, who distinguishes between (1) the bound judicial decision making [*die gebundene richterliche Rechtsfindung*]; (2) the judicial further development of the law [*die Rechtsfortbildung*]; and (3) the free judicial decision making [*die freie richterliche Rechtsfindung*] (Hugo Uyterhoeven, *Richterliche Rechtsfindung und Rechtsvergleichung. Eine Vorstudie über die Rechtsvergleichung als Hilfsmittel der richterlichen Rechtsfindung im Privatrecht* (Verlag Stämpfli 1959)).

[189] Most French authors now recognize *la jurisprudence* as a source of law; see, for example, Philippe Malaurie and Patrick Morvan, *Droit civil: introduction générale* (2nd ed.,

puts it aptly: "[f]ew people in Europe, if any, today deny that courts make law in *some* important sense. The key question is, in *what sense* and *how* it differs from lawmaking by legislators, not *whether* it happens."[190] Nevertheless, even if one rejects the judicial-legislating thesis (the strongest thesis) and the judicial-law-making thesis (the moderate thesis), one can hardly deny that judges enjoy significant discretion in *interpreting* the law (the weak thesis). In Europe, the judges' interpretation powers are strengthened by the ability to invoke the "Convention-conforming,"[191] the "EU-law-conforming,"[192] and the "constitution-conforming" interpretation.

The second answer is more normative and focuses on what objectives are sought by judicial accountability. Some authors invoke the rule of law,[193] public confidence in the courts,[194] institutional responsibility,[195] a well-functioning judiciary,[196] and broader social responsiveness[197] as

Defrénois 2005) 265 (with further references). The authors who deny the law-making powers of judges (see, for example, Jean Carbonnier, *Droit civil. Introduction* (21st ed., Presses Universitaires de France 1992) 263–282) are now in the minority. This debate has recently been replicated in English between Lasser and Komárek. Contrast Lasser, above note 86, at 173, with Komárek 2009, above note 181, at 805, 809–810 and 824. See also Olivier Beaud, "Reframing a Debate among Americans: Contextualizing a Moral Philosophy of Law" (2009) 7 *International Journal of Constitutional Law* 53, 59; and Sébastien Platon, Dr. "Law-Discoverer" and Mr. "Law-Maker": the Strange Case of Case-Law in France, VerfBlog, 2015/4/24, available at www.verfassungsblog.de/en/dr-law-discoverer-and-mr-law-maker-the-strange-case-of-case-lawin-france/ (both explaining the shift in perception of judges and judging in France since the nineteenth century).

[190] Jan Komárek, "When Umpires Strike Back: Some Distinctions between (Judicial) Lawmaking and Legislation" in LAWTE (eds.), *Liber Amicorum Tom Eijsbouts* (Amsterdam: Asser Press 2011), 132–140 at 138. See also Symposium Roundtable "An Exchange with Jeremy Waldron" published in *International Journal of Constitutional Law* (Volume 7, Issue 1, 2009).

[191] By the "Convention-conforming" interpretation is meant interpretation conforming to the European Convention on Human Rights.

[192] The principles of direct effect and supremacy of EU law allow national courts to go even further and apply EU law *instead of* national law. Note that this power of national courts is constrained by the doctrines of "acte claire" and "acte éclairé" (otherwise the national court is obliged to submit a preliminary reference to the ECJ). Nevertheless, national courts enjoy a significant leeway in interpreting these two doctrines.

[193] Voigt, above note 53, at 96; and Charles Gardner Geyh, "Rescuing Judicial Accountability from the Realm of Political Rhetoric" (2006) 56 *Case Western Reserve Law Review* 911, 916.

[194] Geyh 2006, above note 193, at 916; and Jonathan Soeharno, *The Integrity of the Judge: A Philosophical Inquiry* (Ashgate Pub 2009) 41.

[195] Geyh 2006, above note 193, at 917.

[196] John Ferejohn and Larry Kramer, "Independent Judges, Dependent Judiciary: Institutionalizing Judicial Restraint" (2002) 77 *New York University Law Review* 962, 963–964.

[197] Geyh 2006, above note 193, at 917; Owen Fiss, "The Right Degree of Independence" in Irwin P. Stotzky (ed.), *Transition to Democracy in Latin America: The Role of the Judiciary*

meta-goals of judicial accountability. However, the "rule of law" is a loaded term that does not lead us very far; the link between judicial accountability and public confidence in the courts is too indirect; invoking "institutional responsibility" as an ultimate end suffers from tautology; and "well-functioning" and "social responsiveness" are notoriously ambiguous terms.[198]

Impartiality is another goal that is often mentioned in connection with judicial accountability.[199] It can be defined as "impartiality between the government or executive and the citizen *and* between citizen and citizen that means that the judiciary is indifferent to any disparity between the relative power, strength and coincident advantages of the participants."[200] Authors invoking impartiality as an ultimate goal claim, in a nutshell, that accountability should serve as a necessary means to the end of the adjudication of cases by an impartial and neutral third party.[201] However, this aim is also problematic since judicial accountability and judicial impartiality appear to be sometimes in tension with one another. This tension arises, for instance, when judges are held to account by litigants, when judges have to meet stringent performance criteria regarding the number of disposed cases, or when judges adjust their views in order to succeed in retention election.[202]

(Westview Press 1993) 56–58; Holmes, above note 87, at 7 and 12; Antoine Garapon, "Une Justice 'Comptable' de ses Decisions?" in Guy Canivet, Mads Andenas, and Duncan Fairgrieve (eds.), *Independence, Accountability, and the Judiciary* (British Institute of International and Comparative Law 2006) 250; Pérez-Perdomo, above note 18, at 208; and Vanberg 2005, above note 1. Another scholar, Mauro Cappelletti, proposed a socially responsible justice system, based on the idea of "responsive law" (Cappelletti, above note 80, at 61–62) and, more recently, Gar Yein Ng coined the term "social accountability" of the judiciary (Gar Yein Ng, *Quality of Judicial Organisation and Checks and Balances* (Intersentia 2007)). On the idea of "responsive law," see Philippe Nonet and Philip Selznick, *Law & Society in Transition: Toward Responsive Law* (Transaction Publishers 2001) 73–114. Cf. Peter H. Russell and David M. O'Brien (eds.), *Judicial Independence in the Age of Democracy: Critical Perspectives from around the World* (University Press of Virginia 2001) 12; and the French version of Art. 2 of the Universal Statute of Judge adopted by IAJ: "Le juge, en tant que dépositaire de l'autorité judiciaire, doit pouvoir exercer ses fonctions *en toute indépendance* par rapport *à toutes forces sociales, économiques et politiques*, par rapport aux autres juges et par rapport à l'administration de la justice" (emphasis added).

[198] For a similar line of criticism, see Susan Bandes, "Judging, Politics, and Accountability: A Reply to Charles Geyh" (2006) 56 *Case Western Reserve Law Review* 947

[199] Voigt, above note 53, at 96; and Contini and Mohr, above note 69, at 28.

[200] Thomas, above note 131, at 79 (emphasis added).

[201] Contini and Mohr, above note 69, at 28.

[202] For a more theoretical discussion of this tension, see, for example, Guarnieri and Pederzoli, above note 123, at 158–160 (discussing the need to balance judicial impartiality with

Finally, the last meta-goal of judicial accountability that is invoked is the general legitimacy of the courts. It is argued that accountability mechanisms may contribute to the legitimacy of courts in two general ways: (1) by examining such matters as the openness and transparency of the judicial system to ensure that they are respected; and (2) by the very process of calling the judiciary to account.[203] Put differently, the extent to which the judiciary is subject to accountability mechanisms is itself an indicator of legitimacy.[204] This meta-goal seems the most promising one despite the fact that matters such as openness and transparency are not, according to my definition of judicial accountability, measures of accountability. However, legitimacy is a complex notion that cannot be examined in detail here.[205]

It is thus more appropriate to move from these abstract and noble terms (the "meta goals") to more practical goals (the "mid-level goals"). The practical goals include: (1) enabling principals to monitor and evaluate the performance of judges and to induce them to modify that performance in accordance with the principals' preferences; (2) guarding against the abuse of power by judges and sifting out good judges from bad ones; and (3) maximizing judges' individual development.[206] The first two goals are

judicial accountability); and Elaine Mak, "The European Judicial Organisation in a New Paradigm: The Influence of Principles of 'New Public Management' on the Organisation of the European Courts" (2008) 14 *European Law Journal* 718 (discussing the tension between the rule of law principles and the new public management principles in court administration).

[203] Denis Galligan, "Principal Institutions and Mechanisms of Judicial Accountability" in Rudolf V. Van Puymbroeck (ed.), *Comprehensive Legal and Judicial Development: Towards an Agenda for a Just and Equitable Society in the 21st Century* (World Bank Publications 2001) 31. *Cf.* Mak, above note 202, at 730 and 734; Marc A. Loth, "Courts in Quest for Legitimacy: A Comparative Approach" in Marijke Malsch and Niels van Manen (eds.), *De begrijpelijkheid van de rechtspraak* (Boom Juridische Uitgevers 2007); and Paterson 2006, above note 51, at 17.

[204] Galligan, above note 203, at 31.

[205] For a discussion on legitimacy of the ordinary courts, see the previous three notes. See also James Gibson, "Judicial Institutions" in R. A. W. Rhodes and others (eds.), *The Oxford Handbook of Political Institutions* (USA, OUP 2006) 524–528; Pérez-Perdomo, above note 18, at 209–211; and Nick Huls and others, *The Legitimacy of Highest Courts' Rulings: Judicial Deliberations and Beyond* (T.M.C. Asser Press 2009) 163–172 and 192–194.

[206] In pinning these "lower level goals" down, I build on Bovens 2007, above note 24; Mark Bovens and others., "Does Public Accountability Work? An Assessment Tool" (2008) 86 *Public Administration* 225; and on Stephen Colbran, "The Limits of Judicial Accountability: The Role of Judicial Performance Evaluation" (2003) 6 *Legal Ethics* 55, 68. See also John Cunliffe and Andrew Reeve, "Dialogic Authority" (1999) 19 *Oxford Journal of Legal Studies* 453, 455; and Peter Aucoin and Ralph Heintzman, "The Dialectics of Accountability for Performance in Public Management Reform" (2000) 66 *International Review of Administrative Sciences* 45.

beneficial for society, whereas the third goal is beneficial also to judges themselves.[207]

These three goals go hand in hand with the primary focus of this chapter – that is, on individual judges. As emphasized earlier, the judiciary is not measured by its best, but by its worst member. Judges can abuse their power, judges can make mistakes, judges can be rude to the parties in dispute, and judges can be or become lazy. It simply cannot be guaranteed that judges will always act properly. It is thus important to check judges' performance. In fact, what accountability mechanisms should primarily aim for is to raise the "lowest common denominator" of performance[208] of individual judges and, eventually, purge the judiciary of those members who do not meet that standard. But these mechanisms also have a preventive function, since they can provide an early warning of potential problems in a judge's performance.[209] Last but not least, mechanisms of judicial accountability can improve the judicial independence of good judges and shield them from unsubstantiated attacks such as fabricated disciplinary charges or mala fide case overloading.

These three goals also bring to the forefront the quality of the service provided by the judiciary.[210] Accountability may improve the quality of judges' work and their professionalism in three ways.[211] First, the very fact that accountability mechanisms exist may influence judges to implement better decision-making processes and may improve their extrajudicial conduct.[212] Second, when judges' behavior or decision making and the performance of the judiciary are scrutinized by "accounting agents" a change for the better is likely. Third, scrutiny in a specific case may have consequences beyond the case itself. For instance, disciplinary motion against a judge and his or her subsequent punishment or acquittal may

---

[207] Some commentators (e.g., Colbran, above note 206, at 69) and judges (James Burrows Thomas, *Judicial Ethics in Australia* (2nd ed., LBC Information Services 1997) 43–44) even claim that there is a professional *duty* to judicial self-improvement that implies two obligations. First, a continuing duty to improve competence in areas where weakness is detected raises an obligation to participate in continuing judicial education. Second, once a judge realizes that he is incurably incompetent there is a duty to resign (see James Thomas, *Judicial Ethics in Australia* (3rd ed., Lexis Nexis 2009) 43–44).

[208] Term "performance" should be considered broadly in this sentence since it encompasses both decisional and behavioral aspects of the judicial role (see Section III.C).

[209] Pérez-Perdomo, above note 18, at 214.

[210] See Garoupa and Ginsburg 2009, above note 82, at 57; Soeharno, above note 194, at 69; and, more generally, Ng, above note 197, at 9–34.

[211] See generally Galligan, above note 203, at 31–32.

[212] Obviously, judges *must* know that their performance will be *routinely* evaluated.

send a general message to the judiciary about the kind of conduct that is considered appropriate. Similarly, complaints against judges may have broader implications and contain more general advice about how some aspects of decision-making and of administration of the judiciary should be conducted.

Finally, these three "mid-level goals" serve as a safe harbor since, even if disagreement exists with respect to whether judicial accountability ultimately serves the rule of law or a broader social responsiveness, few would contest the claims that incompetent judges should not sit on the bench, that judges should not abuse their power, and that they should educate themselves in order to keep pace with legal and societal developments. Put differently, a general theory of judicial accountability is not necessary[213] in order to agree on "mid-level principles."[214] Hence, even if the dispute on the meta-level remains unresolved,[215] it is nevertheless clear that holding judges to account is important.

V. De Jure versus De Facto Judicial Accountability

It is generally accepted that institutional engineers must acknowledge that outcomes are influenced by informal rules and norms.[216] Institutional mechanisms may function differently on paper and in practice. This banal statement has important consequences for the study of judicial accountability. Some mechanisms of judicial accountability that exist on the books may not be used at all, whereas others may have been captured by a

---

[213] A general theory of judicial accountability demands a normative theory of what judges are supposed to take into account when deciding cases, how they should behave, and to what extent judicial accountability can and should be balanced against other objectives and considerations. In fact, such theory must stipulate what the role of judges and courts is in contemporary society. However, I do not have this ambition and thus I will proceed with the mid-level goals. See also David Law, "Judicial Independence" in Bertrand Badie and others (eds.), *The International Encyclopedia of Political Science* Vol. 5 (SAGE 2011), 1369–1372 (who discusses the same problem with regard to judicial independence).

[214] Here I rely significantly on the theory of "incompletely theorized agreements" (associated with Cass Sunstein) and on the theory of "overlapping consensus" (associated with John Rawls). See Cass R. Sunstein, "Incompletely Theorized Agreements" (1995) 108 *Harvard Law Review* 1733, 1739–1740; and John Rawls, *Political Liberalism* (Columbia University Press 1993) 133–172.

[215] Such dispute is further complicated by the fact that "meta-goals" are inevitably country-specific. See Soeharno, above note 194, at 137.

[216] Mariana Prado and Michael Trebilcock, "Path Dependence, Development, and the Dynamics of Institutional Reform" (2009) 47 *University of Toronto Law Journal* 341, 367.

different principal from the one originally planned. Both phenomena may affect the delicate balance between the four principals.

The importance of the distinction between de jure and de facto judicial accountability was confirmed by previous research. For instance, Voigt observed that while de jure judicial accountability[217] does not have any economically or statistically relevant effect on economic growth, de facto judicial independence and de facto judicial accountability affect economic growth in a very robust fashion.[218] For this reason, Voigt focused primarily on de facto rather than on de jure aspects of judicial accountability. This book will deal with both de facto and de jure aspects, because the legal text (the de jure aspect) serves as a constraint for a de facto practice and because it is valuable to identify the gap between them.[219]

The examples that follow are restricted to the context of the Czech Republic and Slovakia since I know them best. The other reason I limit the discussion to the judiciaries in these two countries is the fact that addressing the gap between de jure and de facto judicial accountability requires a lot of insider information that is not at my disposal with regards to other judiciaries. However, I presume that a gap between de jure and de facto judicial accountability is not a peculiar feature of the Czech and Slovak judicial systems, but rather a common phenomenon.[220] Of course, the width of the gap varies from one country to another and over time.

[217] Voigt, above note 53. Note that Stefan Voigt made the same argument also with regards to judicial independence; see Stefan Voigt and Lars Feld, "Economic growth and judicial independence: Cross country using a new set of indicators" (2003) 19 *European Journal of Political Economy* 497; and Stefan Voigt and Lars Feld, "Making Judges Independent – Some Proposals Regarding the Judiciary" in Roger D. Congleton and Birgitta Swedenborg (eds.), *Democratic Constitutional Design and Public Policy – Analysis and Evidence* (The MIT Press 2006).

[218] Voigt, above note 53, at 103 and 118–120.

[219] For this reason, the Czech and Slovak case studies first provide a description of mechanisms of judicial accountability on the books and only then discuss how they operated in action. See Chapters 5 and 6.

[220] See, for instance, a role of the General Secretariat of the Supreme Court of Japan that to a significant extent controls the Japanese judiciary. However, the literature disagrees on who is the principal of Japanese judges: whether judges are controlled by the Liberal Democratic Party (a dominant party on the Japanese political scene) via the General Secretariat or whether they are controlled by the General Secretariat *itself*. Ramseyer claimed the former [see Ramseyer 1994, above note 78; and J. Mark Ramseyer and Eric Rasmusen, *Measuring Judicial Independence: The Political Economy of Judging in Japan* (University of Chicago Press 2003)], but other commentators persuasively argued for the latter [see David M. O'Brien and Yasuo Ohkoshi, "Stifling Judicial Independence from Within: The Japanese Judiciary" in Peter H. Russell and David M. O'Brien (eds.), *Judicial Independence in the Age of Democracy: Critical Perspectives from around the World* (University of Virginia Press 2001) and John O. Haley, "The Japanese Judiciary: Maintaining Integrity, Autonomy, and

For instance, the Czech Constitution read in conjunction with the Law on Courts and Judges stipulates that judges are to be promoted by the Minister of Justice after consultation with the president of the court to which the promoted judge is to be promoted. However, this de jure description of the promotion process is misleading since it fails to acknowledge fully the role of court presidents. In fact, the Minister of Justice rarely promotes a candidate without the prior consent of the president of the court to which the candidate will be assigned after the promotion.[221] Some scholars thus claim that court presidents are the most important players in the promotion process, which is a significant departure from de jure accountability.

Similarly, the Czech Law on Courts and Judges provided that court presidents should have been consulted by the Minister of Justice in the event of a temporary assignment to a position outside the judiciary. However, these de jure consultative powers soon turned into de facto decision-making powers since the Minister of Justice rarely made a temporary assignment without the prior consent of the president of the court whose judge asked for an assignment. In Slovakia, the de jure rules on the composition of ad hoc committees that select court presidents and on the composition of the nominating bodies[222] are unhelpful unless one can discern whom these nominating bodies actually appoint to the ad hoc committees.

Furthermore, the standards regarding many important mechanisms of judicial accountability are left de jure undefined. In such situations, de facto rules govern. For instance, both in the Czech Republic and in Slovakia it is for each court to decide how to divide judges among panels (e.g., according to their specialization) and how to assign cases among

---

the Public Trust in Law" in Daniel H. Foote (ed.), *Law in Japan: A Turning Point* (University of Washington Press 2008)]. Most recently, David Law argued that the principal–agent relationships of Japanese judges are more complex than initially thought but, in general, he supports Ramseyer's thesis (Law 2009, above note 73).

[221] Each candidate is appointed a judge and assigned to a particular court at the same time. Therefore, there is no chance of being appointed a judge unless one makes a prior arrangement with the president of the court where one wants to be assigned.

[222] By "nominating bodies" I mean people or organs who appoint or elect the members of these ad hoc committees. The ad hoc committee for selection of the president of the District Court consists of five members: two judges elected by the court over which the selected president is intended to preside, one member appointed by the Judicial Council of the Slovak Republic, one court president of a higher court and one member appointed by the Minister of Justice. Therefore, nominators include the court presidents, senior judges, the Judicial Council of the Slovak Republic, and the Minister of Justice (there is a small modification in the composition of ad hoc committees for selecting presidents of the Regional Courts).

those panels.[223] Similarly, the appointment of judges to grand chambers at the Czech Supreme Court and the Czech Supreme Administrative Court is only very vaguely set out. Therefore, it is important to look beyond the text of the procedural codes and the relevant statutes and explore who in fact exercises these powers.

This gap between de jure and de facto judicial accountability poses a significant challenge for institutional design. Obviously, de facto accountability is of greater interest. In the ideal scenario, it would be possible to go further and to study the width of the gap between de jure and de facto accountability, the dimension of accountability at which the gap is the widest, and to what extent the legal texts constrain de facto accountability.

VI.   Accountability Perversions

Finally, one more issue must be addressed in this chapter. Most authors who argue in favor of judicial accountability tend to perceive it as a positive quality and thus overlook its potential negative side effects. On the other hand, critics of judicial accountability tend to reject the idea of holding judges to account outright and thus they also fail to identify perversions of judicial accountability, albeit for a different reason. As a result, little attention has been paid to accountability perversions. These phenomena may take many forms and can be both defensive and proactive. I will mention only four of these: judicial accountability avoidance, simulating judicial accountability, output excesses of judicial accountability, and selective judicial accountability.

Judicial accountability avoidance, in short, conveys the following message: if no one knows what judges are doing, no one can hold them to account. In the United States,[224] as early as in 1820, Thomas Jefferson, in response to Chief Justice Marshall's edict that the Supreme Court issue a single opinion in his name, lamented that "secret, unanimous opinions"

---

[223] I am aware that there are constitutional limits to this discretion. However, it is still very broad.

[224] The examples from the United States that follow are taken from William Li and others, "Using Algorithmic Attribution Techniques to Determine Authorship in Unsigned Judicial Opinions" (2013) 16 *Stanford Technology Law Review* 503, 508–509. On per curiam opinions see also Ira P. Robbins, "Hiding behind the Cloak of Invisibility: The Supreme Court and Per Curiam Opinions" (2012) 86 *Tulane Law Review* 1197; Laura Krugman Ray, "The Road to Bush v. Gore: The History of The Supreme Court's Use of the Per Curiam Opinion" (2000) 79 *Nebraska Law Review* 517; and Stephen L. Wasby and others, "The Per Curiam Opinion: Its Nature and Functions" (1992) 76 *Judicature* 29.

written on behalf of the Court would undermine judicial accountability.[225] Later on, he further noted that per curiam opinions are "certainly convenient for the lazy, the modest, and the incompetent."[226] James Madison shared Jefferson's views and called for a return to seriatim opinions.[227] More recently, Justice Ginsburg admitted that "when anonymity of pronouncement is combined with security in office, it is all too easy, for the politically insulated officials to lapse into arrogant ipse dixits,"[228] and asserted that "[p]ublic accountability through the disclosure of votes and opinion authors puts the judge's conscience on the line."[229] Another prominent U.S. judge, Richard Posner, agreed, arguing that signed opinions elicit the greatest effort from judges and make "the threat of searing professional criticism an effective check on irresponsible judicial actions."[230] The issue of unsigned opinions is even more relevant in the states where judges are not appointed for life and must face retention review.[231] The stakes are simply higher. Not surprisingly, in those states judges resort to per curiam more often.[232]

In contrast to the United States, most civil law countries do not allow judges of ordinary courts to attach a separate opinion. However, that does

---

[225] James Markham, "Against Individually Signed Judicial Opinions" (2006) 56 *Duke Law Journal* 923, 930 (quoting Letter from President Thomas Jefferson to Justice William Johnson (October 27, 1820)).

[226] *See* John P. Kelsh, "The Opinion Practices of the United States Supreme Court 1790–1945" (1999) 77 *Washington University Law Quarterly* 137, 145–146 (citing Letter from Thomas Jefferson to William Johnson (October 27, 1822)).

[227] Ibid., at 145–146. On the path from seriatim opinions to an "opinion of the court" and then to a tradition of writing separately in the United States, see M. Todd Henderson, "From Seriatim to Consensus and Back Again: A Theory of Dissent" (2007) *Supreme Court Review* 283.

[228] Ruth Bader Ginsburg, "Remarks on Writing Separately" (1990) 65 *Washington. Law Review* 133, 139.

[229] Ibid.

[230] Richard A. Posner, *The Federal Courts: Challenge and Reform* (Harvard University Press 1999) 349.

[231] In 2010, nineteen states in the United States employed some form of the retention system to select judges for the state supreme courts (Canes-Wrone, Clark, and Jee-Kwang, above note 114, at 212). On retention reviews, see Chapter 2.

[232] William Li and others in their article report that during the 2006–2007 term, an astounding 57 percent of the opinions issued by the Supreme Court of Texas were unsigned per curiam opinions, and that, over a ten-year period, per curiam opinions constituted 40 percent of the opinions issued by the Supreme Court of Texas; Li and others, above note 224, at 508 (citing to "In the Shadows: A Look into the Texas Supreme Court's Overuse of Anonymous Opinions" (*Texas Watch*, May 2008) <www.texaswatch.org/ wordpress/ wp-content/uploads/2009/12/PerCuriamReportFinal.pdf> 1) [accessed August 1, 2013].

not mean that judicial accountability avoidance is less relevant there. For instance, if the data about the productivity of individual judges (e.g., the number of cases disposed of per month or per annum) are not collected, a poorly performing judge who in the long term may cause significant delays in the delivery of justice can easily escape any consequences. This accountability avoidance can be further reinforced by short statutory limits for issuing a sanction. For example, if the relevant statute allows a disciplinary motion to be initiated only within one year from the moment a judge commits a given act, a judge has only to sweep his misconduct under the carpet for a year and then he is "safe" forever.[233]

Another negative phenomenon is *simulating judicial accountability*. By this I mean the situation where judges pretend that they are held to account, but all judges involved know that they are "safe" and that they will not face any consequences. In other words, there are nominal mechanisms of judicial accountability in place, but there is no real accounting. A declawed complaints mechanism, where complaints by court users are dealt with internally and the results are not publicized, is a typical example of this phenomenon.[234] Another example is judicial performance evaluation that is almost always positive.[235]

The third negative phenomenon is *output excesses of judicial accountability*. By this I mean principals' excessive expectations regarding the number of cases disposed per month or regarding the average length of proceedings. Sometimes the principals do not even care how productive judges are, but rather about how many leftovers they have. Hence, even highly productive judges can end up in problems, if they are unlucky and sit on overburdened courts. This practice is particularly widespread in many postcommunist countries, where many judges are guilty of delaying decisions. This situation can be easily exploited by actors who initiate disciplinary proceedings, because they can use this tool selectively.[236] Excessive productivity expectations may even force judges to issue the verdicts and write the reasoning later on, which can be used as another ground for a disciplinary motion. These quantitative "output" or "productivity" measures also create counterproductive incentives for judges to

---

[233] Of course, in every established democracy such judge would be forced to resign due to peer pressure and the judgment of public opinion. However, this does not always happen in post-authoritarian and post-totalitarian countries.

[234] See the situation in the Czech Republic and Slovakia addressed especially in Chapter 8, Section IV.

[235] This example comes from Italy; see Guarnieri 2013, above note 123, at 348.

[236] See selective accountability discussed subsequently.

behave in ways that can be metered or measured, rather than in ways that promote overall fairness or justice. The most obvious output perversion is splitting a case into separate case files with the aim of artificially multiplying a judge's productivity. For instance, if a plaintiff sues for claims based on fifteen similar invoices, a judge who wants to boost his output will simply divide the case into fifteen separate case files, write a "model decision" for one invoice, "copy and paste" it fourteen times, and end up having fifteen "points" instead of one.[237]

Finally, by *selective accountability* I mean the disguising of favoritism and clientelism as performance-based rewarding and punishing. In practice, it can take many forms. A typical example is the disciplinary prosecution of "disfavored" judges for failure to meet unreasonable output standards, while leaving untouched other judges, even though they do not meet the standards either. In other words, while many judges are guilty of delaying decisions, only a few are disciplined for it. Especially in post-Soviet republics disciplinary motions on this count are very selective and are often a powerful political tool for punishment of politically inconvenient judges.[238] Conversely, disciplinary prosecutors might refrain from initiating disciplinary motion against "loyal" judges or against a friend on the bench, even if their conduct amounts to a punishable offence. Other mechanisms of judicial accountability are also susceptible to abuse. The relevant principals can rig case assignment (both initial assignment and subsequent reassignment of cases) in order to please "loyal" judges and intimidate critics or use promotion to favor their allies and deny this carrot to judges with different political views.[239] Salary bonuses and nonmonetary perks can be distributed selectively too.[240] In other words, both "sticks" and "carrots" can be used arbitrarily.

These four phenomena attest that judicial accountability is a not a mere "buzz word" for all that is positive in the judiciary. As mentioned earlier, one may use judicial accountability in the sense of virtue and reserve this term only for properly holding judges to account. Nevertheless, such analysis would require the formulation of a set of substantive standards of good judging and appropriate judicial behavior. Only then would it be

---

[237] For real life examples of this artificial multiplication, see Chapter 5, Section III.E.

[238] For examples of selective disciplinary motions in Russia, see Olga Schwartz and Elga Sykiainen, "Judicial Independence in the Russian Federation" in Anja Seibert-Fohr (ed.), *Judicial Independence in Transition* (Springer 2012) 971–1064, at 1050–1054. See also Slovak examples in Chapter 6.

[239] For examples of such practice in Slovakia, see Chapter 6.

[240] Ibid.

possible to assess whether judges complied with these standards. However, I do not believe that I can find universally acceptable standards of good judging and appropriate judicial behavior in the near future. Hence, it is more helpful to look at how mechanisms of judicial accountability actually work, discern both their positive and negative effects, and leave the defining of substantive standards of judicial accountability for later.

2

Mechanisms of Judicial Accountability

In Chapter 1 I adopted the following definition of judicial accountability: "judicial accountability is a negative or positive consequence that an individual judge expects to face from one or more principals (from the executive and/or from the legislature and/or from the court presidents and/or from other actors) in the event that his behavior and/or decisions deviate too much from a generally recognized standard." This book thus studies only those institutional mechanisms that are ex post, that may entail sanctions or rewards, and that target individual judges.

In this chapter I identify mechanisms that fall within the ambit of my definition of judicial accountability. Before I start discussing individual mechanisms of judicial accountability, I briefly explain what judges care about, because it tells a lot about which sanctions and rewards are effective. Then I divide mechanisms of judicial accountability into three groups according to their consequences. "Sticks" are mechanisms that result in sanctions. These include impeachment, disciplinary motions, complaints, retention reviews, reassignment, relocation, demotion, civil liability, and criminal liability. "Carrots" are mechanisms that bring about rewards. They may take the form of promotion to a higher court, promotion to the position of a chamber president, promotion to the Grand Chamber at top courts, secondment, temporary assignment outside the judiciary, and appointment to the position of a court president or vice president. "Dual mechanisms" are mechanisms of judicial accountability that can be used both as a stick and as a carrot. They include judicial performance evaluation, volatile salary, volatile nonmonetary benefits, and case assignment.

In order to see the contours of mechanisms of judicial accountability more clearly, I subsequently address those mechanisms that do not fall within the ambit of my definition of judicial accountability, but that either operate as the contingent circumstances of judicial accountability or can be employed in order to rig the judiciary. These mechanisms include (1) ex post mechanisms that affect court officials, entire courts, all judges, or the judiciary as a branch of government rather than individual judges;

(2) screening mechanisms; (3) transparency mechanisms; (4) appeals and quasi-appellate mechanisms; and (5) criminal mechanisms and genuinely pathological mechanisms of judicial accountability. Finally, this chapter explains the differences in holding judges to account between recognition (common law) jurisdictions and career (civil law) jurisdictions.

I.   What Do Judges Maximize?

Richard Posner provocatively argued that judges are rational, and they pursue instrumental and consumption goals of the same general kind and in the same general way that private persons do.[1] Therefore, they maximize money, leisure time, popularity and prestige.[2] This means that judges consider a salary rise, a smaller docket, promotion, or appointment to a prestigious post such as the position of a court president a reward. In contrast, a salary decrease, extra work, dismissal from office, or nonrenewal of appointment to a prestigious post is perceived as sanction. Some mechanisms provide only one of these incentives, while the other might provide a bundle of them. For instance, promotion to a higher court usually brings with it more money, higher status, lesser docket as well as better working conditions.

However, judges are also concerned about the legal quality of their opinions.[3] They like their job and want to do it well. Hence, a "joy" in doing a good job is another goal judges pursue. This insight should not be underestimated especially in civil law countries, where judges are specialists. For instance, if a judge is a competition law expert and has worked in this field for decades, he naturally sees his professional realization in deciding competition law cases. If he is suddenly transferred to a court section dealing with social security law, he will not only need more time to decide cases in this new area of law before he becomes fully acquainted with it (which means less leisure time), but he will also feel frustrated and no longer find a joy in his work. Reassignment of judges to another section is thus a powerful tool in civil law judiciaries,[4] even if it does not lead to a salary decrease,

---

[1] Richard A. Posner, "What Do Judges and Justices Maximize? (The Same Thing Everybody Else Does)" (1993) 3 *Supreme Court Economic Review* 1. See also Christopher Drahozal, "Judicial Incentives and the Appeals Process" (1998) 51 *Southern Methodist University Law Review* 469, 503.

[2] Posner, R. A. 1993, above note 1.

[3] This is in fact the mainstream view among lawyers both in civil law and common law countries. Note that while numerous studies found evidence that political attitudes influence judicial decision making in the United States, they did not rule out the possibility that judges care also about the legal quality of their opinions.

[4] In contrast, in common law world reassignment should not make much difference, because common law judges are universalists.

a higher docket, or lower prospects of promotion.[5] The other way how to reduce the "joy" of judges in doing their job is to worsen, or to refuse to improve, their working conditions. No one wants to work in a shabby office on a slow computer with limited access to Internet, with no secretarial support and no air-conditioning.

In sum, judges care about money, leisure time, popularity, prestige, and a "joy" in doing a good job. This summary draws primarily from studies on motivation of judges conducted in the United States,[6] because literature on what civil law judges maximize is minimal. But despite this drawback, the insights from common law world help us to understand which sanctions and rewards are effective in the context of the judiciary and why particular mechanisms of judicial accountability hit judges so hard.

II. What Is "In": Taxonomy of Mechanisms of Judicial Accountability

Certain mechanisms can be found in virtually any judicial system. It is difficult to imagine a judicial system where judges are never promoted and are not subject to disciplinary sanctions. Other mechanisms are country-specific. For instance, only some countries allow judges to be impeached outside "regular" disciplinary proceedings, only a few countries stipulate retention mechanisms for judges and even fewer countries permit judges' salaries to depend on their performance. Some mechanisms tend to appear only in specific legal cultures. For instance, measures such as assigning a judge outside the judiciary, promoting a judge to the position of a chamber president, or the temporary assignment of a judge to a higher court (secondment) are typical measures for civil law systems.

All in all, hardly any country employs all of the mechanisms of judicial accountability addressed in the following sections. This list thus provides a pool of mechanisms from which each country can choose. It explains why each mechanism *is* a mechanism of judicial accountability and identifies its specific features. Mechanisms entailing negative sanctions are addressed first, followed by those that reward judges and dual mechanisms that can be used both as a "stick" and as a "carrot."

---

[5] It will be shown later that arbitrary case assignment can also reduce judges' "joy" in a similar way; see Section II.C of this chapter.

[6] The literature has become too vast to cite. For three seminal works, see Lawrence Baum, *The Puzzle of Judicial Behavior* (University of Michigan Press 1997); Jeffrey A. Segal and Harold J. Spaeth, *The Supreme Court and the Attitudinal Model Revisited* (Cambridge University Press 2002); and Richard A. Posner, *How Judges Think* (Harvard University Press 2008).

At this stage it is also important to emphasize that all mechanisms of judicial accountability can be used in good faith, but also disingenuously.[7] Sticks are particularly prone to abuse. Typical examples include politically motivated disciplinary motions, punishing judges by relocation to rural areas for holding against the government too often, and prosecuting judges on fabricated charges. However, "carrots" and dual mechanisms are also susceptible to misuse. Principals can buy judges through salary bonuses or subsidized housing, deny their promotion for having a too high acquittal rate, or punish disloyal judges by an increased case load. In other words, they may punish judges who go astray and reward judges who are loyal to their cause, irrespective of the merit. This insight should be borne in mind when reading the taxonomy of mechanisms of judicial mechanisms that follows.

A.   Sticks

Impeachment is a typical mechanism of judicial accountability. The impeachment process is set in motion when a judge breaks a generally agreed upon standard. Even though, in theory, a judge can be impeached on the basis of his decisions, most impeachments in developed countries are based on allegations of legal or ethical misconduct, not on judicial performance. Put differently, judges usually face impeachment for their off-the-bench behavior. A successful impeachment process usually results in the judge being removed.[8]

The process itself varies from country to country, but the legislature generally plays the most important role. In the United States, the initiative rests with the House of Representatives and the Senate, presided over by the Chief Justice of the Supreme Court, decides.[9] In Canada, judges of the superior courts are removable by the Governor General on Address of the Senate and House of Commons.[10] A similar procedure is laid down in India.[11] In Germany, it is the Federal Constitutional Court that decides, upon application of the Bundestag, on the impeachment of federal judges.[12]

---

[7] For specific examples of both categories in the Czech Republic and Slovakia, see Chapters 5 and 6. See also examples from other countries in Chapter 1.

[8] But see Article 98(2) of Basic Law (Germany) that stipulates that the Federal Constitutional Court may order either that the judge be transferred or retired *or*, in the case of an intentional infringement, it may dismiss him.

[9] Art. II Section 4 of the United States Constitution.

[10] Art. 99(1) of Constitution Act 1867 (Canada).

[11] Art. 124(2) of Indian Constitution.

[12] Art. 98(2) of Basic Law (Germany).

For the purposes of this book, the term "impeachment" includes also "quasi-impeachment" procedures such as that in force in Ireland, where a joint resolution of both houses of the Parliament (*Oireachtas*) may remove a judge.[13] Although this Irish procedure does not technically involve impeachment, it operates in a similar fashion.

Disciplinary motion is another widely accepted mechanism of judicial accountability. Like impeachment, disciplinary motions are used to hold judges to account more often for their legal or ethical misconduct rather than for their judicial performance. Initiating disciplinary motions for "bad decision-making," that is for the substance of a decision, is rare and limited to cases of extreme incompetence. However, disciplinary motions are relatively often initiated against judges who repeatedly fail to meet the required quota of judgments and, consequently, cause unreasonable delays in the delivery of justice. Hence, decisional accountability cannot be entirely discarded, when it comes to disciplinary offenses.

As to behavioral accountability, judges are held to account both for their actions in their official capacity and for offenses committed in their personal capacity. The standard is usually defined vaguely, either positively as "good behavior" or negatively as "anything that infringes the dignity of the judicial office or undermines confidence in independent, impartial, professional and just decision-making." The process itself is extremely diverse, both with regard to the bodies that have the power to initiate disciplinary motions and with regard to the decision-making body.[14] The list of disciplinary punishments that can be imposed is also very long. It includes, among other things, reprimands, salary reductions, removal from the position of a chamber president, suspension of a judge, relocation, demotion, forced retirement, and dismissal from judicial office.

Complaints against individual judges can give affected parties the opportunity to complain about the behavior of a judge, while on or off the bench. The body that typically decides on these complaints ranges from the ombudsman[15] to the Ministry of Justice.[16] Occasionally, the agencies that receive complaints have the competence to impose minor sanctions on misbehaving judges. But even if the complaint agency cannot impose

---

[13] Art. 35(4) of Constitution of Ireland.

[14] For an overview of disciplining judges in six European countries, see Giuseppe Di Federico (ed.) *Recruitment, Professional Evaluation and Career of Judges and Prosecutors in Europe* (IRSIG-CNR 2005).

[15] For instance, the "Judges Ombudsman's Office" started to operate in Israel in 2003 (see the Ombudsman for Complaints against Judges Law, 2002).

[16] This complaint system is in force in the Czech Republic.

legal sanctions, the result of a successful complaint is an informal sanction such as disapproval or loss of prestige. This sanction is even stronger when decisions of the complaint agencies are published.

A complaint mechanism differs from other accountability mechanisms, because it provides a "fire-alarm" rather than "police-patrol" oversight.[17] In the former, principals actively seek evidence of misbehavior by agencies: principals look for trouble as a method of control much as does a prowling patrol car. In the latter, principals wait for signs that agencies are improperly executing policy: they use complaints from concerned groups to trigger concern that an agency is misbehaving.[18] By creating a complaint mechanism against judges, politicians decentralize the monitoring function to their constituents, who can lodge complaints to inform them of misconduct of judges and other failures within the judiciary. Fire-alarm oversight has several characteristics that are valuable to principals. Most importantly, it is less costly and time-consuming than a comprehensive police-patrol oversight and, if designed properly, brings about targeted sanctions and rewards.[19] This is particularly important in civil law judiciaries that consist of thousands of judges, because the costs of a comprehensive police-patrol oversight become excessive in such an environment. For instance, if the Ministry of Justice wants to actively search for and punish disciplinary misconduct and send its representatives to sit at court hearings or screen the case files, it will be very expensive and highly likely to be also inefficient.

Retention reviews refer to a periodic process the aim of which is to decide whether a judge should stay in office. Not being retained is the ultimate sanction – because it has the same effect as dismissal. Retention review mechanisms take various forms, of which reappointment and reelection are the most common, but other techniques are available as well. Usually, the process of retention review replicates the mode of initial selection. A typical example of retention review is a judicial retention election[20] in

---

[17] See Matthew D. McCubbins and Thomas Schwartz, "Congressional Oversight Overlooked: Police Patrols Versus Fire Alarms" (1984) 28 *American Journal of Political Science* 165.

[18] Matthew D. McCubbins, Roger G. Noll, and Barry R. Weingast, "Political Control of the Bureaucracy" in P. Newman (ed.) *The New Palgrave Dictionary of Law and Economics* (Palgrave Macmillan 1998) 50, 53.

[19] For other advantages of fire-alarm oversight, see McCubbins, Noll, and Weingast 1998, above note 18, at 53–54; Joel D. Aberbach, *Keeping a Watchful Eye: The Politics of Congressional Oversight* (The Brookings Institution Press 1990); or Morris S. Ogul and Bert A. Rockman, "Overseeing Oversight: New Departures and Old Problems" (1990) 15 *Legislative Studies Quarterly* 5.

[20] This procedure is sometimes also referred to as retention referendum.

the state court systems in many U.S. states, where judges are periodically subject to a referendum held at the same time as a general election.[21] In 2010, nineteen states in the United States employed some form of the retention system to select judges for the state supreme courts.[22] A similar structure was established in Japan, where every ten years the judges of the Supreme Court are subject to retention election by the people.[23] Yet another retention scheme applies to lower court judges in Japan as they face reappointment every ten years, which is effectively controlled by the Supreme Court judges.[24] In Europe, communist regimes adopted periodic retention review mechanisms that ran the gamut from retention referenda via reelection to reappointment. Most postcommunist regimes in the CEE abandoned these techniques due to their misuse during the communist era, but many post-Soviet republics decided to keep them.[25]

Apart from periodic retention review mechanisms, there are also "one-and-for-all" retention reviews that cannot be repeated. They usually take place at the beginning or at the end of judge's tenure. The so-called

[21] A judicial retention vote differs from a regular election in that voters are not asked to choose from a list of candidates. In other words, the judges on the ballot paper do not have opponents. Rather, the voters choose whether or not to elect the incumbent judge for another term in office. A judge is deemed to have been retained if ballots cast in favor of retention outnumber those against.

[22] More specifically, fifteen out of these nineteen states employed the so-called Missouri Plan (Alaska, Arizona, Colorado, Florida, Indiana, Iowa, Kansas, Maryland, Missouri, Nebraska, Oklahoma, South Dakota, Tennessee, Utah, and Wyoming) and four additional states (California, Illinois, New Mexico, and Pennsylvania) utilized retention elections but employed other means for initial selection or multiple methods for reselection; Brandice Canes-Wrone, Tom S. Clark, and Jee-Kwang Park, "Judicial Independence and Retention Elections" (2012) 28 *Journal of Law, Economics, & Organization* 211, 212.

[23] See Art. 79 para. 2 of the Constitution of Japan (Kenpo) ("The appointment of the judges of the Supreme Court shall be reviewed by the people at the first general election of members of the House of Representatives following their appointment, and shall be reviewed again at the first general election of members of the House of Representatives after a lapse of ten years, and in the same manner thereafter."). But note that according to Ramseyer and Rosenbluth the retention elections have in practice been marginal; see J. Mark Ramseyer and Frances McCall Rosenbluth, *Japan's Political Marketplace* (rev. ed., Harvard University Press 1997), 152–153.

[24] See Art. 80 para. 1 of the Constitution of Japan (Kenpo) ("The judges of the inferior courts shall be appointed by the Cabinet from a list of persons nominated by the Supreme Court. All such judges shall hold office for a term of ten (10) years with privilege of reappointment, provided that they shall be retired upon the attainment of the age as fixed by law.") On the deleterious effect of this type of retention review on the Japanese judiciary, see Section IV of this chapter.

[25] Moldova (see ECtHR, July 11, 2006, *Gurov v. Moldova*, no. 36455/02), Azerbaijan (see ECtHR, April 22, 2010, *Fatullayev v. Azerbaijan*, no. 40984/07), and Georgia (see Art. 86(2) of the Georgian Constitution) belong to this category.

judges on probation (*Richter auf Probe*) in Germany who face a retention review only once in their career (after the first three to five years on the bench) are an example of the former,[26] whereas retention review in the Czech Republic of judges who have reached the age of 65 years[27] represents the latter.[28]

Reassignment to a different panel is available only at large courts that are divided into smaller units. At courts such as the U.S. Supreme Court reassignment within the same court is impossible. Another important factor is whether judges in a given country are generalists or specialists. For a generalist, reassignment to another panel triggers fewer changes than for a specialist who, if assigned to a panel dealing with other area of law, has to exercise a lot of effort to become an expert in the new area of law. Note that if judges are specialized, even individual judges can be affected by reassignment, because they can be reassigned, for instance, from a corporate law to a family law specialization.

Specialization and assigning a judge to a specific panel of the court is a typical feature of civil law courts, where even top courts consist of dozens of judges.[29] Once assigned to a particular panel, a judge may either stay on the panel indefinitely or be transferred to another panel after some time. Such reshuffling of the panels, or changing the type of cases individual judges hear, is not necessarily wrong. It can be argued that it is healthy for every judge to change environment from time to time and be exposed to ideas from new colleagues. It prevents long-serving judges from "burning out." This again applies in particular to civil law judiciaries

[26] See Art. 12 *Deutsches Richtergesetz.*; and Anja Seibert-Fohr, "Judicial Independence in Germany" in Anja Seibert-Fohr (ed.), *Judicial Independence in Transition* (Springer 2012) 447–519, at 472–472. Similar systems of "judges on probation" exist in Estonia (Timo Ligi, "Judicial Independence in Estonia", in ibid., at 762–763), Moldova (Nadejda Hriptievschi and Sorin Hanganu, "Judicial Independence in Moldova", in ibid., 1119–1196, at 1143) and fifteen other European countries (see the 2012 CEPEJ Report, 274–275). However, Slovakia abolished the four-year probation period of judges in 2001 (see Chapter 6). Russia followed in 2009 (Olga Schwartz and Elga Sykiainen, "Judicial Independence in the Russian Federation", in ibid., 971–1064, at 1004–1005) and in Poland the system of "judges on probation" was struck down by the Constitutional Court (see Adam Bodnar and Lukasz Bojarski, "Judicial Independence in Poland", in ibid., 667–738, at 695–699).

[27] The Czech Law on Courts and Judges of 1991 set maximum retirement age of seventy years that could not be extended under any circumstances. In addition to this maximum retirement age it also granted discretion to the Minister of Justice to decide whether a judge could retain his judicial office when he reached the age of sixty-five years.

[28] See Art. 46(1)(b) of the Czech Law on Courts and Judges of 1991. Note that this act was replaced by the Czech Law on Courts and Judges of 2002, which does not include a similar provision.

[29] For instance, the French *Cour de Cassation* consists of 80–90 judges.

run according to the career model, in which judges often join the judiciary in their mid-twenties.

However, reassignment can also be misused to intimidate "recalcitrant" judges. For instance, when a judge is known for his knowledge of competition law, he will most likely be assigned to the panel that deals primarily[30] with disputes involving competition law. If this judge is without his consent reassigned to a panel that specializes in cases on social security law and if he is not given sufficient time to study this new area of law, he will inevitably work more slowly and be less productive.[31] As a result, it is significantly more likely that he will face a disciplinary motion for causing delays in delivering justice. In conclusion, when reassignment is done *ex post*, it operates as a mechanism of judicial accountability because it is yet another way of sanctioning judges.[32] In contrast, when reassignment is determined *ex ante*, for example that judges of a given court will be randomly reassigned every three years, it cannot be used as a stick and thus does not count as a mechanism of judicial accountability.

Relocation from one court to another court of the same level is a more severe stick than reassignment within the same court, because a relocated judge must either commute or move to the seat of his new court. A change of this nature also increases a judge's expenditures. The use of this measure is usually tolerated only temporarily and for good cause, for instance because of a shortage of judges or because of a reorganization of the judiciary. Several countries have (mis)used this mechanism. Communist regimes often employed this measure to intimidate recalcitrant judges.[33] But they are not alone. For instance, a mass transfer of judges occurred during the "Emergency" period in India, leading to a judicial challenge to the transfers that succeeded on the grounds that the president had not consulted the Chief Justice before making these transfers.[34] Relocation to undesirable locations

---

[30] Even the specialized panels in the civil law systems often have some kind of "common agenda" that is shared across all panels.

[31] I leave aside negative repercussions on the court as a whole and on litigants. For instance, reassignment of a competent judge may cause delays in his "new" panel (because he is slow and incompetent in the new area of law) as well as in his "original" panel (which loses a competent judge).

[32] In theory, reassignment can be used both to reward and to punish judges. However, in practice the former rarely happens since reassignment to the desired panel (i.e., to desired specialization) is usually done *with the consent* of the reassigned judge.

[33] See, for example, Jaroslav Vorel, Alena Šimáková a kol. *Československá justice v letech 1948–1953 v dokumentech. Díl I.* (Praha, Úřad dokumentace a vyšetřování zločinů komunismu 2003) 174–175 (discussing relocation and other techniques used by the Communist Party of Czechoslovakia in the 1950s).

[34] See M. P. Singh, "Securing the Independence of the Judiciary: The Indian Experience" (2000) 10 *Indiana International and Comparative Law Review* 245, 267.

has been reported even in Japan, where it is used against judges who rule against the national government on sensitive issues.[35]

Demotion is even harsher than relocation to another court of the same level. It not only involves commuting or moving to another city, but also causes other negative consequences. Demotion may trigger a significant salary or pension cut, reduce the prestige, or go along with a higher case load at the lower court. If any principal has the power to decide on the demotion of a professional judge without providing any reasons, demotion becomes a pathological mechanism of judicial accountability that is incompatible with the modern understanding of the role of courts. However, some democratic states stipulate demotion as a possible result of impeachment[36] or disciplinary proceedings.[37]

Civil liability entails potential responsibility for the payment of damages to the aggrieved party. If a judge has to pay damages for making an incorrect decision, he is held to account since he is punished for his failures in decision making. Judges may be liable in damages not only for errors contained in a judgment, but also for defamatory utterances made in court or for defamatory statements contained in a judgment.[38] This form of accounting for the content of a decision has become rather rare.[39] However, judges may also incur civil liability for undue delays in delivering their decisions. For instance, Article 6(1) of the European Convention of Human Rights guarantees, among other things, the right to a fair trial within a reasonable time[40] and the European Court of Human Rights regularly awards damages for violations of this provision. Finally, the individual civil liability of a judge must be distinguished from state liability. The latter does not involve individual accounting and, hence, does not count as a mechanism of judicial accountability.

Criminal liability that is specific to judicial office is a particularly crude mechanism of judicial accountability, which is rarely applied. Judges are,

---

[35] See J. Mark Ramseyer and Eric Rasmusen, *Measuring Judicial Independence: The Political Economy of Judging in Japan* (University of Chicago Press 2003), 41–47; David Law, "The Anatomy of a Conservative Court: Judicial Review in Japan" (2009) 87 *Texas Law Review* 1545, 1560–1562; and David Law, "How to Rig the Federal Courts" (2011) 99 *Georgetown Law Journal* 779, 799. See also Section IV of this chapter.

[36] See, for example, Art. 98(2) of Basic Law (Germany).

[37] See, for example, Art. 45 of Law on Magistrates (France).

[38] See Report on Civil Liability of Judges, International Association of Judges (IAJ-UIM), Study Commission II, 2003.

[39] See, for example, ECtHR, *Kobenter and Standard Verlags Gmbh v. Austria*, November 2, 2006, no. 60899/00.

[40] In fact, this is the most often invoked provision before the ECtHR.

of course, subject to the same criminal liability as other citizens. No one wants judges who beat their wives, take part in robberies, take bribes,[41] or engage in brutal sadomasochistic practices.[42] However, criminal liability in the context of judicial accountability concerns criminal offenses that apply specifically to judges for their behavior on the bench and, theoretically, also for their decisions.

B. Carrots

So far, only the mechanisms entailing negative sanctions have been addressed. However, not only "sticks," but also "carrots," may serve as an incentive for judges.[43] *Promotion* is perhaps "the carrot of carrots," especially within the career judiciaries, where judges enter the judiciary at a relatively young age and from then on they try to climb the ladder as high and as fast as possible. As Adolf Leonhardt, the Minister of Justice of the German Empire and a major architect of the 1877 *Gerichtsverfassungsgesetz* (Constitutional Law on Courts), famously stated: "I have nothing against the independence of judges, as long as I promote them."[44] The landscape in Germany has changed a lot, but several commentators observed that the denial of promotion is a real threat to judges since it deprives them of the social status and economic benefits that go along with promotion.[45] Moreover, promotion to a higher court often translates into a lower caseload or even a control over the docket via leave to appeal mechanisms, a highly appreciated asset within the judiciary. Conversely, denial of promotion is equivalent to punishment.[46] Judges are arguably promoted because of their knowledge of the law, but other factors come into play too. Hence,

---

[41] All of these examples (and many more) can be found in James Thomas, *Judicial Ethics in Australia* (3rd ed., Reed International Books 2009).

[42] See ECtHR, *K.A. and A.D. v. Belgium*, February 17, 2005, nos. 42758/98 and 45558/99.

[43] On how carrots and sticks work in general, see Ian Ayres, *Carrots and Sticks: Unlock the Power of Incentives to Get Things Done* (Bantam 2010).

[44] Cited from Neil Chisholm, "The Faces of Judicial Independence: Democratic versus Bureaucratic Accountability in Judicial Selection, Training, and Promotion in South Korea and Taiwan", 62 *American Journal of Comparative Law* 893, 893.

[45] Martina Künnecke, "The Accountability and Independence of Judges: German Perspectives" in Guy Canivet, Mads Andenas, and Duncan Fairgrieve (eds.), *Independence, Accountability, and the Judiciary* (British Institute of International and Comparative Law 2006) 217, 226. A personal account of a maverick judge in Berlin, Rüdiger Warnstädt, confirms this view; see Stephen Ross Levitt, "The Life and Times of a Local Court Judge in Berlin" (2009) 10 *German Law Journal* 169, 197–198. Denial of promotion is a real threat also in France; see Chapter 1, Section III.B.

[46] See, for example, ECtHR, August 2, 2001, *N. F. v. Italy*, no. 37119/97, § 13.

decisional accountability plays a dominant role. The only way of avoiding a potential abuse of promotions, that is, limiting the discretion of the promoting body, is to prohibit promotions altogether, decide on promotions by flipping a coin, or to adopt a system that relies on ex ante criteria such as seniority. However, all of these solutions are problematic.[47]

Apart from being promoted to a higher court, judges can be promoted to other positions. This chapter will refer to the following five mechanisms as "quasi-promotion mechanisms" in order to distinguish them from promotion to a higher court. For instance, judges can be *promoted to the position of a chamber president* within the same court or, in the case of top courts, *selected to sit in the Grand Chamber*. How do these mechanisms operate in practice? For instance, in the Czech Republic a promotion to the position of chamber president is considered as advancement in one's judicial career.[48] It increases a judge's prestige, as chamber presidents can preside over trials heard by a panel of judges, as well as his salary.[49] The Grand Chamber is a necessary evil that results from the fact that top courts in civil law countries consist of dozens of judges. Large courts cannot decide cases in plenary session[50] and, hence, these courts create Grand Chambers that usually convene when the case law of various panels starts to diverge. The procedure for selecting judges to the Grand Chamber and the number of those judges vary from one country to another, but all countries have something in common – the judges that sit on the Grand Chamber have significant influence over the development of the law. This is the reason that position is prestigious and why it matters who chooses those judges.

Promotion to the position of a chamber president and to the Grand Chamber exists in most civil law countries. There are two main differences between these two mechanisms. First, promotion to the position of chamber president is usually accompanied by both prestige and a salary increase, whereas serving on the Grand Chamber is only a matter of

---

[47] The first solution is incompatible with the career model of the judiciary; the second is difficult to justify both normatively and on the grounds of efficiency; and the third is highly problematic as it leads to corporativism.

[48] The fact that many judges in civil law countries emphasize the title "chamber president" in their CVs and some of them even require others to address them as "Mr. chamber president" or "Mrs. chamber president" attests to the importance of this career advancement.

[49] For instance, this salary increase amounts to approximately 10% in the Czech Republic (it varies according to the number of years in practice of a given judges and the level of the court he sits at).

[50] One can hardly imagine how eighty or even more judges (which is a standard number of judges at top civil law courts; see above note 29) could produce a unanimous decision (note that most civil law countries do not allow *ordinary* judges to cast a separate opinion).

prestige. Second, promotion to the position of a chamber president is once and for all and judges can be stripped of this position only by a disciplinary panel. In contrast, judges entitled to sit on the Grand Chamber are usually selected for a fixed renewable term.

Secondment, a temporary assignment to a higher court, is another example of a "carrot" since this "temporary promotion" not only increases the chances of a seconded judge being promoted indefinitely, but also comes with a higher salary during the period of secondment.[51] Judges in civil law countries can also ask for a *temporary assignment outside the judiciary*,[52] for instance to the Ministry of Justice or to another position in the civil service.[53] Why do some judges long for these assignments? Their motivation differs. Some judges want to embark on political career,[54] some want to leave their imprint on the law,[55] some want to increase their chances of being promoted,[56] and others simply need a break from their routine. Note also that temporary assignment outside the judiciary means that the assigned judge remains a judge and can return to the judiciary after the end of his assignment.[57]

Temporary assignments outside the judiciary raise difficult questions of separation of powers[58] and may impinge upon the right to a fair trial.[59] That

---

[51] There is a growing case law of the European Court of Human Rights on problematic aspects of secondment of judges: see, for example, ECtHR, *Iwańczuk v. Poland* (dec.) no. 39279/05, November 17, 2009; and ECtHR, *Richert v. Poland*, October 25, 2011, no. 54809/07, § 44–57.

[52] By temporary assignment outside the judiciary I mean only a voluntary assignment. Forced assignments, even if "only" temporary, are a pathological mechanism. Hence, this mechanism of judicial accountability always operates as a carrot.

[53] This practice is very common, for instance, in France and Spain.

[54] A famous Spanish investigative judge, Baltasar Garzón, is a typical example of this group. See also discussion on "superjudges" in Chapters 5 and 6.

[55] For instance, by drafting a new code under the auspices of the Ministry of Justice.

[56] In the Czech Republic and Slovakia, temporary assignment to the Ministry of Justice increased the chances of promotion by the very fact that an assigned judge was "singled-out" from hundreds of other judges of the same rank. In the case of Japan, temporary assignment to the Ministry of Justice as a prosecutor (*hanken koryu*) is also a promising career sign.

[57] In fact, it is the return to judicial ranks and not the initial assignment outside the judiciary that is the most dangerous feature of this mechanism. It will be shown in Chapters 5 and 6 that this "travelling among branches" can create "super-judges" who retain links to the Ministry of Justice even after their return to the judicial ranks, and thus may easily intimidate other judges.

[58] The Czech Constitutional Court twice struck down the provision allowing temporary assignment outside the judiciary for a violation of the principle of separation of powers. See Judgment No. Pl. ÚS 7/02; and Judgment No. Pl. ÚS 39/08, §§ 46–49.

[59] See, for example, ECtHR, *Sacilor-Lormines v. France*. no. 65411/01, September 11, 2006 (where the ECtHR dealt with a situation where the French Council of State found against the applicant (in the case between the applicant and the Ministry for Economic Affairs,

is why certain countries stipulate a special "freezing period" during which a judge who returns to the judiciary from an elected or appointed position outside the judiciary cannot take part in deciding cases.[60] However, for the purposes of this chapter it suffices to say that temporary assignments outside the judiciary can help a judge in his career and hence operates as a mechanism of judicial accountability.

These four types of quasi-promotion should not be underestimated. While they arguably provide lesser incentives than a permanent promotion to a higher court, they have several "advantages." First, apart from secondment, they can all be used to reward judges of top courts who cannot be promoted any further.[61] Second, with the exception of promotion to the position of a chamber president, they can all be employed repeatedly. In contrast, a promotion to a higher court is irreversible under normal circumstances.[62] This means that once the principal promotes a judge to a higher court, he loses all his leverage, but when he applies quasi-promotion mechanisms, he retains his influence.

A very specific type of promotion is *appointment to the position of a court president or vice president*.[63] It is often accompanied by significant monetary and nonmonetary benefits. Especially in civil law countries, these benefits include a significant salary rise[64] and broad administrative powers.[65] In all judicial systems, becoming the court president is also a matter of prestige, in particular at top courts. Criteria for selecting court presidents are often opaque[66] and usually consist of a mix of legal craftsmanship, exemplary behavior, and managerial skills. Hence,

---

Finance and Industry) and where only seven days after the delivery of that judgment, one of the members of the French Council of State panel was appointed to the post of Secretary General at the very same ministry.

[60] See, for example, John Bell, *Judiciaries within Europe: A Comparative Review* (CUP 2006) 204 (discussing a three-year "freezing period" in Spanish context).

[61] But this is no longer true in Europe. A judge of a top *ordinary* court can still long to become a Justice of the Constitutional Court, a judge of the ECtHR, a judge or an Advocate General of the Court of Justice, a judge of the General Court (former Court of First Instance), or a judge of the Civil Service Tribunal.

[62] Exceptionally, judges can be demoted to a lower court by decision of a disciplinary tribunal or an impeachment court. See above notes 36–37.

[63] For a more detailed discussion of the role of the court officials, see Section III.A.

[64] This increase can be as high as 30% in the Czech Republic (it depends on the number of years of practice and on the court level).

[65] Powers of the court officials are addressed in Section III.A.

[66] Not surprisingly, there is no comparative study on the powers of court presidents. For a rare attempt, limited to the Chief Justices, see Clifford Wallace, "Comparative Perspectives on the Office of Chief Justice" (2005) 38 *Cornell International Law Journal* 219.

both decisional and behavioral accountability are considered. Moreover, politics plays a far more significant role in selecting court officials than in other types of promotion. It is worthy of mention that, like other mechanisms, "accounting" can be avoided in selecting court officials. For instance, court officials can be selected on the basis of seniority, all judges of a given court can rotate[67] and hold this position for a short period of time, or court officials can be selected from all judges at a given court by a lot. However, these modalities come with a heavy price and thus they are rarely employed.

C. Dual Mechanisms

The third group of mechanisms of judicial accountability is comprised of mechanisms that operate as "double-edged swords" because they may result in both positive and negative consequences. Four mechanisms that fall into this category are performance evaluations, volatile salaries, volatile nonmonetary benefits, and nonrandom case assignment.

Judicial performance evaluations have become increasingly popular in Western democracies. Their popularity results from increasing pressure to apply "new public management" to the court administration.[68] Judicial performance evaluation is ex post in nature since it assesses retrospectively how a judge has performed his tasks.[69] The role of judicial performance evaluations can be reinforced if they are coupled with formal sanctions, but even if they are not they still count as a mechanism of judicial accountability since any formal assessment has reputational effects. Hence, an accounting element is inevitably present. As suggested earlier, individual judicial performance evaluation is a "double-edged sword" since it pinpoints the best judges as well as the worst. Sanctions can be either negative (such as compulsory additional training, suspension of promotion, or/ and loss of prestige) or positive (such as higher chances of promotion or reputational gain) or both. Finally, one must distinguish between performance evaluation of individual judges and entire courts. Only the former

---

[67] This system operates on the state level in several U.S. States.

[68] On the rise of "new public management" in court administration in Europe, see Elaine Mak, "The European Judicial Organisation in a New Paradigm: The Influence of Principles of 'New Public Management' on the Organisation of the European Courts" (2008) 14 *European Law Journal* 718; or Gar Yein Ng, *Quality of Judicial Organisation and Checks and Balances* (Intersentia 2007).

[69] Even if criteria for evaluation are stipulated in advance they can never be defined at such a level of precision that they can avoid discretion in their eventual application.

falls within my definition of judicial accountability, since the latter does not involve individualized accounting.

From the modern new-public-management evaluation of judges, which is primarily skills-based,[70] it is important to distinguish the Soviet-era version of evaluation that was based on quantitative indicators of performance, especially the infamous rate of reversal (stability of sentences), which encourages judges to conform to the desires of their superiors (inter alia by avoiding acquittals).[71] In the Soviet evaluation system the high reversal rate may negatively affect a judge's prospects of promotion or even lead to a reduction in his salary.[72] This requires from a lower court judge to look over his shoulder and avoid decisions that might be overturned. While the civil law tradition arguably emphasizes consistency over originality, the Soviet-style evaluation system interferes with independence of individual judges far more than the new-public-management system. For this reason, the use of reversal rates disappeared from the evaluation of judges in most European countries decades ago, to be replaced by a skills-based approach.[73] However, the Soviet system must be mentioned here, because some postcommunist countries in the CEE retained some of its features.

A *volatile salary* is another mechanism that allows for both punishing and rewarding judges. "Bad judges" suffer from lower remuneration and "good judges" benefit from a higher salary. Salaries can be volatile in both directions or just in one direction. For instance, if a judge's salary or part of it depends on individual productivity, it can be both increased and decreased.[74] In theory, one can also imagine a system that punishes "bad

---

[70] See Peter H. Solomon, "The Accountability of Judges in Post Communist States: From Bureaucratic to Professional Accountability" in Anja Seibert-Fohr (ed.), *Judicial Independence in Transition* (Springer 2012) 909–935, 915–922. However, even the new public management evaluation may collide with the rule of law principles; see Elaine Mak, "The European Judicial Organisation in a New Paradigm: The Influence of Principles of 'New Public Management' on the Organisation of the European Courts" (2008) 14 *European Law Journal* 718.

[71] See Solomon 2012, above note 70, 911–913; Olga Schwartz and Elga Sykiainen, "Judicial Independence in the Russian Federation" in Anja Seibert-Fohr (ed.), *Judicial Independence in Transition* (Springer 2012) 971–1064, at 1003, 1008–1009, 1012, 1030–1033, and 1254–1255; Maria Popova, *Politicized Justice in Emerging Democracies: A Study of Courts in Russia and Ukraine* (CUP 2012), 134–139.

[72] The latter is a common practice in China; see Peter H. Solomon, "Authoritarian Legality and Informal Practices: Judges, Lawyers and the State in Russia and China" (2010) 43 *Communist and Post-Communist Studies* 351, 357.

[73] See Solomon 2012, above note 70, 915–922.

[74] Such system was implemented in Spain, but it was eventually abolished by the Spanish Supreme Court; see STS, 3ª, March 7, 2006 (Rec. 2004\30; MP: Margarita Robles Fernández

judges" but does not reward "good judges." However, reducing the salaries of individual judges (outside the disciplinary proceedings) is a sensitive issue and systems that reward "good judges" with bonuses are more
common. The French *prime modulable* (flexible bonus), which is designed
to take better consideration of the individual merit of each judge and his
contribution to the good performance of the judiciary, is a good example
of such system. This bonus is based on monthly gross salary and ranges
from 5% to 9 % depending on the judge's position and evaluation of the
performance of his duties.[75] Such a system was also in place in Slovakia.[76]
According to the recent study on European judicial systems, salary
bonuses are available in five countries (Albania, Malta, Montenegro, San
Marino, and Turkey) and bonuses for specific important responsibilities
can be awarded in the other five (Cyprus, Denmark, France, Hungary, and
Turkey).[77]

The related issue is what part of a judge's salary is volatile. In theory, the
whole of a judge's salary can be volatile, but today it is very difficult to find
a judicial system in which that is so.[78] If volatile salaries are stipulated at
all, the volatility applies only to a small part of the judge's salary.[79] Finally,
one must also take into account criteria used to change a judge's salary.
Volatile parts of judicial salaries can be based on individual productivity or tied to complex judicial performance criteria, which can be either
formal or informal. Nevertheless, judicial performance cannot be easily
converted into numbers, and thus any criteria, even if they are announced
ex ante, leave significant discretion to the body that decides on volatile

---

(Supreme Court of Spain). See also Francesco Contini and Richard Mohr, "Reconciling
Independence and Accountability in Judicial Systems" (2007) 3 *Utrecht Law Review* 34–35.

[75] For further details, see Antoine Garapon and Harold Epineuse, "Judicial Independence
in France" in Anja Seibert-Fohr (ed.), *Judicial Independence in Transition* (Springer 2012)
273–305, at 287.

[76] For further details, see Chapter 6.

[77] The 2012 CEPEJ Report, 272.

[78] Justices of the Peace (*Giudice di Pace*), who decide, among other things, on detention
of asylum seekers in Italy, serve as a rare current example. They do not have an employment relationship with the State and are paid a benefit in relation to the work effectively
carried out (i.e., hearings held and measures taken). As of 2014, for every validation of
detention they received 10 euro and for every hearing 20 euro (see Alessia Di Pascale
and Pier Luigi di Bari, "Completed Questionnaire for the Project Contention National
Report – Italy" (2014), available at http://contention.eu/docs/country-reports/ItalyFinal
.pdf, at pp. 5–6). Justices of the Peace in the United States may serve as a historical example. These judges were paid by litigants for issuing writs and did not have a fixed salary
from the state.

[79] The Spanish system referred to in note 74 operated in this fashion.

parts of judicial salary.[80] Finally, some countries may use salary bonuses to persuade judges to work in remote parts of the country. For instance, in order to encourage mobility overseas, the salaries of judges appointed to France's overseas departments and territories are substantially increased with a rise ranging from 40% for the islands of Guadeloupe and Martinique to 105% for the islands of Wallis and Futuna.[81]

Volatile nonmonetary benefits are less visible and less quantifiable than judge's salary, but they operate in a similar manner. These benefits span from air-conditioning and other working conditions to subsidized housing and vacation packages.[82] It is a common sense that a slow computer, a slow Internet connection, or the lack of secretarial support can significantly impinge upon a judge's work and eventually affect his performance. No or dispersed vacation time and poor or remote housing may have the same effect. To be sure, distribution of nonmonetary benefits among individual judges depends on the allocation of resources among courts and on the budget of the entire judiciary. However, the distribution of resources within each court can be used to reward or punish judges, because statutes rarely stipulate in detail how nonmonetary benefits allocated to each court should be distributed. This is usually the task of another body – the court officials, the court administration, or the Ministry of Justice.

Nonmonetary benefits play a particularly important role in holding judges to account in post-Soviet republics. For example, judges in Russia and Ukraine are often entitled to subsidized housing, and, since the available housing is not unlimited and not all housing is equal, this perk is often used by court presidents to please or intimidate judges.[83] "Disloyal" judges thus can be denied an apartment for several years or "can suddenly face eviction or transfer to another apartment, which in the best-case scenario is a huge hassle."[84] In fact, Russian and Ukrainian court presidents have even wider powers and may help judges with other perks that affect their well-being, such as judges' vacation packages and the access to day care for

---

[80] That is also the reason the Spanish system of volatile parts of judicial salaries referred to in note 74 was eventually struck down. *Cf. Provincial Judges Reference* [1997] 3 S.C.R. 3 (Supreme Court of Canada).

[81] Garapon and Epineuse, above note 75, at 287.

[82] For a succinct summary of these nonmonetary benefits, see Vicki C. Jackson, "Judicial Independence: Structure, Content, Attitude" in Anja Seibert-Fohr (ed.), *Judicial Independence in Transition* (Springer 2012) 19–86, at 53–56.

[83] See Maria Popova, *Politicized Justice in Emerging Democracies: A Study of Courts in Russia and Ukraine* (CUP 2012), at 134.

[84] Ibid.

their children.[85] Other postcommunist countries leave generally less room for holding judges to account by nonmonetary benefits, but Chapter 6 will show that some Slovak court presidents managed to exploit this room effectively and used nonmonetary benefits to reward and punish judges.

Case assignment represents the last mechanism of judicial accountability that can bring about both positive and negative sanctions.[86] Principals can use case assignment as a "carrot" by assigning interesting and novel cases to "favored" judges. Conversely, they can use it as a "stick" by assigning mundane and repetitive cases to "recalcitrant" judges. Similarly, a principal can help his "favored" judges by assigning to them only cases within their area of expertise. Interestingly, principals can also please their "favored" judges by assigning them easy cases and punish "recalcitrant" judges by assigning them difficult cases.[87] The risk of manipulation of case assignment can be avoided if cases are distributed among judges on a random basis or according to unchangeable criteria set in advance. When such system of case assignment is put in effect, it cannot be used as a mechanism of judicial accountability.

Many countries in the Germanic legal family as well as postcommunist countries adopted a concept of the right to a legal judge (*gesetzlicher Richter*), which requires a blind distribution of cases according to the criteria set in advance that eliminate the discretion of court presidents.[88] These criteria are usually set in the "work schedule." The "legal judge" is then the judge who is supposed to decide the case according to the criteria set in the work schedule. If another judge eventually decides the case – because the rules set in the work schedule were not followed *or* because the work schedule itself allowed for the discretionary assignment of cases – then the case was not decided by a "legal judge" and the right to a legal judge was violated. The rationale behind the concept of a "legal judge" is to ensure, to the maximum extent possible, random case assignment. Put differently, according to the concept of a legal judge, no actor is allowed to use his or her discretion in assigning cases. This concept

---

[85] See Solomon 2010, above note 72, at 354; or Solomon 2012, above note 70, at 912.

[86] There is a huge variety among the models of case assignment. However, court presidents play the decisive role in most civil law countries. See Philip M. Langbroek and Marco Fabri, *The Right Judge for Each Case: A Study of Case Assignment and Impartiality in Six European Judiciaries* (Intersentia 2007).

[87] By "difficult cases" I mean time-consuming cases; see Chapter 1, note 157.

[88] For further details regarding the German principle of *gesetzlicher Richter*, see Anja Seibert-Fohr, "Judicial Independence in Germany" in Anja Seibert-Fohr (ed.), *Judicial Independence in Transition* (Springer 2012) 447–519, at 481–483.

was adopted in response to the abuse of case assignment by totalitarian regimes and has remained alien to many legal cultures. For instance, in the United Kingdom case assignment is done by court presidents who distribute cases on a discretionary basis and their decisions are not subject to any review.

However, the right to a legal judge, even if it is firmly embedded in the judicial system, is not a panacea as the need for flexibility requires that in certain situations – such as a shortage of judges, illness of a judge, appointment of a new judge, or secondment of a judge – departure from the general rule stipulated ex ante is allowed. As with many other mechanisms, the proverbial devil lies in the detail. Unless there is a check on those who may trigger these exceptions,[89] there is a high potential for abuse of initial case assignment as well as of subsequent reassignment.[90]

III.   What Is "Out": Contingent Circumstances of Judicial Accountability

Mechanisms of individual judicial accountability are not the only mechanisms that may influence the functioning of the judiciary. A battery of other measures is available to actors who want to control judges and ensure that they do not go astray. These additional mechanisms can be roughly divided into five groups: (1) *ex post* mechanisms that affect court officials, judges as a group, entire courts, or the judiciary as a branch of government rather than *individual* judges, (2) screening mechanisms, (3) transparency mechanisms, (4) appeals and quasi-appellate mechanisms, and (5) pathological mechanisms of judicial accountability. This section analyzes these five groups in more detail and explains why none of them meets the criteria of my definition of judicial accountability. In doing so I draw inspiration not only from democratic regimes, but also from techniques totalitarian and authoritarian regimes employed to control their judges and to ensure the smooth implementation of their agendas. The aim of broadening the pool of available mechanisms is to remedy the "drawback" of exclusive reliance on democratic regimes, where some

---

[89]   One may invoke here a famous phrase of Carl Schmitt: "Sovereign is he who decides on the exception."

[90]   See ECtHR, *Daktaras v. Lithuania*, no. 42095/98, October 10, 2000, §§ 35–38; ECtHR, *Bochan v. Ukraine*, no. 7577/02, May 3, 2007, §§ 67–75; ECtHR, October 9, 2008, *Moiseyev v. Russia*, no. 62936/00, §§ 182–184; and ECtHR, *DMD GROUP, a.s. v. Slovakia*, no. 19334/03, October 5, 2010, §§ 65–72.

mechanisms capable of influencing judges have not been explored at all and most mechanisms have not been stretched to their limits.[91]

A.   Ex Post Mechanisms That Do Not Affect Individual Judges

This book studies ex post institutional mechanisms that influence individual judges in their decision making and in their behavior. This means that only those mechanisms that are ex post, entail positive or negative consequences, and target individual judges fall within the ambit of my definition of judicial accountability. All three conditions must be met simultaneously. This section addresses mechanisms that might meet the first two conditions, but fail to fulfill the third since they do not primarily affect individual judges. These mechanisms can be roughly divided into four groups: (1) ex post mechanisms that affect entire courts; (2) ex post mechanisms that affect all judges within a particular jurisdiction; (3) ex post mechanisms that affect the judiciary as a branch of government; and (4) ex post mechanisms that affect court officials.

The first group comprises mechanisms that target entire courts. Many mechanisms that can be employed to reward or sanction individual judges cannot be applied to courts. One cannot impeach the court, initiate disciplinary motions against it, promote it, or temporarily assign it outside of the judiciary. While other mechanisms such as relocating the court, retaining the whole court, or "degrading" the court are quite a stretch, they may happen. For instance, the Ukrainian President Yushchenko abolished the Kyiv City Administrative Court and set up two new courts instead.[92] Vladimir Putin showed a different version of achieving the same aim. He merged Russian commercial courts that were generally considered more independent than the civil and criminal courts with the rest of the judiciary and replaced the Supreme Commercial Court by an Economic Collegium at the new "super" Supreme Court.[93] On the other hand, holding a court liable for civil or criminal infractions is impossible. One can

---

[91] Charles Gardner Geyh, "Rescuing Judicial Accountability from the Realm of Political Rhetoric" (2006) 56 *Case Western Reserve Law Review* 911, 925.

[92] Alexei Trochev, "Meddling with Justice: Competitive Politics, Impunity, and Distrusted Courts in Post-Orange Ukraine" (2010) 18 *Democratizatsiya* 122, 135.

[93] See, for example, William Partlett, "Judicial Backsliding in Russia", JURIST – Academic Commentary, September 30, 2014, http://jurist.org/academic/2014/09/william-partlett-russia-reform; and Kathrin Hille, "Putin Tightens Grip on Legal Systém" *Financial Times* (London, November 27, 2013).

find only individual judges or the state liable, but not the court. In other words, no carrots[94] and only a few sticks are available.[95]

So what mechanisms can be used? Interestingly, all four dual mechanisms discussed in the previous section can be applied to entire courts. After an adjustment, applicable mechanisms are the performance evaluation of courts, volatile court budgets, volatile nonmonetary support, and the transfer of jurisdiction among courts. Each of these mechanisms usually operates under the radar of constitutional and human rights scholars, but all of them can be employed with great success. Performance evaluation of entire courts does not vary much from performance evaluation of individual judges. The only difference is that court evaluations are based on aggregated data. Similarly, volatile budgets do not affect the salaries of individual judges, but impinge upon the salaries of the support staff and clerks. Moreover, budget allocations have significant ramifications for IT support and other working conditions such as computers, equipment, and components that affect the maintenance of the court building. Meddling with nonmonetary support is closely related. A lack of subsidized housing for judges, no air-conditioning in the court building, or providing only a few secretaries may undermine performance of a given court. All three mechanisms thus can have a tremendous indirect impact on judges in a given court, but do not involve individual accounting.

The fourth mechanism, the transfer of jurisdiction to a different court, is even more subtle. This measure can punish judges of a particular court by stripping them of jurisdiction over certain types of cases and transferring those cases to another, more "principal-friendly," court.[96] However, this punishment is only marginal and indirect. Furthermore, transferring jurisdiction is a very crude measure. Usually, only the legislature can resort to this technique and once one accepts the fact, that the legislature can create entirely new courts with special jurisdiction,[97] one can hardly

---

[94] In theory, a principal may reward all judges in a particular court by paying for their "judicial tourism" (judicial training abroad) or by increasing their salaries, but it is also a stretch of the imagination.

[95] For instance, the executive may refuse to fill the vacancies at a given court in order to increase the workload of the sitting judges.

[96] Note the difference between transfer of jurisdiction *among* courts and "jurisdiction stripping." The latter "strips" *all* courts of jurisdiction on certain issues and channels these issues *outside* the judiciary. "Jurisdiction stripping" is addressed later among mechanisms that affect the judiciary.

[97] Note that certain constitutions explicitly list all types of courts in the country and, hence, implicitly prohibit the creation of special courts. See, for example, Article 91(1) of the Czech Constitution. On the creation of new courts and the abolishment of existing courts, see the following Section.

argue that division of jurisdiction among existing courts is settled once and for all. The danger of this measure is that it can be always cloaked in positive terms by invoking the need for specific qualification to decide certain disputes, the necessity of easing the case load of overburdened courts, or pragmatic concerns such as proximity to the central organs of the State,[98] even though the real motivation is to influence the outcome of certain cases or to fill the new posts with the protégés.

The second group of mechanisms consists of those that affect all judges of a given jurisdiction instead of merely affecting the judges of a particular court. There are only two mechanisms that fall into this category: the introduction or the reduction of a compulsory retirement age and statutory salary reduction. Both of these mechanisms operate across the board and do not allow for individualized accounting. Therefore, they do not count as mechanisms of judicial accountability according to my definition. Adopting both of these mechanisms may be the result of desirable or acceptable motives as well as of malicious ones. The decision to reduce the salaries of all judges may be triggered by an economic crisis[99] or a nationwide natural catastrophe,[100] but also by mistrust and dissatisfaction with the judiciary.[101] Similarly, introducing or lowering the compulsory retirement age may rest on reasonable social science analysis, such as a genuine effort to prevent decrepitude on the bench, or may stem from the need to get rid of unwanted judges.

However, there is one difference between these two mechanisms. Salary reductions apply to all judges and can never be used to target a particular group. In contrast, introducing or lowering the retirement age, under specific circumstances, allows the State to target a particular group of judges. In particular, when the State undergoes a transition

---

[98] All of these rationales were invoked by the Communist Party of Czechoslovakia in 1948 when it created the State Court (claiming that the new judicial body would be more efficient in dealing with crimes against the republic), moved the seat of the Supreme Court of Czechoslovakia from Brno to Prague (so that it was closer to the Communist Party Secretariat) and changed the jurisdiction of other ordinary courts.

[99] For instance, Estonia and Ireland decided to reduce judicial salaries in the wake of European financial crisis; see Chapter 1, note 97.

[100] For instance, in 2002 the Czech Parliament passed a statute reducing judicial salaries in order to improve the economic situation of the Czech Republic after the catastrophic floods in the same year.

[101] For instance, the Bulgarian cabinet has been using its discretion regarding the end-of-the-year bonuses in this way. As a result, Bulgarian judges have been offered or denied a thirteenth salary around Christmas. For further details, see Maria Popova, "Why the Bulgarian Judiciary Does Not Prosecute Corruption?" (2012) 59 *Problems of Post Communism* 35, 40.

from one regime to another, introducing or lowering the retirement age leads to the dismissal of judges of the old regime and paves the way for packing the courts with judges who share the values of the new regime. However, as mentioned in the foregoing, both introducing and lowering the retirement age can be abused. For instance, Russia's introduction of the retirement age of sixty-five in 2001 was perceived by many as a political decision driven by the Presidential Administration to get rid of some unwanted judges in higher courts, especially Constitutional Court judges, who were about sixty-five.[102] The recent judicial reform of Viktor Orbán in Hungary that reduced the retirement age of judges from seventy years to sixty-two years virtually overnight is another example of the abuse of this mechanism.[103]

The third group of mechanisms operates on an even higher level as it affects the judiciary as a branch of government. These mechanisms raise different concerns, namely issues of separation of powers and checks and balances. It is almost impossible to list all the mechanisms that belong to this category. They run the gamut from statutory overrides, constitutional amendments, and jurisdiction-stripping through the creation of special courts or the abolition of existing courts to the decision to increase the number of judges or the decision to increase the number of lay judges on the panels. A huge amount of literature has been devoted to these mechanisms and, more broadly, to the relationship between the judiciary and the other two branches of government. But, despite incessant talk about these measures and their impact on judges, these mechanisms have little to do with individual judicial accountability.

The three aforesaid groups of ex post mechanisms cover measures that operate on a higher level of generality than mechanisms targeting individual judges. If these categories were placed on a continuum, mechanisms affecting individual judges would be at the one end and mechanisms that can sway the judiciary as a branch of government at the other. The higher the level of mechanisms, the lower the impact that these mechanisms have on individual judges. But there is one more group of mechanisms, often overlooked, which does not fit into this hierarchical structure, because it remains "aside" – mechanisms that affect court presidents and vice presidents.

The powers of court officials vary from country to country, but in every jurisdiction court presidents and vice presidents play a dual role. On the

---

[102] Schwartz and Sykiainen, above note 26, at 971–1064, at 1008.

[103] See Judgment of the Hungarian Constitutional Court on Reduction of Retirement Age of Judges (from seventy years to sixty-two years) of July 16, 2012; and Judgment of the Court of Justice of November 6, 2012, C-286/12 Commission v Hungary.

one hand they are regular judges. On the other hand, they are managers vested with administrative tasks.[104] In the first role, their job does not differ from the tasks of other judges. They sit on the bench and decide cases.[105] In the second role, they exercise administrative functions. These functions vary from organizing training for judges to allocating material support among sections of the court and overseeing the nonjudicial staff. In their first role, in theory court officials can be held to account in the same way and by the same mechanisms as ordinary judges.[106] But in practice the court officials decide on several mechanisms of judicial accountability by themselves[107] and thus they are immune from many accountability mechanisms. Nevertheless, court officials can also be held to account for their performance of administrative tasks.[108] It is the latter group of mechanisms that are *specific* to the court officials I will focus on here.

Court officials can be appointed for a fixed renewable term. Some countries have introduced specific disciplinary proceedings for court officials. These procedures are governed by different rules from those for disciplinary motions for regular judges.[109] Other countries allow court officials to be dismissed without cause.[110] In such cases, the dismissed court official is

---

[104] In many systems, court presidents possess formal or at least informal powers in the appointment and promotion of judges.

[105] In most civil law systems, court officials have a reduced case load, because they have numerous administrative tasks.

[106] Some exceptions apply. For instance, a court official cannot be rewarded by being promoted to the position of court official.

[107] Court officials may decide on case assignment, promotions of judges, secondment of judges, and on temporary assignments outside the judiciary.

[108] I am aware of the fact that the two roles of court officials are sometimes difficult to distinguish and that each role can have a significant spill-over effect on the other. However, the fact that several countries adopted *specific* disciplinary proceedings for court officials suggests that it is possible to distinguish judicial acts and administrative acts of court officials (see the following footnote).

[109] Specific disciplinary proceedings for court officials were adopted in France and in the Czech Republic. The French law accepts that a court president can be recalled from the position of court president without his judicial capacity being called into question. The doctrine distinguishes between judicial acts [*actes à caractère judiciaire*] and administrative acts [*actes à caractère administratif*] of judicial officials. For further details, see Philippe Lemaire, "Le Contrôle Fonctionnel de Gestion (1)" in Guy Canivet, Mads Andenas, and Duncan Fairgrieve (eds.), *Independence, Accountability, and the Judiciary* (British Institute of International and Comparative Law 2006) 335. On the Czech Republic, see Art. 87(2) and Art. 88(2) of the Czech Law on Courts and Judges.

[110] Such situation exists in Slovakia, where a complicated procedure of selecting judicial officials was set up, but the Minister of Justice was left with power to dismiss court officials without the requirement to justify it; see Chapter 6.

allegedly affected only in his administrative capacity and he stays in judicial office as a regular judge. One can also imagine specific performance evaluation of court officials or volatile salaries for them. In theory, complaints may target court officials specifically for their failures in executing administrative tasks, but in practice it is impossible to draw the line between complaining against the court official as a judge and complaining against the court official as an administrator.

A specific feature of court officials as a group is that almost no carrots are available for them. To be sure, they care about the prestige and the well-being of their courts and, if they do not manage to secure enough funds, it can make their job as court leaders harder. Judges who complain to the court president that they do not have enough toners for printing are clearly a hassle for the court president.[111] Vice versa, when court presidents are particularly good at raising funds, for instance for large-scale renovations of the court building, they may be perceived by regular judges as doing their jobs properly. However, delaying or providing funds for the entire court affects court presidents only remotely and indirectly.

Therefore, the only real carrot for court presidents is promotion to a higher court. Nevertheless, even this carrot suffers from several drawbacks when applied to court officials. First, it does not work for court officials at the top courts. Second, even promotion to a higher court sometimes does not pay off. Many court officials prefer being "primus inter pares" at a lower court rather than becoming "one out of many" at a higher court. What is even more striking is that in several civil law countries the court president at a lower court has a higher salary than a regular judge at a higher court, which is one level up in the judicial hierarchy. For instance, in the Czech Republic the court official is always better off in financial terms when he refuses to become a regular judge at a higher court. Put differently, the salary bonus for the president of the district court is higher than the salary increase that accompanies promotion to the regional court. The same rule applies to promotions to the high court and even to promotions to the Supreme Court and to the Supreme Administrative Court of the Czech Republic.

What remains is to address the question why mechanisms affecting court officials do not count as mechanisms of judicial accountability. In order to answer this question one must return to the dual role of court officials. Court officials are judges as well as administrators. The specific

---

[111] See Maria Popova, *Politicized Justice in Emerging Democracies: A Study of Courts in Russia and Ukraine* (CUP 2012), 145.

measures addressed so far hold court officials to account for their performance in pursuing *administrative* tasks that they are vested with and not for their decision making or behavior in fulfilling their judicial duties. The nature and scope of these administrative tasks depend on many factors such as history and legal culture as well as the political and social context. These factors translate into distinct models of court administration. The typology of these models will be addressed in more detail in Chapter 3. Here it suffices to say that in the judicial council model and in the courts service model, court officials tend to share their powers with the judicial council or with the court service, whereas in the Ministry of Justice model they act as public servants and are bound by instructions issued by Ministers of Justice.[112]

What all these models have in common is that court officials are sooner or later emancipated from their principals. This phenomenon occurs irrespective of the large-scale structure, be it the judicial council, the Court Service or the Ministry of Justice. A typical scenario unfolds as follows. Initially, principals handpick their court officials and they are able to exercise control over the judiciary through those officials for some time. However, court officials gradually gain power and become players who have interests of their own, which are not necessarily aligned with the interests of their principals. As a result, the court officials no longer serve as mere transmission belts for their principals. Hence, court officials should be treated as a separate group of principals that may hold regular judges to account. For this reason one cannot mix together accountability mechanisms affecting regular judges and specific accountability mechanisms affecting court officials qua court officials.

To be sure, the level of emancipation of court presidents may vary. On the one side of the continuum is China, where the Communist Party carefully selects court presidents and vice presidents from the apex courts level all the way down to the local courts. These court presidents are then in charge of the Chinese Communist Party's oversight of judicial operations.[113] However, even under these circumstances, strenuous as they are, court presidents can carve out some room for maneuver.[114] In Ukraine and Russia, the links between the presidential administration and judiciary's

---

[112] On the hybrid models (that lie somewhere in between) and on the "communist model" (which is, roughly, a distorted "Ministry of Justice" model), see Chapter 3.

[113] Zhu Suli, "The Party and the Courts" in Randall Peerenboom (ed.), *Judicial Independence in China: Lessons for Global Rule of Law Promotion* (CUP 2009), 52–68, at 56.

[114] See, for example, Xin He, "Judicial Innovation and Local Politics: Judicialization of Administrative Governance in East China" (2013) 69 *China Journal* 1.

leadership are also strong and the court presidents have a variety of ways of dealing with noncompliant judges.[115] Western democracies can be placed on the other side of the continuum. The role of court presidents, who once held strong powers, has gradually changed there and they can no longer interfere with decision making of individual judges and affect their well-being.[116] The Czech Republic,[117] Slovakia,[118] Poland,[119] Hungary,[120] and Croatia[121] fall somewhere in the middle. In these countries, court presidents who operated as prolonged hands of the Communist Party before democratization emancipated themselves from the executive and pursued to a greater or lesser extent their own agenda. Therefore, in order to understand the role of court presidents in each country, it is important to take into account to what extent court presidents emancipated from their original principals.[122]

B.   Screening Mechanisms

There are several genuine screening mechanisms that have a significant effect on the functioning of the judiciary, but that do not involve the accounting of judges. The selection of judges is by far the most important.[123] The power to nominate and appoint or elect judges, although it involves individual judges, is not a mechanism of judicial accountability,

---

[115] See, for example, Alena Ledeneva, "From Russia with *Blat*: Can Informal Networks Help Modernize Russia?" (2009) 76 *Social Research* 257, 276; or Maria Popova, *Politicized Justice in Emerging Democracies: A Study of Courts in Russia and Ukraine* (CUP 2012), in particular at 139–145.

[116] See Chapter 8, Section I.

[117] See Chapter 5.

[118] See Chapter 6.

[119] See Adam Bodnar and Lukasz Bojarski, "Judicial Independence in Poland" in Anja Seibert-Fohr (ed.), *Judicial Independence in Transition* (Springer 2012) 667, 678–679 and 708–711.

[120] See, for example, Zoltán Fleck, "Judicial Independence in Hungary" in Anja Seibert-Fohr (ed.), *Judicial Independence in Transition* (Springer 2012) 793, 812–817.

[121] See Alan Uzelac, "Amendments to the Law on Courts and Law on the State Judicial Council – Elements of the Reform of the Organizational Judicial Legislation" in Goranka Lalić (ed.), *Croatian Judiciary: Lessons and Perspectives* (Netherlands Helsinki Committee 2002) 37–69, at 54–61; and Alan Uzelac, "Role and Status of Judges in Croatia" in Paul Oberhammer (ed.), *Richterbild und Rechtsreform in Mitteleuropa* (Manzsche Verlags 2001) 23–65, at 43–57.

[122] See Chapter 8, Section I.

[123] For a good overview of the judicial appointment process in various countries, see Kate Malleson and Peter H. Russell (eds.), *Appointing Judges in an Age of Judicial Power: Critical Perspectives from around the World* (University of Toronto Press 2006).

because it is not concerned with past judicial behavior that is now sanctioned or rewarded.

Codes of judicial conduct represent another example of a mechanism that does not involve accounting. They usually have no formal normative force, but even if they do, they define reproachable behavior of judges ex ante and only the body that applies such codes engages in holding judges to account. With a certain degree of simplification, one may say that codes of judicial conduct operate like quasi-statutes. Furthermore, several ex post mechanisms can operate so as to avoid accounting if designed accordingly.[124] In order to avoid confusion, this part will refer to those measures that can be used, depending on their particular institutional setup, as both ex ante and ex post mechanisms as "mixed mechanisms." Case assignment, salaries of judges, and reassignment of judges within the same court are the most prominent examples of "mixed mechanisms." The Parliament can stipulate that cases must be assigned as well as reassigned on a random basis among a sufficient number of individual judges or panels.[125] Volatile salaries can be prohibited and the whole of salaries thus fixed in advance.[126] Reassignment within the same court can be subjected to the approval of an affected judge, panels can be reshuffled on a random basis only, or the statute may grant those judges who are reassigned outside their previous specialization a few months to retrain in the new area of law.[127]

C. Transparency Mechanisms

Judges' decision making and behavior can also be influenced by transparency mechanisms. These include, among other things, the compulsory publication of all judgments, the openness of judicial proceedings to the public, the recording of the trial proceedings, the wide distribution of vacancies within the judiciary, publishing lists of candidates for judicial office and candidates for promotion and/or the publication of interviews with those candidates, the publication of judicial statistics,[128] and compulsory disclosure of judges'

---

[124] See Section II of this chapter.

[125] The Slovak Parliament attempted to introduce such system of random case assignment in April 2002, but to a great extent it failed. See Chapter 6 for further details.

[126] This is a typical arrangement in most democratic countries.

[127] This is what the Slovak Parliament did in 2011 in the wake of abusing this mechanism of judicial accountability; see § 51a(2) of Law No. 757/2004 Z. z., on Courts, as amended by Law No. 33/2011 Z. z. (which laid down that any judge reassigned to a new specialization against their will must be granted two months for requalification).

[128] Judicial statistics must be distinguished from judicial performance evaluation. The mere publication of how many cases were decided does not in itself involve any evaluation; it

property and annual earnings. What these measures have in common is that they provide useful information about the judges' work and are essential for assessing their performance. Financial disclosures also provide information about the extrajudicial behavior of a given judge and potential conflicts of interests that may lead to his recusal.

However, these mechanisms differ from mechanisms of judicial accountability, because they entail neither positive nor negative sanctions.[129] Transparency is a prerequisite for effective "accounting," but transparency mechanisms in themselves do not hold judges to account. It is only the *subsequent* step based on information generated from transparency mechanisms, such as a disciplinary motion against a given judge, his reassignment or promotion, or the reduction of his salary, which actually punishes or rewards him.[130] Nevertheless, transparency mechanisms still play an important role. Put bluntly, if a principal does not have sufficient information about the performance of his agent, he can hardly hold him to account. When studying the judiciary of a particular country, it is thus important to take into account the interplay between transparency and accountability mechanisms. The lack of the former may make the latter toothless or even distort them.

For instance, when judicial decisions are not published at all or when they are published only selectively, this may have significant ramifications for many mechanisms of judicial accountability. Actors who decide on the promotion and quasi-promotion of judges do not have enough information on which to base their decisions. It is also impossible to conduct meaningful judicial performance evaluation or decide on volatile salaries. Similarly, when the body that is vested with the power to initiate disciplinary motion or the power to impeach does not have access to materials that it needs to initiate these procedures, it becomes a mere bystander. Therefore, transparency is important for fighting information asymmetry, which is particularly high in the context of the judiciary. To be sure, one should always ask who possesses information about judges, because the identity of the information holder suggests who benefits from a lack of transparency. Nevertheless, despite the fact that transparency mechanisms play an important role in every judicial system, they are not mechanisms of judicial accountability.

---

merely provides information that may be used for evaluation or criticism. Hence, publishing judicial statistics is similar to publishing judicial decisions.

[129] For further explanation of this position, see Chapter 1.

[130] See, for example, the situation in China, where high reversal rates may lead to a reduction in a judge's salary; for further details see note 72.

D. Appeals and Quasi-Appellate Mechanisms

Another set of mechanisms that do not fall within the ambit of the definition of judicial accountability consists of appeals and quasi-appellate mechanisms such as "extraordinary appeals," en banc proceedings, and "interpretative guidelines" issued by top courts. These four mechanisms are difficult to define generically, because the specific procedures for using them, including the basic questions of who initiates them and against which types of decisions they can be used, vary greatly from country to country.[131] However, I may tentatively define them as follows.

An *appeal* is a process for requesting a higher court for formal change to a judicial decision, which has not yet become final, by one of the parties. The so-called *extraordinary appeals* operate differently, since they empower privileged actors to request the Supreme Court to review any ruling of the lower court, including rulings that have already become final.[132] The power to lodge an extraordinary appeal is usually vested with an actor distinct from the parties involved in the dispute and the judges who sat on the case. Most often, the General Prosecutor, the Minister of Justice, or the court presidents trigger this procedure. The *en banc procedure* refers to a procedure where a judicial decision which has not yet become final is reviewed by the same court sitting "as the full court."[133] The en banc procedure is usually triggered by judges of that court and not by the parties, even though the parties can suggest a hearing en banc. Finally, the so-called *interpretative guidelines* empower judges of top ordinary courts to consolidate the case law of lower courts without a link to a specific case. In other words, this procedure does not require the existence of the "case and controversy."[134] "Interpretative guidelines" can be either binding or merely advisory, but in both cases this procedure significantly constrains the discretion of lower court judges.[135]

---

[131] Not to mention that even within the *same* jurisdiction, the nature of these mechanisms can vary greatly depending on the type of the case.

[132] See Lech Garlicki, "Politics and Political Independence of the Judiciary" in András Sajó and L. R. Bentch (eds.), *Judicial Integrity* (Brill Academic Publishers 2004) 125, 129.

[133] In rarer instances, an appellate court will order a hearing *en banc* as an initial matter, instead of the panel hearing. In such case, the *en banc* hearing operates as an ordinary appeal, just with a different composition of the bench.

[134] For further details, see Zdeněk Kühn, "The Authoritarian Legal Culture at Work: The Passivity of Parties and the Interpretational Statements of Supreme Courts" (2006) 2 *Croatian Yearbook of European Law and Policy* 19.

[135] Ibid.

One may distinguish these four mechanisms on the basis of several criteria, but classifying them according to the body that usually initiates them is the most illuminating approach: an appeal is brought by one of the parties, an en banc decision is triggered by the very same court that originally decided the impugned case, an extraordinary appeal is lodged by the General Prosecutor, and an interpretative guideline is initiated by top ordinary courts. But given the breadth of the possible configurations of these mechanisms, even this crude classification often becomes blurred. For instance, in some countries the right to appeal is limited by writ of certiorari or leave to appeal procedures. Thus, the judges (deciding on writ of certiorari or leave to appeal) decide whether the case reaches the merits on the appellate or top court. In other countries, an extraordinary appeal can be initiated not only by the General Prosecutor, but also by court presidents. Hence, judges once again play a role in this mechanism.

It is also important to stress that while virtually every state allows appeals against judicial decisions, the other three mechanisms are not so widespread. One may roughly conclude that en banc decisions exist in some common law countries, whereas "extraordinary appeals" and "interpretative guidelines" can be found primarily in civil law countries and in the postcommunist legal systems in particular. One more caveat must be added with regard to en banc decisions. In civil law systems[136] with huge top ordinary courts that consist of dozens of judges, the en banc hearing is sometimes replaced by the "Grand Chamber." Given the sheer number of judges, these courts cannot sit en banc and, thus, they create "Grand Chambers" that are significantly larger than ordinary panels, but that do not include all of the judges of the court.[137] These Grand Chambers can be triggered in two different ways. The first group of Grand Chambers operates in a similar way to the en banc procedure, the sole difference being that the body that decides is not "the full court" but the Grand Chamber.[138] In such scenario, the Grand Chamber operates as another instance within the same court. The second type of Grand Chamber procedure differs

---

[136] It is also possible to find "Grand Chambers" at the European Court of Human Rights and the Court of Justice.

[137] Note that even in the United States the law stipulates that "[a]ny court of appeals having more than 15 active judges ... may perform its en banc function by such number of members of its en banc courts as may be prescribed by rule of the court of appeals" (Section 6 of Pub. L. No. 95–486, October 20, 1978, 92 Stat 1629). So far, only the United States Court of Appeals for the Ninth Circuit has utilized this procedure. The Ninth Circuit has twenty-eight judges in total and its "en banc panel" consists of eleven judges.

[138] A referral to the Grand Chamber of the ECtHR under Article 43 ECHR50 is an example of such procedure.

significantly from the en banc procedure since the Grand Chamber is convened only in the *subsequent* case, when the regular panel arrives at the conclusion that is inconsistent with a judgment *previously* delivered by the court. If such situation occurs, the regular panel relinquishes its jurisdiction in favor of the Grand Chamber, which is supposed to decide which of the two positions prevails. However, the Grand Chamber decides only on the issue regarding which the regular panels disagree. Hence, if there are other issues, the case is remanded to the regular panel, which renders the judgments on the merits.[139]

Now it is possible to move to the question of why appeals and quasi-appellate mechanisms are not mechanisms of judicial accountability. The answer is "no" for all four mechanisms, because none of these four mechanisms results in a sanction or reward. This conclusion begs further explanation. Only appeals will be discussed in more detail subsequently, but the conclusions with regard to appeals apply mutatis mutandis to the other three mechanisms.

If the decision is appealed, it can be either reversed or affirmed. When a decision is reversed on appeal, what does it mean for the judge who issued the reversed decision? Will his salary be reduced? Will someone initiate a disciplinary motion or an impeachment against him? Will he be reassigned to another panel, relocated to another court, or demoted to a lower court? Will it increase his chances of losing his retention election or being promoted? In democratic societies it is hardly so.[140] Conversely, when a decision is affirmed on appeal, what does it mean for the judge who issued it? Will it increase his chances of promotion? Maybe. But maybe not.[141] Many reversals reflect differences in judicial philosophy or legal policy rather than mistake or incompetence by the lower court judges and thus they are not perceived as criticism.[142] Moreover, the body that decides on the promotion of judges might want to increase diversity on the appellate court and, hence, the judge whose decisions are always affirmed on appeal is considered unsuitable. The promoting body might also disagree with prevailing judicial philosophy or trends in the case law of the

---

[139] Procedure governing the Grand Chamber of the Supreme Administrative Court of the Czech Republic belongs to this group.

[140] But *cf.* the situation in China discussed in note 72 above.

[141] For instance, in the United States Higgins and Rubin found that reversal rates do not affect district judges' chances of promotion. See Richard S. Higgins and Paul H. Rubin, "Judicial Discretion" (1980) 9 *J Legal Stud* 129. But *cf.* Stephen J. Choi and others, "What Do Federal District Judges Want? An Analysis of Publications, Citations and Reversals" (2012) 28 *Journal of Law, Economics, & Organization* 518, 521–522.

[142] See Posner, R. A. 1993, above note 1, at 14–15.

appellate courts and thus it is looking for someone who holds different views from the current appellate judges. To be sure, judges of apex courts might sit on promotion panels and consider a low reversal rate to be the most important factor for promotion. In the post-Soviet states, reversal rates are taken even more seriously and can be sufficient grounds for disciplinary action or even dismissal.[143] However, this is an exception to the rule and, more importantly, in such cases reversal rates are becoming a part of judicial performance evaluation or a disciplinary offence and for *that* reason, not in itself, appeals may operate as a mechanism of judicial accountability.

What about a judge's prestige? Does it suffer when his decision is reversed? And does it increase when his decision is affirmed? The answer depends on whether principals agree with the decision of the first instance court or with that of the appellate court. Moreover, many things can happen between the moment when the lower court delivers its decision and the moment when the appellate court decides on appeal. For instance, new facts can emerge. The Supreme Court can change its previous position or even overrule the governing precedent. Hence, even if one were to presume that the appellate court decides all cases correctly (which is hardly a sustainable position), it does not mean that the trial court's decision was incorrect *at the time that it was delivered*. Put differently, the fact that the decision was reversed or affirmed does not in itself say anything about whether the initial decision was right or wrong. This leads to the inevitable conclusion that an appeal does not differ much from a statutory override[144] in its impact. Both of these mechanisms are ex post in nature, but neither of them has a significant reputational or other effect on judges who decided cases that were reversed or overridden.

Furthermore, there are additional factors that significantly limit the role of appeals. First, most decisions are not appealed. Second, many appeals are dismissed on admissibility criteria or on quasi-procedural criteria such as leave to appeal or a writ of certiorari. Third, many countries prioritize the principle of collegiality, which means that most cases are decided by panels and not by single judges, and, at the same time, prohibit judges from delivering separate opinions. In this scenario, the judge's responsibility is significantly minimized, since judges can invoke confidentiality of deliberation and can make the claim that no outsider can know for sure how a

---

[143]   See note 72 above.
[144]   On statutory overrides, see William N. Eskridge, "Overriding Supreme Court Statutory Interpretation Decisions" (1991) 101 *The Yale Law Journal* 331.

particular judge voted.[145] The remaining two factors are country-specific, but, given the focus of this book, they should be mentioned as well. Fourth, in Europe, judges of the ordinary courts have more than one master. Even the Supreme Court is not the highest court. It is overseen by the constitutional court and by the European Court of Human Rights and constrained by the Court of Justice of the European Union. Given this setup, a lower court judge can "outsmart" the Supreme Court by submitting a preliminary reference to the Court of Justice or by initiating a concrete review of constitutionality before the constitutional court. Even if he does not or cannot do so, the fact that his decision was reversed by the Supreme Court is not the end of the matter since the decision of the Supreme Court is still subject to review by the constitutional court and the European Court of Human Rights.

Finally, in transitional countries, one can often witness the following phenomenon that I call a "sandwich scenario." Most postcommunist states in the CEE established specialized constitutional courts after their respective revolutions. These constitutional courts act as agents of change and "downstream consolidators of democracy."[146] Even though these constitutional courts formally stay outside the ordinary judiciary, in practice they are above the ordinary courts and act as top appellate courts. Purges within the ordinary courts were limited in most postcommunist countries and judges who were active during the communist era usually hold positions at the higher echelons of the judiciary due to their seniority. Slowly but gradually new judges who graduated from postcommunist law schools, some of which also studied law abroad, are starting to fill the lower echelons of the judiciary. This means that judges appointed after the fall of communism sit on the lower courts and on the constitutional court, whereas judges who were appointed in the communist era occupy the seats at appellate courts and at the Supreme Court. In other words, communist old timers are "sandwiched" by the new blood.[147] It is not difficult to guess what often happens in this configuration. Alliances emerge between natural partners. Decisions of lower courts are often reversed by the appellate courts and

---

[145] Top common law courts sometimes issue per curiam opinions the aim of which is, among other things, to hide the author of the opinion. Nevertheless, per curiam opinions are exceptions to the rule. Moreover, recently some scholars came with techniques how to determine authorship in unsigned opinions; see William Li and others, "Using Algorithmic Attribution Techniques to Determine Authorship in Unsigned Judicial Opinions" (2013) 16 *Stanford Technology Law Review* 503.

[146] See Tom Ginsburg, "Courts and New Democracies: Recent Works" (2012) 37 *Law & Social Inquiry* 720, 729–735.

[147] I admit that this is a huge simplification, but it illustrates the unreliability of reversal rates.

decisions of the appellate courts are often affirmed by the Supreme Court, but the constitutional court often steps in and sides with the lower court. Reversal rates mean little in this scenario.[148]

E.   Criminal and Pathological Mechanisms of Influencing Judges

So far only mechanisms that have failed to meet at least one of the three requirements of judicial accountability have been addressed in this section. However, I argued in Chapter 1 that judicial accountability contains an irreducible normative element and, hence, I exclude certain mechanisms from my definition of judicial accountability even though these mechanisms meet all three requirements – namely criminal mechanisms and genuinely pathological mechanisms.

Examples of criminal forms of rigging judges are numerous. They include bribes, threats to judges and their families, and other forms of intimidation. In a nutshell, criminal mechanisms cover everything that can be considered a criminal act. These criminal mechanisms cannot be included among mechanisms of judicial accountability, irrespective of which standard they promote, because they are unacceptable under any circumstance and in any jurisdiction. For instance, one may take for granted that democratic societies prohibit bribery and other criminal forms of intimidation even if some members of society occasionally resort to these techniques. Criminal mechanisms can be employed by various actors, including the mafia, the oligarchy, and members of the executive, but they do not have explicit backing from the State.

In contrast, totalitarian and authoritarian regimes use pathological methods to promote their ideological agendas.[149] But totalitarian and authoritarian regimes do not resort only to genuinely pathological mechanisms. They also distort mechanisms that are employed to great success in democratic regimes.[150] The "good" thing is that experiences from totalitarian and authoritarian regimes remedy the "drawback" of reliance on

---

[148] But see note 141 above.
[149] Note that criminal mechanisms do not appear in totalitarian regimes. The ruling party does not have to bribe its judges in order to achieve the desired result, since it can easily tame them without monetary incentives. Furthermore, totalitarian regimes do not approve of a judiciary that is overly responsive to *alternative* centers of power and thus cautiously seal off the judiciary from other influences.
[150] I am aware that there is a fine line between genuinely pathological mechanisms and a pathological use of accepted mechanisms, but this book defines pathological mechanisms narrowly.

democratic regimes, where some mechanisms have not been explored at all and most mechanisms have not been stretched to their limits.

"Telephone justice" is a good starting point for the discussion of pathological mechanisms. The expression "telephone justice" is meant to describe the situation where a government official calls a judge in order to convince him to rule in a way that pleases the administration.[151] In practice, judges in totalitarian regimes were expected to "call" the relevant officers of the ruling party themselves and ask how the case ought to be decided. Of course, only important cases had to undergo this procedure. There was no reason, for example, to discuss the outcome of an ordinary divorce trial with representatives of the ruling party. On the other hand, the most important cases, in particular "show trials," were orchestrated from A to Z by the ruling party. If a judge did not follow the orders of the ruling party, he was dismissed or, in the worst case scenario, had to undergo a criminal trial.[152]

Later, totalitarian and authoritarian regimes developed more sophisticated procedures for controlling the judiciary. They ensured that politically sensitive cases were assigned exclusively to a small group of reliable judges. This was done by channeling politically sensitive cases either to specific panels of the ordinary courts or to special courts that operated in parallel to the ordinary courts.[153] Totalitarian regimes tend to opt for the former, because they can easily control the ordinary judiciary, whereas authoritarian regimes opt for the latter.[154] Under both scenarios, only

---

[151] For a more detailed discussion of this phenomenon, see Kathryn Hendley, "'Telephone Law' and the 'Rule of Law': The Russian Case" (2009) 1 *Hague Journal on the Rule of Law* 241.

[152] For instance, the Communist Party of Czechoslovakia was very harsh on "disobedient" judges in the early years after the 1948 coup d'état. R. Hartych, judge of the State Court, was sentenced to eighteen years in prison, for his refusal to exercise his function according to "class criteria" and for not following the orders of Rudolf Slánský, the General Secretary of the Communist Party of Czechoslovakia (Vorel and Šimáková, above note 33, at 14). Another judge of the State Court, J. Solnař, was sentenced to five years in prison for his alleged collaboration with Nazis during the Protectorate (Vorel and Šimáková, above note 33, at 14).

[153] The third option is to circumscribe the jurisdiction of courts. However, this technique can never *in itself* achieve the same results as the previous two options.

[154] Franco's Spain and Pinochet's Chile are examples of regimes that opted for the latter. See José J. Toharia, "Judicial Independence in an Authoritarian Regime: The Case of Contemporary Spain" (1975) 9 *Law & Society Review* 475; Christopher M. Larkins, "Judicial Independence and Democratization: A Theoretical and Conceptual Analysis" (1996) 44 *The American Journal of Comparative Law*, 612–613; and Lisa Hilbink, "Agents of Anti-Politics: Courts in Pinochet's Chile" in Tom Ginsburg and Tamir Moustafa (eds.), *Rule by Law: The Politics of Courts in Authoritarian Regimes* (CUP 2008).

selected prescreened judges could decide politically sensitive cases. What was common to both totalitarian and authoritarian regimes was that if a judge did not follow the "advice" of the ruling party or the dictator, he faced reprisals.

Often, the judge was not the only person affected by the reprisals. Totalitarian regimes were smart enough to use the "leverage effect" of reprisals imposed on the judge's family members and even on his colleagues. For instance, the communist regime could expel a judge's children from university or fire his spouse from her job within hours. The probability that a judge's children could start studying elsewhere was close to zero. Similarly, any chance that the judge's spouse would find a decent job was gone. As for indirect reprisals against colleagues, a totalitarian regime could easily have reduced the budget of the whole court in which a judge who issued a "recalcitrant opinion" sat. The result would be no bonus payments and no equipment for any judge within the court. Not surprisingly, fellow judges exercised significant pressure on a "recalcitrant judge" to prevent this from happening. Thus, it comes as no surprise that most judges knew the rules of the game and voluntarily agreed to follow the "advice" they were given.[155]

The techniques used against a "recalcitrant" judge varied from country to country and over time. They included, among others, removal from the bench, forced retirement, temporary suspension, criminal prosecution for not following the orders of the ruling party, disciplinary motion on fabricated charges, no chance of reelection, no chance of promotion, withdrawal of the volatile part of the judge's salary, relocation to a court in a geographically isolated area,[156] demotion to a lower court, reassignment to a different panel with a mundane or at least politically neutral agenda (such as divorces), and overloading "recalcitrant" judges with hundreds of small cases with no politically significant content.[157]

This list of possible forms of reprisals includes two types of mechanisms – pathological mechanisms per se and regular mechanisms of judicial accountability used in a pathological way. The former group comprises

---

[155] For a masterful portrayal of these "case-assignment techniques" in Communist Czechoslovakia, see Ivan Klíma's fiction book *Judge on Trial* (I. Klíma, *Judge on Trial* (Knopf 1993)). For a description of the role and functioning of the judiciary in the early years of the communist regime (1950s) in Czechoslovakia, see also Otto Ulč, *The Judge in a Communist State. A View from Within* (Ohio University Press 1972).

[156] See, for example, Law 2009, above note 35, at 1561–1562 with further references (on the effective use of the relocation technique in Japan).

[157] For real life examples, see, for example, Hilbink 2008, above note 154, at 123–126.

the dismissal of judges without a cause,[158] forced retirements,[159] and criminal prosecution of judges for not following the orders of the ruling party.[160] No one can deny that these mechanisms are incompatible with the role of the judiciary as a neutral third among the two parties to the dispute.[161] These mechanisms are excluded from the definition of judicial accountability on the same grounds as criminal mechanisms. The latter group covers mechanisms that are not pathological as such, but that can be used by totalitarian regimes to further their cause. These mechanisms cannot be excluded from the definition of judicial accountability on the mere ground that they can be subject to abuse. To hold otherwise would render the notion of judicial accountability meaningless since virtually any mechanism of judicial accountability can potentially be misused and, hence, would have to be excluded.

A few more insights can be learned from how totalitarian regimes controlled the judiciary. First, experience under totalitarian regimes attests that the judiciary can be relatively easily controlled through a few reliable judges installed in the right places.[162] Even totalitarian regimes that aimed

---

[158] For instance, when the Chilean military took the power in 1973 inspired by conservative values and a strong right wing ethos, it dismissed about 10 percent of the judges, mainly in the lower echelons, for being allegedly left-wing supporters; see Juan E. Vargas and Mauricio Duce, 2000. *Informe sobre independencia judicial en Chile*, Due Process of Law Foundation. For other examples in Latin America, see Nuno Garoupa and Maria Maldonado, "The Judiciary in Political Transitions: The Critical Role of U.S. Constitutionalism in Latin America" (2011) 19 *Cardozo Journal of International and Comparative Law* 593.

[159] Forced retirement has been particularly popular in Central and Latin America; see, for example, Garoupa and Maldonado, above note 158, at 619 and 630 (discussing forced retirements of judges in Argentine and Mexico); or Raul A. Sanchez Urribarri, "Courts between Democracy and Hybrid Authoritarianism: Evidence from the Venezuelan Supreme Court" (2011) 36 *Law & Social Inquiry* 854, 873 (discussing forced retirements of two justices of the Electoral Chamber orchestrated by Hugo Chávez in Venezuela). However, forced resignations of judges took place also in Japan (see J. Mark Ramseyer, "The Puzzling (In)Dependence of Courts: A Comparative Approach" (1994) 23 *The Journal of Legal Studies* 721, 735 and 737), Turkey (Ceran Belge, "Friends of the Court: The Republican Alliance and Selective Activism of the Constitutional Court of Turkey" (2006) 40 *Law & Society Review* 653, 660) or, more recently, in Hungary (see László Sólyom, The Separation of Powers Is Integral to the Fabric of Democracy, Journal of Parliamentary and Political Law July (2013) 7 *Journal of Parliamentary and Political Law* 159).

[160] See note 152 above.

[161] For a more detailed analysis of the logic of the triad in conflict resolution and the role of a judge as an impartial third, see Martin Shapiro, *Courts: A Comparative and Political Analysis* (University of Chicago Press 1981) 1–17.

[162] Stephen Holmes, "Judicial Independence as Ambiguous Reality and Insidious Illusion" in Ronald Dworkin (ed.), *From Liberal Values to Democratic Transition: Essays in Honor of János Kis* (Central European University Press 2004) 9.

at total control of society and, consequently, also at total control of the judiciary, rarely achieved this goal completely. Hence, they had to use two second-best alternatives. These were channeling sensitive disputes beyond the reach of the courts or assigning sensitive cases to reliable judges.[163] As certain disputes, such as criminal trials involving dissidents, could not be "channeled out" without a total loss of legitimacy of the ruling regime, the only option was to rig the case assignment. In other words, the ruling party had to control case assignment in order to assign politically sensitive cases exclusively to reliable judges.[164] How could a totalitarian regime do that? The answer lies primarily with the court officials. The regime hand-picked the most reliable judges and appointed them to the positions of court presidents and vice presidents, granted these court officials power to assign cases and retained the residual power to remove these court officials at will. The higher the court, the tighter the control that the ruling party exercised. This control reached its apex at the level of supreme courts.[165] Put differently, the supreme courts acted as agents of the principal (the ruling party) and kept the lower courts (with the help of presidents of inferior courts) in line with the will of the ruling party.[166]

The second insight is that no regime, irrespective of how strong it is, can control the judiciary without having its own people *within* the judiciary. One may say that only judges can beat judges. This is so for several reasons. In order to rig the courts, one has to know the internal dynamics within the judiciary. This knowledge is hard to acquire without insider experience. Furthermore, courts are difficult to control from the outside, because they handle too many cases and because the information asymmetry is too

---

[163] As long as the totalitarian or authoritarian regime manages to get the politically sensitive cases before reliable judges, it does not have to control the rest of the judiciary. In fact, it should invite independent decision making in *other* cases as it creates a helpful façade of judicial independence. See David Dyzenhaus, *Judging the Judges, Judging Ourselves: Truth, Reconciliation and the Apartheid Legal Order* (Hart Publishing 2003) (on the South Africa during apartheid); Kim Lane Scheppele, "Declarations of Independence: Judicial Responses to Political Pressure" in Stephen B. Burbank and Barry Friedman (eds.), *Judicial Independence at the Crossroads: An Interdisciplinary Approach* (SAGE Publications 2002) 237 (on the U.S.S.R); and Solomon 2010, above note 72, at 354 and 357–358 (on Russia and China).

[164] Besides case assignment, the Communist regimes employed two more techniques: the so-called interpretative guidelines and the so-called extraordinary appeals. Section II.E describes how these two mechanisms work in practice.

[165] Michal Bobek, "Quantity or Quality? Re-Assessing the Role of Supreme Jurisdictions in Central Europe" (2009) 57 *American Journal of Comparative Law* 33, 44.

[166] See a similar pattern in the Chilean judiciary during the Pinochet era (see Hilbink 2008, above note 154, at 122–123).

high. Even the omnipotent *prokuratura* in the Soviet Union and its satellites could not oversee every case that appeared before the courts and had to rely on the help of cooperating judges and court presidents. Furthermore, even though cases that were "wrongly decided" from the point of the ruling party could be appealed and the decisions reversed, once a problematic decision leaves the courtroom, it has a life of its own and may cause trouble for the ruling regime. In sum, totalitarian regimes had a strong incentive to get the verdicts "right" the first time and they wanted to have the "right" verdicts delivered under the façade of legality.

IV.   Mechanisms of Judicial Accountability in Recognition and Career Judiciaries

The previous two sections analyzed available mechanisms of judicial accountability and contingent circumstances that influence the functioning of these mechanisms. Each country then chooses its own set of mechanisms and designs them accordingly. A particular set depends on answers to three key questions – who is accountable, to whom, and for what[167] – which to a great extent determine how judges are held to account and may even lead to country-specific "cultures of judicial accountability." However, there are certain patterns behind the answers to these three questions that roughly correspond to models of judicial organization. As Sophie Boyron has argued, "[d]ifferences in organizational structures will lead to different types of identity being developed," which "[in] turn ... will impact on the structures for accountability that will need to be put into place."[168] The distinction between "career" and "recognition" judiciaries[169] is thus particularly useful to identify general approaches to judicial accountability, because each of these two models raises different challenges in terms of incentives and performance.

Distinctive features of the career model are well known.[170] New judges join the judiciary soon after the law school at the bottom of the judicial

---

[167] See Chapter 1.

[168] Sophie Boyron, "The Independence of the Judiciary: A Question of Identity" in Guy Canivet, Mads Andenas, and Duncan Fairgrieve (eds.), *Independence, Accountability, and the Judiciary* (British Institute of International and Comparative Law 2006) 77, 78 (both citations).

[169] See Nicholas Georgakopoulos, "Independence in the Career and Recognition Judiciary" (2000) 7 *University of Chicago Law School Roundtable* 205; or Nuno Garoupa and Tom Ginsburg, "Hybrid Judicial Career Structures: Reputation Versus Legal Tradition" (2011) 3 *Journal of Legal Analysis* 411.

[170] For the overview of the traditional features of the career model, see John Henry Merryman and Rogelio Perez-Perdomo. *The Civil Law Tradition? An Introduction to the Legal Systems*

hierarchy. Selection of judges is apolitical, based primarily on technical criteria such as the grades from the law school. Due to their early entry, career judges have little experience outside the courtroom and judging usually becomes their first and at the same time last vocation. As most career judges stay in the judicial office until retirement, they spent their entire career with the judiciary, where they work their way up through the judicial system. Hence the "career model." It is also claimed that career judges prefer to stick to legal positivism in their decision making and perceive themselves as "guardians of the law" who do not do anything else than apply the preexisting legal rules.[171]

The career model has been traditionally contrasted to the recognition model. The recognition model rests on the merit-based selection of judges who join the judiciary not sooner than in the middle of their career. This model stresses the importance of the life wisdom and experience; judging becomes only the second or the third vocation and promotions of judges are rather rare. Selection of judges in this model is based on the performance at the Bar and takes into account political criteria. For the latter characteristics this model is often referred to as the "recognition model."[172] Judges in the recognition model are often portrayed as more open in explaining their personal views in their judgments and more prone to judicial law-making.

In order to understand the difference between recognition and career judiciary more clearly, it is helpful to introduce Damaška's two visions of officialdom. Mirjan Damaška distinguishes between the hierarchical ideal of the officialdom and the coordinate ideal of officialdom.[173] The hierarchical ideal relies on a professional corps of officials, organized into a clear hierarchical structure and making decisions according to technical standards. This system requires an extensive control and oversight of activities of the lower levels of the system. Hence, it roughly corresponds to conceptions of classical bureaucracy. In contrast, the coordinate ideal envisions

---

of Europe and Latin America (3rd ed., Stanford University Press 2007) 34–38; David S. Clark, "The Organization of Lawyers and Judges" in Mauro Capelletti (ed.), *International Encyclopedia of Comparative Law, Volume XVI: Civil Procedure* (Mohr Siebeck 2002) 164–186; or Carlo Guarnieri, "Appointment and Career of Judges in Continental Europe: The Rise of Judicial Self- Government" (2004) 24 *Legal Studies* 169, 169–173.

[171] This view has been heavily criticized as misleading. See Shapiro, above note 161, at 135–148 (on judicial law-making in civil law systems in general); or literature cited in Chapter 1, Section IV.

[172] Sometimes it is also referred to as the "political model" of the judiciary.

[173] See Mirjan R. Damaška, *The Faces of Justice and State Authority: A Comparative Approach to the Legal Process* (Yale University Press 1986) 16–46 and 181–239.

an amorphous machinery of justice with not so strict hierarchy that relies on lay officials or democratically elected officials who apply standards of substantive justice rather than technical norms. The decision making in this system rests on shared visions and common understanding of ethical and political norms, and thus the system does not require extensive control and review of individual decisions. Due to this horizontal distribution of authority, it is called a "coordinate" ideal.

This categorization reflects the abovementioned differences between career and recognition models of the judiciary. As career judges enter the judiciary as "greenhorns" at the bottom of the judicial hierarchy they tend to defer to senior judges and to court presidents. They gradually become socialized within the judicial ranks and once they climb the ladder of judicial hierarchy, they just switch their roles and reproduce the same pattern. Not surprisingly, career judges tend to "look down" at other legal professions and at advocates in particular, since they consider them biased and partial. Conversely, when "recognition judges" enter the judiciary, they are already experienced lawyers and strong personalities. Furthermore, once they are appointed, they have little prospect for promotion. These two factors, taken together, limit the influence of the senior judges and court presidents in common law systems. The court presidents still play an important role, but the mentality is different as they are not considered "superiors" of other judges. Lastly, there is a strong link between the Bar and the Bench in common law countries, which is missing in most civil law countries.

The hierarchical officialdom and career model have been associated with civil law judicial structures, whereas the coordinate officialdom and recognition model have been prevalent in common law jurisdictions. More recently, scholars have argued that the career/recognition distinction does not correspond perfectly to the civil law/common law distinction, but rather that pockets of career judiciary develop in legal systems dominated by recognition judiciaries and vice versa.[174] In other words, they suggest that most legal systems favor the mix of the two models, rather than a pure institutional design.[175] However, despite this convergence between civil law and common

---

[174] Garoupa and Ginsburg 2011, above note 169.
[175] See also Robert Reed, "Le contrôle informel: L'institution judiciaire, les juges et la societé (1)" [Informal Control: The Judiciary, Judges and Society (1)], in Guy Canivet, Mads Andenas, and Duncan Fairgrieve (eds.), *Independence, Accountability, and the Judiciary* (British Institute of International and Comparative Law 2006) 401, 402 (who has suggested that the French and British judiciaries have been converging and that the judiciary in the United Kingdom is becoming a career judiciary).

law jurisdictions, if one leaves aside specialized courts and constitutional courts and focuses only on the ordinary judiciary, the career/recognition distinction still corresponds to the civil law/common law distinction pretty well.

Each of these two models, civil law (career) judiciary and common law (recognition) judiciary, approaches differently two fundamental sources of the need to hold judges to account. One is that the preferences of the judiciary may be isolated from the rest of society, which is a standard adverse selection problem. The other potential problem is that the judiciary is not sufficiently incentivized to perform well, which may result in shirking, judicial development of doctrines that benefit the judiciary directly rather than society,[176] and corruption. These moves can be referred to as a moral hazard problem.[177]

The key difference between civil law and common law models of judicial organization is that the recognition model emphasizes ex ante screening to deal with adverse selection and external monitoring to deal with moral hazard, whereas the career model emphasizes hierarchical supervision to deal with moral hazard and internal professional norms and promotion to deal with adverse selection.[178] This explains why court presidents are not considered "superiors" of other judges in recognition models. It also shows that promotion (in a broad sense) plays a very different role in each model. As becoming a court president is not considered promotion in common law models, usually only one carrot, promotion to a higher court, is available and even this carrot is a marginal accountability mechanism, because it is very rare. There are no positions of chamber presidents, no secondment of judges to a higher court, and no temporary assignments outside the judiciary. In contrast, carrots are critical accountability tools in career judiciaries. In a sense, promotion in career judiciaries plays the same role as ex ante screening in recognition judiciaries. While in common law jurisdictions the main channel of political influence has been recruitment, in civil law systems the executive and to some extent also the legislature exerts influence on the judiciary through promotion.[179]

---

[176] Such doctrines include rules that empower judges or force the society to allocate more resources to the judiciary, excessive formalism leading to dismissals of cases on procedural grounds, rules that curb the cases that require oral hearings, deciding the case on procedural grounds rather than addressing the merits, or splitting a case into separate case files with the aim of artificially multiplying a judge's productivity,

[177] This terminology comes from Garoupa and Ginsburg 2011, above note 169, at 427–428.

[178] See also Garoupa and Ginsburg 2011, above note 169, at 430.

[179] Carlo Guarnieri, Judicial Independence in Europe: Threat or Resource for Democracy? (2013) 49 *Representation* 347, 347. But note that the judicial council model might erode even the role of promotion in civil law systems if judges from lower courts have majority on the judicial council (which seems to be the case of Italian *Consiglio de la Magistratura*;; see ibid., at 348 and 353–354). However, it very much depends on the design and competences of the judicial council.

Examples from two civil law and two common law jurisdictions that fol-low confirm these patterns. To start with the French judiciary, it has been "structured as a collective entity and takes decisions as a collegiate body"[180] and "the whole system [in France] tends to deny individual identities to judges."[181] Boyron also points out that "in most cases it is impossible to identify a judge with a specific solution in the case law, because it will be identified with a court."[182] In France, the judiciary is considered to be more than a loose confederation of individual judges. In addition, it is generally perceived that most judicial "accidents" or malfunctioning of justice are caused by an accumulation of errors or mistakes by different actors (e.g., a judge, a prosecutor, and/or civil servants) and that the only remedy for the victim in such cases is to bring a liability action against the state. The French "culture of judicial accountability" thus ensures that external actors can hold "the judiciary [...] collectively accountable in various ways but few processes and mechanisms are in place to render judges individually accountable."[183] The key accountability mechanism is promotion which is controlled by bodies where senior judges have an upper hand. The *Conseil supérieur de la magistrature*, the French judicial council, controls promo-tion to higher courts and *commissions d'avancément* (promotion commis-sions) decide on promotion at lower echelons of the French judiciary.[184]

In contrast, "[t]he organization of the judiciary in England revolves largely around the notion of individuality."[185] The appointment process is the search for an individual who possesses specific qualities, judgments are written by individual judges, and it is easy to isolate the work of each judge and criticize his decisions.[186] Thus, one may say that the British "culture of judicial accountability" emphasizes the accountability of indi-vidual judges, who can, in extreme cases, even become the target of vicious personal attacks by the media – so-called judge bashing.[187]

Additional differences between these two countries stem from the well-known specifics of the common and civil law judiciaries. Most judges in the United Kingdom enter the judiciary in the later stages of their careers

---

[180] Boyron, above note 168, at 78.
[181] Ibid., at 96 n. 91.
[182] Ibid., at 96 n. 91.
[183] Ibid., at 93.
[184] See Jean-Francois Weber, "Conseil supérieur de la magistrature (CSM)" in Thierry Renoux (ed.), *La Justice en France* (La documentation française 2013) 219, 221–222.
[185] Boyron, above note 168, at 97.
[186] Ibid., at 97–98.
[187] This term was coined by Stephen Sedley in Foreword to Michael Addo (ed.), *Freedom of Expression and the Criticism of Judges: A Comparative Study of European Legal Standards* (Ashgate 2000).

and have fewer prospects of promotion than French career judges.[188] "Travelling of judges among branches," which is quite common for judges of the *Conseil d'État*[189] who can be temporarily assigned to the ministries or other public offices,[190] is prohibited in the United Kingdom.[191] Last but not least, the civil law concept of the right to a legal judge that requires random case assignment has not found its way to the United Kingdom.[192] To be sure, several authors have recently suggested that the French and British judiciaries have been converging and that the judiciary in the United Kingdom is becoming a career judiciary.[193] However, there are still profound differences regarding judicial accountability in these two countries and the British and French judiciaries are still the ideal types in the Weberian sense.

So is the United States judiciary, where profoundly different systems operate at the federal and state levels. At the federal level, apart from impeachment there are almost no mechanisms that can be used to hold Art. III judges[194] to account.[195] Promotions are very rare and other carrots

---

[188] See Reed, above note 175, at 402.

[189] Note that according to the French doctrine, the *Conseil d'État* is not, strictly speaking, a court, but a part of the *function publique*, and hence the temporary assignment of judicial members of the *Conseil d'État* to other posts within the public service is formally considered to be travelling within the *same* branch of the French State. For more details on the functioning of the French *Conseil d'État*, see Jean-Paul Costa, *Le Conseil d'État dans la societé contemporaine* [The *Conseil d'État* in Contemporary Society] (1993); Bruno Latour, *The Making of Law: An Ethnography of the Conseil d'État* (Polity 2010), available also in French (*La Fabrique de Droit: Une ethnographie du Conseil d'État* (2002)); Jean Massot and Thierry Girardot, *Le Conseil d'État* (1999); or Bernard Stirn, *Le Conseil d'État: Son rôle, sa jurisprudence* [The Conseil d'État: Its Role and Jurisprudence] (1991).

[190] This practice may even result in a violation of the right to an impartial court; see, for example, ECtHR, September 11, 2006, *Sacilor Lormines v. France*, no. 65411/01.

[191] See Reed, above note 175, at 402.

[192] See Diana Woodhouse, "Judicial Independence and Accountability within the United Kingdom's New Constitutional Settlement" in Guy Canivet, Mads Andenas, and Duncan Fairgrieve (eds.), *Independence, Accountability, and the Judiciary* (British Institute of International and Comparative Law 2006) 121, 138.

[193] Boyron, above note 168, at 97.

[194] It is important to remember that within the U. S. federal judiciary one must distinguish between the so-called Article III judges (judges of district courts and circuit courts and Justices of the Supreme Court of the United States), who are subject to very few mechanisms of judicial accountability, and other federal judges (such as magistrates, bankruptcy judges, or administrative judges), who are usually appointed for specified terms of office and face additional forms of accountability. See, for example, Edwin L. Felter, "Accountability in the Administrative Law Judiciary: The Right and the Wrong Kind" (2008) 86 *Denver University Law Review* 157.

[195] See, for example, Posner, R. A. 1993, above note 1, at 4–7. But see Charles Gardner Geyh, "Informal Methods of Judicial Discipline" (1993–1994) 142 *University of Pennsylvania Law Review* 243.

or sticks are not available. Salaries of Article III judges are fixed, there are no meaningful nonmonetary benefits, cases are assigned on random basis, and there is no formal judicial performance evaluation. Dual mechanisms are thus not utilized at all. On the other hand, many states appoint judges for only a limited term and use retention elections to hold them to account,[196] and have developed comprehensive judicial performance evaluation programs. Hence, there are distinct cultures of judicial accountability at the federal and state levels.

Yet another different peculiar culture of judicial accountability exists in Japan, where the judiciary is effectively controlled by a nuanced combination of rigorous screening of candidates for judicial positions, extensive socialization of selected candidates in the judicial school, regular retention review by members of the House of Representatives every ten years, comprehensive assessment of judges, careful selection of judges nominated for promotion and for assignment outside the judiciary, and the selection of top court judges whose age is close to a compulsory retirement age.[197] Moreover, Japanese judges are not appointed to a particular court and thus can be relocated to any part of Japan.[198] Several scholars then argued that he who controls the appointment of the Chief Justice and members of the General Secretariat of the Supreme Court that controls the training school for new judges controls the entire Japanese judiciary.[199]

Each of these four jurisdictions has developed a distinctive "culture of judicial accountability," but the career and recognition models are still clearly visible within them. This short comparison also shows that what American scholars know about the United States judiciary will not help them in assessing civil law systems. Despite increasing convergence between common law and civil law systems, the significant differences

---

[196] For an overall picture of how these retention elections operate, see, for example, Canes-Wrone, Clark, and Jee-Kwang, above note 22.

[197] See Law 2009, above note 35.

[198] See examples in Law 2009, above note 35; and Law 2011, above note 35.

[199] Law 2009, above note 35. See also Ramseyer, above note 159; Ramseyer and Rasmusen, above note 35; David M. O'Brien and Yasuo Ohkoshi, "Stifling Judicial Independence from Within: The Japanese Judiciary" in Peter H. Russell and David M. O'Brien (eds.), *Judicial Independence in the Age of Democracy: Critical Perspectives from around the World* (University of Virginia Press 2001); John O. Haley, "The Japanese Judiciary: Maintaining Integrity, Autonomy, and the Public Trust" in Daniel H. Foote (ed.), *Law in Japan: A Turning Point* (University of Washington Press 2007); and Frank K. Upham, "Political Lackeys or Faithful Public Servants: Two Views of the Japanese Judiciary" (2005) 30 *Law & Social Inquiry* 421.

remain and each system employs different accountability techniques. Most importantly, as common law countries recruit judges in the latter stage of their careers and know well whom they choose they do not need many accountability mechanisms after judges are appointed. In contrast, civil law countries appoint their judges at the early age and thus need more accountability mechanisms to induce judges to not deviate too much from generally recognized standards.

3

Judicial Accountability and Judicial Councils

In Chapter 2 I identified mechanisms of judicial accountability that fit into my definition of judicial accountability. However, these mechanisms do not operate in a vacuum and it is important to take into account the environment judges operate in. The model of court administration in a given country plays a key role here, as it to a great extent determines how judges are held to account. Different models of court administration may even change a "culture of judicial accountability" in a given country.[1]

Based on this assumption, the European Union (EU) and Council of Europe (CoE) hoped that their new model of court administration, the judicial council, would bring about necessary positive changes in the CEE and find a new balance between judicial independence and judicial accountability. As the impact of the Judicial Council of the Slovak Republic on holding Slovak judges to account will be the central inquiry in the case studies, it is important to explain the relationship between judicial councils and judicial accountability and to define the Judicial Council Euro-model that I will put to the test in Chapters 4–7.

I. The Rise of Judicial Councils and Their Effects

Historically, in Europe, court administration was in the hands of sovereign kings and emperors. Later on, republicanism transferred these powers from the sovereign rulers to the Ministry of Justice or a similar body. Thus, these powers were vested with *Oberste Justizstelle* in Austria, the Lord Chancellor in England, *Le Ministère de la Justice* in France, *Reichskanzler* in Germany, and with *Il Ministero della Giustizia* in Italy.[2] Self-governmental

---

[1] Carlo Guarnieri, "Judicial Independence in Europe: Threat or Resource for Democracy?" (2013) 49 *Representation* 347, 350. On "cultures of judicial accountability," see Chapter 2, Section IV.

[2] For a succinct summary of this development, see Nicola Picardi, "La Ministère de la Justice et les autres modèles d´administration de la justice en Europe" in Giovanni E. Longo (ed.), *L'indipendenza della giustizia, oggi* (Judicial independence today: liber amicorum in onore di Giovanni E. Longo 1999) 269–273. For a more historical account, see Martin Shapiro,

bodies of judges did not exist[3] and court presidents were subordinate to the Minister of Justice rather than players on their own. Ministers of Justice thus controlled virtually all mechanisms of judicial accountability. This arrangement prevailed, by and large, until the end of World War II.

It was only in the wake of World War II, when the first two judicial councils as we understand them today – as independent and autonomous bodies endowed with significant powers in the management of the judiciary – appeared. In 1946, the French Constitution of October 27, 1946 entrenched the *Conseil supérieur de la magistrature*. A year later, the Italian Constitution of December 27, 1947 laid the foundations of the Italian *Consiglio superiore della magistratura*. These two judicial councils resulted from different historical, cultural, and social contexts and they sought different aims,[4] but they formed the "first wave" of judicial councils.

The "second wave" of judicial councils took place in the late 1970s, when Spain, Portugal, and Greece established theirs. It is not surprising that these changes coincided with the fall of authoritarian regimes in those countries. Judicial councils, like the newly created constitutional courts, were supposed to facilitate the transition of these countries to democracy. The "third wave" of judicial councils followed a decade later. This time it spanned two continents, because the fall of communism in Europe and the collapse of many authoritarian regimes in Latin America happened more or less at the same time. As a result, several countries in postcommunist Europe[5] as well as in Latin America[6] established judicial councils in the late 1980s or the early 1990s.

Courts: A Comparative and Political Analysis (University of Chicago Press 1981) 126–156; or John Philip Dawson, *The Oracles of the Law* (University of Michigan Press 1968).

[3] To be sure, some independent bodies dealing with the management of the judiciary, such as the *Consiglio superiore della magistratura* in Italy, came into being as early as in 1907, but these bodies had only consultative powers at that time. See, for example, Simone Benvenuti, "The French and the Italian High Councils for the Judiciary Observations Drawn from the Analysis of Their Staff and Activity (1947–2011)" (2012 IPSA World Congress, Madrid, July 8–12, 2012). For a more detailed exposition into the functioning of *Consiglio superiore della magistratura*, see Daniela Piana and Antoine Vauchez, *Il Consiglio superiore della magistratura* (Il Mulino 2012). Similarly, some disciplinary bodies such as the French *Conseil supérieur de la magistrature* were also created before the World War II, but they had no powers in other agendas; see the Law of August 30, 1883 (*Réforme de l'organisation judiciaire*).

[4] This is often forgotten and these two judicial councils are put in the same basket. For further details, see Benvenuti, above note 3; or Thierry S. Renoux (ed.), *Les Conseils superieurs de la magistrature en Europe* (Paris: La documentation francaise 1999).

[5] These countries include Bulgaria, Poland, and Romania. For further details, see the following sect ion.

[6] See Linn A. Hammergren, "Do Judicial Councils Further Judicial Reform? Lessons from Latin America Carnegie Endowment Rule of Law Series" Working Paper No. 28; or Rebecca Bill Chavez, "The Appointment and Removal Process for Judges in Argentina: The Role of

However, the debate on whether or not to introduce a judicial council crossed the borders of individual states and became a transnational issue only with the prospect of the enlargement of the EU in the mid-1990s.[7] The European Commission, supported by the CoE and various advisory bodies, had the necessary leverage at its disposal and started to exercise significant pressure on the postcommunist states that sought accession to the EU to adopt particular judicial reforms. These "pan-European" bodies identified the judicial council model as the most appropriate means of reforming the judiciary. Most of the states in the CEE that had not adopted the judicial council model during the "third wave" buckled under the increasing pressure and eventually adopted a judicial council. Hungary and Slovenia established judicial councils in 1997, followed by Slovakia, Estonia, and Lithuania in 2002. Romania and Bulgaria had already created their judicial councils in the previous wave, but they were forced to modify their existing models in order to meet the "pan-European" standards laid down by the EU and the CoE. Due to efforts of the CoE, which has a broader membership than the EU, strong judicial councils were introduced also in Georgia, Moldova, and Ukraine.[8] It is in this "fourth wave" of judicial councils that Judicial Council Euro-model, which is crucial for this book, came into being.

Judicial councils changed the landscape of court administration. For the first time in history judges were granted significant autonomy in managing the judiciary. The composition, competences, and powers of judicial councils vary from one state to another, but each state that opted for this model of court administration transferred certain powers from political branches to this newly established body. Nuno Garoupa and Tom Ginsburg summarize the typology of judicial councils (in the broad sense) nicely according to two criteria – their competence and composition (see Table 3.1).[9]

Judicial Councils and Impeachment Juries in Promoting Judicial Independence" (2005) 49 *Latin American Politics & Society* 33.

[7] The CoE gave preference to the judicial council model as early as in 1994. See Committee of Ministers, Recommendation No. R (94) 12, October 13, 1994, printed in: 37 Yearbook of the European Convention on Human Rights 453 (1994), Principle I 2 (c).

[8] See Lydia F. Müller, "Judicial Administration in Transitional Eastern Countries" in Anja Seibert-Fohr (ed.), *Judicial Independence in Transition* (Springer 2012) 937–969.

[9] Nuno Garoupa and Tom Ginsburg, "Guarding the Guardians: Judicial Councils and Judicial Independence" (2009) 57 *American Journal of Comparative Law* 103, figure 2. For an alternative typology, which is limited to selected judicial councils in Europe, see Cristina Parau, "Explaining Judiciary Governance in Central and Eastern Europe: External Incentives, Transnational Elites and Parliament Inaction" (2015) 67 *Europe-Asia Studies* 409, table 1.

Table 3.1. *Typology of judicial councils*

Competences	Judges from Supreme Court dominate	Judges from lower courts dominate	Nonjudges dominate
Extensive (discipline, removal, promotion, appointments)	Strong hierarchical judicial council (Japan, Mexico, Thailand)	Strong nonhierarchical judicial council (Italy, France)	Politicized judicial council (Ecuador, Barbados, Singapore)
Intermediate (appointments only)	Hierarchical self-regulating judicial appointments commission (Bangladesh)	Nonhierarchical self-regulating judicial appointments commission (Belgium)	Judicial appointments commission (USA, UK, Canada, Netherlands, Germany)
Minimal (housekeeping functions)	Weak judicial council (Panama)	Weak judicial council (Brazil, Hungary)	Weak judicial council (Paraguay)

Source: Nuno Garoupa and Tom Ginsburg, "Guarding the Guardians: Judicial Councils and Judicial Independence" (2009) 57 *American Journal of Comparative Law* 103.

Due to this transfer of competences, accountability arrangements also underwent a significant change. The Minister of Justice was no longer the key principal of judges and he lost control over several, if not the majority, of accountability mechanisms. Judicial councils may, depending on their powers, decide on all types of promotions, removal and disciplining of judges, set criteria for case assignment, and reassignment or decide on salary bonuses.

This institutional change begs the question: what do judicial councils actually do? Or, more specifically, did the judicial councils actually deliver "the goods" they promised? The proponents of judicial councils among politicians and judges tend to evade this question. They take an unjustifiably rosy view of judicial councils and make normative claims without any empirical evidence.[10] Scholars were also silent on this issue for

---

[10] See, for example, Violane Autheman and Sandra Elena, *Global Best Practices-Judicial Councils: Lessons Learned from Europe and Latin America*'(IFES 2004) (arguing that

a long time. It was only the long-term dubious effects of judicial councils in Latin America that led to the first critical studies.[11] More recently, European scholars have started to question the view that the judicial council is a panacea for the postcommunist judiciaries. These voices come from Hungary,[12] Romania,[13] Bulgaria,[14] Slovakia,[15] as well as from former Soviet republics.[16] These authors claim that judicial councils may have negative effects in the new democracies and that several judicial councils indeed went astray. Nevertheless, most of these studies lack empirical evidence

judicial councils should be composed of a majority of judges elected by their peers and should be tasked with selection, promotion, discipline, and training); or guidelines developed by organs of the EU and the CoE discussed subsequently.

[11] See, for example, Hammergren, above note 6.

[12] See Károly Bárd, "Judicial Independence in the Accession Countries of Central and Eastern Europe and the Baltics" in András Sajó and Lorri Rutt Bentch (eds.), *Judicial Integrity* (Martinus Nijhoff 2004) 265; Zoltán Fleck, "Judicial Independence and Its Environment in Hungary" in Jiří Přibáň, Pauline Roberts, and James Young (eds.), *Systems of Justice in Transition: Central European Experiences since 1989* (Ashgate 2003); Béla Pokol, "Judicial Power and Democratization in Eastern Europe" in Proceedings of the Conference Europanisation and Democratisation: The Southern European Experience and the Perspective for the New Member States of the Enlarged Europe (2005) 165; or Zoltán Fleck, "Judicial Independence in Hungary" in Anja Seibert-Fohr (ed.), *Judicial Independence in Transition* (Springer 2012) 793.

[13] See Bogdan Iancu, "Constitutionalism in Perpetual Transition: The Case of Romania" in Bogdan Iancu (ed.), *The Law/Politics Distinction in Contemporary Public Law Adjudication* (Eleven International Publishing 2009) 187, 196–198; Cristina Parau, "The Drive for Judicial Supremacy" in Anja Seibert-Fohr (ed.), *Judicial Independence in Transition* (Springer 2012) 619; and Ramona Coman and Cristina Dallara, "Judicial Independence in Romania" in Anja Seibert-Fohr (ed.), *Judicial Independence in Transition* (Springer 2012) 835.

[14] See Daniel Smilov, "EU Enlargement and the Constitutional Principle of Judicial Independence" in Wojciech Sadurski, et al. (eds.), *Spreading Democracy and the Rule of Law?: The Impact of EU Enlargement on the Rule of Law, Democracy and Constitutionalism in Post-Communist Legal Orders* (Springer 2006) 313; Diana Bozhilova, "Measuring Success and Failure of EU-Europeanization in the Eastern Enlargement: Judicial Reform in Bulgaria" (2007) 9 *European Journal of Law Reform* 285; Maria Popova, "Be Careful What You Wish For: A Cautionary Tale of Post-Communist Judicial Empowerment" (2010) 18 *Demokratizatsiya* 56; Thierry Delpeuch and Margarita Vassileva, "Lessons from the Bulgarian Judicial Reforms: Practical Ways to Exert Political Influence on a Formally Very Independent Judiciary" in Leny E. de Groot-van Leeuwen and Wannes Rombouts (eds.), *Separation of Powers in Theory and Practice: An International Perspective* (Wolf Legal Publishers 2010) 49; and Maria Popova, "Why the Bulgarian Judiciary Does Not Prosecute Corruption?" (2012) 59 *Problems of Post Communism* 35.

[15] See Ján Svák, "Slovenská skúsenosť s optimalizáciou modelu správy súdnictva" in Jan Kysela (ed.) *Hledání optimálního modelu správy soudnictví pro Českou republiku* (Kancelář Senátu 2008) 54.

[16] See in particular Müller 2012, above note 8, at 937–969 (critically reviewing strong judicial councils in Georgia, Ukraine, and Moldova, as well as weak judicial councils in Armenia, Azerbaijan, and Kazakhstan).

that would prove their assertions, and advocates of judicial councils can easily dismiss these studies as biased, misleading, or at least incomplete.

In sum, opposing views emerged regarding the functioning of judicial councils. It is thus high time to study judicial councils thoroughly and without bias.[17] While I cannot generalize about all types of judicial councils in all possible environments I believe that I can make a reasonably robust empirical analysis of the functioning of the judicial council model of court administration in the CEE which scholars working in other parts of the world can build on. This empirical analysis will be conducted in Chapters 4 through 7 by means of case studies on the Czech Republic and Slovakia. Now I must identify features of the Judicial Council Euro-model that was heavily promoted and eventually implemented in the CEE and narrow down the accountability issues I will focus on in the case studies.

II.   The Judicial Council Euro-model of Court Administration

Dozens of judicial councils came into being during the four waves mentioned in the previous section. It is not surprising that their composition, competences, and powers vary from one state to another.[18] Therefore, I must make clear what I mean by "judicial council" or, more precisely, which type of judicial council I want to study. In a nutshell, the empirical part of this book focuses on the Judicial Council Euro-model, which played a key role in the fourth wave of judicial councils in the late 1990s and the early years of the twenty-first century.

Two caveats must be made here. First, I must make clear at the outset that there is no formal document that would define the Judicial Council Euro-model. Therefore, I must excavate the parameters of this model from various documents originating from diverse bodies of the EU and the CoE. One may even object that there is no single model of judicial council jointly advocated by the EU and the CoE and that

---

[17] There are few law review articles that study judicial councils thoroughly (see the literature in the three notes that follow), but they tend to overlook the systems *without* judicial councils and, moreover, do not cover Slovakia.

[18] For a succinct categorization of judicial councils, see Nuno Garoupa and Tom Ginsburg, "The Comparative Law and Economics of Judicial Councils" (2009) 27 *Berkeley Journal of International Law* 53; Garoupa and Ginsburg 2009a, above note 9; or Renoux 1999, above note 4.

these two organizations do not necessarily agree on the requirements of such a model. However, a number of the European Commission documents[19] and the institutional dialogue between the relevant bodies of the EU and the CoE[20] clearly rebut this objection and reveal that there is a mutual agreement on this issue. Most recently, the chapter on the judiciary of the 2013 Action Plan for Montenegro, which contains the EU accession commitments, employs the CoE standards as benchmarks for virtually all aspects of judicial reforms required from Montenegro.[21] A high ranking official of the European Commission responsible for judicial reforms in the former Yugoslavia also confirmed that the EU agrees with the CoE's standards and promotes its judicial council model in the accession countries.[22]

Second, the aim of this section is merely to identify the features of the Judicial Council Euro-model. This book does not trace the development of this standard[23] or its legal basis[24] and it does not question the "double standards" applied by the European Commission during the EU accession process.[25] Similarly, it does not describe the complex web of organs, committees, subcommittees, and affiliated entities of the EU and the CoE involved in the process of defining those standards.[26] For this reason I also do not question the legitimacy and democratic pedigree of those bodies. Nor I challenge the normative justification of the

---

[19] See, for example, Anja Seibert-Fohr, "Judicial Independence in European Union Accessions: The Emergence of a European Basic Principle" (2009) 52 *German Yearbook of International Law* 405.

[20] *See* Daniela Piana, *Judicial Accountabilities in New Europe: From Rule of Law to Quality of Justice* (Ashgate 2010) chapter 2; Anja Seibert-Fohr, "Judicial Independence – The Normativity of an Evolving Transnational Principle" in Anja Seibert-Fohr (ed.), *Judicial Independence in Transition* (Springer 2012) 1279–1360, at 1333–1345; Hammergren, above note 6, at 940; and Guarnieri 2013, above note 1, at 351.

[21] See Government of Montenegro, *Action Plan: Chapter 23 Judiciary and Fundamental Rights*, June 23, 2013, 15–59.

[22] Interview with a senior official at DG JUST, Brussels, April 8, 2014.

[23] On this aspect of the Judicial Council Euro-model, see Seibert-Fohr 2009, above note 19; Lydia F. Müller, "Judicial Independence as a Council of Europe Standard" (2009) 52 *German Yearbook of International Law* 461; and Michal Bobek and David Kosař, "Global Solutions, Local Damages: A Critical Study in Judicial Councils in Central and Eastern Europe" 15 *German Law Journal* 1257, 1258–1262 (2014).

[24] Seibert-Fohr 2009, above note 19, at 407–419.

[25] Generally on the double or even multiple standards in the accession process, see, for example, Dimitry Kochenov, *EU Enlargement and the Failure of Conditionality* (Kluwer 2008) 264–266, 271–290.

[26] For a comprehensive overview of these bodies, see Piana 2010, above note 20, chapter 2.

substantive content of the Euro-standards.[27] All I want to do is to define the components of the Judicial Council Euro-model.

There are five key requirements of the Judicial Council Euro-model that may be distilled from the plethora of documents produced by numerous organs and affiliated bodies of the EU and the CoE: (1) A judicial council should have constitutional status;[28] (2) at least 50% of the members of the judicial council must be judges and these judicial members must be selected by their peers; that is by other judges;[29] (3) a judicial council ought to be vested with decision-making and not merely advisory powers;[30] (4) a judicial council should have substantial competences in all matters concerning the career of a judge including selection, appointment, promotion, transfer, dismissal, and disciplining;[31] and (5) a judicial council must

---

[27] See Smilov, above note 14, at 323–325 (referring to European Commission's concept of judicial independence as a myth); and Bobek and Kosař, above note 23, at 1269–1273 (criticizing the "Euro-model" of judicial council for the lack of democratic legitimacy, ignoring the growing power of courts, neglecting the threats coming from within the judiciary, ignoring the reluctance of established European democracies to embrace the "Euro-model," and ignoring local specifics in the receiving states).

[28] The European Network of Councils for the Judiciary (ENCJ), Councils for the Judiciary Report 2010–2011 para. 1.4; and CCJE, Opinion no.10 (2007) to the attention of the Committee of Ministers of the Council of Europe on the Council for the Judiciary at the service of society (Strasbourg, November 21–23, 2007) para. 11. See also European Charter on the Statute for Judges [Strasbourg, July 8–10, 1998] para. 1.2.

[29] ENCJ, Councils for the Judiciary Report 2010–2011 para. 2.1; and CCJE, Opinion no.10 (2007) to the attention of the Committee of Ministers of the Council of Europe on the Council for the Judiciary at the service of society (Strasbourg, November 21–23, 2007) para. 18. See also European Charter on the Statute for Judges [Strasbourg, July 8–10, 1998] para. 1.3; Resolution of ENCJ on "Self Governance for the Judiciary: Balancing Independence and Accountability" (May 2008) para. 4 (b); and Recommendation CM/Rec (2010)12 of the Committee of Ministers to member states on judges: independence, efficiency and responsibilities, adopted by the Committee of Ministers on November 17, 2010 para. 27. See also the first attempts to read this requirement into the right to an independent tribunal guaranteed by Article 6(1) ECHR in ECtHR, January 9, 2013, *Volkov v. Ukraine*, no. 21722/11, §§ 109–112.

[30] ENCJ, Councils for the Judiciary Report 2010–2011 paras 3.4 and 3.13; CCJE, Opinion no.10 (2007) to the attention of the Committee of Ministers of the Council of Europe on the Council for the Judiciary at the service of society (Strasbourg, November 21–23, 2007) paras 48, 49, and 60. See also European Charter on the Statute for Judges [Strasbourg, July 8 -10, 1998] paras 3.1, 4.1., and 7.2.; and Recommendation CM/Rec (2010)12 of the Committee of Ministers to member states on judges: independence, efficiency and responsibilities, adopted by the Committee of Ministers on November 17, 2010, para. 46.

[31] ENCJ, Councils for the Judiciary Report 2010–2011 para. 3.1; and CCJE, Opinion no.10 (2007) to the attention of the Committee of Ministers of the Council of Europe on the Council for the Judiciary at the service of society (Strasbourg, November 21–23, 2007) para. 42. See also European Charter on the Statute for Judges [Strasbourg, July 8–10, 1998] para. 1.3.

be chaired either by the President or Chief Justice of the Highest Court or the neutral head of state.[32]

This set of five criteria is by no means the definitive list of requirements and recommendations proposed by the EU and the CoE. Many documents produced by these two organizations demand more stringent criteria and additional requirements.[33] The above-mentioned set is, rather, the lowest common denominator of what is expected and what the EU and the CoE advocate for.

It is clear from the "should" language of the documents that these five criteria may not always been framed as "must" requirements. However, the language should not obfuscate the obligatory nature of these requirements for the so-called new European democracies. In fact, most of the documents of the EU and the CoE use the "should" language for two reasons. First, the "should" language carves out exceptions for the so-called old European democracies, which are not willing to modify their current models of court administration. Second, the "should" language is employed in order to make these documents as inclusive as possible and also to speak to the bodies in some European states that represent different styles of court administration, such as the Court Service model[34] and hybrid models of court administration that have different rationales and play a different role.[35]

These five criteria also capture the "invisible rationale" of the Judicial Council Euro-model – to concentrate as much power as possible in one institution that is dominated by judges. This "self-government" of judges is a golden thread running through all five criteria. Some documents make this claim more explicitly by stressing that the judicial council must

---

[32] ENCJ, Councils for the Judiciary Report 2010–2011 para. 4.1; CCJE, Opinion no.10 (2007) to the attention of the Committee of Ministers of the Council of Europe on the Council for the Judiciary at the service of society (Strasbourg, November 21–23, 2007) para. 33.

[33] For instance, some documents preclude the participation of the Minister of Justice in the judicial council or require judicial councils to have budgetary powers, oversee judicial training, process complaints from the users of courts, comment on bills affecting the judiciary or propose new legislation. See, for example, ENCJ, Councils for the Judiciary Report 2010–2011 paras 3.5–3.9 and 3.14–3.18; or CCJE, Opinion no.10 (2007) to the attention of the Committee of Ministers of the Council of Europe on the Council for the Judiciary at the service of society (Strasbourg, November 21–23, 2007) paras 65–90.

[34] The Court Service model is sometimes referred to as a "Northern European Model" of judicial council [See, for example, Wim Voermans and Pim Albers, "Councils for the Judiciary in EU Countries" (2003) European Council for the Efficiency of Justice, CEPEJ]. I reject this label (as well as the "Southern European Model" label) as unhelpful and misleading; see also Garoupa and Ginsburg 2009a, above note 9, at 109, note 20.

[35] On the Court Service model and hybrid models of court administration see below.

"secure the independence of the judiciary 'from every *other* power'" that is from the executive and the legislature – not from the judiciary – and "ensure effective self-governance."[36] I might also reverse this "invisible rationale" – the flipside of judicial self-government is distrust in politicians and discomfort with democracy in general.[37] I will show below that this "invisible rationale" is not shared by all the European countries that adopted the judicial council model.

Interestingly, the Judicial Council Euro-model completely overlooks the threats from within the judiciary and does not stipulate any checks against the capture of this model by a narrow group of judicial leadership. More specifically, court presidents and vice presidents are not precluded from becoming members of the judicial council and no maximum ratio of these judicial officials among judicial members of the judicial council is generally set.[38] Similarly, any rule ensuring the representation of all echelons of the judiciary in the judicial council is missing. This omission means that there are no checks and balances between the judicial leadership and regular judges. Internal independence of an individual judge vis-à-vis the judicial leadership who may decide through the Judicial Council Euro-model on their careers is thus left unprotected.

In order to see the specific features of the Judicial Council Euro-model more clearly it is helpful to juxtapose this model with other models of court administration. This short detour should also save this book from a common vice in the scholarship on judicial systems, namely that scholars tend to compare only countries *with* judicial councils and debates therein while ignoring countries *without* judicial councils and debates therein.[39]

---

[36] ENCJ, Councils for the Judiciary Report 2010–2011 § 1.4.

[37] See, for example, Seibert-Fohr 2009, above note 19, at 432–433. On a more general level, see Roberto Unger, *What Should Legal Analysis Become* (Verso 1998), 72–73; or Jeremy Waldron, "Dirty Little Secret" (1998) 98 *Columbia Law Review* 510.

[38] CCJE, Opinion no. 10 (2007), para. 26. Contrast, however, ENCJ, Councils for the Judiciary Report 2010–2011, para. 2; European Charter on the Statute for Judges, Strasbourg, July 8–10, 1998, para. 1.3; "Budapest Resolution," para. 4 (b); and Recommendation CM/Rec (2010)12, para. 27. Similarly, the Judicial Council Euro-model does not set any limit on the number of senior judges of appellate and top courts.

[39] A rare exception is the synthesis report on states without judicial councils compiled by Lord Thomas; see "Councils for the Judiciary: States without a High Council" *preliminary report* (CCJE 2007) 4, Strasbourg, March 19, 2007. In fact, debates in countries that have resisted the introduction of judicial councils (e.g., Germany) are particularly illuminating as they discuss the pros and cons of both solutions more openly. See, for example, Beschluss "Selbstverwaltung' der Bundesvertreterversammlung des Deutschen Richterbundes" [Motion for Self-Administration by the Assembly of Federal Representatives of the German Association of Judges], adopted on November 15, 2002 in Kiel (summary of the motion published in *Neue Juristische Wochenschrift* 2002, Heft 42, XXVII–XXXIV). See also papers

There are five models of court administration in use in Europe:[40] (1) the "Ministry of Justice" model, (2) the judicial council model, (3) the courts service model, (4) hybrid models, and (5) the socialist model.

The "Ministry of Justice" model is the longest-standing one. Under this framework, the Ministry of Justice plays a significant role in both the appointment and promotion of judges and in the administration of courts and court management. This model exists in Austria, the Czech Republic, Finland, and Germany, among others. Still, it is misleading to claim that judges themselves play no role in the appointment and promotion of judges or in the administration of courts and court management in this model and that the Ministry of Justice controls these processes unilaterally.[41] In the ministerial model, it is also other bodies, such as the legislature, the President of a given country, judicial boards, and the ombudsman or professional organizations, which often play a significant role or at least have their influence as well. Moreover, a crucial role in these systems is in fact played by presidents of appellate and supreme courts, who are consulted regarding judicial promotion, appointments, and other key issues. Some of the appointments or promotions cannot even be carried out without their consent. Thus, albeit called the "Ministry of Justice model," it does not mean that the executive runs it all exclusively. The strong criticism one may encounter with respect to this model in a number of international documents and academic writings, and which the proponents of the judicial council model often criticize with fervor, is a parody of the Minister of Justice model that no longer exists in Europe.[42]

The judicial council model is a model in which an independent intermediary organization positioned between the judiciary and the politically

---

delivered by the (then) president of the *Bundesverfassungsgericht* [Federal Constitutional Court] Hans-Jürgen Papier (Hans-Jürgen Papier, "Zur Selbstverwaltung der Dritten Gewalt" (2002) Neue Juristische Wochenschrift 2585) and by the (then) president of the German Judges' Association Geert Mackenroth (Geert W. Mackenroth and H. Teetzmann, "Selbstverwaltung der Justiz: Markenzeichen zukunftsfähiger Rechtsstaaten" (2002) *Zeitschrift für Rechtspolitik* 337). For a brief overview of this debate in English, see Martina Künnecke, *Tradition and Change in Administrative Law an Anglo-German Comparison* (Springer 2007), 47–72.

[40] Different classifications are equally plausible. My classification relies heavily on Picardi, above note 2.

[41] In fact, other bodies such as the legislature, the President of a given republic, judicial boards, the ombudsman or professional organizations often play a role or at least have their say in the Ministry of Justice model as well.

[42] What many critics attacked in Central and Eastern Europe was in fact the "state administration of courts," which was based on the socialist model (on this model of court administration see below) rather than the genuine Ministry of Justice model.

responsible administrators in the executive or the parliament has significant powers primarily in appointing and promoting judges and in exercising disciplinary powers vis-à-vis judges. Judicial councils my also play a role in the areas of administration, court management, and budgeting for the courts, but these powers are only secondary to their "personal competences" regarding a career of individual judges. Belgium, Bulgaria, France, Hungary (until Orbán's 2011 judicial reform), Italy, Lithuania, the Netherlands, Poland, Portugal, Romania, Slovakia, Slovenia, and Spain belong to this group. As will be shown subsequently, however, not all of these judicial councils meet the criteria of the Euro-model.

In contrast, in the court service model the primary function of an independent intermediary organization is in the area of administration (supervision of judicial registry offices, caseloads and case stocks, flow rates, the promotion of legal uniformity, quality care etc.), court management (e.g., housing, automation, recruitment, training, etc.), and budgeting the courts. In contrast to judicial councils, the court services have a limited role in the appointment and promotion of judges and do not exercise disciplinary powers vis-à-vis judges. These powers are sometimes vested in independent organs – such as judicial appointment commissions – that operate separately from the court service. Denmark, Ireland, Norway, and Sweden are examples of countries that have adopted the court service model.

By hybrid models, I mean any model that combines various components of the previous three models in such a way that it is significantly distinct from each of them. Hybrid models operate in England and Wales, Estonia, Hungary (since 2011), Iceland, Switzerland, Cyprus, Liechtenstein, and Luxembourg. These models are so specific that one cannot generalize about them in order to create one clear box. They include judicial appointment commissions that deal only with the selection of judges up to a certain tier of the judicial system, whereas the rest of the court administration is vested in another organ (England and Wales); countries where the judicial council coexists with another strong nationwide body responsible for court administration (Hungary since 2011); countries where the Minister of Justice shares power with judges of the Supreme Court (Cyprus); federal countries where the court administration varies from one state to another (Switzerland); and microstates that have peculiar systems of court administration tailored to their specific needs (Liechtenstein and Luxembourg).

Finally, the socialist model of court administration[43] concentrated the power generally in three institutions – the General Prosecutor, the

---

[43] For a more detailed exposition of how the socialist model of court administration works, see John Hazard, *Communists and Their Law* (University of Chicago Press 1969); Attila Rácz,

Supreme Court, and court presidents – which are then themselves controlled by the Communist Party. Therefore, it is the Party controlling the courts through these institutions. Specific features of this model varied from one communist country to another and changed as they got further from the communist revolution.[44] The following mechanisms were nonetheless quite common: the relocation and demotion of judges without a decision of the disciplinary court, arbitrary assignment of cases by court presidents, the reassignment at will of judges within their courts or deciding on salary bonuses of judges, and the power of the Supreme Court to remove any case from the lower courts and decide it itself. Apart from these mechanisms available within the judiciary, judges were subject to frequent retention reviews, the Communist Party had a residual power to dismiss judges who did not exercise judicial office in line with the Party policies, and the General Prosecutor had the right to ask for the review by the Supreme Court of any judicial decision, including those that had already became final.[45] The pure socialist model of court administration no longer exists in Europe.[46] However, it is important to mention this model,[47] because some postcommunist countries in Central

---

Courts and Tribunals: A Comparative Study (Akadémia Kiadó, 1980), 41–100; René David and John Brierley, *Major Legal Systems in the World Today* (3rd ed., Stevens 1985) 155–306; or Zdeněk Kühn, *The Judiciary in Central and Eastern Europe: Mechanical Jurisprudence in Transformation?* (Brill 2011), in particular 52–62.

[44] See also Chapter 8, Section III.

[45] For descriptions of the office of the Procurator and its functions in English, see, for example, Gordon B. Smith, *The Soviet Procuracy and the Supervision of Administration* (Sijthoff & Noordhoff 1978); or Glenn G. Morgan, *Soviet Administrative Legality: The Role of Attorney General's Office* (Stanford University Press 1962). A comparative East/West assessment is offered in J. A. Jolowicz (ed.), *Public Interest Parties and the Active Role of the Judge in Civil Litigation* (Milano, Giuffrè 1974); or Vera Lange, "Public Interest in Civil Law, Socialist Law, and Common Law Systems: The Role of the Public Prosecutor" (1988) 36 *American Journal of Comparative Law* 279. For further references, see Christopher Osakwe's review of the aforementioned Smith's book in (1980) 28 *American Journal of Comparative Law* 700, in particular note 5.

[46] Only the Belarusian model of court administration gets close. On the state of the Belarusian judiciary, see Alexander Vashkevich, "Judicial Independence in the Republic of Belarus" in Anja Seibert-Fohr (ed.), *Judicial Independence in Transition* (Springer 2012) 1065, in particular at 1068–1071, 1101–1103, 1109–1110 and 1115–1118. However, the socialist model is still alive outside Europe, for instance in China; See, for example, Peter H. Solomon, "Authoritarian Legality and Informal Practices: Judges, Lawyers and the State in Russia and China" (2010) 43 *Communist and Post-Communist Studies* 351; Xin He, "Black Hole of Responsibility: The Adjudication Committee's Role in a Chinese Court" (2012) 46 *Law & Society Review* 681; Ling Li, "The 'Production' of Corruption in China's Courts: Judicial Politics and Decision Making in a One-Party State" (2012) 37 *Law & Social Inquiry* 848.

[47] Alternatively, we may perceive the socialist model of the administration of courts as a perverse version of the classic "Ministry of Justice" model. However, the merging of these two models into one would ignore important differences between the two.

and Eastern Europe did not get rid of all features of the socialist model[48] and, even more importantly, because the legacy of the omnipotent Supreme Court and court presidents has lasted until today.

A quick glance at the models of court administration in Europe suggests that a great number of current EU Member States have opted for the judicial council model. This does not, however, mean that all of them would have indeed taken on board and introduced the promoted Euro-model outlined earlier and advocated by the EU and the CoE. The composition, competences, as well as the power of judicial councils vary widely among the countries that established the judicial council model,[49] and many of these judicial councils do not meet the criteria of the Judicial Council Euro-model. For instance, French, Dutch, and Portuguese judges are in the minority on their judicial councils. In Spain, judicial members of the judicial council are not selected by their peers. Judicial councils in Belgium, Poland, and Slovenia do not play any role in disciplining judges. Finally, the Hungarian Judicial Council met the requirements of the Judicial Council Euro-model only until Orbán's government passed the 2011 judicial reform that took many powers from the Hungarian High Council for the Judiciary (*Magyar Köztársaság Bíróságai*) and transferred them to the newly established National Judicial Office.[50] Therefore, the European consensus on the criteria stipulated by the Judicial Council Euro-model is rather wishful thinking. On the contrary, a closer look shows a variety of rationales and features of judicial councils in Europe.

The Judicial Council Euro-model is thus in fact only a subset of judicial councils that exist in Europe. The key feature that distinguishes the promoted Euro-model from its competing alternatives, including other types of judicial councils, is that it centralizes competences affecting virtually *all* matters of the career of judges at one place and grants control over this body to the judges. The Euro-model is built on the premise that judges are reliable, solid actors who know their duties and are able to administer it. It is therefore considered wise to insulate the judiciary from the democratic process. If we compare the Euro-model with the

---

[48]   In fact, these "remnants" of the socialist model of court administration have been the prime targets of criticism raised by the EU and the CoE.

[49]   For a helpful taxonomy of judicial councils, see Garoupa and Ginsburg 2009a, above note 9, at 122; and Renoux 1999, above note 4.

[50]   The Hungarian model of court administration after the 2011 judicial reforms thus belongs to the category of "hybrid models."

existing judicial councils in the EU Member States, it is evident that the Euro-model had been heavily inspired by the Italian judicial council rather than that of France, Spain, or Portugal, because in the latter countries, the national Ministries of Justice have preserved some influence over judicial recruitment.[51]

Most studies on judicial councils thus suffer from a serious flaw. They use the term "judicial council" as a generic label that refers to any independent intermediary organization positioned between the judiciary and the politically responsible administrators in the executive or the legislature. However, this use of the term "judicial council" generates confusion and simplifies the differences among hybrid models, the Court Service model, and judicial council models in the narrow sense. I disagree with this over-simplification[52] and define the "judicial council" more narrowly.[53] This approach is also more appropriate from the methodological point of view, because it prevents the overgeneralization of the results of the Slovak case study.

This book reveals what consequences the Judicial Council Euro-model brought about in Slovakia, but it does not tell us anything about how the Court Service model or a hybrid model would have fared there if either of them had been chosen instead of the Judicial Council Euro-model. Similarly, since the Judicial Council of the Slovak Republic meets the criteria of the Judicial Council Euro-model, this shows only how a *particular* model of the judicial council – the model advocated by the EU and the CoE – operates in the postcommunist environment. It does not tell us how *other* types of judicial councils would have fared in Slovakia or in other countries in the CEE. Put differently, we should not want to "throw out the baby with the bathwater" and claim that any type of judicial council would have worked the way the Judicial Council Euro-model worked in Slovakia between 2003 and 2010.

---

[51] For further details, see Parau 2012, above note 13, at 643–644.

[52] It is also tempting to perceive the Ministry of Justice model and the judicial council model as two ends of the same continuum and claim that the hybrid models and the Court Service model are intermediary steps toward the judicial council model. However, this view again simplifies the complex nature of court administration and ignores important historical and cultural differences between European countries. In fact, the Court Service model and the judicial council model are two distinct solutions that address different problems and do not seem to converge toward the latter model.

[53] See also Garoupa and Ginsburg 2009a, above note 9 (who omit Denmark, Finland, Norway, and Sweden from their comprehensive study of judicial councils and thus they do not consider the Court Service as a "subtype" of judicial councils).

III.   The Impact of the Judicial Council Euro-model on Judicial Accountability

What are the effects of the Judicial Council Euro-model? We do not know the answer to this question, because judicial councils have not so far been subjected to a rigorous empirical analysis.[54] The scholarly literature and the relevant documents of international and supranational organizations usually tell us what the judicial council is supposed to do, but rarely study whether the particular judicial council actually "delivered the goods" it promised. Those few studies that attempt to assess the effects of the judicial council model often lack empirical evidence for their conclusions.

We may thus summarize that international and supranational organizations devote most of their resources to the creation of judicial councils and pay less attention to what happens afterward. This is unfortunate for several reasons. First, we should not forget that a judicial council is only a means to an end, namely improving the functioning of the judiciary and eradicating the existing shortcomings within the given judicial system,[55] and not an end in itself.[56] If the judicial council does not achieve the envisaged goals, it should be modified or even disbanded. Second, even if the judicial council model works well in general, it may – like any other institution – need fine-tuning after the first couple of years of its existence and perhaps even thereafter at regular intervals. Finally, the reluctance to study the actual effects of judicial councils invites suspicion. For instance, politicians, scholars, and lay people may start wondering why the EU and the CoE avoid monitoring and assessing the "post-judicial council" period and speculating that these two organizations would have troubles in coming to terms with the fact that the Judicial Council Euro-model, which they so vigorously argued for in new European democracies, has failed to "deliver the goods." Put differently, the EU and the CoE have too much to lose if the rosy picture of the Judicial Council Euro-model falls apart, because they presented that model as a "universal good" and if they are proved wrong their credibility will suffer.

---

[54]   Many commentators lament this lack of empirical evidence on judicial councils; See, for example, Seibert-Fohr 2009, above note 19, at 433; Smilov, above note 14; and Garoupa and Ginsburg 2009a, above note 9, at 119.

[55]   I bypass here what is meant by "improving the functioning of the judiciary" and "shortcomings of the judicial system."

[56]   See also Anja Seibert-Fohr, "European Perspective on the Rule of Law and Independent Courts" (2012) 20 *Journal für Rechtspolitik* 161, 166 (who argues that the problem of recent documents produced by the CoE is that they have gradually shifted the emphasis from obligations of *results* to obligations of *means*).

Due to the lack of empirical research on judicial councils I must infer potential effects of judicial councils from the scholarly literature and from goals identified by the "founding fathers" of judicial councils, including goals set by international and supranational bodies such as the CoE and the EU. It goes without saying that assertions of scholars and goals set by advocates of judicial councils discussed subsequently on the one hand and the actual effects of the judicial council model on the other may differ. I exploit these sources merely in order to identify the potential consequences of introducing the judicial council model that are worthy of further inquiry in the empirical part of this book.

In my search for the effects of the introduction of the Judicial Council Euro-model, I focus only on institutional and personal consequences for the judiciary and judges. I thus leave aside the potential impact of this model on various values external to the judiciary such as "the rule of law, civil liberties, individual freedoms [and]basic human rights."[57] This is intentional: As important and grandiose as these values are, they are also either contested terms and/or so vague that they are in practice impossible to measure to any reasonable degree.[58]

Therefore, I can narrow down the question to be answered as follows: which values or characteristics of the judiciary was the introduction of the Judicial Council Euro-model supposed to enhance? There is one value which stands out in the policy documents produced under the auspices of the CoE and the EU: judicial independence. In fact, virtually all of the documents of these two bodies claim that the Euro-model improves judicial independence.[59] Unfortunately, none of these documents spell out what they mean by judicial independence. They usually acknowledge the difference

---

[57] See, for example, ENCJ, Councils for the Judiciary Report 2010–2011 § 1.2 *in fine*.

[58] See, for example, Tom Ginsburg, "Pitfalls of Measuring the Rule of Law" (2011) 3 *Hague Journal on the Rule of Law* 269; or Jeremy Waldron, "Is the Rule of Law an Essentially Contested Concept?" (2002) 21 *Law and Philosophy* 137 (both discussing the possibility to measure the rule of law). The same problems permeate the other grandiose values stated earlier.

[59] See ENCJ, Councils for the Judiciary Report 2010–2011 para. 1.7; CCJE, Opinion no.10 (2007) to the attention of the Committee of Ministers of the CoE on the Council for the Judiciary at the service of society (Strasbourg, November 21–23, 2007) para. 8; Resolution of the ENCJ on "Self Governance for the Judiciary: Balancing Independence and Accountability" (May 2008) para. 1; European Charter on the Statute for Judges [Strasbourg, July 8–10, 1998] para. 1.3; Resolution of the ENCJ on "Self Governance for the Judiciary: Balancing Independence and Accountability" (May 2008) para. 1; and Recommendation CM/Rec (2010)12 of the Committee of Ministers to member states on judges: independence, efficiency and responsibilities, adopted by the Committee of Ministers on November 17, 2010 para. 26.

between the independence of individual judges and the independence of the judiciary and claim that judicial councils enhance both of these facets of judicial independence.[60] It would appear nonetheless that the documents clearly prioritize the latter aspect, the autonomy of the judiciary.[61] It is thus possible to conclude that the "general mission"[62] of the Judicial Council Euro-model has been to safeguard and improve judicial independence.

Other potential values of the judicial council model are mentioned far less frequently. As early as in 1994, the CoE stressed the importance of the efficiency of judges.[63] Later on, both the CoE and the EU contended that judicial councils improve the efficiency of the judiciary.[64] In fact, speeding up judicial procedures and reducing workloads became a mantra of the EU Accession Reports. Later on, the quality of justice was added as a separate value, which the judicial council model is supposed to deliver.[65]

Surprisingly, much less attention has been paid, until very recently, to other generally acceptable values such as transparency, participation, and accountability. During the accession process the European Commission

[60] See CCJE, Opinion no.10 (2007) to the attention of the Committee of Ministers of the Council of Europe on the Council for the Judiciary at the service of society (Strasbourg, November 21-23, 2007) para. 8; or Recommendation CM/Rec (2010)12 of the Committee of Ministers to member states on judges: independence, efficiency and responsibilities, adopted by the Committee of Ministers on November 17, 2010 para. 26.

[61] See, for example, ENCJ, Councils for the Judiciary Report 2010-2011 para. 2.2; CCJE, Opinion no.10 (2007) to the attention of the Committee of Ministers of the Council of Europe on the Council for the Judiciary at the service of society (Strasbourg, November 21-23, 2007) paras 12-13; or Recommendation CM/Rec (2010)12 of the Committee of Ministers to member states on judges: independence, efficiency and responsibilities, adopted by the Committee of Ministers on November 17, 2010 para. 4.

[62] CCJE, Opinion no.10 (2007) to the attention of the Committee of Ministers of the Council of Europe on the Council for the Judiciary at the service of society (Strasbourg, November 21-23, 2007) title of Part II.

[63] See Committee of Ministers, Recommendation No. R (94) 12, October 13, 1994 in: "37 Yearbook of the European Convention on Human Rights" (1994) 453.

[64] See Resolution of the ENCJ on "Self Governance for the Judiciary: Balancing Independence and Accountability" (May 2008) para. 1; ENCJ, Councils for the Judiciary Report 2010-2011 para. 1.7; CCJE, Opinion no.10 (2007) to the attention of the Committee of Ministers of the Council of Europe on the Council for the Judiciary at the service of society (Strasbourg, November 21-23, 2007) para. 10; or Recommendation CM/Rec (2010)12 of the Committee of Ministers to member states on judges: independence, efficiency and responsibilities, adopted by the Committee of Ministers on November 17, 2010 para. 26.

[65] See ENCJ, Councils for the Judiciary Report 2010-2011 para. 1.7; CCJE, Opinion no.10 (2007) to the attention of the Committee of Ministers of the Council of Europe on the Council for the Judiciary at the service of society (Strasbourg, November 21-23, 2007) para. 10.

was mostly preoccupied with judicial independence and the efficiency of the judiciary and side-lined transparency mechanisms.[66] So was the CoE.[67] Recently, both of these international organizations have stressed the importance of transparency in their documents on judicial councils.[68] They nonetheless tend to focus on the transparency of the judicial council itself and not on the transparency of the judiciary.[69] Participation has undergone similar development. For instance, the EU as well as the CoE, after initial reluctance, relaxed their position on composition of the judicial council and accept the parity between judges and nonjudges.[70]

What is most striking, given the well-known problems of venality of CEE judiciaries and their low ethical standards, is how little attention the EU and the CoE paid to judicial accountability. The relevant policy documents that define the JC Euro-model mention this value only in passing.[71] Despite the fact that judicial accountability has gradually emerged as the second most important goal of judicial councils in the scholarly literature, competing with judicial independence,[72] the relevant policy documents of the EU and the CoE focused until very recently on (limited) accountability of the judicial council instead of accountability of the judiciary and/or

---

[66] See the EU Accession Reports of the CEE countries.

[67] See, for example, Committee of Ministers, Recommendation No. R (94) 12, October 13, 1994 in: "37 Yearbook of the European Convention on Human Rights" (1994) 453; or European Charter on the Statute for Judges [Strasbourg, July 8–10, 1998] (which do not mention transparency at all).

[68] See, for example, ENCJ, Councils for the Judiciary Report 2010–2011 paras 1.7 and 7.2; or Resolution of the ENCJ on "Self Governance for the Judiciary: Balancing Independence and Accountability" (May 2008) in fine.

[69] See CCJE, Opinion no.10 (2007) to the attention of the Committee of Ministers of the Council of Europe on the Council for the Judiciary at the service of society (Strasbourg, November 21–23, 2007) Part VI; or ENCJ, Councils for the Judiciary Report 2010–2011 para. 2.5.

[70] Compare the most recent documents (e.g., ENCJ, Councils for the Judiciary Report 2010–2011 para. 2.2; or Recommendation CM/Rec (2010)12 of the Committee of Ministers to member states on judges: independence, efficiency and responsibilities, adopted by the Committee of Ministers on November 17, 2010 para. 27) that accept "only" 50% of judicial members in the judicial council with older documents that claim that "a substantial majority of the members should be judges" (CCJE, Opinion no.10 (2007) to the attention of the Committee of Ministers of the Council of Europe on the Council for the Judiciary at the service of society (Strasbourg, November 21–23, 2007) para. 18).

[71] See CCJE, Opinion no.10 (2007) to the attention of the Committee of Ministers of the Council of Europe on the Council for the Judiciary at the service of society (Strasbourg, November 21–23, 2007) Part VI; or Resolution of the ENCJ on "Self Governance for the Judiciary: Balancing Independence and Accountability" (May 2008) para. 10.

[72] See Garoupa and Ginsburg 2009a, above note 9, at 110.

individual judges,[73] or make clear that "the accountability of the judiciary can in no way call into question the independence of the judge when making judicial decisions."[74] It was only after the end of the period studied by this book, the years between 1993 and 2010, when the European Network of Councils for the Judiciary (ENCJ) and the Consultative Council of European Judges (CCJE) started to address judicial accountability more comprehensively.[75]

The fact that not a single document of the consultative organs of the CoE or the EU produced over the years sets standards for how judicial councils and self-administrating judiciaries ought to address corruption of judges is also quite telling.[76] All in all, the values promoted and goals set deeply reflect the way in which the standards were created – by (senior) judges and for (largely also senior) judges. Thus, great attention is being paid to institutional and power-enhancing elements, whereas somewhat meager attention has been paid to the less comfortable – but for the functional judiciary – extremely important "housekeeping" elements.

Given the importance attached to judicial accountability by growing literature on judicial councils and the lack of empirical studies on judicial accountability, the empirical component of this book focuses on the impact of the Judicial Council Euro-model on mechanisms of judicial accountability. The two concepts define the scope of empirical analysis in the next four chapters. First, the pair of empirical case studies on the Czech Republic and Slovakia tells us something only about the impact of one type of judicial council, Judicial Council Euro-model, which both the EU and the CoE advocate for, and not about judicial councils with different composition and powers than the Euro-model. However, the Euro-model

---

[73] See CCJE, Opinion no. 10 (2007), Part VI. But cf. ENCJ, Councils for the Judiciary Report 2010–2011, para. 2.2.

[74] Budapest Resolution, para. 10.

[75] See in particular ENCJ, Independence and Accountability of the Judiciary, ENCJ Report, 2013–2014, adopted by the General Assembly of the ENCJ held in Rome in June 11–13, 2014; and CCJE, Opinion no. 17 (2014) on the evaluation of judges' work, the quality of justice and respect for judicial independence (Strasbourg, October 24, 2014).

[76] Note that the CoE has recently started to address the issue of judicial corruption more comprehensively and there is a new resolution of the Parliamentary Assembly of the CoE in the making. There have been some efforts made in the late 2000s. See PACE, Committee on Legal Affairs and Human Rights, "Judicial corruption", Rapporteur: Mr. Kimmo Sasi (Finland), Report, Doc. 12058, November 6, 2009; PACE, Committee on Legal Affairs and Human Rights, "Corruption as a threat to the rule of law", Rapporteur: Ms Mailis (Estonia), Report, Doc. 13228, June 10, 2013, pp. 12–13; and PACE, Committee on Legal Affairs and Human Rights, "Judicial Corruption: urgent need to implement the Assembly's proposals", Rapporteur: Mr Kimmo Sasi (Finland), AS/Jur (2014) 19, May 15, 2014.

was adopted by many similarly situated states in the CEE more or less at the same time, and thus the results from Slovakia can be corroborated by the results from other countries in the region. Second, the empirical case studies study judicial accountability as a mechanism and not as a virtue.[77] Therefore, I narrowed my case studies on the Czech Republic and Slovakia to the analysis of the impact of the Judicial Council Euro-model on mechanisms of judicial accountability, which I identified in Chapter 2. Through these two case studies based on the "most similar cases" logic,[78] the four chapters that follow attempt to answer the questions about judicial councils posed in the introduction.

---

[77] The reasons why I prefer studying judicial accountability as a mechanism are stated in Chapter 1.
[78] For the justification of this research design see Chapter 4.

PART TWO

Holding Czech and Slovak Judges Accountable

Prologue to the Case Studies: Methodology
and Data Reporting

Part Two of this book offers a small-N longitudinal analysis of the use of mechanisms of judicial accountability in the Czech Republic and Slovakia from 1993 to 2010. It is based primarily on archival materials and interviews conducted in both countries during summer visits in 2010 and 2011 and then during a one-year period from May 2012 until April 2013. This chapter explains the research design of my case studies and my methodology, provides information about data collection and, finally, addresses potential inaccuracies of my empirical analysis.

I.   Research Design of My Case Studies

For the purposes of my case studies, I fine-tuned the four research questions defined in the introduction to the specifics of the Czech Republic and Slovakia. The result is the following four research questions that delineate the scope of my analysis in the case studies:

Q.1 Did the Judicial Council of the Slovak Republic (JCSR) disempower dominant principals from the "pre-JCSR" era (the Minister of Justice, the legislature, and court presidents) and empowered regular judges?

Q.2 Did the JCSR reduce the use of mechanisms of judicial accountability (quantitative dimension)?

Q.3 Did the JCSR reduce the imposed sanctions and granted rewards (qualitative dimension)?

Q.4 Did the JCSR reduce accountability perversions?

Keeping in mind the competing claims regarding the impact of judicial councils on judicial accountability,[1] I identified three alternative hypotheses for each question. The first hypothesis is always based on the conventional wisdom about the role of judicial councils among their proponents. The alternative hypothesis builds on the historical experience with holding

---

[1] See Chapter 3.

judges to account in Czechoslovakia and takes into account the views of scholars who question the conventional wisdom about the effect of judicial councils on the ground. However, there may be a third answer to my research questions – that there was no change at all after the introduction of a judicial council in Slovakia. Therefore, I added the third hypothesis to each research question – the JCSR made no difference.

These sets of competing hypotheses read as follows:

Q.1   Did the JCSR disempower dominant principals from the "pre-JCSR" era (the Minister of Justice, the legislature, and court presidents) and empowered regular judges?

H.1a The JCSR disempowered all dominant principals from the "pre-JCSR" era and empowered regular judges.

H.1b The JCSR disempowered the Minister of Justice and the legislature but, instead of empowering regular judges, it enhanced the power of court presidents.

H.1c The JCSR made no difference.

Q.2   Did the JCSR reduce the use of mechanisms of judicial accountability (quantitative dimension)?

H.2a The JCSR reduced the use of mechanisms of judicial accountability.

H.2b The JCSR increased the use of mechanisms of judicial accountability.

H.2c The JCSR made no difference.

Q.3   Did the JCSR reduce the sanctions/rewards (qualitative dimension)?

H.3a The JCSR reduced the sanctions/rewards imposed.

H.3b The JCSR increased the sanctions/rewards imposed.

H.3c The JCSR made no difference.

Q.4   Did the JCSR reduce accountability perversions?

H.4a The JCSR reduced accountability perversions.

H.4b The JCSR increased accountability perversions.

H.4c The JCSR made no difference.

In sum, there are three possible answers to each of the four research questions: (1) my empirical analysis will prove the claims of the proponents of judicial councils; or (2) it will refute their claims and show that the Slovak judicial system moved in the opposite direction; or (3) it will show that the introduction of the judicial council in Slovakia made no difference. I think that all possible results[2] are valuable. If my empirical analysis proves the claims of advocates of judicial councils, it will mean that the judicial

---

[2]   In fact, there are twelve possible results since there are three answers to each research question and the answers to the research questions are not dependent on each other.

council model delivers the goods it was envisaged to deliver. If my analysis shows that the judicial council had the opposite effect, it will debunk a widely held view that the judicial council model of court administration improves the independence of individual judges and reduces their accountability. Finally, if my analysis shows that the introduction of the judicial council model in Slovakia made no difference, it would still be a valuable observation as it will seriously question, given the huge costs of such a large-scale institutional change, the desirability of introducing a judicial council model.

A few more words must be said about the design of my case studies. The aim of the two case studies on the Czech Republic and Slovakia is to examine the impact of introducing the Judicial Council Euro-model on the use of mechanisms of judicial accountability. However, in order to discern which changes were caused by the JCSR in Slovakia, it is not enough to compare the results between 1993 and 2002 in Slovakia with those between 2003 and 2010 in the same country. The comparison of the "pre-JCSR" period with the "post-JCSR" period in Slovakia is critical for an understanding of the impact of the JCSR, but in order to eliminate false inferences it is also necessary to examine the cross-country results and the parallel development in the Czech Republic.

For this reason I divide the period between 1993 and 2010 into two phases, the creation of the JCSR in 2002 being the critical juncture. "Phase I" covers the years between 1993 and 2002. "Phase II" consists of the years between 2003 and 2010. Following a two (countries) by two (phases) matrix, there are four mini-case studies: (1) 1993–2002 in the Czech Republic (*CR I*); (2) 1993–2002 in Slovakia (*SR I*); (3) 2003–2010 in the Czech Republic (*CR II*); and (4) 2003–2010 in Slovakia (*SR II*). Mini-case studies CR I, CR II and SR I cover periods when the Czech Republic and Slovakia retained the Ministry of Justice model, whereas SR II deals with the period when the judicial council model applied in Slovakia.

Four comparisons can be made among these four mini-case studies. Each of them will serve a different purpose:

(1) *CR I with SR I*: This comparison will demonstrate how mechanisms of judicial accountability were used in the Czech Republic and Slovakia when both states retained the same model of court administration (the MoJ model) and will assess whether any differences existed between the two countries. If this comparison shows that the results regarding mechanism of judicial accountability in *CR I* and *SR I* were the same or substantially similar (hence both countries were by and large in the same position before the introduction of the Judicial Council

Euro-model in Slovakia), then it will be more likely that the differences between *CR II* and *SR II* were caused by the JCSR. On the other hand, if there was a significant difference between CR I and SR I, it must be taken into account when interpreting the *CR II with SR II* comparison.

(2) *CR I with CR II*: This comparison will show how mechanisms of judicial accountability were used in the Czech Republic before and after 2002. This comparison has an instrumental value since it serves as a check on whether it was the judicial council that caused the difference under consideration in Slovakia after 2002. If there was a substantial change in holding Czech judges to account after 2002, it must be taken into account in interpreting the effects of the Judicial Council Euro-model in Slovakia. Vice versa, if the results in the Czech Republic in 1993–2002 and 2003–2010 yield similar results, it will be more likely that the change in Slovakia was caused by the JCSR.

(3) *SR I with SR II*: This comparison is a central part of this book, because it analyzes what happened in Slovakia after the introduction of the Judicial Council Euro-model of court administration. It will show what changes, if any, took place in Slovakia after the introduction of the Judicial Council Euro-model.

(4) *CR II with SR II*: This comparison will show how mechanisms of judicial accountability were used in a period when the Czech Republic retained the MoJ model and Slovakia switched to the JC model of court administration and whether there were differences between these two countries. This comparison serves as an additional check on whether it was the judicial council that caused the difference under consideration in Slovakia after 2002. For instance, if this comparison reveals that the use of mechanisms of judicial accountability in the Czech Republic (with the MoJ model) after 2002 moved in the same direction as in Slovakia (with the JC model), it will be evident that a variable or variables other than the introduction of the judicial council made the difference.[3]

For the sake of clarity, I will proceed by country and not by period. *CR I with CR II* comparison is conducted in Chapter 5, followed by *SR I with SR II* comparison in Chapter 6, whereas the remaining two comparisons will be conducted in Chapter 7. These four comparisons ensure that I can distinguish between a mere correlation and causation and identify those

---

[3] For instance, both countries joined the European Union in 2004.

changes after the introduction of the JCSR in Slovakia that were indeed *caused* by the JCSR.

II. What Is Measured?

Part Two of this book identifies all mechanisms of judicial account-ability available in the Czech Republic and Slovakia between 1993 and 2010 and measures them. It looks both at formal standards of mecha-nisms of judicial accountability and at how judges were actually held to account. Nevertheless, I focus primarily on the latter, because I believe that what really matters is not what the law says about mechanisms of judicial accountability (de jure judicial accountability), but how mecha-nisms of judicial accountability operate in practice (de facto judicial accountability).[4] For instance, regarding disciplinary motions what mat-ters is not who can initiate disciplinary motions against judges and for what, but who actually initiated disciplinary motions, how often, for what conduct, how many of these motions resulted in sanctions, and what sanc-tions were actually imposed. However, both case studies deal with both de facto and de jure aspects, because the legal text (the de jure aspect) serves as a constraint for a de facto practice and because it is valuable to iden-tify the gap between them. For that reason, each case study starts with the description of mechanisms of judicial accountability on the books and only then it discusses how these mechanisms operated in action.

The following mechanisms existed in the Czech Republic and/or Slovakia between 1993 and 2010, some of them for the entire period and some of them only temporarily: disciplinary proceedings, once-and-for-all retention reviews for new judges (the so-called judges on probation[5]), complaint mechanisms, reassignment (within the same court), promo-tion (to a higher court), promotion to the position of chamber president (within the same court), secondment (to a higher court), temporary assignment outside the judiciary, grand chamber appointment (at top courts), appointment of a judge to the position of court president or vice president, case assignment, a judge's volatile salary, and judicial perfor-mance evaluation.

The focus of this book is on instances of the observable use of mecha-nisms of judicial accountability. By "observable use" I mean instances in

---

[4] On the distinction between *de jure* judicial accountability and *de facto* judicial accountabil-ity, see Chapter 1.
[5] On "judges on probation," see Chapter 2, Section II.A.

which the relevant principal holds a judge overtly to account and there is an official record of that action; for instance, when a litigant submits a complaint, when the Minister of Justice initiates a disciplinary motion, or when the court president prepares a judicial performance evaluation. Therefore, instances of holding judges to account that cannot be traced back and corroborated with evidence such as verbal reprimands by court presidents, a change in the working conditions of judges, or indirect pressure that eventually forces a judge to retire involuntarily are not measured.[6]

My longitudinal analysis is primarily a qualitative one, but it builds heavily on quantitative analysis. It assesses patterns of holding Czech and Slovak judges to account. The first three research questions inquire into who holds Czech and Slovak judges to account, how often, and how intensively. The last research question is slightly more normative as it focuses on accountability perversions such as judicial accountability avoidance, simulating judicial accountability, output excesses of judicial accountability, and selective accountability. Nevertheless, this book passes no judgment on whether the particular conduct of a judge should be considered a disciplinary offense or whether the relevant decision of the disciplinary court was right. Similarly, I presume that there is no hierarchy among the mechanisms of judicial accountability. All of them are treated as equally important.[7] In other words, this book does not set any normative benchmark – ideal set of mechanisms of judicial accountability and their relative importance, what behavior of judges is permitted and what is not, or who should hold judges to account – against which to compare the situation in the Czech Republic and Slovakia.

III.   Data Collection

The way in which the empirical analysis in Part Two is carried out differs with respect to disciplinary motions and complaints on the one hand and other mechanisms of judicial accountability on the other.

As regards disciplining judges, for the Czech Republic as well as for Slovakia I went through all disciplinary motions[8] initiated in the period between 1993 and 2010 and indexed all decisions of disciplinary panels that dealt with those motions.[9] In the Czech Republic all disciplinary

---

[6] See the discussion of potential inaccuracies that follow.
[7] See the section on method and evaluation that follow.
[8] Note that not every disciplinary motion led to a decision by the disciplinary panel as several judges died or resigned before the disciplinary panel could deliver its decision.
[9] Some of these motions were decided only in 2012 as many disciplinary proceedings (especially in Slovakia) lasted several years.

files are stored at the Ministry of Justice and I accessed them during my research trip in summer 2011. In Slovakia the majority of disciplinary files are stored at the Supreme Court of Slovakia, but some files from the 1990s are archived at the regional courts. I accessed the disciplinary files of Slovak judges during several research trips that took place in January 2012, December 2012, and January 2013. Regarding complaints lodged by litigants, I went through a sample of complaints at the Czech Ministry of Justice in summer 2011, but this exercise turned out to be futile as most complaints did not make sense and, even if they had, only rarely complaints triggered a disciplinary motion or other mechanism of judicial accountability anyway. I found the same pattern in Slovakia during my research trips in 2012 and 2013. Moreover, both in the Czech Republic and in Slovakia more serious complaints against judges were included in separate folders among disciplinary files. Yet again only very few of these complaints led directly[10] to a disciplinary motion. I complemented this data on disciplinary motions and complaints with interviews with judges, their support staff, public servants at the Czech and Slovak Ministries of Justices, politicians (including former Ministers and Vice Ministers of Justice), scholars and advocates. Finally, I examined all secondary (doctrinal) sources dealing with disciplining judges or complaints against judges between 1993 and 2010.

For all mechanisms of judicial accountability, I collected as many primary materials as possible such as the work schedules for assignment of judges and case assignment (in the Czech Republic as well as in Slovakia) or samples of judicial performance evaluation (in Slovakia). Subsequently, I corroborated these primary materials from secondary sources. I searched the newspapers and databases of judicial decisions (of the ordinary courts as well as constitutional courts) and looked for "judicial accountability issues." In addition, I examined all doctrinal sources discussing the use of these mechanisms of judicial accountability between 1993 and 2010 and beyond, and conducted interviews with judges, their support staff, public servants at the Czech and Slovak Ministries of Justices, politicians (including former Ministers and Vice Ministers of Justice), scholars and advocates. The analysis of these mechanisms of judicial accountability is thus less "bullet-proof" than measuring the complete datasets of disciplinary

---

[10] I am not claiming that complaints were completely useless. It is conceivable that the outcomes of complaints attracted attention to a problematic judge, as a result of which the Minister of Justice or a court president followed that judge's work more closely. However, it is not possible to measure this indirect impact of complaints.

motions and samples of complaints, but the wide array of materials consulted gives a reasonable picture of them.

IV.   Method and Evaluation

This book examines a vast array of primary and secondary materials that
provide a reasonably accurate[11] picture of the use of mechanisms of judicial
accountability in both countries. First, mechanisms of judicial accountability, both those that were explicitly laid down by law and those that lacked
a clear legal basis, available in a given year are identified. This exercise is
repeated for every year of the period studied (1993–2010) and for each of the
two countries under examination. As I do not stipulate a hierarchy of available mechanisms of judicial accountability,[12] each such mechanism is given
the same default weight, which is 1.

Subsequently, the method differs for each research question. Regarding
the core research question – who held judges to account – the default
weight for each mechanism is divided among the principals who actually
used them in a given year. The default weight for each mechanism of judicial accountability is 1. If the principal alone could use a given mechanism, the entire default weight would be assigned to him. For instance,
in 1997 the Czech court presidents decided unilaterally on promotion of
judges to the position of chamber presidents and thus they received the
entire default weight of 1. If two principals had to agree on the use of a
given mechanism of judicial accountability, the default weight would be
divided equally between them. For instance, both the relevant court presidents and the Minister of Justice had to consent to secondment of a judge
in the Czech Republic in 2006, and thus court presidents and the Minister
of Justice each received 0.5 for that mechanism. Finally, if one of the principals had a major say, but his discretion was limited by another actor, the
default weight was divided accordingly. For instance, in 2006 the Czech
court presidents had a major say in the reassignment of judges, but their
discretion was limited by judicial boards and therefore court presidents
received 0.75 and judicial boards (that are included in the tables among
"Other actors") received 0.25 for this mechanism.

---

[11] See the discussion of potential inaccuracies that follow.

[12] It is impossible to create an *abstract* hierarchy of mechanisms of judicial accountability
that would rank these mechanisms at a different weight based on their impact on individual judges. Such hierarchy would inevitably be subjective and, moreover, each judge values aspects of his status differently (someone is more concerned about his salary, someone
cares about the power to shape the law, someone strives for promotion, someone may not
be interested in promotion at all as he does not want to move etc.).

Finally, the division of the default weight in disciplinary proceedings is the most complex as disciplinary proceedings consist of two stages – various disciplinary prosecutors could initiate disciplinary motion and then the different body, a disciplinary panel, decided on this motion. Therefore the default weight is first divided equally between the disciplinary prosecutors as a whole and the disciplinary panel (the latter is included in the tables among "Other actors"). Then the weight received by the disciplinary prosecutors as a whole is further divided between those disciplinary prosecutors who in a given year actually initiated disciplinary motions. For instance, 40 disciplinary motions were initiated in the Czech Republic in 2006. Out of these 40 motions 38 were initiated by the court presidents and only two by the Minister of Justice. As mentioned above, the default weight for each mechanism of judicial accountability is 1. Hence, the default weight for disciplinary motions is also 1. This default weight is first divided between the disciplinary prosecutors (who received 0.5) and the disciplinary panel (that received 0.5). Subsequently, the default weight of disciplinary prosecutors as a whole is distributed between the two active[13] disciplinary prosecutors: court presidents are given 0.475 (as 95% of disciplinary motions were initiated by court presidents) and the Minister of Justice is given 0.025 (as only 5% of disciplinary motions were initiated by the Minister of Justice).

Once the default weight of each available mechanism of judicial accountability in a given year is distributed among the relevant principals, I can quantify which principals held judges to account in that year and which of them had a major say. This exercise is repeated for every year of the period studied (1993–2010) and for each of the two countries under examination.

Regarding the second research question – how often were mechanisms of judicial accountability used – I had to bracket out those mechanisms the frequency of use of which was fixed by law and no actor could increase or reduce the number of instances they were used in a given year. This applies, for instance, to annual salary bonuses in Slovakia (which could be awarded only once a year), to judicial performance evaluation in Slovakia (which, until 2009, was supposed to be conducted every five years), to once-and-for-all retention reviews of new judges in Slovakia (which could take place only once after the initial four years in judicial office), and to the appointment of judges to the position of court president or vice president

---

[13] Note that this does not mean that only these two disciplinary prosecutors had the power to initiate disciplinary motions. However, what matters is who actually used this "stick" and not who might have used it.

in both countries (the number of these positions was fixed by law). For the remaining mechanisms of judicial accountability, I examined the available data and determined how often each mechanism was used in a given year. This exercise is repeated for every year of the period studied (1993–2010) and for each of the two countries under examination.

The third research question inquiries into the seriousness of the consequences (which means the severity of sanctions or the magnitude of rewards) resulting from the use of mechanisms of judicial accountability. Again certain such mechanisms have sanctions or rewards fixed by law. These mechanisms include promotion, chamber president appointment, secondment, temporary assignment outside the judiciary, and the appointment of a judge to the position of court president or vice president. Therefore, only six mechanisms could be examined under this research question – complaints, judicial performance evaluation, salary bonuses, reassignment of judges, case assignment, and disciplinary motions. For these six mechanisms[14] I examined the available data and focused on the consequences of each mechanism used in a given year.

Finally, the last research question – the occurrence and frequency of accountability perversions – did not require the studying of additional sources. The answer to this question is contained in the data and materials studied for the previous three research questions. I combined the quantitative data as well as secondary sources to determine which accountability perversions emerged and how often they occurred in a given year.

The aforementioned combination of qualitative and quantitative methods gives me a solid basis that allows me to evaluate the use of the mechanism of judicial accountability both across time and across countries. More specifically, in each country it is possible to observe:

(1) how many mechanisms of judicial accountability were available in a given year and over time;
(2) who actually held judges to account;
(3) the number of instances of the use of individual mechanisms of judicial accountability in a given year and the reduction or increase in these instances over time;
(4) the seriousness of consequences resulting from the use of individual mechanisms of judicial accountability in a given year and the reduction or increase in these consequences over time; as well as

---

[14] Two of these mechanisms (salary bonuses and judicial performance evaluation) were available only in Slovakia, which fact must be taken into account when comparing Slovakia with the Czech Republic.

(5) the emergence of accountability perversions in a given year and their increase or decrease over time.

This framework combined with the four comparisons – Slovakia 1993–2002 with Slovakia 2003–2010, the Czech Republic 2003–2010 with Slovakia 2003–2010, the Czech Republic 1993–2002 with Slovakia 1993–2002, and the Czech Republic 1993–2002 with the Czech Republic 2003–2010 – is sufficient for testing the hypotheses of my book.

V. Potential Inaccuracies

Throughout the course of the book, I came across the following potential inaccuracies. First, it is not possible to measure empirically certain mechanisms of judicial accountability such as working conditions of individual judges, because either the relevant data are not available or their assessment would be purely subjective.[15] Second, regarding mechanisms of judicial accountability I can measure, I must still acknowledge that I can never measure the use of these mechanisms perfectly since sometimes it is impossible to observe certain acts or the motivation behind them. For instance, a judge may voluntarily resign if he knows that a disciplinary motion, which is likely to succeed, will otherwise be initiated against him. It is quite obvious that such a judge will never state the true reasons for his decision to leave the judiciary.[16] Therefore, I cannot observe from outside whether such resignation was truly voluntary or whether he was actually held to account and forced to leave the bench. Similarly, even without the fear of disciplinary motions some judges may be "forced to retire" by their peers or by external actors such as the media or legislators, if their presence on the bench is considered problematic.[17]

---

[15] For instance, it is impossible to observe (and assess objectively) a change in the standard of "working conditions of judges" over a period of years. Such inquiry would be blatantly subjective.

[16] In fact, the Czech laws as well as the Slovak statutes provide certain incentives for this self-purging behavior. If a "tainted" judge steps down before the disciplinary motion is initiated or before the disciplinary panel gives its decision, he may join the Bar and start his private practice with a clean slate. However, when he is found guilty of disciplinary offense, the Bar can refuse his membership application and he may be barred from private practice forever.

[17] See, for example, J. Mark Ramseyer, "The Puzzling (In)Dependence of Courts: A Comparative Approach" (1994) 23 *The Journal of Legal Studies* 721, 734–735 (on "bribing" judges in Japan with high pensions in exchange for their agreeing to retire); Donald P. Kommers, "Autonomy versus Accountability: The German Judiciary" in Peter H. Russell and David M. O'Brien (eds.), *Judicial Independence in the Age of Democracy: Critical*

All these limits to my empirical analysis of mechanisms of judicial accountability may distort the true picture of how Czech and Slovak judges are held to account. Nonetheless, I still believe that my analysis provides a reasonably accurate picture of holding Czech and Slovak judges to account.

First of all, my book is about patterns of how are judges held to account and not an exact quantitative analysis. Even though there may be occasional inaccuracies with one or a few mechanisms of judicial accountability, my analysis is correct regarding the general trends. Put differently, even if my data are not entirely right in units, they provide an accurate picture about the overall order of magnitude. It is not important whether, within a given year there were in reality eight and not just seven disciplinary motions initiated or salary bonuses in reality amounted to ten thousand five hundred euro and not just ten thousand four hundred and ninety five. The important finding is that disciplinary motions were in the range of a few motions, not of hundreds, and salary bonuses were in the range of thousands of euro, not the hundreds.

Secondly, where such information was available, I took into account instances of discreet holding judges to account. One may still object that court presidents meet with judges in person and discuss the problems regarding judge's work informally, Ministers of Justice have their own channels via which they send the signals to problematic judges, and so on. However, Slovak as well as Czech judges have not been shy to go public when they felt that their independence was threatened and thus problematic instances of the use of mechanisms of judicial accountability usually attracted significant media attention. In addition, Czech and Slovak judges are very litigious people and they challenged virtually every measure that affected them before the ordinary courts or before the constitutional court. Hence, notwithstanding the fact that there might be instances of more discreet forms of personal communication between judges and their principals, the impact such informal encounters have on holding judges to account is limited.

Finally, one more caveat must be added here. There is no purely independent variable in the political system. Any institution in the

Perspectives from around the World (University of Virginia Press 2001) 132–133 (discussing the fate of Judge Rainer Orlet in Germany); or Ceran Belge, "Friends of the Court: The Republican Alliance and Selective Activism of the Constitutional Court of Turkey" (2006) 40 *Law & Society Review* 653, 660 (pinpointing early retirement of Turkish judges in the 1950s).

political system is a result of various endogenous and exogenous forces and depends on multiple factors. These factors include strategic interests of domestic political actors, pressure from international actors, as well as institutional, cultural, and historical factors. This logic also applies to the judicial council. Therefore, one must treat the assertion that the judicial council is an independent variable with caution. This issue is addressed in depth in Chapter 7, where I examine alternative explanations for changes that took place in Slovakia after the introduction of the Judicial Council Euro-model of court administration.

5

The Czech Republic

This chapter tells the story of holding Czech judges to account in the years of 1993 to 2010. The aim of this chapter is to show what mechanisms of judicial accountability were used during this period and what actors controlled those mechanisms. However, this chapter also serves a higher-level purpose in my book. It is instrumental for understanding the impact of introducing the Judicial Council Euro-model of court administration in Slovakia in 2003, which will be addressed in the following chapter. For that reason, the discussion in this chapter is divided into two periods: 1993–2002 and 2003–2010. This division into two phases allows me to compare the use of mechanisms of judicial accountability in the Czech Republic and Slovakia before and after the critical juncture of my book, the creation of the Judicial Council of the Slovak Republic in 2003.

The structure of this chapter is as follows. Section I addresses general issues that have permeated the Czech judiciary since the division of Czechoslovakia. Section II explains major institutional changes adopted between 1993 and 2010 and the political vectors behind them. It also provides the necessary background for understanding how the Czech judiciary operates. Sections III and IV contain the core findings of this chapter. Section III shows how Czech judges were held to account in the first decade after the split of Czechoslovakia (1993–2002). Section IV studies mechanisms of judicial accountability in the eight subsequent years (2003–2010). Finally, Section V provides conclusions regarding the use of mechanisms of judicial accountability in the Czech Republic.

I.   The Czech Judiciary in Context

This section addresses the issues that the Czech Republic had to solve after the split of Czechoslovakia. The aim of this part is to provide a broader picture of the environment in which Czech judges operate. It starts with sketching the political development in the Czech Republic after the dissolution and discussing the immediate consequences of the dissolution of Czechoslovakia upon Czech legal institutions. Subsequently, it focuses on two specific themes related to the postdissolution Czech judiciary: dealing with the past within the Czech judiciary and the impact of the EU accession process upon Czech judicial reforms. Finally, it identifies key players within Czech judicial politics.

A.   Politics of the Czech Republic

Courts do not operate in a political vacuum. It is thus increasingly accepted that, in order to understand the role of judges in a particular country, it is important to pay attention to the political environment in which they operate. Two major figures on the Czech political scene after the split were the same as in the presplit era – Václav Havel and Václav Klaus. Václav Havel, a former president of the Czech and Slovak Federal Republic, was elected president of the independent Czech Republic, whereas Václav Klaus' Civic Democratic Party (ODS) won the first elections in 1992 and Klaus became the first Prime Minister of the independent Czech Republic. Both Václavs played critical roles in the political transition from Federal Czechoslovakia. However, they were like *yin* and *yang*.[1] Havel, a playwright and dissident, distrusted political parties and preferred apolitical politics.[2] He called for establishing the rule of law, warned of too hasty economic reforms, and was willing to listen to lawyers.[3] In contrast, Klaus, an economist by profession, looked down on lawyers and wanted to privatize state property and adopt economic reforms as soon as possible. Klaus

---

[1] For a concise summary of their relationship, see Muriel Blaive and Nicolas Maslowski, "The World of the Two Václavs: European-Minded vs. National(ist) Intellectuals in Czechia" in Justine Lacroix and Kalypso Nicolaïdis (eds.), *European Stories: Intellectual Debates on Europe in National Contexts* (OUP 2010) 257.

[2] See Delia Popescu, *Political Action in Václav Havel's Thought: The Responsibility of Resistance* (Lexington Books 2011), 106–107. See also Aviezer Tucker and others, "From Republican Virtue to Technology of Political Power: Three Episodes of Czech Nonpolitical Politics" (2000) 115 *Political Science Quarterly* 421; or Gil Eyal, "Anti-Politics and the Spirit of Capitalism: Dissidents, Monetarists, and the Czech Transition to Capitalism" (2000) 29 *Theory and Society* 49.

[3] But note that according to Tucker et al., Havel also paid little attention to institution-building, albeit for different reasons than Klaus: "Havel's Republicanism and Klaus's belief in unregulated markets share a disregard of institutional designs. Havel presumed that if people are good, institutions are insignificant. Klaus held that anything goes as long as it is profitable; institutions only get in the way. Neither of them understood the significance of the rule of law, radical restructuring, and expansion of law schools, the court system, and the police." (Tucker and others, above note 2, at 443).

strongly disagreed with Havel's concept of apolitical politics; instead he believed in political parties and partisan politics.

Klaus eventually prevailed and proceeded with his economic reforms. Nevertheless, the rivalry endured. Klaus, as a Prime Minister, controlled the majoritarian institutions, namely the Chamber of Deputies and the Government. In contrast, Havel, holding the office of President of the Czech Republic, had a significant impact on nonmajoritarian institutions, in particular on the Constitutional Court and the Czech National Bank.

The Czech Republic was doing relatively well in the first years after the split. The coalition of centrist and right-wing parties under the leadership of the Civic Democratic Party adopted major economic reforms and the political situation was relatively stable.[4] Some commentators even referred to the Czech Republic as the "economic tiger of Central Europe."[5] Due to this economic success in the early 1990s, Klaus won the 1996 elections and remained Prime Minister. However, the economy started to deteriorate in late 1996, when the Czech Republic went into recession. The recession, together with a corruption scandal, triggered a split within the Civic Democratic Party, which eventually led to the fall of Václav Klaus' second government in 1997. These events resulted in the worst political crisis in postsplit Czech history and caused huge animosity between major political leaders.

In the 1998 elections the Social Democratic Party (ČSSD) came out as winner, followed by the Civic Democratic Party, which was again led by Klaus. Nevertheless, neither Social Democrats nor the Civic Democratic Party were willing to enter into a coalition with smaller parties and, thus, none of them could achieve a majority in the Chamber of Deputies. This stalemate was, surprisingly, solved by agreement between the Social Democratic Party and the Civic Democratic Party – the so-called Opposition Pact (*opoziční smlouva*). Social Democrats formed a minority government with the support of the Civic Democratic Party, which in return was granted many positions within the state organs and companies and agreed to adopt a new election law favoring large parties.

In 2002, the Social Democrats won the election again. This time they formed a coalition government with centrist parties, while the Civic Democratic Party became the opposition. Due to the electoral defeat, Václav Klaus resigned as chairman of the Civic Democratic Party.

---

[4] Of course, this is a huge simplification. For a critical analysis of this period, see Abby Innes, *Czechoslovakia: The Short Goodbye* (Yale University Press 2001).

[5] Jonathan Lynn, "Czech Republic Called Potential Economic Tiger" *Journal of Commerce* (September 2, 1993).

Nevertheless, he did not retire from mainstream politics for long. He soon celebrated his successful comeback. After the protracted presidential elections in the Czech Parliament he replaced Václav Havel in that office and became the second President of the Czech Republic in 2003. In contrast, Havel retired from politics for good.

Between 2003 and 2006 Klaus "cohabited"[6] with the government led by the Social Democrats. In 2006 and 2010, the Civic Democratic Party under the new leadership won the elections and formed coalition governments. But the Civic Democratic Party diverged from the path envisaged by its founder, Václav Klaus, and thus Klaus entered into a new period of de facto "cohabitation," even though his former party had a major role in the government. In the meantime, the Czech Parliament reelected Klaus who served his second presidential term until 2013.

This brief description of the Czech postsplit political environment reveals several important features of the Czech political scene in the 1990s and 2000s. The Czech party system was bipolar and had a transparent conflict structure as the party competition revolved around a unique cleavage: economy.[7] Two major parties emerged after the split – a left leaning Social Democratic Party (ČSSD) and a right leaning Civic Democratic Party (ODS) – and "the structure of inter-party competition in the Czech Republic has been characterized by the alternation between ODS-liberal government and ČSSD-social-democratic cabinets."[8] Nevertheless, due to the existence of the Communist Party which blocks the Czech political scene,[9] neither of these two major parties ever achieved a majority within the Chamber of Deputies. Each of these parties thus had to find coalition partners. What is worse, even today if one of these two parties joins with all the centrist parties that make it to the Parliament,[10] it often obtains only a tiny majority, if one at all. For

---

[6] Note that the standard political science literature uses this term to refer to a period when the president faces a hostile Parliament only in *semipresidential* systems (such as France). In this book, I use the term "cohabitation" more freely to refer to a period when the Czech president faces a hostile Parliament, even though the Czech Republic is technically considered a parliamentary *system*, and not a semipresidential one. This departure from the standard usage of this word is justified by a relatively strong position of the Czech presidents in practice. In other words, the Czech political *régime* lies somewhere in between parliamentarism and semipresidentialism.

[7] Fernando Casal Bértoa, "Party Systems and Cleavage Structures Revisited: A Sociological Explanation of Party System Institutionalization" (2014) 20 *Party Politics* 16, 24.

[8] Ibid., at 25.

[9] The Communist Party is a nonsystemic party, but it consistently attracted 10–18% votes in the elections held between 1992 and 2010.

[10] That is all parliamentary parties apart from the Communists.

instance, the 2006 elections led to a total stalemate – the Civic Democratic Party and its coalition partners obtained 100 seats within the Chamber of Deputies and the Social Democrats with the Communist Party also won 100 seats. These weak parliamentary majorities also explain why the Czech Constitutional Court is so strong and why it has been able to interfere with the so-called megapolitics[11] without any meaningful threat from the political forces.[12]

However, notwithstanding this fragile stability,[13] the Czech party system continued to be among the most institutionalized in Eastern Europe in general, and the Visegrad region[14] in particular, for most of the period of 1993–2010.[15] This changed only toward the end of the studied period due to the meltdown of the Czech party system at the end of the 2000s, which implied primarily the downfall of the Civic Democratic Party (ODS) and of the small liberal parties.[16] This meltdown opened up the possibility for new alliances, increased electoral volatility, and fragmentation of the Czech political scene.[17]

B.   Consequences of the Division of Czechoslovakia

In a nutshell, there was strong continuity between the Federal Czechoslovakia of 1992[18] and the Czech Republic of 1993. Czechs looked favorably on the postcommunist federal regime and when they decided to change their institutions, they looked for inspiration to the interwar era. A strong attachment to the First Czechoslovak Republic has two

---

[11]   On the judicialization of "megapolitics," see Ran Hirschl, "The Judicialization of Mega-Politics and the Rise of Political Courts" (2008) 11 *Annual Review of Political Science* 93.

[12]   See the section that follows dealing with key actors of Czech judicial politics.

[13]   See Kevin Deegan-Krause and Tim Haughton, "A Fragile Stability: The Institutional Roots of Low Party System Volatility in the Czech Republic, 1990–2009" (2010) 17 *Czech Journal of Political Science* 227.

[14]   The notion of "Visegrad states" refers to the Czech Republic, Slovakia, Hungary, and Poland. The Visegrad group, comprising of the four aforesaid states, is named after a castle and town in Hungary, where the group was formed on February 15, 1991.

[15]   Bértoa 2014, supra note 7, 25 (with further references).

[16]   Zsolt Enyedi and Fernando Casal Bértoa (2015), 'Brothers in Arms? Party-blocs and party system closure', paper presented at the ECPR Joint Sessions in Warsaw on March 29 – April 2, 2015, (available at http://whogoverns.eu/brothers-in-arms-party-blocs-and-party-system-closure/), at 29.

[17]   Ibid.

[18]   The formal title of the common state of Czechs and Slovaks at that time was "The Czech and Slovak Federal Republic."

explanations. This regime was revered as the "success story" of modern Czech statehood[19] and the interwar institutional models had inherent value because they existed prior to the advent of the communist regime.[20] One may even say that Czech politicians revived the "theory of continuity" advanced by Edvard Beneš after World War II.[21] Within the judiciary, this continuity was both personal and institutional as "defederalization" had little impact on the judicial system.

In fact, all but one Czechoslovak federal organ were abolished without a successor and the relevant republican organs took over their competencies. The only top federal institution that was actually transformed instead of being replaced or abolished without replacement was the Federal Supreme Court. Transformation of the Federal Supreme Court begs a question. The republican Supreme Court of the Czech Republic was already in place and it could easily take over the agenda of the Federal Supreme Court, as republican organs in other areas of government did. In fact, the republican Supreme Court of the Slovak Republic became the top Slovak court after the dissolution of Czechoslovakia. So why did the Czechs opt for the trans-formation alternative? And what happened to the republican Supreme Court of the Czech Republic?

The answers to these two questions are intertwined. At the moment of the dissolution of Czechoslovakia, the post of President of the Federal Supreme Court was held by Otakar Motejl who enjoyed an unquestion-able reputation and it was considered unacceptable to leave him with-out a major position within the Czech judiciary. In addition, Motejl was also a major ally of Václav Havel. At the same time, it was considered inappropriate to fire the president of the republican Supreme Court of the Czech Republic, Antonín Mokrý, just because there was a need to find a position for Motejl. In other words, it was a "two roosters and one

---

[19] Remember that the First *Czechoslovak* Republic (1918–1938) was run predominantly by Czechs.

[20] Zdeněk Kühn, "The Democratization and Modernization of Post-Communist Judiciaries" in Alberto Febbrajo and Wojciech Sadurski (eds.), *Central and Eastern Europe After Transition* (Ashgate Publishing 2010) 177, at 187.

[21] Under the so-called "theory of legal continuity," advocated by the once-and-future Czechoslovak President Edvard Beneš, the German invasion of March 1939 and the Franco-British failure to uphold their guarantees of rump Czechoslovakia had violated, and thereby invalidated, the Munich Pact of 1938. As Frommer puts it, "according to this theory, Beneš remained president, the First [Czechoslovak] Republic still existed, and, . . ., Czechoslovakia's . . . laws applied throughout the occupation to all of the dismembered country's citizens" (Benjamin Frommer, *National Cleansing: Retribution against Nazi Collaborators in Postwar Czechoslovakia* (CUP 2005) at 80).

hen house" scenario. Politicians eventually found the most pragmatic solution for this conundrum – to create another hen house.

Again, a return to the interwar arrangement served as a pretense. There were four tiers of general courts in Czechoslovakia from 1918 until 1949. In 1949 the Communist regime abolished high courts, allegedly in order to "simplify" the Czechoslovak judicial system.[22] The post-Velvet Revolution politicians skillfully used this historical argument and claimed that a return to "normalcy" requires the resurrection of high courts. As a result, a new tier of the high courts was entrenched in the 1993 Constitution of the Czech Republic. The federal-era Supreme Court of the Czech Republic was transformed into the High Court of Prague and Mokrý became its president. This move created room for Motejl and "his" Federal Supreme Court. The Federal Supreme Court, short of its Slovak judges, was transformed into the Supreme Court of the Czech Republic and Motejl became the Chief Justice. This story is worth telling for two reasons. First, it shows extremely strong path-dependence within the judiciary. Second, it shows that the reintroduction of high courts was driven primarily by the need to create the new office for a key pro-Havel figure within the ordinary judiciary[23] and was not a carefully engineered and thought-out institutional change.

To sum up, the dissolution of Czechoslovakia brought about one major institutional change in the Czech Republic. The Parliament created a new tier of high courts and, thus, the Czech Republic had a four-tier judicial system after the split, which consisted of district courts, regional courts, high courts, and the Supreme Court. Other than that, changes within the judiciary were minimal. The 1993 Czech Constitution envisaged the creation of the Supreme Administrative Court (again pursuant to the interwar model), but this court came into being only in 2003. The Ministry of Justice model of court administration, which underwent "decommunization" as early as in 1991, was also left untouched.[24]

---

[22] On the ideal of simplicity in communist law, see John Hazard, *Communists and Their Law* (University of Chicago Press 1969) 103–126.

[23] The rationale behind the creation of high courts is confirmed by the fact that the second high court (in Olomouc) was created only in 1996 (until then the High Court of Prague exercised the jurisdiction of both high courts). In other words, the urgent "two roosters and one hen house" stalemate was fixed and no one missed the other high court.

[24] For more details, see Section II.A of this chapter.

C. The Impact of the EU Accession Process upon Czech Judicial Reforms

In sum, the EU Accession Process[25] had little impact on Czech judicial reforms that dealt with the issues of court administration and judicial independence. In 1997, the European Commission concluded that "[t]he Czech judiciary [was] independent."[26] Thereafter it devoted little attention to the system of court administration and separation of powers in the accession progress reports on the Czech Republic. Instead, the European Commission decided to focus on three different issues: the serious backlog of unresolved cases, the large number of unfilled vacancies for judges,[27] and the insufficient qualification of judges in EU law. In other words, the Commission's top priorities were the speeding-up of judicial proceedings, filling the vacancies within the judiciary, and improving the training of judges in the EU law,[28] and not improving judicial independence or increasing the self-governance of the judiciary.[29]

---

[25] For further details on the EU Accession Process and the so-called EU's conditionalities, see, for example, Dimitry Kochenov, *EU Enlargement and the Failure of Conditionality* (Kluwer 2008).

[26] Agenda 2000 – Commission Opinion on the Czech Republic's Application for Membership of the European Union, DOC/97/17 (Brussels, July 15,1997) at 12.

[27] There were 390 vacancies out of a total number of judges' posts of 2,726 in 1998. By January 1, 2002 the number of judges' posts had increased to 2,941; 2,669 judges were in active service (as of April 1, 2002) while 272 judicial vacancies remained. See the 1998 Accession Progress Report on the Czech Republic, 8; and the 2002 Accession Progress Report on the Czech Republic, 23. See also Annex C.

[28] See, for example, the 2000 Accession Progress Report on the Czech Republic that started with the following sentence: "The 1999 Accession Partnership established as a short term priority the implementation of a programme to reform the judiciary by filling vacancies, simplifying procedures, and stepping up the training of judges in EC" (at p. 19). See also the 2001 Accession Progress Report on the Czech Republic, 20: "The key areas for further improvement of the judicial system remain the speeding-up of court proceedings, the enforcement of court judgements, training of judges and prosecutors and administrative support for judges and courts."

[29] What is more, the Accession Progress Reports on the Czech Republic included erroneous and misleading information. For instance, from 1999 until 2001 the European Commission maintained that "formally [Czech] judges ... [could] be recalled by the Minister of Justice" [the 1999 Accession Progress Report on the Czech Republic, p. 13; see also the 2000 Accession Progress Report on the Czech Republic, 20; and the 2001 Accession Progress Report on the Czech Republic, 19]. Apparently, the European Commission failed to distinguish between judges and judicial officials (court presidents and vice presidents) in the 1999 and 2001 Reports. The Commission got it right only in the 2002: "The Constitution enshrines the independence of judges, although the Minister of Justice is

The 2000 and 2002 Regular Reports on the Czech Republic's Progress toward Accession illustrate this phenomenon eloquently. Even though Motejl's fully fledged judicial reform, which attempted to establish the Judicial Council Euro-model of court administration and increase judicial self-government, failed in 2000, the 2000 Report merely stated that "... draft constitutional amendments regarding judicial self-administration and the functional structure of the courts ... have been rejected by the Parliament as insufficiently prepared."[30] Two years later, the European Commission praised the Czech Republic in its 2002 Report for introducing "judicial boards," which the European Commission misleadingly labeled "Judicial Councils,"[31] even though the system of court administration remained virtually the same.

This soft stance of the European Commission[32] toward the Czech system of court administration confused Czech scholars and judges. Some scholars noted that the European Commission adopted a considerably "tougher" attitude as regards other accession states from Central Europe. For instance, Zdeněk Kühn observed that "[w]hen we look at [parts of] the EU [Accession Progress R]eports dealing with the court administration, we can see a puzzle which is difficult to explain. While the European Commission heavily criticized Latvia for its system of court administration which is very similar to the Czech one, it did not raise such criticism against the Czech Republic at all."[33] The following chapter will show that the European Commission was considerably "tougher" on Slovakia as well. These findings confirm that the European Commission failed to make any consistent assessment of the candidate countries' reforms.[34] However,

responsible for appointing, transferring and terminating the appointment of the *President and Vice-Presidents of courts*" (the 2002 Accession Progress Report on the Czech Republic, 22, emphasis added).

[30] The 2000 Accession Progress Report on the Czech Republic, p. 19.

[31] "The ... [2002 Law on Courts and Judges] introduced a first step toward self-government of the judiciary by the creation of *Judicial Councils* which have the status of consultative bodies at all court levels" (emphasis added). The 2002 Accession Progress Report on the Czech Republic, 22. See also Comprehensive monitoring report on the Czech Republic's preparations for membership, 12.

[32] *Cf.* the comprehensive review of the current situation regarding judicial independence in ten EU accession countries in the country studies prepared by the OSI EU Accession Monitoring Program www.soros.org/resources/articles_publications/publications/judicialind_20011010, which was far more critical of the Czech model of court administration.

[33] See, for example, Zdeněk Kühn, "Historický a komparativní kontext domácí diskuse o postavení soudní moci" in Jan Kysela (ed.), *Hledání optimálního modelu správy soudnictví pro Českou republiku* (2008) 46, at 52, note 26.

[34] See Kochenov, above note 25, at 264–266, 271–290; Anja Seibert-Fohr, "Judicial Independence in European Union Accessions: The Emergence of a European Basic

I leave this issue of "double standards" aside as it is not central to this book. It suffices to conclude that the European Commission exercised minimal pressure on Czech politicians with regard to changes in the court administration and, hence, the EU Accession Process did not play a significant role in the decisions on the large-scale design of the Czech judicial system.

D. Dealing with the Past within the Czech Judiciary

Several authors have claimed that there are strong links between purging the judiciary by the newly established democratic regimes and judicial accountability. For instance, Yusuf pinpoints corruption as the most prominent form of misgovernance permeating the Nigerian judiciary[35] and claims that "the persistence of real or imagined corruption in the judiciary is *a product* of the existential continuity of the institution in the transition process [and t]his will arguably remain the case as long as the matter of accountability of the judiciary for complicity in misgovernance during the country's authoritarian past remains completely ignored or under-addressed at best."[36]

Similarly, Piana makes claims regarding the impact of decommunization of the judiciary and judicial accountability in the CEE.[37] More specifically, she has argued that the Czech Republic was an outlier among the judiciaries in the CEE, because "[s]tarting from 1991, a long process of lustration was responsible for the dismissal of the greater part of the bench"[38] and "only 30% of judges remained on the bench after transition."[39] Later on, she suggests that "[b]y lustrating the judicial staff, the new political

---

Principle" (2009) 52 *German Yearbook of International Law* 405; Daniel Smilov, "EU Enlargement and the Constitutional Principle of Judicial Independence" in Adam Czarnota, Martin Krygier, and Wojciech Sadurski (eds.), *Spreading Democracy and the Rule of Law: The Impact of EU Enlargement on the Rule of Law, Democracy, and Constitutionalism in Post-communist Legal Orders* (2006) 313; and Diana Bozhilova, "Measuring Success and Failure of EU-Europeanization in the Eastern Enlargement: Judicial Reform in Bulgaria" (2007) 9 *European Journal of Law Reform* 285; or Cristina Parau, "The Drive for Judicial Supremacy" in Anja Seibert-Fohr (ed.), *Judicial Independence in Transition* (Springer 2012) 619; and Ramona Coman and Cristina Dallara, "Judicial Independence in Romania" in Anja Seibert-Fohr (ed.), *Judicial Independence in Transition* (Springer 2012) 835.

[35] See Hakeem Yusuf, *Transitional justice, Judicial Accountability and the Rule of Law* (Routledge 2010), at 174–175.

[36] Ibid., at 177 (emphasis added).

[37] See Daniela Piana, *Judicial Accountabilities in New Europe: From Rule of Law to Quality of Justice* (Ashgate 2010), 97–102.

[38] Ibid., at 100. See also ibid., at 92, 108, 110 (footnote 33), and 164.

[39] Ibid., at 98.

elite maximized its capacity to control the high levels of the judicial systems."[40] In other words, Piana makes three claims. The first is that there was a *widespread purge* within the Czechoslovak judiciary after the fall of the communist regime. The second is that this purge happened *because* of the so-called lustration laws.[41] The third is that judges from the communist era lost control over the *higher* echelons of the Czech judiciary. These three specific aspects of the dealing with the past, according to Piana, have influenced judicial accountability in the Czech Republic.

I disagree with Yusuf and do not think that there is necessarily a link between accountability of judges for corruption and their accountability for gross violations of human rights.[42] However, it is possible that ex-communist judges may be more prone to follow the habits from the communist regime – such as meritless disciplinary motions initiated by court presidents, subservience to the executive, court presidents, and senior judges, or shirking habits – than judges appointed after the fall of the communist regime who do not carry the "communist baggage" with them. In addition, the breadth of purges after the fall of the communist regime may also explain the level of judicial complicity with the communist regime[43] and the stance of the new democratic political elites toward the judiciary. This means that if the Czech Republic and Slovakia significantly differ regarding their reckoning with the past, this must be taken into account when interpreting the results of the empirical analysis of the use of mechanisms of judicial accountability. For these reasons, it is important to address the issue of dealing with the past within the Czech judiciary and scrutinize Piana's claims.

In sum, all Piana's claims about the Czech Republic mentioned earlier are problematic and provide a misleading picture of how the past was dealt

---

[40] Ibid., at 108.

[41] These two claims are repeated by other authors as well. See also Alexei Trochev, "Meddling with Justice: Competitive Politics, Impunity, and Distrusted Courts in Post-Orange Ukraine" (2010) 18 *Democratizatsiya* 122, 134–135.

[42] It is quite possible that judges who were complicit in gross violations of human rights under the authoritarian or totalitarian regime did not take bribes under the democratic regime, and vice versa. Likewise, young judges, who joined the judiciary after the fall of the authoritarian and totalitarian regime and thus could not be complicit in gross violations of human rights in their judicial roles, could be more corrupt than their older colleagues. For further details, see David Kosař, "The least accountable branch" (review essay) (2013) 11 *International Journal of Constitutional Law* 234, 251–252.

[43] See Paloma Aguilar, "Judiciary Involvement in Authoritarian Repression and Transitional Justice: The Spanish Case in Comparative Perspective" (2013) 7 *International Journal of Transitional Justice* 245, 258–260.

with within the Czech judiciary. Regarding the first claim, most sources agree that there were only limited purges within the Czechoslovak judiciary after the Velvet Revolution. According to these sources, 484 out of 1460 Czech judges on the bench in 1990 left the judiciary between January 1990 and December 1992.[44] This means that two thirds of judges from the communist era remained on the bench, and not 30% as Piana claims.

Regarding the second claim, it is highly unlikely that all 484 judges left the judiciary because of lustration laws.[45] First, the Large Lustration Law[46] came into effect only in November 1991 and judges who left the judiciary from January 1990 until October 1991 could hardly decide to do so *because* of the Large Lustration Law, whose adoption was by no means clear at that time. Secondly, many judges left the judiciary in order to improve their financial situation, as working as an attorney became an easy bonanza in the early 1990s due to the booming economy and general shortage of lawyers.[47] To sum up, although the precise number of judges who left the Czech judiciary on the ground of or in order to avoid the Large Lustration Law cannot be determined,[48] most sources agree that the number of such judges was relatively small, and most judges who left the Czech judiciary after the Velvet Revolution of 1989 did so for other reasons.[49]. Therefore, the Czech lustration laws had only a marginal impact on the judiciary.

Finally, the third claim that the Czech judges from the communist era lost their influence within the judiciary is equally problematic. On the contrary, the data provided by the Czech Ministry of Justice in January

---

[44] Eliška Wagnerová, "Position of Judges in the Czech Republic" in Jiří Přibáň, Pauline Roberts, and James Young (eds.), *Systems of Justice in Transition: Central European Experiences since 1989* (Ashgate 2003) 163, 170 (according to her, out of 1,460 Czech judges on the bench in 1990, approximately one-third (484) left the judiciary within three years: 185 judges left the judiciary in 1990, followed by 148 judges in 1991, and 151 judges in 1992). *See also* Kühn 2010, above note 20, at 181.

[45] Lustration is a specific vetting process for selected position (mostly) in the public sector. For a recent take on how the Czech lustration laws operate, *see* David Kosař, "Lustration and Lapse of Time: Dealing with the Past in the Czech Republic" (2008) 4 *European Constitutional Law Review* 460.

[46] Act No. 451/1991 Coll., on standards required for holding specific positions in state administration of the Czech and Slovak Federal Republic, Czech Republic, and Slovak Republic of October 4, 1991.

[47] See, for example, Kühn 2010, above note 20, at 181; Michal Bobek, "The Fortress of Judicial Independence and the Mental Transitions of the Central European Judiciaries" (2008) 14 *European Public Law* 99, at 118–119 (2008).

[48] Note that there were other transitional measures taken in the Czech Republic (at that time still a part of federal Czechoslovakia) after the Velvet Revolution; see Wagnerová, above note 44, at 169.

[49] See above note 47.

2011 showed a very different picture. All court officials of the Supreme Administrative Court (president and vice president) and of the High Court in Prague (president and three vice presidents) were former members of or candidates for the Communist Party.[50] The situation at the Supreme Court was not much different. Even though the court officials of the Supreme Court were not ex-communists, almost half the judges of the Supreme Court (31 out of 66) were former members of the Communist Party. The numbers at other top courts were also striking. Almost a third of the judges of the Supreme Administrative Court and of the High Court in Olomouc and an even higher percentage of judges of the High Court of Prague joined the Communist Party prior to 1989.[51] So did a significant number of judges of the regional courts. In contrast, the percentage of ex-communists among judges of district courts is relatively low. One may thus speak of an inverse pyramid: "the higher one goes in the structure of the judiciary, the higher the percentage of ex-communists."[52] This inverse pyramid has little to do with the way lustration was carried out; it is simply a consequence of the fact that lower-court judges are younger. In sum, the communist-era judges retained their influence within the Czech judiciary.

Interestingly, in stark contrast to the Slovak scenario, the call for reckoning with the past within the judiciary and hunger to know more about communist judges have never waned in the Czech Republic. On the contrary, insufficient dealing with the past within the judiciary is a proverbial "skeleton in the cupboard," which has become a recurring issue that attracts significant attention in the Czech media. The whole discussion culminated in a call for disclosure of ex-communists on the bench. As judges were not willing to do that voluntarily, one staunch anti-communist initiated an action before the administrative courts under the Freedom of Information Act.[53] The ordinary courts (the Municipal Court in Prague as well as the Supreme Administrative Court) rejected this action, primarily on the ground that a judge's membership in political party is sensitive information and providing such information would violate a judge's privacy. Hence, the dispute again wound up before the Constitutional Court.

---

[50] Note that all Czech judges had to undergo lustration, but a mere membership in the Communist Party of Czechoslovakia is not an obstacle for holding the judicial office according to the Large Lustration Law.

[51] All data are taken from the list of ex-communist judges compiled by the Czech Ministry of Justice and originally published on January 7, 2011 (note that this list was revised several times).

[52] Kühn 2010, above note 20, at 181.

[53] Law No. 106/1999 Coll., on the Free Access to Information (Freedom of Information Law).

The Constitutional Court quashed the judgments of the ordinary courts and held that information about judges' membership of the Communist Party prior to November 17, 1989 belonged to the public sphere. What is even more interesting is what happened after the Constitutional Court's judgment. The public and scholars applauded the Constitutional Court's stance and submitted numerous requests for information under the Freedom of Information Act to the court presidents. Not surprisingly, judges fought back. They argued that they had not hurt anybody,[54] that judges' membership in the Communist Party[55] in itself could not influence their work in the democratic environment, that it was too late to address this issue[56] and that there was no other choice in the early 1990s due to the shortage of judges. They also invoked the ultimate trick – no law requires the collection of information about judges' membership of political parties and thus no body possesses reliable information about judges' communist past. On this ground, court presidents refused many requests for information. In a nutshell, judges again tried to portray themselves as small cogs in the wheels of the communist regime preventing the worst from happening and tried to brush the issue under the carpet.

However, this argument this time succeeded only in part. A few weeks after the judgment of the Constitutional Court, the Ministry of Justice published online the list of judges who were members of the Communist Party before 1989.[57] The Ministry did so despite the fact that, until then, it had consistently claimed that it did not possess this information. Journalists and ordinary people immediately started to check who was on the list. The fact that the original list published by the Ministry of Justice was both overinclusive (it mistakenly included several judges who were never members of the Communist Party) and underinclusive (the list omitted a few

---

[54] See, for example, Vladimír Stibořík, "Všechno jsem soudil podle svědomí" interview (*Mladá fronta DNES*, March 18, 2010) 2 (attached to Luděk Navara, "Šéf vrchního soudu rozhodoval v 80. letech v politických procesech" in Vladimír Stibořík, "Všechno jsem soudil podle svědomí" interview (*Mladá fronta DNES*, March 18, 2010)) http://zpravy.idnes.cz/sef-vrchniho-soudu-rozhodoval-v-80-letech-v-politickych-procesech-phs-/domaci.aspx?c=A100317_215456_domaci_abr accessed August 15, 2013.

[55] Note that according to reliable sources there were 1,701,085 members of the Communist Party as of January 1, 1989.

[56] For instance, Tomáš Lichovník, the President of the Judicial Union, expressed this opinion on a nationwide TV channel; see "Ministerstvo vydalo seznam soudců z KSČ, čtyři jména poté vyškrtlo" (*Česká televize*, January 7, 2011) www.ceskatelevize.cz:8001/ct24/domaci/111953-ministerstvo-vydalo-seznam-soudcu-z-ksc-ctyri-jmena-pote-vyskrtlo/ accessed August 15, 2013.

[57] See the list of ex-communist judges compiled by the Czech Ministry of Justice and originally published on January 7, 2011 (note that this list was revised several times).

members of the Communist Party and it did not cover the so-called candidates for membership in the Communist Party) added more fuel to the fire. Judges who were correctly included in the list downplayed the importance of membership of the Communist Party,[58] whereas judges who were included mistakenly vigorously protested and threatened the Ministry of Justice with defamation claims for damaging their reputation.[59] The genie was out of the bottle and no one could put it back.

The list of ex-communist judges compiled by the Minister of Justice in 2011 also disproved a myth that the judges from the communist era had lost their influence within the judiciary.[60] To be sure, according to this list there were 598 ex-communists out of approximately 3,000 judges within the Czech judiciary in 2011, which amounts to a mere 20%, and thus it is technically incorrect to characterize Czech judges as "former communist judges."[61] However, as mentioned earlier, most court officials and a significant portion of regular judges of the Czech apex courts were ex-communists.[62]

In sum, three conclusions can be made about dealing with the past within the Czech judiciary. First, the Czech Republic is not an outlier in the region regarding the purges within the judiciary. There was no widespread cleansing of the judiciary and the results of the Czech way of dealing with the past within the judiciary thus did not differ significantly from the outcomes in Poland, Hungary, Bulgaria, Romania, and Slovakia.[63] In fact, the only country that conducted significant purges within the judiciary in the CEE region was the reunified Germany that conducted thorough administrative purges within the whole of the GDR judiciary and criminal prosecution of selected GDR judges.[64] Second, since many of the communist-era judges still sit on the bench and hold important positions within the judiciary, the transition of the Czech judiciary is far

---

[58] See, for example, Stibořík, above note 54.
[59] See, for example, "Mezi soudci z KSČ se ocitli neprávem. Zvažují žaloby" (*Lidové noviny*, January 12, 2011) 4; or "Soudkyně v KSČ být nemohla, v roce 1989 jí bylo 14 let" (*Mladá fronta DNES Kraj Moravskoslezský*, January 11, 2011), 1 http://zpravy.idnes .cz/soudkyne-se-nasla-na-seznamu-ksc-v-roce-1989-ji-ale-bylo-teprve-ctrnact-11u-/ domaci.aspx?c=A110111_1512947_ostrava-zpravy_jog accessed August 15, 2013.
[60] This further disproves Piana's portrayal of dealing with the past within the Czech judiciary; see notes 37–40.
[61] Kühn 2010, above note 20, at 181.
[62] See above notes 50–52.
[63] On the Slovakian way of dealing with the past within the judiciary, see Chapter 6, Section I.D.
[64] See Kosař 2013, above note 42, at 255 (with further references).

from over.[65] Instead, it is an ongoing process.[66] Third, dealing with the past within the judiciary between 1993 and 2010 was still an issue that attracted significant attention in the Czech Republic and the "sex appeal" of this topic did not wane in this period. This never-ending reckoning with the past, coupled with the "defensive" position of ex-communist judges, also had negative spill-over effects on the judiciary as a whole. The communist past of key judicial figures was an easy target and provided impetus for attacks on individual judges and for a continued distrust of the Czech judiciary.

E. "Superjudges" and Other Key Actors in Czech Judicial Politics

In order to understand the Czech judicial politics it is important to introduce the most influential individuals within the judiciary who played an important role in shaping judicial power in the Czech Republic. Only then it makes sense to discuss four major constitutional actors and three formal and informal institutions that exercise influence over the Czech judiciary.

In identifying key figures within the Czech judiciary between 1993 and 2010 I will focus primarily on a special category of judges whom I refer to as "superjudges." By a "superjudge" I mean a professional judge who at some point of his or her career joined the executive power and then returned to the judiciary. The sequence is important. A "superjudge" was a judge before he moved to the executive branch and then returned to the judiciary, empowered by all the knowledge and contacts he made within the executive branch. This "travelling among branches" is not specific to the Czech Republic. It exists, to a greater or lesser extent, in most civil law systems. But for historical reasons this practice is particularly troubling in postcommunist judicial systems.

There are two superjudges who still hold important positions within the Czech judiciary – Jaroslav Bureš and Josef Baxa.[67] Jaroslav Bureš has a particularly rich record. He became a district court judge in 1980. In 1986 he was promoted to the Municipal Court in Prague and yet again in 1991

---

[65] For a similar claim in the postcommunist context, see Kora Andrieu, "An Unfinished Business: Transitional Justice and Democratization in Post-Soviet Russia" (2011) 5 *International Journal of Transitional Justice* 198.

[66] See A. James McAdams, "Transitional Justice: The Issue that Won't Go Away" (2011) 5 *International Journal of Transitional Justice* 304, at 312.

[67] It is also worthy of mention that Bureš was a member of the Communist Party from 1986 until 1989.

to the High Court in Prague (the then republican Supreme Court[68]). Few years later, he became the Supreme Court judge (1996–1999), but in 2000 he decided to take the job of the President of the High Court in Prague (2000–2001) and just one year later left the judiciary entirely in order to become the Minister of Justice (2001–2002). In 2003 he unsuccessfully ran for the office of President of the Czech Republic and then he served as Minister for Legislation (2004–2005) and as counsel at White & Case in Prague (2005–2006). Nevertheless, after his political stint he wanted to return to the judiciary.

The details of Bureš's return are striking and made it to the headlines of all major Czech newspapers. On January 30, 2006 the President of the Czech Republic, Václav Klaus, dismissed Mrs Iva Brožová from the position of President of the Supreme Court,[69] by a short letter that did not contain any reasons for her dismissal, and appointed Bureš to that post instead. More specifically, Václav Klaus (1) removed Iva Brožová from the position of the Supreme Court president; (2) appointed Bureš a judge; (3) assigned Bureš, with the consent of the Vice President of the Supreme Court, to the Supreme Court; and (4) appointed Bureš to the vacant position of the President of the Supreme Court. However, Iva Brožová challenged steps (1), (3), and (4) before the Constitutional Court.[70]

As to the step 1, the Constitutional Court found Brožová's dismissal unconstitutional in July 2006.[71] As a result, Bureš's subsequent appointment to the position of the President of the Supreme Court (step 4), was also unconstitutional. However, Bureš still remained a regular judge of the Supreme Court. But that did not last long. Two months later, the Constitutional Court held that the assignment of Bureš to the Supreme Court as a regular judge (step 3) was also unconstitutional,[72] since it was

---

[68] Note that after the dissolution of Czechoslovakia in 1992, the federal-era Supreme Court of the Czech Republic was transformed into the High Court of Prague (whereas the Federal Supreme Court became the Supreme Court of the Czech Republic). For further details, see Section I.B of this chapter.

[69] Note that Brožová was recalled "only" from the position of *court president*. She was not dismissed from *judicial office* and thus she still remained a judge of the Supreme Court.

[70] Note that Brožová could not challenge step (2), as it did not affect per se the Supreme Court composition.

[71] Judgment of the Constitutional Court of the Czech Republic of July 11, 2006, case no. Pl. ÚS 18/06, in conjunction with Judgment of the Constitutional Court of the Czech Republic of September 12, 2006, case no. II. ÚS 53/06. For further details, see Michal Bobek, "The Administration of Courts in the Czech Republic – In Search of a Constitutional Balance" (2010) 16 *European Public Law* 251, at 263–265.

[72] Judgment of the Constitutional Court of the Czech Republic of December 12, 2006, case no. Pl. ÚS 17/06.

made without the consent of the President of the Supreme Court (Iva Brožová). According to the Constitutional Court, the Vice President of the Supreme Court could not act on behalf of the president of the Supreme Court in such matters.[73] But Klaus did not give up and appointed Bureš to the position of Vice President of the Supreme Court. The Constitutional Court fought back again[74] and, this time with highly dubious reasoning, found that appointment unconstitutional as well.[75] As a result of these events, there was no avenue left for Bureš to return to the Supreme Court. Nevertheless, Bureš was still a judge (step 2), albeit only "floating in the orbit" as he was not assigned to any court. The Minister of Justice solved this problem soon. He assigned Bureš to the High Court of Prague and immediately made Bureš its Vice President. Hence, Bureš eventually found his way back into the judiciary.[76]

Josef Baxa started as a judge at the district court in 1984. In 1989 he was promoted to the Regional Court in Pilsen, where he subsequently held the position of vice president. In 1998 Otakar Motejl, then the Minister of Justice, brought him to Prague and Baxa became a Deputy Minister of Justice. Baxa served as Deputy Minister of Justice for several ministers (including the abovementioned Bureš) between 1998 and 2002. As of January 2, 2003 he was appointed the President of the newly created Supreme Administrative Court.

These are the successful (Baxa) or at least partly successful stories (Bureš). Other judges planned a similar path, but they failed. Jiří Vyvadil is an example of the latter group. Vyvadil had a rich career as a politician as well as a judge. He was an MP (1992–1996), Senator (1996–2000), and a judge at the district court (2001–2005). In March 2005 he was temporarily assigned to the Supreme Administrative Court, but as early as in

[73] Ibid.
[74] Judgment of the Constitutional Court of the Czech Republic of September 12, 2007, case no. Pl. ÚS 87/06.
[75] Note that Art. 63(f) of the Czech Constitution stipulates that the President of the Czech Republic "shall appoint *from among judges* the President and *Vice-Presidents* of the Supreme Court" (emphasis added). Despite this wording, the Constitutional Court held that the President of the Czech Republic may choose Vice Presidents of the Supreme Court only from among *judges of the Supreme Court*. As Bureš's assignment to the Supreme Court had been earlier found unconstitutional (see Judgment of the Constitutional Court of the Czech Republic no. Pl. ÚS 17/06, cited above in note 72), he was not a judge of the Supreme Court and hence he could not be appointed to the position of a vice president of the Supreme Court. See Judgment of the Constitutional Court of the Czech Republic of September 12, 2007, case no. Pl. ÚS 87/06, §§ 40–41 and 70.
[76] Bureš eventually became the President of the High Court in Prague in 2013.

September 2005 he was further assigned to the Ministry of Justice, where he was supposed to work on judicial reform. However, he went too far during his assignment to the Ministry of Justice. He was allegedly involved in various suspicious political deals and his private meeting with a controversial entrepreneur finally finished him. Baxa, then already the President of the Supreme Administrative Court, initiated disciplinary motion against Vyvadil in 2006, and Vyvadil decided to resign in order to avoid disciplinary trial. Later on, he earned his living as an advocate and political advisor.

Both of these two stories of "superjudges" suggest one thing. Judges knew that their temporary assignment to the Ministry of Justice could help them to climb up the "judicial ladder" faster than under normal circumstances. Temporary assignment had other positive effects as well. Judges assigned to the Ministry of Justice were more visible to the media as well as to the public. This "singling-out" from the crowd is a highly precious asset for judges in the civil law system, where regular judges are often perceived as "grey mice." Furthermore, contacts and information accumulated at the Ministry of Justice also count. Contacts mean information and information means power. Not surprisingly, "superjudges," especially if they wanted to settle scores with their opponents within the judiciary, presented a grave danger to the Czech judicial system. The Constitutional Court soon recognized this danger and struck down the provisions of the Law on Courts and Judges that allowed temporary assignment to the Ministry of Justice.[77]

Now it is possible to explain the role of constitutional organs and other formal or informal entities in the Czech judicial politics. Historically, the Czechoslovak models of court administration always rested on two pillars – the Ministry of Justice and the court presidents.[78] This has not changed since the split. Hence, the Ministry of Justice as well as judicial officials remained the key institutional players in the Czech judicial system. In addition to these two pillars, two more constitutional actors have increasingly intervened in judicial matters – the President of the Czech Republic and the Constitutional Court.

The President of the Czech Republic is not merely a representative figure. On the contrary, he has particularly wide powers vis-à-vis the judiciary. According to the Czech Constitution, he appoints all judges of the

---

[77] See Judgment of the Constitutional Court of the Czech Republic of June 18, 2002, case no. Pl. ÚS 7/02; and Judgment of the Constitutional Court of the Czech Republic of October 6, 2010, case no. Pl. ÚS 39/08, §§ 46–49. Both of these judgments are addressed subsequently.
[78] See Bobek 2010, above note 71, 252–254.

ordinary courts, appoints presidents and vice presidents of the Supreme Court and Supreme Administrative Court,[79] and appoints, upon approval by the Senate, all judges of the Constitutional Court.[80] Hence, he exercises a significant influence both over the ordinary courts and over the Constitutional Court. Since 2008 the President has also appointed presidents of high courts and regional courts, in both cases upon nomination by the Minister of Justice.[81] But these powers also beg a question: what is the extent of the President's discretion in staffing the courts and selecting judicial officials? This question has permeated the Czech constitutional discourse and led to several fierce battles before administrative courts and the Constitutional Court.[82] The Supreme Administrative Court and the Constitutional Court eventually curtailed the President's discretion in appointing judges of the ordinary courts,[83] but his discretion in selecting Justices of the Constitutional Court is, leaving aside basic criteria such as age, legal education, and sufficient experience, almost unlimited. The precise width of the President's discretion in selecting court presidents and vice presidents is unclear.[84] In addition to appointment powers, since 2008 the President has also held a "stick" against judges as he can initiate disciplinary motions against any judge of the ordinary courts.[85]

In addition, one must also take into account historical legacy of strong Czechoslovak and Czech presidents who often had the ambition to run the country instead of the Prime Minister or at least steer it into another direction. This applies not only to Václav Havel, the first Czech president (1993–2003), and his major rivals and eventually also successors at the presidential office, Václav Klaus (2003–2013) and Miloš Zeman (from 2013 until now), but also to the first Czechoslovak president, Tomáš Garrigue Masaryk (1918–1935), and Edvard Beneš (1935–1938 and 1940–1948), a Czechoslovak longtime foreign minister and later president. It was in fact Masaryk and Beneš who created an informal political organization known as the *Hrad* or "Castle"

---

[79] See Sections III and IV of this chapter.
[80] The Czech Constitution thus transplanted the U.S. model of appointment of federal judges for appointment of Justices of the Czech Constitutional Court.
[81] See Section IV of this chapter.
[82] See Bobek 2010, above note 71; or Zdeněk Kühn, "Judicial Administration Reforms in Central-Eastern Europe: Lessons to be Learned" in Anja Seibert-Fohr (ed.), *Judicial Independence in Transition* (Springer 2012) 603, 607–610.
[83] See Bobek 2010, above note 71, at 260–263. See also notes 70–76.
[84] Ibid., at 263–265.
[85] Art. 8(2)(b) of the Code of Procedure in Matters of Judges, State Prosecutors, and Executors. As will be shown in Section IV.D of this chapter, the President of the Czech Republic did not use this power between 2008 and 2010.

to set the country's political agenda,[86] and since then he who occupied the Prague Castle had de facto far more power than what the Czechoslovak and Czech constitutions envisaged for the presidential office.

The Czech Constitutional Court is a powerful institution based upon the German centralized model of constitutional adjudication. The fragmented political scene makes the Constitutional Court even stronger. The interferences of the Constitutional Court in "judicial design issues" are so numerous that I cannot deal with them here.[87] Virtually any "judicial design issue" ends up before the Constitutional Court and that Court has adopted the most stringent intensity of judicial review in these matters. This means that without knowledge of and taking into account the case law of the Constitutional Court the overall picture of the Czech judiciary would be incomplete and misleading. I will address the case law of the Czech Constitutional Court subsequently, in connection with a particular mechanism of judicial accountability.

The power of these four constitutional actors, the Ministry of Justice, judicial officials, the President of the Czech Republic, and the Constitutional Court, comes directly from the Czech Constitution. However there are other formal and informal actors that possess significant power within the judiciary. These actors include judicial boards, the Judicial Union, and the "kolegium of presidents of regional courts."

Judicial boards[88] (*soudcovské rady*) were established in 2002 at all Czech courts.[89] They have a statutory basis and comment primarily on the promotion or temporary assignment of judges to a given court, on the division of the court's case load and on the system of case assignment.[90] Judicial boards are "self-governing" bodies, but they have only advisory powers and court presidents are not bound by their advice.[91] The real role of these boards in the administration of a particular court depends on the

---

[86] See Andrea Orzoff, *Battle for the Castle: The Myth of Czechoslovakia in Europe, 1914–1948* (OUP 2009).

[87] For a snapshot of these interventions, see Bobek 2010, above note 71.

[88] Given the nature and composition of these bodies, the more appropriate translation into English would be "judicial assemblies," but all materials on the Czech judiciary in English, including the accession reports of the European Union, use the term "judicial board." Hence, in order to avoid confusion, I will refer to these bodies as "judicial boards" as well.

[89] Small district courts are an exception as there is no judicial board at district courts with fewer than eleven judges. Instead, the plenary session of all judges fulfills the tasks of a judicial board. For further details, see Arts. 46–59 of Law no. 6/2002 Coll., on Courts and Judges.

[90] Arts. 50–53 of Law No. 6/2002 Coll., on Courts and Judges.

[91] The central position of court presidents is further buttressed by the fact that they set the agenda of judicial board meetings.

relationship between the board and the court president and, perhaps more importantly, on the personality of the court president. If the court president is a strong personality, the role of the judicial boards diminishes or, in the worst-case scenario, the board becomes a mere bystander. This rule applies also vice versa: the weaker the court president, the more powerful the judicial board. In sum, the powers of judicial boards are narrow and limited to a particular court. They should not be confused with a country-wide judicial *council*.[92]

The Judicial Union (*Soudcovská unie*) is a professional association of judges, which was established in 1990. The Judicial Union claims that it represents approximately one third of Czech judges.[93] The main goals of the Judicial Union include protecting judicial independence, participating in the continuous education of judges and judge-trainees, representing the interests of the judiciary, contributing to the democratic legal order, promoting modern models of court administration, and cooperation with similar bodies abroad. The Judicial Union has been particularly vocal in promoting the judicial council model of court administration and its members have taken a leading role in challenging judicial reforms before the Constitutional Court. Not surprisingly, judicial accountability does not rank high in its agenda. In terms of its representativeness, the Judicial Union does not publish how many judges from each tier of the Czech court system it represents. However, on the basis of the composition of the executive organs of the Judicial Union and its rhetoric one may reasonably assume that the Judicial Union represents primarily the interests of lower courts judges, that is, judges of district courts and regional courts.

Finally, the so-called kolegium of presidents of regional courts (*kolegium předsedů krajských soudů*) is an informal group that consists of all eight presidents of regional courts.[94] The group of eight court presidents convenes regular meetings, where the regional court presidents discuss current issues within the judiciary. The number of their meetings varies, but they usually meet four times a year and the venue rotates among the regional courts seats.[95] Even though it has no statutory basis,[96] the costs of

---

[92] This mistake was made even by the European Commission; see note 31 above.

[93] Interview with the First Vice President of the Judicial Union, Daniela Zemanová, conducted on October 9, 2012 (on file with author).

[94] Note that there are eight regional courts in the Czech Republic.

[95] Interview with a former president of a regional court (who was one of the co founders of the kolegium) from May 6, 2015.

[96] Note that in 2007 presidents of regional courts attempted to formalize the kolegium and add it to the Law on Courts and Judges. However, both the Minister of Justice and the

these meetings are covered by the regional court budgets. Interestingly, the creation of the kolegium is a postcommunist phenomenon. While regional court presidents used to meet with the Minister of Justice already in the communist era and then in the 1990s, they have not held separate meetings just for themselves at that time. They established the kolegium and regularized their meetings only in 2002.[97] They soon started to distribute the minutes of their meetings to the Minister of Justice, who later on promised to the regional court presidents that these minutes will be discussed at the ministerial meetings.[98]

Most sources agree that regional court presidents decided to create the kolegium for two reasons – to discuss practical issues that affected all regional courts[99] and the need to take the lead in judicial reforms.[100] Initially, the kolegium focused on the former, but it soon shifted its attention to the latter, which culminated by announcing the program of "Emancipation of the Czech judiciary" on January 27, 2005. Despite the fact that the kolegium has no statutory underpinning and operates on a purely informal basis, it is one of the most influential bodies in the Czech judicial system. Minutes from their meetings are regularly discussed at the Ministry of Justice and are taken seriously. The media also often refer to the position of the kolegium. In private, not only officials at the Ministry of Justice, but even presidents of top courts (the Supreme Court and the Supreme Administrative Court) and presidents of high courts admit that it is extremely difficult to push forward any change without the approval of the kolegium (i.e., without the backing from regional court presidents). The vast powers of presidents of regional courts must also be understood in their historical context. Presidents of regional courts grew in importance after the Communist Party abolished high courts, the bastions of the First Czechoslovak Republic, in 1952[101] and due to increasing insulation

---

presidents of the top courts rejected that idea and the relevant amendment the Law on Courts and Judges was not adopted (ibid.).

[97] According to one of the "founding fathers" of the kolegium, the idea of creating an informal association of regional court presidents was suggested to them by Mr Jean-Michel Peltier, a French liaison magistrate in Prague (ibid.).

[98] Ibid.

[99] For instance, they discussed whether attorneys had to undergo X-ray scanning at the entrance to the court building like other citizens or not.

[100] Ibid. This view was confirmed by the President of the Supreme Administrative Court (Interview with the President of the Supreme Administrative Court from April 27, 2015).

[101] As mentioned above in Section I.A, high courts were reestablished in 1993 (only in the Czech Republic, not in Slovakia). However, they never rose to the prominent position, which they had held in the interwar period. On the contrary, high courts became "pariahs"

of the top courts (the Supreme Court and the Supreme Administrative Court) from the rest of the ordinary judiciary after 1993. In a nutshell, the importance of the kolegium as well as of individual presidents of regional courts cannot be overestimated.

II.   Court Administration after the Split (1993–2010): Two Decades of Calibrating the Ministry of Justice Model

The previous section sketched the background against which the Czech courts operate and addressed major events within the postsplit history of the Czech Republic. This section focuses in more detail on judicial reforms adopted between 1993 and 2010 and on their repercussions. It draws attention to significant institutional changes within the Czech judicial system and the motivation behind them. It is divided into two periods: 1993–2002 and 2003–2010. The rationale of this division is to see more distinctly the contrast between Slovakia's Judicial Council Euro-model and the Czech Republic's Ministry of Justice model of court administration. The aim of this part is to explain why the changes in the Czech judicial system occurred, which "political vectors" and individuals were behind them, and what these changes meant for the Czech judiciary.

A.   Ministry of Justice Model Retained (1993–2002)

In a nutshell, the Czech Republic retained the "Ministry of Justice" model of court administration inherited from Federal Czechoslovakia, which means that the executive branch and court presidents played a central role within the system. Besides the model of court administration, very few changes were introduced into the Czech judicial system. The Czech Constitution of 1993 reintroduced a new tier of courts (high courts),[102] abolished all military courts (as of December 31, 1993),[103] and changed the mode of selection of judges (judges are no longer elected, but appointed by the President of the Czech Republic).[104] The two major federal statutes

---

of the Czech judicial system and there have been influential voices seeking to abolish them again.

[102] For further details, see Section I.A.

[103] Art. 110 of the Constitutional Law No. 1/1993 Coll., the Constitution of the Czech Republic.

[104] Art. 63(1)(f) in conjunction with Art. 93(1) of the Constitutional Law No. 1/1993 Coll., the Constitution of the Czech Republic.

governing the judiciary, the 1991 Law on Courts and Judges and the 1991 Disciplinary Code for Judges, were left almost untouched. The "defederalization" amendments to these two statutes merely reflected the changes brought by the Czech Constitution and deleted all references to federal judicial bodies. Other changes were marginal. The only change that is worthy of mention is that politicians decided that the seat of the Supreme Court of the Czech Republic would be in Brno[105] and thus the "geographic separation of powers" was preserved.[106]

The years between 1993 and 1998 were relatively uneventful.[107] The only major problem was a shortage of judges,[108] but it was gradually addressed by the increased appointment of new judges.[109] However, it was the proverbial "calm before the storm." In 2000 the Minister of Justice Otakar Motejl prepared a proposal for the creation of a High Council of the Judiciary that would consist of sixteen members – eight judges and eight members of other legal professions – elected for five years. The High Council of the Judiciary was supposed to be granted broad powers concerning matters of the selection and nomination of candidates for judicial office, the appointment and dismissal of judicial officials, as well as the training of judges. Given these broad powers the High Council of the Judiciary was supposed to be entrenched in the Constitution.

---

[105] Symbolically, the communist regime moved the seat of the Supreme Court of Czechoslovakia from Brno to Prague in 1950 so that the top court was closer to the Communist Party Secretariat. The Federal Supreme Court of Czechoslovakia returned to Brno only in 1991, after the Velvet Revolution.

[106] Note that Brno lies next to the borders with Slovakia and is located approximately 200 km east of Prague.

[107] The 1995 Amendment to the 1991 Law on Court and Judges brought the most significant changes of that period. Among other things, it reintroduced the relocation and demotion of judges (but only if the change in the court organization required it) and finished the "defederalization" of the Czech judicial system (it abolished *kolegia* and "interpretational guidelines" at the level of high courts).

[108] For reasons for this shortage, see Section I.D of this chapter.

[109] Unfortunately, the shortage of judges also led to the unfortunate practice when less than stellar, to put it diplomatically, candidates entered the Czech judiciary. See, for example, Wikileaks, cable 08PRAGUE499, CZECH JUSTICE SYSTEM: INCOMPLETE REFORMS, § 5: "The shortage of judges was gradually addressed by increased hiring, but many of the new entrants, who were rushed into the profession, were poorly prepared for the job"; or the interview with the Czech Minister of Justice from September 9, 2011: "There was a huge shortage of judges in the 1990s and de facto everybody who fulfilled formal criteria could become a judge"("U některých soudců pochybuji, jestli vůbec znají platné právo" (*Hospodářské noviny*, September 9, 2011) 25). For a more detailed discussion on the repercussions of this hasty appointment in the early 1990s, see David Kosař, "Transitional Justice and Judicial Accountability: Lessons from the Czech Republic and Slovakia" (2010) (unpublished manuscript, available at http://ssrn.com/abstract=1689260).

By this judicial reform package,[110] which consisted of the Constitutional Amendment[111] and two brand new laws[112] on courts and judges, Motejl wanted to replace the Ministry of Justice model of court administration with the Judicial Council Euro-model. However, his proposal eventually failed. The Constitutional Bill was rejected in the second reading in the Chamber of Deputies by a strong majority (114 MPs voted for the rejection of the bill, 68 MPs voted for the bill)[113] and the other two laws soon followed its fate. Only members of the Social Democratic Party eventually voted for the Constitutional Bill. All other political parties were against the proposed Constitutional Amendment.

There are various explanations for this failure. The most widely accepted one is that politicians did not consent to the transfer of such broad powers to the judiciary, because they were afraid of judicial corporativism and elitism.[114] Mrs Vlasta Parkanová, a former Minister of Justice (1997–1998) and the rapporteur on all three laws, voiced this criticism most clearly during the parliamentary debate.[115] She also suggested that the Czech judiciary belongs to the Austrian tradition and the Czech Republic should rather adopt a moderate reform built on the Austrian model of "personal senates" and, like many other MPs, raised the lack of democratic accountability of the judiciary.[116]

However, several commentators suggested that these official explanations were not the main reasons for rejecting the reform package. They claim that this proposal was too far-reaching and radical and thus it required a significant amendment of the Czech Constitution,[117] that

---

[110] See the document entitled *Návrh koncepce reformy soudnictví* [The Conception of the Reform of the Judiciary] of June 16, 1999 (no. 1097/99-L), approved by the Czech Government by the decision no. 686 of July 7, 1999. An outline of the reform proposal was published in the law journal *Právní rozhledy*, special supplement to no. 5/1999, 1–8.

[111] See the Constitutional Bill No. 541/0.

[112] These two statutes were Law on Courts (Bill No. 539/0) and Law on Judges and Lay Judges (Bill No. 540/0).

[113] To complete the figures, two MPs abstained and fifteen MPs were absent.

[114] See Michal Bobek, "The Administration of Courts in the Czech Republic – In Search of a Constitutional Balance" (2010) 16 *European Public Law* 251, 269.

[115] See Mrs Vlasta Parkanová's comments in the first reading of the Bill No. 539/0 on June 28, 2000 (27th session of the Chamber of Deputies on June 28, 2000).

[116] See Mrs Vlasta Parkanová's comments in the first reading of the Constitutional Bill No. 541/0 (22nd session of the Chamber of Deputies on March 1, 2000).

[117] The Constitutional Bill, apart from introducing the High Council of the Judiciary, also introduced a maximum age limit for ordinary judges and Constitutional Court Justices, prohibited a renewal of the term of Constitutional Court Justices, changed the status of the Czech National bank, and amended several other provisions of the Czech Constitution.

Motejl was an independent minister without sufficient political support even within the Social Democratic Party which appointed him, that judges themselves were divided and many of them disagreed with the judicial reform package that persuaded politicians that it was not the right time to transfer such wide powers to the judiciary, that many politicians (including the Social Democrats themselves) feared that Motejl had become "too big" and successful and another major accomplishment would elevate him to prominent status, or that his far-reaching reform of the judiciary was submitted prematurely.[118] Motejl also alienated regional court presidents, key players within the Czech judiciary,[119] by dismissing the five of them in 1999.[120] He himself on retrospect blamed this "judicial oligarchy" for the failure of his judicial reform.[121]

Interestingly, the reaction of the European Union was minuscule. The 2000 Regular Report on the Czech Republic's Progress devoted just one sentence to this event which merely described that "... draft constitutional amendments regarding judicial self-administration and the functional structure of the courts ... have been rejected by the Parliament as insufficiently prepared."[122] This indifference of the European Commission regarding the failed reform of the Czech system of court administration has perplexed Czech scholars and judges ever since.[123]

Motejl's proposal is the only serious attempt to change the large-scale structure of the Czech judiciary. Since the failure of Motejl's reform in 2000 no other Minister of Justice has submitted a reform of a similar scale to the Parliament. However, there have been incessant talks among judges about the need for the judicial council model. The Judicial Union has been a particularly active voice in suggesting various reform proposals. The Constitutional Court also repeatedly pleaded for the abandoning of the Ministry of Justice model and the introduction of the judicial council model of court administration.[124] Nevertheless, this pressure has not

---

[118] These explanations are based on informal interviews with former and current politicians and court presidents, but they cannot be corroborated by the hard data.

[119] See Section I.E of this chapter.

[120] See Jana Kolomazníková and Luděk Navara, "Pravým důvodem odvolání soudců je zřejmě jejich minulost", IDnes.cz, March 17, 1999.

[121] Otakar Motejl, "Pohled ministrů spravedlnosti" in Jan Kysela (ed.) *Hledání optimálního modelu správy soudnictví pro Českou republiku* (Kancelář Senátu 2008) 13–16, at 14.

[122] The 2000 Accession Progress Report on the Czech Republic, p. 19.

[123] See above notes 31–34.

[124] See in particular Judgment of the Constitutional Court of the Czech Republic of June 18, 2002, case no. Pl. ÚS 7/02; Judgment of the Constitutional Court of the Czech Republic of July 11, 2006, case no. Pl. ÚS 18/06, § VII; and Judgment of the Constitutional Court of the Czech Republic of October 6, 2010, case no. Pl. ÚS 39/08, §§ 60–61.

materialized into any meaningful proposal that would find support from a substantial part of any major political party. What is worse, over two decades, perhaps in despair, the voices within the judiciary as well as the Judicial Union, and to a certain extent also the Constitutional Court, radicalized, which makes the finding of a solution acceptable to politicians as well as for judges even more difficult.

For these reasons, there has not been any other major critical juncture capable of changing the large-scale structure of the judiciary in the Czech Republic. Judicial reforms adopted between 1993 and 2002 only modified the existing Ministry of Justice model and did not touch upon the large-scale issues. The most far reaching reform took place in 2002, when Minister of Justice Jaroslav Bureš, a successor to Otakar Motejl, prepared the new Law on Courts and Judges,[125] which established the so-called judicial boards (*soudcovské rady*) at each court,[126] introduced compulsory examination of all judges of district courts, regional courts, and high courts, established the Council for Testing Competence of Judges (*Rada pro odborné znalosti soudců*), stipulated the compulsory continuing education of judges, and introduced the compulsory retirement age of seventy years for all judges.[127] Nevertheless, the Constitutional Court struck down most of these innovations. It abolished the compulsory examination of all judges (including its repercussions on promotion and on dismissal from judicial office), the Council for Testing Competence of Judges as well as compulsory continuing education of judges.[128] In other words, the Constitutional Court sealed the status quo and the 2002 Law on Courts and Judges eventually brought few changes to the existing model of court administration. Other reforms brought only small-scale changes that will be discussed in more detail in connection with a relevant mechanism of judicial accountability.

B.   Updating the Ministry of Justice Model (2003–2010)

As mentioned above, the only serious attempt to alter the model of court administration took place in 2000, when the Minister of Justice Otakar Motejl, prepared a proposal for the creation of a High Council of the Judiciary, and it failed. Three years later, the 2002 Law on Courts and

---

125   Law No. 6/2002 Coll., on Courts and Judges.
126   See above, Section I.E of this chapter.
127   For further details, see Section III of this chapter.
128   Judgment of the Constitutional Court of the Czech Republic of June 18, 2002, case no. Pl. ÚS 7/02.

Judges (prepared by Jaroslav Bureš) made more modest innovations, but most of these innovations had a short life-span due to the intervention of the Constitutional Court. The only step toward self-administration of the judiciary was thus the creation of judicial boards (*soudcovské rady*) at all high courts and regional courts and at the district courts with more than ten judges. But judicial boards serve merely as advisory bodies to the court president at each court and play a relatively marginal role.[129] They should not be confused with the nationwide judicial council with broad competences such as the Judicial Council of the Slovak Republic in Slovakia.

The debacle of Motejl's reform in the Parliament and Bureš's reform before the Constitutional Court led to a stalemate. No significant amendment to the 2002 Law on Courts and Judges affecting the model of court administration took place until 2008. The only change in the Czech judicial system was that the Supreme Administrative Court, envisaged already by the 1993 Czech Constitution, finally came into being in January 2003. Since then, the Czech Republic has had two top ordinary courts.

It was only in 2008 that the Parliament decided to calibrate the "Ministry of Justice model" of court administration and passed the amendment to the 2002 Law on Court and Judges which introduced limited terms for all judicial officials.[130] Until 2008, judicial officials (i.e., court presidents and vice presidents) were appointed by the Minister of Justice for an unlimited period. The only exception applied to judicial officials of the two highest courts, the Supreme Court and the Supreme Administrative Court. These four judicial officials were also appointed for an unlimited period, but by the President of the Czech Republic. The 2008 Amendment to the Law on Courts and Judges[131] changed that and introduced a time limit for the mandate of judicial officials.[132] As a result, since 2009 judicial officials of district courts, regional courts, and high courts have been appointed for seven years, whereas the Presidents and Vice Presidents of the Supreme Court and the Supreme Administrative Court are appointed for a term of ten years. During this term judicial officials can be removed only following a decision of a disciplinary panel. Therefore, the 2008 Amendment to

---

[129] Competences of these judicial boards were described above in Section I.E of this chapter.

[130] Another important institutional change contained in the 2008 Amendment to Law on Courts and Judges concerns a paradigmatic shift of the institutional design of disciplinary proceedings concerning judges. This change will be described in more detail in Section IV.B of this chapter.

[131] Law No. 314/2008 Coll., amending Law No. 6/2002 Coll., on Courts and Judges, Lay Judges, and the State Administration of Courts.

[132] For further details, see Bobek 2010, above note 71, at 263–265.

the Law on Courts and Judges in fact did two things. It introduced term limits for judicial officials and at the same time guaranteed them security of tenure.

The introduction of term limits for judicial officials caused an outcry among current judicial officials. This is not surprising since their position was shaken for the first time since the independence of the Czech Republic. Some judicial officials soon realized that they would have to become "regular judges" again at some point down the road. The lament of judicial officials eventually succeeded and a group of senators challenged this part of the 2008 Amendment before the Constitutional Court. However, the Constitutional Court, to the surprise of many judicial officials, not only found that the introduction of limited terms for judicial officials was constitutional, but also struck down the provision that allowed the reappointment of the same judicial officials for successive terms.[133] This means that *all* judicial officials, including presidents and vice presidents of both top ordinary courts, were *required* to leave their post within ten years from the date on which the 2008 Amendment to the Law on Courts and Judges entered into force, which is by October 2018. In particular, the change in the post the President of the Supreme Administrative Court in 2018 is capable of having a major impact on the Czech judiciary.[134]

In sum, the Czech postcommunist model of court administration returned to the precommunist era arrangement and proved to be impermeable until 2010. As one scholar aptly put it, "an almost identical model of state administration of courts to that in place ... in the Czech Republic can be found in the Austrian codification of the law on this matter, in the Law on the Organization of Courts of 1896."[135] The only change that may reshuffle the cards within the Czech judiciary in future was adopted in 2008 and its full consequences will be revealed only in 2018.

III.   Mechanisms of Judicial Accountability from 1993 to 2002

The core of this section identifies mechanisms of judicial accountability that were used in this period, explains what the law[136] said about these

---

[133] Judgment of the Constitutional Court of the Czech Republic of October 6, 2010, case no. Pl. ÚS 39/08.

[134] Note that Iva Brožová, the President of the Supreme Court resigned voluntarily already in January 2015.

[135] Bobek 2010, above note 71, at 252–253.

[136] The term "law" is understood broadly so as to encompass the Constitution, statutes, as well legal norms of lesser force.

mechanisms, and then analyzes how these mechanisms operated in practice. It also addresses selected institutional measures that may influence the use of mechanisms of judicial accountability, namely the recruitment of judges, transparency mechanisms, appeals and quasi-appellate mechanisms, and the training of judges. These measures do not fall within the ambit of my definition of judicial accountability. They operate as "the contingent circumstances or additional requirements that might influence whether a certain form of accountability will bring about a certain set of results."[137]

The inclusion of these contingent circumstances increases the persuasiveness of the pivotal contrast between Slovakia's judicial council based on the Judicial Council Euro-model and the Czech Republic's Ministry of Justice model. If the training and recruitment of judges, the level of transparency, and available appellate mechanisms turn out to be similar in the two countries, this similarity will reinforce the contrast between these two models of court administration and vice versa.

A.   Contingent Circumstances

The following four categories of mechanisms that may influence the functioning of mechanisms of judicial accountability, even though they do not count as such, will be addressed here: (1) the recruitment and selection of judges, (2) transparency mechanisms, (3) appeals and quasi-appellate mechanisms, and (4) the training of judges.

Regarding the *recruitment and selection* of judges, the Czech law is very succinct. The Czech Constitution stipulates that all judges of the ordinary courts are appointed by the President of the Czech Republic.[138] The 1991 Law on Courts and Judges stipulated only basic criteria for judicial office: Czech nationality, full legal capacity, finished legal education, a clean criminal record, a minimum age of twenty-five years, and a very vague requirement that a candidate must have "experience and moral characteristics that ensure that he will exercise his function properly."[139] In addition, every judge had to submit a negative lustration certificate as defined by the Large Lustration Law.[140] No further guidance on criteria for

---

[137] Mark Philp, "Delimiting Democratic Accountability" (2009) 57 *Political Studies* 28, 32.

[138] However, the President's appointment decree must be contrasigned by the Prime Minister (see Art. 63(1)(i) in conjunction with Art. 63(3) of the Constitutional Law No. 1/1993 Coll., the Constitution of the Czech Republic).

[139] Art. 34(1)–(2) of Law No. 335/1991 Coll., on Courts and Judges.

[140] For further information on the applicability of the Large Lustration Law to judges, see Section I.C.

the recruitment and appointment of judges was provided by the legislation of that era.

This de jure recruitment standard begs the question, did the head of the Czech Republic personally select and handle appointments of dozens or hundreds of judges every year?[141] The answer is "of course not." In practice, the responsibility for the recruitment of new judges rested on the shoulders of the "usual suspects" of the Czech judicial system – the Ministry of Justice and court presidents. There were two tracks to the judiciary – the "career" track and the "lateral" track. The "career" track was the rule and the "lateral track" rather an exception, but it is important to address both of them.

The "career" track was open primarily to law school graduates. According to the internal instruction of the Ministry of Justice,[142] the selection of these young candidates was vested in with the presidents of regional courts. Once selected, they became so-called "judicial candidates" (*justiční čekatelé*) and their status as well as training was governed by the 1991 Law on Courts and Judges.[143] Judicial candidates spent three years as "apprentices" at various levels of the judicial system, and at the end of this three-year period they were required to pass a comprehensive "judicial exam" (*justiční zkouška*). Due to the shortage of judges in the early 1990s, judicial candidates who succeeded in the judicial exam had a very high chance of being appointed judges. As to their placement, judicial candidates who passed the judicial exam were assigned predominantly to the lower courts (district courts and regional courts).

The "lateral" track to the judiciary was even more opaque. The 1991 Law on Courts and Judges did not preclude the appointment of lawyers who had not gone through judicial apprenticeship. Unfortunately, apart from the general rules described above,[144] the 1991 Law did not stipulate any

---

[141] Václav Havel appointed 170 judges in 1993, 194 judges in 1994, 142 judges in 1995, 94 judges in 1996, 96 judges in 1997, 131 judges in 1998, 110 judges in 1999, 137 judges in 2000, 134 judges in 2001, and 129 judges in 2002. These new judges in part replaced the judges who left the judiciary after the Velvet Revolution and in part filled the newly created vacancies.

[142] Internal instruction of the Ministry of Justice No. 125/92-Inst. Note that such important issues as who selects "judicial candidates" (i.e., future judges) were not stipulated in the Constitution or the statute, but in the ministerial instruction, which could be changed on a whim.

[143] Again, note that the most important issue – who selects judicial candidates – was governed by the ministerial instruction, whereas the bureaucratic issues such as the length of their training and details of the judicial exam were regulated by the statute.

[144] See note 138.

rules governing such entry into the judiciary. The only rule was that there were no rules. These "lateral candidates" for judicial office were formally recommended to the President of the Czech Republic by the Minister of Justice, but it is unclear who actually handpicked these candidates. Regarding their placement, it was for the Minister of Justice to assign "lateral judges" to any court, subject to one important caveat. The president of the Supreme Court and presidents of high courts had to consent to the assignment of any judge to "their" respective courts. Put differently, the Minister of Justice had an unfettered discretion to assign judges to district courts and regional courts, whereas if he or she wanted to assign a judge to one of the two high courts or to the Supreme Court, the presidents of those courts could veto such assignment.

In sum, the Czech Constitution vested the power to select judges only in the President of the Czech Republic, but in practice there were four players with a de facto veto power: (1) court presidents; (2) the Minister of Justice, (3) the Government, and (4) the President of the Czech Republic. In fact, court presidents and the Minister of Justice played a far more important role in the recruitment of judges on the ground than the President of the Czech Republic and the Government. Interestingly, the abovementioned opaque model of selecting judges worked relatively well until the late 1990s due to a mix of the following factors: a shortage of judges, relatively low salaries for judges,[145] poor material support of judges, large caseloads awaiting the new judges,[146] and a relatively small number of candidates for judicial office. However, this model started collapsing once judges' salaries and material support improved and once private practice ceased to be a bonanza for every law school graduate. Due to these factors, the pool of lawyers interested in judicial office increased dramatically.

The increased demand for judicial office began creating pressure on the existing model of appointment of Czech judges. Neither the Ministry of Justice nor the court presidents were able to come up with any meaningful reform. Eventually, they adopted a very "original" solution. In 1999 they delegated the task of sifting through potential candidates to psychologists. According to the new model, every candidate had to undergo comprehensive psychological testing. The instruction of the Ministry of Justice stipulated that the results of the psychological tests were only advisory,

---

[145] Salaries of judges could not compete with the profits of private lawyers at that time. Note that there was a severe shortage of advocates in the early 1990s and thus they could charge high fees even for routine services.

[146] This huge case load resulted from two factors: (1) the shortage of judges; and (2) the new entrepreneurial environment that led to increased litigation before the courts.

but in practice they soon degenerated into a compulsory requirement for judicial candidates and became a very important factor in evaluating "lateral" candidates. What is worse, psychological testing was carried out in such a way that almost 70% of candidates[147] did not pass it.[148] As a result, since 1999 we have been able to speak of five players with a de facto veto power: (1) psychologists; (2) court presidents; (3) the Minister of Justice, (4) the Government, and (5) the President of the Czech Republic. As in the pre-1999 era, the President of the Czech Republic and the Government were the marginal actors.

Apart from the recruitment of judges, I concluded in Chapter 2 that several mechanisms (such as case assignment, judicial salaries, reassignment within the same court, and promotion) can be designed to avoid accounting if the relevant criteria are stipulated in advance and are not subject to ex post change. In the Czech Republic, none of case assignment, reassignment within the same court or promotion is based purely on ex ante criteria. Therefore, these three mechanisms may be used to hold individual judges to account. Judicial salaries are an exception. The salary of each judge in the Czech Republic is determined by statute as a fixed sum[149] with no fluctuating part. Discretionary bonuses or extra payments are prohibited and the only body that can reduce the salary of an individual judge is the disciplinary court. As a result, leaving aside disciplinary motions which are discussed separately, the way in which the Czech law determines judicial salaries does not allow any actor to use that mechanism against individual judges.[150]

---

[147] This is the most common estimate mentioned in the literature. There are no objective and comprehensive data about the success rates in the psychological testing of candidates for judicial office. For a partial view (presented by a person who tested judicial candidates), see Jiří Dan, "Psychologická vyšetření uchazečů o přijetí na pozice právních čekatelů a státních zástupců v letech 1998–2010" No. 10/2011 Státní zastupitelství 11–18.

[148] No one has suggested that the psychological testing was politically motivated or rigged so as to leave in the contest only the candidates "preselected" by someone else. However flawed the testing was, it served as a "neutral" filter. Nevertheless, there might have been an implicit political assignment of a different kind – to design the psychological testing in such a way that only a few candidates (irrespective of which) passed it. I refer to the latter phenomenon as "outsourcing of responsibility."

[149] The Czech formula for determining judicial salaries is a complex one. The salary of an individual judge depends in particular on the level of the court he is assigned and a number of years he has been practicing law. However, several additional criteria (e.g., chamber presidents and judicial officials earn more than regular judges) and exceptions (judges of both top ordinary courts earn the same salary irrespective of the length of their experience) apply.

[150] But note that the Czech Parliament attempted to reduce judicial salaries *across-the-board* several times.

Regarding *transparency mechanisms*, the Czech Republic did not fare well between 1993 and 2002. It was already mentioned earlier that the recruitment of judges was opaque. There was no requirement to inform the public about vacancies within the judiciary. Neither the lists of candidates for judicial office nor the interviews with these candidates were published. Promotion of judges was even less transparent and the decision was usually reached between the relevant court presidents and the Minister of Justice in private. No vacancies were advertised and no open selection procedures took the place.

As regards other potentially available transparency mechanisms, the situation can be summarized as follows. The requirement of compulsory annual disclosure of property and annual earnings did not apply to judges. Judicial statistics were compiled in an ad hoc manner by the Ministry of Justice or court presidents, but the results were rarely published and, if they were, these statistics never focused on individual judges. Judicial proceedings were public, but presiding judges often prohibited the recording of these proceedings.[151]

Finally, access to judicial decisions was extremely difficult to obtain. The Supreme Court published only a small proportion of its decisions in the official Collection of Judgments and Opinions of the Supreme Court. Decisions of lower courts (district courts, regional, courts and high courts) were virtually inaccessible, with a few exceptions selected for publication in the Supreme Court's official Collection or in law reviews. The mental transition of Czech judges regarding the publication of all judgments of all courts was very slow. The communist culture of centralized official collections of judgments that contained only the "correct" decisions selected by the Supreme Court judges (not surprisingly, a majority of the published decisions were those issued by the Supreme Court) still prevailed.[152] This situation improved only in 2000, when the Supreme Court finally started to publish its decisions online. Unfortunately, the lower courts did not follow and access to their decisions remained severely limited for the entire period.

---

[151] The 2002 Law on Courts and Judges explicitly allowed this practice; see Art. 8(3) of Law No. 6/2002 Coll., on Courts and Judges. Some court presidents went even further. For instance, in 2008 one district court president issued an order prohibiting the use of cell phones and recording devices in the entire court building. She eventually resigned from the position of court president (due to public pressure as well as in order to "preempt" disciplinary sanction), but this example illustrates how far court presidents were willing to go in order to prevent any "disruption" from the public.

[152] Zdeněk Kühn and Hynek Baňouch, "O publikaci a citaci judikatury aneb proč je někdy judikatura jako císařovy nové šaty" (2005) 13 *Právní rozhledy* 484–491.

The availability of *appeals and quasi-appellate mechanisms* can be summarized as follows. As far as appeals were concerned, access to appellate courts as well as to the Supreme Court was very generous. Similarly to most civil law courts, Czech courts cannot control their docket. In other words, there is no leave to appeal or writ of certiorari mechanism that would grant the appellate courts the power to select the cases it wants to hear.

As to quasi-appellate mechanisms, "extraordinary appeals" (*stížnost pro porušení zákona*) in civil law matters were abolished in 1991. They were retained in criminal law matters, but the use of "extraordinary appeals" was severely limited by the Code of Criminal Procedure so as to avoid the abuse of that mechanism. Since 1995 only the Minister of Justice has been able to lodge an "extraordinary appeal"[153] and such "extraordinary appeal" cannot, except in extreme cases, challenge the court's decision regarding the sentence imposed.[154] Due to this development, "extraordinary appeals" have played only a marginal role in the postsplit Czech Republic. On the other hand, the Supreme Court[155] could still issue so-called interpretative guidelines in order to unify divergent case law. Neither the equivalent of *en banc* proceedings nor referral to the grand chamber of the Supreme Court "à la Strasbourg"[156] exists in the Czech Republic.

Finally, the *training* of judges was extremely eclectic in the 1990s. The Ministry of Justice, with the help of regional court presidents, organized thorough training only for judicial candidates. Once judicial candidates, or members of other legal professions, were appointed to the bench, no systematic training was provided. The Judicial Academy did not exist at that time,[157] and thus it was for the Ministry of Justice and the Supreme Court to develop courses for sitting judges. This system did not work well. Courses were organized on an ad hoc basis and did not reflect the needs of most judges. In addition to training provided by Czech organs, the European Commission and various international organizations provided their own training session to Czech judges. This training organized by foreign bodies also suffered from many drawbacks. It focused only on a few areas of the law, was insufficiently tied to the Czech legal context, and, if

---

[153] Until 1995, both the General Prosecutor and Minister of Justice were vested with this power.

[154] See Art. 266(2) and (4) of Law No. 141/1961 Coll., Code of Criminal Procedure.

[155] Until 1995, high courts could also issue their own "interpretative guidelines." However, this power was rather a residuum of hasty transformation of the republican Supreme Court into the High Court of Prague in 1993.

[156] For further details on these two procedures, see Chapter 2.

[157] It was established only in 2002.

the foreign lecturers did not speak Czech, the transmission of knowledge was impaired by the language barrier. Off the record, Czech judges also suggest that these sessions led by foreign experts were often primitive and assumed that Czech judges just "climbed down from trees." Hence, foreign training had only a limited impact on the Czech judiciary.[158]

B.   Which Mechanisms of Judicial Accountability Were Used?

In Chapter 2 I identified three categories of mechanisms of judicial accountability: "sticks," "carrots," and dual mechanisms, which can operate both as "sticks" and "carrots." The Czech Republic did not apply all of these mechanisms between 1993 and 2002. The impeachment of judges as well as regular retention reviews were abolished immediately after the fall of the communist regime[159] and no one in the Czech Republic dared to reintroduce these measures. The involuntary relocation and demotion of judges were also prohibited.[160] Mechanisms of complaint against individual judges did not exist. There was no special ground for the criminal liability of judges and civil liability was so severely limited[161] that it could not be used as a separate mechanism of judicial accountability.[162] Hence, only two "sticks" were available: disciplinary motions and reassignment within the same court.

Most dual mechanisms did not exist either. There was neither the new-public-management nor the Soviet-style system of judicial performance evaluation.[163] Salaries of judges were fixed in advance.[164] Similarly, no formal discretionary nonmonetary benefits were available. All Czech judges receive a special benefit for purchasing professional literature and representative clothes, but its amount is fixed by a statute.[165] There was no

---

[158]   The impact of training is often exaggerated; see Piana 2010, above note 37.

[159]   These two mechanisms were perceived as the major weapons of the Communist Party vis-à-vis "recalcitrant" judges.

[160]   Note that *temporary* relocation of judges was allowed until December 31, 1993.

[161]   Art. 57 of Law No. 335/1991 Coll., on Courts and Judges set out the state liability regime. That means that the State was responsible for miscarriages of justice and the State had to pay the damages.

[162]   The State could recover the paid damages from the judge *only* if a judge was found guilty in a disciplinary or criminal trial. See Art 17(2) of Law No. 82/1998 Coll.

[163]   More specifically, the Soviet-style system was abandoned, but the new-public-management system was not introduced for the lack of consensus on its criteria. For the difference between these two systems, see Chapter 2, Section II.C.

[164]   Arts 28–31 of Law No. 236/1995 Coll. on the Salary and Other Indemnities Associated with the Execution of the Office of Representatives of State Power and Some State Bodies and Judges

[165]   It amounts to 5.5% of the salary of a given judge. See Art. 32(1) of Law No. 236/1995 Coll.

right of all judges to subsidized housing. Each court usually had few flats reserved for its judges, but these served primarily for temporary housing of new judges. Moreover, due to the constitutional protection against involuntary relocation, gradual deregulation of rents in state-owned housing and growing salaries of judges meant that judges preferred to buy their own housing anyways. Similarly, no special vacation packages for judges or preferential access to the day care for judges' kids were available. The presidents and vice presidents of the Supreme Court and the Supreme Administrative Court receive somewhat broader set of nonmonetary benefits, including subsidized housing and a car with a driver, but all of these perks are determined by the statute which leaves no room for discretion.[166] Altering working conditions of a judge at the court building was thus the only nonmonetary benefit that could have been used to please or cause hassle to judges. However the use of this mechanism cannot be traced back and corroborated with evidence and thus it will not be measured here.[167] Therefore, the only dual mechanism in place was case assignment.[168]

In contrast to the lack of "sticks" and minimal use of dual mechanisms, a plethora of "carrots" awaited judges. These carrots included promotion to a higher court, promotion to the position of chamber president, appointment to the grand chamber, secondment, temporary assignment outside the judiciary, and the appointment of a judge to the position of court president or vice president. Some of these carrots were accompanied only by a rise in prestige, whereas others brought also monetary (salary increase) or leisure (reduced case load) benefits. The former include, for instance, appointment to the grand chambers. Typical examples of the latter are promotion to a higher court or becoming a judicial official.

It is not my intention to categorize these carrots according to the value of the perks that accompanied each of them, but it is worth briefly mentioning what perks were attached to each mechanism. Two carrots, promotion to a higher court and appointment to the position of court president or vice president, included all three aforementioned perks – a significant salary increase, reduced case load, and higher prestige. In contrast, chamber presidents did not benefit from a reduced case load and the increase in prestige was negligible. On the other hand, the salary increase was still notable. Two more quasi-promotions within the judicial ranks

---

[166] See Arts. 32(2) and 33 of Law No. 236/1995 Coll.
[167] For further explanation, see Chapter 4, Section V.
[168] Even though the Czech Charter of Fundamental Rights entrenched the right to a legal judge, the Parliament adopted basic rules on case assignment only in 2000 and even the new system of case assignment failed to introduce truly random case assignment.

could be used to hold judges to account – secondment to a higher court and appointment to the grand chamber. The former was accompanied by a salary increase, but was by its nature only temporary.[169] The latter was merely a matter of prestige as it did not come with any monetary benefit and resulted in higher case load. In addition to promotions within the judiciary, there was one additional carrot – temporary assignment outside the judiciary. Such assignments yielded particularly promising results for judges in the 1990s.[170]

In sum, nine mechanisms of judicial accountability were employed in the Czech Republic between 1993 and 2002: disciplinary motions, reassignment within the same court, case assignment, promotion to a higher court, promotion to the position of chamber president,[171] appointment to the grand chamber of the Supreme Court, secondment, temporary assignment outside the judiciary, and the appointment of a judge to the position of court president or vice president. To see the difference throughout the years of 1993–2002, I include a concise table (Table 5.1).

C.   Mechanisms of Judicial Accountability on the Books

This section addresses what the law said about mechanisms of judicial accountability that were used between 1993 and 2002 and what legal standards it laid down. I start with "sticks" and then I proceed to "carrots" and "dual mechanisms."

The most obvious stick in this period was *disciplinary motions*. Before the dissolution of Czechoslovakia the disciplining of judges was governed by a separate statute.[172] After the split the Czech Republic decided to retain the same statute, with minor amendments, and it used it until the 2002 judicial reform. In order to understand the disciplining of judges, four issues must be addressed: who could initiate a disciplinary motion, who ruled on that motion, actions for which judges were disciplined, and the available sanctions.

Regarding the first issue, the Ministry of Justice supervised all the ordinary courts and court presidents looked after their own courts as well

---

[169] In addition to a temporary salary increase, secondment also increased the chances of a given judge being promoted indefinitely.

[170] See Section I.E of this chapter.

[171] "Promotion" to the position of "kolegium chairman" (at the Supreme Court) worked on a similar principle. However, there were only three such positions within the judiciary and thus I do not consider it a separate mechanism of a judicial accountability.

[172] Law No. 412/1991 Sb., on Disciplinary Liability of Judges.

Table 5.1. *Mechanisms of judicial accountability available in the Czech Republic between 1993 and 2002*

Mechanisms of judicial accountability available in the Czech Republic between 1993 and 2002	
1993–2000	2001–2002
Sticks	
Disciplinary proceedings	Disciplinary proceedings
Reassignment	Reassignment
Carrots	
Promotion to a higher court	Promotion to a higher court
Chamber president appointment	Chamber president appointment
Secondment	Secondment
Temporary assignment outside the judiciary	Temporary assignment outside the judiciary
Appointment of a judge to the position of court president or vice president	Appointment of a judge to the position of court president or vice president
–	*Grand chamber appointment*
Dual mechanisms	
Case assignment	Case assignment

as lower courts. This means that only the Minister of Justice and court presidents could trigger disciplinary motions.[173] The system of disciplining judges was strictly hierarchical. The Minister of Justice could initiate a disciplinary motion against any judge; the president of a high court could initiate a disciplinary motion against any judge of his court as well as against judges of regional courts that fell under the high court's jurisdiction; the president of a regional court could initiate a disciplinary motion against any judge of his court and judges of districts courts that fell under the jurisdiction of his regional court; and, finally, the president of a district court could initiate a disciplinary motion against any judge of his court. The only exception to this rule applied to the president of the Supreme Court who could initiate a disciplinary motion only against judges of the Supreme Court and thus he was not involved in overseeing lower courts.

[173] Here I bypass specific rules applicable to administrative offences committed by judges. In such cases, the administrative organs (e.g., the Police or the municipality) could act as disciplinary prosecutors.

However, neither the Minister of Justice nor court presidents could discipline judges. The court president and the minister were entitled only to supervise judges, detect errors and initiate disciplinary motions. Judges could be censured or removed only following the decision of a disciplinary panel, which between 1993 and 2002 consisted exclusively of professional judges.[174] Before the disciplinary panel it was either the Minister of Justice or the president of the court who acted as disciplinary prosecutor. Disciplinary panels were assembled pursuant to a hierarchical pattern: disciplinary panels at regional courts decided on motions against judges of district courts; disciplinary panels at high courts decided on motions against judges of regional courts as well as against judges of the relevant high court; and disciplinary panels at the Supreme Court decided on motions against judges of the Supreme Court. For judges of the Supreme Court, there was only a single-instance procedure before the disciplinary panel of the Supreme Court, whereas judges of regional and high courts could appeal the decision of the first instance disciplinary court to a higher disciplinary court. The precise composition of the disciplinary panels was defined in the so-called work schedule (*rozvrh práce*), an internal document of the court which determines the composition of chambers, including disciplinary chambers, as well as criteria according to which cases are assigned to single judges and chambers within the relevant court.[175] The work schedules were issued by court presidents who thus, in fact, determined also the composition of the disciplinary panels.

As regards the nature of actions for which judges could be disciplined, the 1991 Disciplinary Code was very succinct. It defined a disciplinary misdemeanor as an "intentional violation of ... judicial duties or behavior that infringes upon dignity of [the judicial] office or threatens public confidence in independent, impartial and just decision-making of courts."[176] If the importance of the duty violated, type of conduct, the judge's degree of culpability, repetitiveness of the conduct, or other aggravating factors occurred, it increased the harmfulness of the judge's conduct and the offense was considered a serious disciplinary misdemeanor.[177] Disciplinary sanctions followed this disciplinary misdemeanor/serious disciplinary

---

[174] It is worth mentioning that court presidents, who acted as disciplinary prosecutors, could not sit on the disciplinary panels.

[175] For further details on how "work schedules" operated in this period, see notes 198–200 and 220.

[176] Art. 2(1) of the 1991 Disciplinary Code.

[177] Art. 2(2) of the 1991 Disciplinary Code.

misdemeanor dichotomy. For disciplinary misdemeanors, disciplinary panels had to choose between the following two types of sanction:[178] a reprimand and several categories of salary reduction.[179] Serious disciplinary misdemeanors[180] led to harsher sanctions: dismissal from the position of chamber president, longer salary reduction,[181] relocation to another court of the same level, demotion to a lower court, or dismissal from judicial office. No further criteria for sanctioning were defined by the law. As a result, disciplinary panels had broad discretion in imposing sanctions and rules for disciplining judges became judge-made law.

In contrast to the relatively detailed rules governing the disciplining of judges, neither the Czech Constitution nor other laws defined standards for *reassignment* within the same court. The 1991 Law on Courts and Judges laid down that the Minister of Justice would decide on the assignment of each judge to a particular court, but this law did not mention to which division (in case of single judges) or chamber of a given court a newly appointed judge would be assigned. No rules on reassignment were mentioned either. Judges were assigned and reassigned within each court pursuant to the so-called work schedule (*rozvrh práce*), an internal document of the court issued by the court president.[182] Czech law thus vested the power to reassign judges (and, indirectly, also to decide on their specialization) in court presidents. However, it was silent on two key aspects of reassignment: the reasons for which judges could face reassignment and the criteria for reassignment. This lack of legal standards was particularly troubling, because Czech judges are not generalists. On the contrary, single judges at lower courts as well as panels of judges at higher courts decide only cases in certain areas of the law designated to them. As a result,

---

[178] Art. 3(1) of the 1991 Disciplinary Code.

[179] Until July 1997, only two types of salary reduction were available: salary deduction of up to 15% for up to three months (in the case of a repetitive misdemeanor carried out for up to six months) or assignment to a lower salary bracket for up to three years. From August 1997, four types of salary reductions could be imposed: (1) removal of salary increase belonging to chamber presidents, (2) salary deduction of up to 25% for up to six months (in the case of a repetitive misdemeanor carried out for up to one year); (3) suspension of salary increase (which was based on the number of years of legal practice) for up to three years, and (4) reduction of years of legal practice (used for calculation of judges' salaries) of up to three years for a period of up to three years.

[180] Art. 3(3) of the 1991 Disciplinary Code.

[181] This sanction, which entitled disciplinary panels to impose significant salary reductions for up to three years, was introduced only in 1997. Note also that this sanction did not apply to judges of the Supreme Court.

[182] For further details on how "work schedules" operated in this period, see notes 198–200 and 220.

reassignment outside their area of specialization may have serious consequences for Czech judges.

Promotion to a higher court is a particularly important carrot in civil
law judiciaries, because judges enter the judiciary at a relatively young age
and then try to climb the ladder as high and as fast as possible.[183] Given
the importance of this mechanism, Czech law said surprisingly little on
this issue. The Czech Constitution did not address this issue at all and the
1991 Law on Courts and Judges only briefly mentioned that assignment
to a particular court is to be decided upon by the Minister of Justice.[184]
Regarding promotion to regional courts, no further rules were laid down
and, thus, the Minister of Justice was not de jure constrained by any other
actor. Promotion to the Supreme Court was an exception. The 1991 Law on
Courts and Judges set an important limit on the discretion of the Minister
of Justice – promotion to the Supreme Court could proceed only with
the consent of the president of the Supreme Court. The same rule applied
to promotion to high courts until 1995,[185] but since 1996 the Minister of
Justice has not needed the consent of high court presidents and has been
able, according to de jure standard, to act unilaterally.

Another important carrot was *appointment to the position of court president or vice president*. The Czech Constitution was silent regarding judicial officials of district courts, regional courts, and the high courts. This
issue was regulated by the 1991 Law on Courts and Judges which gave
this power to the Minister of Justice.[186] The de jure standard of appointment of judicial officials of the Supreme Court is more difficult to discern.
According to the Czech Constitution, the President of the Czech Republic
"shall appoint from among judges the President and Vice Presidents of the
Supreme Court."[187] This quotation suggests two things. First, the President
of the Czech Republic may elevate any judge (from any level of the judicial system) to the position of President or Vice President of the Supreme
Court. Second, the plural "Vice *Presidents*" implies that there can be more
than one vice president of the Supreme Court.

However, the Constitutional Court did not accept this textual interpretation and adopted a different position vis-à-vis both issues. Regarding the

---

[183] See Chapter 3 for a more detailed discussion of this phenomenon.
[184] Art. 40(1) of Law No. 335/1991 Coll., on Courts and Judges.
[185] Note that this power of presidents of the high courts was not a product of conscious institutional design, but rather an anomaly that resulted from the hasty transformation of the
republican Supreme Court (from the "federal era") into the High Court of Prague in 1993.
For further details of this transformation, see Section I.A.
[186] Art. 39(3) of Law No. 335/1991 Coll., on Courts and Judges.
[187] Art. 62(1)(f) of the Constitutional Law No. 1/1993 Coll., the Constitution of the Czech
Republic.

first issue, the Constitutional Court held that the President of the Czech Republic may appoint the president and vice presidents of the Supreme Court only from among the judges of the Supreme Court.[188] It is important to recall here that a sitting president of the Supreme Court must consent to the appointment of any judge to the Supreme Court, which means that the president of the Supreme Court may block the appointment of any person outside the pool of judges of the Supreme Court to the position of vice president of the Supreme Court. Regarding the second issue, the Constitutional Court opined that as long as the statutory law does not specify precisely how many vice presidents can be appointed to the Supreme Court it is not possible to appoint more than one vice president. The Constitutional Court thus set its seal on the status quo.[189]

In contrast to the appointment of judicial officials, the 1991 Law on Courts and Judges was clear regarding *promotion to the position of chamber president* within the same court.[190] This power belonged to the president of a given court.[191] The only exception applied to chamber presidents at district courts who were appointed by presidents of regional courts and not by presidents of district courts. For instance, the President of the Supreme Court[192] decided on promotion of the Supreme Court judges to the position of chamber president. Interestingly, the 1991 Law on Courts and Judges did not set any criteria for promotion.

Regarding *promotion to grand chambers*,[193] the 2000 Amendment[194] to the 1991 Law on Courts and Judges, which introduced grand chambers,

---

[188] Judgment of the Constitutional Court of the Czech Republic of September 12, 2007, case no. Pl. ÚS 87/06.

[189] Judgment of the Constitutional Court of the Czech Republic of October 6, 2010, case no. Pl. ÚS 39/08, § 57–61.

[190] For the sake of simplicity, I treat promotion to the position of kolegium chairman and promotion to the position of chamber president as one mechanism. The kolegium is a larger body that consists of all judges who deal with a particular area of law (such as civil law and criminal law). The rise in salary as well as in prestige that accompanied appointment to the position of kolegium chairman is by nature slightly higher than in the case of appointment to the position of chamber president, but the essence of this promotion is the same.

[191] Art. 39(2) and Art. 39(4) of Law No. 335/1991 Coll., on Courts and Judges.

[192] Until 1995, *kolegia* operated also at high courts. However, this power was rather a remnant of the hasty transformation of the republican Supreme Court into the High Court of Prague in 1993.

[193] The 2000 Amendment to the 1991 Law on Courts and Judges stipulated that the grand chamber would be established for each *kolegium* of the Supreme Court. In 2000, there were three *kolegia*: the criminal law kolegium, the civil law kolegium and the commercial law kolegium. On January 1, 2007, the civil law kolegium and the commercial law kolegium were merged into a single "kolegium for civil and commercial law."

[194] This means that grand chambers did not exist until 2000 and thus this mechanism of judicial accountability was not available between 1993 and 2000.

provided no guidance on who appoints judges to the grand chambers, by what standards, and for how long. Put differently, there was no legal standard at all.

The de jure standard for the remaining two carrots, secondment of judges and temporary assignment of judges outside the judiciary, is straightforward. The power to *second* a judge (to a higher court) was vested with the Minister of Justice and court presidents. The Minister of Justice decided on secondment to the high courts, whereas presidents of regional courts decided on secondment to "their" regional courts.[195] Finally, secondment to the Supreme Court required the consent of both the Minister of Justice and the President of the Supreme Court.[196] No criteria for secondment were laid down by law.

In contrast to secondment, *temporary assignment outside the judiciary* was fully in the hands of the Minister of Justice.[197] Only the number of available places changed over time. Until 1995, judges could be assigned to various functions outside the judiciary, including the Ministry of Justice, the Office of the Government of the Czech Republic, the Office of the Parliament,[198] and the Constitutional Court. All of the aforementioned positions were prestigious, but assignment to the Ministry of Justice was particularly valuable as the Minister of Justice decided on promotion of judges. After 1996, the rules on temporary assignment were tightened and the only place outside the judiciary that remained on the list was the Ministry of Justice. As with secondment, no further criteria for temporary assignment outside the judiciary were laid down by law.

The last available mechanism was *case assignment*. In Chapter 2 I showed that nonrandom case assignment can be used as an accountability mechanism since the relevant principals may assign cases so as to punish or reward judges. In the Czech Republic, the de jure standard of case assignment is closely tied to the concept of a legal judge.[199] Article 38(1) of the Czech Charter of Fundamental Rights provides that "[n]o one may be removed from the jurisdiction of his legal judge" and "[t]he jurisdiction of courts and the competence of judges shall be provided for by law." This emphasis on the right to a legal judge is not surprising given the long

---

[195]   See Art. 42(1) of Law No. 335/1991 Coll., on Courts and Judges.
[196]   Art. 42(2) of Law No. 335/1991 Coll., on Courts and Judges.
[197]   Art. 42(1)(a) of Law No. 335/1991 Coll., on Courts and Judges.
[198]   Note that the Czech parliamentary system is bicameral, but the Senate (the upper chamber) was not established until 1996.
[199]   On the concept of a legal judge, see Chapter 3.

experience of abuse of case assignment during the communist era.[200] But entrenching this right in the norm of a constitutional rank does not in itself solve the problem. When it comes to case assignment, the proverbial devil lies in the details. The main issue is how an abstract ideal of a "legal judge" translates into more specific rules that prevent, or at least minimize, the opportunity for the misuse of this mechanism by court presidents.

The Czech Parliament did not lay down such rules in the early 1990s and court presidents could still use case assignment as a "stick" or as a "carrot." Until 2000, neither the 1991 Law on Courts and Judges nor any other law specified the criteria for and the method of case assignment. The method of case assignment within each court was based on the so-called work schedule (*rozvrh práce*) issued by its court president. The work schedule is an internal document of the court, which determines the composition of chambers as well as criteria according to which cases are assigned to single judges and chambers within the relevant court.

The 2000 Amendment to the 1991 Law on Courts and Judges introduced basic rules regarding the work schedule that had repercussions, among other things, on case assignment. By granting the power to define the rules for case assignment to court presidents and leaving great room for their discretion it turned the de facto standard into law. More specifically, the new Article 4a of that Law stipulated that court presidents had to issue the work schedule for each calendar year, that every person had the right to see the work schedule upon request and that the work schedule had to include specific rules for substitution[201] of the originally designated decision-making formation (a chamber or a single judge). This was significant progress.

Nevertheless, the 2000 Amendment still did not say anything about which rules the work schedule had to follow and about the actual method of case assignment (whether it had to be based on software developed according to the actual work schedule or whether the human factor was allowed).

---

[200] The court presidents used several techniques in order to achieve the desired result in sensitive cases during the communist era. For instance, they assigned sensitive cases to themselves or to panels over which they presided, or to specific panels composed of "reliable" judges. After the fall of communism, new rationales for rigging case assignment emerged (court presidents could use case assignment as a "carrot" by assigning interesting and novel cases to "favored" judges or as a "stick" by assigning mundane and repetitive cases to "recalcitrant" judges), but the techniques remained the same.

[201] By substitution I mean the situation where one of the judges on the original decision-making formation can no longer decide on a particular case (e.g., due to his long-term illness or because of his recusal).

The key failure, from the "concept of a rightful judge" point of view, was that it did not require case assignment to be random. Furthermore, Article 4a explicitly granted the court presidents the power to change the work schedule during the relevant calendar year, if that was deemed "necessary." Therefore, court presidents could continue to use initial case assignment as well as subsequent reassignment as a "stick" or as a "carrot" even after the 2000 Amendment.

D. Mechanisms of Judicial Accountability in Action

The previous section described what the law on the books said about mechanisms of judicial accountability available between 1993 and 2002. This section will analyze how these mechanisms operated in practice.

Between 1993 and 2002, 253 *disciplinary motions* were initiated against judges. According to de jure standards, apart from specific rules applicable to administrative offences committed by judges,[202] only two actors could initiate disciplinary motions – the Minister of Justice and court presidents. These two actors shared the responsibility for supervising judges, detecting their errors and, ultimately, initiating disciplinary motions. However, in practice court presidents dominated the domain of disciplining judges and thus held the most important "stick" firmly in their hands. Court presidents initiated 215 out of 253 disciplinary motions (85%). More specifically, 181 disciplinary motions (72%) were initiated by the presidents of the very same court in which the judge being disciplinarily prosecuted worked; 34 motions (13%) were lodged by the presidents of the superior courts; whereas only 26 disciplinary proceedings (10%) were initiated by the Minister of Justice and 12 (5%) by other actors.[203] These numbers prove the old proverb "near is my shirt, but nearer is my skin."

However, statistics regarding the number of disciplinary motions and their initiators provide only a limited insight into how disciplinary proceedings operate. It is important also to address the following questions: for what were judges disciplinarily prosecuted, what was the success rate of disciplinary motions, and what sanctions did disciplinary panels impose? Regarding the typology of misconducts, the most common

---

[202] If a judge committed an administrative offence (such as speeding or bad parking), he could choose whether he wanted to have his case tried by the administrative authority or by the disciplinary panel.

[203] The "other actors" include the Police and other administrative organs that could trigger disciplinary motions against judges only if judges committed an administrative offense.

reason for initiating disciplinary motions was delays in delivering justice[204] (62%), followed by administrative offences (13%) and alcohol-related issues (9%). In contrast, disciplinary motions for violating judicial independence, judicial impartiality, or judicial ethics were relatively rare (7%).

The overall success rate of disciplinary motions was relatively high. Disciplinary panels issued a disciplinary sanction in 143 cases (57%) and, in addition, in 32 cases (13%) the disciplinarily prosecuted judges voluntarily resigned from judicial office. This means that disciplinary prosecutors employed this stick successfully in 70% of the motions. In contrast, in only 40 cases (16%) did disciplinary panels acquit the judges completely. The number of cases in which disciplinary panels found judges guilty, but refrained from imposing a sentence was marginal. There were only 6 cases of absolute discharge, which amounts to 2% of the disciplinary motions. Hence, we may say that judges escaped a sanction in 46 cases (18%). In the remaining 32 cases (13%), the proceedings ended without a decision on the merits. Out of the 143 imposed sanctions, the most common sanction was a salary reduction (58 cases, 41%), followed by reprimand (53 cases, 37%), fine (14 cases, 10%), and dismissal from judicial office (12 cases, 8%). The other available sanctions such as dismissal from the position of chamber president, relocation and demotion were used only sparingly or not at all.

These are the overall numbers. However, it is worth considering the success rates of court presidents on the one hand, and the Minister of Justice on the other. According to my data, disciplinary panels issued a sanction in 62% of the motions initiated by court presidents, whereas the Minister of Justice was successful in only 15% of his motions. In addition to those motions that led to disciplinary sanctions, we must also address those that forced judges to resign voluntarily. Out of 32 resignations, 30 resulted from disciplinary motions initiated by court presidents (94%) and only 2 were triggered by the Minister of Justice (6%). In other words, court presidents were fifteen times more successful in forcing judges to resign. True, we must keep in mind that the Minister of Justice initiated seven times fewer disciplinary motions than court presidents. However, even if this difference is taken into account, court presidents were still twice as effective in forcing judges to resign.[205]

---

[204] The term "delay in delivering justice" encompassed several types of delays such as inaction in certain cases or delays in writing reasoned opinions (it is possible to announce the result of the case orally at the hearing and submit the written judgment within thirty days from the hearing).

[205] More specifically, court presidents forced 30 judges to resign in 215 disciplinary motions they initiated (14%), whereas the Minister of Justice succeeded in 2 cases out of 26 (7.6%).

In conclusion, the empirical study of disciplinary proceedings against judges in 1993–2002 shows that court presidents were not only more active in using this "stick" than the Minister of Justice, but also far more successful in employing it. It reveals, contrary to general wisdom, that court presidents dominated this mechanism of judicial accountability, whereas the Minister of Justice played a less important role.

Regarding *reassignment* within the same court, I concluded that Czech law provided little guidance on the use of this mechanism. Thus, I must look into practice to determine who decided on reassignment of judges and according to what criteria. The answer to the first part is straightforward – this power belonged to court presidents. The answer to the second part of this question is also unambiguous – there were no criteria at all. Until 2000, the only informal limit on the discretion of court president was that they could not arbitrarily reassign too many judges at the same time. Individual judges had little chance to fight back. For instance, when a judge of the district court in Prague resisted her reassignment from a civil law to a criminal law panel, the court president immediately initiated disciplinary motion against her and the disciplinary panel mercilessly imposed the harshest sentence – dismissal from judicial office – for violation of judicial duty.[206]

Later, this almost unfettered discretion of court presidents was slightly curbed by the entrenching of the rules governing annual work schedules which determined in advance which type of cases would go to each judge and, if a panel decision was required, who would sit on which panel. Nevertheless, the power to issue work schedules was vested in court presidents who could, furthermore, deviate from them during the year if they deemed such deviation necessary. What is more, regular judges lacked the necessary information to counter the arguments of court presidents since there was huge information asymmetry. Only court presidents had precise information about the productivity of each judge or panel, about the case load as well as about the number of unfinished cases. For instance, when a court president said that there should be more panels dealing with commercial law as the commercial law docket or the number of unfinished cases had increased, no one could effectively challenge his claim.

It is important to realize that reassignment happens quite often within the Czech judiciary, which consists of three thousand judges.[207] In addition

---

[206] See Decision of the High Court of Prague of June 29, 1994 *Judge S. W.*

[207] This number varied significantly between 1993 and 2010. On the number of judges in the Czech Republic see Annex C of this book.

to the aforesaid internal reasons, there are also many "external" reasons that trigger reassignment – when a new judge is appointed, promoted, or seconded to a given court, when a judge goes on maternity or parental leave,[208] when a judge leaves the judiciary (voluntarily when he retires, or by the decision of the disciplinary court), when a judge becomes seriously ill, or when a judge dies. In all these circumstances, panels must be filled or reshuffled and sometimes their docket has to be changed as well. Single judges may also be forced to move to another specialization, either temporarily or permanently. Thus, court presidents have many opportunities to use reassignment to punish judges within their courts.[209]

The practice of *promotion* to higher courts was, in general, in line with the de jure standard, with one important caveat. Even though the Minister of Justice could, with the exception of promotion to the Supreme Court, decide unilaterally on the promotion of judges to a higher court, this rarely happened in practice. Court presidents managed to fight successfully the unilateral actions of the ministers until a new custom slowly emerged. According to this new de facto standard, the promotion of judges required the consent of both the Minister of Justice and two court presidents, the president of the court where a given judge sat and the president of the higher court to which it was proposed that the judge be promoted. Under this new arrangement, court presidents soon took control over the promotion of judges and the model that de jure applied only to promotion to the Supreme Court was extended to all tiers of the Czech judicial system.

This seems puzzling. If the Ministers of Justice could unilaterally promote judges to regional courts and since 1996 also to high courts[210], why would not they do it in practice? There is no easy answer to that question. However, three factors played in favor of court presidents: high turnover of ministers of justice, information asymmetry, and increasing political costs of fighting the court presidents. First, there were eleven ministers of justice between 1993 and 2010, the average length of their term was 622 days (1 year, 8 months

---

[208] It is important to keep in mind that the Czech judiciary is a "career" judiciary and lawyers become judges in their twenties or thirties. Therefore, Czech judges go on a maternity leave (or a parental leave) more often than in countries where judging is a second or a third job and lawyers enter the judiciary in their forties or fifties.

[209] In theory, reassignment can also be used to reward judges if a given judge wants to move to another specialization. However, given high specialization of Czech judges this scenario is very rare in practice.

[210] Note that until 1995 the president of the High Court in Prague had to consent to promotion to his court as well. See note 184 above.

and 13 days),[211] and none of the ministers stayed in the office for more than four years. In contrast, virtually all court presidents served for much more than two years and many of them held the office of a court president for more than a decade. Second, ministers of justice had not sufficient information about individual judges to make informed decisions on promotion. There was no individualized judicial statistics, no performance evaluation of individual judges, no complaint mechanism, and virtually no judgments of the lower courts were published. In such scenario, the only available option for the ministers of justice was to rely on judgment of the regional court presidents who had the hands-on experience with individual judges. Third, when ministers attempted to promote judges against the will of the court presidents, court presidents went public, which caused an unnecessary hassle for the ministers. Such confrontation immediately attracted the media attention and became the subject of intense public scrutiny, which empowered the opposition parties and complicated the work of the ministry on other issues. Later on, court presidents even challenged the rare minister's attempt to promote a judge unilaterally before administrative courts on the ground that the judge concerned was not good enough for being promoted.[212] These three factors explain why virtually all ministers of justice between 1993 and 2002 treated the presidents of regional courts as partners and only rarely rejected their proposals for promotion. Pavel Rychetský, the Vice Prime Minister (1998–2003) and the Minister of Justice (2002–2003), put it frankly. When asked "What is the personal politics of a minister of justice?" he replied "The one that fulfils the wishes of the regional court presidents."[213]

Similarly, according to available information, no Minister of Justice attempted to threaten the President of the Supreme Court that, if the Supreme Court President refuses to consent to promotion of minister's nominees, the Minister will veto the Supreme Court President's candidates for promotion too. Again, information asymmetry, threat of media

---

[211] My own calculation based on the length of the term of each Minister of Justice between 1993 and 2010. Note that four intermezzos, when there was no minister of justice and the Prime Minister or the Vice Minister took care of the Ministry of Justice, and the second term of Jiří Pospíšil (July 2010 to June 2012) are intentionally excluded from this calculation.

[212] See Judgment of the Supreme Administrative Court of the Czech Republic of April 16, 2009, No. 5 As 13/2009.

[213] Pavel Rychetský, "Pohled ministrů spravedlnosti" in Jan Kysela (ed.) *Hledání optimálního modelu správy soudnictví pro Českou republiku* (Kancelář Senátu 2008) 20–24, at 22. The contributions of other three ministers of justice – Otakar Motejl (1998–2000), Karel Čermák (2003–2004), and Jiří Pospíšil (2006–2009 and 2010–2012) – further confirm Rychetský's view (see ibid., at 15, 18, and 28–31).

outcry, high turnover of ministers of justice,[214] and strong personalities at the helm of the Supreme Court prevented this from happening.

The de facto rules of *promotion to the position of chamber president* within the same court do not differ from the de jure standards. In practice, promotion to the position of chamber president was fully in the hands of court presidents. Presidents of regional courts were particularly influential in this type of promotion since the president of a regional court administered not only his own court and judges assigned to it, but also all the district courts within the jurisdiction of that regional court. As to *appointments to the grand chambers* of the Supreme Court, I concluded that Czech law did not provide clear standards. In practice, the president of the Supreme Court took control over this mechanism. The only limit to his discretion was the informal pressure of his fellow judges at the Supreme Court.

The *secondment* of judges followed the same path as the permanent promotion of judges. According to de jure standards, the power to second judges was shared by the Minister of Justice and court presidents. However, court presidents soon started to dominate the discussion on secondment. Court presidents controlled secondment to regional courts as well as to the Supreme Court and soon encroached upon the powers of the Minister of Justice to second judges to high courts. A similar shift happened with *temporary assignment of judges outside the judiciary*. Even though the Minister of Justice could act unilaterally according to de jure standards, in fact court presidents had the power of veto.

However, there was one mechanism, which Ministers of Justice controlled with an iron fist and over which other actors had no say. Not surprisingly, this mechanism was the *appointment of judges to the position of court president or vice president*. In fact, the selection of judicial officials became one of the few mechanisms that in practice remained fully in the hands of the Ministers of Justice. But this does not mean that court presidents were transmission belts of Czech Ministers of Justice.[215] Virtually all court presidents and vice presidents from the communist era were removed shortly after the Velvet Revolution in 1990. They were replaced by judges chosen by the democratic political elites. These new court presidents appointed after the fall of the communist regime were

---

[214] Note that while there were eleven ministers of justice between 1993 and 2010 (see note 210), there were only three presidents of the Supreme Court in the same period: Otakar Motejl (1993–1998), Eliška Wagnerová (1998–2002), and Iva Brožová (2002–2015).

[215] See also discussion in Chapter 2, Section III.A and Chapter 8, Section I.

appointed for an indefinite period,[216] and thus the vacancies at these posts were very rare.[217]

Even though Law on Courts and Judges gave power to the Minister of Justice to dismiss court presidents of the district, regional, and high courts, the rule "he who appoints judicial officials may also dismiss them" has been rarely used for the following reasons. First, the political costs of dismissing court presidents became extremely high. Most ministers desperately wanted to avoid this type of confrontation, because these confrontations gave the proverbial stick to the opposition parties to beat the minister as well as the ruling coalition. Even Otakar Motejl, whose stature and reputation was unquestionable in the 1990s, faced severe criticism of the Supreme Court president and the media, when he, as the Minister of Justice, dismissed five court presidents in 1999. Court presidents also fought back and heavily criticized Motejl's proposal of the High Council of the Judiciary, which eventually failed.[218] Second, ministers needed regional court presidents for making informed decisions on promotion and other personnel matters. As mentioned earlier, there was no individualized judicial statistics, no performance evaluation of individual judges, and no complaint mechanism. The only available option for the ministers of justice was thus to rely on judgment of the regional court presidents who had the hands-on experience with individual judges. As a result, they started to treat the presidents of regional courts as partners.[219] In fact, only Otakar Motejl, who had been the President of the Supreme Court (1993–1998) before he became the Minister of Justice (1998–2000), dared to dismiss regional court presidents. Third, court presidents later on started to challenge their dismissals before the Constitutional Court and the Supreme Administrative Court and eventually won these disputes.[220]

Regarding *case assignment*, the Czech statute law provided no criteria until 2000. In practice, this was the realm of court presidents.[221] The 2000 Amendment to the 1991 Law on Courts and Judges only legalized this de facto situation. Hence, it is possible to conclude that court presidents

---

[216] Note that the limited term of court presidents and vice presidents were introduced in the Czech Republic only in 2008. See Sections II.B and IV.C of this chapter.

[217] The vacancy opened only if a sitting court president died, retired, or was promoted.

[218] See Section II.A of this chapter.

[219] See above note 212.

[220] See notes 69–75. See also Section IV.D of this chapter.

[221] For further details, see David Kosař, "Rozvrh práce: opomíjený předpoklad soudcovské nezávislosti a klíčový nástroj pro boj s korupcí soudců" [Case Assignment: The Overlooked Precondition of Judicial Independence and the Tool against Judicial Corruption], (2014) 153 *Právník* 1049.

dominated case assignment throughout the whole period between 1993 and 2002. How did they do it? In order to answer this question, we must distinguish between two phases of case assignment – the creation of the work schedule for a given year and the subsequent use of the work schedule during that year. But in order to understand the practice of case assignment in the Czech Republic it is necessary to recall the specific features of the Czech judicial system.

The Czech judicial system consists of relatively large courts at all levels of the judiciary, including the Supreme Court.[222] Cases are never decided in plenary sessions and the en banc procedure does not exist. That means that cases are assigned either to single judges (at the first instance courts) or to small panels of judges (at appellate courts as well as at the Supreme Court). With minor exceptions, between 1993 and 2002 all panels consisted of three judges. In such an environment, case assignment is extremely important.

The first phase of case assignment, the creation of work schedules, was fully in the hands of court presidents. The only informal curb on court presidents was peer pressure from other judges. However, regular judges in practice had little leverage vis-à-vis their court presidents. When the court president said that panels A, B, and C would hear cases dealing with contracts and panels D, E, and F would deal with corporations, there was little room for debate. The same rule applied to civil, criminal, and administrative law panels. Therefore, court presidents could easily draft the work schedule so as to reward or punish judges.

However, this institutionalized practice was not the only way to misuse case assignment, because the initial design of case assignment had only limited precommitment effects. First, Article 4a of the 1991 Law on Courts and Judges authorized court presidents to depart from the original rules if they deemed it necessary. This still was not the worst option as such departure from the original rules had to be announced to the parties to a given dispute as well as to other judges. Therefore, the parties could invoke their right to a legal judge and challenge the change in the composition of the decision-making formation before a higher court. In addition, judges who were not persuaded by the necessity for case reassignment could at least signal to the media that reassignment of the case was suspicious.

It is the remaining option that was more dangerous. In theory as well as in practice, it was possible to rig case assignment at the court registry. Since no law laid down a concrete method of case assignment, every

---

[222] Note that the Supreme Administrative Court started to operate only from January 1, 2003.

court president adopted his or her own system. None of these systems was designed to ensure random case assignment. Instead, court presidents often delegated the task of case assignment to employees at the court registries. The relevant employees were supposed to assign cases according to the rules set by the work schedule. However, the work schedule laid down only very crude criteria. A typical rule read as follows: "all cases dealing with contracts shall be assigned to panels A, B, and C in alphabetical order and then again from panel A."

But what happens if the postman brings twenty case files on the same day? According to what criteria should the court registry assign these twenty files? Neither the law nor the work schedule contemplated this situation. Recall that the work schedule stipulated only that case no. 1 should go to panel A, case no. 2 to panel B, case no. 3 to panel C, case no. 4 again to panel A, and so on. However, there is a hitch. Someone has to decide *which* case out of the twenty cases that arrived the same day will be labeled "case no. 1" and *which* case will be labeled "case no. 2." In other words, the court registrars could always use hidden criteria in distributing cases among panels A, B, and C. Here the human factor came in – everything depended on the character of the court registrars. If the court president gave instructions to the relevant court registrar that certain cases, for instance "easy cases" or "interesting cases," should go to panel A and the rest to panels B and C, no one else learned about this practice and no one could challenge it.

E.   Brief Summary of Years 1993–2002

Based on the analysis of mechanisms of judicial accountability used from 1993 to 2002, the following tentative conclusions relevant for the first research question emerge. First, there were two major principals of judges – the Minister of Justice and court presidents. The other principals were marginal. Neither the Chamber of Deputies nor the Senate had any role in holding judges to account. Other potential actors (such as the public, the ombudsman, or the Bar) had no say either. Second, court presidents, and not the Minister of Justice, dominated the Czech judiciary in practice. Court presidents entirely controlled the following four mechanisms: reassignment, case assignment, chamber president appointment, and appointment to grand chambers. They also dominated disciplinary motions[223] and had an equal say with the Minister of Justice in three other

---

[223]   However, note that disciplinary panels, which were composed of professional judges, served as a check on the power of court presidents.

mechanisms (promotion, secondment, and temporary assignment outside the judiciary). Contrary to general wisdom, there was only one mechanism which was controlled entirely by the Minister of Justice – appointment to the position of court president or vice president. Third, the powers of all the principals remained quite stable in 1993–2002. Table 5.2 quantifies the "accountability-to-whom question."

Regarding the second and third research questions, how frequently and how severely were judges held to account, I do not address them here, since I do not have any normative benchmark on how often and how intensively Czech judges should have been held to account between 1993 and 2002. Therefore these numbers do not have any "stand alone" value. They make sense only when compared with what happened in the other three mini-case studies. All four intercountry and intracountry comparisons[224] will be conducted only in Chapter 7.

Finally, out of the four accountability perversions I identified in Chapter 1 two emerged in the Czech Republic between 1993 and 2002: judicial accountability avoidance and output excesses of judicial accountability. Regarding judicial accountability avoidance, Czech judges resisted the introduction of individualized statistics, judicial performance evaluation, measures to improve the transparency of judicial decision-making, and personal financial disclosures. At the same time, they vigorously defended short statutory limits for initiating disciplinary motions. This environment left significant room for judicial accountability avoidance.

Czech judges also quickly adapted to the judicial metrics and adopted several techniques to meet the monthly "soft quota" for finished cases. For instance, they artificially split the case into separate case files with the aim of artificially multiplying their productivity. The prime example is the conduct of a judge of the regional court who divided one appeal challenging seventy-six decisions of the tax authority into seventy-six separate case files in order to boost the number of disposed cases. However, the Supreme Administrative Court identified the real rationale for splitting the original appeal and rebuked the judge concerned.[225] The "soft quotas" also led some judges to adopt an attitude that can be described as "get rid of the case as soon as possible and with the least resources." This meant that such judges preferred dismissing the case on procedural grounds, which is usually the

---

[224] For further details on the research design of my case studies, see Chapter 4, Section I.
[225] The Supreme Administrative Court criticized this conduct as uneconomical, unconstitutional, and unethical. See Judgment of the Supreme Administrative Court of the Czech Republic of February 1, 2006, No. 1 Afs 24/2005. See also Judgment of the Supreme Administrative Court of the Czech Republic of April 21, 2005, No. 2 Afs 53/2004.

Table 5.2. *Who controlled de facto mechanisms of judicial accountability in the Czech Republic between 1993 and 2002?* Czech Republic (1993–2002)

Year	Who controlled de facto mechanisms of JA?				
	Number of available mechanisms	Number of mechanisms controlled by MoJ	Number of mechanisms controlled by CP	Number of mechanisms controlled by LEG	Number of mechanisms controlled by OTHERS
1993	8	2.63	4.87	–	0.50
1994	8	2.53	4.95	–	0.52
1995	8	2.53	4.95	–	0.52
1996	8	2.52	4.98	–	0.50
1997	8	2.51	4.97	–	0.52
1998	8	2.52	4.92	–	0.56
1999	8	2.53	4.91	–	0.56
2000	8	2.52	4.94	–	0.54
2001	9	2.69	5.81	–	0.50
2002	9	2.50	5.97	–	0.53
Average	8.2	2.55	5.13	0	0.52
Average [%]		**31%**	**63%**	**0%**	**6%**

* MoJ = Minister of Justice, CP = court presidents, LEG = Legislature, OTHERS = other actors (e.g., judges other than court presidents, judicial boards, ombudsman, the Bar, the public)

easiest way how to "finish" the case, and then waited whether the appeal is lodged and what the appellate court would do.

On the other hand, there were few opportunities for simulating judicial accountability in this period and I could not find any traces of systematic misuse of mechanisms of judicial accountability in order to punish critics and reward allies within the judiciary in this period. To be sure, there were some problematic instances of reassignment of judges and case assignment by court presidents. Similarly, promotion of some judges was debatable. But none of these incidents affected the Czech judiciary as such and no group within the judiciary was systematically targeted. In sum, selective accountability was on the low ebb in this period.

IV.   Mechanisms of Judicial Accountability from 2003 to 2010

This section focuses on the period between 2003 and 2010 and follows the same structure as the analysis of the period between 1993 and 2002. To avoid repetition, the discussion will focus primarily on new mechanisms introduced in 2003–2010 and on the existing mechanisms that were altered in this period.

A.   Contingent Circumstances

The screening mechanisms were subject only to minor changes. The de jure system of recruitment and selection of judges remained essentially the same, subject to two minor adjustments. The 2002 Law on Courts and Judges explicitly stipulated the number of years of practice required for appointment to a particular level of the judicial system.[226] This change reduced the discretion of the Minister of Justice in the assignment of newly appointed judges. One year later, the Czech Parliament increased the minimum age for judges from twenty-five to thirty years. This change resulted from heavy criticism of the so-called kindergarten judiciary and the growing consensus that "twenty-something judges" lack sufficient experience to fulfill judicial tasks in the twenty-first century.

---

[226] More specifically, Art. 67 of Law No. 6/2002 Coll., on Courts and Judges stipulated that only candidates with no less than eight years of legal practice can be appointed to regional courts or high courts. Regarding the Supreme Court, Law No. 6/2002 Coll., on Courts and Judges required ten years of legal practice.

The latter change was only a half-way solution aimed at silencing the most vocal critics. Increasing the minimum age just kicked the can a little further down the road. I mentioned in the previous section that two exogenous factors began exercising significant pressure on the Czech system of appointment of judges – increasing judicial salaries and fewer opportunities in private practice. These two factors led to fierce competition for each vacancy within the judiciary. However, the existing system failed to provide clear criteria for the selection of judges from a larger pool of candidates and the higher minimum age did not do anything to solve this issue either. This pressure resulted in two phenomena. One of them, the growing importance of psychological testing,[227] was discussed in the previous section. The second phenomenon, which emerged only after the adoption of the 2002 Law on Courts and Judges, was the increase in litigation over judicial appointments. The new circumstances called for a systematic overhaul of the recruitment and selection of judges, but the Czech Parliament responded with only cosmetic changes.

Apart from these two minor modifications, the process of appointing judges remained the same. The major "veto players" did not change. President of the Supreme Court, and also President of the newly established Supreme Administrative Court, continued to control the staffing of their courts. This meant that the president of the Supreme Court could veto any judge whom the President of the Czech Republic intended to appoint to the Supreme Court.[228] The president of the Supreme Administrative Court had the same power.[229] At the lower courts, the relevant court president and the Minister of Justice usually made a "deal" and each of them chose his own candidates.[230] As a result, a fragile balance between court presidents and the executive power was maintained.

Regarding mechanisms such as case assignment, judicial salaries, reassignment, and promotion, which can be designed so as to avoid accounting, the 2002 Law on Courts and Judges made only minor adjustments. Criteria for case assignment, reassignment within the same court and for

---

[227] The psychological testing met both criteria of an "easy solution" to the problem of too many candidates for each vacancy. First, it was quasi-scientific and difficult to challenge. Second, the Ministry of Justice was not directly involved in the testing and thus it could easily rebuff any accusations that it wanted to rig the courts.

[228] Art. 70 of Law No. 6/2002 Coll., on Courts and Judges.

[229] Art. 124 of the Law No. 150/2002 Coll., the Code of Administrative Justice.

[230] Note that judges of lower courts were usually appointed in bigger groups. Therefore, if there were four vacancies at the regional court, it was possible to reach a deal whereby the regional court president would choose two candidates and the Ministry of Justice would nominate its own two candidates.

promotion continued to be determined by ex-ante criteria only to a limited extent, if at all. The rule governing judicial salaries remained the same too.

The system of *appellate and quasi-appellate mechanisms* did not change much either. The rules governing "extraordinary appeal" (*stížnost pro porušení zákona*) remained the same. "Extraordinary appeals" were allowed in criminal law matters and only the Minister of Justice could lodge such appeals. The Supreme Court[231] as well as the newly established Supreme Administrative Court[232] could still issue "interpretative guidelines" in order to unify divergent case law. Finally, neither the equivalent of an en banc procedure nor referrals to the grand chamber of the Supreme Court "à la Strasbourg" were introduced in the Czech Republic between 2003 and 2010.

In contrast, the *training* of judges underwent significant change. Most importantly, the 2002 Law on Courts and Judges established the Judicial Academy, a centralized institution that provides training to both judicial candidates and sitting judges. The 2002 Law on Courts and Judges, as passed by the Parliament, went even further. It introduced compulsory education for all judges, regular examination of all judges, and the Council for Testing the Competences of Judges. However, the Constitutional Court did not accept such far-reaching changes and "killed" these three innovations.[233] As a result, the only innovation that survived the constitutional challenge was the Judicial Academy itself.

The Judicial Academy remedied two major problems of judicial training that existed in the 1990s. First, it reduced the influence of the Ministry of Justice and court presidents over judicial training and, in particular, over invited speakers. Second, it increased the quality as well as the variety of courses. In the meantime, the number of courses provided or facilitated by foreign actors, in particular on EU law related issues, skyrocketed. This was not surprising given the expectation of the imminent accession of the Czech Republic to the EU, which took place in 2004.

Despite significant institutional changes and the increased efforts of EU agencies, the impact of judicial training provided by foreign experts on the ground was still limited. Most of the problems from the 1990s did not fade away. Training sessions were usually attended by the same small number of judges, whereas a majority of judges ignored them.[234] In addition, talks

---

[231] Art. 14(3) of Law No. 6/2002 Coll., on Courts and Judges.

[232] Art. 12(2) in conjunction with Art. 19 of the Law No. 150/2002 Coll., the Code of Administrative Justice.

[233] Judgment of the Constitutional Court of the Czech Republic of June 18, 2002, case no. Pl. ÚS 7/02.

[234] The numbers of judges who attended seminars organized by the Judicial Academy of the Czech Republic is not available for the entire period between 2003 and 2010. However,

delivered by foreign experts often did not meet the needs and expectations of Czech judges, because foreign experts did not understand the specifics of the Czech legal environment and failed to address its actual problems.

The reform of *transparency mechanisms* stopped halfway down the road. On the one hand, the appointment and promotion of judges remained opaque. There was still no requirement to inform the public about vacancies within the judiciary. Neither lists of candidates for judicial office nor interviews with those candidates were published. Similarly, vacancies at higher courts were not advertised and the selection procedure was not open. As regards the requirement of compulsory annual disclosure of property and annual earnings, judges successfully fought the proposal to extend this obligation to them. Judicial statistics followed the same pattern. They were compiled mostly in an ad hoc manner and their results were rarely published.

On the other hand, access to judicial decisions improved. As mentioned in the previous section, the Supreme Court began publishing all its decisions online in 2000. The newly established Supreme Administrative Court followed this path and started publishing all of its decisions online soon after its establishment in September 2005. However, access to the decisions of lower courts remained severely limited until 2010.[235]

B.   Which Mechanisms of Judicial Accountability Were Used?

In a nutshell, all mechanisms of judicial accountability that were used between 1993 and 2002 remained available between 2003 and 2010 as well. In addition to the existing mechanisms, the 2002 Law on Courts and Judges established a new complaint mechanism, allowed involuntary relocation as well as demotion under specific circumstances, and introduced the so-called judicial competence evaluation. However, only the complaint mechanism could be employed as a mechanism of judicial accountability, because demotion and relocation were designed in such a way as to leave no room for discretion[236] and the "judicial competence

---

59% judges did not participate in a single seminar in 2010. Out of 1,270 judges who took part in Judicial Academy's seminars, a majority (55.2%) attended more than one event. For all of these figures, see Výroční zpráva Justiční akademie za rok 2010 [The 2010 Annual Report of the Judicial Academy of the Czech Republic], p. 8.

[235]   This situation improved only in 2011. In January 2011, the Supreme Administrative Court began publishing all decisions of regional courts in administrative matters on its Web site. A few months later, the Ministry of Justice announced that it would launch a new Web site that would include major decisions of regional and high courts.

[236]   Relocation and demotion cannot be used as a mechanism of judicial accountability in the Czech Republic, since they can be triggered, roughly, only when a court a given judge

Table 5.3. *Mechanisms of judicial accountability available in the Czech Republic between 2003 and 2010*

Mechanisms of judicial accountability available in the Czech Republic between 2003 and 2010
Sticks
Disciplinary proceedings
Reassignment
Complaint mechanism
Carrots
Promotion to a higher court
Chamber president appointment
Secondment
Temporary assignment outside the judiciary
Appointment of a judge to the position of court president or vice president
Grand chamber appointment
Dual mechanisms
Case assignment

evaluation" was struck down by the Constitutional Court in 2003.[237] Other than that, no major change took place. The 2002 Law on Courts and Judges did not include impeachment; civil liability was still conditioned by prior disciplinary or criminal sanctions;[238] there was no separate ground for the criminal liability of judges;[239] judicial salaries were still fixed in advance and no formal discretionary nonmonetary benefits were available.[240] In sum, ten mechanisms of judicial accountability were employed in the Czech Republic between 2003 and 2010 (see Table 5.3).

C.   Mechanisms of Judicial Accountability on the Books

As mentioned in Section II, in the late 1990s Otakar Motejl, the Minister of Justice and former President of the Supreme Court, decided that it was time to replace the laws governing the judiciary that dated back to the federal

is assigned to is abolished. In addition, further safeguards apply; see Art. 72 of Law No. 6/2002 Coll., on Courts and Judges.
[237] For further details, see notes 247–250 below.
[238] See Art. 78 of Law No. 6/2002 Coll., on Courts and Judges.
[239] See Art. 76 of Law No. 6/2002 Coll., on Courts and Judges.
[240] See Section III.B of this chapter.

era. However, his full-fledged reform failed in 2000 and it was only his successor, Jaroslav Bureš, who pushed the new laws through Parliament in 2002. The 2002 Law on Courts and Judges as well as the 2002 Disciplinary Code remained in force until 2010 and most de jure standards of judicial accountability thus can be found there.

The 2002 judicial reform slightly altered the design of *disciplinary proceedings*. Most importantly, it unified and centralized the disciplining of judges. According to the new 2002 Disciplinary Code, the same rules applied to all judges, irrespective of the tier of the judiciary they belonged to. A two-stage procedure newly applied to all judges. The first instance proceedings took place at the high court and appellate review was conducted by the Supreme Court. Initially, disciplinary panels still consisted of professional judges only.

Rules governing the initiation of disciplinary motions were amended as well. The 2002 Law on Courts and Judges bolstered the already hierarchical system and empowered the president of the Supreme Court and the president of the Supreme Administrative Court. Under the new arrangement, they could initiate disciplinary motions not only against judges of their courts, but also against lower court judges.[241] The powers of the Minister of Justice and presidents of district courts, regional courts, and high courts remained the same. As a result, the hierarchical pattern of disciplining Czech judges was perfected.

As regards the actions for which judges were disciplined, the 2002 Disciplinary Code was as succinct as its predecessor. It defined disciplinary misconduct as an "intentional violation of ... judicial duties as well an intentional behavior or conduct, which infringes upon dignity of judicial office or threatens public confidence in independent, impartial and just decision-making of courts."[242] Nevertheless, the 2002 Disciplinary Code abolished the dichotomy between misconduct and serious misconduct. The new law merely laid down that according to the seriousness of the misconduct, four sanctions could be imposed: reprimand, salary reduction of up to 25% for up to six months (or for up to one year in the case of repetitive misconduct), recall from the position of chamber president, and dismissal from judicial office. This means that several disciplinary sanctions from the previous decade, such as relocation to another court of the same level or demotion to a lower court, were no longer available.

---

[241] See Art. 8 of Law No. 7/2002 Coll., the Code of Disciplinary Procedure with Judges and Prosecutors (hereinafter only "the 2002 Disciplinary Code").
[242] Art. 87 of the 2002 Disciplinary Code.

This system survived until 2008, when the Parliament adopted the 2008 Amendment to the Law on Courts and Judges, which again altered the institutional design of disciplinary motions against judges. The new mixed disciplinary panels were moved to the Supreme Administrative Court and the disciplinary proceedings became single instance only. The Parliament also decided to include nonjudges on disciplinary panels, heretofore an unacceptable move. The mixed disciplinary panels are composed of six members – three judges[243] and three members of other legal professions[244] – chosen for five years by lot from the basket for each profession. Not surprisingly, this legislative move was met with fierce criticism from the judiciary, whose members claimed that "judges should be judged only by judges." Nevertheless, the Czech Constitutional Court eventually upheld the new institutional design of disciplinary proceedings.[245] In addition, the 2008 Amendment empowered the President of the Czech Republic to initiate a disciplinary motion against any judge of the ordinary courts.

The 2002 Law on Courts and Judges also amended rules governing the *reassignment* of judges. It explicitly set out that court presidents should decide on the assignment and reassignment of judges, in both cases after consultation with judicial boards.[246] Furthermore, new safeguards were introduced in order to minimize misuse of this mechanism. A court president could still change the work schedule if he deemed it necessary, but was limited by two new requirements. He or she had to consult on such change with a judicial board and the reassignment could not affect "live" cases.[247] In other words, reassignment was allowed only pro futuro and could not be used retroactively to change the composition of a chamber or the identity of a single judge in a given case.

In addition to amending the existing "sticks," the 2002 Law on Courts and Judges introduced a brand new system of *complaints* against individual judges. Every natural and legal person could lodge a complaint

---

[243] Three judicial members must include one judge of the Supreme Court, one judge of the Supreme Administrative Court, and one judge from the lower courts. Each judicial member of the panel is chosen by a lot from a separate basket of candidates.

[244] Three nonjudicial members must include one state prosecutor, one attorney, and one academic. Each nonjudicial member is chosen by a lot from a separate basket of candidates from the same profession.

[245] Judgment of the Constitutional Court of the Czech Republic of October 1, 2010, case no. Pl. ÚS 33/09.

[246] See Art. 41(2) and Art. 42(4) in conjunction with Art. 42(1)(a) of Law No. 6/2002 Coll., on Courts and Judges.

[247] Art. 42(4) of Law No. 6/2002 Coll., on Courts and Judges.

with regard to delays in delivering justice, improper behavior of judges, or violation of dignity of judicial proceedings. The system of processing the complaints mirrored the hierarchical system of disciplining judges. The president of the Supreme Court dealt with complaints against judges of the Supreme Court, presidents of high courts dealt with complaints against judges of high courts, presidents of regional courts dealt with complaints against judges of regional courts, and presidents of district courts dealt with complaints against judges of district courts. On top of that, the Minister of Justice decided on complaints against court presidents as well as on "complaints about the improper processing of complaints" brought by complainants who alleged that court presidents did not handle their original complaints adequately.

Another innovation brought by the 2002 Law on Courts and Judges was the system of "judicial competence evaluation," which was a peculiar mix of the new-public-management and the Soviet-style systems of judicial performance evaluation.[248] It involved regular compulsory examination of all judges, including judges of the Supreme Court. Every newly appointed judge was supposed to undergo such examination thirty-six months after his or her appointment, whereas sitting judges had to pass re-examination every five years. The examination was supposed to test the expertise of judges and consisted of the following components: (1) knowledge of statutes and other legal norms, (2) knowledge of case law published in the Official Collection edited by the Supreme Court, (3) the ability to apply knowledge and skills in conducting trials and in decision making, (4) level of theoretical knowledge, (5) management skills in organizing the work of the judicial department, and (6) publications, research, and pedagogical activities.[249]

This initial assessment was supposed to be conducted by court presidents. There were three possible grades: excellent, satisfactory, and unsatisfactory (a failing grade). A failing grade triggered extensive review of the decisions given by an allegedly "incompetent" judge within the period studied. This review was conducted by a special panel of three judges appointed by the relevant court president. If this review did not disprove the initial negative assessment, the whole file was referred to the Council for Testing Competence of Judges, a newly established specialized body designed to evaluate the expertise of judges. The Council for Testing Competence of Judges then decided whether or not a given judge had sufficient expertise. A negative decision of the Council resulted in dismissal

[248] For the difference between these two systems, see Chapter 2, Section II.C.
[249] Art. 136 of Law No. 6/2002 Coll., on Courts and Judges.

from judicial office.[250] This decision was subject to appeal to the special chamber of the Supreme Court. In a nutshell, this highly peculiar system of judicial competence evaluation gave court presidents another "stick" with which to beat regular judges. Nevertheless, the system of judicial competence evaluation was immediately struck down by the Constitutional Court[251] and thus it never came into being.[252] Since then no attempt to introduce a comprehensive system of judicial performance evaluation has been made in the Czech Republic.

Regarding *promotion* to a higher court, the 2002 Law on Courts and Judges closed the gap between the de jure and de facto standards as it explicitly acknowledged the role of court presidents at all levels of the Czech judicial system. Under the new arrangement, the Minister of Justice can no longer unilaterally decide on promotion to regional and high courts, because he has to consult the relevant court president on every promotion.[253] For instance, if he intends to promote a judge to a regional court, he must consult the president of that regional court about that promotion. The rules for promotion to the Supreme Court and the Supreme Administrative Court granted even more power to court presidents. The 2002 Law on Courts and Judges retained the previous model and thus the presidents of these two top courts had to consent to every promotion to their respective court.[254] In other words, they did not have merely consultative powers, but the power to veto any candidate.[255] In addition to the diffusion of the promotion competences of the Minister of Justice, the 2002 Law on Courts and Judges also explicitly laid down the number of years of practice required for promotion to a particular level of the judicial system.[256] This move was supposed to prevent the "wild promotion" of inexperienced judges to higher courts.

---

[250] Art. 94(d) of Law No. 6/2002 Coll., on Courts and Judges.

[251] Judgment of the Constitutional Court of the Czech Republic of June 18, 2002, case no. Pl. ÚS 7/02.

[252] Unfortunately, the Constitutional Court "threw out the baby with the bathwater," because it also abolished the obligation of judges to participate in further professional education. See Bobek 2008, above note 47, at 111.

[253] Art. 73(1) of Law No. 6/2002 Coll., on Courts and Judges.

[254] Art. 73(3) of Law No. 6/2002 Coll., on Courts and Judges.

[255] See Arts. 50–53 of Law No. 6/2002 Coll., on Courts and Judges, and Art. 25(1)(b) of Law No. 6/2002 Coll., on Courts and Judges

[256] More specifically, Art. 71 stipulated that only candidates with no less than eight years of legal practice can be promoted to regional courts or to high courts. Regarding the Supreme Court and the Supreme Administrative Court, the 2002 Law on Courts and Judges required ten years of legal practice.

The *appointment of judges to the position of court president or vice president* remained the same until 2008. This means that the Minister of Justice, except in both top courts, played a major role in this process. The appointment process changed in 2008, with the Parliament's riposte to the Constitutional Court's hostile position on the rule "he who appoints judicial officials may also dismiss them." Due to the unconstitutionality of this rule,[257] the Parliament introduced limited terms for judicial officials. In addition to introducing limited terms,[258] the 2008 Amendment also altered the mode of appointment. This change primarily affected presidents of regional courts and high courts. From 2009 onward, these court presidents have no longer been appointed by the Minister of Justice, but by the President of the Czech Republic upon the nomination of the Minister of Justice.

Presidents of district courts were still appointed by the Minister of Justice, as in the 1993–2002 era, but the Minister can no longer act unilaterally as he was constrained by the president of the relevant regional court who nominates the candidate. A similar change affected the appointment of court vice presidents. All vice presidents up to the level of the high courts were appointed by the Minister of Justice upon nomination of the president of a given court. Only the rules governing the appointment of judicial officials of the Supreme Court and the Supreme Administrative Court remained the same. Presidents and vice presidents of these two courts are appointed by the President of the Czech Republic. The sole limit on the discretion of the President of the Czech Republic is set by the Constitutional Court, which held that the President *must* choose from judges of a given top court.

Rules governing *promotion to the position of chamber president* remained almost the same. This power was vested in court presidents.[259] The only change regarding this quasi-promotion concerned the new consultative

---

[257] See Judgment of the Constitutional Court of the Czech Republic of July 11, 2007, case no. Pl. ÚS 18/06 (discussed in more detail in Section I.E of this chapter).

[258] Judicial officials of district courts, regional courts and high courts are appointed for seven years, whereas the Presidents and Vice Presidents of the Supreme Court and the Supreme Administrative Court are appointed for a term of ten years; see Arts. 103(2), 104(2), 105(2), and 106(2) of Law No. 6/2002 Coll., on Courts and Judges after the 2008 Amendment; and Art. 13(3) of the Law No. 150/2002 Coll., the Code of Administrative Justice. During this term judicial officials can be removed only following a decision of a disciplinary panel. Special transitional provisions apply to judicial officials who were in office on October 1, 2008; see Arts II and IV of Law No. 314/2008 Coll.

[259] Arts. 102(2)–(3), 103(2), 104(2), and 105(2) of Law No. 6/2002 Coll., on Courts and Judges.

powers of judicial boards. These newly established bodies were entitled to comment on candidates for this position.[260] However, the opinion of judicial boards was not binding upon court presidents[261] and thus court presidents still had the power to make the final decision.

Appointments to the grand chambers became even more important in 2003, since grand chambers were established also at the Supreme Administrative Court. However, neither the 2002 Law on Courts and Judges nor the Code of Administrative Justice defined precise rules governing such appointments.[262] Both statutes set out how many judges sit on grand chambers, but neither determines by what standards are grand chamber judges selected and for how long.[263] Hence, we may conclude that the situation remained roughly the same as before the creation of the Supreme Administrative Court.

As to the *secondment* judges, the 2002 Law on Courts and Judges "legalized" the existing de facto standard. As a result, the Minister of Justice lost most of his powers in this area and the power to second a judge was vested primarily with court presidents. Regarding secondment to regional courts, the Minister of Justice had no powers at all as presidents of regional courts alone decided on secondment to "their" respective regional courts. In the case of secondment to higher courts (i.e., to high courts, the Supreme Court, and the Supreme Administrative Court), the Minister of Justice decided upon proposals made by the relevant court presidents. This means that the Minister had a veto power, but could not initiate such secondment unilaterally.[264]

Temporary assignment outside the judiciary still remained primarily in the hands of the Minister of Justice, whose decision-making power was limited only by the requirement to consult with the relevant court president on such assignment.[265] However, the importance of this "carrot" decreased significantly over time. First, after 2002 there were just two potential places outside the judiciary. The 2002 Law on Courts and Judges

---

[260] See Arts. 50–53 of Law No. 6/2002 Coll., on Courts and Judges and Art. 25(1)(a) of Law No. 6/2002 Coll., on Courts and Judges.

[261] See Section I.E of this chapter.

[262] See Art. 19 of Law No. 6/2002 Coll., on Courts and Judges and Art. 16 of Law No. 6/2002 Coll., on Courts and Judges.

[263] It is difficult to explain why judicial boards at the Supreme Court and the Supreme Administrative Court were not granted the power to comment on candidates for grand chamber.

[264] See Art. 68 of Law No. 6/2002 Coll., on Courts and Judges, and Art. 25(1)(b) of Law No. 6/2002 Coll., on Courts and Judges.

[265] Art. 68 of Law No. 6/2002 Coll., on Courts and Judges.

permitted assignment only to the Judicial Academy and to the Ministry of Justice. Second and more importantly, temporary assignment to these two bodies was no longer perceived as a positive career move. On the contrary, work with the Judicial Academy (located in Kroměříž, a small town far away from Prague and with no major court) did not enjoy a high reputation and assignment to the Ministry of Justice was perceived as a problematic practice due to the previous case law of the Constitutional Court.[266] This perception eventually turned out to be correct as, only a few years later, the Constitutional Court again held that the assignment of judges to the Ministry of Justice violates the principle of separation of powers.[267] As a result, the assignment to the Judicial Academy was (apart from suspension of the judicial office for judges serving a term at international courts and tribunals) the only option and temporary assignment outside the judiciary has become a marginal mechanism.

The core document that contained rules on *case assignment* was still the "work schedule." Basic rules governing the adoption of work schedules were inserted into the statute as early as in 2000. The 2002 Law on Courts and Judges supplemented these basic rules with additional details. Most importantly, it explicitly required that each work schedule contain a method of case assignment and that cases must be assigned according to their subject matter. Nevertheless, the 2002 Law on Courts and Judges failed to establish an objective and transparent method for the assignment and reassignment of cases. It did not even specify the method to be used. Rather, it laid down various aspirational rules and general conditions that provided only vague guidance to case assignment.

For instance, it provided that cases should be assigned so that all panels have the same workload and that cases must be assigned on the day they arrive at the court. Neither of these rules is objectionable, but it is fallacious to think that they can prevent the rigging of the case assignment procedure. The obligation to assign cases on the day they arrive is simply not a sufficient safeguard, especially in courts, where dozens of case files reach the court every day. The requirement that each panel have the same workload is similarly toothless. This is merely an aspirational goal and the only person who has information about the caseloads is the court president anyway.

---

[266] Judgment of the Constitutional Court of the Czech Republic of June 18, 2002, case no. Pl. ÚS 7/02.

[267] Judgment of the Constitutional Court of the Czech Republic of October 6, 2010, case no. Pl. ÚS 39/08, § 46–49.

Finally, the 2002 Law on Courts and Judges made one more institutional change. It stipulated that court presidents must discuss a draft of the work schedule with judicial boards before its adoption. Similar constraints apply to reassignment. If the court president wants to reassign cases during the calendar year, he or she must consult a judicial board. In sum, the new law curtailed the court presidents' unlimited discretion, while, at the same time, leaving them significant room for maneuver.

D.   Mechanisms of Judicial Accountability in Action

The previous section explained what the Czech law laid down about the mechanisms of judicial accountability that were used between 2003 and 2010. This section will analyze how these mechanisms operated in practice, with one exception. I will not discuss the system of "judicial competence evaluation," because this mechanism was outlawed by the Constitutional Court in 2003 and "judicial competence evaluation" never took place in practice. Again I start with "sticks," followed by "carrots" and "dual mechanisms."

Regarding *disciplinary motions*, data from 2003 to 2010 show a very similar pattern to the one we saw in the years between 1993 and 2002. The average number of disciplinary motions per annum was slightly higher than in the previous decade, but the increase was not dramatic. As in the previous era, court presidents were the dominant principals in disciplinary proceedings. Of the 246 disciplinary motions lodged in 2003–2010, court presidents initiated 213 (87%), whereas the Minister of Justice initiated only 21 (9%). The remaining 12 motions (5%) were initiated by other organs[268] for administrative offences such as speeding or bad parking. Interestingly, the President of the Czech Republic, who became the third disciplinary prosecutor in October 2008, did not initiate a single disciplinary motion until December 2010. I may thus conclude that the distribution of disciplinary motions among disciplinary prosecutors in 2003–2010 differed only minimally from that in 1993–2002.

As regards the typology of misconduct, the most common reason for initiating disciplinary motions in 2003–2010 was delay in delivering justice (67%), followed by violations of judicial independence, judicial impartiality, or judicial ethics (8%), administrative offences (6%), and alcohol-related issues (2%). These statistics are similar to the data

---

[268] Most of these motions were initiated by the Police for driving offences.

from 1993 to 2002. Two caveats must be added here. The first concerns alcohol-related issues. In 2003–2010 we can see a sharp decline in disciplinary motions based on this ground. It is difficult to make causal inferences here, but this decline was most probably caused by the fact that the number of judges with drinking problems decreased.[269] The second caveat relates to motions for administrative offences. The decrease in these offences can be explained more easily. The main reason behind this decrease was the 2008 Amendment to the 2002 Law on Courts and Judges, which abolished the judges' privilege of having their administrative offences tried by disciplinary courts. As a result, administrative offences committed by judges in 2009 and 2010 were tried by the relevant administrative bodies and were not heard by disciplinary panels.

Two more statistics are worthy of mention. The overall success rate of disciplinary motions was relatively high. Disciplinary panels issued a disciplinary sanction in 143 cases (58%) and, in addition, in 28 cases (11%) judges resigned voluntarily. This means that the success rate was 69%. In contrast, disciplinary panels acquitted judges completely in only 20 cases (8%). The number of cases in which disciplinary panels found judges guilty, but refrained from imposing a sentence, was also relatively low – 24 cases (10%). Hence, judges were exonerated in 18% of cases. In the remaining 31 cases (13%), the disciplinary motion ended without a decision on the merits. Of 143 sanctions imposed between 2003 and 2010, the most common was a salary reduction (85 cases, 59%), followed by reprimand (42 cases, 29%), dismissal from judicial office (9 cases, 6%) and fines (6 cases, 4%). The remaining sanction – dismissal from the position of chamber president – was imposed only once.

The last statistic regarding disciplinary motions compares the success rate of court presidents, on the one hand, and that of the Minister of Justice, on the other. Data for the years 2003–2010 shows that disciplinary panels issued sanctions in 62% of the motions initiated by court presidents, whereas the Minister of Justice was successful in only 19% of his motions. Once again, court presidents were also far more successful in forcing judges to resign. Out of 28 resignations, 23 resulted from disciplinary motions initiated by court presidents (82%), whereas only 5 can be attributed to the Minister of Justice (18%).

---

[269] This decrease may have two explanations. First, sitting judges who had a drinking problem were forced to leave the judiciary in the previous period. Second, new judges with drinking problems knew that disciplinary panels handed out severe sentences for this misconduct and thus they either resigned voluntarily or were forced to leave the judiciary informally.

In conclusion, the results of the empirical study of disciplinary proceedings against judges between 2003 and 2010 show that court presidents, once again, dominated this mechanism of judicial accountability. Court presidents were not only more active in using this "stick," but were also far more successful in employing it. Furthermore, all statistics concerning disciplinary proceedings in 2003–2010 show a pattern similar to the statistics from the previous decade. In other words, there has been a strong path-dependence in the disciplining of Czech judges.

The second "stick" was *reassignment* within the same court. Many concerns raised in connection with the de facto use of this mechanism in 1993–2002 apply with equal force to the period between 2003 and 2010. Most importantly, there were no set criteria for reassignment. De jure, there was a shift in who decided on reassignment. Court presidents could no longer reassign judges unilaterally as they were required to discuss both reassignment at the beginning of each calendar year (determined by the work schedule) and reassignment during the calendar year with judicial boards. In practice, court presidents were still the most important actors in the process of reassignment as only they could trigger it, even though their discretion as well as their information advantage was reduced.

The last "stick" to be addressed is the new *complaint* mechanism. Complaints were the only means by which someone other than the Minister of Justice or court presidents could hold judges to account. Nevertheless, complaints against individual judges have been toothless. All complaints were in practice processed by court presidents without any intervention from the Ministry of Justice. The results of these complaints were not publicized and thus complaints had only a limited impact on the reputation of a given judge. Furthermore, I could not trace any link between complaints and triggering disciplinary motions. In other words, the accountability effect of this mechanism was minimal.

Regarding the *promotion* of judges to a higher court, the de facto standard did not differ from that in the previous period. As in the period from 1993 to 2002, the Minister of Justice shared his power to decide on promotions with court presidents. The major difference from the 1993–2002 era is that the 2002 Law on Courts and Judges explicitly acknowledged the joint decision-making and thus closed the gap between the de jure and the de facto standards. The practice that emerged in the 1990s thus found its way into the law and de jure rules were aligned with de facto rules.

Two additional mechanisms experienced similar development – the *secondment* of judges and *temporary assignment outside the judiciary*. In both cases, the de facto standard from 1993–2002, that is, the dominance of court presidents over the secondment of judges and their significant influence on temporary assignment outside the judiciary, not only prevailed in practice, but was also newly entrenched in the 2002 Law on Courts and Judges. As a result, the de jure and de facto standards applicable to these two mechanisms converged.

De facto rules governing the *promotion to the position of chamber president* and *appointments to the grand chamber* also remained the same. In practice, court presidents decided on both of these "carrots." Thus, there was no difference between the de facto standards applicable to these two mechanisms in 1993–2002 and those existing in 2003–2010. There was no de jure standard governing appointment to the grand chamber. Court presidents thus had wide discretion regarding the composition of grand chambers. Regarding promotion to the position of chamber president, the 2002 Law on Courts and Judges said that judges are promoted to the position of chamber president by court presidents following consultation with the judicial board of a given court. However, the opinions of judicial boards were not binding upon court presidents and the latter still had significant influence. Path dependence thus again prevailed and judicial boards had only a marginal influence on the appointment of chamber presidents.

The last "carrot" was the *appointment of judges to the position of court president or vice president*. The appointment of presidents of the Supreme Court and the Supreme Administrative Court did not change. It remained fully in the hands of the President of the Czech Republic until 2010. However, he de facto could not use this power between 2003 and 2010 as there was no vacancy at either court at all in this period. As to the other echelons of the Czech judiciary, until 2008 the Minister of Justice played a dominant role in selecting judicial officials, but he had to make more and more concessions to court presidents, which culminated in the new custom that created a delicate balance between the Minister of Justice and court presidents.[270] According to the new custom, which was later "legalized" by the 2008 Amendment to the 2002 Law on Courts and Judges,[271] the Minister of Justice appointed district court presidents only from candidates nominated by regional court presidents. The Minister enjoyed greater discretion in appointing regional court presidents and high court presidents, but he had to discuss his choice with the "kolegium of regional court presidents"[272] and secure the approval of the President

---

[270] See Section III.D of this chapter.
[271] See Section IV.C of this chapter.
[272] For further details regarding the kolegium, see Section I.E of this chapter.

of the Czech Republic, who formally appointed regional court and high court presidents.

This development must be understood in the context of high-profile litigation over the power to dismiss court presidents and vice presidents. The attempt of the President of the Czech Republic to dismiss the president of the Supreme Court was found unconstitutional by the Constitutional Court,[273] which rejected the rule "he who appoints judicial officials may also dismiss them."[274] The lower court presidents also successfully fought rare attempts to recall them before the administrative courts. When the Minister of Justice removed the President of the District Court for Prague-West, she challenged her dismissal and the Municipal Court allowed the action and annulled the decision of the Minister.[275] In addition, the 2008 Amendment to the Law on Courts and Judges made a concession to court presidents and in particular to regional court presidents. It recognized the power of presidents of all courts up to the level of the high courts to select "their" vice presidents and empowered presidents of regional courts to nominate candidates for the office of district court president. In other words, court presidents have definitely emancipated from the executive branch, namely from the Ministry of Justice and the President of the Czech Republic.

The President of the Czech Republic de jure unilaterally appointed all judicial officials of the Supreme Court and the Supreme Administrative Court. But vacancies for these positions were extremely rare. In fact, between 2003 and 2010 there was no vacancy at either court at all. Due to these specific circumstances, Havel's successor, Václav Klaus, had to live with Havel's appointees at both top courts for the entire period between 2003 and 2010.[276]

The only available dual mechanism of judicial accountability in the period between 2003 and 2010 was *case assignment*. The de facto practice of case assignment did not change much from that in the previous decade, despite the fact that the 2002 Law on Courts and Judges tightened the rules governing the creation of work schedules and limited the discretion of

---

[273] See notes 69–75.

[274] See Section III.D of this chapter.

[275] Judgment of the Municipal Court in Prague (Administrative Division) of July 24, 2005, Case 5 Ca 37/2005–42, Unpublished. For further details, see Bobek 2010, above note 71, 259–260.

[276] Klaus had only one occasion during his two successive terms as a President of the Czech Republic (2003–2013) to select a judicial official of one of the two top ordinary courts. In 2011, the Vice President of the Supreme Court reached the mandatory retirement age and Klaus appointed his successor.

court presidents in departing from the work schedule. In sum, de facto standards from the previous era prevailed to a large extent.

However, one important change took place in practice. Until 2002, case assignment operated in the shadow of the law and no one outside the judiciary paid much attention to it. This is no longer the case. As a result of several scandals, case assignment has increasingly come to the forefront of debates about the Czech judiciary. The first scandals appeared in 2007 and 2008, when the Minister of Justice discovered that the president of the Municipal Court of Brno had rigged the case assignment procedure. In 2007, she assigned a highly publicized criminal trial to a judge in violation of the order of assignment set by the work schedule. A year later, it turned out that the same court president had rigged case assignment again, this time with the aim of assigning only "easy cases" to herself.[277] These two disciplinary motions confirmed that case assignment could easily be manipulated by judicial officials. Furthermore, it is increasingly accepted that these two cases were only the tip of the iceberg.[278]

E.   Brief Summary of Years 2003–2010

The following tentative conclusions flow from the analysis of the use of mechanisms of judicial accountability between 2003 and 2010. First, the two major principals of judges – the Minister of Justice and court presidents – remained the same. The other principals were still marginal, but their role slightly increased. The 2002 Law on Courts and Judges empowered the public and in particular judicial boards. The public was allowed to lodge formal complaints against judges and judicial boards were granted a consultative role regarding several mechanisms controlled by court presidents. Second, court presidents again dominated the Czech judiciary in practice. They decided unilaterally on appointments to grand chambers and dominated the following four mechanisms:[279] reassignment, case assignment, chamber president appointment, and disciplinary proceedings. In addition, they decided jointly with the Minister of Justice on promotion, secondment, and temporary assignment outside the judiciary.

---

[277] By "easy cases" I mean cases that are not time-consuming.

[278] Another scandal, on much larger scale, arose in September 2011, when the Czech domestic national intelligence agency, the Security Information Agency (*Bezpečnostní informační služba*), issued its annual report for the year 2010. Its 2010 Report contained, among other things, allegations of manipulation of case files and violations of case assignment rules.

[279] In case assignment, reassignment, and chamber president appointment, court presidents were limited only by the requirement to consult on these issues with judicial boards.

Last but not least, court presidents also processed all complaints against judges. There was only one mechanism in which court presidents did not play a major role – appointment of judicial officials.[280] Third, the powers of all principals remained quite stable in 2003–2010. Table 5.4 quantifies the "accountability-to-whom question."

Regarding the second and third research questions, how frequently and how severely were judges held to account, I do not address them here, since answering them makes sense only when compared with what happened in the other three mini-case studies. All four intercountry and intracountry comparisons[281] will be conducted only in Chapter 7. Here it suffices to say that the frequency as well as the intensity of most mechanisms of judicial accountability available in the Czech Republic in this period remained roughly the same.

Regarding accountability perversions, judicial accountability avoidance and output excesses of judicial accountability remained problematic in the Czech Republic between 2003 and 2010. As to the former phenomenon, Czech judges still resisted the introduction of individualized statistics, judicial performance evaluation, and personal financial disclosures. Short statutory limits for initiating disciplinary motions also remained in the books. Hence, there was still significant room for judicial accountability avoidance. As to the latter, the access of the Czech Republic to the European Union further increased the pressure on judges to improve their performance and reduce delays in delivering justice. Due to the lack of any qualitative assessment of judicial decisions and relatively low *l'esprit de corps* of the Czech judiciary, various "output tricks"[282] for boosting judges' performance still existed.

Czech judges were also responsive to the judicial metrics and adopted several techniques to meet the monthly "soft quota" for finished cases. The main techniques remained the same. Judges artificially split the case into separate case files with the aim of artificially multiplying their productivity, or dismissed the case on procedural grounds instead of issuing judgment on the merits.[283] Despite significant efforts of the appellate courts to eradicate this practice, it continued to flourish.

---

[280] But note that since 2009 court presidents have played a significant role even in selecting judicial officials.

[281] For further details on the research design of my case studies, see Chapter 4, Section I.

[282] The techniques used by judges remained the same as between 1993 and 2002.

[283] See examples in Section III.E of this chapter.

Table 5.4. *Who controlled de facto mechanisms of judicial accountability in the Czech Republic between 2003 and 2010?* Czech Republic (2003–2010)

Year	Who controlled de facto mechanisms of JA?				
	Number of available mechanisms	Number of mechanisms controlled by MoJ	Number of mechanisms controlled by CP	Number of mechanisms controlled by LEG	Number of mechanisms controlled by OTHERS
2003	10	2.54	5.68	–	1.79
2004	10	2.54	5.96	–	1.50
2005	10	2.53	5.94	–	1.53
2006	10	2.53	5.98	–	1.50
2007	10	2.54	5.90	–	1.56
2008	10	2.58	5.89	–	1.53
2009	10	2.34	6.16	–	1.50
2010	10	2.25	6.23	–	1.52
Average	10	2.48	5.97	0.00	1.55
Average [%]		**25%**	**60%**	**0%**	**15%**

* MoJ = Minister of Justice, CP = court presidents, LEG = Legislature, OTHERS = other actors (e.g., judges other than court presidents, judicial boards, ombudsman, the Bar, the public)

As to selective judicial accountability, there were still some problematic instances of reassignment of judges and case assignment by court presidents. However, Czech judges were even more vigilant between 2003 and 2010 than in the previous period and some court presidents even attempted to challenge debatable promotions before administrative courts.[284] Hence, the room for selective judicial accountability further decreased. In sum, I could not find any traces of systematic misuse of mechanisms of judicial accountability in order to punish critics and reward allies within the judiciary in this period. I may thus conclude that selective accountability was minimal in this period. Finally, there was only one mechanism where simulating judicial accountability took place, which was the new complaint mechanism that remained toothless for the entire period.

V.   Overall Conclusion on the Czech Case Study

In conclusion, the analysis of the use of mechanisms of judicial accountability between 1993 and 2010 shows strong path-dependence. Both periods, 1993–2002 and 2003–2010, yield similar results regarding all four research questions.[285] This means that if there was a change between the years 1993–2002 and the years 2003–2010 in Slovakia, it is more likely that this change was *caused* by the introduction of the Judicial Council Euro-model rather than by other variables. The findings of this chapter have thus to a significant extent eliminated the option that there may be something other than the Judicial Council of the Slovak Republic behind the changes that took place in Slovakia after 2003.

---

[284] See, for example, Judgment of the Supreme Administrative Court of the Czech Republic of April 16, 2009, No. 5 As 13/2009–61.

[285] For more details, see Chapter 7.

6

Slovakia

This chapter tells the story of holding Slovak judges to account between 1993 and 2010. It is the central chapter of this book, because it analyzes what happened after the introduction of the Judicial Council of the Slovak Republic. In order to see the difference between the Judicial Council Euro-model and the Ministry of Justice model of court administration more clearly, this chapter follows the structure adopted in the previous chapter with respect to the Czech Republic. Section I addresses general issues that have permeated the Slovak judiciary since the split of Czechoslovakia. Section II explains major institutional changes adopted between 1993 and 2010 and the political vectors behind them. It also provides the necessary background for understanding how the Slovak judiciary operates. Sections III and IV contain the core findings of this chapter. Section III shows how Slovak judges were held to account in the first decade after the dissolution of Czechoslovakia (1993–2002). Section IV studies mechanisms of judicial accountability in the eight subsequent years (2003–2010), when Slovakia used the Judicial Council Euro-model. Finally, Section V briefly summarizes conclusions regarding the use of mechanisms of judicial accountability in Slovakia.

I. The Slovak Judiciary in Context

This section addresses common issues that Slovakia had to resolve after the split of Czechoslovakia. The aim of this section is to provide a broader picture of the environment in which Slovak judges operate. It starts by sketching the political scene in the Slovak Republic after the dissolution and discussing the immediate consequences of the split of Czechoslovakia. Subsequently, it focuses on the impact of the EU accession process upon Slovak judicial reforms and dealing with the past within the Slovak judiciary. Finally, it identifies key players in the Slovak judicial system.

A. Politics of the Slovak Republic

As with the Czech Republic, there was strong path-dependence in the political leadership in the first years after the dissolution of Czechoslovakia. Vladimír Mečiar, the winner of the 1992 elections, held a firm grip on the Slovak political scene until the late 1998, when his Movement for Democratic Slovakia (HZDS) won the elections again, but due to its minimal coalition potential it went into opposition.

Mečiar was a controversial figure. He was heavily criticized for his autocratic methods, both in Slovakia and on the international scene. In addition, he was accused of collaborating with the State Secret Service (ŠtB) during the communist era and substantial evidence was gathered to support this claim. In terms of an overarching political theme, Mečiar played successfully on the nationalist string. He projected himself as "the defender of Slovak interest within Czechoslovakia and later as the protector of the newly independent Slovakia within a hostile world."[1] As a result, a connecting thread of Slovak party politics in the 1990s was the politics of independence.

For these reasons in the first decade of Slovak party politics everything revolved around HZDS and its domineering leader. The dividing line was between those who were willing to cooperate with Mečiar and those who opposed him.[2] Under Mečiar's rule, Slovakia also became increasingly isolated and prospects of the accession of the Slovak Republic to the EU looked dim in the mid-1990s as the European Union decided not to extend an invitation to Slovakia at the Luxembourg summit in 1997 to begin accession negotiations.[3] Nevertheless, an anti-Mečiar broad-based coalition of liberals, conservatives, and social democrats under the leadership of Mikuláš Dzurinda (the Slovak Democratic Coalition, later on Slovak Democratic and Christian Union – Democratic Party), acting together, managed to defeat Mečiar in the 1998 elections and repeated their victory four years later.[4] During these two terms Slovakia changed course, adopted

---

[1] Kevin Deegan-Krause, "Uniting the Enemy: Politics and the Convergence of Nationalisms in Slovakia" (2004) 18 East European Politics and Societies 651, 684.

[2] See Tim Haughton, "Exit Choice and Legacy: Explaining the Patterns of Party Politics in Post-communist Slovakia" (2014) 30 East European Politics 210.

[3] Ibid., 222.

[4] As mentioned earlier, Mečiar's Movement for Democratic Slovakia (HZDS) won the 1998 as well as 2002 elections, but the centrist parties together obtained a smooth majority of the seats in the National Council.

a pro-EU policy, speeded up reforms, and eventually joined the EU in 2004,[5] the very same year as the Czech Republic did.[6]

After successful accession to the EU, the centrist parties lost the 2006 elections. Róbert Fico, the leader of the left-wing party Direction (Smer[7]), emerged the winner and he formed a coalition with the Slovak National Party, an extremist nationalist party, and with Mečiar's HZDS. This change at helm brought Mečiar again to the forefront of Slovak politics, but his influence has gradually waned. He twice ran unsuccessfully for President of Slovakia (in 1999 and 2004), he was not offered a post in Fico's cabinet after the 2006 elections even though his party was a part of Fico's coalition, and his star fell finally to earth in the 2010 parliamentary elections, when his HZDS for the first time in its history did not win any seats in the National Council, since it failed to obtain enough votes to pass the 5% electoral threshold. Fico's Smer thus eventually replaced HZDS and started to play a dominant role in the Slovak politics.

We may thus conclude that the first Slovak party system in the 1990s was anchored by the presence of a sizable nationalist force (Mečiar's HZDS) that was opposed by the colorful bloc of liberals, conservatives, and social-democrats, whereas the second system that emerged around the millennium continued the bipolar pattern, but it transformed the nationalist camp (HZDS) into a more standard leftist pole (Smer).[8] With the steady rise of Smer the closure index increased in Slovakia and fragmentation has also declined in the last years.[9] In economic terms, Slovakia lagged behind the Czech Republic in the 1990s, but was soon on the mend. The gap in performance between the two countries significantly decreased and Slovakia eventually joined the Eurozone on January 1, 2009.

The Slovak political system and the form of government to a large extent mirror the Czech ones.[10] Two major differences exist between these two

---

[5] The same year Slovakia joined NATO (five years later than the Czech Republic).

[6] For further details, see Haughton 2014, above note 2, 221–222.

[7] The full title of this party is "Direction-Social Democracy" (*Smer – sociálna demokracia*). However, Slovaks as well as the scholarly literature refers to it just as "Smer" and hence I will stick to the short title.

[8] Zsolt Enyedi and Fernando Casal Bértoa (2014), "Elite and Mass Dynamics: The East Central European Example," paper presented at the OPPR Workshop on "Parties and Democracy in Post-communist Europe" at EUI on September 18–19, 2014, (available at http://whogoverns.eu/elite-and-mass-dynamics-the-east-central-european-example/), at 25.

[9] Zsolt Enyedi and Fernando Casal Bértoa (2015), "Brothers in Arms? Party-blocs and Party System Closure," paper presented at the ECPR Joint Sessions in Warsaw on March 29–April 2, 2015, (available at http://whogoverns.eu/brothers-in-arms-party-blocs-and-party-system-closure/), at 39.

[10] See Ladislav Cabada, Vít Hloušek, and Petr Jurek, *Party Systems in East Central Europe* (Lexington Books 2014), 74–75.

countries. First, despite the fact that the Slovak president is directly elected since 1999,[11] he is slightly weaker than the Czech one. While both of them rule from the castle dominating the respective capital, the "Prague Castle" has definitely a greater stature, which dates back to the First Czechoslovak Republic[12] and perhaps even further in history.[13] Moreover, for the purpose of this book it is critical that the Slovak President has been vested with less powers vis-à-vis the judiciary. He had no say in selecting Slovak judges until 2001 at all since Slovak judges were elected by the legislature.[14] After the creation of the JCSR he formally appoints judges, but it is the JCSR, to which the Slovak President nominates only three out eighteen members, that actually selects the new judges.[15] Similarly, the JCSR elects the President of the Supreme Court and the Slovak President has no discretion whether to appoint the nominee of the JCSR or not, and the court presidents of the lower courts are appointed by the Minister of Justice, not the Slovak President.[16] Finally, the Slovak President, unlike the Czech President, is not the only nominator of Justices of the Constitutional Court. Instead, he must choose from the list of candidates submitted by the National Council. Therefore, the Czech President is far more influential than his Slovak counterpart vis-à-vis the judiciary. Second, the Slovak parliament is unicameral, whereas Czechs opted for bicameralism. The lack of a second chamber, coupled with a weaker president, means that Slovak politics is slightly more majoritarian.[17]

In sum, Slovakian politics shares several similar features with the Czech politics. No Slovak political party was able to win an absolute majority between 1993 and 2010[18] and no coalition has ruled for more than two consecutive terms. Both countries have very similar scores regarding parliamentary fragmentation, party system closure, and

---

[11] Note that the Czech Republic switched from the indirect election of the President by the Parliament to direct elections as well, but only in 2012 which is after the period studied in this book.

[12] See Chapter 5, note 86.

[13] There has always been a strong historical narrative of the Prague Castle, which was the seat of Bohemian kings and under Charles IV and Rudolph II also the seat of the Holy Roman Emperor.

[14] See Section III of this chapter.

[15] See Section II.B and IV of this chapter.

[16] See Section IV of this chapter.

[17] This issue will be addressed in more detail in Chapter 7.

[18] Mečiar's HZDS came close in the 1992 elections, winning 74 seats out of 150 on the National Council (two seats short of an absolute majority). In the 2012 elections, Fico's Direction-Social Democracy became the first party since the breakup of Czechoslovakia to win an absolute majority of seats.

electoral volatility.[19] The Slovak party system is also bipolar and consists of two camps. However, two aspects of this division are specific to Slovakia. First, one camp has been dominated by a large party with others playing minor supportive roles (although the party playing the starring role changed from HZDS in the 1990s to Smer in more recent times), whereas the other camp has been much more of a patchwork of parties.[20] Second, while there has been a stability of blocs and camps, there has been fluidity in terms of the carriers of that message.[21] For these reasons, Slovakia has been considered "stable in its instability"[22] and has achieved, in contrast to the Czech Republic, only a weak level of institutionalization.[23] In addition, cleavages are more complex in Slovakia. From the moment of its independence in 1993, the Slovak party system has been characterized by the presence of two cleavages (centre–periphery and economy) and one structural divide (religion).[24] Finally, Slovakia belongs to the least ideologically polarized countries in the region, while polarization in the Czech Republic is high.[25] These differences will be revisited in more detail in Chapter 7.

B.   Consequences of the Division of Czechoslovakia

The consequences of the split of Czechoslovakia in Slovakia were different from those in the Czech Republic.[26] Slovak political elites did not feel strong attachment to the First Czechoslovak Republic. According to them, the First Czechoslovak Republic was primarily a Czech enterprise. Symbolically, Mečiar deleted October 28 – the most important national holiday in Czechoslovakia and in the Czech Republic, which marks the beginning of an independent Czechoslovak state in 1918 – from the list of national

---

[19] Fernando Casal Bértoa, "Post-Communist Politics: On the Divergence (and/or Convergence) of East and West Government and Opposition" (2013) 48 *Government and Opposition* 398, 402–413, and 417. See also more recent data in Zsolt Enyedi and Fernando Casal Bértoa, "Party System Closure and Openness: Conceptualization, Operationalization and Validation" (2014) 20 *Party Politics* (forthcoming); and Enyedi and Bértoa 2014a, supra note 8.

[20] Haughton 2014, above note 2, 214.

[21] Ibid., 214.

[22] Ibid., 212.

[23] Fernando Casal Bértoa, "Party Systems and Cleavage Structures Revisited: A Sociological Explanation of Party System Institutionalization" (2014) 20 *Party Politics* 16, 18.

[24] Ibid., 26. See also Cabada, Hloušek, and Jurek, above note 10, 92–95.

[25] Bértoa 2013, supra note 19, 409.

[26] For a more detailed analysis of the consequences of the "Velvet Divorce," see Abby Innes, *Czechoslovakia: The Short Goodbye* (Yale University Press 2001).

holidays.[27] In practical terms, this denouncing of the First Czechoslovak Republic had one consequence – there was little incentive to look for institutional inspiration in the democratic period between the two world wars.[28] In contrast to the Czech political leadership, Mečiar also disagreed with many reforms adopted between 1989 and 1992 and showed his antipathy toward Slovaks serving in the organs of the postsplit federal regime.[29]

At the same time, Slovak political leaders showed little interest in "decommunization." They could afford a lenient stance toward ex-communists, because Slovaks took a less dim view of the post-Prague-Spring communist regime and did not call for decommunization of the public sector. It is not possible to discuss here in more detail why Slovaks perceived the communist regime differently from Czechs, but I agree with Nedelsky "that the communist regime had different levels of legitimacy in the Czech and Slovak Republics [at least from the Prague Spring of 1968 onward] and that this has had implications for developments in the post-communist period."[30] More specifically, purges after the 1968 Soviet invasion were less severe in Slovakia, repression was weaker, the Slovak economy flourished in the 1970s and 1980s, and the decimation of the Czech intelligentsia left many vacancies available for Slovaks. The "pressure" in the "cooker" was thus lower in Slovakia and the communist regime was viewed more positively among Slovaks. Due to these factors, the communist regime's elites managed to relegitimize themselves and erode the public interest in "decommunization."[31] For instance, when several influential commentators in the early 1990s raised serious allegations that Mečiar himself

---

[27] See Law No. 241/1993 Z. Z., on National Holidays, Days of Rest, and Memorial Days. October 28 was added to the list of Memorial Days (not to the list of National Holidays) in Slovakia only in 1999, that is, after the end of Mečiar's rule.

[28] One caveat must be added here. As Svák correctly argues, both the 1993 Czech Constitution and the 1992 Slovak Constitution were *in general* based on the 1920 Czechoslovak Constitution, because there was nothing else to build on in either country. See Ján Svák, "Slovenská skúsenosť s optimalizáciou modelu správy súdnictva" in Jan Kysela (ed.) *Hledání optimálního modelu správy soudnictví pro Českou republiku* (Kancelář Senátu 2008) 54, 55.

[29] For instance, while most Justices of the Federal Constitutional Court of the Czech nationality were appointed to the newly established Czech Constitutional Court in 1993, Mečiar did not nominate a single Slovak member of the Federal Constitutional Court to the first Constitutional Court of Slovakia.

[30] Nadya Nedelsky, "Divergent Responses to a Common Past: Transitional Justice in the Czech Republic and Slovakia" (2004) 33 *Theory and Society* 65, 67.

[31] Ibid., 88–94. For further details, see Herbert Kitschelt, Zdenka Mansfeldova, Radoslav Markowski, and Gabor Tóka, *Post-Communist Party Systems: Competition, Representation, and Inter-Party Cooperation* (CUP 1999); and Gil Eyal, *The Origins of Postcommunist Elites: From the Prague Spring to the Breakup of Czechoslovakia* (University of Minnesota Press 2003).

was implicated in cooperation with the State Security Police during the communist era,[32] nothing happened.[33] In sum, the new political elites in Mečiar's milieu, many of whom were the communist era managers and technocrats, had no interest in decommunization and the Slovak people did not demand it either.

The lack of interest in "decommunization" had several effects. First, lustration laws were not enforced in Slovakia after the split.[34] Second, the 1992 Slovak Constitution "undid" one important change adopted by the Czechoslovak Parliament between 1989 and 1992 – it reestablished retention reviews of new judges. Finally, the Ministry of Justice model of court administration was left untouched. As a result, the Slovak judiciary in 1993 looked very much the same as the Slovak judiciary before the Velvet Revolution.

Two more factors must be mentioned here. First, Slovak postsplit leaders could not build on prior experience with an independent statehood. The only example of Slovak political independence prior to the break-up of Czechoslovakia in 1993, the wartime clero-fascist Slovak State (1939–1945), did not serve as a source of inspiration for both ideological and pragmatic reasons.[35] Second, as most federal institutions, including the Federal Supreme Court and the Federal Constitutional Court, had their seats in the Czech part of the federation, Slovak leaders did not have to decide whether to transform them or not. These specifics of transition from the postcommunist federal Czechoslovakia to separate Slovak statehood – antifederal bias, little attachment to the First Czechoslovak Republic, little interest in "decommunization" and resulting institutional changes, the nonexistence of the prior separate Slovak statehood which Slovak leaders could build on, and no need to decide on the fate of federal institutions – each in its own way, influenced the postdivision institutional design of the Slovak judiciary.

As there was no need to transform the Federal Supreme Court, which had its seat in the Czech provinces, there was no need to create a new tier

---

[32] See Pavel Žáček, ""Sachergate": první lustrační aféra", *Paměť a dějiny*, No. 01/2007, at 53; see also Nedelsky 2004, above note 30, at 89–90.

[33] Note that similar allegations would have meant the end of a political career in the Czech Republic.

[34] See Section I.D of this chapter.

[35] However, this does not mean that a study of the wartime Slovak State might not explain certain patterns in the Slovak mode of governance. For a thoughtful discussion of these issues that go beyond this book, see Nadya Nedelsky, "The Wartime Slovak State: A Case Study in the Relationship between Ethnic Nationalism and Authoritarian Patterns of Governance" (2001) 7 *Nations and Nationalism* 215.

of courts. The presplit republican Supreme Court of the Slovak Republic became the top Slovak court after the dissolution of Czechoslovakia and that was it. This also explains why there are no high courts in Slovakia and the Slovak judicial system consists of three tiers only – district courts, regional courts, and the Supreme Court. The Supreme Administrative Court was neither established nor envisaged by the 1992 Slovak Constitution, partly due to the lack of motivation to revive the interwar institutions.

In sum, mental path-dependence with reformed communism in Slovakia has been stronger than in the Czech Republic and Slovak postdivision leaders were less bound by strong historical narratives. As Nedelsky has put it, "Slovaks tended to see the [Czechoslovak] communist regime more favorably and the [Czechoslovak] post-communist regime less favorably, than Czechs did."[36] Due to this peculiar configuration, Slovak postsplit leaders had a significant leeway in structuring the institutions of the new Slovak Republic. As Haughton has argued, "[in the 1990s], the two other components of the triple transition: democratisation and marketisation were subordinated to the process of state-building."[37] Slovakia's exit from federalism was thus different from the exit of the Czech Republic, which relied on the existing Czechoslovak structures and the interwar institutional legacy. Put differently, it was politically less costly to move away from the precommunist institutional arrangements as no one wanted to revive the institutions from the First Czechoslovak Republic. This insight may partly explain why the Judicial Council Euro-model passed so smoothly through the Slovak Parliament, whereas a similar proposal met with strong resistance in the Czech Chamber of Deputies.

C.   The Impact of the EU Accession Process upon Slovak Judicial Reforms

The EU Accession Process had a visible impact on Slovak judicial reforms and no doubt contributed to the introduction of the Judicial Council Euro-model of court administration. From the outset, the European Commission was far tougher on Slovakia than on the Czech Republic. The very first line of the relevant part of the 1997 Commission Report started with the following sentence: "The independence of the judicial

---

[36] Nadya Nedelsky, "Czechoslovakia, and the Czech and Slovak Republics" in Lavinia Stan (ed.), *Transitional Justice in Eastern Europe and the Former Soviet Union: Reckoning with the Communist Past* (Routledge 2008) 37, 50.

[37] Haughton 2014, above note 2, 219.

system in Slovakia is impeded in a number of respects."[38] The criticism of the European Commission was threefold. The European Commission rebuked Slovakia for the election of judges by the legislature, the existence of a "probationary period" for new judges and for the excessive powers of the Minister of Justice.[39]

Regarding the last, the European Commission emphasized that "[t]he Minister for Justice also has the power, which he has already used, to transfer the presidents and vice presidents of judicial districts at his discretion."[40] This line of criticism is puzzling since the Czech Ministers of Justice had the same power vis-à-vis judicial officials and they used it in practice. Yet the Commission's Report on the Czech Republic was silent on this issue. The 1997 Commission Report on Slovakia also mentioned problems with the staffing of courts, the competences of judges, and excessive delays,[41] but the main focus of the report was on judicial independence and court administration.[42]

In the annual Accession Progress Reports that followed, the European Commission repeatedly lambasted Slovakia for not dealing with the aforementioned issues.[43] Even when Slovakia complied with the required standards of judicial independence de facto, the European Commission did not consider it enough. In the 1999 Accession Progress Report the European Commission not only pushed for the transfer of powers from the Minister of Justice to judicial boards,[44] but it also explicitly required Slovakia to amend the Constitution: "The independence of the judiciary has improved de facto but needs to be consolidated de jure, notably through an amendment to the constitution eliminating the probation period for judges and modifying

---

[38] Agenda 2000 – Commission Opinion on Slovakia's Application for Membership of the European Union, DOC/97/20, Brussels, July 15, 1997, at p. 18.

[39] Agenda 2000 – Commission Opinion on Slovakia's Application for Membership of the European Union, DOC/97/20, Brussels, July 15, 1997, at p. 18. Note that all of these three mechanisms exist in several EU/EEC Member States.

[40] Agenda 2000 – Commission Opinion on Slovakia's Application for Membership of the European Union, DOC/97/20, Brussels, July 15, 1997, at p. 18.

[41] Agenda 2000 – Commission Opinion on Slovakia's Application for Membership of the European Union, DOC/97/20, Brussels, July 15, 1997, at pp. 19 and 120.

[42] See Agenda 2000 – Commission Opinion on Slovakia's Application for Membership of the European Union, DOC/97/20, Brussels, July 15, 1997, at pp. 18–19, 23, and 109, and, in particular conclusion of the Agenda 2000 Opinion at p. 126.

[43] See, for example, the 1998 Accession Progress Report on Slovakia, p. 10; or the 1998 Composite Paper which confirmed that one of the main challenges in the field of democracy and the rule of law in Slovakia remained the independence of its judges (cited in the 1999 Accession Progress Report on Slovakia, p. 14).

[44] See the 1999 Accession Progress Report on Slovakia, p. 14.

the nomination and removal procedures."[45] The 2000 Accession Progress Report again emphasized the need to amend the Slovak Constitution and eradicate the "probationary period" for judges. Other important milestones,[46] such as the adoption of the 2000 Law on Judges and Lay Judges or the unsuccessful attempt to dismiss Štefan Harabin from the Presidency of the Supreme Court, were mentioned only in passing.[47]

Once Slovakia adopted the 2001 Constitutional Amendment,[48] the European Commission softened its stance significantly. Two major goals were accomplished – the constitutional amendment abolished the four-year probationary period and established the Judicial Council Euro-model of court administration.[49] The 2000 and 2001 Accession Progress Reports also mentioned widespread corruption within the Slovak judiciary,[50] but failed to address why the powers concerning the court administration should be transferred to the judiciary (via the Euro-model), which was generally perceived as corrupt.

The 2002 and 2003 reports of the European Commission were generally positive. The Commission praised the adoption of the 2002 Law on the Judicial Council and other judicial reforms, such as the installation of "electronic registries" at all ordinary courts.[51] In general, the emphasis of these two reports shifted from issues of judicial independence toward efficiency issues such as reducing the length of proceedings and judicial training. Interestingly, the 2003 report also criticized the secretiveness and leniency of the Slovak disciplinary courts.[52]

---

[45] The 1999 Accession Progress Report on Slovakia, p. 18 (repeated word by word at p. 70).
[46] See the 2000 Accession Progress Report on Slovakia, p. 81: "Certain legal steps were taken to strengthen the independence of the judiciary. However, key parts of the reform, in particular the constitutional amendment with regard to the nomination and probationary system, which were set as a short term priority, have not yet been adopted. Therefore, continued efforts are needed to ensure the independence of the judiciary."
[47] See the 2000 Accession Progress Report on Slovakia, pp. 16–17.
[48] Constitutional Law No. 90/2001 Z. z. that amends the Slovak Constitution (hereinafter only the "2001 Constitutional Amendment").
[49] See the 2001 Accession Progress Report on Slovakia, p. 24: "Important steps were taken to strengthen the independence of the judiciary. In particular, the constitutional amendment abolished the four-year probationary period for judges and provided for setting up a Judicial Council. This amendment now needs to be implemented by primary legislation and at a practical level to guarantee the judiciary's professional impartiality and political neutrality."
[50] See the 2000 Accession Progress Report on Slovakia, p. 17; and the 2001 Accession Progress Report on Slovakia, p. 18.
[51] See the 2002 Accession Progress Report on Slovakia, pp. 22–24; and the 2003 Accession Progress Report on Slovakia, pp. 12–13.
[52] See the 2003 Accession Progress Report on Slovakia, p. 12.

In sum, the impact of the EU Accession Process on Slovak judicial reforms was far more significant and visible than in the Czech Republic. This is not surprising, given the fact that the European Commission adopted much "tougher" stance toward Slovakia and required Slovak leaders to adopt far-reaching institutional changes, including the constitutional amendment. It is clear that the pressure from the European Commission contributed to the introduction of the Judicial Council Euro-model of court adminis-tration in Slovakia.[53] However, it is not entirely clear how significant this contribution was. The main target of the European Commission was the "probationary period" for new judges. A partial transfer of powers from the Ministry of Justice to judicial boards by the 2000 Law on Judges and Lay Judges thus might have satisfied it.[54] Most sources in Slovakia thus agree that "anti-mečiarism" played the more significant role in the debate on the JCSR, whereas the pressure of the European Commission merely legitimized this process.[55] However, the EU argument was still important since Slovak politi-cal elites wanted to prove to the EU that Slovakia is a trustworthy candidate for the integration.

D.   Dealing with the Past within the Slovak Judiciary

In general, Slovaks paid less attention to the reckoning with the past than Czechs.[56] The fate of the lustration law serves as a good example. When the vote on the lustration bill was taken in the Federal Assembly, all mem-bers of Mečiar's HZDS voted against it. Despite Mečiar's objections, the bill was eventually adopted and the 1991 Lustration Law became appli-cable to the entire territory of Czechoslovakia. However, Mečiar and his allies managed to limit the impact of lustration in Slovakia, both before and after the dissolution. Prior to the split, the 1991 Lustration Law "had only a formal effect" in Slovakia.[57] Given the fact that Mečiar won

---

[53]   See Alexander Bröstl, "At the Crossroads on the Way to an Independent Slovak Judiciary" in Jiří Přibáň, Pauline Roberts, and James Young (eds.), *Systems of Justice in Transition: Central European Experiences since 1989* (Ashgate 2003) 141, 147; or Pavol Rohárik, "The Judiciary and Its Transition in Slovakia after 1989" in Jiří Přibáň, Pauline Roberts, and James Young (eds.), *Systems of Justice in Transition: Central European Experiences since 1989* (Ashgate 2003) 213, 217.

[54]   I revisit this issue in Section II.B of this chapter.

[55]   For further details, see Section II.B of this chapter.

[56]   The reasons why the Slovak approach toward dealing with the past has been so different from the Czech approach are complex and go beyond this chapter. For potential explana-tions, see Nedelsky 2004, above note 30.

[57]   Jozef Darski, "Decommunization in Eastern Europe" (1993) 6 *Uncaptive Minds* 73, 78.

the first Slovak elections in 1992, the hostility of the Slovak leadership toward lustration continued. Immediately after the dissolution, Mečiar's government challenged the 1991 Lustration Law before the Slovak Constitutional Court on the ground of its incompatibility with international human rights treaties. When the Slovak Constitutional Court dismissed his petition, Mečiar decided simply not to enforce that law[58] and wait until it expired in 1996.[59]

This story is in stark contrast to the perception of the 1991 Lustration Law in the Czech Republic, where it still applies today and has become a part of national mythology, which makes it virtually untouchable.[60] In other words, "although passage of the 1991 lustration law was a 'Czechoslovak' decision, lustration itself has been largely a Czech pursuit."[61] Nevertheless, I argued in the previous chapter that due to the specific design of the 1991 Lustration Law it had only a marginal impact on the Czech *judiciary*. As a result, the impact of lustration on the Czech and Slovak judiciaries has been similar, despite different attitudes toward lustration as such. It is thus possible to conclude that both in the Czech Republic[62] and in Slovakia[63] the number of judges who resigned or were removed on the ground of lustration was small.

However, the reluctance of Slovak elites to deal with the past has an impact beyond the lustration context. Neither politicians nor the media have been eager to learn about the communist past of the Slovak judiciary. Criticism of individual judges for their wrongdoing during the communist era did not occur either. Slovak judges adopted a "Don't ask, don't tell" policy, the Slovak people accepted it, and Slovak judges, in turn, embraced this acquiescence. That is why we do not even know how many judges from the communist era still sit on the Slovak bench. Given this tacit acceptance of the past, it is not surprising that judging the communist judges has not

---

[58] No Ministry in Slovakia was given authority to issue lustration certificates and so no lustration certificates were issued between 1993 and 1996.

[59] Note that the 1991 Lustration Law was initially adopted only for a period of five years. While in Slovakia it was not renewed, the Czech Parliament prolonged its applicability for another five years in 1996, and in 2001 it was eventually prolonged indefinitely.

[60] The Lustration Law, this time with indefinite application, was upheld by the Czech Constitutional Court in 2001 (Judgment of the Czech Constitutional Court of December 5, 2001, No. Pl. 09/01 *Lustration II*). For a recent analysis of the 1991 Lustration Law, Roman David, *Lustration and Transitional Justice: Personnel Systems in the Czech Republic, Hungary, and Poland* (University of Pennsylvania Press, 2011).

[61] Nadya Nedelsky 2004, above note 30, at 77.

[62] See Chapter 5.

[63] See also Rohárik, above note 53, at 215.

been a significant issue in Slovak politics and that there have not been any calls for further purges within the judiciary.

In sum, as with the Czech situation many of the communist-era judges still sit on the bench in Slovakia and they hold important positions within the judiciary. The precise numbers are not available, but given the "softer" stance of Slovaks toward the communist regime, it is likely that the ratio of communist-era judges in Slovakia is even higher than the relatively high number in the Czech Republic. However, the Slovak postsplit scenario significantly differs from the Czech one, since dealing with the past within the judiciary is not an issue that attracts particular attention in Slovakia.

E.   "Superjudges" and Other Key Actors in Slovak Judicial Politics

In this section I will first briefly introduce the most influential individuals within the judiciary who played an important role in shaping judicial power in Slovakia. I will again focus primarily on "superjudges," that is on professional judges who at some point in their career join the executive power and then return to the judiciary.[64] Sketching the trajectories of these important figures is essential for understanding the key events that took place within the Slovak judiciary between 1993 and 2010. Subsequently, I will identify six constitutional actors and additional formal and informal institutions that have taken or took part in Slovak judicial politics.

Four judges from the 1993–2010 era stand out in Slovakia: Milan Hanzel, Jozef Liščák, Milan Karabín and Štefan Harabin. Milan Hanzel was the first Slovak superjudge. He was a military judge since 1977, became the Minister of Justice in March 1994, after the end of his days as a minister he returned to the military court, and later on became the General Prosecutor. However, he stayed in the office of the Minister of Justice only until December 1994 and hence he could have made only little difference. It was only Jozef Liščák, the second Slovak judge-turned-Minister-of-Justice, who fully exploited his previous experience and a status of a judge. He was serving as a judge of the Regional Court in Banská Bystrica, when he was appointed Minister of Justice by Vladimír Mečiar in 1994. The Slovak judiciary initially put its faith in him, because it believed that he had been a judge before and thus he would represent the interests of the judiciary. Nevertheless, Liščák soon resorted to authoritative personal management, and, he eventually lost the support of judges, who even signed a petition for his resignation. Despite these efforts, he served as Minister of Justice for almost four years, from December 13, 1994 until October 30, 1998. Note that Liščák was not a

[64] For further exposition of the role of "superjudges," see Chapter 5, Section I.E.

"superjudge" according to my definition, as he did not return to the judicial ranks after his term at the Ministry (he became a notary), but he still heavily influenced the Slovak judiciary in the 1990s.

In contrast to Liščák, Štefan Harabin, a most controversial Slovak judge who has divided the Slovak judiciary since the late 1990s, was a true "super-judge" and his story shows how a judge-turned-Minister-of-Justice who returns to judicial ranks from his ministerial position can fully exploit his power and contacts from the Ministry in his favor. Harabin became a judge in 1983 and gradually climbed up within the Slovak judiciary until he reached the Supreme Court in 1991. In 1998 the National Council con-trolled by Mečiar elected Harabin to the position of the President of the Supreme Court of Slovakia, despite opposition from the judicial board of the Supreme Court and the Council of Judges of the Slovak Republic. He held this position until 2003, when his five-year term ended. He ran for another five-year term, but in a fierce battle he eventually lost to Milan Karabin.[65] Thus, he became a regular judge of the Supreme Court again. However, this did not last long. In July 2006 Harabin became Minister of Justice. He held this office until June 2009, when he returned to the Supreme Court. His return was spectacular as he was elected the President of the Supreme Court by the JCSR and at the same time he became the Chairman of the JCSR.

The third key figure within the Slovak judiciary was Milan Karabin. He became a judge of the district court in 1974 and, like most judges in the career model, was subsequently promoted to the regional court and eventu-ally in 1982 to the Supreme Court of Slovakia. In 1996, the National Council elected him to the position of the President of the Supreme Court of Slovakia. He resigned only a year later, in 1997, for health reasons and paved the way for Harabin to the presidency of the Supreme Court. However, his health got better and in 2003 competed against Harabin for the presidency of the Supreme Court, a battle which Karabín eventually won after a protracted election at the newly established Judicial Council of the Slovak Republic.[66] After the end of his five-year term, Karabín ran for the presidency of the Supreme Court again. However, he did not manage to win the nomination at the Judicial Council of the Slovak Republic in May 2009. Instead, it was Harabin who won the nomination a month later and became the President the Supreme Court of Slovakia for the period between 2009 and 2014.[67] Karabín remained on the Supreme Court as a regular judge.

[65] For further details on the 2003 contest between Harabin and Karabín, see Section IV.D of this chapter.
[66] See ibid.
[67] For further details on the 2009 contest between Harabin and Karabín, see ibid.

Importantly, even though the rivalry between Harabin and Karabin was primarily about different visions of the Slovak judiciary, there was also a political side to the story. Harabin allegedly had close ties with Mečiar's HZDS, whereas Karabin was associated with Christian Democrats.[68] This brings us to the constitutional actors and other entities that have played a significant role in the Slovak judicial politics.

As to the constitutional actors involved in judicial politics, the starting line for Slovakia was the same as for the Czech Republic. Historically, the Czechoslovak models of court administration always rested on two main pillars – the Ministry of Justice and the court presidents.[69] The Slovak Parliament buttressed this two-pillar model in 1992 by adopting the Law on the State Administration of Courts.[70] However, in contrast to the Czech Republic, Slovak leaders vested certain personal decisions regarding judges with the National Council, the legislative branch. These three bodies, the Ministry of Justice, judicial officials, and the National Council remained the key institutional players in Slovak judicial politics until 2002. The 2001 Constitutional Amendment introduced a new element into the system, the Judicial Council of the Slovak Republic, and disempowered the National Council in judicial matters. I will discuss this critical juncture in the next section.[71] In this section I will focus primarily on other actors.

Two more constitutional actors, the President of the Slovak Republic and the Slovak Constitutional Court, increasingly intervened in judicial matters. Between 1993 and 2002, the President of the Slovak Republic played no role in staffing the ordinary courts, as all judges were also elected by the National Council.[72] He had no say in selecting the President and Vice

---

[68]   However, recall that not only Harabin (in 1998), but also Karabín (1996) were elected to the office of the President of the Supreme Court of Slovakia by the National Council thanks to the votes of Mečiar's HZDS. Some Slovak sources suggest that it was the Slovak National Party, the coalition partner of Mečiar's HZDS between 1994 and 1998, that, according to the informal coalition agreement, hand-picked the President of the Supreme Court of Slovakia This means that both Harabin and Karabín had to appeal to the Slovak National Party, if they wanted to be elected.

[69]   See Zdeněk Kühn, *The Judiciary in Central and Eastern Europe: Mechanical Jurisprudence in Transformation?* (Brill 2011), in particular at 31–62; and Michal Bobek, "The Administration of Courts in the Czech Republic – In Search of a Constitutional Balance" (2010) 16 *European Public Law* 251.

[70]   Law No. 80/1992 Zb., on the State Administration of Courts.

[71]   See Section II.B of this chapter.

[72]   The explanation why the postsplit Slovak political leaders vested personnel decisions with parliament, but Czech leaders did not is simple. The Czech leaders revived the interwar arrangement from the First Czechoslovak Republic, whereas the Slovak leaders had no incentives to find inspiration in the interwar era, because they considered the First Czechoslovak Republic as primarily a Czech enterprise (see Sections I.A, I.B, and I.D of this chapter). The Slovak leaders thus retained the federal arrangement from the late 1980s and early 1990s.

President of the Supreme Court either. The National Council elected these two judicial officials too. The President of the Slovak Republic had his say only in appointing judges of the Constitutional Court. He appointed all ten constitutional Justices from the basket of twenty candidates nominated by the National Council. Constitutional Justices served only a seven-year term, which was three years shorter than in the Czech Republic. The 2001 Constitutional Amendment strengthened the position of the President of the Slovak Republic, as he was vested with the power to appoint all regular judges as well as judicial officials of the Supreme Court. However, he could not act alone. The JCSR nominated and he affirmed.

The Slovak Constitutional Court was also weaker than its Czech "brother." A shorter term of office for Justices, their election by the legislature, limited jurisdiction over individual constitutional complaints, and strong majorities in the National Council, each in its own way, led to a more deferential constitutional court. The jurisdiction regarding individual constitutional complaints was eventually expanded and Justices' terms extended to twelve years, but the Slovak Constitutional Court never achieved the stature of its Czech counterpart and its involvement in Slovak judicial politics, with one notable exception,[73] was relatively modest.

The power of the abovementioned six constitutional actors, the Ministry of Justice, judicial officials, the National Council, the JCSR, the President of the Slovak Republic, and the Constitutional Court, emanates directly from the Slovak Constitution. However, there are other formal and informal actors that exercised significant influence within the Slovak judiciary. These actors include judicial boards, the Council of Judges of the Slovak Republic, the Association of Slovak Judges, and other professional organizations of judges.

Judicial boards (*sudcovské rady*) were established at all Slovak courts from the regional court level above in 1995.[74] They have a statutory basis and comment primarily on the promotion or temporary assignment of judges, on the selection of court presidents and vice presidents, on the division of the case load and the system of case assignment, and on the division of the court's budget.[75] While the competences of judicial boards in Slovakia were broader than in the Czech Republic, Slovak judicial boards still served only as advisory bodies and their recommendations were not binding on court presidents. As in the Czech Republic, the real role of these boards in the administration of a particular court thus depended on the relationship between the judicial board and the court

---

[73] This exception was the judgment that abolished the Special Court (Judgment of the Slovak Constitutional Court of May 20, 2009, No. Pl. 17/08-238).

[74] See Art. 58 in the 1991 Law on Courts and Judges, as amended by Law No. 307/1995 Z.z.

[75] See Art. 58(8) of the 1991 Law on Courts and Judges, as amended by Law No. 307/1995 Z.z.

president. If the court president was a strong personality, the role of the judicial board diminished and vice versa. According to Rohárik, "court presidents ... not only failed to take many recommendations of judicial [boards] into account, without giving any reason, but they even failed to consult the [boards] as prescribed by law."[76] In sum, the powers of judicial boards were narrow and limited to a particular court.

The 1995 judicial reform also introduced another body, the Council of Judges of the Slovak Republic (*Rada sudcov Slovenskej republiky*),[77] which had no equivalent in the Czech Republic. The Council consisted of chairs and vice-chairs of judicial boards and thus operated as an umbrella entity for judicial boards at individual courts. Its task was to coordinate the activity of judicial boards, to comment on the budget of the judiciary and on the laws affecting judges, and to provide an opinion on candidates for promotion to the Supreme Court and on candidates for positions at international courts.[78] From the conceptual point of view, it was a true self-governing body composed exclusively of judges. Therefore, it should not be confused with a nationwide judicial *council* and cannot be considered even as a precursor to the JCSR.[79] Nor it was an equivalent to the informal "kolegium of presidents of regional courts" that operated in the Czech Republic in the same period.[80] As mentioned earlier, judicial boards were advisory bodies to the court presidents and all the representatives of judicial boards were regular judges. This means that the representatives of judicial boards in the Council of Judges of the Slovak Republic were also regular judges, and not court presidents. The only court president sitting on the Council of Judges of the Slovak Republic was the President of Supreme Court of Slovakia, who acted as a chair of this Council. Hence, in a sense the Council of Judges of the Slovak Republic was a counterweight to court presidents rather than the guardian of the interests of court presidents. However, in practice, the Council of Judges of the Slovak Republic, despite its broad consultative powers, also had only a limited impact on the ground, as the President of the Supreme Court, Štefan Harabin, repeatedly ignored its recommendations.[81]

---

[76] Rohárik, above note 53, at 216. Rohárik speaks of the situation in the 1990s and in the first years of twenty-first century, but his description captures the practice between 2003 and 2010 too.

[77] See a new Art. 58a in the 1991 Law on Courts and Judges introduced by Law No. 307/1995 Z.z.

[78] See Art. 58a(4) of the 1991 Law on Courts and Judges, as amended by Law No. 307/1995 Z.z.

[79] This confusion was widespread in Slovakia. See Svák, above note 28, at 56.

[80] See Chapter 5, Section I.E.

[81] For further details, see Section III of this chapter.

The Association of Slovak Judges (*Združenie sudcov Slovenska*) is the oldest and the largest judicial union in Slovakia. It was established in 1990 and played an important role especially in the 1990s, when the Slovak judiciary was united against Mečiar's interferences. According to Rohárik, the Association of Slovak Judges was far more influential than the Czech Union of Judges in the 1990s.[82] At that time, it represented the majority of Slovak judges.[83] However, the return of Štefan Harabin to the position of President of the Supreme Court in 2009 led to a split within the Association of Slovak Judges. Members of the Association of Slovak Judges who criticized Harabin's return did not achieve a majority in the Association and decided to leave. As a result, membership of the Association of Slovak Judges dropped to 350,[84] which amounts to approximately one quarter of the Slovak judiciary. What is more, this split took a West versus the East shape. Judges from the West left, whereas judges from the East stayed and consolidated their position. Since most judges from West Slovakia left, including several former chairmen and vice-chairmen of the Association, the seat of the Association moved from Bratislava, the capital located in Western Slovakia, to Košice, a city close to eastern border. Tellingly, the meeting of the Association in April 2011 was attended by only fifty judges, of whom only one member came from Bratislava and one from Banská Bystrica, a regional city in Western Slovakia.[85]

Some of the former members of the Association from Western Slovakia established a new organization called "For Transparent Judiciary" (*Za otvorenú justíciu*) and became vocal critics of Harabin's methods. In addition to the Association of Slovak Judges and the "For Transparent Judiciary" movement, there is one more professional organization of judges in Slovakia – the Slovak Union of Independent Judiciary (*Slovenská únia nezávislého súdnictva*), which is far less visible than the other two associations. It was established in 2000 and it allegedly consists of approximately 100 judges.[86]

---

[82] Rohárik, above note 53, at 228.

[83] Some sources claim that even 70% of Slovak judges used to be members of this Association. See, for example, Lukasz Bojarski and Werner Stemker Köster, *The Slovak Judiciary: Its Current State and Challenges* (Open Society Fund 2011) 14.

[84] Günter Woratsch, *Zpráva o stavu slovenské justice – fenomén Štefan Harabin*, Pecs, April 23, 2011.

[85] Ibid.

[86] Bojarski and Köster, above note 83, at 15.

II.   Court Administration after the Split (1993–2010): The Road from the Ministry of Justice Model to the Judicial Council Euro-model

Section I sketched the background against which the Slovak courts operate and addressed major events within the postsplit history of the Slovak Republic. This section focuses in more detail on judicial reforms adopted between 1993 and 2010 and on their repercussions. As the Judicial Council of the Slovak Republic started to operate fully only in 2003, this part is divided into periods covering the years 1993–2002 and 2003–2010. The aim of this part is to explain why the changes in the Slovak judicial system occurred, which "political vectors" and individuals were behind them, and what these changes meant for the Slovak judiciary.

A.   *Ministry of Justice Model Retained (1993–2002)*

Slovakia decided to retain the "Ministry of Justice" model of court administration in 1993.[87] The only significant "novelty" was the re-introduction of retention reviews for new judges through the concept of "judges on probation." In fact, the 1992 Slovak Constitution introduced even fewer changes concerning the judicial system than the 1993 Czech Constitution. In contrast to the Czechs, the Slovaks did not change the mode of selection of judges, did not create a new tier of courts (high courts) and did not abolish the military courts. Slovakia retained the election of judges by the National Council (the legislature) as well as the three-tier system of the judiciary. The three major statutes governing the judiciary, the 1991 Law on Courts and Judges, the 1991 Disciplinary Code for Judges and the 1992 Law on State Administration of Courts, were left almost untouched. The "defederalization" amendments to these statutes merely reflected the changes brought about the Slovak Constitution and deleted all references to federal judicial bodies.

The years between 1993 and 1998 under Mečiar's rule were years of state-building.[88] With a certain degree of simplification, Slovakia in 1993 was in similar situation to the new-born Czechoslovakia in 1918 and faced very similar problems. Most importantly, the Slovak judiciary suffered from a severe shortage of judges. The reasons behind the departure

---

[87]   For further details, see Arts. 7–16 of Law No. 80/1992 Zb., on the State Administration of Courts; and Rohárik, above note 53, at 217–220.

[88]   See Haughton 2014, above note 2, 219.

of many judges from the Slovak judiciary in the early 1990s were roughly the same as in the Czech Republic,[89] but the situation was much worse in Slovakia. First, another exodus of Slovak judges took place in the mid-1990s, when many judges of the district courts as well as regional courts and the Supreme Court who were dissatisfied with their material conditions left the judiciary.[90] Second, further seats within the judiciary became empty in 1997, when Mečiar's government decided to "improve effective access of citizens to judicial protection by reducing the physical distance between their place of residence and court building"[91] and created five new regional courts and thirteen new district courts virtually overnight. Due to these three factors, the Slovak judiciary was severely understaffed during the whole of 1990s. As a result, pupillage of judicial candidates had to be shortened[92] and "wild promotion" flourished.[93]

No serious attempt to revise the existing "Ministry of Justice" model took place between 1993 and 1998. The judiciary was run according to standards laid down in the 1992 Law on State Administration of Courts,[94] which granted the key powers to the Minister of Justice and court presidents. The Slovak legislature established judicial boards in 1995, which is seven years earlier than the Czech Republic, but these boards played a marginal role.[95] The Ministry of Justice was headed by Josef Liščák who "acted as though the entire Slovak judiciary was one big court and he its president."[96] Liščák had a tense relationship with some judges and he became famous by referring to young judges who criticized his methods as "buggers and frats stupid as cues" ("*smradov a frackov blbých ako tágo*").[97] This dissatisfaction with his performance came to a head in April 1997 when the Association of Slovak Judges and more than 100 judges from all over Slovakia signed a petition for his resignation. But Liščák refused to resign and remained in office until the 1998 parliamentary elections.

---

[89] See Chapter 5.
[90] For further details, see Bröstl, above note 53, at 145 (who claims that twenty-two regional court judges and seven Supreme Court judges left the judiciary in the mid-1990s).
[91] Rohárik, above note 53, at 217.
[92] Bröstl, above note 53, a 145.
[93] See Rohárik, above note 53, at 217. This period of "wild promotion" of judges is discussed in more detail later; see notes 202–205.
[94] For further details, see Arts. 7–16 of Law No. 80/1992 Zb., on the State Administration of Courts; and Rohárik, above note 53, at 217–220.
[95] See Section I.E.
[96] Rohárik, above note 53, at 216. See also Section I.E.
[97] *Minister spravodlivosti J. Liščák označil sudcov za "smradov" a "frackov blbých ako tágo,"* Sme.sk, April 16, 1997, available at www.sme.sk/c/2071456/minister-spravodlivosti-j-liscak-oznacil-sudcov-za-smradov-a-frackov-blbych-ako-tago.html.

During the Mečíar's regime, the executive repeatedly interfered with the Slovak judiciary. In 1997, Mečiar's cabinet refused to recommend twelve judges of the first group of "judges on probation" to the National Council for their indefinite reelection. The Government did not give any reasons for this move and simply returned the proposals for the reelection of those twelve judges to the state court administration and judicial boards for reconsideration.[98] Mečiar's period was also an era of "wild promotion" of judges, which allowed his cabinet to install its own people at the top of the Slovak judicial hierarchy.[99] Josef Liščák also dismissed several court presidents[100] and openly criticized some of the young judges.[101]

The tension between the Minister of Justice and top judicial officials continued after the 1998 elections with one difference – the key players switched sides. The centrist coalition replaced Mečiar's coalition in the autumn of 1998, but the incumbent National Council controlled by Mečiar managed to elect Mečiar's nominee – Štefan Harabin – to the post of the President of the Supreme Court shortly beforehand (in February 1998). Harabin heavily criticized reforms proposed by the new centrist government and some judges started to perceive him as a political counterweight to the Minister of Justice, whereas other judges – including the then influential Association of Slovak Judges – supported the reforms. The division within the judiciary gradually became wider and this rupture within the judicial community has never closed.[102]

The new centrist government eventually prepared the 2001 Constitutional Amendment that, among other things, created the JCSR and introduced the Judicial Council Euro-model of court administration in Slovakia. The JCSR as well as the motivation behind its adoption will be discussed in the following section. In this section I will focus on two events that took place between 1998 and 2002 and were to a large extent unrelated to the process of establishing the JCSR.

First, according to the polls conducted in the late 1990s the Slovak judiciary suffered from endemic corruption. The poll by the World Bank conducted in 2000 confirmed this finding. According to the respondents of this poll, "courts and prosecutors rank[ed] second in the list of public institutions with widespread corruption and seventh in the list of

---

98 Rohárik, above note 53, at 216.
99 Ibid., at 217. For further details, see Section III.D of this chapter
100 *Minister Liščák zavádza a nemá dôveru sudcov*, Sme.sk, May 5, 1997, available at www.sme .sk/c/2073444/minister-liscak-zavadza-a-nema-doveru-sudcov.html.
101 See above note 97.
102 For further details, see Rohárik, above note 53, at 218–219.

institutions to whose officials the respondents claimed to have given a bribe."[103] These findings led to the adoption of anticorruption measures that had the following impact on the court administration. On the personal level, the Minister of Justice dismissed several judicial officials for manipulation of case assignment.[104] On the institutional level, the Slovak Government prepared the project of the so-called electronic registries that were supposed to ensure the random assignment of cases by software at all ordinary courts.[105]

Second, the National Council passed a new Law on Judges and Lay Judges in 2000. This statute left the overall structure of the court administration intact, but introduced several important changes. It laid down the rights and responsibilities of judges as well as rules concerning the commencement and termination of judicial office, the disciplinary liability of judges, the remuneration of judges, and their entitlements after termination of judicial office. The most important innovations were as follows. It introduced competitive selection procedures for the initial recruitment and subsequent promotion of judges, dealt with certain shortcomings in the rules governing disciplinary motions, and enhanced the powers of judicial boards (vis-à-vis court presidents) in the appointment and promotion of judges. It also imposed new restrictions on judges. It established regular performance evaluation of all judges, prohibited their membership of political parties, and required judges to submit annual written declarations regarding their activities other than judging as well as annual financial declaration.[106]

One more caveat must be added here. It is a cliché to say that tiny details sometimes matter. But the "geographic separation of powers" or the lack thereof is a prime example of such small details. In the Czech Republic, both top ordinary courts, the Supreme Court and the Supreme Administrative Court, have their seats in Brno, which is located 200 km from Prague, the seat of the Parliament and all ministries. In contrast, the Supreme Court of Slovakia[107] shares the very same building with the Ministry of Justice on Župné námestie no. 13 in the center of Bratislava. In sum, the geographic

---

[103] Rohárik, above note 53, at 226 (referring to the 2000 World Bank Report).
[104] For further details, see Rohárik, above note 53, at 226.
[105] For further details, see notes 275–279 in this chapter.
[106] All of these mechanisms will be discussed in more detail later. For a succinct summary of the 2000 Law on Judges and Lay Judges, see Rohárik, above note 53, at 221–222.
[107] Note that there is no "Supreme Administrative Court" in Slovakia. Judicial review of administrative acts is carried out within the ordinary courts by specialized chambers dealing with administrative law.

separation of powers in Slovakia is zero, whereas the geographic separation of powers in the Czech Republic is 200 km. These 200 km can make a world of difference. For instance, when the then Minister of Justice, Štefan Harabin, was appointed President of the Slovak Supreme Court in 2009, he literally took the elevator and entered his new office.

B.   The Judicial Council Euro-model Takes Over (2003–2010)

The Judicial Council of the Slovak Republic (JCSR) was introduced into Slovakia by the 2001 Constitutional Amendment and started to operate fully in 2003.[108] This section briefly discusses how the Judicial Council Euro-model of court administration came into being in Slovakia, then it analyzes the composition and powers of the JCSR, and finally it focuses on the most serious problems that emerged during the operation of the JCSR.

The 2001 Constitutional Amendment that erected the judicial council model was submitted to the National Council by the group of MPs. Peter Kresák, an MP for SOP (Party for Civic Understanding) which was a member of a governing coalition, acted as a rapporteur for this constitutional bill. The debate in the National Council on the JCSR was intensive, but the 2001 Constitutional Amendment was eventually adopted by a broad majority. The dividing line between those who were in favor and those against was clear. It followed the bipolar structure of the Slovak political scene of that time.[109] All MPs from an anti-Mečiar broad-based coalition of liberals, conservatives, and social democrats under the leadership of Mikuláš Dzurinda voted in favor of the constitutional bill. All members of HZDS and SNS (Slovak National Party), coalition partner in Mečiar's government in 1992–1998, voted against the bill. The final vote on the Constitutional Bill on February 23, 2001 was as follows: ninety MPs for, fifty-seven MPs against, one MP abstained and two MPs were missing. Few months later, Law on the JCSR was passed as well.[110]

Two major factors contributed to the adoption of the JCSR – pressure from the European Commission in Accession Progress Reports and the

---

[108]   Note that first members of the JCSR were appointed or elected between May and September 2002, but it took a while before the JCSR was fully operational. Moreover, the chairman of the JCSR (the President of the Supreme Court) was appointed by the President of the Slovak Republic only in 2003; see Section IV.D of this chapter. Note also that the National Council passed the Law No. 185/2002 Z. z., on the Judicial Council of the Slovak Republic (hereinafter the "2002 Law on the JCSR") only in April 2002.

[109]   See Section I.A of this chapter.

[110]   This time the vote was very much in favor of the bill: 113 MPs for, no MP against, 1 MP abstained, 1 MP did not vote, and 15 MPs were absent.

so-called anti-Mečiarism. The former factor was discussed in Section I.C of this chapter. The latter factor requires further explanation. The period of "mečiarism" refers to years between 1992 and 1998,[111] when Vladimír Mečiar ruled Slovakia with his HZDS.[112] Mečiar was known for his autocratic style of governing the country,[113] and after the broad coalition won the 1998 elections it wanted to ensure that "Mečiar-style interferences"[114] with the judiciary could not be repeated. In order to prevent these interferences, the centrist coalition founded a new institution – the JCSR.

Slovakia thus perhaps had a greater need for some institutional restructuring of the judiciary than the Czech Republic. However, the 2001 constitutional reform did not result from the collapse of the previous model of court administration. Nor was it a well-prepared institutional change resulting from pressure from scholars and policy-makers. It was a quick political decision influenced by both supranational and domestic actors. Most sources agree that "anti-mečiarism" played the more significant role, whereas the pressure of the European Commission merely legitimized this process.[115] Some authors even claim that the creation of the JCSR was an "oversensitive reaction to the so-called 'mečiarism.'"[116] This is also in line with the prevailing view of political scientists on Slovakia who suggest that the critical 1998 election and the years that followed were first and foremost a battle to remove an illiberal government from power and "it is best to see the EU here as a reinforcement agent, entrenching the ... divides [between the two Slovak political camps] and giving an extra incentive to the anti-Mečiar forces to coalesce."[117]

The introduction of the JCSR was also hastily done. There was no political discussion. There was no consultation with experts. The centrist coalition presented the Judicial Council Euro-model as the "right" solution that should eradicate the vices of the Ministry of Justice model of court administration. It was supposed to enhance judicial independence, insulate the

---

[111] Note that some authors use the term "Mečiarism" in a more narrow sense to refer only to the years 1994–1998. See Svák, above note 28, at 54.

[112] See Section I.A of Chapter 5.

[113] See Section I.A of this chapter.

[114] These interferences included refusal to renominate some probationary judges after the expiration of their probation period, dismissals of court presidents, and wild promotion of judges with a short experience on the bench to the regional courts and to the Supreme Court. For further details, see Section II.A and Section III.D of this chapter.

[115] Interviews with politicians and judges who promoted the creation of JCSR (on file with author).

[116] Svák, above note 28.

[117] Haughton 2014, above note 2, 221.

judiciary from the political tumult, and improve the overall performance of judges.[118] This lack of deliberation has haunted the JCSR ever since. Several constitutional issues soon arose. What is the function of the JCSR? How does the JCSR fit into the existing paradigm of the Slovak separation of powers? Is the JCSR part of any of the three classical powers – the legislative, the executive, or the judicial – or is it a *sui generis* organ such as the National Bank? Neither the explanatory memorandum to the 2001 Constitutional Amendment nor the scholarly writings of that time provided answers to these questions. The prevailing attitude was that the JCSR was simply a "good" thing and the abovementioned issues could be figured out later.[119]

The Slovak Constitution stipulated that the JCSR was supposed to consist of eighteen members: the President of the Supreme Court who acted as chairman of the JCSR,[120] eight judges elected by the judiciary,[121] three members elected by the National Council of the Slovak Republic (the legislature), three members appointed by the President of the Slovak Republic, and three members appointed by the Government of the Slovak Republic.[122] All members of the JCSR serve a five-year term which is renewable only once.[123] It is not entirely clear why Slovakia opted for this composition. According to Svák, Slovakia wanted to meet a minimum standard set by the Council of Europe that asserts that judges should not be in the minority on the judicial council – that is why half of the members of the JCSR are judges.[124] The plan was that nine judges on the JCSR would be the President of the Supreme Court and eight judges representing eight

---

[118] See Bröstl, above note 53, at 147.
[119] Even the Constitutional Court of the Slovak Republic has struggled to classify the JCSR. In some rulings it held that the JCSR is a constitutional organ sui generis (Decision of the Constitutional Court of the Slovak Republic No. I. ÚS 62/06 of 1 March 2006; Decision of the Constitutional Court of the Slovak Republic No. I. ÚS 162/09 of 24 June 2009; and Judgment of the Constitutional Court of the Slovak Republic No. II. ÚS 5/03 of 19 February 2003. For more details on these issues, see ÚS 29/2011 of 13 December 2012), while in others it opined that it is a constitutional organ of the judicial power (Judgment of the Constitutional Court of the Slovak Republic No. Pl. ÚS 10/05 of 21 April 2010; and Judgment of the Constitutional Court of the Slovak Republic No. II. ÚS 79/04 of 21 October 2004). See also Svák, above note 28, at 55–56.
[120] Note that this rule was changed by the Constitutional Amendment No. 161/2014 Z.z., which stipulates that the chairman of the JCSR shall be elected by the JCSR from among its members and that a court president cannot be a chairman of the JCSR. However, this constitutional amendment was adopted only in 2014 and hence it does not affect the period studied in this book.
[121] Since 2014 there are nine judges elected by the judiciary (this results from the Constitutional Amendment No. 161/2014 discussed in the previous note).
[122] Art. 141a(1) of the Slovak Constitution.
[123] Art. 141a(2) of the Slovak Constitution.
[124] For further details, see Svák, above note 28, at 57.

circuits of regional courts, and the remaining nine members would be nonjudges picked by other branches of the Government.[125]

That was the plan. However, the actual composition of the JCSR has from the outset been very different, because the 2001 Constitutional Amendment did not explicitly stipulate the precise number of judges and nonjudges in the JCSR or their ratio. Due to this omission, all nominating organs (i.e., not only the judiciary) could nominate judges to the JCSR.[126] This happened in practice and judges eventually had a majority in the "first" JCSR (2002–2007) as well as in the "second" JCSR (2008–2013). The "first" JCSR was composed of twelve judges and six nonjudges and the "second" JCSR consisted of sixteen judges and two nonjudges, because on both occasions certain "non-judicial" nominators chose judges as their candidates and nominated them to the JCSR.

This begs the question why did the political branches chose judges if they did not have to? There are several explanations for this phenomenon. Some politicians believed that only judges truly understand the mechanisms within the judiciary and the judicial politics, some politicians thought that to counterweight the judges elected within the judiciary they must nominate "their" own judges, some politicians wanted to please particular judges with the expectation of return favors in future, and sometimes judges themselves informally approached the politicians and offered to serve on the JCSR.[127] Here it is important to stress that Slovakia's legal milieu is very small and everybody knows everybody.[128] Especially "super-judges" like Štefan Harabin, who traveled across branches,[129] brought the lists of their protégés with themselves. In addition, Robert Fico, the Slovak Prime Minister in 2006–2010 is a lawyer by profession, served as the Agent of the Slovak Government before the European Court of Human Rights in 1994–2000, and has taught at the Bratislava Law School. Hence, Fico has maintained his own contacts within the Slovak legal milieu.

In addition, the electoral districts for judicial candidates eventually did not correspond to the circuits of regional courts. Instead, there was one nationwide electoral district for the entire period between 2003 and 2010.[130] As a result, some circuits were not represented at all in the JCSR, whereas other circuits had more than one representative. What is more, several judges of

---

[125] For further details, see ibid.
[126] According to Svák, this was the critical mistake of the 2001 Constitutional Amendment. See ibid.
[127] Interview with a Judge of the Supreme Court of Slovakia from April 23, 2015.
[128] I revisit this point in Chapter 7, Section IV.
[129] On Slovak "superjudges," see Section I.E of this chapter.
[130] This changed only in 2010.

lower courts appointed to the JCSR were promoted to the Supreme Court during their term at the JCSR and, thus, the lower courts became disproportionally unrepresented on the JCSR. Last but not least, many judges sitting on the "first" JCSR (2002–2007) as well the "second" were in fact former or current judicial officials (i.e., court presidents and vice presidents) and not regular judges. In sum, the JCSR turned out to be a very different body from the organ envisaged by its creators. This development also shows how important it is to decide who selects judicial members of the judicial council and how the electoral law to the judicial council is designed.[131]

The JCSR has broad powers particularly in matters regarding a career of individual judges, including the selection of judges, promotion of judges, disciplining of judges, and appointment and dismissal of judicial officials.[132] In addition to these "personal competences," it also oversees training judges, providing advisory opinions on the budget allocated to the judiciary as a whole, and appointing members of the disciplinary panels. The JCSR can also comment on bills affecting the judiciary and influence the education of judges.[133] Most of the aforementioned mechanisms will be discussed in more detail later. Here it suffices to say that the JCSR has the final word in selecting and promoting judges. This means that no candidate can be appointed a judge without the consent of the JCSR and no judge can be promoted without its approval. The JCSR's role is different in the disciplining of judges and the appointment and dismissal of judicial officials, because it does not directly decide these issues. The Disciplinary Court decides on the former and the Minister of Justice on the latter. But the JCSR can still significantly influence the result of disciplinary motions, since it decides on the composition of disciplinary panels and can act as a disciplinary prosecutor. The JCSR's role in the staffing of the posts of court presidents and vice presidents is also far from marginal, as it has an advisory role in the appointment procedure and can initiate the dismissal of a judicial official. As Bröstl put it, the JCSR reminds one of a "Southern European model" of judicial council.[134]

---

[131] The mode of selection of judicial members had great consequences also on the operation of the Hungarian judicial council (before Orbán's 2011 judicial reform) – see Béla Pokol, "Judicial Power and Democratization in Eastern Europe" in *Proceedings of the Conference Europeanisation and Democratisation: The Southern European Experience and the Perspective for the New Member States of the Enlarged Europe* (2005) 165, 188–189.

[132] Art. 141a(4) of the Slovak Constitution.

[133] For a more detailed list of competences of the JCSR, see Bröstl, above note 53, at 147. See also Rohárik, above note 53, at 222–223.

[134] Bröstl, above note 53, at 147. Note I rejected the labels "Southern European model" and "Northern European model" as unhelpful and misleading; see Chapter 3.

Now I can return to the vexing issues that arose after the creation of the JCSR. The first issue is what the JCSR actually *is*. There is no clear answer to that question. The Constitutional Court has avoided this issue so far.[135] Most Slovak judges still do not see the difference between judicial boards[136] on the one hand and the JCSR on the other, and they think of the JCSR as an organ of self-government of the judiciary.[137] Members of the JCSR no longer hold this opinion – according to them the JCSR is a constitutional organ that is the source of the legitimacy of the judiciary. Among Slovak scholars, only Svák grappled with this issue in more detail. He agrees with the view of members of the JCSR. According to him, the JCSR is neither an organ of judicial self-government nor the highest organ representing the judiciary, but a source of the legitimacy of a judge, and he sees the JCSR as a consequence of a shift from the perception of a judge as a "civil servant" to the perception of a judge as a person finding law and justice.[138] He explicitly criticizes the de facto departure from the parity of judges and nonjudges on the JCSR, as the legitimacy of judges then stems from the judicial power itself, and not from the people (represented by the legislature) and from the political power (represented by the President and the Government).[139]

However, far more problems popped up during the functioning of the JCSR. Most importantly, the President of the Supreme Court who chairs the JCSR became an omnipotent figure under Harabin's presidency.[140] Scholars and public officials also accused the JCSR of *per rollam* voting,[141] secretiveness, holding its meetings in awkward locations that dissuaded the public and journalists from attending them, and a lack of transparency.[142]

---

[135] See Judgments of the Slovak Constitutional Court No. II. ÚS 5/03 of February 19, 2003; and No III. ÚS 79/04 of October 21, 2004; and Decisions of the Slovak Constitutional Court No. II. ÚS 258/03 of December 17, 2003; No. II. ÚS 119/04 of May 5, 2004; and No. IV. ÚS 162/05 of June 1, 2005.

[136] On the nature and competences of judicial boards in Slovakia, see Section I.E.

[137] *Cf.* Svák, above note 28, at 55 (who argues that inserting the JCSR within the part of the Slovak Constitution that deals with the Judicial Branch is in fact *the least* persuasive).

[138] Svák, above note 28, at 56.

[139] Ibid., at 57–58.

[140] One may borrow Rohárik's words (that were originally employed to describe the term of Josef Liščák, the Minister of Justice in the mid-1990s; see above note 96) and say that Harabin "acted as though the entire Slovak judiciary was one big court and he its president."

[141] Voting done by the so called "per rollam" (by letter) means that it is a voting without calling a meeting (e.g., by correspondence), which meant that nobody could attend the JCSR's meetings.

[142] See, for example, Jana Dubovcová, "Umožňuje súčasný stav súdnictva zneužívanie disciplinárneho konania voči sudcom, zneužívanie výberových konaní a dáva výkonnej moci

Others pointed to the dual role of the JCSR in the disciplining of judges, where the JCSR serves as a disciplinary prosecutor and at the same time decides on the composition of disciplinary panels. Last but not least, a collective action problem emerged in the JCSR's decision-making on the promotion of judges, because the JCSR simply does not have enough information to decide whether the transfer of a judge to another district or regional court will have a positive effect on the administration of justice. Svák put it aptly: "It is not clear whether the JCSR is an organ that 'works' or an organ that 'chats.'"[143]

Despite the growing criticism of the functioning of the JCSR, none of these problems were dealt with until 2010. On the contrary, Štefan Harabin attempted to increase the powers of the JCSR during his term as Minister of Justice. With the benefit of hindsight, we know that he did so with the prospect of becoming the President of the Supreme Court and the chairman of the JCSR. Harabin's proposal included the transfer of the power to appoint court presidents and vice presidents from the Ministry of Justice to the JCSR, eliminating the role of the Minister of Justice in disciplining judges, the transfer of further competences concerning judicial training to the JCSR, and transfer of the power to suspend judges of district and regional court judges to the President of the Supreme Court. This bill, which would have made the President of the Supreme Court a ruler of the Slovak judiciary with unlimited powers, eventually failed.[144]

III.   Mechanisms of Judicial Accountability from 1993 to 2002

This section first briefly addresses contingent circumstances that might have influenced the effectiveness of mechanisms of judicial accountability. Then it identifies mechanisms of judicial accountability that were used between 1993 and 2010, explains what the law[145] said about those mechanisms and analyzes how these mechanisms operated in practice.

---

oprávnenie zasiahnuť do súdnej moci?" in Transparency International Slovensko (ed.), *Výzvy slovenského súdnictva a možnosti zlepšenia existujúceho stavu* (2010) 50, 53–56; Bojarski and Köster, above note 83, at 94 and 107–109; or Woratsch, above note 84.

[143]   Svák, above note 28, at 61.

[144]   Ministerstvo chce opäť posilniť Najvyšší súd a Súdnu radu, *Sme*, May 19, 2010 [www.sme .sk/c/5383676/ministerstvo-chce-opat-posilnit-najvyssi-sud-a-sudnu-radu.html].

[145]   The term "law" is understood broadly so as to encompass the Constitution, statutes, as well legal norms of lower force.

A. Contingent Circumstances

The same four categories of contingent circumstances that I addressed in the chapter on the Czech Republic will be discussed here: (1) the recruitment and selection of judges, (2) transparency mechanisms, (3) appeals and quasi-appellate mechanisms, and (4) the training of judges. Due to space constraints, only the most important aspects of these mechanisms will be discussed.

Regarding the *recruitment and selection* of judges, the Slovak politicians decided not to follow the principles of the federal reform of 1991 and reintroduced the election of judges. New Slovak judges were elected by the National Council (the legislature) upon nomination by the Government.[146] Moreover, all new judges were initially elected for only four years and after this period they faced reelection. If they were reelected, they became judges for an indefinite period.[147] Other than that, Slovaks kept the 1991 Law on Courts and Judges from the federal era that laid down additional criteria for the judicial offices, which were already described in the chapter on the Czech Republic. All Slovaks judges also, at least in theory, had to provide a negative lustration certificate as defined by the Large Lustration Law.[148] Nevertheless, the Large Lustration Law had another trajectory in Slovakia. Lustration was detested by the post-split Slovak political leadership, which decided not to enforce the Large Lustration Law until it expired in 1996.[149]

The postsplit system of "judges on probation," which loosely reminds one of the German concept of "Richter auf probe,"[150] caused several problems in the mid-1990s and came under close scrutiny from the European Commission during the accession process.[151] Due to pressure from both domestic circles and the EU agencies, the National Council eventually passed a constitutional amendment in 2001 that, besides introducing the JCSR, also revamped the mode of recruitment and selection of judges. Under the revised Slovak Constitution judges are no longer elected by the legislature to a probationary period of four years, but appointed by the President of the Slovak Republic upon the nomination of the JCSR for an

---

[146] Art. 145(1) of the 1992 Slovak Constitution.
[147] Art. 145(1) of the 1992 Slovak Constitution.
[148] For further information on the applicability of the Large Lustration Law to judges, see Section I.C of this chapter and Chapter 4.
[149] For details, see Section I.C. of this chapter.
[150] On the concept of "Richter auf probe," see Chapter 2, Section I.A.
[151] See Section I.D of this chapter.

indefinite period.[152] The 2001 Constitutional Amendment also introduced a minimum age requirement of thirty years.[153] This constitutional arrangement has remained unchanged until today.

The key question was again who de facto selected new judges in Slovakia. Until the 2001 Constitutional Amendment Slovak judges were appointed formally by the National Council upon nomination from the Government, but in fact two other players dominated this selection process – the Minister of Justice and court presidents. Thus, there were four players with a de facto veto power: (1) court presidents; (2) the Minister of Justice; (3) the Government; and (4) the National Council. Interestingly, psychological testing never became as influential in selecting new judges as in the Czech Republic. Perhaps, the key players who selected new judges did not need to sift through an oversupply of law graduates interested in joining the bench. One more difference from the Czech environment may explain this. Slovak judges were extremely hostile to the possibility of a lateral track to the judiciary and they did everything possible to prevent it. They also believed that every judge should start at the district court and only then could try to climb up the ladder of the judicial hierarchy. As a result, a strong barrier between judges and other legal professions soon emerged and transfers of members of other legal professions to the judiciary were extremely rare.

Several problems permeated the recruitment of judges in the early years of the Slovak Republic. The shortage of judges was so severe that the National Council had to shorten the pupilage of judicial candidates.[154] This problem was further exacerbated after the creation of new courts in 1997. Furthermore, the selection process itself was very opaque and marred by cronyism. By "coincidence" new judicial candidates were often recruited from among the family members of sitting judges. According to the 2013 data, 277 out of 1,383 judges (20%) have at least one family member among judges or court employees.[155] Moreover, 55% out of these 277 judges have a family member among judges only. This means that 11%

---

[152] Art. 145(1) of the 1992 Slovak Constitution after the 2001 Constitutional Amendment. Note that when a judge reaches sixty-five years, the President of the Slovak Republic may in theory recall a judge upon the proposal of the JCSR. However, the JCSR in practice proposed a renewal of the term of all judges who reached the age of sixty-five years. Hence, Slovak judges were de facto appointed for an indefinite period.

[153] Art. 145(2) of the 1992 Slovak Constitution after the 2001 Constitutional Amendment.

[154] See Bröstl, above note 53, at 145.

[155] Transparency International Slovakia, *Kto je s kým rodina na našich súdoch*, Sme.sk (Bratislava, November 10, 2013). See also an interactive map of these family ties at http://sudy.transparency.sk/.

of the Slovak judiciary has family ties among themselves. In the Slovak language, there is even a special term for this "family members placement business" – *rodinkárstvo*.[156] There was no visible improvement in this area until the 2001 Constitutional Amendment.

Apart from the recruitment of judges, I concluded in Chapter 2 that several mechanisms (such as case assignment, judicial salaries, reassignment within the same court, and promotion) can be designed so as to avoid accounting if the relevant criteria are laid down in advance and are not subject to ex post change. In Slovakia, none of case assignment, reassignment within the same court, and promotion was based purely on ex ante criteria between of 1993 and 2001.[157] Therefore, these three mechanisms could be used to hold individual judges to account. In contrast to what happened in the Czech Republic, the salaries of Slovak judges were not fixed in advance either. The Slovak law allowed for the awarding of special salary bonuses in addition to a fixed salary for judges and thus judicial salaries could also be used as a mechanism of judicial accountability.

Regarding *transparency mechanisms*, Slovakia did not perform well between 1993 and 2000. The recruitment of judges was opaque. There was no requirement to inform the public about vacancies within the judiciary. Neither lists of candidates for judicial office nor interviews with these candidates were published. The promotion of judges was even less transparent and the decision was usually reached between the relevant court president and the Minister of Justice behind closed door. No vacancies were advertised and no open selection procedures took place. The situation improved only in 2000 after the adoption of the new Law on Judges and Lay Judges,[158] which improved the transparency in the selection as well as promotion of judges.

As regards other potentially available transparency mechanisms, the situation can be summarized as follows. Judicial statistics were compiled only in an ad hoc manner, by the Ministry of Justice and court presidents, and their results were rarely published. Moreover, those statistics contained only aggregate data for entire courts and did not focus on individual judges. Judicial proceedings were public, but presiding judges often prohibited the recording of those proceedings.[159] Until

---

[156] This term can be roughly translated as "favoritism of family members." On this phenomenon, see, for example, Dubovcová 2010, above note 142, at 53–56.

[157] For details, see Sections III.C and III.D of this chapter.

[158] Law No. 385/2000 Z. z., on Judges and Lay Judges.

[159] This practice changed only in the subsequent period (2003–2010) after the Slovak Minister of Justice initiated four disciplinary motions (two motions in 2003 and two more motions

2000, the requirement of compulsory annual disclosure of property and annual earnings did not apply to judges. However, the 2000 Law on Court and Judges changed that and required judges to submit to the National Council the so-called Income and Property Declaration[160] and a "Written Statement"[161] mentioning all other functions of a judge[162] on an annual basis.

Finally, access to judicial decisions was almost nonexistent. The Supreme Court published only a small proportion of its decisions in the official Collection of Judgments and Opinions of the Supreme Court. The decisions of district and regional courts were virtually inaccessible, with a few exceptions selected for publication in the Supreme Court's official Collection or law reviews. The mental transition of Slovak judges regarding the publication of all judgments of all courts was even slower than in the Czech Republic. As in the Czech Republic, the communist culture of centralized official collections of judgments that contained only "correct" decisions selected by the Supreme Court judges still prevailed. What is more, neither the Slovak courts nor the Slovak Ministry of Justice developed an *internal* system for collecting and indexing case law. That led to an awkward situation, where one chamber of the Supreme Court did not have access to decisions of other chambers of the Supreme Court. This problem was not dealt with until 2002.

The availability of *appeals and quasi-appellate mechanisms* in Slovakia was similar to that in the Czech Republic. Access to the appellate courts as well as to the Supreme Court was very generous. There was no leave to appeal or writ of certiorari mechanism that would grant the Supreme Court the power to select the cases it wanted to hear. The Slovak courts thus could not control their dockets. "Extraordinary appeals" in civil law matters were abolished in 1991, but they were retained in criminal law matters. The use of "extraordinary appeals" was significantly limited by the Code of Criminal Procedure so as to avoid abuse of this mechanism, but "extraordinary appeals" played a somewhat more important role in the postsplit Slovakia than in the Czech Republic. In Slovakia, both the Minister of Justice and the General Prosecutor could lodge an "extraordinary appeal" and such "extraordinary appeal" was permitted in more

---

in 2004) against presiding judges who prohibited the parties to use a dictaphone in the courtroom.

[160]   Art. 32 of Law No. 385/2000 Z. z., on Judges and Lay Judges.
[161]   Art. 31 of Law No. 385/2000 Z. z., on Judges and Lay Judges.
[162]   The other functions included public functions as well as functions outside the public sector (e.g., teaching at private universities).

scenarios than in the Czech Republic.[163] As in the Czech Republic, the Slovak Supreme Court could still issue so-called interpretative guidelines in order to unify divergent case law, whereas the equivalent of en banc procedure or referral to the grand chamber of the Supreme Court "à la Strasbourg"[164] did not exist in Slovakia at this period.

Finally, the *training* of judges did not differ from the situation in the Czech Republic in 1993–2002. The Judicial Academy did not exist[165] and no systematic training was provided to or required from sitting judges in Slovakia. The only part of judicial education that worked reasonably well was the training of judicial candidates organized by the Ministry of Justice and regional court presidents. Training sessions provided by supranational or foreign organizations also had only a limited impact for reasons described in the previous chapter.[166]

B. Which Mechanisms of Judicial Accountability Were Used?

Between 1993 and 2002 Slovakia did not apply all the mechanisms of judicial accountability I identified in Chapter 2, but it adopted a wider range of accountability mechanisms vis-à-vis its judges than its Czech counterparts. Most importantly, the 1992 Slovak Constitution reintroduced the retention review.[167] In addition, the Slovak system allowed salary bonuses to be paid to judges. The amount of these salary bonuses was not fixed at advance and the National Council thus in theory enjoyed unlimited discretion in awarding them. As a result, this "carrot" could be used to hold individual judges to account. Finally, Slovakia established a complaints mechanism in 1992[168] and judicial performance evaluation in 2001.[169]

Apart from these novelties, the list of mechanisms of judicial accountability resembled the Czech one. As regards the "sticks," the involuntary

---

[163] See Art. 266 of the Code of Criminal Procedure (Law No. 141/1961 Coll.), as amended in Slovakia. For further details, see Milan Lipovský, "Sťažnosť pre porušenie zákona a konanie o nej – niekoľko poznámok" (2004) 56 *Justičná revue* 671.

[164] For further details on these procedures, see Chapter 2.

[165] The Slovak Judicial Academy was established only in 2003.

[166] See Chapter 5, Section II.A *in fine*.

[167] The motivation behind reintroducing retention, which was abused during the communist era and immediately repealed by the Czechoslovak leaders after the 1989 Velvet Revolution, is unclear. The most plausible explanation is that the initial four-year period was supposed to serve as a guarantee of the quality of judges and create a more flexible personnel policy during a transitional period (see Bröstl, above note 53, at 147; and Rohárik, above note 53, at 216, note 3).

[168] See Art. 17–27 of Law No. 80/1992 Zb., on the State Administration of Courts.

[169] See Art. 27 of Law No. 385/2000 Z. z., on Judges and Lay Judges.

relocation and demotion of judges were prohibited, there was no special ground for the criminal liability of judges, and civil liability was so severely limited[170] that it could not be used as a separate mechanism of judicial accountability.[171]

In sum, three "sticks" were available between 1993 and 2000: disciplinary proceedings, a one-and-for-all retention review after the first four years in judicial office, and reassignment within the same court. In 2001, the large-scale constitutional overhaul[172] abolished the nonrecurring retention review and reduced the number of available "sticks" to two. As regards dual mechanisms, Slovakia eventually applied three of them. Between 1993 and 2000, only case assignment[173] and the volatile part of a judge's salary could be used to hold Slovak judges to account. Later on, the 2000 Law on Judges and Lay Judges introduced a new system of judicial performance evaluation. In contrast, there were no formal discretionary nonmonetary benefits. Slovak judges did not have the right to subsidized housing and could not be pleased by discretionary vacation packages or by preferential placement of their kids to the nurseries. Altering working conditions of a judge was the only potential reward or a threat, but for reasons discussed in Chapter 4 the use of this mechanism cannot be measured.[174] Regarding nonmonetary benefits the situation in Slovakia was thus very similar to that one in the Czech Republic.

Finally, a plethora of "carrots" awaited judges. These carrots included promotion to a higher court, promotion to the position of chamber president, secondment, temporary assignment outside the judiciary, and the appointment of a judge to the position of court president or vice president. Most of these carrots were accompanied not only by a rise of prestige, but also by a salary increase and reduced case load. Like the situation in the Czech Republic, promotion to a higher court and appointment to the position of court president or vice president came with the best perks. Regarding quasi-promotion within the judiciary, the only major difference from

---

[170] Art. 57 of the 1991 Law on Courts and Judges set out the state liability regime. That means that the State was responsible for miscarriages of justice and the State had to pay the damages. The 2000 Law on Judges and Lay Judges retained this model as well (see Arts. 104–106 of Law No. 385/2000 Z. z., on Judges and Lay Judges).

[171] The State could recover the damages paid from a judge *only* if that judge was found guilty in disciplinary or criminal trial. See Arts. 13 and 19 of Law No. 58/1969 Zb.

[172] For details, see Section II.B of this chapter.

[173] Even though the Slovak Constitution guarantees the right to a legal judge, the National Council adopted basic rules on case assignment only in the 2000 Law on Judges and Lay Judges, and even this statute failed to introduce a truly random case assignment.

[174] See Chapter 4, Section V.

Table 6.1. *Mechanisms of judicial accountability available in Slovakia between 1993 and 2002*

Mechanisms of judicial accountability available in Slovakia between 1993 and 2002	
1993–2000	2001–2002
Sticks	
Disciplinary proceedings	Disciplinary proceedings
Reassignment	Reassignment
Complaint mechanism	Complaint mechanism
Once-and-for-all retention reviews for new judges	~~Once-and-for-all retention reviews for new judges~~
Carrots	
Promotion to a higher court	Promotion to a higher court
Chamber president appointment	Chamber president appointment
Secondment	Secondment
Temporary assignment outside the judiciary	Temporary assignment outside the judiciary
Appointment of a judge to the position of court president or vice president	Appointment of a judge to the position of court president or vice president
Dual mechanisms	
Case assignment	Case assignment
Salary bonuses	Salary bonuses
-	*Judicial performance evaluation*

the Czech Republic was that a grand chamber did not exist at the Slovak Supreme Court between 1993 and 2002. Finally, there was one additional carrot – temporary assignment outside the judiciary. In sum, Slovakia used twelve different mechanisms of judicial accountability between 1993 and 2002, but only eleven of them were available at the same time (see Table 6.1).

C.   Mechanisms of Judicial Accountability on the Books

This section addresses what the law said about mechanisms of judicial accountability that were used between 1993 and 2002 and what legal standards it laid down. To see the difference between Slovakia and the Czech Republic more clearly, I again start with "sticks," followed by "carrots" and "dual mechanisms."

Regarding the *disciplining* of judges, Slovakia decided to retain the federal-era statute until 2000, when the Slovak Parliament passed a new Law on Judges and Lay Judges.[175] Under the federal statute, the system of disciplining judges was strictly hierarchical. The Ministry of Justice supervised all the ordinary courts, whereas court presidents (with one exception) looked after their own courts as well as after lower courts.[176] The Minister of Justice could initiate a disciplinary motion against any judge, the president of a regional court could initiate a disciplinary motion against any judge of his court and against judges of districts courts that fell under the jurisdiction of his regional court and, finally, the president of a district court could initiate a disciplinary motion against any judge of his court.[177] The only exception to this rule applied to the president of the Supreme Court who could initiate a disciplinary motion only against judges of the Supreme Court.

Therefore, only the Minister of Justice and court presidents could trigger disciplinary motions.[178] However, neither the Minister of Justice nor court presidents could discipline judges. The court president and the minister were entitled only to supervise judges, detect errors, and initiate disciplinary motions.[179] Judges could be removed only by the National Council[180] following the decision of a disciplinary panel, which between 1993 and 2002 consisted exclusively of professional judges.[181] Before the disciplinary panel, it was either the Minister of Justice or the president of the court who acted as disciplinary prosecutors. Disciplinary panels were set up pursuant to a hierarchical pattern: disciplinary panels at regional courts decided on motions against judges of district courts, while disciplinary panels at

---

[175] See Section II.A of this chapter.

[176] See Art. 6(2) of Law No. 412/1991 Sb., as amended by Law No. 149/1993 Z. z.

[177] Note that, in contrast to the Czech Republic, Slovakia did not abolish military courts immediately after the dissolution of Czechoslovakia (it did so only in 2009). However, special rules applicable for military judges will not be addressed here.

[178] Here I do not deal with specific rules applicable to administrative offences committed by judges. In such cases, the administrative organs (e.g., the Police or the municipality) can act as disciplinary prosecutors.

[179] However, note that court presidents not only acted as disciplinary prosecutors, but also decided on the composition of disciplinary panels. Many judges criticized this dangerous concentration of power. See, for example, Rohárik, above note 53, at 220.

[180] This is the major difference between the Slovak and the Czech systems of disciplining judges. In the Czech Republic, judges who were convicted of committing a disciplinary offense which was deemed incompatible with judicial office were dismissed by the disciplinary court itself.

[181] It is important to mention that court presidents who acted as disciplinary prosecutors could not sit on the disciplinary panels.

the Supreme Court decided on motions against judges of regional courts and the Supreme Court.[182] For judges of regional courts and the Supreme Court there was only a single-instance procedure before the disciplinary panel of the Supreme Court, whereas judges of district courts could appeal the decision of disciplinary panels established at regional courts to the Supreme Court. Notably, being a member of a disciplinary panel did not carry an extra salary, but it was considered prestigious and many judges considered it an honor to sit on the disciplinary panels.[183]

The 2000 Law on Judges and Lay Judges changed this model and introduced the Disciplinary Court which has decided on all disciplinary motions against Slovak judges since January 2001. The Disciplinary Court was officially attached to the Supreme Court, but it was designed rather as a sui generis court. Its members, all being professional judges, were elected by the Council of Judges of the Slovak Republic for a three-year-term. The Disciplinary Court decided in five-member panels[184] in the first instance and in seven-member panels[185] on appeals. A few months later, the 2001 Constitutional Amendment made a small adjustment to the new system. It laid down that the Constitutional Court should decide on disciplinary motions against the president and vice president of the Supreme Court.[186] As a result, these two judicial officials did not fall under the jurisdiction of the Disciplinary Court.[187]

Regarding conduct for which judges could be disciplined, the 1991 Disciplinary Code was very succinct.[188] It defined a disciplinary misdemeanor as an "intentional violation of ... judicial duties or behavior that infringes upon dignity of [the judicial] office or threatens public confidence in independent, impartial and just decision-making of courts."[189] If the nature of the violated duty, type of conduct, the judge's degree of

---

[182] See Art. 5(2) of Law No. 412/1991 Sb., as amended by Law No. 149/1993 Z. z.

[183] Interview with a Judge of the Supreme Court of Slovakia from April 23, 2015.

[184] The composition of this five-member panel was as follows: two district court judges, two regional court judges, and one judge of the Supreme Court. The Supreme Court judge always acted as a panel chairman. See Art. 119(6) of Law No. 385/2000 Z. z., on judges and Lay Judges.

[185] The appellate panel consisted exclusively of Supreme Court judges. See Art. 119(6) of Law No. 385/2000 Z. z., on Judges and Lay Judges.

[186] Art. 136(3) of the Slovak Constitution after the 2001 Constitutional Amendment.

[187] The rules (such as rules on who could initiate a disciplinary motion, for what, and which sanctions were available) applicable to the disciplining of the president and vice president of the Supreme Court were the same ones that applied to other judges.

[188] The 1991 Disciplinary Code, the federal-era law, was already described in Chapter 5, Section III.C.

[189] Art. 2(1) of the 1991 Disciplinary Code.

culpability, repetitiveness of the conduct, or other aggravating factors increased the harmfulness of the judge's conduct, the offense was considered a serious disciplinary misdemeanor.[190] Slovakia decided to retain the federal-era definitions after the split, but it slightly changed the scope of the disciplinary misdemeanor in 1995,[191] in 2000,[192] and again in April 2002.[193] Furthermore, the definitions of disciplinary offenses changed in one more aspect in 2000. The 2000 Law on Judges and Lay Judges departed from the existing dichotomy of disciplinary offenses – instead of two types of disciplinary offences (disciplinary misdemeanor and serious disciplinary misdemeanor), Art. 117 of the 2000 Law on Judges and Lay Judges explicitly distinguished three types of disciplinary offences (disciplinary misdemeanor, serious disciplinary misdemeanor, and, serious disciplinary misdemeanor that is incompatible with judicial office).

Disciplinary sanctions between 1993 and 2000 followed the disciplinary misdemeanor/serious disciplinary misdemeanor dichotomy. For a disciplinary misdemeanor, disciplinary panels had to choose between a reprimand and a salary reduction.[194] A serious disciplinary misdemeanor[195] led to harsher sanctions: dismissal from the position of chamber president, relocation to another court of the same level, demotion to a lower court, or dismissal from the judicial office. As mentioned earlier, the 2000 Law on Judges and Lay Judges changed from the existing dichotomy to trichotomy of disciplinary offenses, but it did not change the palette of available sanctions.

[190] Art. 2(2) of the 1991 Disciplinary Code.
[191] The revised definition of a disciplinary misdemeanor after the 1995 amendment was as follows: "intentional non-fulfillment or violation of ... a judicial duties or behavior that is capable of casting doubts on independence of a judge, on conscientiousness and impartiality of a judge in decision-making of courts, on lack of bias toward parties to the dispute and on an effort to finish the judicial proceeding justly and without delays, or such behavior of a judge that is incompatible with principles of judicial ethics" [Art. 2(1) of Law No. 412/1991 Sb., as amended by Law No. 307/1995 Z. z.].
[192] The new definition of a disciplinary misdemeanor in the 2000 Law on Judges and Lay Judges was as follows: "intentional non-fulfillment or violation of ... a judicial duties, behavior that is capable of casting doubts on independence of a judge, on conscientiousness and impartiality of a judge in decision-making of courts, on lack of bias toward parties to the dispute and on an effort to finish the judicial proceeding justly and without delays" [Art. 116(1) of Law No. 385/2000 Z. z., on Judges and Lay Judges].
[193] The Parliament added to the existing definition of a disciplinary misdemeanor in the 2000 Law on Judges and Lay Judges two new counts: (1) unsatisfactory performance based on judicial performance evaluation; and (2) intentional submission of incomplete or false information in financial declaration or in a personal declaration.
[194] Art. 3(1) of the 1991 Disciplinary Code. More specifically, the 1991 Disciplinary Code laid down that salary deduction can reach up to 15% for up to three months (and in case of a repetitive misdemeanor for up to six months).
[195] Art. 3(3) of the 1991 Disciplinary Code.

The 2000 Law on Judges and Lay Judges thus brought about only one change in sanctioning judges – as a result of the new tier of disciplinary offenses, dismissal from judicial office could be imposed only for a serious disciplinary misdemeanor that was incompatible with judicial office. No further criteria for sanctioning were set out in the 1991 Disciplinary Code or the 2000 Law on Judges and Lay Judges. As a result, disciplinary panels had broad discretion in imposing sanctions and the disciplining of judges became a judge-made law.

The second "stick" was the *complaint mechanism*, which was introduced in Slovakia as early as in 1992.[196] These complaints were the only means by which consumers of justice could hold judges to account. The system of processing the complaints was based on the hierarchical pattern similar to the one applicable to disciplining judges. The president of the Supreme Court dealt with complaints against judges of the Supreme Court, presidents of regional courts dealt with complaints against judges of regional courts and against presidents of district courts, and presidents of district courts dealt with complaints against judges of district courts. The Minister of Justice decided on complaints against presidents of regional courts as well as on "complaints about the improper processing of complaints" brought by complainants who alleged that presidents of district and regional courts did not handle their original complaints adequately. Somewhat surprisingly, the 1992 Law on State Administration of Courts did not permit a complaint against the president of the Supreme Court. Similarly, it was not possible to lodge a complaint challenging the way the president of the Supreme Court processed a complaint against a Supreme Court judge. In other words, the president of the Supreme Court was exempted from this mechanism of judicial accountability.

The third "stick" that allowed the holding of judges to account was the once-and-for-all *retention* election for new judges. This stick operated as follows. Every new judge was elected initially only for four years and after the expiration of this period he faced reelection, this time for an indefinite period. No criteria for retention were stipulated by law until 2000.[197]

---

[196] See Arts. 17–27 of Law No. 80/1992 Zb., on the State Administration of Courts. Note that a similar system of complaints against individual judges was adopted in the Czech Republic only in 2002.

[197] Note that the 2000 Law on Judges and Lay Judges to a significant extent formalized the process of retention (see Arts. 7–8 of this Law). It introduced judicial performance evaluation of "judges on probation," required consultations with judges of higher courts as well as with the Council of Judges of the Slovak Republic, and granted "judges on probation" the right to object to the results of judicial performance evaluation. However, this revamped retention process applied only in the short interim period before the abolition of the one-and-for-all retention review of new judges, that is from January 1, 2001 until April 15, 2002.

According to the Slovak Constitution, the decision to retain or not to retain a judge after the initial four years was a purely political decision of the National Council. One may say that, until reelection, new judges were on "probation." This technique is not totally alien to civil law systems,[198] even though it has been on the decline in Europe. However, the Slovak model of "judges on probation" was very specific in one aspect – *all* new judges, irrespective of the level of the judicial hierarchy they were assigned to – had to undergo a probationary period. That meant that not only young career judges entering the lower echelons of the judiciary, but also senior candidates assigned to the Supreme Court were subject to the four-year probationary period.[199]

The last "stick" available in Slovakia was the *reassignment* of judges within the same court. The Slovak de jure rules governing reassignment of judges were similar to the Czech ones – there were no rules. In contrast to the relatively detailed rules governing the disciplining of judges, neither the Slovak Constitution nor other laws defined standards for the reassignment of judges within the same court. This lack of legal standards was particularly important since Slovak judges are not generalists. Like their Czech counterparts, single judges at lower courts as well as panels of judges at higher courts in Slovakia decide only cases in certain areas of the law designated to them. This division of case load within each court was also based on the so-called "work schedule," an internal document of the court issued by the court president. However, Slovak law did not stipulate any criteria for reassignment.

Since Slovakia historically belongs to countries with a career judiciary, *promotion* to a higher court is an important carrot for Slovak judges. Until 2000, Slovak legislation retained the system from the federal era. The Slovak Constitution did not address the promotion of judges at all and the 1991 Law on Courts and Judges only briefly mentioned that assignment to a particular court was to be decided upon by the Minister of Justice.[200] Regarding promotion to regional courts, no further rules were stipulated and, thus, the Minister of Justice was not de jure constrained by any other actor. Promotion to the Supreme Court was governed by a different rule as the 1991 Law on Courts and Judges set one important limit

---

[198] See, for example, the concept of *Richter auf Probe* in Germany discussed in Chapter 2, Section I.A.

[199] For more details regarding retention review in Slovakia, see Rohárik, above note 53, at 216; or Bröstl, above note 53, at 147.

[200] Art. 40(1) of the 1991 Law on Courts and Judges.

on the discretion of the Minister of Justice – promotion to the Supreme Court could proceed only with the consent of the president of the Supreme Court. Since 2001 the brand new system of promotion has been at place. The new system brought two major changes. First, all promotions had to result from open competition run according to the rules set in advance.[201] Second, promotion to the Supreme Court required the consent of the Council of Judges of the Slovak Republic and any candidate for such promotion had to be over thirty-five years old.[202]

The second carrot was *appointment to the position of court president or vice president*. The Slovak Constitution explicitly addressed only the selection of the president and the vice president of the Supreme Court. Until 2000, the president and the vice president of the Supreme Court were elected for five years by the National Council (the legislature) among Supreme Court judges.[203] The same person could serve as a judicial official at the Supreme Court for only two consecutive terms.[204] All other judicial officials (presidents and vice presidents of district courts and regional courts) were appointed by the Minister of Justice.[205] The 2001 Constitutional Amendment that introduced the JCSR changed the mode of appointment of judicial officials at the Supreme Court. The new arrangement is as follows. The president and the vice president of the Supreme Court are appointed for five years among Supreme Court judges by the President upon the nomination of JCSR.[206] The maximum limit of two consecutive terms was preserved.[207] The mode of appointment of judicial officials at lower courts remained the same until 2002.[208] The Minister of Justice thus still played a key role in selecting judicial officials at district and regional courts.

The third carrot available between 1993 and 2002 was *promotion to the position of chamber president*. The Slovak Parliament initially decided to retain the federal-era arrangement, and thus it vested the power to promote judges to the position of chamber president exclusively in the court presidents. More specifically, the president of a regional court appointed

---

[201] Art. 14(3) of Law No. 385/2000 Z. z., on Judges and Lay Judges.
[202] Art. 14(2) of Law No. 385/2000 Z. z., on Judges and Lay Judges.
[203] Art. 145(2) of the Slovak Constitution.
[204] Art. 145(2) of the Slovak Constitution.
[205] Art. 39(3) of the 1991 Law on Courts and Judges, as amended by Law No. 12/1993 Z. z.
[206] Art. 145(3) of the Slovak Constitution after the 2001 Constitutional Amendment.
[207] Art. 145(3) of the Slovak Constitution after the 2001 Constitutional Amendment.
[208] These rules were changed only in 2004 by the new Law on Courts (see Section IV.C of this chapter).

chamber presidents at "his" regional court as well as at the district courts belonging to "his" region, whereas the President of the Supreme Court appointed chamber presidents at the Supreme Court.[209]

The 2000 Law on Judges and Lay Judges changed the existing arrangement, and to a great extent limited the powers of court presidents. Court presidents still had the power to appoint chamber presidents, but the new Law required open competition for each vacancy for a chamber president and prior consultation with a judicial board.[210] Furthermore, the procedure of appointment of chamber presidents was abolished altogether at district courts and every judge assigned to the district court became a chamber president *ex lege*.[211]

The de jure standard for the remaining two carrots, secondment of judges and the temporary assignment of judges outside the judiciary, is straightforward. The power to *second* a judge was vested with court presidents and the Minister of Justice. More specifically, presidents of regional courts decided on secondment to "their" regional courts,[212] whereas secondment to the Supreme Court required the consent of both the Minister of Justice and the President of the Supreme Court.[213] The 2000 Law on Judges and Lay Judges confirmed these rules.

In contrast to secondment, *temporary assignment outside the judiciary* was fully in the hands of the Minister of Justice,[214] with the exception of temporary assignment of the Supreme Court judges which required consultation with the President of the Supreme Court.[215] However, the number of available places changed over time. Until 2000, judges could be assigned to the following positions outside the judiciary: the Ministry of Justice, the Office of the Government of the Slovak Republic, the Office of the President, and the Office of the National Council of the Slovak Republic.[216]

---

[209] Arts. 39(2) and (4) of the 1991 Law on Courts and Judges, as amended by Law No. 12/1993 Z. z. The same principle applied to the selection of chamber presidents at military courts, but this issue is not dealt with here.

[210] Art. 15(1) of Law No. 385/2000 Z. z., on Judges and Lay Judges. At the Supreme Court, the President of the Supreme Court had to consult the relevant kolegium as well.

[211] Art. 15(3) of Law No. 385/2000 Z. z., on Judges and Lay Judges.

[212] See Art. 42(1) of the 1991 Law on Courts and Judges.

[213] Art. 42(e) of the 1991 Law on Courts and Judges, as amended by Law No. 12/1993 Z. z.

[214] Art. 42(1)(a) of the 1991 Law on Courts and Judges.

[215] Art. 42(1)(b) of the 1991 Law on Courts and Judges.

[216] Moreover, in addition to temporary assignment to the positions outside the judiciary mentioned earlier, Slovak judges could run for seats in the National Council (the legislature) as well as for the positions of president and vice president of the Supreme Audit Office. If they succeeded, they did not lose judicial office. Instead, their judicial post was suspended

All of the aforementioned positions were prestigious, but assignment to the Ministry of Justice was particularly valuable as the Minister of Justice decided on the promotion of judges.

Interestingly, Slovak rules governing temporary assignment outside the judiciary subsequently took a different path from the one in the Czech Republic. While temporary assignment outside the judiciary was increasingly treated with suspicion in the Czech Republic and this mechanism was curtailed over time, Slovaks held the opposite view and thus the 2000 Law on Judges and Lay Judges expanded the number of positions outside the judiciary that judges could be temporarily assigned to. Under the 2000 Law on Judges and Lay Judges, judges could be assigned not only to the Ministry of Justice, the Office of the Government of the Slovak Republic, the Office of the President and the Office of the National Council of the Slovak Republic, but also to the institution responsible for judicial training and to the Constitutional Court.[217] On the other hand, the length of temporary assignment for most positions was limited to one year out of three consecutive years.[218] This one-year-rule did not apply to temporary assignment to the Ministry of Justice and to the judicial training institutions. As in the Czech Republic, no further criteria for temporary assignment outside the judiciary were laid down by law between 1993 and 2002.

There were three dual mechanisms available in Slovakia between 1993 and 2002: volatile salaries, case assignment, and judicial performance evaluation. However, only volatile salaries and case assignment were available for the entire period, as judicial performance evaluation was introduced only in 2001.

Regarding the *salaries* of judges, postcommunist federal laws set fixed salaries for judges and prohibited any individualization of judicial salaries by way of salary bonuses.[219] However, the Slovak parliament soon after the dissolution amended the federal-era statute and introduced salary bonuses that could be paid in three occasions: (1) the successful completion of extra tasks that were not related to judicial decision-making;

until the end of their mandate in the legislature or at the Supreme Audit Office (Art. 51a of the 1991 Law on Courts and Judges, as amended by Law No. 12/1993 Z. z.). From 1995 judges could also run for other public offices as well as in municipal elections. Note that such practice was expressly prohibited in the Czech Republic.

[217] Art. 12(2) of Law No. 385/2000 Z. z., on Judges and Lay Judges.
[218] Art. 12(5) of Law No. 385/2000 Z. z., on Judges and Lay Judges.
[219] See Law No. 420/1991 Zb., on Salaries of Judges and Judicial Candidates.

(2) when a judge reached the age of fifty years or at the date of his retirement; and (3) in other exceptional cases.[220] The National Council decided on salary bonuses under the first two counts, whereas the Minister of Justice issued salary bonuses on the third count. No further criteria were laid down by law. That means that the National Council and the Minister of Justice enjoyed absolute discretion as to the amount and periodicity of judicial salary bonuses. This scheme operated without any change until the 2001 Constitutional Amendment, which transferred the power to decide on salary bonuses to the newly created Judicial Council of the Slovak Republic.[221]

The de jure standard of *case assignment* is closely tied to the concept of a legal judge in Slovakia.[222] Article 48(1) of the Slovak Constitution stipulates that "[n]o one shall be removed from his legal judge." However, as I stressed in the previous chapter,[223] in case assignment the proverbial devil lies in the details. Slovak law did not pay sufficient attention to the detail and left the system of assigning cases to a large extent unregulated between 1993 and 2002. Two periods must be distinguished. Until 2000, neither the 1991 Law on Courts and Judges nor any other law specified the criteria for and method of case assignment. The method of case assignment within each court was based on the "work schedule" issued by its court president.[224] Hence, court presidents decided on case assignment.

It was only the 2000 Law on Judges and Lay Judges that explicitly set out the right of a judge to be assigned cases according to the work schedule and allowed judges to challenge violations of the work schedule before the court president and ultimately before the judicial board.[225] Nevertheless, the 2000 Law on Judges and Lay Judges still did not specify the criteria for and method of case assignment. Most importantly, it did not require case assignment to be random. In addition, the process of creation of the work schedule was also not addressed explicitly. The key role of the court president in preparing the work schedule could be inferred from the new statute at least implicitly, but no further criteria were laid down. As a result,

---

[220] Art. 11a of Law No. 420/1991 Zb., on Salaries of Judges and Judicial Candidates, as amended by Law No. 148/1993 Z. z.

[221] For a brief overview of the issues relating to the judicial salaries of Slovak judges, albeit somewhat one-sided, see Bröstl, above note 53, at 150–152.

[222] For a more detailed discussion on the concept of a legal judge, see Chapter 2.

[223] See Chapter 5.

[224] For a more detailed description of how a work schedule works, see Chapter 5.

[225] Art. 34(2) of Law No. 385/2000 Z. z., on Judges and Lay Judges.

court presidents could continue to use case assignment as a "stick" or as a "carrot" until 2002.

All of this changed in April 2002, when the 2002 Law on the JCSR laid down detailed rules on the content of the work schedule as well as on the method of case assignment. Under the new arrangement, the work schedule was still prepared by the court president, but he had to discuss it with other judges and consult a judicial board about it.[226] The 2002 Law on the JCSR for the first time in Slovak history also explicitly required random case assignment. More specifically, it provided that "[c]ases shall be assigned to judges according to the work schedule on random basis with the use of technical means and software ... so that the possibility of rigging case assignment is excluded."[227] This led to the creation of the so-called electronic registry at each court, which assigned cases on a random basis by software without any interference by human beings.[228] The same statute also provided that the annual work schedule had to contain, among other things, the following information: the subject matter specialization of each judge and each chamber, the composition of each chamber, the rules governing the substitution of judges, how to proceed if the composition of a court changed or if a legal judge was recused, and how to proceed if the software used for case assignment did not work temporarily.[229] In addition, the 2002 Law on the JCSR increased the transparency of case assignment as it required the work schedules to be available to the public.[230] All of these changes reduced the influence of court presidents on case assignment.

Nevertheless, one must distinguish among three phases of case assignment – the creation of the work schedule, assigning case files at the court registry according to the existing work schedule, and subsequent reassignment of cases. The 2002 Law on the JCSR reduced as far as possible the risk of the manipulation of case files in the second phase – that is at the court registry. Nevertheless, court presidents still had a major part in creating the work schedule and their power to reassign cases was left largely intact. Most importantly, that law did not explicitly require the random

---

[226] Art. 27(1) and (3) of the 1991 Law on Courts and Judges, as amended by Law No. 185/2002 Z. z.

[227] Art. 26(2) of the 1991 Law on Courts and Judges, as amended by Law No. 185/2002 Z. z.

[228] For further details, see Katarína Staroňová, "Projekt 'Súdny manažment' ako protikorupčný nástroj" in Emília Sičáková-Beblavá and Miroslav Beblavý (eds.), *Jedenásť statočných: prípadové štúdie protikorupčných nástrojov na Slovensku* (2008) 215; and notes 275–279.

[229] Art. 26(3) of the 1991 Law on Courts and Judges, as amended by Law No. 185/2002 Z. z.

[230] Art. 27(4) of the 1991 Law on Courts and Judges, as amended by Law No. 185/2002 Z. z.

method to be used also for reassigning cases. In other words, case assignment could still be used as a "carrot" or as a "stick."

Formal *judicial performance evaluation* did not exist in Slovakia until 2000. It was introduced only by the 2000 Law on Judges and Lay Judges. The so-called assessment of judges took place in three different scenarios: (1) every five years for each judge; (2) if a judge was a candidate in any open competition within the judiciary; and (3) if a judge himself asked for such assessment.[231] Similarly to the Czech system of judicial competence evaluation introduced in the Czech Republic in 2002, the new Slovak assessment of judges was a peculiar mix of the new-public-management and the Soviet-style system of judicial performance evaluation,[232] because it focused not only on skills, but presumably also on the correctness of the decisions under review. More specifically, judges were assessed by their court presidents who based their assessment on the following information: (1) the review of decisions delivered by a judge under evaluation and the review of the smoothness and dignity of judicial proceedings conducted by a judge under evaluation (conducted by a special committee appointed by a judicial board of given court.); (2) the opinion of appellate judges who decide on appeals against decisions delivered by a judge under evaluation; and (3) the court president's own knowledge about a judge under evaluation.[233] It means that all three principals involved in judicial performance evaluation – the court president, senior judges from higher courts, and judges sitting on a special review committee – were judges. Members of other legal professions had no say in this exercise. This model of purely internal judicial performance evaluation, based on the hierarchical ideal of authority,[234] thus further empowered primarily court presidents and strengthened the bureaucratic patterns within the Slovak judiciary.

D.   Mechanisms of Judicial Accountability in Action

The previous section described what the law on the books said about mechanisms of judicial accountability that were used between 1993 and 2002. This section will analyze how those mechanisms operated in practice.

---

[231] Art. 27(1) of Law No. 385/2000 Z. z., on Judges and Lay Judges. In the interim period, before the abolition of the once-and-for-all retention review of new judges, the assessment took place also at the end of the four-year probation period of the new judges.

[232] For the difference between these two systems, see Chapter 2, Section II.C.

[233] Art. 27(2) of Law No. 385/2000 Z. z., on Judges and Lay Judges.

[234] On the distinction between the hierarchical and coordinate ideals of authority, see Chapter 2, Section IV.

Between 1993 and 2002, ninety-eight *disciplinary motions* were initiated against Slovak judges. According to de jure standards, only two actors could initiate such motions – the Minister of Justice and court presidents. These two actors shared responsibility for supervising judges, detecting their errors and, ultimately, initiating disciplinary motions. However, in practice court presidents dominated the sphere of disciplining judges and thus held the most important "stick" firmly in their hands. Court presidents initiated 72 out of 98 disciplinary motions (73%). More specifically, 68 disciplinary motions (69%) were initiated by the presidents of the very same court where the judge being disciplinarily prosecuted worked, 4 motions (4%) were lodged by presidents of the superior courts, whereas only 25 disciplinary motions (26%) were initiated by the Minister of Justice and 1 motion (1%) by other actors.

Regarding the typology of misconducts, the most common reason for initiating disciplinary motions was delays in delivering justice[235] (47%), followed by other issues (20%), administrative offences (19%), and alcohol-related issues (8%). In contrast, disciplinary motions for violating judicial independence, judicial impartiality, or judicial ethics were relatively rare (5%).

The overall success rate of disciplinary motions was relatively low. Disciplinary panels issued disciplinary sanctions in only 39 cases (40%) and only in 2 cases (2%) did the impugned judges resign from judicial office voluntarily. This means that disciplinary prosecutors were successful in only 42% of disciplinary motions. Judges were acquitted in 10 cases (10%) and no judge was absolutely discharged between 1993 and 2002. Most motions (47 cases or 48%) were dismissed on procedural grounds, mostly for exceeding statutory limit for initiating disciplinary motion.[236] Out of the 39 sanctions imposed, the most common were a reprimand (17 or 44%) and a salary reduction (14 cases or 36%). The other available

---

[235] The term "delay in delivering justice" encompassed several types of delays such as inaction in certain cases or delays in writing reasoned opinions (it is possible to announce the result of the case orally at the hearing and submit the written judgment within thirty days of the hearing).

[236] Note that disciplinary panels adopted a "protective" interpretation of the amendment that expanded this time limit (due to its alleged retroactivity) and by this move saved many disciplinarily prosecuted judges from disciplinary decisions on the merits. Many commentators asserted that only the Constitutional Court can set aside the law duly passed by the Parliament. However, the Constitutional Court adopted the dubious position that disciplinary panels cannot initiate concrete review of constitutionality (Decision of the Constitutional Court of Slovakia of March 4, 2002, No. Pl. ÚS 7/02) and thus created a gap, which was filled by a "protective" interpretation of disciplinary panels.

sanctions such as fines (3 cases, 8%), relocation (2 cases, 5%), demotion (2 cases, 5%) and dismissal from the position of chamber president (1 case, 2%) were used sparingly. Interestingly, not a single judge was dismissed from judicial office by a disciplinary court in the entire decade. Slovak disciplinary panels were thus much softer on their colleagues than their Czech counterparts.[237]

These are the overall numbers. However, it is worth considering the success rates of court presidents on the one hand, and the Minister of Justice on the other. Before delving into the results it is necessary to provide some insight into how a judge attracted the attention of the Ministry of Justice to the extent that the Minister of Justice would open a disciplinary motion, and not the court president. First, the Minister could get the information about the potential disciplinary behavior from various sources that were not available to a court president – from the media in high profile cases, via the personal letters of litigants addressed to the minister complaining about a given judge, or from the results of occasional missions of the Ministry's officials to the problematic courts. Nevertheless, this does not necessarily mean that if the Minister initiated the disciplinary motion, he learned about the transgression of a judge before a given court president. Sometimes court presidents knew about the behavior concerned, but were not willing to lodge a disciplinary motion in border-line cases, were persuaded that the relevant behavior was not a disciplinary offense, or were not willing to discipline their protégés. Second, ministers also initiated few disciplinary motions against the court presidents who had no incentive to fight each other.

Now we can return to the data results. If we look at the data, we will see that disciplinary panels issued a sanction in 43% of the motions initiated by court presidents, whereas the Minister of Justice was successful in only 32% of his motions. In addition to these motions that led to disciplinary sanctions, we must also look at those that forced judges to resign voluntarily. Only two resignations took place between 1993 and 2002 and both of them resulted from disciplinary motions initiated by court presidents. Court presidents were thus more successful than the Minister of Justice both in imposing sanctions and in forcing judges to resign.

---

[237] In the Czech Republic, twelve judges were stripped of the judicial robe and another thirty-two judges resigned voluntarily between 1993 and 2002. In contrast, only two Slovak judges resigned from judicial office and none was dismissed by a disciplinary panel. Even if one takes into account the fact that there is approximately twice more judges in the Czech Republic, the disparity between the two countries is striking.

In conclusion, the results of the empirical study of disciplinary proceedings concerning Slovak judges in 1993–2002 are twofold. First, the
results show that, contrary to general wisdom, court presidents controlled
this mechanism of judicial accountability, whereas the Minister of Justice
played a secondary role. Court presidents were not only more active in
using this "stick," but they were also more successful in employing it.
Second, the disciplinary process was relatively toothless, especially in
comparison with that of the Czech Republic. Not a single Slovak judge was
dismissed by a disciplinary panel between 1993 and 2002. Even the most
egregious conduct of a judge, such as heavy drinking at the workplace
which resulted in the rescheduling of several hearings, was not enough to
strip him or her of the judicial robe. Most other sanctions imposed by the
disciplinary court were also mild. Given this protective approach by disciplinary panels, it is not surprising that judges prosecuted for disciplinary
offences were unwilling to step down voluntarily from judicial office and
instead fought until the end.

The *complaint mechanism* was even more declawed in practice. I could
not trace any significant link between the complaints lodged and the initiation of disciplinary motions against a judge complained of. According
to the disciplinary case files, not a single disciplinary motion against a
judge was triggered exclusively or predominantly by a complaint from the
litigants or the public. In practice, complaints were almost exclusively processed by court presidents, with a minimal intervention from the Ministry
of Justice. The results of the complaint process were not publicized and,
thus, complaints had only a limited impact on the external reputation of
a given judge. On the other hand, the internal accountability effect of this
mechanism was beyond doubt. In addition, due to the secrecy of the whole
process, the complaint mechanism had an important residual effect – it
increased information asymmetry between court presidents and regular
judges as well as between court presidents and the Ministry of Justice. In
other words, the court presidents had more complete information about
the behavior and performance of judges than anyone else.[238]

The de facto standards of the once-and-for-all *retention* review for new
judges took a peculiar course. According the 1992 Slovak Constitution,
every new judge was elected initially for four years and after that expiration

---

[238] This information asymmetry slightly decreased in 2002, when the Slovak Parliament
introduced compulsory judicial performance evaluation. However, that was supposed to
be conducted only every five years and was eventually abolished in 2009; see below Section
IV.C of this chapter.

of this period he faced reelection. The first group of "judges on probation" who fell within the ambit of this rule were elected in the first months of 1993. Therefore, retention review did not take place until 1997 and operated rather as a "sleeping" mechanism of judicial accountability. Once the initial four-year term of the first group of judges expired at the beginning of 1997, problems arose immediately. The Constitution said that National Council was to decide on their reelection, this time for an indefinite term. Nevertheless, the Government stepped in and refused to recommend twelve judges of that group to the National Council. The Government did not give any reasons for this move and simply returned the proposals for the reelection of those twelve judges to the state court administration and judicial boards for reconsideration.[239]

The judiciary immediately fought back and expressed a "concern about the Government's ambition to assume Parliament's competence to [re] elect judges."[240] The Government eventually buckled under media pressure, but the very first reelection of judges in postcommunist Slovakia exposed the complexity of the use of the retention mechanism. According to the Slovak Constitution, the Government was not supposed to play any formal role in reelecting judges. However, de facto it played a critical role in the retention of new judges. The criteria for reelection were purely political and never crystallized into a constitutional convention governed by stable rules. The politicization of the retention election soon attracted the attention of the European Commission and eventually led to the 2001 Constitutional Amendment that put an end to this practice.

Regarding *reassignment* within the same court, I concluded that de jure the power to decide on reassignment belonged to court presidents. However, the key question – according to what criteria were judges reassigned – was governed by de facto standards set out by court presidents. In practice, the limits of court presidents' discretion were minimal. The only informal limit on the discretion of court presidents was not to reassign arbitrarily too many judges at the same time. An individual judge could hardly challenge his reassignment.

One may object that reassignment was to a great extent prevented by the work schedule. However, Slovak law between 1993 and 2000 did not contain any rules governing annual work schedules and the content of the work schedule varied from one court to another. In this legal vacuum, court presidents took control over the work schedule. Not only did

---

[239] Rohárik, above note 53, at 216.
[240] Ibid.

they have the power to issue the annual work schedule, but they could also deviate from the work schedule during the given year if they deemed such deviation necessary. It is also important to remember that, as with the situation in the Czech Republic in the same era, information asymmetry favored court presidents and further bolstered their powers. Only court presidents had precise information about the productivity of each judge or panel, about their case load as well as about the number of unfinished cases. As a result, regular judges lacked the necessary information to counter the arguments of court presidents. Finally, given the number of judges in Slovakia,[241] there were many opportunities for court presidents to punish judges by reassignment.[242]

This almost unfettered power of court presidents to reassign judges was affected by the 2002 Law on the JCSR, which touched upon the composition of chambers. However, these new rules started to operate in practice only in 2003 and so they will be described in the following section that deals with standards applicable between 2003 and 2010.

The practice of *promotion* of judges to higher courts took a similar course to that in the Czech Republic. De facto rules on the promotion of judges were in general in alignment with the de jure standard, with one important caveat. Even though the Minister of Justice could, with the exception of promotion to the Supreme Court, decide unilaterally on the promotion of judges, this rarely happened in practice. Court presidents managed successfully to fight the unilateral actions of the ministers until a new custom slowly emerged. According to this new de facto standard, the promotion of judges required the consent of both the Minister of Justice and two court presidents, the president of the current court where a given judge sat and the president of the higher court to which the judge was proposed to be promoted.[243] Under this new arrangement, court presidents soon took control over the promotion of judges and the model that de jure applied only to promotion to the Supreme Court was extended to all tiers of the Slovak judiciary. The process of promotion took place behind closed doors and criteria for promotion were opaque. For instance, the president of the Supreme Court, Štefan Harabin, rejected the promotion of a judge

---

[241] This number varied significantly between 1993 and 2010. On the number of judges in Slovakia see Annex C of this book.

[242] For more details on this aspect, see chapter on the Czech Republic (Chapter 5, Sections III.D and IV.D). The situation in Slovakia was very similar.

[243] There is a historical explanation of this custom. In a nutshell, court presidents have formed a "special caste" within the judiciary. This phenomenon can be traced back to the era of the Austro-Hungarian Empire.

to the Supreme Court despite the fact that that judge had been recommended by the Council of Judges of the Slovak Republic.

However, this system applied only from 1993 until 2000. In 2001, de facto rules followed the change of de jure rules, namely the adoption of the 2000 Law on Judges and Lay Judges. All promotions had to result from open competition run according to the rules set out in advance. In addition, the promotion of a judge to the Supreme Court was conditional upon the consent of the Council of Judges of the Slovak Republic instead of the consent of the President of the Supreme Court. This institutional change was supposed to increase transparency, limit the discretion of court presidents, and curtail the powers of the President of the Supreme Court in particular. Conversely, the involvement of the Council of Judges of the Slovak Republic improved peer review and empowered regular judges, which means judges who were *not* court presidents or vice presidents. Nevertheless, these new rules had little impact in practice because they had too short a life span. The new Judicial Council Euro-model abolished the Council of Judges of the Slovak Republic and returned significant powers in the promotion of judges to court presidents.[244]

The 1990s was a period of "wild promotion" in Slovakia. Many judges left the judiciary after 1989 for better posts in the private sector, which contributed to a shortage of judges in Slovakia in the early 1990s.[245] Another exodus of judges took place in the mid-1990s, when many judges of the appellate courts and the Supreme Court, who were dissatisfied with their material conditions, left the judiciary.[246] Finally, territorial reorganization of the court system in 1997 had significant repercussions on the promotion of Slovak judges as well, since five new regional courts were created. These three factors, each on its own, led to numerous vacancies at appellate courts that had to be filled hastily from a relatively small pool of candidates.[247] One of the side effects of this period of "wild promotion" was that very young judges became judges of appellate courts, and sometimes even reached the Supreme Court.[248] This also allowed Mečiar's cabinet to

---

[244] See below in Section IV.D.

[245] For further details, Bröstl, above note 53, at 145.

[246] For further details, see Bröstl, above note 53, at 145.

[247] For further details, see Rohárik, above note 53, at 217.

[248] This period of "wild promotion" also explains why the Parliament later set strict minimum age limits for each tier of the Slovak judiciary. See also notes 337–338.

install its own people at the top of the Slovak judicial hierarchy. Sometimes judges with three-year experience on the bench were promoted directly from the District Court to the Supreme Court.[249]

The *appointment of judges to the positions of court president or vice president* in practice followed de jure rules. This meant that the selection of judicial officials at district and regional courts was fully in the hands of the Minister of Justice, whose discretion was virtually unlimited. The selection of the president and vice president of the Supreme Court also did not depart from standards laid down by the Slovak Constitution and thus these judicial officials were elected by the National Council for five years. Nevertheless, the battle for the position of the president of the Supreme Court led to several bitter constitutional disputes.

After the then-president of the Supreme Court, Milan Karabín, resigned in December 1997, the National Council of the Slovak Republic, controlled by Vladimír Mečiar, elected Štefan Harabin, President of the Supreme Court for a five-year period. However, Mečiar lost the prime ministership in the September 1998 elections and went into opposition. One of the side effects of Mečiar's fall was that various controversial acts by Štefan Harabin came under close scrutiny. On August 16, 2000 the Government eventually adopted a resolution under which it initiated the revocation of Harabin's appointment for, among other things, his failure to initiate disciplinary motions with the Vice President of the Supreme Court who had forcibly entered premises belonging to the Ministry of Justice, aggrandizing his powers, arbitrary decisions on promotion and secondment to the Supreme Court, misrepresenting the views of the judiciary on the constitutional amendment bill, and commenting on a Supreme Court decision prior to its delivery to the parties.[250] On December 19, 2000 in the National Council of the Slovak Republic the motion that Harabin's appointment be revoked was defeated by sixty-two votes to sixty, with fifteen abstentions. According to many sources,[251] the result of this motion was heavily influenced by the urgent mission of the UN Special Rapporteur on the independence of judges and lawyers, Param Cumaraswamy, to Slovakia

---

[249] Interview with a former president of the regional court from April 29, 2015. See also Section II.A of this chapter.
[250] For further details, see ECtHR, *Harabin v. Slovakia* (dec.), no. 62584/00, July 9, 2002; or Report of the Special Rapporteur on the Independence Of Judges And Lawyers On His Mission To The Slovak Republic (November 27–29, 2000), E/CN.4/2001/65/Add.3, § 27–33.
[251] See, for example, Rohárik, above note 53, at 218–219.

in November 2000,[252] and Cumaraswamy's subsequent criticism of the Government's motion.[253]

However, the controversy over the position of the Supreme Court president did not end in 2000. As mentioned earlier, following the entry into force, on July 1, 2001, of the 2001 Constitutional Amendment the post of President of the Supreme Court was to be filled by the candidate favored by the President of the Slovak Republic, upon the proposal of the JCSR, from among the judges of the Supreme Court for a five-year period.[254] Štefan Harabin was a successful candidate for that post in an election held by the JCSR on December 20, 2002. Nevertheless, the Constitutional Court subsequently invalidated his election on the ground that the other candidate had been at a disadvantage compared with Štefan Harabin, who in his capacity as the head of the JCSR could cast a vote for himself.[255] The subsequent elections having failed to result in the appointment of the President of the Supreme Court, Harabin held the post until February 2003, when the five-year term for which he had been appointed in 1998 expired.

It remains to address whether and to what extent the court presidents acted as the conduit of the will of the Slovak politicians at the National Council and at the Ministry of Justice. It seems that even though there were several interferences coming from both of these political actors, Slovak court presidents did not operate as straightforward transmission belt of the Slovak political elite. Like in the Czech Republic, virtually all Slovak court presidents and vice presidents from the communist era were removed shortly after the Velvet Revolution in 1990 and were replaced by judges chosen by the democratic political elites. These new court presidents appointed after the fall of the communist regime were appointed for an indefinite period.[256] Hence, the number of vacancies on these posts was limited. True, some court presidents were recalled by the Ministers

---

[252] See Report of the Special Rapporteur on the Independence of Judges and Lawyers on His Mission to the Slovak Republic (November 27–29, 2000), E/CN.4/2001/65/Add.3.

[253] Notably, at the end of his mission, Param Cumaraswamy, allegedly "in view of the intense media interest on the issue of Dr. Harabin's removal," held a press conference on November 29, 2000 on the premises of the Supreme Court, where he commended the deputies of the Slovak Parliament for having defeated the Government's motion to remove Štefan Harabin as President of the Supreme Court. For a sober account of Param Cumaraswamy's term as the Special Rapporteur on the Independence of Judges and Lawyers, see Lorne Neudorf, "Promoting Independent Justice in a Changing World" (2012) 12 *Human Rights Law Review* 107, 108–112.

[254] See Article 145(3) of the Slovak Constitution after the 2001 Constitutional Amendment.

[255] Judgment of the Constitutional Court of Slovakia of February 19, 2003, case no. II. ÚS 5/03.

[256] Note that the limited term of court presidents and vice presidents were introduced in Slovakia only in 2005. See Section IV.C of this chapter.

of Justice Liščák[257] and Čarnogurský.[258] However, these dismissals were justified by the manipulation of the case assignment process by the given court presidents[259] or limited in number.[260] The unsuccessful impeachment of Štefan Harabin in 2000 also shows that a Supreme Court president was able to openly resist the politicians currently in power. Hence, even though Slovak court presidents perhaps lagged slightly behind their Czech colleagues in terms of emancipation from the politicians at power, they had significant room for maneuver.

De facto rules of *promotion to the position of chamber president* did not differ from de jure standards until 2000. In practice, promotion to the position of chamber president was fully in the hands of court presidents. Presidents of regional courts were particularly influential in this type of promotion since the president of a regional court administered not only his own court and the judges assigned to it, but also all the district courts within the jurisdiction of that regional court.

Like de facto rules on promotion to a higher court, this arrangement changed after the adoption of the 2000 Law on Judges and Lay Judges. After 2001, court presidents still formally decided on this carrot, but all promotions to the position of chamber president resulted from open competition and required consultation with judicial boards. In addition, the position of chamber president at district courts was abolished. The aims of these institutional changes were the same as those behind the changes in the promotion of judges to higher courts – to increase transparency, limit the discretion of court presidents, and curtail the powers of the President of the Supreme Court. Conversely, the involvement of judicial boards and election by their peers empowered regular judges. Nevertheless, these new rules operated for only two years, because the Judicial Council Euro-model changed the rules again.

The *secondment* of judges followed the same path as the permanent promotion of judges. According to de jure standards, the power to second judges to regional courts was vested in the presidents of regional courts. The power to second judges to the Supreme Court was shared by the Minister of Justice and the President of the Supreme Court. However, court presidents in fact controlled secondment not only to regional courts, but also to

---

[257] *Minister Liščák zavádza a nemá dôveru sudcov*, Sme.sk, May 5, 1997, available at www.sme .sk/c/2073444/minister-liscak-zavadza-a-nema-doveru-sudcov.html.

[258] See Rohárik, above note 53, at 226; or *Judges fired for mismanagement*, The Slovak Spectator, August 23,1999, available at http://spectator.sme.sk/articles/view/3914/1/.

[259] Ibid. See also note 273 below.

[260] Liščák dismissed only two court presidents in 1999; see note 257 above.

the Supreme Court. The criteria were nonexistent, which often led to arbitrariness. For instance, the president of the Supreme Court, Štefan Harabin, proposed to assign temporarily to the Supreme Court a district court judge who had clearly failed to meet the professional and moral requirements for holding a post at the Supreme Court, while he rejected the transfer of a judge recommended by the Council of Judges of the Slovak Republic.[261] A similar shift happened with the *temporary assignment of judges outside the judiciary*. Even though the Minister of Justice could act unilaterally according to de jure standards, in fact court presidents had a power of veto.

The practice of awarding *salary bonuses* was relatively uneventful until 2000. The National Council decided on most salary bonuses, as provided by law. The criteria were unclear, but the bonuses were relatively stable and the amounts of bonuses awarded were in reasonable relation to the basic salary. For instance, the bonuses awarded to the president of the Supreme Court amounted to between 10% of his average salary in 1997 and 28% of his average salary in 1998 (see Table 6.2).

In June 2001, the National Council lost its power to decide on judicial salary. The 2001 Constitutional Amendment transferred this power to the JCSR. However, the JCSR started to operate fully only in August 2003. In the meantime, many court presidents exploited the legal vacuum in 2001 and 2002 and unilaterally gave themselves the power to decide on salary bonuses. Some of these court presidents also abused the lack of maximum limits for salary bonuses and awarded high bonuses to themselves and their "friends" on the bench.

For instance, the president of the Supreme Court, Štefan Harabin, in 2001 and 2002 awarded himself bonuses that were higher than his annual basic salary (see Table 6.2). But Harabin also used his new power to reward his favorite judges at the Supreme Court. In September 2002, he gave out salary bonuses totaling 2,234,000 SKK and again in December totaling 2,756,000 SKK.[262] The precise distribution of these bonuses among individual judges is not publicly available, but according to reliable sources, the bonuses varied from zero for "disfavored" judges to several hundred thousand Slovak crowns for his "favorite" judges.[263]

In other words, de facto rules for awarding salary bonuses to judges significantly departed from de jure rules in 2001 and 2002. In practice, court presidents and not the JCSR, which was not operating at that time, unilaterally

---

[261] See ECtHR, *Harabin v. Slovakia* (dec.), no. 62584/00, July 9, 2002.
[262] Odmeny udelené sudcom Najvyššieho súdu v roku 2002, *Pravda*, December 20, 2002.
[263] Ibid.

Table 6.2. *Regular salary and salary bonuses of the President of the Supreme Court of Slovakia between 1993 and 2002*

Year	1993	1994	1995	1996	1997	1998	1999	2000	2001	2002
Average salary [thousand SKK]	162	211	211	259	294	332	332	386	411	445
Bonuses [thousand SKK]	30	45	54	35	30	92	66	57	420	685
Bonuses/Ave.Salary [%]	19%	21%	26%	14%	10%	28%	20%	15%	102%	154%

Source: Katarína Staroňová, Rovní a rovnejší Štefana Harabina, June 1, 2009).

decided on salary bonuses. What is more, their discretion regarding to whom to award a bonus and how big a bonus to award was virtually unlimited.

As mentioned above, Slovak law did not lay down any criteria regarding *case assignment* until 2000. In practice, court presidents prepared the annual work schedules, and thus they also decided on case assignment. The 2000 Law on Judges and Lay Judges, which came into force in January 2001, only legalized this de facto situation.[264] Thus, I may conclude that court presidents dominated case assignment throughout the whole period between 1993 and 2002.

I described in detail how the work schedule was prepared and how case assignment and reassignment worked in practice in the chapter on the Czech Republic.[265] Work schedules and case assignment operated in the same way in Slovakia. Therefore, the potential dangers of vesting the power to create annual work schedules and to decide on reassignment during the year to court presidents without stipulating any criteria in law were the same as in the Czech Republic. First, court presidents could easily manipulate the work schedule so as to reward or punish judges.[266] Second, court presidents could depart from the existing work schedule, if they deemed it necessary.[267] As the European Court of Human Rights observed, the latitude of court presidents in reassigning cases was "significant" in Slovakia at that time.[268] Sometimes court presidents did not even bother with justifying reassignment and applying generic criteria and simply reassigned individual cases.[269] In the most blatant cases, court presidents reassigned cases to themselves so that they could control their outcome.[270] Third, given the fact that Slovak law neither laid down a concrete method of case assignment nor required the case assignment to be random, there was an ample room for court registrars to use "invisible" criteria in assigning cases.[271]

---

[264] The right of judges to challenge violations of the work schedule before the court president and the judicial board proved to be toothless.

[265] See also Chapter 5, Sections III.D and IV.D.

[266] For further details on how to do it, see the chapter on the Czech Republic (Chapter 5, Sections III.D and IV.D).

[267] For an example of misuse of this power, see ECtHR, *DMD GROUP, a.s. v. Slovakia*, no. 19334/03, October 5, 2010, §§ 15–21 and §§ 65–72.

[268] ECtHR, *DMD GROUP, a.s. v. Slovakia*, no. 19334/03, October 5, 2010, § 68.

[269] ECtHR, *DMD GROUP, a.s. v. Slovakia*, no. 19334/03, October 5, 2010, § 69.

[270] ECtHR, *DMD GROUP, a.s. v. Slovakia*, no. 19334/03, October 5, 2010, § 71. For another example, see Bröstl, above note 53, at 153.

[271] The available techniques of rigging case assignment at the court registry were described in the chapter on the Czech Republic (Chapter 5, Sections III.D and IV.D).

There is general consensus in Slovakia that abuse of case assignment was widespread in the 1990s[272] and that it involved courts at all echelons of the Slovak judiciary.[273] Interestingly, the public poll taken at one district court revealed that the motivation behind rigging case assignment was twofold – to influence the outcome of the case and to speed up the delivery of the judgment.[274]

The importance of case assignment explains the battle over the installation of the so-called electronic registry at the Supreme Court.[275] The "electronic registry" is the name for the process of assigning cases on a random basis by software without any interference from human beings.[276] "Electronic registries" were required by the 2002 Law on the JCSR[277] and were introduced at all district and regional courts by the end of 2002. The only court that resisted the introduction of the "electronic registry" was the Supreme Court, whose president, Štefan Harabin, did everything to forestall the process of disempowering court presidents in assigning cases.[278]

---

[272] See, for example, Rohárik, above note 53, at 223; or Staroňová, above note 228, at 217. The results of the 2002 poll are notable: 60% of respondents stated that corruption at courts and prokuratura existed and was widespread, 25% of respondents stated that corruption at courts and prokuratura existed but they did not know how widespread it was, and only 1% stated that corruption at courts and prokuratura did not exist (Transparency International Slovakia (2004), cited from Staroňová, above note 228, at 217).

[273] On the Supreme Court, see below. Regarding regional courts, for instance, the president and the vice president of the Regional Court of Bratislava were dismissed for manipulation of the case assignment process in the summer of 1999 and three more judicial officials of Žilina were dismissed for similar reasons toward the end of 1999. See Rohárik, above note 53, at 226; or "Judges fired for mismanagement," The Slovak Spectator, August 23, 1999, available at http://spectator.sme.sk/articles/view/3914/1/.

[274] Jana Dubovcová, "Sudnictvo a korupcia" in Emília Sičáková-Beblavá and Daniela Zemanovičová (eds.), Protikorupčne nastroje (TIS, 2003) (cited from Staroňová, above note 228, at 222). See also Rohárik, above note 53, at 226.

[275] The installation of "electronic registries" at each court was a part of a broader project called "Judicial Management" (Súdný manažment). The "Judicial Management" project was implemented in 1999–2005 and its aim was twofold – to reduce corruption and to increase the efficiency of courts.

[276] The project of "electronic registries" was partially funded and its implementation facilitated by the Swiss Government and by ABA-CEELI; see Staroňová, above note 228, at 226–227.

[277] Law No. 185/2002 on the JCSR.

[278] Harabin raised various objections that either lacked any substance (for instance, he asserted that the case assignment could be rigged anyway by lodging repetitive motions) and were eventually rebutted or were only minor (for instance, he voiced the criticism that random case assignment did not take into account the level of difficulty of each case); see, for example, Staroňová, above note 228, at 225–226. However, the main point here is that he basically ignored the law that was properly passed by the Slovak Parliament and acted as someone who is above the law.

Štefan Harabin repeatedly clashed on this issue not only with the Minister of Justice, but also with the vice president of the Supreme Court, Juraj Majchrák. Majchrák was a staunch supporter of the "electronic registry," which he perceived as a necessary tool in the fight against corruption.[279] Despite the external and internal pressure, Štefan Harabin managed to prevent the installation of the "electronic registry" at the Supreme Court until his term expired in February 2003 and thus cases at the Supreme Court were not assigned on a random basis for the entire period between 1993 and 2002.

In sum, it is possible to conclude that between 1993 and 2002, court presidents at all courts had significant latitude in assigning cases. They dominated the process of creating the annual work schedule[280] as well as the actual assignment of individual cases. Similarly, their power to reassign cases was very broad, despite the attempts of the Constitutional Court of the Slovak to enforce the right to a legal judge. The only difference was that the president of the Supreme Court retained this power until December 2002, whereas the discretion of presidents of the lower courts has been curtailed in the second half of 2002.[281]

The first *judicial performance evaluation* took place in 2001. As mentioned earlier, three principals were involved in it: (1) court presidents; (2) senior judges from higher courts; (3) judges sitting on a special review committee. Nevertheless, court presidents played the key role in assessing judges and treated the other two actors as mere providers of necessary information rather than coevaluators of judges. Moreover, the results of judicial performance evaluation were not published and so this mechanism in practice increased the information asymmetry that favored court presidents. Criteria of judicial performance evaluation were vague and court presidents thus enjoyed broad discretion. Finally, the link between judicial performance and disciplining judges was unclear. No statute forced court presidents to initiate disciplinary motions against poorly performing judges. This again left significant latitude for court presidents in deciding how to proceed in such cases.

---

[279] As will be shown subsequently, Harabin did not forget Majchrák's criticism and retaliated against him once he became the president of the Supreme Court again in 2009.

[280] Note that the first annual work schedules adopted according to the new rules laid down by the 2002 Law on the JCSR were the work schedules for 2003, since the 2002 Law on the JCSR was adopted in April 2002 and thus it could not affect the annual work schedule for 2002 prepared in the early months of 2002.

[281] Note that even the "electronic registry" did not remove all discretion from court presidents. For more details, see notes 400–409 in this chapter.

E.   Brief Summary of Years 1993–2002

The following tentative conclusions can be drawn from the analysis of mechanisms of judicial accountability used between 1993 and 2002. First, there were three major principals of judges – the Minister of Justice, the National Council, and court presidents. Other actors played a very limited role in holding judges to account. Judicial boards had no decision-making powers and court presidents in practice often disregarded even their consultative powers. The public could use a complaint mechanism, but these complaints were eventually processed by court presidents. The remaining potential actors, such as the ombudsman and the Bar, had no say at all.

Second, court presidents, and not the Minister of Justice, dominated the Slovak judiciary in practice. Court presidents entirely controlled the following four mechanisms: reassignment, case assignment, chamber president appointment, and secondment. They also initiated most disciplinary motions,[282] processed complaints from the public, and had an equal say with the Minister of Justice in two other mechanisms, namely promotion and temporary assignment outside the judiciary. The legislature controlled two mechanisms completely – once-and-for-all retention reviews of new judges[283] and salary bonuses. It also the elected the President and the Vice President of the Supreme Court of the Slovak Republic, but vacancies at these posts were extremely rare.[284] Contrary to general wisdom, there was only one mechanism which was controlled entirely by the Minister of Justice – appointment to the position of court president or vice president. Third, the powers of all principals remained quite stable between 1993 and June 2001. It was only the 2001 Constitutional Amendment that changed the balance of powers among the three major principals. Table 6.3 quantifies[285] the "accountability-to-whom question."

Regarding the second and third research questions, how frequently and how severely were judges held to account, I do not address them here, since I do not have any normative benchmark on how often and how

---

[282] However, note that disciplinary panels, which were composed of professional judges, served as a check on the power of court presidents.

[283] Note that the Government increasingly interfered with the retention review and so the legislature did not control this mechanism completely.

[284] There were two Presidents of the Slovak Supreme Court elected by the National Council between 1993 and 2002: Milan Karabin in 1996 and Štefan Harabin in 1998 (both were elected during the Mečiar's regime). Between 1993 and 1996 the seat of the President of the Slovak Supreme Court was occupied by Karol Plank (1990–1996) who was selected already in the federal era.

[285] For explanation of the method used to calculate this table, see Chapter 4.

Table 6.3. *Who controlled de facto mechanisms of judicial accountability in Slovakia between 1993 and 2002? Slovakia (1993–2002)*

Year	Who controlled de facto mechanisms of JA?				
	Number of available mechanisms	Number of mechanisms controlled by MoJ	Number of mechanisms controlled by CP	Number of mechanisms controlled by LEG	Number of mechanisms controlled by OTHERS
1993	10	1.90	6.00	1.10	1.00
1994	10	1.90	6.00	1.10	1.00
1995	10	1.98	5.92	1.10	1.00
1996	10	1.90	6.00	1.10	1.00
1997	11	2.07	5.83	1.60	1.50
1998	10	1.90	5.50	1.60	1.00
1999	11	2.09	5.81	1.60	1.50
2000	11	2.15	5.75	1.60	1.50
2001	11	2.00	7.55	–	1.45
2002	11	2.03	7.51	–	1.46
Average	10.5	1.99	6.19	1.08	1.24
Average [%]		**19%**	**59%**	**10%**	**12%**

* MoJ = Minister of Justice, CP = court presidents, LEG = Legislature, OTHERS = other actors (e.g., judges other than court presidents, judicial boards, ombudsman, the Bar, the public)

intensively Slovak judges should have been held to account between 1993 and 2002. As I mentioned already in Chapter 5, these numbers do not have any "stand alone" value. They make sense only when compared with what happened in the other three mini-case studies. All four intercountry and intracountry comparisons[286] will be conducted in Chapter 7.

Finally, regarding accountability perversions two of them emerged in Slovakia between 1993 and 2002: judicial accountability avoidance and output excesses of judicial accountability. As to the former, Slovak judges resisted the introduction of individualized statistics, judicial performance evaluation (until 2000), measures to improve the transparency of judicial decision-making, and personal financial disclosures. They also managed to successfully invoke and defend short statutory limits for initiating disciplinary motions. As to the latter, Slovak adopted the same techniques to meet the monthly "soft quota" for finished cases as their Czech colleagues. They either artificially split the case into separate case files with the aim of artificially multiplying their productivity or preferred, if possible, short procedural decisions instead of the judgment on the merits.[287]

On the other hand, simulating judicial accountability was rare in this period as the only toothless mechanism of judicial accountability was the complaint system. Finally, I could not find any traces of systematic misuse of mechanisms of judicial accountability in order to punish critics and reward allies within the judiciary. Similarly to the Czech Republic, there were some problematic instances of reassignment of judges and case assignment by court presidents, promotion of certain judges was debatable (especially during the period of "wild promotion"[288]) and Mečiar's government used one time retention reviews to retaliate against young judges. But none of these incidents affected the Slovak judiciary as such and there was no pattern to target a particular group within the judiciary. In sum, selective accountability was relatively low.

IV. Mechanisms of Judicial Accountability from 2003 to 2010

This section discusses contingent circumstances in Slovakia from 2003 to 2010 and then it analyzes what the law on the books said about holding Slovak judges to account and how they were actually held to account in

---

[286] For further details on the research design of my case studies see Chapter 4, Section I.
[287] For further details see Chapter 5.
[288] See Section III.D of this chapter.

this period. It follows the same structure and looks at the same issues as the previous section which focused on the period between 1993 and 2002. To avoid repetition, the discussion will focus primarily on new mechanisms introduced in 2003–2010 and on the existing mechanisms that were altered in this period.[289]

A. Contingent Circumstances

The only group of measures that remained relatively static and followed the pattern from the previous decade was *appeals and quasi-appellate mechanisms*. "Extraordinary appeals" were allowed in criminal law matters and only the Minister of Justice could lodge such appeals. The Supreme Court[290] could still issue "interpretative guidelines" in order to unify divergent case law and the grand chamber of the Supreme Court had not been created.

The remaining three groups of measures underwent significant modifications between 2003 and 2010. The *recruitment and selection of judges* changed due to the introduction of the JCSR, which started to play a key role in selecting judges from 2003.[291] As mentioned in Section III.A, under the revised Slovak Constitution judges are appointed for an indefinite period by the President of the Slovak Republic upon the nomination of the JCSR.[292] However, the constitutional rules do not fully capture the complexity of the selection of judges in Slovakia.

First, the statutory law provided that each vacancy within the judiciary had to be filled on the basis of open competition and established an additional body that played a role in selecting judges – an ad hoc "judicial

---

[289] The literature in English on the state of the Slovak judiciary in this period is scarce; for a brief overview, see Bojarski and Köster, above note 83. The key publications in Slovak are Svák, above note 28; Drgonec 2006a, above note 119; Ján Drgonec, "Disciplinárna zodpovednosť sudcov – Mechanizmus a podmienky jej uplatnenia: Druhá časť: Uplatňovanie disciplinárnej zodpovednosti v praxi disciplinárneho súdu" (2006) 58 *Justičná revue* 601; Eva Kovačechová and Peter Wilfling (eds.), *Presvedčivosť a transparentnosť rozhodovania súdov*, VIA IURIS, 2012; Zuzana Čaputová (ed.), *Zodpovednosť sudcu: Sudcovská etika a disciplinárna zodpovednosť*, VIA IURIS, 2011; and Eva Kovačechová and Zuzana Čaputová (eds.), *Vybrané aspekty disciplinárního súdnictva*, VIA IURIS, 2012.

[290] Arts. 8(3), 20(1)(b), 21(3)(a)–(b) and 22 of the 2004 Law on Courts.

[291] Note that the 2001 Constitutional Amendment that introduced the JCSR came into effect in July 2001, but the JCSR started to operate only in January 2003 and thus these changes became effective on the ground only after 2003.

[292] Art. 145(1) of the 1992 Slovak Constitution after the 2001 Constitutional Amendment. For a more detailed account of the new model of selection and recruitment of judges, see Section IV.A.

selection committee."[293] This committee was created for each vacancy within the judiciary and consisted of five members. The rules for the creation of ad hoc "judicial selection committees" changed over time. Initially, all five members were appointed by the court president upon the nomination of a judicial board of a court where the vacancy was. From November 2003 until December 2008, the court president appointed only three members of the committee upon the nomination of a judicial board, while one member was appointed by the JCSR and one by the Minister of Justice. From January 2009 until December 2010, yet another arrangement applied. The ad hoc "judicial selection committees" still consisted of five members, but its composition was as follows: the president of the court with a vacancy, one member selected by a judicial board of a court with a vacancy, one member appointed by the JCSR, one member appointed by the Minister of Justice, and one member appointed by a collegium of chairmen of judicial boards.[294]

Second, soon after its establishment, a debate about the role of the JCSR in the process of appointment of judges arose within it. The key issue was whether the JCSR should operate as a mere "postman" between the ad hoc "judicial selection committee" and the Slovak President or whether it could review the results submitted by the "judicial selection committee." The latter position eventually prevailed and every candidate for a judicial office had to obtain at least ten out of eighteen votes from the JCSR in order to be nominated by it to the President.[295] This meant that the JCSR controlled the appointment of new judges since it not only nominated one member to "judicial selection committees," but also had the power to block any candidate from the list provided by those.

In a nutshell, despite different de jure standards, court presidents and the JCSR de facto dominated the selection and recruitment of judges until 2009. In 2009, court presidents lost their control of the ad hoc "judicial selection committees," but they could still exercise their influence within the JCSR. Not surprisingly, in 2009 and 2010 the JCSR often clashed with the ad hoc "judicial selection committees" and with the Minister of Justice.

[293] Art. 28 of Law No. 385/2000 Z. z., on Judges and Lay Judges.

[294] Art. 29(2) of Law No. 385/2000 Z. z., on Judges and Lay Judges, as amended by Law No. 517/2008 Z. z. and Law No. 520/2008 Z. z. Note that judicial candidates enjoyed preferential treatment in appointment to district courts throughout this period. It meant that when there was a judicial candidate (who passed a judicial exam) working at the district court where a vacancy opened, there was no open competition and the vacancy was filled by this judicial candidate.

[295] See Svák, above note 28, at 59. This power of the JCSR was confirmed by the Constitutional Court (see Judgment No. III. US 79/04).

These skirmishes eventually led to a stalemate – the JCSR refused to nominate any judge selected by an ad hoc "judicial selection committee" to the President of the Slovak Republic.

Regarding mechanisms such as case assignment, judicial salaries, reassignment, and promotion, which can be designed so as to avoid accounting, Slovakia made significant efforts between 2003 and 2010 to limit potential ex post interference, but all of these four mechanisms included the element of discretion. This means that all four mechanisms could be used to hold individual judges to account and will be thus discussed in Sections IV.C and IV.D.

Many *transparency mechanisms* were introduced as early as by the 2000 Law on Judges and Lay Judges, but they started to operate fully only in 2003. Most importantly, the 2000 Law on Judges and Lay Judges increased transparency in the selection and promotion of judges. It introduced open competitions for vacancies within the judiciary[296] and laid down that each vacancy had to be advertised in advance. Moreover, sitting judges were required to disclose their nonjudicial activities (via personal declaration) as well as their property and income (via financial declaration) on an annual basis.

Access to judicial decisions also improved between 2003 and 2010. The Supreme Court of Slovakia started publishing all decisions on the merits online in August 2008. The broadening of access to decisions of lower courts proceeded only halfway. The Ministry of Justice started to publish all decisions of district and regional courts in civil and commercial law cases online in 2006, but access to decisions in criminal and administrative matters remained almost nonexistent until 2010.[297] Similarly, the transparency of judicial statistics remained poor. Judicial statistics were still compiled mostly in an ad hoc manner and their results were rarely published.[298]

---

[296] Another major increase in transparency took place in 2011, when the Law No. 33/2011 Z. z. and Law No. 100/2011 Z. z. laid down, among other things, that the selection process should be public, that the CVs of candidates for judicial office had to be published online in advance, that candidates for judicial office had to disclose their family ties within the judiciary, and the transparency of judicial performance evaluation was improved. Similar conditions were also required from candidates for the positions of court presidents and vice presidents.

[297] This situation improved only in 2011, when the Slovak Parliament passed the law that requires online publication of all judgments of Slovak courts. See Art. 82a of Law No. 757/2004 Z. z., on Courts, as amended by Law No. 33/2011 Z. z. and Law No. 467/2011 Z. z.

[298] This practice changed only in 2011, when the Law No. 33/2011 Z. z. and Law No. 100/2011 Z. z. provided that statistical data about the work of courts, chambers, and individual

Finally, the *training of judges* underwent similar development as in the Czech Republic. The Judicial Academy of the Slovak Republic was established in 2003 and became responsible for the training of sitting judges as well as judicial candidates. The Judicial Academy had the same effects as in the Czech Republic. It reduced the influence of the Ministry of Justice and court presidents over judicial training and, in particular, over invited speakers. It also increased the quality and variety of courses. The other developments also mirrored the situation in the Czech Republic. On the one hand, the number of courses provided by foreign actors increased due to the expected accession of Slovakia to the European Union. On the other hand, two chronic problems relating to judicial training persisted from the previous period. One was that training sessions were usually attended by the same small number of judges. This was to a great extent remedied in 2009, when the amendment to the 2004 Law on Courts introduced a general duty of judges to attend training at the Judicial Academy.[299] The second problem was that many Slovak judges still held the view that "judges must be trained only by judges," which was strengthened by a hierarchical pattern within the Slovak judiciary. Combination of these two factors led to the "balkanization of judicial education," where judges of lower courts ranked highest the seminars in which judges of the Supreme Court told them how to solve legal issues in "their" cases.[300]

B. Which Mechanisms of Judicial Accountability Were Used?

In a nutshell, all mechanisms of judicial accountability that were used in 2002 remained available between 2003 and 2010 and no new mechanisms were established throughout this period. For the sake of clarity, they are included in the concise table (see Table 6.4).

C. Mechanisms of Judicial Accountability on the Books

The Slovak Parliament eventually succumbed to pressure from domestic actors and the European Commission and decided to replace the existing Ministry of Justice model of court administration with the Judicial Council Euro-model. This effort materialized in the 2001 Constitutional

judges had to be published online on an annual basis and explicitly stated that judicial statistics were a factor in judicial performance evaluation.
[299] Art. 30(7) of Law No. 757/2004 Z. z., on Courts, as amended by Law No. 517/2008 Z. z.
[300] Svák, above note 28, at 62.

Table 6.4. *Mechanisms of judicial accountability available in Slovakia between 2003 and 2010*

Mechanisms of judicial accountability available in Slovakia between 2003 and 2010
Sticks
Disciplinary proceedings
Reassignment
Complaint mechanism
~~Retention for new judges~~
Carrots
Promotion to a higher court
Chamber president appointment
Secondment
Temporary assignment outside the judiciary
Appointment of a judge to the position of court president or vice president
Dual mechanisms
Case assignment
Salary bonuses
Judicial performance evaluation

Amendment, which introduced the Judicial Council of the Slovak Republic. However, it was a further eighteen months before all necessary statutes were passed and the JCSR started to operate fully. This large scale institutional overhaul resulted in, among other things, extensive amendments to the 2000 Law on Judges and Lay Judges[301] and the adoption of several new statutes governing the judiciary such as Law on the Judicial Council of the Slovak Republic,[302] the statute that created the Special Court,[303] and a brand new Law on Courts.[304] De jure standards of most mechanisms of judicial accountability can be found in these four statutes.

The introduction of the Judicial Council Euro-model in Slovakia significantly affected the *disciplining* of judges. The basic design of courts involved in the disciplining of Slovak judges remained the same between 2003 and 2010. The Constitutional Court decided on disciplinary motions

[301] Law No. 385/2000 Z. z., on Judges and Lay Judges.
[302] Law No. 185/2002, on the Judicial Council of the Slovak Republic.
[303] Law No. 458/2003, on the establishment of the Special Court and The Office of Special Prosecutor.
[304] Law No. 757/2004, on Courts.

against the president and vice president of the Supreme Court, whereas the Disciplinary Court, a *sui generis* court attached to the Supreme Court, decided on motions against all other judges. The procedure before the Constitutional Court also remained the same between 2003 and 2010.

However, the procedure before the Disciplinary Court changed several times. Immediately after its creation, the JCSR acquired an important role in the disciplining of judges. First, the JCSR elected all members of the panels of the Disciplinary Court from judges nominated by judicial boards. Second, the JCSR decided on the composition of the panels of the Disciplinary Court as well as on the "work schedule" of the Disciplinary Court. Finally, the JCSR was also granted the power to initiate disciplinary motions against judges, and thus became a disciplinary prosecutor as well.[305] These changes gave tremendous power to those groups who control the JCSR. Two more changes started to function in late 2002. Another disciplinary prosecutor was introduced into the Slovak disciplinary system – the Ombudsman.[306] The number of judges on the panels of the Disciplinary Court was reduced to three (for first instance panels[307]) and five (for appellate panels[308]).

Yet another overhaul of the disciplining of judges took place in October 2003. The 2003 overhaul changed both the definitions of disciplinary offenses and the composition of the Disciplinary Court.[309] Apart from a minor amendment in 2004, this model survived until December 2008, when the composition of the Disciplinary Court changed again. Hence, I distinguish three models[310] of disciplining judges applicable between 2003 and 2010 – the model applicable in 2003, that applicable

---

[305] Art. 120(2)(c) of Law No. 385/2000 Z. z., on Judges and Lay Judges, as amended by Law No. 185/2002 Z. z. This power of the JCSR created a huge constitutional problem, since the JCSR acted as a disciplinary prosecutor and at the same time had a major role in staffing the Disciplinary Court (see Drgonec 2006a, above note 119, 419–420; and Svák, above note 28, at 60).

[306] Art. 120(2)(b) of Law No. 385/2000 Z. z., on Judges and Lay Judges, as amended by Law No. 185/2002 Z. z.

[307] The composition of the three-member panel was as follows: one district court judge, one regional court judge, and one judge of the Supreme Court. The Supreme Court judge always acted as a panel chairman. See Art. 119(6) of Law No. 385/2000 Z. z., on Judges and Lay Judges, as amended by Law No. 185/2002 Z. z..

[308] The appellate panel still consisted exclusively of Supreme Court judges. See Art. 119(6) of Law No. 385/2000 Z. z., on Judges and Lay Judges, as amended by Law No. 185/2002 Z. z.

[309] See Law No. 426/2003 Z. z.

[310] Note that the 2003 Amendment (Law No. 426/2003 Z. z.) to the 2002 Law on Judges and Lay Judges came into effect in November 2003. Nevertheless, for the sake of simplification, I will divide the periods into "full years."

between 2004 and 2008, and that applicable between 2009 and 2010. The perception of membership at the Disciplinary Court among Slovak judges has also changed. Being a member of a disciplinary panel still did not carry an extra salary, but especially after Harabin's return to the presidency of the Supreme Court in 2009 the prestige of this position waned.[311] Members of the Disciplinary Court were subjected to the constant pressure from various groups within the Slovak judiciary as well as from the Minister of Justice and the media. Everybody knew that many disciplinary motions in 2009–2010 were lodged against Harabin's major critics, and this sense of selective disciplining further degraded the perception of the Disciplinary Court in the eyes of judges and the public in large.

This part will again focus on only four issues: who could initiate a disciplinary motion, who decided on that motion, actions for which judges were disciplined, and the available sanctions. I start with disciplinary prosecutors. In 2003 and 2004, the Minister of Justice, the Ombudsman, and the JCSR could trigger disciplinary motion against any judge. In addition, the president of the Supreme Court and presidents of district courts could initiate disciplinary motions against judges of "their" courts and presidents of regional courts could initiate disciplinary motions both against judges of "their" courts and against judges of district courts within "their" regions.[312] In 2005, judicial boards were added to the list of disciplinary prosecutors.[313] Until 2008, judicial boards could initiate disciplinary motions both against regular judges of a given court and against the president of the relevant court. However, they lost the power to trigger the disciplining of the latter in 2009 and so they could prosecute only regular judges in 2009 and 2010. This small change reduced the peer review of court presidents.

Regarding the second issue, the Disciplinary Court decided on disciplinary motions against all judges, apart from the president and vice president of the Supreme Court who were tried before the Constitutional Court. The composition of the Disciplinary Court changed twice between 2003 and 2010. In 2003, the JCSR elected all members of the panels of the Disciplinary Court from judges nominated by judicial boards.[314] Between

---

[311] Interview with a Judge of the Supreme Court of Slovakia from April 23, 2015.

[312] Art. 120(2) of Law No. 385/2000 Z. z., on Judges and Lay Judges, as amended by Law No. 185/2002 Z. z.

[313] Art. 120(2)(f) of Law No. 385/2000 Z. z., on Judges and Lay Judges, as amended by Law No. 757/2004 Z. z.

[314] For details, see Section III.C.

2004 and 2008, professional judges were in the minority on disciplinary panels. The first instance disciplinary panels consisted of three members: one member of the judiciary nominated by the judicial boards, one member nominated by the National Council, and one member nominated by the Minister of Justice.[315] The appellate disciplinary panel consisted of five members: one member of the judiciary nominated by the judicial boards, two members nominated by the National Council, and two members nominated by the Minister of Justice.[316]

The JCSR still had a significant role in the creation of disciplinary panels because it elected all members of disciplinary panels from a pool of candidates which was twice larger as large as the required number of members of disciplinary panels.[317] Moreover, it asserted that it has the power to refuse the candidates submitted by the nominating body.[318] The JCSR also decided on the number of disciplinary panels and on their work schedules and selected the presidents of disciplinary panels.[319] Finally, in 2009 and 2010 the disciplinary panels were composed in the same way, but the law required there to be a majority of judges on each panel. So, at least two judges had to sit on the first instance disciplinary panel and at least three on the appellate panel.

As regards the conduct for which judges could be disciplined, the definitions from the previous period remained in force only until 2003.[320] As early as in late 2003, the Slovak Parliament, dissatisfied with the decision-making practice of disciplinary panels, decided to depart from all-encompassing general definitions for each category of disciplinary offence and instead opted for comprehensive lists of disciplinable conduct. This redefinition of all three categories of disciplinary offenses resulted in extremely convoluted definitions of a "disciplinary offense," a "serious disciplinary offense," and a "serious disciplinary offense incompatible with

---

[315] Art. 119(10) of Law No. 385/2000 Z. z., on Judges and Lay Judges, as amended by Law No. 426/2003 Z. z.
[316] Art. 119(10) of Law No. 385/2000 Z. z., on Judges and Lay Judges, as amended by Law No. 426/2003 Z. z.
[317] Art. 119(3) of Law No. 385/2000 Z. z., on Judges and Lay Judges, as amended by Law No. 426/2003 Z. z. In practice, each nominator (judicial boards, the National Council, and the Minister of Justice) nominated twice as many candidates as the JCSR announced it had to fill and the JCSR chose the members of disciplinary panels from each nominator's "sub-pool" of candidates so that the required composition of the disciplinary panels was met.
[318] See Svák, above note 28, at 60.
[319] Art. 119(9) of Law No. 385/2000 Z. z., on Judges and Lay Judges, as amended by Law No. 426/2003 Z. z.
[320] For further details on these definitions, see Section III.C.

the function of a judge" that cannot be reproduced verbatim here. A summary of these new definitions must suffice.

The definition of "disciplinary offense" included the following counts: violation of judicial duties, behavior incompatible with judicial independence and judicial impartiality, delays, poor performance, failure to submit the financial declaration or to prove an increase in assets, and a violation of the principles of the state administration of courts.[321] All these counts except for the last applied to all judges. The last count targeted only judicial officials. The "serious disciplinary offense" comprised: intentional violation of the judicial duty to decide impartially and without a bias, misconduct covered by the definition of "disciplinary offense" that caused significant harm, repetitive violations of the principles of the state administration of courts, repetitive failure to submit the financial declaration or to prove an increase in assets, arbitrary decision-making that was manifestly inconsistent with the legal order, and fraudulent delays.[322] Finally, three categories of behavior were considered a "serious disciplinary offense incompatible with the function of a judge": drinking alcohol at work, the repeated commission of a serious disciplinary offense, and inability to prove a significant increase in assets.[323] These definitions stayed in force, with minor modifications, until 2010.[324]

Regarding the available sanctions, two periods must be distinguished. Until December 2003, the set of sanctions from the previous period remained in force. In 2004, the list of available sanctions was expanded. For disciplinary misdemeanors, disciplinary panels had to choose between the following four types of sanctions:[325] a reprimand, a salary reduction,[326] dismissal from the position of a judicial official, and publishing the decision

---

[321] Art. 116(1) of Law No. 385/2000 Z. z., on Judges and Lay Judges, as amended by Law No. 426/2003 Z. z.

[322] Art. 116(2) of Law No. 385/2000 Z. z., on Judges and Lay Judges, as amended by Law No. 426/2003 Z. z.

[323] Art. 116(3) of Law No. 385/2000 Z. z., on Judges and Lay Judges, as amended by Law No. 426/2003 Z. z.

[324] The two minor modifications that entered into force in 2009 are worth mentioning: (1) the refusal of a judge to undergo the "breath or blood tests" for alcohol became a new count in the definition of a "disciplinary offense"; and (2) the standard for the "arbitrary decision of a judge" count was no longer "*manifest* inconsistency with the legal order," but a mere "arbitrary decision of a judge that is inconsistent with the law."

[325] Art. 117(1) of Law No. 385/2000 Z. z., on Judges and Lay Judges, as amended by Law No. 426/2003 Z. z..

[326] More specifically, the salary deduction for "standard" disciplinary misdemeanor could amount up to 15% for up to three months (and in the case of repetitive misdemeanor for up to six months).

that a judge had failed to submit his financial declaration. A serious disciplinary misdemeanor led to harsher sanctions:[327] significant salary reduction,[328] dismissal from the position of a judicial official, publishing the decision that a judge had failed to submit his financial declaration, demotion to a lower court, or a dismissal from judicial office. Finally, only one sanction could be imposed for a "serious disciplinary misdemeanor that is incompatible with the judicial office" – dismissal from judicial office.

Nevertheless, the amended 2000 Law on Judges and Lay Judges still did not define further criteria for sanctioning judges. Disciplinary panels thus again enjoyed broad discretion in imposing sanctions and rules for disciplining judges remained judge-made law. However, one more aspect of disciplining judges underwent significant development. Under pressure from civil society the JCSR started to publish most decisions of disciplinary panels on its Web site and so the general public as well as scholars could collect these decisions and study them.

De jure standards applicable to the second stick – the *complaint mechanism* – underwent minimal changes. Until March 2005 the scheme from the previous period was applicable.[329] In April 2005, the 2004 Law on Courts came into force, but the rules governing complaints remained the same.[330] Consequently, court presidents were still vested with the power to process the complaints, the whole system was again based on a hierarchical pattern, and the president of the Supreme Court was exempted from this mechanism.

Finally, as regards the *reassignment* of judges, the 2002 Law on the JCSR legalized the existing de facto practice by laying down new detailed rules on the creation and content of "work schedules." These "work schedules" included primarily rules on case assignment,[331] but they also touched upon the reassignment of judges, since each work schedule had to determine, among other things, the composition of each chamber and the subject matter specialization of each judge and each chamber.[332] According to that statute, the annual work schedule was prepared by the court president, after prior discussion with other judges and consultation with a given

[327] Art. 117(5) of Law No. 385/2000 Z. z., on Judges and Lay Judges, as amended by Law No. 426/2003 Z. z..
[328] More specifically, the salary deduction for a serious disciplinary misdemeanor was 50–70% reduction for 3–12 months.
[329] For further details, see Section III.C above.
[330] For further details, see Arts. 62–70 of Law No. 757/2004 Z. z., on Courts.
[331] See Section III.C.
[332] Art. 26(3)(a)–(b) of the 1991 Law on Courts and Judges, as amended by Law No. 185/2002 Z. z.

judicial board.[333] Despite these advisory powers of judicial boards, court presidents had broad discretion in reshuffling the composition of chambers and reassigning individual judges, both in the phase of preparing the work schedule and during the year. This meant that the existing de facto standard applicable to the reassignment of judges was "legalized." These loose de jure rules on reassignment eventually prevailed until 2010.[334]

The same five "carrots" were available in Slovakia between 2003 and 2010: promotion, the appointment of a judge to the position of court president or vice president, chamber president appointment, secondment, and temporary assignment outside the judiciary.

Not surprisingly, the introduction of the JCSR altered the rules governing several carrots. *Promotion* of judges was one of the carrots the de jure standards of which were changed significantly. The Ministry of Justice lost its power to decide on the promotion of judges and this competence was transferred to the JCSR.[335] Other rules remained the same. Open competition had to precede any promotion[336] and promotion to the Supreme Court was allowed only if a judge had reached the age of thirty-five.[337] The age rules changed only in 2009, when the minimum age for promotion to the Supreme Court was raised to forty and the minimum age of thirty-five was introduced for promotion to regional courts.[338] Open competition for each vacancy at a higher court followed the same rules as competition for a vacancy within the judiciary. As with the appointment of judges, an ad hoc "judicial promotion committee" was created for each vacancy. Interestingly, only judges could apply for a vacancy at a higher court. In other words, the "lateral" appointment of a member of another legal profession to a higher court was prohibited.

The "judicial promotion committee" consisted of five members for the entire period between 2003 and 2010, but its composition changed over

---

[333] Art. 52 of Law No. 757/2004 Z. z., on Courts.

[334] The new 2004 Law on Courts, which replaced the federal era 1991 Law on Courts and Judges, did not modify the existing regime. See Art. 52 of Law No. 757/2004 Z. z., on Courts; for further requirements laid down by the 2004 Law on Courts regarding "work schedules," see the discussion on de jure standards of case assignment later in this chapter.

[335] Art. 14(1) of Law No. 385/2000 Z. z., on Judges and Lay Judges, as amended by Law No. 185/2002 Z. z.

[336] Art. 14(3) of Law No. 385/2000 Z. z., on Judges and Lay Judges, as amended by Law No. 185/2002 Z. z.

[337] Art. 14(2) of Law No. 385/2000 Z. z., on Judges and Lay Judges, as amended by Law No. 185/2002 Z. z.

[338] Art. 14(2) of Law No. 385/2000 Z. z., on Judges and Lay Judges, as amended by Law No. 290/2009 Z. z. and Law No. 290/2009 Z. z. Special rules for assignment to the Special Court are left aside here.

time. Initially, all five members were appointed by the court president of the court where the vacancy opened upon the nomination by a judicial board of a given court. From November 2003 until December 2008, a court president appointed only three members of the committee upon the nomination of a judicial board, while one member was appointed by the JCSR and one by the Minister of Justice. In January 2009 the composition of the ad hoc promotion committees changed again. From 2009 until 2010, the ad hoc committee for promotion to a regional court consisted of the following five members: the president of the regional court which had the vacancy, one member selected by a judicial board of the regional court which had the vacancy, one member appointed by the JCSR, one member appointed by the Minister of Justice, and one member appointed by a collegium of chairmen of judicial boards.[339] The composition of the ad hoc committee for promotion to the Supreme Court was slightly different: the president of the Supreme Court, two members selected by a judicial board of the Supreme Court, one member appointed by the JCSR, and one member appointed by the Minister of Justice.[340]

When speaking about *appointment to the position of court president or vice president* it is necessary distinguish between the appointment of judicial officials of the Supreme Court on the one hand and that of judicial officials of the lower courts on the other. The appointment of the president and vice president of the Supreme Court between 2003 and 2010 was governed by the Slovak Constitution, as amended by the 2001 Constitutional Amendment. These rules were described in Section III.C and will not be repeated here. No further amendment to this part of the Slovak Constitution was adopted between 2003 and 2010.

However, the rules for the appointment of presidents and vice presidents of district courts and regional courts changed several times between 2003 and 2010.[341] Until March 2005, the rules from the previous period remained in force.[342] In April 2005, the 2004 Law on Courts that modified the process of selection of judicial officials at district courts and regional courts entered into force. Different rules applied to court presidents and vice presidents.

---

[339] Art. 29(2) of Law No. 385/2000 Z. z., on Judges and Lay Judges, as amended by Law No. 517/2008 Z. z. and Law No. 520/2008 Z. z.
[340] Art. 29(2) of Law No. 385/2000 Z. z., on Judges and Lay Judges, as amended by Law No. 517/2008 Z. z. and Law No. 520/2008 Z. z.
[341] The special rules applicable to the selection of presidents and vice presidents of military courts (2003–2009), the Special Court (2004–2009), and the Special Criminal Court (2009–2010) are not dealt with here.
[342] For more details, see Section III.C.

Under the new scheme it was still the Minister of Justice who appointed court presidents, but the selection process was significantly modified. Importantly, the 2004 Law on Courts also introduced limited terms as well as term limitations for court presidents – like the president of the Supreme Court, presidents of the lower courts could be appointed only for five years and they could serve only two consecutive terms.[343] Regarding the selection process, for each vacancy for the position of court president, open competition was required. A call for applications had to be made in advance and any judge of the same-court-level or of a higher court could apply. As with the appointment and promotion of judges, an ad hoc "selection committee" was established.

The composition of the "selection committee" for presidents of district courts was as follows: the president of the relevant regional court, two members nominated by a judicial board of a given court, one member nominated by the JCSR, and one member nominated by the Ministry of Justice.[344] The composition of the "selection committee" for presidents of regional courts was slightly different: the president of the Supreme Court, one member nominated by a judicial board of a given court, one member appointed by a collegium of chairmen of judicial boards, one member nominated by the JCSR, and one member nominated by the Ministry of Justice.[345] Importantly, all "selection committees" prepared a list of candidates in order of preference and the Ministry of Justice had to select the new court president among the top three candidates.[346]

These detailed rules governing appointment of court presidents contrast with the minimal attention paid to their dismissal. Presidents of the regional and district courts could be dismissed by the Minister of Justice on his own motion for failure to fulfill their duties as laid down by the 2004 Law on Courts,[347] or upon petition submitted by the JCSR, by the judicial board of a given court or by the president of a higher court.[348]

---

[343] Art. 36 of Law No. 757/2004 Z. z., on Courts. Note that under the previous scheme (governed by the 1991 Law on Courts and Judges) court presidents at district and regional courts were appointed for an indefinite period. The transitional provisions of the 2004 Law on Courts provided that sitting court presidents would stay in office for two years and sitting vice presidents for one year from the entry into force of that act (see Arts 93–94 of Law No. 757/2004 Z. z., on Courts).

[344] Art. 37(5) of Law No. 757/2004 Z. z., on Courts.

[345] Art. 37(5) of Law No. 757/2004 Z. z., on Courts.

[346] Art. 37(4) of Law No. 757/2004 Z. z., on Courts.

[347] These duties, stipulated in Art. 42 of the 2004 Law on Courts, are vague and numerous.

[348] Art. 38(3)–(5) of Law No. 757/2004 Z. z., on Courts.

Regarding the appointment of vice presidents of district courts and regional courts, neither the JCSR nor the judicial boards participated in their selection. All vice presidents of lower courts were appointed by the Minister of Justice for five years upon nomination of the president of a given court.[349] Interestingly, the 2004 Law on Courts set no limit on consecutive terms for vice presidents of lower courts. As with court presidents, the Minister of Justice could dismiss vice presidents of the regional and district courts either on his own motion or upon petition submitted by one of the following four bodies: the JCSR, the judicial board of a given court, the president of a higher court, or the president of a given court.[350]

The mode of appointment and dismissal of court presidents and vice presidents of the lower courts introduced by the 2004 Law on Courts remained in force, with few changes, until 2010. The two significant modifications were brought about in 2009. First, judicial boards could no longer propose a dismissal of court presidents and vice presidents of the lower courts.[351] Second, the power of the Minister of Justice to dismiss court presidents and vice presidents was expanded. Under the new rule the Minister of Justice could dismiss court presidents and vice presidents not only for nonfulfillment of their duties explicitly laid down in the 2004 Law on Courts, but also for other serious reasons.[352]

Rules governing *promotion to the position of chamber president* remained the same until 2010. This meant that regional court presidents and the Supreme Court president still played a key role in deciding on this carrot.[353] Open competition for each vacancy as a chamber president and prior consultation with a judicial board were required by law, but court presidents had the final word.[354]

As regards the *secondment* of judges, this power was completely transferred from court presidents and the Minister of Justice to the JCSR in November 2003.[355] Under this arrangement, the JCSR both initiated and decided on the secondment of judges. However, the Slovak Parliament

---

[349] Art. 40 of Law No. 757/2004 Z. z., on Courts.

[350] Art. 41 in conjunction with Art. 38(3)–(5) of Law No. 757/2004 Z. z., on Courts.

[351] Art. 38(3) of Law No. 757/2004 Z. z., on Courts, as amended by Law No. 527/2008.

[352] Art. 38(5) of Law No. 757/2004 Z. z., on Courts, as amended by Law No. 527/2008.

[353] However, promotion to the position of chamber president was not available at district courts as all judges assigned to district courts were chamber presidents. Art. 15(3) of Law No. 385/2000 Z. z., on Judges and Lay Judges.

[354] Art. 15(1) of Law No. 385/2000 Z. z., on Judges and Lay Judges. At the Supreme Court, the President of the Supreme Court had to consult the relevant collegium as well.

[355] Art. 12(2) of Law No. 385/2000 Z. z., on Judges and Lay Judges, as amended by Law No. 426/2003 Z. z.

changed this scheme again in 2005 and returned certain powers to court presidents. Under the new scheme, secondment was initiated by the court president of the "receiving" court, that is the court to which a judge was proposed to be seconded, and the JCSR decided upon such proposal. Furthermore, the JCSR also had to discuss secondment with the president of the "sending" court, which is the court which a judge was proposed to be seconded from. In other words, the JCSR shared the power to second judges with court presidents. This scheme remained in force until 2010.

The 2000 Law on Judges and Lay Judges also laid down a time limit for the secondment of judges. Initially, no judge could be seconded to a higher court for more than one year out of three consecutive years.[356] This time limit was supposed to prevent abusing temporary secondment and turning it into de facto permanent secondment. This time limit was expanded in 2009. From January until July 2009, only criminal law judges could be seconded for up to two years out of three consecutive years[357] and since July 2009 it has been possible to second all judges for up to two out of three consecutive years.[358]

Temporary assignment outside the judiciary remained in the hands of the Ministry of Justice between 2003 and 2008.[359] The only exception was newly established temporary assignment to the Office of the JCSR, where the JCSR decided on the assignment. The available places outside the judiciary were thus as follows: the Ministry of Justice, the Office of the Government of the Slovak Republic, the Office of the President, the Office of the National Council of the Slovak Republic, the Judicial Academy, the Constitutional Court, and the JCSR. This scheme applied until December 2008. However, most powers were transferred from the Ministry of Justice to the JCSR in 2009. Under the new scheme, the Minister of Justice decided only on temporary assignment to the Ministry of Justice and to the Judicial Academy. For all other places it was the JCSR that decided on temporary assignment. In all cases, relevant court presidents had to be consulted, but their view was not binding.[360] The new scheme remained in force until December 2010.

---

[356] Art. 12(4) of Law No. 385/2000 Z. z., on Judges and Lay Judges, as amended by Law No. 426/2003 Z. z.

[357] The explanatory memorandum to the relevant amendment to Law No. 385/2000 Z. z., on Judges and Lay Judges does not explain why only criminal law judges enjoyed this preferential treatment.

[358] Art. 12(4) of Law No. 385/2000 Z. z., on Judges and Lay Judges, as amended by Law No. 290/2009 Z. z. and Law No. 291/2009 Z. z.

[359] Art. 13(5) of Law No. 385/2000 Z. z., on Judges and Lay Judges, as amended by Law No. 426/2003 Z. z.

[360] Art. 13(3) of Law No. 385/2000 Z. z., on Judges and Lay Judges, as amended by Law No. 517/2008 Z. z. and Law No. 520/2008 Z. z.

There were three dual mechanisms available in Slovakia between 2003 and 2010: volatile salaries, case assignment, and judicial performance evaluation. Regarding *salary bonuses*, Slovakia switched policies between 2003 and 2010.[361] Initially, salary bonuses were not allowed at all.[362] Later on, the grounds for awarding salary bonuses were limited to the situation when a judge reached the age of fifty years.[363] However, after September 2004 the system of salary bonuses reverted to the scheme from the 1990s since it allowed bonuses to be paid not only when a judge reached the age of fifty or at the date of his retirement, but also for successful completion of extra tasks that were not related to the judicial decision-making. In other words, discretionary awarding of salary bonuses was back. In all instances, court presidents decided on salary bonuses. Finally, a new scheme was set up from January 2009 (when Harabin was the Minister of Justice). This scheme yet again expanded the grounds for which the discretionary bonuses could be granted. Besides the two existing grounds, salary bonuses could be awarded also for exceptional performance of judges and of judicial officials, and for the completion of a specific task during temporary assignment.[364] Court presidents still decided on salary bonuses in most cases.[365] The exceptions to this general rule was bonuses for judicial officials and for temporarily assigned judges – these were awarded by presidents of higher courts, by the Minister of Justice, or by the organs to which a judge was temporarily assigned.[366]

As regards *case assignment*, the 2002 Law on the JCSR legalized the existing de facto practice by laying down new detailed rules on the creation and content of "work schedules." Under the new arrangement, the work schedule was still prepared by the court president, but he had to discuss it with other judges and consult it with a judicial board.[367] The 2002 Law on the JCSR also for the first time in Slovak history explicitly required random case assignment. More specifically, it provided that "cases shall be

---

[361] Note that salary bonuses were abolished only in 2011 by Law No. 33/2011 Z. z. & Law No. 100/2011 Z. z.

[362] See Art. 79 of Law No. 385/2000 Z. z., on Judges and Lay Judges. This scheme was in force until June 2003.

[363] This scheme was in force until August 2004.

[364] Art. 79(1) of Law No. 385/2000 Z. z., on Judges and Lay Judges, as amended by Law No. 517/2008 Z. z. and Law No. 520/2008 Z. z.

[365] Art. 79(3) of Law No. 385/2000 Z. z., on Judges and Lay Judges, as amended by Law No. 517/2008 Z. z. and Law No. 520/2008 Z. z.

[366] Art. 79(4)-(5) of Law No. 385/2000 Z. z., on Judges and Lay Judges, as amended by Law No. 517/2008 Z. z. and Law No. 520/2008 Z. z.

[367] Art. 27 of the 1991 Law on Courts and Judges, as amended by Law No. 185/2002 Z. z.

assigned according to the work schedule ... on random basis with the use of technical means and software ... so that the possibility of influencing case assignment is excluded."[368] In addition, the 2002 Law on the JCSR increased the transparency of case assignment. It required work schedules to be available to the public and to contain, among other things, the following information: the subject matter specialization of each judge and each chamber, the composition of each chamber, the rules governing the substitution of judges in case of recusal, how to proceed if a judge was not available due to a long-term illness or for other reasons, how to proceed if any judge or chamber was overloaded, and how to proceed if the software used for case assignment did not work temporarily.[369]

Nevertheless, court presidents still could change the general rules of case assignment in the work schedule during a given year and had broad discretion in reassigning individual cases. The following section will show that this exception became the rule at some courts and thus case assignment could still be used as "carrot" or as a "stick."[370] The Slovak Parliament addressed this issue once more in the 2004 Law on Courts, which provided for a random method also for reassigning cases.[371] However, the Slovak Parliament at the same time felt the need to allow certain exceptions to the general rule on random case assignment for the sake of preserving flexibility. Therefore, court presidents were still allowed to change the work schedule during the calendar year, if they deemed it necessary.[372]

Finally, the system of *judicial performance evaluation* remained the same until December 2008. From January 2009, the modified rules applied to the assessment of judges. Compulsory regular performance evaluation for each judge every five years was abolished and the powers of court presidents were further widened. Under the new rules, court presidents could rely on the results of the so-called revisions of judges' work and could also take into account factors that were not explicitly listed in the 2002 Law on Judges and Lay Judges.[373] Judges who disagreed with the assessment made by the court president could raise objections before the judicial board, but the court presidents still had the major say.

---

[368] Art. 26(2) of the 1991 Law on Courts and Judges, as amended by Law No. 185/2002 Z. z.

[369] Art. 26(3) of the 1991 Law on Courts and Judges, as amended by Law No. 185/2002 Z. z.

[370] For an example of misuse of this power, see ECtHR, *DMD GROUP, a.s. v. Slovakia*, no. 19334/03, October 5, 2010, §§ 15–21 and §§ 65–72 (which will be discussed in more detail later).

[371] Art. 51(4) of Law No. 757/2004 Z. z., on Courts.

[372] Art. 52(7) of Law No. 757/2004 Z. z., on Courts.

[373] Art. 27(2) of Law No. 385/2000 Z. z., on Judges and Lay Judges, as amended by Law No. 517/2008 Z. z. and Law No. 520/2008 Z. z.

D.   Mechanisms of Judicial Accountability in Action

The previous section explained what the Slovak law stated about the mechanisms of judicial accountability that were available between 2003 and 2010. This section will analyze how these mechanisms operated in practice.

Regarding *disciplinary proceedings*, data from 2003–2010 show a pattern that is very different from what we saw between 1993 and 2002. The number of disciplinary motions increased significantly in 2003 and remained high in the following seven years.[374] As in the previous era, court presidents were the most active principals in disciplinary proceedings. Out of 225 disciplinary motions lodged in 2003–2010, court presidents initiated 122 (55%), the Minister of Justice initiated 76 (34%) and the JCSR 5 (2%). The remaining 22 motions (9%) were initiated by other organs.[375] I can thus conclude that the distribution of disciplinary motions among disciplinary prosecutors in 2003–2010 is similar to that in 1993–2002. What is striking is that the number of disciplinary motions during the eight years between 2003 and 2010 was more than twice higher than that (98) in the previous decade.

As to the typology of misconduct, the most common reason for initiating disciplinary motions in 2003–2010 was delay in delivering justice (43%), followed by other violations of judicial duty (36%), administrative offences (10%), violations of judicial independence, judicial impartiality, or judicial ethics (8%), and alcohol-related issues (3%). These statistics differ from the data for 1993–2002 in several respects. First, the absolute number of disciplinary motions for delays doubled from 46 to 96. Second, the absolute number of disciplinary motions for other violations of judicial duty quadrupled from 20 to 82. Third, the absolute number of disciplinary motions for violations of judicial independence, judicial impartiality or judicial ethics more than tripled from 5 to 17. In contrast to the increase in the three aforementioned motions, the absolute numbers of administrative offenses and alcohol-related issues among disciplinary motions in 2003–2010 remained very similar to the absolute numbers in 1993–2002.

The overall success rate of disciplinary motions was very low. Disciplinary panels issued a disciplinary sanction in 58 cases (26%) and only in six cases (3%) did judges resign voluntarily before the decision of

---

[374] The number of disciplinary motions in Slovakia was almost as high as in the Czech Republic, even though there are more than twice as many judges in the Czech Republic.

[375] Most of these motions were initiated by the Police for driving offences.

the disciplinary panel could be delivered. This means that the success rate of disciplinary prosecutors was as low as 29%. In contrast, 100 motions (44%) were dismissed on procedural grounds. In addition, disciplinary panels acquitted judges completely in 52 cases (23%) and in another 9 (4%) they found judges guilty, but refrained from imposing a sentence. This means that in 72% of the disciplinary motions the impugned judges did not face any sanction. Out of 58 sanctions imposed in 2003–2010, the most common was a salary reduction (27 cases, 47%), followed by reprimand (21 cases, 37%) and fines (5 cases, 9%). The other available sanctions such as demotion (2 cases) and dismissal from the position of chamber president (1 case) were used sparingly or not at all (relocation). Only two judges were dismissed between 2003 and 2010. However, both of those dismissals were rather special. The first judge was dismissed by the President and not by the disciplinary panel, because he was convicted of a criminal offense, and the second judge was not reappointed rather than dismissed.[376] I may thus summarize, that yet again not a single Slovak judge was dismissed from judicial office by the disciplinary court.

The last statistics in this study of disciplinary proceedings compares the success rate of court presidents, on the one hand, and that of the Minister of Justice, on the other. My data from 2003–2010 show that 30% of motions initiated by court presidents led to disciplinary sanctions, whereas the success rate of the Minister of Justice was 22%. Thus, court presidents were still more successful than the Minister of Justice, but the difference in the success rates was not as high as between 1993 and 2002. Court presidents were also more successful in forcing judges to resign. Out of 6 resignations in 2003–2010, 5 resulted from disciplinary motions initiated by court presidents (83%) and only 1 was triggered by the Minister of Justice (17%).

In conclusion, the results of the empirical study of disciplinary proceedings with judges between 2003 and 2010 vary significantly from the statistics concerning disciplinary proceedings in 1992–2002. The only statistics that remained relatively constant was that court presidents, once again, dominated this mechanism of judicial accountability. They were not only more active than the Minister of Justice or other actors in using this "stick," but also more successful in employing it. The differences were as follows. First of all, number of disciplinary motions skyrocketed. That in 2003 and

---

[376] This was a residual application of retention review. The impugned judge was elected for a four-year initial term in 2001 under the old regime (before the 2001 Constitutional Amendment) and when his term expired he was not reappointed under the new regime (after the 2001 Constitutional Amendment).

2004 alone was almost as high as the number of disciplinary motions during the entire previous decade. Second, the success rate of disciplinary
motions was extremely low. Even if we count voluntary resignations, only
29% of motions led to any sanction. What is more, yet again not a single Slovak judge was dismissed by disciplinary panels and the sanctions
imposed were relatively mild. Third, this mechanism was effectively used
by Štefan Harabin to intimidate judges who disagreed with him, including
his opponents at the Supreme Court. As Harabin was a President of the
Supreme Court, he also chaired the JCSR, which decides on the composition of disciplinary panels.

This concentration of powers gave him tremendous influence, even
if disciplinary motions did not eventually lead to disciplinary sanctions
being imposed on the judges, because the very fact of initiating a disciplinary motion had a negative reputational effect on an impugned judge.
Moreover, judges against whom disciplinary motions were pending faced
several "collateral" consequences. They could not work as they were
often suspended and their salaries were significantly reduced during this
interim period. Intentionally or not, disciplinary panels did not decide on
several disciplinary motions for years and thus exacerbated the financial
and psychical harms done to the judges being prosecuted for disciplinary
offences. Given the concentration of power at the JCSR[377] and the defective
institutional design of disciplinary motions,[378] there was no opportunity to
challenge this practice.

The rise in disciplinary motions against Supreme Court judges in 2009
and 2010 suggests that Harabin was particularly eager to silence his critics at the Supreme Court.[379] Harabin himself initiated 12 disciplinary
motions against Supreme Court judges in 2009 and 2010 and one more
motion was triggered by the JCSR, which was chaired by Štefan Harabin.[380]
This is a sharp rise from the previous years. Only 18 disciplinary motions
against Supreme Court judges were initiated throughout the entire period
between 2003 and 2010 and only 10 such motions took place in the entire
previous decade (1993 and 2002). To sum up, Harabin, as a Minister of
Justice, initiated one disciplinary motion against the President of the

---

[377] As mentioned above in Section IV.C, the JCSR has accumulated two functions: it served as
a disciplinary prosecutor *and* it decided on the composition of disciplinary panels.

[378] Most importantly, there was no chance to review whether the initiation of the disciplinary
motion was justified. For further details, see Svák, above note 28, at 60.

[379] See Bojarski and Köster, above note 83; Dubovcová 2010, above note 142, at 54–56; or
Woratsch, above note 84.

[380] Some of these cases are reported in Bojarski and Köster, above note 83, at 102–105.

Supreme Court Milan Karabin in 2006, and within eighteen months of 2009 and 2010, as a Supreme Court President, he was involved in 13 other motions against Supreme Court judges. In other words, he was behind 14 out of 18 disciplinary motions against Supreme Court judges. The absolute number of his disciplinary motions against the Supreme Court judges is in itself high. However, if we compare this number with previous years, it is becoming clear that these disciplinary motions were selective and were supposed to punish his opponents at the Supreme Court. Several lower court judges who dared to criticize Harabin also faced disciplinary trial, as a result of which they were often suspended and their salaries were significantly reduced during this interim period.[381]

Regarding the *complaint mechanism*, no significant change took place in practice between 2003 and 2010. This mechanism was dominated by court presidents who processed almost all complaints against judges. The link between the complaints lodged and the initiation of disciplinary proceedings against a judge complained was minimal in this period and the results of the complaint process were also not publicized.

Finally, the practice of *reassignment* remained the same. Between 1993 and 2002 the power to decide on reassignment belonged to court presidents and the limits of court presidents" discretion were minimal. This de facto standard prevailed until 2010, despite the adoption of the Law on the JCSR in 2002 and the new Law on Courts in 2004. These two statutes only codified existing practice and explicitly granted the power to reassign judges to court presidents. The other legal changes brought about by these two statutes had little impact in practice. These statutes granted court presidents significant latitude in reshuffling the composition of chambers and reassigning individual judges, both in the phase of preparing the work schedule and during the year,[382] and court presidents used this latitude in practice.

The methods employed by Štefan Harabin after his return to the Supreme Court in 2009 will again serve as an example of the vast powers of court presidents in this area. Soon after Harabin became the President of the Supreme Court, he reshuffled the composition of the chambers at the Supreme Court, "contained" recalcitrant judges in two chambers of the administrative law division and made sure that these two chambers could decide on only certain categories of cases (such as detention cases, asylum,

---

[381] Dubovcová 2010, above note 142, at 54–55.
[382] See Section III.D.

social security cases).[383] In other words, all cases with a significant monetary aspect such as competition law or tax law cases went to other chambers of the administrative law division. A similar practice took place also at the lower courts, albeit on the smaller scale. I may thus conclude that all concerns raised in connection with the de facto use of this mechanism between 1993 and 2002 apply with equal, if not greater, force to the period between 2003 and 2010. Most importantly, there were no criteria for reassignment and no safeguards against the abuse of this mechanism.[384]

De facto standards of *promotion* of judges changed between 2003 and 2010. In Section III.D of this chapter I mentioned that the 2000 Law on Judges and Lay Judges altered the de facto rules governing promotion, in particular by introducing formal competitions for each vacancy, reducing the influence of court presidents, and increasing the involvement of regular judges.[385] Three players had de jure power to have their say in promoting judges – the Minister of Justice, court presidents, and judicial boards (composed of regular judges). Court presidents were de facto the most influential actors, but they could not act unilaterally as they had not enough votes to outnumber the remaining two actors. The introduction of the JCSR reshuffled this balance of power. Most importantly, the Ministry of Justice completely lost its say in promoting judges in 2003, since its representatives were not included among the members of "judicial promotion committees." A representative of the Minister of Justice returned to the "judicial promotion committee" in 2004, but the institutional changes resulting from the introduction of the JCSR had the following de facto effects: while the powers of judicial boards remained the same, the JCSR re-empowered court presidents and reduced the influence of the Minister of Justice. I may thus summarize that, until 2008, court presidents[386]

---

[383] Eva Mihočková, *Šikanovanie v talári*, Plus 7 dní, December 12, 2011 [available at www .pluska.sk/plus7dni/vsimli-sme-si/sikanovanie-vtalari.html]. See also Pavol Kubík and František Múčka, *Ako úraduje Štefan I. Čistič: Pôsobenie nového šéfa Najvyššieho súdu SR varuje pred rozširovaním jeho kompetencií*, TREND, September 30, 2009 [available at http://ekonomika.etrend.sk/ekonomika-slovensko/ako-uraduje-stefan-i-cistic-2.html]; or Pavol Kubík, *Keď losuje Štefan Harabin: Na Najvyššom súde majú rozhodnutia predsedu občas väčšiu váhu ako paragrafy*, TREND, March 11, 2010 [available at http://ekonomika .etrend.sk/ekonomika-slovensko/ked-losuje-stefan-harabin-2.html].

[384] Certain mechanisms against the abuse of the reassignment of judges were introduced in 2011. More specifically, Law No. 33/2011 Z. z. lays down that cases from a different specialization can be assigned to a judge only under specific circumstances (with his consent or after consulting the judicial board) and that a special two-month period must be granted to a reassigned judge to prepare for his new agenda.

[385] See Section III.D.

[386] Court presidents appointed three out of five members of each "judicial promotion committee" upon nomination of the relevant judicial boards. In addition, the member of the

shared powers over promotion with judicial boards, while the single vote of the representative of the Minister of Justice in the "judicial promotion committees" was marginal.

Here it is important to remember that the JCSR is not an "it," but a "they," and that the composition of the JCSR makes a huge difference to the de facto standards governing promotion. As mentioned earlier, the composition of the JCSR eventually turned out to be different from what the creators of the JCSR envisaged, because court presidents soon gained the upper hand in the JCSR.[387] This specific trajectory in composition of the JCSR proved to be critical in 2009 and 2010. A slight change in the composition of "judicial promotion committees" disempowered judicial boards and buttressed the influence of court presidents. Court presidents sat on each "judicial promotion committee" ex officio and another two proponents of court presidents were nominated by the JCSR and by the collegium of chairmen of judicial boards. Therefore, the members nominated by the judicial board and the Ministry of Justice were always outvoted, even if they voted together. The composition of "judicial promotion committees" for vacancies at the Supreme Court was slightly different, but since Harabin had already packed the judicial board of the Supreme Court, the result was the same – he had the final word.

The *appointment of judges to the positions of court president or vice president* in practice followed de jure rules. Until March 2005, de facto rules from the previous period prevailed. This meant that the selection of judicial officials at district and regional courts was fully in the hands of the Minister of Justice, both de jure and de facto. The discretion of the Minister of Justice was virtually unlimited at that time. This changed de jure in April 2005. Under the new statutory rules, the ad hoc selection committees nominated the list of three candidates from which the Minister of Justice had to choose the court president. Under the new regime, court presidents were appointed for five years instead of an indefinite period. All vice presidents of lower courts were then appointed for five years by the Minister of Justice upon the nomination of the president of a given court.

However, there was a loophole in the 2004 Law on Courts, because it allowed the Minister of Justice to dismiss judicial officials quite easily. Štefan Harabin, when he became the Minister of Justice in 2006, fully

"judicial promotion committee" nominated by the JCSR was de facto a candidate of judicial officials, who de facto dominated both the "first" (2002–2007) and the "second" JCSR (2008–2013).

[387] See Section II.B above.

exploited this loophole. He dismissed – allegedly for mismanagement – seven presidents of the regional and district courts in two days.[388] This lack of safeguards against the dismissal of judicial officials in practice meant that, despite the change of de jure standards regarding the appointment of judges to the positions of court president or vice president, the Minister of Justice still could to a certain extent control this mechanism of judicial accountability.

However, this does not mean that all Slovak court presidents were transmission belts of the Minister of Justice. First, only Štefan Harabin, who was a former Supreme Court president and still de facto a Supreme Court judge (as he was only temporarily assigned to the Ministry of Justice), dared to use this power. Second, even Harabin could not unilaterally pick his own court presidents. He could only dismiss those he did not like. Third, the political costs of the dismissal of court presidents were very high and Harabin became a target of severe criticism from the media, his fellow judges, as well as many politicians for this move. Finally, as will be shown subsequently, the Minister of Justice could neither dismiss the President of the Supreme Court, who was at that time automatically a Chairman of the JCSR, nor appoint him. Harabin himself suffered a defeat at the JCSR in 2003 before he recovered in 2009. To this analysis I move next.

The process of selecting the president and vice president of the Supreme Court also remained the same. Not surprisingly, the battle over the position of the President of the Supreme Court did not fade away. I mentioned in the previous section that due to the inability of any candidate for this position to find enough votes within the JCSR, the incumbent President of the Supreme Court, Štefan Harabin, completed his five-year term and stepped down only in February 2003. The first election of the President of the Supreme Court after the February Judgment of the Constitutional Court[389] took place on May 7, 2003. Three candidates competed for this position – Štefan Harabin, Juraj Majchrák (the Vice President of the Supreme Court), and Milan Karabín (a Supreme Court judge and former Supreme Court President in 1996–1997).

The JCSR was divided and no candidate managed to get enough votes. The second election was scheduled for June 23, 2003. As no candidate from the previous election could participate, three new – allegedly

[388] *Harabin odvolal predsedov súdov, spustil kontroly.* Sme.sk, October 4, 2006, available www .sme.sk/c/2929137/harabin-odvolal-predsedov-sudov-spustil-kontroly.html. See also *Harabin odvolal ďalších sudcov,* Topky.sk, October 5, 2006, available at www.topky.sk/ cl/10/127310/Harabin-odvolal-dalsich-sudcov.
[389] See above note 255.

324   HOLDING CZECH AND SLOVAK JUDGES ACCOUNTABLE

"second-rate" – candidates were nominated. None of them succeeded. The third election was held on September 30, 2003. The "heavy-weights" of the Slovak judiciary – Štefan Harabin, Juraj Majchrák, and Milan Karabín – clashed again. However, this time Majchrák withdrew a few minutes before the final vote and asked members of the JCSR to vote for Karabín. As a result of this move, Karabín gained enough votes to win the nomination of the JCSR and a few days later he became the President of the Supreme Court.

The same protracted dispute took place when Karabín's five-year term expired on October 7, 2008. The selection of the next President of the Supreme Court was initially scheduled for September 30, 2008. The incumbent, Milan Karabín, was supposed to be the only candidate. However, no elections were eventually held in 2008 since the JCSR decided to postpone them until the allegations of Karabín's financial mismanagement had been refuted. Many commentators asserted that this postponement had no basis in law and alleged that this move was made in order to prepare for the smooth transition of Štefan Harabin from the post of Minister of Justice to the presidency of the Supreme Court.[390] Further delays occurred in 2009 and the first election of the JCSR took place only on May 6, 2009. The incumbent, Milan Karabín, was the only candidate. However, he did not manage to win the nomination. In fact, not a single member of the JCSR cast a vote for him. The second election was scheduled for June 22, 2009. Two candidates competed for the nomination of the JCSR – Štefan Harabin (who was still the Minister of Justice at that moment) and Eva Babiaková (a judge of the Supreme Court). As candidates from the previous elections cannot compete in the election that immediately follows, Harabin did not have to face Karabín in this election. Harabin eventually won fifteen votes out of eighteen at the JCSR. The Slovak President appointed Harabin to the office a day later.

The de facto rules of *promotion to the position of chamber president* (within the same court) did not differ much from the de jure standards. Court presidents shared this power with judicial boards, but the role of the former was stronger. As regards the *secondment* of judges, court presidents also played a key role between 2003 and 2010. Formally, court presidents shared this power with the JCSR. However, they dominated both the "first"

---

[390] Note that the review of Karabín's alleged economic mismanagement of the Supreme Court was initiated by the Ministry of Justice, which was headed by Karabín's main rival, Štefan Harabin.

Table 6.5. *Regular salary and salary bonuses of the President of the Supreme Court of Slovakia between 2003 and 2006*

Year	2003	2004	2005	2006
Average salary [thousand SKK]	578	672	741	809
Bonuses [thousand SKK]	0	132	287	109
Bonuses/Ave.Salary [%]	0%	20%	39%	13%

Source: Katarína Staroňová, Rovní a rovnejší Štefana Harabina, June 1, 2009.

(2002–2007) and the "second" JCSR (2008–2013) and thus the power of court presidents to second judges was de facto unlimited.

Finally, de facto standards of *temporary assignment outside the judiciary* remained the same. Even though the Minister of Justice could act unilaterally according to de jure standards (between 2003 and 2008), in fact court presidents had the power of veto. This status quo was confirmed in 2008 by the formal change that transferred the power to assign judges to most positions outside the judiciary to the JCSR. As a result, after 2009 the following de facto standard emerged – the Minister of Justice shared with court presidents the power to assign judges to the Ministry of Justice and to the Judicial Academy, whereas the JCSR, controlled by court presidents, decided on all other temporary assignments unilaterally.

Salary bonuses did not exist in 2003 and thus they were not awarded in practice. They were reintroduced only in 2004. Under the presidency of Milan Karabín at the Supreme Court (2003–2008), all regular judges of the Supreme Court received the same annual salary bonus in the amount of 2,000 EUR.[391] Karabín's salary bonus was higher, but it never reached the amount Harabin awarded himself in 2001 and 2002, either in nominal terms or in comparison with a basic salary(see Table 6.5).[392]

This practice changed in 2009, when Štefan Harabin moved from the position of the Minister of Justice to the post of President of the Supreme Court. The precise amount of salary bonuses awarded to individual judges of the Supreme Court is not made public, but according to the media,[393] Štefan Harabin earned 69,443 EUR for six months (June-December

---

[391] Ľuboš Kostelanský and Vanda Vavrová, "Harabinovi sudcovia zarobili viac ako premiér," *Pravda*, August 12, 2010.

[392] Official data for 2007–2010 are not available.

[393] Kostelanský and Vavrová, above note 391; and Mihočková, above note 383.

2009) at the Supreme Court,[394] even though the standard monthly salary of a Supreme Court judge was 2,900 EUR (which is 34,800 EUR per annum and 17,400 EUR for six months). However, Harabin did not award high salary bonuses only to himself. His "allies" at the Supreme Court received generous bonuses as well.

According to the Slovak daily *Pravda* the following four judges received an annual salary well above the average: Daniela Švecová (her annual salary amounted to 76,797 EUR), Jana Bajánková (75,523 EUR), Anna Marková (59,181 EUR) and Ida Hanzelová (57,621 EUR).[395] All these four judges held crucial positions and Harabin needed their support. Daniela Švecová was a member of the JCSR and the Vice President of the Supreme Court. Jana Bajánková was the chairman of the civil law division at the Supreme Court. Ida Hanzelová was a member of the JCSR and the chairman of the administrative law division at the Supreme Court. Anna Marková was also a member of the JCSR. Although the precise amount of salary bonuses cannot be deduced from the annual salaries of individual judges, it is clear that some judges received salary bonuses in the amount of tens of thousands of euro in 2009.[396]

In other words, Harabin revived the practice of the selective awarding of generous bonuses he had already used in 2001 and 2002. He awarded generous salary bonuses to his allies and denied them to his critics.[397] As one of the Supreme Court judges, Peter Paluda, who was on Harabin's "black list," aptly put it, "Harabin produces loyal judges by threatening them and at the same time by pleasing them with salary bonuses and allowing them to function normally if they are obedient."[398] According to this Supreme Court judge, the salary bonuses of the Supreme Court judges in 2009 and 2010 varied from 50 EUR per annum for "recalcitrant" judges to tens of thousands euro for "obedient" judges.[399]

---

[394] Harabin earned additional 25,336 EUR as a Minister of Justice for January–June 2009 and his total salary for 2009 was 94,779 EUR (see ibid). Due to special bonuses, his salary was significantly higher than that of the Chief Justice of the Constitutional Court (37,835 EUR), the General Prosecutor (44,191 EUR), and the Prime Minister (45,124 EUR).

[395] Kostelanský and Vavrová, above note 391.

[396] The data for 2010 is not available since the President of the Supreme Court of Slovakia refused to make this information public.

[397] For further details, see Bojarski and Köster, above note 83, at 111–112; Kostelanský and Vavrová, above note 391; or Mihočková, above note 383.

[398] Cited from Mihočková, above note 383. See also Kubík and Múčka, above note 383; or Kubík, above note 383.

[399] Cited from Mihočková, above note 383. See also Kubík and Múčka, above note 383; or Kubík, above note 383. Another Judge of the Supreme Court of Slovakia confirmed this

Regarding *case assignment*, one must distinguish between the Supreme Court on the one hand and the lower courts on the other. The practice of assigning cases at the Supreme Court underwent significant development between 2003 and 2010. The issue with the "electronic registry" was not resolved even when Harabin stepped down and Milan Karabín became the president of the Supreme Court in February 2003. Due to protracted technical problems the "electronic registry" did not work at the Supreme Court until January 2005. Therefore, random case assignment at the Supreme Court's registry operated only between 2005 and 2008. However, even Karabín did not accept random case assignment wholeheartedly. He decided that in order to prevent delays, certain election matters would not be assigned by the "electronic registry" (i.e., on a random basis[400]), but pursuant to the rules set out in the work schedule (which did not guarantee random case assignment). Karabín, in his capacity as a President of the Supreme Court, also had a major say in creating annual work schedules and could reassign cases if he deemed it necessary.

This changed after Harabin's return to the presidency of the Supreme Court 2009. Soon after he had been elected president, he dismissed the head of the Supreme Court registry and replaced her with a person of his own choice.[401] This move was interpreted by Slovak media as an attempt

view and added that judges of the Supreme Court of Slovakia were divided into three groups for the purpose of distributing salary bonuses: (1) judges against whom a disciplinary motion was pending (these judges received 0 EUR); (2) judges who were critical of Harabin (these judges received 50 EUR); and (3) judges who either openly supported Harabin or were at least silent (these judges received salary bonuses in the range of 3,000–10,000 EUR, sometimes even several times a year). This judge also explained where this extra money came from – there were several vacant seats at the Supreme Court, but the Supreme Court received money from the state budget even for the salaries of judges to be appointed to these vacancies (Interview with a Judge of the Supreme Court of Slovakia from April 23, 2015).

[400] Note that even the "electronic registry" (software assigning cases on random basis) can be defeated. Several Slovak lawyers asserted that some parties used the following technique – they repeatedly lodged and withdrew the petitions to the court (action/appeals) until the case was finally assigned to a "convenient" judge (i.e., a judge who was on good terms with the party to the dispute). See also Kubík, above note 383.

[401] Kubík, above note 383. See also follow-up articles on rigged case assignment in Trend: *Lietajuce spisy*, TREND, April 28, 2010 [available at: www.etrend.sk/trend-archiv/ rok-2010/cislo-17/lietajuce-spisy.html]; Pavol Kubík, *Najvyšší reaguje: Sedem trestných sudcov tvrdí, že spisy dostávajú "neexistujúce senáty,"* TREND, March 17, 2010 [www .etrend.sk/trend-archiv/rok-2010/cislo-11/najvyssi-reaguje.html]; Pavol Kubík, *Bez podateľne: Štefan Harabin sa už pre zákony netrápi,* TREND, March 10, 2010 [www.etrend .sk/trend-archiv/rok-2010/cislo-10/bez-podatelne.html]; *Delenie spisov u Š. Harabina zákon neporušuje, konštatuje Súdna rada: Z kancelárie rady prišla po mesiaci odpoveď na*

to gain control over the court registry.[402] Harabin did not switch off the "electronic registry" though. He did not need to. He reassigned dozens of cases ex post (after initial random assignment by the software), allegedly on efficiency grounds. More specifically, he claimed that these changes were necessary in order to balance the uneven workload of judges and increase the efficiency of the Supreme Court.[403] For instance, in November 2009 Harabin took thirty already assigned cases away from one judge and reassigned them to another. In the commercial law division, Harabin took unfinished cases away from selected judges and reassigned them to other chambers. Similarly, in appeals against decisions of the Special Court, he reassigned cases from the original chamber to another two chambers. Sometimes he changed the work schedule as frequently as twenty-five times per year.[404] As a result, many high-profile cases were not assigned according to the random rule. This tale also shows that initial random case assignment can be easily bypassed by reassigning cases ex post on nonrandom criteria.[405]

In addition to overseeing the Supreme Court registry and having almost unfettered discretion in the reassignment of cases, Harabin also had ex lege a major say in creating the annual work schedule. In sum, Harabin easily gained control over all three phases of case assignment (creating general rules in the work schedule, the actual assignment of cases at the registry, and ex post reassignment) and used this mechanism both as a "carrot" and as a "stick" vis-à-vis the Supreme Court judges. He used both "quantitative"

---

otázky TRENDU, TREND, April 12, 2010 [www.etrend.sk/ekonomika/delenie-spisov-u-harabina-zakon-neporusuje-konstatuje-sudna-rada.html].

[402] Ibid.

[403] Eva Mihočková, above note 383. See also Kubík and Múčka, above note 383; or Kubík, above note 383.

[404] Ibid.

[405] Some of these reassignment techniques were eventually found unconstitutional for a violation of the right to a legal judge (see e.g. Judgments of the Constitutional Court of the Slovak Republic No. III. ÚS 212/2011 of 18 October 2011; No. IV. ÚS 459/2012 of 13 August 2013; and No. II. ÚS 16/2011 of 11 September 2013). However, one must keep in mind that two categories of disputes must be distinguished here – disputes between private parties and disputes between a private party and the state. In the former category of disputes, that is in in civil and commercial cases, both parties can claim before the Constitutional Court that their right to a legal judge was infringed by nonrandom reassignment. But in the latter category of disputes, which consists of criminal and administrative cases, only the private party may lodge an individual complaint to the Constitutional Court, because under the prevailing theory in Slovakia state authorities do not have rights, and thus the authorities cannot rely on the right to a legal judge. This means that when reassignment benefited the party to the dispute against the state, the Constitutional Court had no chance to review the rigged case assignment.

and "qualitative" methods. Regarding the former, it was reported that "recalcitrant" judges were given an extra workload, approximately sixty cases more than "obedient" judges.[406] As regards the latter, "recalcitrant" judges were forced to decide on all detention cases that had to be decided within the statutory limit of seven days.[407] These detention cases were initially supposed to be evenly distributed among all chambers, but Harabin eventually decided that they would be assigned only to the two chambers composed of "recalcitrant" judges.[408] Conversely, "obedient" judges had a lower case load and were assigned interesting cases. The Supreme Court judge Jana Henčeková described this in the following way: "The aim of [these measures] is [twofold:] to overload them [the "recalcitrant" judges] and exclude [them] from decision-making of interesting cases."[409]

Judicial performance evaluation operated in practice in the same fashion as in the previous regime until 2008. Court presidents dominated this mechanism and they enjoyed broad discretion in assessing "their" judges. The criteria were vague and the link between the evaluation of judges and disciplinary motions was unclear. Nevertheless, certain judges did not like the external check on their performance and, Štefan Harabin (in his capacity as a Minister of Justice), eventually bent his ears to these calls and abolished the regular performance evaluation (every five years) of judges.[410] This little statutory change had a huge impact in practice, because after 2009 judges had to undergo performance evaluation only if they competed for a new position or if they explicitly required it.

This move had two practical consequences. First, it de facto exempted judges of the Supreme Court from performance evaluation, since these judges had no incentive to compete for promotion or secondment. Second, any judge who was satisfied with his current position and preferred the status quo was also unaffected by judicial performance evaluation. The same amendment also granted additional de jure powers in assessing judges to court presidents. However, this change only buttressed the existing de facto standards as court presidents already controlled judicial performance evaluation.

---

[406] Mihočková, above note 383. See also Kubík and Múčka, above note 383; or Kubík, above note 383.
[407] Ibid.
[408] Ibid.
[409] Cited from Mihočková, above note 383.
[410] See Section III *in fine* of this chapter.

E. Brief Summary of Years 2003–2010

The following tentative conclusions flow from the analysis of the use of mechanisms of judicial accountability between 2003 and 2010. First, due to the 2001 Constitutional Amendment the National Council no longer plays any role in holding judges to account and hence the number of key principals of judges was reduced from three (the Minister of Justice, the National Council, and court presidents) to two (the Minister of Justice and court presidents). The other principals were still marginal and their role diminished even further in 2009 and 2010. The public was still allowed to lodge formal complaints against judges and members of judicial boards sat on various ad hoc selection committees deciding on promotion, the appointment of judicial officials, and on judicial performance evaluation. Nevertheless, Harabin's reform reduced the number of representatives of judicial boards in ad hoc selection committees and, as a result, judicial boards de facto lost their co-decision-making power in 2009.

These changes beg the question: who gained the powers that the legislature and judicial boards lost? The answer to this question seems obvious – the JCSR. However, the JCSR is not an "it," but a "they." A more careful analysis showed that the JCSR during the entire period between 2003 and 2010 was controlled by court presidents and by the President of the Supreme Court in particular. This became even more apparent after the nomination of the "second" JCSR (2007–2012), where the number of nonjudges as well as judges who were not judicial officials dropped significantly. With a certain degree of simplification I may say that the transfer of powers to the JCSR in fact empowered court presidents and the President of the Supreme Court. Therefore, court presidents again dominated the Slovak judiciary in practice.

But the domination of court presidents in 2003–2010 (and especially in 2009 and 2010) was of a different degree from the domination of court presidents in 1993–2002. Court presidents, acting either unilaterally or through the JCSR, de facto controlled the following mechanisms:[411] reassignment, case assignment, secondment (from 2005), and salary bonuses (from 2004). In addition, they had a major say in promoting judges, appointing chamber presidents, deciding on temporary assignments outside the judiciary, and conducting judicial performance evaluation. They also dominated disciplinary motions and processed complaints from

---

[411] In case assignment, reassignment and chamber president appointment, court presidents were limited only by the requirement to consult these issues with judicial boards.

the public. Their power increased even more in 2009 due to the reform prepared by Štefan Harabin, who paved his way to the presidency of the Supreme Court. This reform allowed court presidents to gain the upper hand in the promotion of judges and solidify their control over judicial performance evaluation and temporary assignment outside the judiciary.

In contrast, the role of the Minister of Justice gradually waned. He still played a key role in appointing judicial officials, but even this mechanism was no longer fully in the hands of Minister of Justice, because after 2005 the Minister of Justice had to choose a court president from three candidates nominated by the ad hoc selection committee, where the Minister of Justice was in the minority. The Minister of Justice became a minority in all other ad hoc selection committees dealing with the promotion and secondment of judges and, in fact, could never outvote court presidents. In 2009 the Minister of Justice lost even this residual power over the temporary assignment of judges. In sum, both the legislature and the Minister of Justice disappeared from the picture by 2009 and court presidents gained control over virtually all mechanisms of judicial accountability. Table 6.6 portrays the "accountability-to-whom question" between 2003 and 2010 in quantifiable terms.

Regarding the second and third research questions, how frequently and how severely were judges held to account, I do not address them here, since answering them makes sense only when compared with what happened in the other three mini-case studies. All four intercountry and intracountry comparisons[412] will be conducted only in Chapter 7 that analyses the effects of the JCSR on mechanisms of judicial accountability. Here it suffices to say that there was a significant rise in disciplinary motions in Slovakia after the introduction of the JCSR, and that in 2009 and 2010, once Harabin and his allies had conquered the Supreme Court of Slovakia as well as the JCSR, court presidents multiplied the use of reassignment of judges and case reassignment. In addition, my analysis revealed that in 2009 and 2010 salary bonuses skyrocketed, reassignment of judges outside their specialization and case assignment techniques entailed more severe consequences, and disciplinary motions had more severe effects than in the previous years. In sum, there was a sharp change in 2009 after Harabin's return to the judiciary, both regarding the frequency of the use of several mechanisms and regarding the intensity of consequences for judges impugned.

---

[412] For further details on the research design of my case studies, see Chapter 4, Section I.

Table 6.6. *Who controlled de facto mechanisms of judicial accountability in Slovakia between 2003 and 2010? Slovakia (2003–2010)*

Year	Who controlled de facto mechanisms of JA?				
	Number of available mechanisms	Number of mechanisms controlled by MoJ	Number of mechanisms controlled by CP	Number of mechanisms controlled by LEG	Number of mechanisms controlled by OTHERS
2003	10	1.69	6.70	–	1.60
2004	11	1.80	6.98	0.10	2.10
2005	11	1.33	7.78	–	1.88
2006	11	1.21	7.94	–	1.86
2007	11	1.10	8.01	–	1.89
2008	11	1.16	8.04	–	1.80
2009	11	0.60	9.16	–	1.22
2010	11	0.63	9.15	–	1.20
Average	10,9	1.19	7.97	0.01	1.69
Average [%]		**11%**	**73%**	**0%**	**16%**
Average in 2009 & 2010 [%]		**6%**	**83%**	**0%**	**11%**

Note: MoJ = Minister of Justice, CP = court presidents, LEG = Legislature, OTHERS = other actors (e.g., judges other than court presidents, judicial boards, ombudsman, the Bar, the public)

Finally, Slovakia witnessed one significant change regarding accountability perversions. While judicial accountability avoidance, simulating judicial accountability, and output excesses of judicial accountability in the "post-JCSR" phase remained on the similar levels to the "pre-JCSR" phase, selective accountability gradually increased once Harabin became the Minister of Justice, and skyrocketed after the capture of the JCSR by Harabin and his allies in June 2009. This development will be described in more detail in Chapter 7, where I distill the causal effects of the JCSR on judicial accountability.

V.   Overall Conclusion on the Slovak Case Study

In Slovakia, the two periods studied, 1993–2002 and 2003–2010, yield very different results. The analysis of the use of mechanisms of judicial accountability between 1993 and 2010 thus shows that there was a sharp break with the past after the introduction of the JCSR. However, in order to claim that these changes in the use of such mechanisms in Slovakia after 2003 were *caused* by the introduction of the Judicial Council Euro-model of court administration, I must also make the cross-country comparison with the Czech Republic and consider other potential independent variables. These alternative causes of the change that took place within the Slovak judiciary after 2003 will be discussed in the Chapter 7.

7

Evaluation: The Czech Republic and Slovakia Compared

The previous two chapters provided intracountry comparison of how Czech and Slovak judges were dealt with between 1993 and 2002 on the one hand and between 2003 and 2010 on the other. However, in order to reveal the real impact of the JCSR on the use of mechanisms of judicial accountability, it is necessary also to conduct cross-country comparisons in both periods. Section I thus compares the use of mechanism of judicial accountability in the Czech Republic and Slovakia in the period before the introduction of the JCSR (1993–2002). Section II then compares the use of such mechanisms in the period after the JCSR's introduction (2003–2010). After that I will have all four comparisons[1] I need to distinguish between what merely *happened* in Slovakia after the introduction of the JCSR and what was *caused* by the JCSR. Therefore, I can test my hypotheses in Section III. Finally, Section IV subjects the results of my empirical analysis to further control. It discusses the alternative explanations for changes that took place in Slovakia after the introduction of the JCSR and challenges the core assumptions of this book.

I. Comparing Results from Slovakia and the Czech Republic between 1993 and 2002

Before I start answering the research questions, it is helpful to summarize which mechanisms of judicial accountability were used in the Czech Republic and in Slovakia between 1993 and 2002. For the sake of the clarity and brevity, I compare the lists of mechanisms available in the two countries in a simple table (see Table 7.1).

A. Who Held Judges to Account?

Regarding the question "Who held Czech and Slovak Judges to Account?" between 1993 and 2002, we can see that the Czech Parliament

---

[1] For the rationale behind conducting these four comparisons, see Introduction. The research design of these comparisons is further elaborated in Chapter 4.

Table 7.1. *Mechanisms of judicial accountability in the Czech Republic and Slovakia between 1993 and 2002*

Mechanisms of judicial accountability available between 1993 and 2002	
Czech Republic	**Slovakia**
Sticks	
Disciplinary proceedings	Disciplinary proceedings
Reassignment	Reassignment
–	Complaint mechanism
–	Retention for new judges (until 2001)
Carrots	
Promotion to a higher court	Promotion to a higher court
Chamber president appointment	Chamber president appointment
Secondment	Secondment
Temporary assignment outside the judiciary	Temporary assignment outside the judiciary
Appointment of a judge to the position of court president or vice president	Appointment of a judge to the position of court president or vice president
Grand chamber appointment (since 2001)	–
Dual mechanisms	
Case assignment	Case assignment
–	Salary bonuses
–	Judicial performance evaluation (since 2001)

did not play any role in holding judges to account, whereas the founding fathers of the Slovak Republic vested significant powers in this area with the legislature (the National Council). Therefore, there were only two major principals of judges in the Czech Republic (the Minister of Justice and court presidents), whereas mechanism of judicial accountability in Slovakia were dominated by three major principals (the Minister of Justice, the National Council, and court presidents). Other principals – regular judges (represented by judicial boards), the Bar, court users, and the public – played a marginal role in both countries throughout the entire period. Tables 7.2 and 7.3 provide details of the mechanisms of judicial accountability in the Czech Republic and Slovakia between 1993 and 2002.

Table 7.2. *Who controlled de facto mechanisms of judicial accountability in the Czech Republic between 1993 and 2002?* Czech Republic (1993–2002)

Year	Who controlled de facto mechanisms of JA?				
	Number of available mechanisms	Number of mechanisms controlled by MoJ	Number of mechanisms controlled by CP	Number of mechanisms controlled by LEG	Number of mechanisms controlled by OTHERS
1993	8	2.63	4.87	–	0.50
1994	8	2.53	4.95	–	0.52
1995	8	2.53	4.95	–	0.52
1996	8	2.52	4.98	–	0.50
1997	8	2.51	4.97	–	0.52
1998	8	2.52	4.92	–	0.56
1999	8	2.53	4.91	–	0.56
2000	8	2.52	4.94	–	0.54
2001	9	2.69	5.81	–	0.50
2002	9	2.50	5.97	–	0.53
Average	8.2	2.55	5.13	0	0.52
Average [%]		31%	63%	0%	6%

Note: MoJ = Minister of Justice, CP = court presidents, LEG = Legislature, OTHERS = other actors (e.g., judges other than court presidents, judicial boards, ombudsman, the Bar, the public)

Table 7.3. *Who controlled de facto mechanisms of judicial accountability in Slovakia between 1993 and 2002? Slovakia (1993–2002)*

Year	Who controlled de facto mechanisms of JA?				
	Number of available mechanisms	Number of mechanisms controlled by MoJ	Number of mechanisms controlled by CP	Number of mechanisms controlled by LEG	Number of mechanisms controlled by OTHERS
1993	10	1.90	6.00	1.10	1.00
1994	10	1.90	6.00	1.10	1.00
1995	10	1.98	5.92	1.10	1.00
1996	10	1.90	6.00	1.10	1.00
1997	11	2.07	5.83	1.60	1.50
1998	10	1.90	5.50	1.60	1.00
1999	11	2.09	5.81	1.60	1.50
2000	11	2.15	5.75	1.60	1.50
2001	11	2.00	7.55	–	1.45
2002	11	2.03	7.51	–	1.46
Average	10.5	1.99	6.19	1.08	1.24
Average [%]		**19%**	**59%**	**10%**	**12%**

Note: MoJ = Minister of Justice, CP = court presidents, LEG = Legislature, OTHERS = other actors (e.g., judges other than court presidents, judicial boards, ombudsman, the Bar, the public)

If we look at the division of powers among the major principals, we can see that court presidents dominated most mechanisms of judicial accountability in both countries (on average, 63% in the Czech Republic and 59% in Slovakia) and the Minister of Justice ranked second (on average, 31% in the Czech Republic and 19% in Slovakia) in both countries. In Slovakia, the legislature also had its say and controlled on average 10% of the mechanisms of judicial accountability. While Slovakia used a slightly higher number of such mechanisms (on average 10.5 mechanisms) than the Czech Republic (on average 8.2 mechanisms) between 1993 and 2002 and the division of power among the principals in each country changed slightly[2] in this period, the aforementioned pattern remained by and large the same.

One might infer from this comparison that the Minister of Justice was much weaker in Slovakia than in the Czech Republic. However, this is not entirely true. Both the Czech Republic and Slovakia are unitary parliamentary republics with the Prime Minister as the head of Government. As a rule, Prime Ministers are heads of the political parties that mustered the majority in the Parliament, either acting alone or together with the coalition partners. Therefore, there is a strong link between the majority in the Parliament and the Government. In fact, Mečiar's coalition (1993–1998) and the centrist coalition (1998–2002) always appointed their own people to the post of Minister of Justice. Therefore, the governing coalition controlled both the legislature and the Ministry of Justice. If we combine the powers of the Slovak legislature and the Slovak Minister of Justice, we see that Slovak politicians representing the governing coalition controlled on average 29% of the mechanisms of judicial accountability, which is almost the same as the Czech Minister of Justice's share (31%). We may thus conclude that politicians representing the governing coalition in both countries controlled almost one-third of the mechanisms of judicial accountability. Finally, in Chapters 5 and 6 I also excluded the option that the Czech and Slovak court presidents operated as the transmission belts of the political actors.[3]

In sum, the answer to the question "Who held judges to account?" is very similar in both countries. In both countries court presidents played

---

[2] The division of powers among principals changed mainly due to two factors: (1) the adoption of new mechanisms that shifted the existing balance of powers (this type of change was relatively rare); and (2) shifts in the use of existing mechanisms such as disciplinary motions (this type of change was relatively insignificant).

[3] This issue will be revisited in Chapter 8.

a dominant role and controlled almost two-thirds of the mechanisms of judicial accountability. In both countries politicians in the governing coalition controlled almost one-third of the available mechanisms. In both countries, the other players such as regular judges, the Bar, the court users, and the public were marginal and controlled less than 12% of mechanisms. In other words, despite de jure differences the Slovak and the Czech Ministry of Justice models de facto divided the power to hold judges to account in a similar fashion.

B.   How Much Were Judges Held to Account?

This question has two aspects, the quantitative and the qualitative. The quantitative aspect refers to how often judges were held to account. This aspect tells us a lot about how much judges were held to account, but it provides only a partial answer to this question. In order to get a better picture, it is necessary to inquire also into how severely judges were held to account. This is what I refer to as the qualitative aspect. Before I start addressing these two aspects, I must add one important caveat. Five mechanisms of judicial accountability existed between 1993 and 2002 either only in Slovakia or only in the Czech Republic, and so I cannot conduct a cross-country comparison regarding their use in the pre-JCSR phase. These mechanisms are: the complaints mechanism, retention review, salary bonuses, judicial performance evaluation (these four mechanisms were available only in Slovakia), and the appointment of top court judges to the grand chamber (which was available only in the Czech Republic).

However, there are further factual and methodological problems that complicate the inquiry into how often judges were held to account. Regarding the quantitative aspect, I must leave aside the so-called fixed mechanisms of judicial accountability. By "fixed" mechanisms I mean mechanisms that set a fixed interval when they can or must be used and thus the relevant principals cannot increase or reduce the number of occasions on which they are used. This issue arises, for instance, with regard to the appointment of judges to the position of court president or vice president.[4] The number of these positions as well as the length of term of

---

[4] The same problem applies also to annual salary bonuses in Slovakia (which can *ex definitio* be awarded only once a year) or to regular performance evaluation of Slovak judges (which, until 2009, was supposed to be conducted every five years). However, these two mechanisms did not exist in the Czech Republic and so I cannot compare them anyway.

judicial officials was fixed by law[5] and, subject to few exceptions,[6] no one could alter it. In addition, the frequency of use of several mechanisms of judicial accountability is to a greater or lesser extent determined by practical exigencies. Most "carrots," reassignment and case assignment belong to this group. For instance, the number of promotions may be influenced, among other things, by the creation of new courts[7] or by the number of judges of higher courts who are dismissed or demoted, reach retirement age, or decide to leave the judiciary for other reasons. Finally, the full data for many mechanisms of judicial accountability are not available (sometimes in one country, sometimes in both) and hence the frequency of their use cannot be determined with a sufficient degree of precision. This problem permeates the following mechanisms: the reassignment of judges, complaints, promotion, chamber president appointment, secondment and temporary assignment outside the judiciary, and case assignment.

In other words, the only mechanism of judicial accountability I am able to compare, with a sufficient degree of precision, in quantitative terms is disciplining judges. Therefore, I will discuss only disciplinary motions in more detail. As regards other mechanisms of judicial accountability that were available in both countries between 1993 and 2002,[8] I must rely heavily on secondary sources such as scholarly papers, newspaper articles and extrajudicial writings, and extrajudicial speeches.[9] None of the Czech and Slovak sources suggest that these mechanisms were used more frequently than necessary. In other words, the silence on these mechanisms in the

---

[5] Czech court presidents and vice presidents were appointed indefinitely until October 2008. Slovak court presidents (apart from the President of the Supreme Court of Slovakia) were appointed indefinitely until April 2005.

[6] In theory, Czech and Slovak court presidents and vice presidents could be dismissed by the body that appointed them. However, these attempts were either unsuccessful or highly controversial. This argument that the court presidents could operate as "transmission belts" was discussed in Chapters 5 and 6 and rejected. It will be revisited in Chapter 8.

[7] New courts were created both in the Czech Republic and in Slovakia. Czechs created the High Court in Olomouc in 1996 and the Supreme Administrative Court in 2003. Slovaks created five new regional courts and thirteen new district courts in 1997 and established the Special Court in 2004.

[8] Apart from disciplinary motions, the following mechanisms of judicial accountability were available both in the Czech Republic and in Slovakia: reassignment of judges, promotion to a higher court, chamber president appointment, secondment, temporary assignment outside the judiciary, and case assignment.

[9] However, I believe that these secondary sources are good proxies, because judges are very touchy about their reassignment or about situations where cases initially assigned to them are reassigned to someone else. Therefore, they almost invariably go public with these irregularities.

media in both countries means that neither in the Czech Republic nor in Slovakia the frequency of the use of the remaining mechanisms of judicial accountability were salient issues between 1993 and 2002. Thus I may presume that these mechanisms operated in a similar fashion.

Regarding the qualitative aspect, I also face factual and methodological problems. Most importantly, the consequences of most mechanisms – the severity of sanctions and/or the scope of rewards – were fixed by law. Those mechanisms with fixed sanctions/rewards include promotion, chamber president appointment, secondment, temporary assignment outside the judiciary, and appointment of a judge to the position of court president or vice president. If I leave these mechanisms aside, only three mechanisms available in both countries remain: disciplinary motions, reassignment, and case assignment. Among these three mechanisms, full data again exist only for disciplinary motions. As regards other mechanisms of judicial accountability that were available in both countries between 1993 and 2002, I must again rely primarily on secondary sources. As with the quantitative aspect, none of these sources reveal significant differences between the Czech Republic and Slovakia in this period.

Now I can turn to the quantitative comparative analysis of disciplinary motions. Figures 7.1 and 7.2 show how many disciplinary motions were initiated in the Czech Republic and Slovakia between 1993 and 2002.

However, if we want to compare these two countries, we must take into account the fact that there were approximately twice as many judges in the Czech Republic as in Slovakia during the entire period. Therefore, to get a better picture, we must divide the number of motions in the Czech Republic by the ratio of Czech to Slovak judges.[10] This corrected comparison yields interesting results. The number of disciplinary motions per judge was significantly higher in the Czech Republic than in Slovakia until 1999. However, since 2000 the number of motions per judge in Slovakia has gradually increased. The number of disciplinary motions almost reached the Czech level in 2000, surpassed it in 2001, and in 2002 was already five times higher.

---

[10] Note that between 1993 and 2002 the number of judicial offices available in the Czech Republic and Slovakia was not fixed by law, so the number of judges changed constantly (due to retirements, new appointments, the creation of new courts, etc.). The exact number of judges in both countries as of December 31 of each year and the resulting ratio of Czech to Slovak judges are mentioned in Annex C. Subsequently, I divide the number of disciplinary motions in the Czech Republic by this ratio to get the adjusted data that reflects the number of judges in each country (Table 7.5).

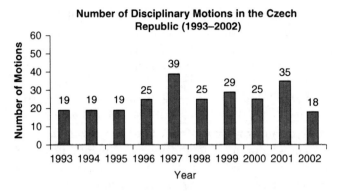

Figure 7.1. *Number of disciplinary motions in the Czech Republic and Slovakia between 1993 and 2002.*

Tables 7.4 to 7.7 reveal the results of disciplinary motions initiated in each country between 1993 and 2002. For each country, I include two tables. The first shows what disposition disciplinary courts in a given country reached as well as the number of resignations (where a disciplinarily prosecuted judge resigned before the disciplinary court reached its decision). The second table focuses on those decisions where disciplinary courts found a judge guilty of a disciplinary offense and imposed a sanction, and provide taxonomy of these sanctions. These four tables show that Czech disciplinary courts were significantly tougher on judges than their Slovak counterparts. Czech disciplinary courts imposed sanction in 57% of motions (against 40% in Slovakia) and in 13% of motions forced Czech judges to resign (against a mere 2% in Slovakia). If we look at the sanctions imposed, we see a similar pattern. Results regarding salary reductions, fines and reprimands are very similar in both countries, but the Czech disciplinary courts dismissed 8% of judges between 1993 and

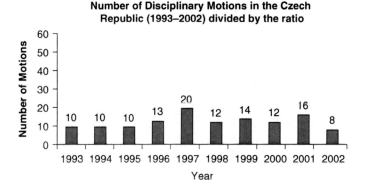

Figure 7.2. *Number of disciplinary motions in the Czech Republic and Slovakia between 1993 and 2002 (corrected comparison).*

2002, whereas not a single judge was dismissed by the Slovak disciplinary courts in that period.

One may object that all of the abovementioned interpretations of the numbers regarding disciplinary motions are based on the assumptions that the merit of disciplinary motions in both countries was the same and that the rate of punishable transgressions committed by judges is the same over time. For instance, a high success rate for principals in one country could mean either that principals there can obtain sanction even if they bring weak cases against judges they want to target or that principals are very weak and bring motions only when they have very solid evidence of transgression. Similarly, number of motions over time may increase because either more judges start committing transgressions or the principals decide to be tougher on judges and start bringing motions more zealously. Unfortunately, there is no reliable indirect proxy for these two

Table 7.4. *Results of disciplinary motions in Slovakia between 1993 and 2002*

Results of disciplinary motions in Slovakia (1993–2002)

Year	resignation	sanction imposed	absolute discharge	acquittal	other	Total number of motions
1993	0	1	0	1	1	3
1994	0	1	0	0	1	2
1995	0	5	0	0	1	6
1996	0	3	0	0	0	3
1997	0	1	0	0	2	3
1998	0	0	0	0	0	0
1999	0	5	0	1	2	8
2000	0	6	0	1	5	12
2001	1	5	0	1	14	21
2002	1	12	0	6	21	40
Total	**2**	**39**	**0**	**10**	**47**	**98**
	2%	40%	0%	10%	48%	100%

Table 7.5. *Disciplinary sanctions imposed in Slovakia between 1993 and 2002*

Disciplinary sanctions imposed in Slovakia (1993–2002)

Year	Dismissal from the office	Salary Reduction	Fine	Reprimand	Other	Total
1993	0	0	0	1	0	1
1994	0	1	0	0	0	1
1995	0	1	0	4	0	5
1996	0	0	1	2	0	3
1997	0	0	0	1	0	1
1998	0	0	0	0	0	0
1999	0	1	1	3	0	5
2000	0	3	1	1	1	6
2001	0	3	0	1	1	5
2002	0	5	0	4	3	12
Total	**0**	**14**	**3**	**17**	**5**	**39**
	0%	36%	8%	44%	13%	100%

Table 7.6. *Results of disciplinary motions in the Czech Republic between 1993 and 2002*

Results of disciplinary motions in the Czech Republic (1993–2002)

Year	resignation	sanction imposed	absolute discharge	acquittal	other	Total number of motions
1993	1	9	0	5	4	19
1994	0	12	0	3	4	19
1995	2	12	1	1	3	19
1996	6	16	0	0	3	25
1997	8	23	1	5	2	39
1998	4	13	1	4	3	25
1999	5	15	1	3	5	29
2000	2	18	0	2	3	25
2001	2	15	0	14	4	35
2002	2	10	2	3	1	18
Total	**32**	**143**	**6**	**40**	**32**	**253**
	13%	57%	2%	16%	13%	100%

Table 7.7. *Disciplinary sanctions imposed in the Czech Republic between 1993 and 2002*

Disciplinary sanctions imposed in the Czech Republic (1993–2002)

Year	Dismissal from the office	Salary reduction	Fine	Reprimand	Other	Total
1993	1	2	1	5	0	9
1994	0	2	0	10	0	12
1995	0	5	0	6	1	12
1996	3	6	1	5	1	16
1997	2	12	1	7	1	23
1998	0	6	3	4	0	13
1999	1	10	1	3	0	15
2000	2	5	3	7	1	18
2001	2	5	3	3	2	15
2002	1	5	1	3	0	10
Total	**12**	**58**	**14**	**53**	**6**	**143**
	8%	41%	10%	37%	4%	100%

unobservable variables (disciplinary motion merit and rate of transgression committed). Hence, it is important to decide which of the two alternative interpretations is more plausible on ad hoc basis. To this analysis I move next.

As to issue of the rate of transgression committed, the higher volume of disciplinary motions in the Czech Republic between 1993 and 2002 may mean either that the Czech principals held Czech judges more accountable or that Czech judges were more likely to commit offenses. However, the second alternative can be dismissed easily as there is ample evidence of higher judicial corruption in Slovakia than in the Czech Republic.[11] As to the disciplinary motion merit, judges in the Czech Republic and Slovakia are very vocal and if there was a significant amount of arbitrary disciplinary motions based on weak evidence, it would have leaked out to the media. However, there is no evidence of this sort in the media in any of the two countries between 1993 and 2002. Hence, I may presume the merit of disciplinary motions in both countries was the same.

Apart from disciplinary motions, there were only two other mechanisms of judicial accountability that were available in both countries and that allowed accounting of judges in various degrees of intensity: reassignment of judges and case assignment. However, none of the Czech and Slovak sources suggest that either of these two mechanisms was employed in order to cause more significant consequences for a judge concerned that were strictly necessary in a given situation. In other words, the silence on these mechanisms in the media means that neither in the Czech Republic nor in Slovakia the intensity of the use of these two mechanisms were salient issues between 1993 and 2002. Thus I may presume that these mechanisms operated in a similar fashion.

C.   Which Accountability Perversions Emerged?

In Chapter 1, I identified four accountability perversions I am interested in: judicial accountability avoidance, simulating judicial accountability, output excesses of judicial accountability, and selective judicial accountability. The analysis of de facto use of mechanisms of judicial accountability in the Czech Republic and Slovakia between 1993 and 2002 showed that while judicial accountability avoidance and output excesses of judicial accountability appeared in both countries, simulating judicial accountability and selective judicial accountability were relatively rare.

---

[11] See Section IV of this chapter.

Regarding judicial accountability avoidance, Czech as well as Slovak judges resisted the introduction of individualized statistics, judicial performance evaluation (in Slovakia until 2000), measures to improve the transparency of judicial decision-making, and personal financial disclosures. At the same time, they vigorously defended short statutory limits for initiating disciplinary motions. This environment left significant room for judicial accountability avoidance.

Similarly, both judicial systems prioritized quantity over quality and some judges quickly adapted to this judicial metrics. They adopted several techniques to meet the monthly "soft quota" for finished cases. For instance, they artificially split the case into separate case files with the aim of artificially multiplying their productivity. These "soft quotas" also led some judges to adopt an attitude that can be described as "get rid of the case as soon as possible and with the least resources." This meant that such judges preferred dismissing the case on procedural grounds, which is usually the easiest way how to "finish" the case, and then waited whether the appeal is lodged and what the appellate court would do.

On the other hand, there were few opportunities for simulating judicial accountability. The only mechanism that proved to be toothless was the complaints mechanism in Slovakia. Finally, I could not find any traces of systematic misuse of mechanisms of judicial accountability in order to punish critics and reward allies within the judiciary in this period. While there were some problematic instances of reassignment of judges and case assignment by court presidents in both countries, Mečiar's government used retention reviews to retaliate against young judges, and promotion of some judges in both countries was debatable, none of these incidents affected the Czech or Slovak judiciaries as such and no group within these two judiciaries was systematically targeted.

II.   Comparing Results from Slovakia and the Czech Republic between 2003 and 2010

In order to set the stage for answering the research questions regarding the period between 2003 and 2010, I again compare the available mechanisms of judicial accountability in the Czech Republic and Slovakia in this period in a simple table.

Table 7.8 shows that there were few changes regarding the available mechanisms of judicial accountability in the two countries. In Slovakia, no such mechanism was created or abolished between 2003 and 2010. Abolition of retention for new judges in Slovakia had taken place already

348 HOLDING CZECH AND SLOVAK JUDGES ACCOUNTABLE

Table 7.8. *Mechanisms of judicial accountability in the Czech Republic and Slovakia between 2003 and 2010*

Mechanisms of judicial accountability available between 2003 and 2010	
Czech Republic	Slovakia
Sticks	
Disciplinary proceedings	Disciplinary proceedings
Reassignment	Reassignment
Complaint mechanism	Complaint mechanism
-	~~Retention for new judges~~
Carrots	
Promotion to a higher court	Promotion to a higher court
Chamber president appointment	Chamber president appointment
Secondment	Secondment
Temporary assignment outside the judiciary	Temporary assignment outside the judiciary
Appointment of a judge to the position of court president or vice president	Appointment of a judge to the position of court president or vice president
Grand chamber appointment	-
Dual mechanisms	
Case assignment	Case assignment
–	Salary bonuses
–	Judicial performance evaluation

in 2001 and was described in the part devoted to the years between 1993 and 2002. I mention it here only in order to see the difference between the two periods in Slovakia more clearly. In the Czech Republic, only one change took place between 2003 and 2010 – a complaints mechanism was established in 2002.[12]

A. Who Held Judges to Account?

If we look at who held Czech and Slovak judges to account between 2003 and 2010, we can see a different picture from that between 1993

---

[12] The system of "judicial competence evaluation" was struck down by the Constitutional Court in 2003 and thus "judicial competence evaluation" never took place in practice. For this reason, I do not include it here.

and 2002. In the Czech Republic the major principals from the previous era (the Minister of Justice and court presidents) remained the same, but Slovakia witnessed a significant change. The 2001 Slovak Constitutional Amendment, which created the JCSR, completely eliminated the role of the legislature in holding Slovak judges to account and reduced the powers of the Minister of Justice. Conversely, it empowered the JCSR and court presidents. It may seem that there were three major principals in Slovakia between 2003 and 2010 – court presidents, the Minister of Justice, and the JCSR. Nevertheless, this is a misleading view. In the previous chapter I showed that Slovak court presidents not only gained new powers, but also got the upper hand in the JCSR. Hence, with a certain degree of simplification, we may say that the transfer of powers to the JCSR turned into the transfer of those powers from the Slovak Ministry of Justice and the Slovak legislature to court presidents in general and to the President of the Slovak Supreme Court in particular. This became even more obvious after Harabin's 2008 judicial reform, which started to yield its results in 2009 and 2010. Other principals – regular judges (represented by judicial boards), the Bar, court users, and the public – still remained weak, albeit that their powers slightly increased in the Czech Republic and in the early years of this period also in Slovakia. (See Tables 7.9 and 7.10.)

More specifically, court presidents still controlled on average 60% of the mechanisms in the Czech Republic, whereas in Slovakia they controlled on average 73% of the mechanisms. The Ministry of Justice was the second major principal of judges in both countries, but its role varied between the Czech Republic and Slovakia. The Czech Ministry of Justice controlled on average 25% of the mechanisms of judicial accountability, whereas the Slovak Ministry of Justice controlled on average only 11%. In neither country did the legislature play any role in holding judges to account in this period. Finally, the other principals controlled on average 15–16% of the mechanisms in both countries.

However, the average numbers mask a significant shift in Slovakia in 2009 and 2010. While the division of power to hold judges to account remained stable in the Czech Republic throughout the whole period, the balance of power among Slovak principals changed in 2009, when the 2008 Harabin's judicial reform bore fruit. That judicial reform, adopted by Harabin who had his prospects of becoming the Supreme Court President and the Chairman of the JCSR already in mind,[13] transferred further

---

[13] For further details, see Chapter 6.

Table 7.9. *Who controlled de facto mechanisms of judicial accountability in the Czech Republic between 2003 and 2010?* Czech Republic (2003–2010)

Year	Who controlled de facto mechanisms of JA?				
	Number of available mechanisms	Number of mechanisms controlled by MoJ	Number of mechanisms controlled by CP	Number of mechanisms controlled by LEG	Number of mechanisms controlled by OTHERS
2003	10	2.54	5.68	–	1.79
2004	10	2.54	5.96	–	1.50
2005	10	2.53	5.94	–	1.53
2006	10	2.53	5.98	–	1.50
2007	10	2.54	5.90	–	1.56
2008	10	2.58	5.89	–	1.53
2009	10	2.34	6.16	–	1.50
2010	10	2.25	6.23	–	1.52
Average	10	2.48	5.97	0.00	1.55
Average [%]		**25%**	**60%**	**0%**	**15%**

Note: MoJ = Minister of Justice, CP = court presidents, LEG = Legislature, OTHERS = other actors (e.g., judges other than court presidents, judicial boards, ombudsman, the Bar, the public)

Table 7.10. *Who controlled de facto mechanisms of judicial accountability Slovakia between 1993 and 2002? Slovakia (2003–2010)*

Year	Who controlled de facto mechanisms of JA?				
	Number of available mechanisms	Number of mechanisms controlled by MoJ	Number of mechanisms controlled by CP	Number of mechanisms controlled by LEG	Number of mechanisms controlled by OTHERS
2003	10	1.69	6.70	–	1.60
2004	11	1.80	6.98	0.10	2.10
2005	11	1.33	7.78	–	1.88
2006	11	1.21	7.94	–	1.86
2007	11	1.10	8.01	–	1.89
2008	11	1.16	8.04	–	1.80
2009	11	0.60	9.16	–	1.22
2010	11	0.63	9.15	–	1.20
Average	10.9	1.19	7.97	0.01	1.69
Average [%]		**11%**	**73%**	**0%**	**16%**
Average in 2009 & 2010 [%]		**6%**	**83%**	**0%**	**11%**

Note: MoJ = Minister of Justice, CP = court presidents, LEG = Legislature, OTHERS = other actors (e.g., judges other than court presidents, judicial boards, ombudsman, the Bar, the public)

powers to the JCSR and the President of the Supreme Court. As a result, in 2009 and 2010 court presidents dominated 83% of the mechanisms of judicial accountability, the Ministry of Justice controlled only 6% and other actors also only 11%.

In sum, the Czech Ministry of Justice model and the Slovak judicial council model yielded different results between 2003 and 2010. Court presidents controlled most mechanisms of judicial accountability in both countries, but the power of Slovak court presidents in 2003–2010 (and especially in 2009 and 2010) was of a different degree from that of Czech court presidents in that period. Slovak court presidents and the President of the Slovak Supreme Court in particular, acting either unilaterally or through the JCSR, controlled or had a veto power over virtually all mechanisms of judicial accountability, and thus they basically ruled the Slovak judiciary. In contrast, the Czech court presidents had significant power, but their powers were counterbalanced by the Minister of Justice and, to a lesser extent, by other actors. Finally, as court presidents in both countries further emancipated from their principals,[14] the "court presidents as transmission belts of the executive" argument does not work in this period either.[15]

B.   How Much Were Judges Held to Account?

As in the period between 1993 and 2002, several mechanisms of judicial accountability used in the Czech Republic and Slovakia between 2003 and 2010 were not available in both countries, and so I cannot conduct a cross-country comparison regarding their use in the post-JCSR phase. These mechanisms were: salary bonuses, judicial performance evaluation (which were available only in Slovakia), and the appointment of top court judges to the grand chamber (which was available only in the Czech Republic). In addition, the same methodological and factual difficulties permeate the quantitative and qualitative aspects of the question.[16]

As a result, the only mechanism of judicial accountability I am able to compare in this period in quantitative and qualitative terms is again the disciplining of judges. As regards other mechanisms that were available in both countries between 2003 and 2010,[17] I must again rely primarily on

---

[14] See Chapters 5 and 6.
[15] This issue will be revisited in Chapter 8.
[16] See Section I of this chapter.
[17] Apart from disciplinary motions, the following mechanisms of judicial accountability were available both in the Czech Republic and in Slovakia: a complaints mechanism, the

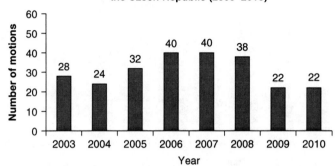

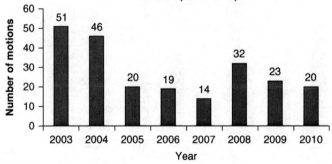

Figure 7.3. *Number of disciplinary motions in the Czech Republic and Slovakia between 2003 and 2010.*

secondary sources such as scholarly papers, newspaper articles, and extrajudicial writings and speeches.[18] I will first address how often judges were held to account, followed by how severely judges were held to account.

Regarding how often judges were held to account, I will start with a quantitative analysis of disciplinary motions. Figures 7.3 and 7.4 show how many disciplinary motions were initiated in the Czech Republic and Slovakia between 2003 and 2010.

---

reassignment of judges, promotion to a higher court, chamber president appointment, secondment, temporary assignment outside the judiciary and case assignment, and appointment to the position of court president or vice president.

[18] I again exclude "fixed" mechanisms of judicial accountability.

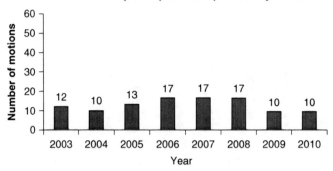

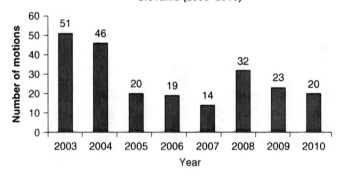

Figure 7.4. *Number of disciplinary motions in the Czech Republic and Slovakia between 2003 and 2010 (corrected comparison).*

As in years 1993–2002, the number of Czech judges was approximately twice as high as the number of Slovak judges between 2003 and 2010.[19] Thus, to get a better picture, I must again divide the number of motions in the Czech Republic by two. This corrected comparison yields the following results. The number of motions per judge in Slovakia was almost four times higher than in the Czech Republic in 2003 and 2004, then the Slovak numbers dropped close to or below the Czech levels in 2005–2007, and again skyrocketed in 2008–2010 when it was approximately twice as high as in the Czech Republic.

---

[19] Note that between 2003 and 2010 the number of judicial appointments available in the Czech Republic and Slovakia was still not fixed by law, so the number of judges changed constantly.

These ups and downs in 2005–2007 and 2008–2010 can be explained by Harabin's move to the Ministry of Justice in 2006 and by his return to the judiciary in 2009.[20] When Harabin became a Minister of Justice in 2006, he had to be "nice" to judges as he wanted to achieve as broad support from among them as possible. Therefore, he stopped pressing judges and initiated very few disciplinary motions against them. However, once he became the President of the Supreme Court and the Chairman of the JCSR, he wanted to settle the score with his critics within the judiciary and thus he initiated – himself, through his allies at lower courts, or through the JCSR – dozens of motions. These motions were aimed in particular at his critics at the Supreme Court.

The alternative interpretation of these ups and downs in 2005–2007 and 2008–2010 is that the Minister of Justice has to be more careful about initiating disciplinary motions even against recalcitrant judges because of the optics for judicial independence, but the JCSR allows court presidents to initiate more politically motivated disciplinary motions under the guise of judicial self-government, because the general public as well as the politicians are more vigilant and rigorous in policing the independence from politicians than internal independence from court presidents. However, these two interpretations are rather complementary as it is always court presidents who can exploit information asymmetry, the veil of legitimacy stemming from their membership of the judicial branch.

If we look at other mechanisms of judicial accountability, there was a significant difference between the Czech Republic and Slovakia in case reassignment and the reassignment of judges in the second half of 2009 and in 2010. The turning point was again June 2009 when Štefan Harabin became the President of the Supreme Court of Slovakia and thus, ex lege, also the Chairman of the JCSR. Within the next eighteen months, as the media as well as the affected judges repeatedly reported, Harabin and his allies among court presidents significantly increased the use of reassignment of

[20] The alternative explanation is that any selection of a President of the Supreme Court of Slovakia (who was between 2002 and 2014 *ex constitutione* also a chairman of the JCSR) is a "constitutional moment" that leads to fights between competing factions within the Slovak judiciary and therefore also increases the use of available mechanisms of judicial accountability in the year preceding and the year following the selection of the President of the Supreme Court of Slovakia. This could also explain high numbers of disciplinary motions in 2002–2004 (Milan Karabín became the President of the Supreme Court of Slovakia in 2003) and 2008–2010 (Štefan Harabin became the President of the Supreme Court of Slovakia in 2009). However, I would need more of such constitutional moments to confirm this hypothesis. But even if this hypothesis proves to be true, this will again show the deleterious effects of the Judicial Council Euro-model (just in a slightly different way).

judges and case reassignment to reward judges loyal to their cause and to punish their critics.[21]

Now I can turn to the qualitative aspect. I will start with disciplinary motions. Tables 7.11 to 7.14 reveal the results of disciplinary motions initiated in each country between 2003 and 2010. For each country, I include two tables. The first shows what conclusions disciplinary courts in a given country reached as well as the number of resignations (where a disciplinarily prosecuted judge resigned before the disciplinary court reached its decision). The second table focuses on those decisions where disciplinary courts found a judge guilty of disciplinary offense and imposed a sanction, and provides a taxonomy of those sanctions. These four tables reveal a similar general pattern to that of the pre-JCSR period. The Czech disciplinary courts were significantly tougher on judges than their Slovak counterparts regarding all aspects of disciplining judges. Czech disciplinary courts imposed sanction in 58% of motions (against 26% in Slovakia) and in a further 11% of motions forced judges to resign (against a mere 3% in Slovakia). If we look at the sanctions imposed, results regarding salary reductions, fines, and reprimands are very similar in both countries. However, there was again a significant difference regarding dismissals from judicial office. Czech disciplinary courts dismissed nine judges, whereas not a single judge was dismissed by Slovak disciplinary courts in this period.[22]

However, these tables to a great extent conceal the intensity of the consequences for Slovak judges against whom the disciplinary motion was initiated, especially in 2009 and 2010. After Štefan Harabin's return to the Presidency of the Supreme Court of Slovakia, he himself as well as pro-Harabin disciplinary prosecutors initiated disciplinary motions against his critics and in most cases proposed the most severe sanction – the dismissal from the office. Therefore, the stakes were very high for the impugned judges. Moreover, the JCSR headed by Harabin often decided to suspend the salaries of disciplinarily prosecuted judges for the period of the disciplinary trial, which took in some cases several years. In addition, several disciplinary motions initiated by Harabin and his allies were withdrawn after the centrist coalition won the 2010 parliamentary elections.

---

[21] For further details, see Chapter 6.
[22] As explained in Chapter 6, Section IV.D, both of the two dismissals of judges between 2003 and 2010 were rather special. The first judge was dismissed by the President and not by the disciplinary panel, because he was convicted of a criminal offense, and the second judge was not reappointed rather than dismissed.

Table 7.11. *Results of disciplinary motions in Slovakia between 2003 and 2010*

Results of disciplinary motions in Slovakia (2003–2010)

Year	Resignation	Sanction imposed	Absolute discharge	Acquittal	Other	Total number of motions
2003	3	14	3	8	23	51
2004	1	14	0	25	6	46
2005	0	4	1	2	13	20
2006	0	1	0	5	13	19
2007	0	3	2	4	5	14
2008	0	10	1	5	16	32
2009	2	3	1	2	15	23
2010	0	9	1	1	9	20
Total	**6**	**58**	**9**	**52**	**100**	**225**
	3%	26%	4%	23%	44%	100%

Table 7.12. *Disciplinary sanctions imposed in Slovakia between 2003 and 2010*

Disciplinary sanctions imposed in Slovakia (2003–2010)

Year	Dismissal from the office	Salary reduction	Fine	Reprimand	Other	Total
2003	0	3	2	8	1	14
2004	0	8	0	6	0	14
2005	2	2	0	0	0	4
2006	0	0	0	1	0	1
2007	0	2	0	1	0	3
2008	0	4	2	3	1	10
2009	0	3	0	0	0	3
2010	0	5	1	2	1	9
Total	**2**	**27**	**5**	**21**	**3**	**58**
	3%	47%	9%	36%	5%	100%

Table 7.13. *Results of disciplinary motions in the Czech Republic between 2003 and 2010*

Results of disciplinary motions in the Czech Republic (2003–2010)

Year	Resignation	Sanction imposed	Absolute discharge	Acquittal	Other	Total number of motions
2003	2	20	2	1	3	28
2004	3	12	3	4	2	24
2005	3	19	6	1	3	32
2006	5	24	3	2	6	40
2007	4	27	2	3	4	40
2008	5	19	5	2	7	38
2009	3	9	2	3	5	22
2010	3	13	1	4	1	22
Total	**28**	**143**	**24**	**20**	**31**	**246**
	11%	58%	10%	8%	13%	100%

Table 7.14. *Disciplinary sanctions imposed in the Czech Republic between 2003 and 2010*

Disciplinary sanctions imposed in the Czech Republic (2003–2010)

Year	Dismissal from the office	Salary reduction	Fine	Reprimand	Other	Total
2003	2	12	1	5	0	20
2004	1	6	0	5	0	12
2005	2	5	2	9	1	19
2006	1	18	0	5	0	24
2007	3	17	2	5	0	27
2008	0	11	1	7	0	19
2009	0	7	0	2	0	9
2010	0	9	0	4	0	13
Total	**9**	**85**	**6**	**42**	**1**	**143**
	6%	59%	4%	29%	1%	100%

Finally, as mentioned earlier, there were instances when a judge died before the disciplinary panel decided upon the disciplinary motion. The case of the Vice President of the Supreme Court, Juraj Majchrák, is a prime example. In sum, despite the Czech disciplinary courts were in general harsher than their Slovak counterparts, the mere initiation of a disciplinary motion against Slovak judges in 2009 and 2010 had more severe negative reputational, monetary, and sometimes even health consequences than in the Czech Republic.

Apart from disciplinary motions, there were only two other mechanisms of judicial accountability that were available in both countries and that allowed accounting of judges in various degrees of intensity: reassignment of judges and case assignment. Regarding these two mechanisms, the situation in the Czech Republic and Slovakia again started to diverge significantly in 2009. While none of the Czech secondary sources suggest that either of these two mechanisms was employed in order to cause more significant consequences for a judge concerned that were strictly necessary in a given situation, the Slovak picture was different after Harabin's return to the judiciary in 2009.

Once Harabin gained control over all three phases of case assignment (creating general rules in the work schedule, the actual assignment of cases at the registry, and ex post reassignment), he started to employ this mechanism both as a "carrot" and as a "stick" vis-à-vis the Supreme Court judges. He gave extra workload to "recalcitrant" judges and decided that "recalcitrant" judges would be assigned all detention cases (detention cases have strict statutory limits for rendering the judgment). Conversely, "loyal" judges had a lower case load and received interesting cases.[23] As one the affected Supreme Court judges suggested: "The aim of [these measures] is [twofold:] to overload them [the "recalcitrant" judges] and exclude [them] from decision-making of interesting cases."[24] Similar changes took place also at the lower courts that were controlled by the pro-Harabin forces.

Harabin also changed the consequences attached to the reassignment of judges. Soon after Harabin became the President of the Supreme Court, he reshuffled the composition of the chambers at the Supreme Court, "contained" recalcitrant judges in two chambers of the administrative law division, and made sure that these two chambers could decide on only certain categories of cases (such as detention cases, asylum, social security

---

[23] For further details, see Chapter 6, Section IV.D.
[24] Cited from Eva Mihočková, *Šikanovanie v talári*, Plus 7 dní, December 12, 2011.

cases).[25] No time was granted to the reassigned judges to prepare for his new agenda.[26] Conversely, all cases with a significant monetary aspect such as competition law or tax law cases were channeled to other chambers of the administrative law division. A similar practice took place also at the lower courts, albeit on the smaller scale.

C.   Which Accountability Perversions Emerged?

In contrast to the previous period, the Czech Republic and Slovakia started to diverge regarding the existence of accountability perversions between 2003 and 2010. While simulating judicial accountability and output excesses of judicial accountability permeated both countries on a roughly similar scale, judicial accountability avoidance was slightly higher in Slovakia and selective judicial accountability plagued only the Slovak judiciary.

As to simulating judicial accountability, complaints mechanisms turned out to be toothless in the Czech Republic as well as in Slovakia. Regular judicial performance evaluation in Slovakia had eventually a similar fate to that in the Czech Republic and the Slovak Parliament, egged on by an influential segment of the Slovak judiciary, eventually abolished it altogether.[27]

As regards output excesses of judicial accountability, it is important to emphasize that the Czech Republic and Slovakia exercised increased pressure on judges to improve their performance and reduce delays in delivering justice. At the same time, no qualitative assessment of judicial decisions existed in either of these two countries. This environment provided fertile soil for inventing various "output tricks" for boosting judges' performance. While this phenomenon cannot be measured, it was a public secret that, especially at lower courts, what mattered was how many decisions a judge delivered per month and the quality of those decisions was secondary. The techniques used by judges, despite a significant effort of the constitutional and top courts in both countries to eradicate them, remained the same as in the previous period.[28]

Regarding judicial accountability avoidance, at first sight it was higher in the Czech Republic, where judges still successfully resisted the

---

[25]   For further details, see Chapter 6, Section IV.D.

[26]   Note that judges of the Supreme Court of Slovakia have a narrow specialization and hence their reassignment to another specialization has serious repercussions for them.

[27]   Note that, given the elements of the outdated Soviet-style evaluation criteria in the Slovak judicial performance evaluation system (see Chapter 6, Section III.C), the resistance of Slovak judges against this system was understandable.

[28]   For further details, see Chapter 5, Section III.E.

introduction of individualized statistics, judicial performance evaluation, and personal financial disclosures. In contrast, Slovak judges had to lodge annual personal financial disclosures and until 2008 were subject to regular judicial performance evaluation. However, a closer look at disciplinary motions shows that Slovak judges, with the tacit support of the disciplinary courts, were more skillful in finding procedural loopholes in disciplinary proceedings and managed to evade the sanctions. Most importantly, a controversial interpretation of statutory limits for the disciplinary liability of judges and other "procedural tricks" caused 45% of disciplinary motions initiated against judges between 2003 and 2010 to be discontinued before reaching the merits stage. Therefore, the level of judicial accountability avoidance was in fact higher in Slovakia.

However, it was concerning selective judicial accountability that the difference between the Czech Republic and Slovakia was greatest, especially after the elevation of Harabin to the presidency of the Supreme Court of Slovakia in June 2009. After June 2009 Harabin and his supporters among court presidents used all mechanisms of judicial accountability that allowed them to punish their critics and reward their allies. The differences between the salary bonuses of "loyal" judges and those of "recalcitrant" judges widened exponentially, the caseloads of individual judges became uneven and all types of promotion became available only for "loyal" judges. Last but not least, "recalcitrant" judges faced further reprisals that are difficult to quantify, such as reassignment to chambers outside the areas of their expertise, poor working conditions, slow computers, or denial of reimbursement for attending judicial training.[29]

III.   Effects of the Judicial Council Euro-model in Slovakia

In Chapter 4, I formulated four research questions. For each of these four questions, I defined three alternative hypotheses, the first one based on the conventional wisdom about the role of judicial councils, the second one based on the historical experience with holding Czechoslovak judges to account and the third one that the JCSR made no difference:

Q.1 Did the JCSR disempower dominant principals from the "pre-JCSR" era (the Minister of Justice, the legislature, and court presidents) and empowered regular judges?

---

[29] On the potential impact of abusing nonmonetary benefits, see Chapter 3, Section II.C.

H.1a The JCSR disempowered all dominant principals from the "pre-JCSR" era and empowered regular judges.

H.1b The JCSR disempowered the Minister of Justice and the legislature, but instead of empowering regular judges it increased the power of court presidents.

H.1c The JCSR made no difference.

Q.2 Did the JCSR reduce the use of mechanisms of judicial accountability (quantitative dimension)?

H.2a The JCSR reduced the use of mechanisms of judicial accountability.

H.2b The JCSR reduced the use of mechanisms of judicial accountability.

H.2c The JCSR made no difference.

Q.3 Did the JCSR reduce the sanctions/rewards imposed (qualitative dimension)?

H.3a The JCSR reduced the sanctions/rewards imposed.

H.3b The JCSR increased the sanctions/rewards imposed.

H.3c The JCSR made no difference.

Q.4 Did the JCSR reduce accountability perversions?

H.4a The JCSR reduced accountability perversions.

H.4b The JCSR increased accountability perversions.

H.4c The JCSR made no difference.

In this Chapter, I will proceed as follows. I will first summarize what happened in Slovakia after the introduction of the JCSR. Then, I will use the Czech case study as a control for the results from Slovakia.

A. What Happened in Slovakia after the Introduction of the JCSR?

Who Holds Judges to Account?

Regarding the first research question, there were three dominant principals of judges in Slovakia before the split: the Minister of Justice, the legislature, and court presidents.[30] These three principals also played a key role in holding Slovak judges to account between years 1993 and 2002, when the Ministry of Justice model was in place in Slovakia. The division of the power to hold judges to account among these three principals in this period was as follows. Court presidents completely controlled the following four mechanisms of judicial accountability: reassignment, case assignment, chamber president appointment, and secondment. They also

---

[30] In the communist Czechoslovakia, the situation was similar, but only nominally, since all three aforementioned principals were controlled by the Communist Party.

initiated most disciplinary motions, processed complaints from the public, and had an equal say with the Minister of Justice in two other mechanisms (promotion and temporary assignment outside the judiciary). The legislature controlled two mechanisms – once-and-for-all retention review of new judges[31] and salary bonuses. Contrary to general wisdom, there was only one mechanism which was controlled entirely by the Minister of Justice: appointment to the position of court president or vice president. Other principals such as judicial boards and the public played a marginal role in this period. In other words, court presidents, and not the Minister of Justice or the legislature, dominated the Slovak judiciary in practice. Table 7.15 quantifies the "accountability-to-whom question" before the introduction of the JCSR.

The answer to the question who controlled the available mechanisms of judicial accountability changed completely after the introduction of the JCSR. The 2001 Constitutional Amendment which created the JCSR eliminated the role of the legislature in holding Slovak judges to account and reduced the powers of the Minister of Justice and judicial boards. Conversely, it empowered the JCSR and court presidents. Court presidents not only gained new powers, but also got the upper hand in the JCSR. Hence, with a certain degree of simplification, we may say that the transfer of powers to the JCSR in fact transferred powers from the Ministry of Justice, the legislature, and judicial boards to court presidents, and to the President of the Slovak Supreme Court in particular. Other players, such as the public and regular judges, remained mere bystanders. As a result, court presidents again dominated the Slovak judiciary in practice. However, the domination of court presidents in 2003–2010 (and especially in 2009 and 2010) was of a different degree from that in 1993–2002. Court presidents, acting either unilaterally or through the JCSR, controlled or had a veto power in virtually all mechanisms of judicial accountability. Table 7.16 portrays the "accountability-to-whom question" between 2003 and 2010 in quantifiable terms.

In conclusion, the answer to the first question is that the JCSR disempowered the Minister of Justice and the legislature, but instead of empowering regular judges it increased the power of court presidents. The regular judges who were supposed to become the key players in the judicial council model in fact remained marginal players. Hypothesis H.1a based upon the conventional wisdom about the impact of the Judicial Council

---

[31] Note that the Government increasingly interfered with retention review and so the legislature did not control that mechanism completely. For further details, see Chapter 6.

Table 7.15. *Who controlled de facto mechanisms of judicial accountability in Slovakia between 1993 and 2002? Slovakia (1993–2002)*

Year	Who controlled de facto mechanisms of JA?				
	Number of available mechanisms	Number of mechanisms controlled by MoJ	Number of mechanisms controlled by CP	Number of mechanisms controlled by LEG	Number of mechanisms controlled by OTHERS
1993	10	1.90	6.00	1.10	1.00
1994	10	1.90	6.00	1.10	1.00
1995	10	1.98	5.92	1.10	1.00
1996	10	1.90	6.00	1.10	1.00
1997	11	2.07	5.83	1.60	1.50
1998	10	1.90	5.50	1.60	1.00
1999	11	2.09	5.81	1.60	1.50
2000	11	2.15	5.75	1.60	1.50
2001	11	2.00	7.55	–	1.45
2002	11	2.03	7.51	–	1.46
Average	10.5	1.99	6.19	1.08	1.24
Average [%]		**19%**	**59%**	**10%**	**12%**

* MoJ = Minister of Justice, CP = court presidents, LEG = Legislature, OTHERS = other actors (e.g., judges other than court presidents, judicial boards, ombudsman, the Bar, the public)

Table 7.16. *Who controlled de facto mechanisms of judicial accountability in Slovakia between 1993 and 2002?* Slovakia (2003–2010)

Year	Who controlled de facto mechanisms of JA?				
	Number of available mechanisms	Number of mechanisms controlled by MoJ	Number of mechanisms controlled by CP	Number of mechanisms controlled by LEG	Number of mechanisms controlled by OTHERS
2003	10	1.69	6.70	–	1.60
2004	11	1.80	6.98	0.10	2.10
2005	11	1.33	7.78	–	1.88
2006	11	1.21	7.94	–	1.86
2007	11	1.10	8.01	–	1.89
2008	11	1.16	8.04	–	1.80
2009	11	0.60	9.16	–	1.22
2010	11	0.63	9.15	–	1.20
Average	10.9	1.19	7.97	0.01	1.69
Average [%]		**11%**	**73%**	**0%**	**16%**
Average in 2009 & 2010 [%]		**6%**	**83%**	**0%**	**11%**

* MoJ = Minister of Justice, CP = court presidents, LEG = Legislature, OTHERS = other actors (e.g., judges other than court presidents, judicial boards, ombudsman, the Bar, the public)

Euro-model thus proved to be wrong and hypothesis H.1b, which was based on historical legacies within the Slovak judiciary, is correct.

How Much Are Judges Held to Account?

The answer to the second question, which asks about the impact of the JCSR on the quantitative use of mechanisms of judicial accountability, is much less straightforward. It is so for three reasons. First, it is very difficult to answer this question in general terms as each mechanism had a different trajectory between 2003 and 2010. Second, certain mechanisms set a fixed interval when they can or must be used, and so the relevant principals cannot increase or reduce the number of occasions on which these mechanisms are used. This applies to annual salary bonuses (which can be awarded only once a year) and to judicial performance evaluation (which, until 2009, was supposed to be conducted every five years). In other words, the JCSR could not affect the frequency of the use of these two mechanisms. A similar issue arises with regard to the appointment of judges to the position of court president or vice president. The number of these positions as well as the length of term of judicial officials was fixed by law and the JCSR could not alter it. I refer to these three measures as "fixed" mechanisms of judicial accountability. Third, for several mechanisms that remain the data are simply not available to prove or disprove the alternative hypotheses H2.a and H2.b. The empirical support for conclusions regarding the remaining mechanisms of judicial accountability ranges from strong (disciplinary motions) via reasonable (reassignment and case assignment) to minimal (all types of promotions, temporary assignment outside the judiciary, and complaints).

However, we can still divide the remaining mechanisms of judicial accountability into four "bundles" according to the impact of the JCSR on them: mechanisms the use of which increased in quantitative terms after the introduction of the JCSR, mechanisms the use of which decreased in quantitative terms after the introduction of the JCSR, mechanisms the use of which in quantitative terms remained constant, and mechanisms the use of which in quantitative terms cannot be determined. The first bundle includes disciplinary motions, reassignment of judges, and case reassignment. Regarding the second bundle, I did not find any mechanism of judicial accountability the use of which in quantitative terms decreased after the introduction of the JCSR. The third bundle includes annual salary bonuses, judicial performance evaluation, and the appointment of judges to the position of court president or vice president. Finally, the use of the following mechanisms cannot be determined in quantitative terms with a reasonable degree of precision: complaints, promotion, chamber president appointment, secondment, and temporary assignment outside the judiciary.

In sum, neither the hypothesis that the JCSR reduced the use of mechanisms of judicial accountability nor that that the JCSR increased the use of these mechanisms is entirely correct. However, if I leave aside the "fixed" mechanisms of judicial accountability the use of which in quantitative terms cannot be changed, I may conclude that the JCSR did increase the use of three mechanisms (two "sticks" and one dual mechanism) in quantitative terms, whereas I could not find any mechanism the use of which decreased after the introduction of the JCSR. One huge caveat must be added here. For many mechanisms of judicial accountability the necessary data are missing and thus we do not know what the JCSR did to these mechanisms in quantitative terms.

The third research question enquires into the impact of the JCSR on the seriousness of the consequences Slovak judges faced when they were subjected to "accounting." I identified two competing hypotheses regarding the sanctions imposed (for sticks and dual mechanisms) and rewards awarded (for carrots and dual mechanisms). According to hypothesis H.3a the JCSR reduced the sanctions and rewards imposed, whereas the alternative hypothesis H.3b suggested that the JCSR increased them. As with the second question, my analysis does not fully support either of these two hypotheses. I must again divide mechanisms of judicial accountability into bundles.

The consequences of most mechanisms remained the same, because the severity of sanctions or the scope of rewards was fixed by law. Those mechanisms with fixed sanctions and rewards include promotion, chamber president appointment, secondment, temporary assignment outside the judiciary, and the appointment of a judge to the position of court president or vice president. There are two more mechanisms for which sanctions or rewards did not change after the introduction of the JCSR – judicial performance evaluation and complaints – even though the law allowed for various consequences. As for judicial performance evaluation, it was introduced only in 2001, which is only one year before the JCSR started to operate, and so it is not possible credibly to compare the "pre-JCSR" and "post-JCSR" application of this mechanism. The complaints mechanism was toothless in both periods.

In contrast, I could trace qualitative changes in the consequences of four mechanisms. Most importantly, salary bonuses went astray between 2003 and 2010. These bonuses reached astronomic sizes, especially in 2009 and 2010, when they became many times higher than in the "pre-JCSR" period. Regarding case (re)assignment and the reassignment of judges, their consequences were also gradually becoming harsher than in the "pre-JCSR" period, albeit in a subtler way. The reassignment of judges outside their area of specialization as well as the arbitrary assignment and reassignment of cases started to be increasingly employed not to tackle systemic problems or uneven caseloads, but rather to complicate the work of "recalcitrant" judges and to increase the unevenness of their caseloads. High caseloads in turn created pressure on these judges and increased the likelihood of their prosecution for delays in providing justice.

Disciplinary liability also underwent significant development. The assessment of this mechanism is complex. While the overall success rate of disciplinary prosecutors dropped from 42% in the "pre-JCSR" period to 29% in the "post-JCSR" period, these numbers obfuscate the amount of pressure put on judges. First, the mere initiation of a disciplinary motion negatively affected the prestige and salary of judges. Second, the length of trials before disciplinary panels increased rapidly, a fact which, together with the aforementioned negative reputational and monetary effects of suspension from judicial office during a disciplinary trial, aggravated the consequences of such trial. Third, several disciplinary motions initiated by Harabin during his term as Minister of Justice were withdrawn after the centrist coalition won the 2010 parliamentary elections. Fourth, several judges died during the disciplinary proceedings. For similar reasons, the fact that the most common sanctions in the "post-JCSR" period were still salary reductions and reprimands conceals the real consequences of disciplinary motions in Slovakia.

Accountability Perversions

Finally, the fourth research question asked whether the JCSR reduced the four accountability perversions: judicial accountability avoidance, simulating judicial accountability, output excesses of judicial accountability, and selective accountability. Again, I identified two competing hypotheses. According to hypothesis H.4a the JCSR reduced accountability perversions, whereas the alternative hypothesis H.4b suggested that the JCSR increased them. The Slovak case study showed that neither of these two hypotheses proved to be entirely correct since these four negative phenomena did not have the same trajectories.

More specifically, judicial accountability avoidance, simulating judicial accountability, and output excesses of judicial accountability in the "post-JCSR" phase remained on the similar levels to the "pre-JCSR" phase, whereas selective accountability increased significantly after the introduction of the JCSR. Selective accountability gradually increased once Harabin became the Minister of Justice and skyrocketed after the capture of the JCSR by Harabin and his allies in June 2009. From June 2009 Harabin and his supporters among court presidents used all the mechanisms of judicial accountability that allowed them to punish their critics and reward their allies. The differences between the salary bonuses of "loyal" judges and those of "recalcitrant" judges widened exponentially, the caseloads of individual judges became uneven, and all types of promotion became available only for "loyal" judges. Last but not least, "recalcitrant" judges faced further reprisals that are difficult to quantify, such as reassignment to chambers outside their areas of expertise, poor working conditions, slow computers, or the denial of funding to attend judicial training. In the most extreme cases, the cumulative effect of these practices of court presidents amounted to overt bullying. The ultimate aim of these bossing techniques was to put the "recalcitrant" judge under severe psychological pressure and force him to make mistakes so that he broke down completely or "at least" a successful disciplinary motion for delays could be initiated against him. In certain cases, the JCSR, led by Harabin, did not stop short of clear heinousness.[32] For instance, it drove the former Vice President of the Supreme Court Juraj Majchrák to suicide.[33]

B. What Changes Were Caused by the JCSR?

So far I have summarized the changes within the Slovak judiciary after the introduction of the JCSR. However, in order to make the conclusions regarding the impact of the JCSR more credible, I must address alternative explanations for changes between the pre-JCSR (1993–2002) and the post-JCSR (2003–2010) periods. In other words, I have to show that the changes in Slovakia after the introduction of the JCSR were not a mere

---

[32] For instance, when Marta Lauková, judge of the District Court of Bratislava I who belonged to the anti-Harabin camp, got ill, the JCSR (upon the motion of Helena Kožíková, the pro-Harabin president of the District Court of Bratislava I, who was herself a member of the JCSR) suspended Lauková's sickness benefit for reasons of her alleged fake inability to work. Two months later Marta Lauková died.

[33] Štefan Harabin, the president of the Supreme Court of Slovakia, initiated three disciplinary motions against the Supreme Court judge Juraj Majchrák in 2009. Persecution of Juraj Majchrák and other "recalcitrant judges" eventually attracted Zuzana Piussi, a Slovak documentarist, who cut a documentary describing problematic disciplinary motions in Slovakia (Zuzana Piussi, "Nemoc tretej moci" [The Disease of the Third Branch], 2011, Slovakia, 52 min.]. This documentary was broadcast widely in Slovakia as well as in the Czech Republic

correlation and that the JCSR is highly likely to have *caused* the changes I identified in the previous section. Put differently, I have to ask: what if the changes in the years between 2003 and 2010 in Slovakia would have taken place anyways, that is *even if* the Judicial Council Euro-model had not been established and the Ministry of Justice model of court administration had remained in place?

Here the case study on the Czech judiciary and the "most similar cases" logic of this book comes to the fore. The Czech Republic and Slovakia share the same essential features: a communist past, a civil law system, a career model of the judiciary, a Kelsenian model of constitutional review, and membership of the EU and the Council of Europe. In addition, Czech and Slovak judges operated under a common institutional structure from the independence of Czechoslovakia in 1918 until its dissolution in 1992. Both countries retained the Ministry of Justice model of court administration until 2002, when Slovakia established the JCSR, whereas the Czech Republic retained the Ministry of Justice model. Luckily, that model remained in force in the Czech Republic for the entire period between 2003 and 2010. What is more, the results for the period between 1993 and 2002 in the Czech Republic and Slovakia were similar. In other words, the Czech Republic and Slovakia as well as their judicial systems were matched on most attributes between 2003 and 2010,[34] but varied on the key independent variable – the model of court administration.

This allows us to use the Czech case study as a control for the results from Slovakia. In Section III.A of this chapter I compared the use of mechanisms of judicial accountability in Slovakia in the pre-JCSR (1993–2002) and the post-JCSR (2003–2010) periods and summarized the changes after the introduction of the JCSR. In order to eliminate false inferences, for each research question I will do two control tests. First, I will examine whether the same changes took place also in the Czech Republic, which kept the Ministry of Justice model of court administration between 2003 and 2010. If similar changes happened in the Czech Republic between 2003 and 2010, then it is less likely that the JCSR was the main cause of those changes, as the judicial council and the Ministry of Justice models led to similar results. However, if there are no signs of similar changes in the Czech Republic, then it is more likely that those changes were indeed caused by the JCSR. Then, I will look to see whether there were significant differences between the Czech Republic and Slovakia in the use of

---

[34] This is of course a huge assumption as two nations are never the same. I challenge this assumption in Section IV of this chapter.

mechanisms of judicial accountability before the introduction of the JCSR in Slovakia, that is, in the period between 1993 and 2002. If I can trace such differences, I must take them into account when interpreting changes in Slovakia after the introduction of the JCSR.

Regarding the first research question, I observed in Chapter 5 that there were no significant changes among the principals of Czech judges. Two major principals – the Minister of Justice and court presidents – were the same in 1993–2002 as well as in 2003–2010. The division of power between them also remained very similar and so, unlike with regard to Slovakia, I do not observe the rise of the power of court presidents and the disempowerment of the Ministry of Justice in the Czech Republic between 2003 and 2010. In other words, this change, which took place in Slovakia after the introduction of the JCSR, had no equivalent in the Czech Republic.

Nevertheless, I must also check whether the principals of Czech and Slovak judges were the same between 1993 and 2002. In Section I of this chapter, I showed that despite several differences between Czech and Slovak law in the pre-JCSR period, the Slovak and the Czech Ministry of Justice models de facto divided the power to hold judges to account in a similar fashion. In both countries court presidents played a dominant role and controlled almost two-thirds of mechanisms of judicial accountability, whereas politicians in the governing coalition controlled almost one-third of available mechanisms and other principals were marginal. The only major difference was that Slovak judges were held to account both by the Slovak Minister of Justice and the Slovak legislature, whereas the Czech parliament could not hold individual judges to account. I do not consider this difference significant, because the governing coalitions in Slovakia controlled both the Slovak legislature and the Slovak Ministry of Justice, and thus the difference between the two countries was in practice minimal. We may thus conclude that it is significantly more likely that the rise in power of court presidents was caused by the JCSR. This means that hypothesis H.1a stating that the JCSR disempowered the Minister of Justice and the legislature, but instead of empowering regular judges increased the power of court presidents is further strengthened.

As to the second research question, I showed that there was a significant rise in disciplinary motions in Slovakia after the introduction of the JCSR and that in 2009 and 2010, once Harabin and his allies had conquered the Supreme Court of Slovakia as well as the JCSR, court presidents multiplied the use of reassignment of judges and case reassignment. More specifically, the average number of disciplinary motions against Slovak judges per annum between 1993 and 2002 was 9.8, whereas in the period between 2003 and 2010 it reached 28.1, which is almost three times as many. In contrast, the average number of disciplinary motions per annum in these two periods remained relatively stable in the Czech Republic, because it increased only marginally from 25.3 motions (in 1993–2002) to 30.75 motions (in 2003–2010). This increase in disciplinary motions in the Czech Republic by 22% in the "post-JCSR" period is thus in stark contrast to the steep rise by 187% in Slovakia. Regarding the reassignment of judges outside their previous specializations and the reassignment of cases, Slovak media repeatedly reported sudden increases in the use of these mechanisms in 2009 and 2010,[35] whereas I could not trace any mention of such practice in the Czech media in these two years. We may thus conclude that the increased use of all three mechanisms took place only in Slovakia, and so it is more likely that this increase was caused by the JCSR.

With regard to the third research question, my analysis revealed that in 2009 and 2010 salary bonuses skyrocketed, reassignment of judges outside their specialization and case assignment techniques entailed more severe consequences, and disciplinary motions had more severe effects than in the previous years. None of these developments took place in the Czech Republic.[36] Therefore, the increase in these sanctions and rewards is highly likely to have been caused by the JCSR.

Finally, I observed that selective accountability increased after Harabin and his allies got the upper hand over the Supreme Court of Slovakia and the JCSR in 2009. From June 2009 they started to use all mechanisms of judicial accountability that allowed them to punish their critics and reward their allies. Again, none of these things happened in the Czech Republic. Therefore, it is more likely that the rise in selective accountability was caused by the JCSR.

IV.   Alternative Explanations

In the previous section I used the Czech case study as a control in order to ascertain whether or not the changes I identified in Slovakia after the introduction of the JCSR (2003–2010) occurred also in the Czech Republic and whether or not the trajectories of the studied dependent variables between 1993 and 2010 were the same in these two countries. This analysis showed that the Czech Republic and Slovakia had a very

---

[35]   See Chapter 6, Section IV.D.
[36]   But note that salary bonuses are prohibited in the Czech Republic.

similar starting position regarding most dependent variables in 2002, when the JCSR was introduced in Slovakia, and that the changes that happened in Slovakia between 2003 and 2010 did not occur in the Czech Republic.[37] This means that it is more likely that these changes were caused by the Judicial Council Euro-model of court administration and not by the change in other independent variables. Most importantly, it eliminated the possibility that those changes were caused by the accession of Slovakia to the European Union in 2004,[38] because no such changes took place in the Czech Republic, which joined the European Union at the same time.

However, in order to make my claim even more credible, I still have to look for alternative explanations of the changes within the Slovak judiciary between 2003 and 2010. I will do this in two steps. First, I will look at the period between 2003 and 2010 and ask what other changes that might have caused or contributed to the effects I identified in Section III of this chapter, *apart from* the introduction of the JCSR, occurred in Slovakia (and not in the Czech Republic) in this period. Second, I will question the key assumption I built my case studies on, namely that the Czech Republic and Slovakia and their judiciaries share the same essential features, and look for the differences between the two countries that might have contributed to the divergent development in the Czech Republic and Slovakia. In other words, I explicitly acknowledge that the JCSR, like any other institution, cannot operate as a purely independent variable in the Slovak political system; instead, it is subject to various forces and depends on multiple factors.

Regarding the first set of alternative explanations, two changes come immediately to mind – the shifts in Slovak politics and the rise of Štefan Harabin. I addressed *the politics* of the postsplit Czech Republic and Slovakia briefly in Chapters 5 and 6. From this analysis it is clear that both countries have bipolar party system and both political regimes are by and large similarly competitive.[39] No political party was able to win

---

[37] Two exceptions, the higher level of corruption and the higher division within the Slovak judiciary will be addressed subsequently.

[38] Note that one can still claim, as I will do later in Chapter 8, that the European institutions indirectly contributed to the changes that occurred in the Slovak judiciary between 2003 and 2010, because the European Commission vigorously advocated the Judicial Council Euro-model in the accession process.

[39] See Fernando Casal Bértoa, "Party Systems and Cleavage Structures Revisited: A Sociological Explanation of Party System Institutionalization" (2014) 20 *Party Politics* 16, 18; Tim Haughton, "Exit Choice and Legacy: Explaining the Patterns of Party Politics in Post-communist Slovakia" (2014) 30 *East European Politics* 210, 214, Sean Hanley, "Dynamics of New Party Formation in the Czech Republic 1996–2010: Looking for the Origins of a 'political earthquake'" (2012) 28 *East European Politics* 119; Ladislav Cabada,

an absolute majority and no coalition ruled for more than two consecutive terms between 1993 and 2010[40] in Slovakia or the Czech Republic. In fact, the timing of changes at the helm of Slovakia in this period was quite similar to timing of shifts in power in the Czech Republic. Mečiar ruled for the first two terms in Slovakia (like the coalitions led by Klaus's Civic Democratic Party in the Czech Republic), followed by coalitions of centrist parties that also governed for two terms (like the coalitions led by the Czech Social Democrats) and then Fico's coalition (that included Mečiar's HZDS) stepped in for one term (at the same time, the Civic Democratic Party, this time without Klaus, returned to power in the Czech Republic). Hence, despite the fact that the Czech party system is to be considered institutionalized, while its Slovak counterpart only achieves a weak level of institutionalization,[41] the Czech and Slovak political systems are much closer to each other than any other two countries in the region, having very similar scores regarding parliamentary fragmentation, party system closure, and electoral volatility.[42] In particular, when one leaves out the first years after the split (1993–1998), when Slovakia took a significantly different trajectory under Mečiar's rule, both systems yield very similar results.

This potentially promising explanation for the divergent paths of the Czech and Slovak judiciaries based on politics thus seems unlikely. This finding is further corroborated by the data. Changes in the use of mechanisms of judicial accountability or changes in other dependent variables I analyzed in Sections I and II of this chapter do not correlate with the changes in power in either of the two countries. None of the political fragmentation measures (electoral volatility, party fragmentation in parliament, and party system closure) correlate well with the observed variation in the dependent variable either. More specifically, despite the fact that

---

Vít Hloušek, and Petr Jurek, *Party Systems in East Central Europe* (Lexington Books 2014), 79 and 86–89.

[40] Mečiar's HZDS came close in the 1992 elections, winning 74 seats out of 150 on the National Council (two seats short of an absolute majority). In the 2012 elections, Fico's Direction-Social Democracy became the first party since the breakup of Czechoslovakia to win an absolute majority of seats in the National Council.

[41] Bértoa 2014, supra note 39, 18.

[42] Fernando Casal Bértoa, "Post-Communist Politics: On the Divergence (and/or Convergence) of East and West Government and Opposition" (2013) 48 *Government and Opposition* 398, 402–413 and 417. See also Cabada, Hloušek, and Jurek, above note 39, 79 and 86–89; and Zsolt Enyedi and Fernando Casal Bértoa, "Party System Closure and Openness: Conceptualization, Operationalization and Validation" (2014) 20 *Party Politics* (forthcoming).

fragmentation fluctuated in the Czech Republic, the use of mechanisms of judicial accountability was relatively stable over the entire period of 1993–2010 and, in fact, when the number of disciplinary motions reached its peak in 2006–2008, the Czech party system was the least fragmented.[43] In Slovakia, fragmentation measures cannot explain the rise of infighting within the judiciary in 2008–2010, because in that period the fragmentation of the Slovak party system decreased and the party system closure increased.[44] I may thus conclude that although politics undeniably affected the functioning of the Czech and Slovak judiciaries, I could not find support for the thesis that differences in Slovak and Czech politics significantly contributed to the divergent results in holding Czech and Slovak judges to account in the years between 2003 and 2010.

As for individuals, they always matter. But the *role of individuals* is particularly strong in the period of transition to democracy. In such periods people often do not think institutionally. They think names. Transitional periods also inevitably generate strong hero-like characters. Unfortunately, they generate villains too. Štefan Harabin can easily be perceived as the proverbial "villain of the piece." Hence, one can plausibly object that it was not the JCSR but Štefan Harabin who caused the effects I described in Section III of this chapter. Nevertheless, three counterarguments rebut or at least significantly moderate this objection.

First, a closer analysis shows that Harabin could never accomplish with the allegedly old-fashioned Ministry of Justice model what he accomplished with the JCSR between 2009 and 2010.[45] Harabin was the President of the Supreme Court also between 1998 and 2003 and thus I can compare what he did at that period. He could not "buy" judges with astronomical salary bonuses, because the legislature controlled that mechanism at that time.[46] As regards other mechanisms, between 1998 and 2003 he arguably controlled case assignment, reassignment, and promotion, but only at the Supreme Court. It was the JCSR that gave him power over the lower courts as well. It is no exaggeration that the JCSR empowered the President of

---

[43] Zsolt Enyedi and Fernando Casal Bértoa (2014), "Elite and Mass Dynamics: The East Central European Example", paper presented at the OPPR Workshop on "Parties and Democracy in Post-communist Europe" at EUI on September 18–19, 2014, (available at http://whogoverns.eu/elite-and-mass-dynamics-the-east-central-european-example/), 20–22.

[44] Ibid.

[45] One might also claim that Harabin in 1998 was a different person than Harabin in 2009. However, his speeches and actions in both periods refute this idea.

[46] He started misusing this mechanism only when the JCSR was entrenched in the Constitution in 2001 (but had not yet started to operate) and the legal vacuum emerged.

the Supreme Court to the extent that the person holding that position could "act as though the entire Slovak judiciary is one big court and he its president."[47] It is an uncomfortable truth that it was just a matter of time before someone seized this opportunity. Harabin did it, but if it had not been Harabin, there would have been someone else. As the classic says, "power corrupts, and absolute power corrupts absolutely."[48]

One can also speculate what would have happened if Harabin was in the Czech Republic, which retained the Ministry of Justice model. Had Harabin become a president of the Supreme Court of the Czech Republic in 2003, it would have been perhaps even more difficult to prosecute him disciplinarily, because, in contrast to Slovakia, disciplinary proceedings with the Supreme Court president did not take place before a constitutional court like, but before the Supreme Court itself.[49] The chances that Supreme Court judges would have disciplined their own president were thus very low.[50] However, Harabin would not have had any influence on the Czech judiciary beyond the Supreme Court. He would have been able to deny promotion to the Supreme Court and perhaps tinker with the Supreme Court work schedule that defined assignment of judges to panels and case assignment, but that was it. The Ministry of Justice model gave him no carrots and no sticks against judges of other courts. In sum, the "Czech Harabin" between 2003 and 2010 would have found himself in a similar position to the one in Slovakia between 1998 and 2003 – he could have shaken up things at the Supreme Court, but had no chance to influence the whole judiciary.

This brings me to the second counterargument, which is embarrassingly simple. Harabin could never have accomplished what he did had he acted alone. In other words, he needed the support of other members of the Slovak judiciary, not only of court presidents but also of a significant

---

[47] Here I am paraphrasing Pavol Rohárik; see Pavol Rohárik, "The Judiciary and Its Transition in Slovakia after 1989" in Jiří Přibáň, Pauline Roberts, and James Young (eds.), *Systems of Justice in Transition: Central European Experiences since 1989* (Ashgate 2003) 213, 216 (for more context, see Chapter 6).

[48] This quotation is usually attributed to Lord Acton.

[49] This has changed only in October 2008, when the Supreme Administrative Court became a disciplinary court for all judges in the Czech Republic.

[50] This is confirmed by the fate of the disciplinary motions against the President of the Czech Supreme Court (for alleged mismanagement) and against the Vice President of the Czech Supreme Court (for an alleged attempt to influence the outcome of the criminal prosecution of Minister of Regional Development), both of which were discontinued by the disciplinary panels of the Supreme Court.

number of regular judges.[51] This is not to say that he had to woo the majority of Slovak judges to his side. In fact, he never mustered such widespread support. It was enough if the majority was not openly against him. It is another uncomfortable truth that in order to control the judiciary it was enough to place relatively few loyal judges on the "right" places – at the Supreme Court, in court presidents' posts, and at the JCSR. One can object that this could happen in the Czech Ministry of Justice model too, but that is not true. In contrast to Slovakia, where court presidents preserved their powers from the pre-JCSR era and controlled the powers previously held by the Slovak Ministry of Justice via the JCSR, there was always a balance of powers between Czech court presidents and the Czech Ministry of Justice and neither could get the upper hand. The Czech Ministry of Justice model, modified by interventions of the Czech Constitutional Court and growing emancipation of court presidents, was perhaps more clumsy and full of tensions, but it was more resistant to capture and resulted in a constitutional balance.[52] Conversely, the JCSR arguably allowed for smoother governance, but could have been "hijacked" much more easily.

Finally, the third counterargument is that the Judicial Council Euro-model resulted in similar problems in other CEE countries, especially in Romania, Hungary, and Bulgaria.[53] The effects of the Judicial Council Euro-model beyond Slovakia will be addressed in more detail in Chapter 8. Here it suffices to say that similar experiences with the Euro-model in other CEE countries also rebut the promising alternative explanation that Harabin made the difference. Instead, similar problems with this model in other CEE countries attest that the Euro-model produces these effects systematically. We may thus conclude that Harabin only exposed and exemplified the flaws that are embedded in the Judicial

---

[51] He managed to achieve significant support among Slovak judges primarily by portraying himself a savior of the Slovak judiciary who protects the interests of judges against the demands of Daniel Lipšic, the Slovak Minister of Justice between 1998 and 2006.

[52] For a similar conclusion, see Michal Bobek, "The Administration of Courts in the Czech Republic – In Search of a Constitutional Balance" (2010) 16 *European Public Law* 251.

[53] See, for example, Zoltán Fleck, "Judicial Independence in Hungary" in Anja Seibert-Fohr (ed.), *Judicial Independence in Transition* (Springer 2012) 793 (on Hungary); Cristina Parau, "The Drive for Judicial Supremacy" in ibid., 619, 643–656; Ramona Coman and Cristina Dallara, "Judicial Independence in Romania" in ibid., 835; Bogdan Iancu, "Constitutionalism in Perpetual Transition: The Case of Romania" in Bogdan Iancu (ed.), *The Law/Politics Distinction in Contemporary Public Law Adjudication* (Eleven International Publishing 2009) 187, 196–198 (on Romania); and Maria Popova, "Why the Bulgarian Judiciary Does Not Prosecute Corruption?" (2012) 59 *Problems of Post Communism* 35 (on Bulgaria).

Council Euro-model and he thus cannot be considered as a primary cause of the changes between 2003 and 2010.

Regarding the second set of alternative explanations, I identified the following ten variables on which Slovakia and the Czech Republic allegedly differ and which must be taken into account in assessing the impact of the Judicial Council Euro-model in Slovakia:[54] the political system, the powers and vigilance of the constitutional court, the way the past was dealt with within the judiciary, the status and material safeguards of judges, contingent circumstances of judicial accountability, the level of division within the judiciary, the level of corruption within the judiciary, previous experience with running the country, the size of the country and its population, and culture. I will evaluate the plausibility of these alternative variables one by one.

First, one can object that the Slovak *political system* differs from the Czech in one important aspect[55] – the Slovak political system is more majoritarian since the Slovak parliament is unicameral (the National Council), whereas the Czech parliament is bicameral (consisting of the Chamber of Deputies and the Senate), and since the President of Slovakia is de facto weaker than his Czech counterpart. While this difference should not be underestimated, it had little effect on the ordinary[56] judiciaries in the Czech Republic and Slovakia between 1993 and 2010. Most importantly, the Senate of the Czech Republic, which came into being only in 1996, never played any role in holding individual judges of ordinary courts to account.[57] It also did not block any significant judicial reform approved by the Czech Chamber of Deputies. All important judicial reforms went smoothly through both the Chamber of Deputies and the Senate, and when they failed – like the 2000 judicial reform that was supposed to introduce the Judicial Council Euro-model in the Czech Republic – they were defeated in the Chamber of Deputies. Similarly, when the Chamber of Deputies passed the laws cutting the salaries of Czech judges, the Senate

---

[54] This list of variables or, rather, factors is based on the existing literature on the Czech and/or Slovak courts as well as on observations made by Czech and Slovak stakeholders (judges, law professors, advocates, and politicians) during my interviews with them.

[55] Other than that, both countries are parliamentary representative democracies with the Prime Minister as head of government.

[56] Note that I do not address accountability of Constitutional Justices, where the Senate of the Czech Republic plays a significant role.

[57] Note that the National Council played a modest role in holding Slovak judges to account between 1993 and June 2001, but the 2001 Constitutional Amendment transferred all of these powers to the newly established JCSR and so the National Council had no chance to hold individual judges to account between June 2001 and 2010.

never fought back.[58] The Czech Senate thus did not act as a significant veto player in this area of law, and this difference cannot explain the divergent paths the Czech Republic and Slovakia took between 2003 and 2010. Similarly, even though the President of the Czech Republic Václav Klaus tried to remove the Chief Justice of the Czech Supreme Court in 2006,[59] this was the only serious attempt of a Czech President to meddle in the judicial mega-politics and, more importantly, this action was stopped by the Constitutional Court of the Czech Republic. Hence, the differences among the de facto powers of the Presidents of both countries can also be ruled out as a possible explanation of different paths of the Czech and Slovak judiciaries after 2003.

Second, one may claim that the Czech *Constitutional Court* had more powers and/or was more vigilant in this area than its Slovak counterpart. Regarding the powers of these two constitutional courts, this argument does not withstand serious scrutiny. Both constitutional courts were vested with almost identical powers. Both of them can exercise both abstract and concrete review of constitutionality and both decide on individual constitutional complaints.[60] As to the level of vigilance, it must be acknowledged that the Czech Constitutional Court proved to be a more stringent guardian of the judiciary than the Slovak, in particular in the period between 2003 and 2010. Nevertheless, the lesser intensity of constitutional review in this area in Slovakia resulted to a large extent from the very introduction of the JCSR. The JCSR in fact disempowered the Slovak Constitutional Court, because the JCSR *was* entrenched in the Slovak Constitution and the Slovak Constitutional Court had to treat the JCSR as a constitutional organ. Therefore, it is not surprising that the constitutional review of acts of the JCSR was less intensive than that of acts of the Ministry of Justice. Had the Slovak Constitutional Court acted differently,

---

[58] In fact, the Czech bicameral parliament adopted twelve laws that either reduced or froze judicial salaries between 1993 and 2010, whereas the unicameral Slovak legislature passed only four such laws.

[59] For further details, see Chapter 5, Section I.E.

[60] On the difference between these three procedures (abstract review of constitutionality, concrete review of constitutionality and individual constitutional complaints), see David Kosař, "Conflicts between Fundamental Rights in the Jurisprudence of the Czech Constitutional Court" in Eva Brems (ed.), *Conflicts Between Fundamental Rights* (Intersentia 2008) 345, 349–350. On the comparison of jurisdictions and the case law of both constitutional courts, see Radoslav Procházka, *Mission Accomplished: On Founding Constitutional Adjudication in Central Europe* (CEU Press 2002); or Wojciech Sadurski, *Rights before Courts: A Study of Constitutional Courts in Postcommunist states of Central and Eastern Europe* (Springer 2005).

it would have defeated the very purpose of establishing the JCSR. The case law of the Czech Constitutional Court confirms this observation. In fact, the Czech Constitutional Court openly advocated the Judicial Council Euro-model[61] and made it clear that it was so vigilant precisely because it was the executive that decided on several mechanisms of judicial accountability.[62] I can thus conclude that regarding judicial design issues and the individual complaints of judges the Slovak Constitutional Court was less vigilant than its Czech counterpart, but this difference was not an independent factor to be taken into account, but rather a direct consequence of the creation of the JCSR in Slovakia.

Third, given the different trajectories of the Lustration Law in the Czech Republic and Slovakia,[63] *dealing with the past within the judiciary* is another obvious suspect. However, in Chapters 5 and 6 I provided conclusive evidence that even though the general impact of the Lustration Law was much stronger in the Czech Republic than in Slovakia, the impact of lustration on the judiciary was very similar in both countries. The assertions made by some scholars that lustration "was responsible for the dismissal of the greater part of the bench"[64] and that "only 30% of judges remained on the [Czech] bench after transition"[65] are flawed[66] and lack any evidential support.[67] On the contrary, most sources agree that the Lustration Law

---

[61] See in particular Judgment of the Constitutional Court of the Czech Republic of June 18, 2002, case no. Pl. ÚS 7/02; Judgment of the Constitutional Court of the Czech Republic of July 11, 2006, case no. Pl. ÚS 18/06, § VII; and Judgment of the Constitutional Court of the Czech Republic of October 6, 2010, case no. Pl. ÚS 39/08, §§ 60–61.

[62] See ibid.

[63] See Nadya Nedelsky, "Divergent Responses to a Common Past: Transitional Justice in the Czech Republic and Slovakia" (2004) 33 *Theory and Society* 65; David Kosař, "Lustration and Lapse of Time: Dealing with the Past in the Czech Republic" (2008) 4 *Eur. Constitutional Law Review* 460; or Roman David, *Lustration and Transitional Justice: Personnel Systems in the Czech Republic, Hungary, and Poland* (University of Pennsylvania Press 2011) in particular at 71, 78, 112–117 and 137–140.

[64] Daniela Piana, *Judicial Accountabilities in New Europe: From Rule of Law to Quality of Justice* (Ashgate 2010), 100. See also ibid., at 92, 108, 110 n. 33, and 164.

[65] Ibid., at 98.

[66] I stressed in Chapter 5 that the fact that many judges left the Czech judiciary after the Velvet Revolution does not necessarily mean that they left *because* of lustration. In fact, many of them left for purely monetary reasons or for more prestigious jobs.

[67] According to Eliška Wagnerová, former President of the Supreme Court and the Vice President of the Constitutional Court, approximately one-third of Czech judges (480 out of 1,460) left the bench between 1990 and 1992 (Eliška Wagnerová, "Position of Judges in the Czech Republic" in Jiří Přibáň, Pauline Roberts, and James Young (eds.), *Systems of Justice in Transition: Central European Experiences since 1989* (Ashgate 2003) 163, 170). In contrast, Piana does not support her claims with data and does not mention any source for her

affected very few Czech judges.[68] The Czech judiciary, like judges in most countries in the CEE[69] as well as in other parts of the world,[70] in fact managed to escape the purges and thus the dealing with the past within the Czech judiciary was minimal. Put differently, as there was no significant difference between the two countries in this aspect, it could not affect the functioning of the Czech and Slovak judiciaries.

Fourth, one may argue that *the status and material safeguards of judges* were lower in Slovakia and, therefore, Slovak judges had a higher incentive to seek additional income elsewhere and were more prone to corruption. This argument also does not withstand serious scrutiny. The salaries of judges were low in both countries in the early 1990s, but the Czech and the Slovak parliaments addressed this issue in the mid-1990s[71] and tied the salaries of judges to average income in a given country.[72] Since the mid-1990s the salaries of judges in both countries have been roughly similar. According to the 2012 CEPEJ report which includes the 2010 data, the gross annual salary of a Slovak judge at the beginning of his career (28,148 EUR) was even higher than the gross annual salary of a Czech judge at the same stage of his career (24,324 EUR),[73] despite the fact the gross annual

assertions. For my detailed criticism of Piana's claims, see David Kosař, "The Least Accountable Branch (Review Essay)" (2013) 11 *International Journal of Constitutional Law* 234.

[68] See Chapter 5, Section I.D.

[69] Eastern Germany (where all GDR judges had to reapply for their jobs and some of them faced criminal prosecution) and to a lesser extent Poland (where the purge affected only the Supreme Court) are exceptions to this rule. For further details on purging the GDR judiciary, *see* Erhard Blankenburg, "The Purge of Lawyers after the Breakdown of the East German Communist Regime" (1995) 20 *Law & Social Inquiry* 223; Inga Markovits, "Children of a Lesser God: GDR Lawyers in Post-Socialist Germany" (1996) 94 *Michigan Law Review* 2270, 2271–2272; or Martina Künnecke, "The Accountability and Independence of Judges: German Perspectives" in Guy Canivet, Mads Andenas, and Duncan Fairgrieve (eds.), *Independence, Accountability, and the Judiciary* (British Institute of International and Comparative Law 2006) 217, 229–230. For further details on limited purges in the Polish judiciary, *see* Wojciech Sadurski, *Rights before Courts: A Study of Constitutional Courts in Postcommunist States of Central and Eastern Europe* (Springer 2005) 43; or Lech Garlicki, "Politics and Political Independence of the Judiciary" in András Sajó and L. R. Bentch (eds.), *Judicial Integrity* (Brill Academic Publishers 2004) 125, 137–138.

[70] See, for example, David Dyzenhaus, *Judging the Judges, Judging Ourselves: Truth, Reconciliation and the Apartheid Legal Order* (Hart Publishing 2003) (on how South African judges from the apartheid era refused to appear before the Truth and Reconciliation Commission and fought back against any attempt to hold them to account); Hakeem Yusuf, *Transitional Justice, Judicial Accountability and the Rule of Law* (Routledge 2010) (on how Nigerian judges managed to escape accountability after the fall of the military regime).

[71] Slovakia did so immediately in 1993 (see Law No. 120/1993 Z.z.) and the Czech Republic followed two years later (see Law No. 236/1996 Sb.).

[72] On the mechanism, for calculating salaries of Czech and Slovak judges, see Chapters 5 and 6.

[73] The 2012 CEPEJ Report, at 261.

salary was lower in Slovakia. The situation at top courts looked different at the first sight. The same report shows that the gross annual salary of a Slovak judge at the end of his career (40,659 EUR) was significantly lower than the gross annual salary of a Czech judge at the same stage of his career (54,384 EUR).[74] However, if we take into account the lower gross annual salary in Slovakia[75] and salary bonuses that were not taken into account by the CEPEJ study,[76] the differences in salaries of Czech and Slovak judges at the top courts become minimal. As regards other material and social benefits, Slovak law is far more generous to judges than Czech legislation.[77] We may thus conclude that the status and material safeguards of Slovak and Czech judges were roughly the same and this variable cannot explain the differences between the two countries.

Fifth, one might argue that the contingent circumstances in Slovakia differed from those in the Czech Republic. However, I showed that all four key contingent measures – the training of judges, the selection and recruitment of judges, the level of transparency, and available appellate mechanisms – turned out to be similar. In both countries, the Judicial Academy was established at the same time (in 2002 in the Czech Republic and in 2003 in Slovakia) and the training was controlled by senior judges and court presidents. Regarding the selection and recruitment of judges, both countries follow the career model of judiciary and the differences between them are either marginal in practice or decreased over time. As to the former, "lateral hiring" of judges in the Czech Republic was rare and ad hoc "judicial selection committees" established in Slovakia after the establishment of the JCSR meant little change on the ground as the court presidents retained their influence over appointment of judges. As to the latter, the system of "judges on probation,"[78] which had been applicable only in Slovakia, was abolished by the 2001 Constitutional Amendment

---

[74] The 2012 CEPEJ Report, at 266.

[75] See the 2012 CEPEJ Report, at 271 (which includes the ratio of the judge's salary to the national average salary for all European countries).

[76] Remember that the standard amount of a judge's salary bonus at the Supreme Court of Slovakia in the pre-Harabin era was 2,000 EUR per annum. For further details, see Chapter 6.

[77] Slovak judges enjoy longer vacations (six weeks per year), have the right to a fully reimbursed one-week stay at the State spa every year (if they have reached forty-five years and been in judicial office for at least ten years) and are granted various additional social security benefits, including special treatment for pregnant judges and female judges who are taking care for young children. See in particular Arts. 45, 50, 53–57, and 93–102 of the 2000 Law on Judges and Lay Judges.

[78] For more details regarding the system of "judges on probation," see Chapter 6.

and thus it could not have contributed to the effects of the JCSR. Regarding transparency mechanisms, Czech Republic and Slovakia scored roughly the same points. The Czech Republic provided a broader access to judicial decisions throughout the entire studied period, but Slovakia fared slightly better regarding transparency of competitions for vacancies within the judiciary and required from all sitting judges to submit to disclose their nonjudicial activities (via personal declaration) as well as their property and income (via financial declaration) on an annual basis. Finally, both countries retained the criminal and civil codes of procedure from the federal era and thus the available appellate and quasi-appellate mechanisms are virtually the same. In sum, contingent circumstances affecting Slovak and Czech judges were roughly the same and this variable cannot explain the differences between the two countries. To the contrary, this finding regarding contingent circumstances increases the persuasiveness of the pivotal contrast between Slovakia's judicial council model based on the Judicial Council Euro-model and the Czech Republic's Ministry of Justice model.[79]

Sixth, the cohesiveness of the judiciary was much lower in Slovakia than in the Czech Republic before the introduction of the JCSR, and thus I have to consider the possibility that the *level of division within the judiciary* contributed to the effects I observed in 2003–2010.[80] It is difficult to counter this argument because I have no means of isolating the impact of this variable. The only counterargument is that the division within the judiciary plays a lesser role in the Ministry of Justice model than in the judicial council one, because judges have fewer powers in the Ministry of Justice model. Put differently, the disease of judges fighting other judges cannot be "transmitted" to the overall administration of courts so easily under the Ministry of Justice model. But I do not know whether the division within the judiciary is a factor that affects how the Judicial Council Euro-model operates. In order to answer this question, I would have to find two countries that shared similar characteristics and both opted for Judicial Council Euro-model, but differed on how divisive their judiciaries were at the moment of introducing the JCSR. The Czech case study cannot

---

[79] For explanation of the reasons for including contingent circumstances in this study, see Chapter 5, Section III.

[80] I am aware of the fact that I am here breaking a sacrosanct methodological rule – to treat each variable as either independent or dependent variable but never both – but I find it important for understanding the impact of the JCSR in real life. As a consolation I repeat what I said earlier – in the real world there are no truly dependent and independent variables – all variables are to a lesser or greater extent interdependent.

be employed for such comparison and thus I have to admit that factionalism within the Slovak judiciary before establishing the JCSR might have contributed to the effects between 2003 and 2010.

Seventh, one may raise another objection – that the *level of corruption among judges* has been higher in Slovakia than in the Czech Republic. This objection is difficult to tackle, because there are limited comparable data regarding corruption within the Czech and Slovak judiciaries. The Global Corruption Barometer produced by Transparency International started to operate only in 2003 and, moreover, did not include Slovakia until 2011. Similarly, the EBRD-World Bank conducted the so-called BEEPS Reports for both countries only in 2005 and 2008. In the Czech Republic, at least the national STEM polls that cover the entire period between 1993 and 2010 are available.[81] Unfortunately, no comparable systematic surveys were done in Slovakia in the 1990s. However, having these caveats in mind, the available data suggest that the level of corruption within the Slovak judiciary may indeed have been higher in 2002. In the 2002 TIS poll 60% Slovak respondents stated that corruption in the courts and prokuratura exists and is widespread and the 2000 World Bank study showed that Slovak courts and prosecutors ranked second in the list of public institutions with widespread corruption. In contrast, in the 2005 Global Corruption Barometer "only" 44% of Czech respondents opined that the Czech judiciary was very or extremely corrupt and the judiciary ranked third among the most corrupt institutions in the Czech Republic. While these differences are not huge and one must also discount them due to the different methodologies employed in surveys conducted by different organizations, I cannot rule out that a higher level of corruption within the Slovak judiciary at the moment of establishment of the JCSR might have contributed to the effects I observed in the period between 2003 and 2010.

The last three variables – previous experience with running the country, the size of the country, and its population and culture – are less tangible and difficult to corroborate with empirical evidence, but I think that none of these three variables had a significant impact on the developments in the Czech and Slovak judiciaries. As regards the *previous experience with running the country*, it is true that, apart from a short period during the World War II, there was no independent Slovak statehood before 1993 and Slovaks had no opportunity to run their country by themselves.[82]

---

[81] Unfortunately, the STEM polls did not differentiate between different tiers of the Czech judicial system until 2004, when a separate question regarding the Supreme Court was introduced.

[82] This issue was briefly addressed also in Chapter 6, Section I.A.

Nevertheless, at least from the federalization of Czechoslovakia in 1969 Slovaks in fact ran their part of Czechoslovakia. Moreover, after the suppression of the 1968 Prague Spring democratization movement, that was supported primarily by Czechs, many Czechs who held key federal posts before and during the Prague Spring were replaced by Slovaks. Thus, many Slovaks had experience of running federal Czechoslovakia. Therefore, this variable does not seem to be important.

The same can be said of *the size of the country and its population*. While Slovakia is slightly smaller (49,035 km²) and has roughly half the population (5.5 million citizens) of the Czech Republic, which has 10.5 million citizens and covers 78,866 km², these differences should not be overestimated. In both countries, the rules that "everybody knows everybody" and that everything important takes place in the capital (in Bratislava and Prague respectively) apply with equal force. The only difference that may matter is that all the Czech top courts have their seats in Brno and not in Prague, which maintains a healthy "geographic separation of powers," whereas the Supreme Court of Slovakia and the Slovak Ministry of Justice have their seats in the very same building on Župné námestie in Bratislava. However, I do not see how this difference in itself could yield such different results in the two countries.

Culture seems to be the most promising ground for distinguishing the two countries among these "intangible" variables. It is generally well known that the Czech Republic is one of the most, if not the most, atheist countries in the world, whereas Slovakia is very religious. Many Czechs like many Slovaks, off the record, observe that Slovak society is more hierarchical and that Slovaks show greater deference to authority. Several Slovaks, surprisingly, also suggest that a rural mentality is still prevalent within Slovak society. In contrast, several Czech judges, not so surprisingly, suggest (off-the-record, of course) that "what" happened with the JCSR in Slovakia (by "what" they mean the hijacking of the JCSR by Harabin and his allies) could never happen in the Czech Republic. While all these observations might have had a bite in the First Czechoslovak Republic (1918–1938), when Slovak identity was far less developed and the Slovak intelligentsia was less numerous, they sound mostly like clichés today. As Abby Innes has put it, "the idea that Czechs are European and the Slovaks are 'Eastern' is a well-known stereotype of the region."[83]

[83] Abby Innes, *Czechoslovakia: The Short Goodbye* (Yale University Press 2001), x.

PART THREE

Conclusions and Implications

8

Perils of Judicial Self-Government

The previous chapter analyzed the results of the case studies that dealt with the use of mechanism of judicial accountability in the Czech Republic and Slovakia. This chapter moves beyond the borders of these two countries and addresses broader implications of these findings for each of the four research questions. These questions can be summarized as follows. The first question inquired into who holds judges to account and whether the Judicial Council Model changed the allocation of power among judges' principals. The second and third questions asked how often and how intensively CEE judges are held to account and whether the Judicial Council Model of court administration increases the accountability of individual judges. Finally, the fourth question concerned how mechanisms of judicial accountability operate, namely whether judicial accountability perversions occur and whether we can observe any change regarding these phenomena after the introduction of the Judicial Council Model.

In this chapter, I will start with the issue related to the first research question, which is the role of court presidents in the CEE. While several scholars pointed to the vast powers of court presidents in this region, I argue that their impact is still underestimated and that they are the invisible masters of the CEE judiciaries. Based on this insight, I subsequently propose the "judicial leadership theory" (JLT) of judicial councils. Then I will move to a more general theme that is related to the second and third research questions – to what extent the Judicial Council Euro-model increases judicial accountability. Here I will juxtapose the normative goals of the European Union and the Council of Europe in CEE and the real consequences of their joint Pan-European model of court administration on the ground. Third, I will provide more insights into the specifics of holding judges to account in societies that are in the process of transition to democracy. This part will address concerns raised by the fourth research question. Fourth, I explain why the fire-alarm oversight did not work in Slovakia and how this affects the way politicians should monitor judges. Fifth, I will revisit the most abstract issue: the distinction between the concepts of judicial accountability as a mechanism and as a virtue. Here I argue that the key problem of the CEE judiciaries is that there is no consensus on judicial virtues and that without at least a basic agreement on what it means to be a good judge mechanisms of judicial accountability will never operate properly.

I.   Court Presidents: Invisible Masters of Central and Eastern European Judiciaries

One of the main arguments put forth in this book is that court presidents have been the most powerful actors in the Czech and Slovak judiciaries, irrespective of the model of court administration in place. They are the key principals of individual judges. They have the best overview of what is going on within the judiciary, and this information asymmetry works in their favor. They dominate most mechanisms of judicial accountability in practice and they are the most active actors among the principals in using these mechanisms. They can use the most important stick in the civil law judiciaries (disciplinary motion) and have a major say in the most important carrot (promotion of judges). They also completely control several "writ-small"[1] mechanisms, which usually escape scholarly attention, such as case assignment, reassignment of judges among the panels, secondment, and temporary assignment outside the judiciary. These mechanisms may seem marginal at first sight, but they have tremendous consequences for the judges affected in the long run. Moreover, court presidents gradually became gatekeepers to the judiciary in both the Czech Republic and Slovakia, as it was they and not the Minister of Justice who handpicked new judges. With a certain degree of simplification, one may say that Czech and Slovak judges were in fact co-opted by court presidents rather than appointed by the executive.

The Czech case study attests[2] that, contrary to general wisdom, court presidents may enjoy significant powers even within the Ministry of Justice model of court administration. While the Czech statutory law granted a major say regarding most mechanisms of judicial accountability to the Minister of Justice, the court presidents step by step eroded the Minister's sphere of influence and managed to enlarge their own powers. Information asymmetry and hasty legislation in the early 1990s, which left

---

[1] See Adrian Vermeule, *Judicial Mechanisms of Democracy: Institutional Design Writ Small* (OUP 2007)

[2] The Slovak case study in the period before the introduction of the JCSR yields similar results.

many gaps in the statutory law, gave court presidents room for maneuver and they fully exploited that opportunity. As their ultimate tactics, when they were losing ground in their confrontation with the Minister of Justice, they went to the public or to the Constitutional Court and raised the flag of judicial independence. This flag flew high, especially during the EU Accession Process, when any claim accusing the executive of impinging upon the principle of judicial independence could potentially become an issue that could have led to a stalemate in the negotiations.

One may object that court presidents were "transmission belts" of Czech and Slovak Ministers of Justice and should not be treated as separate principals.[3] This "accountability nesting" argument goes as follows. The Czech and Slovak Ministers of Justice could, de jure, dismiss any lower court president for most of the period between 1993 and 2010. Hence judges held to account by lower court presidents were indirectly held to account by the Ministers of Justice, because the Ministers of Justice de jure decided who would be the court presidents. Likewise, the President of the Czech Republic and the Slovak National Council could, de jure, recall the Supreme Court presidents in their countries at whim. As a result, the "transmission belts" argument suggests, the Supreme Court presidents in both counties were the conduit of executive influence over individual Supreme Court judges.

However, this argument does not work for the Czech Republic and Slovakia. When the Slovak National Council attempted to impeach the Supreme Court President Štefan Harabin in 2000 it failed. Similarly, when the President of the Czech Republic recalled the Supreme Court President Iva Brožová, the Constitutional Court stopped him and found his act unconstitutional. Lower court president also emancipated themselves from the Ministry of Justice. While ministers in both countries recalled several court presidents in the 1990s, the political costs of dismissing court presidents were becoming extremely high. The ministers actually needed court presidents in order to conduct meaningful personnel decisions. Due to information asymmetry, the ministers simply had to rely on judgment of the regional court presidents who had the hands-on experience with individual judges. In fact, in both the Czech Republic and Slovakia it was primarily those Ministers of Justice who had once been judges who dared to do use this mechanism.[4] They were judges, had the necessary veneer of

---

[3] See also discussion in Chapter 2, Section III.A.

[4] These Ministers of Justice were, namely, Otakar Motejl (formerly President of the Supreme Court, the Czech Republic), Štefan Harabin (formerly President of the Supreme Court, Slovakia) and Jan Liščák (formerly judge of the Regional Court in Banská Bystrica).

legitimacy and information asymmetry worked in their favor. Moreover, later on the Czech court presidents fought back before the Constitutional Court and administrative courts. They eventually won,[5] and, as a result, the dismissal of court presidents outside the disciplinary process is now considered unconstitutional in the Czech Republic. This means that the emancipation of court presidents in the Czech Republic has reached its final stage. To be sure, some court presidents may decide, for various reasons, to rub shoulders with the executive more than it is necessary, but it is their personal choice. Once they decide to withdraw from this informal communication, the Ministers of Justice have very few means how to force them to cooperate. In sum, the teeth of the Ministry of Justice vis-à-vis court presidents are much weaker in the Czech Republic and Slovakia than in the post-Soviet space.[6]

Piana's claims that court presidents in the Czech Republic have little power[7] and that that feature distinguishes the Czech judicial system from the Polish and Hungarian ones are thus not convincing. Contrary to what Piana says, Czech court presidents have a major say in what Piana refers to as mechanisms of institutional and managerial accountability.[8] As mentioned earlier, they control the assignment and reassignment of judges between chambers, case assignment, and the appointment of chamber presidents,[9] and initiate the majority of disciplinary proceedings against judges. In addition, they process complaints from court users and decide jointly with the Minister of Justice on the appointment, promotion, and secondment of judges. Therefore, court presidents in the Czech Republic have similar powers to their counterparts in Poland and Hungary, even though the former operate in the Ministry of Justice model of court administration whereas the latter two work within the judicial council model.[10]

---

[5] For further details, see Chapter 5.
[6] On the latter, see, for example, Alena Ledeneva, "From Russia with *Blat*: Can Informal Networks Help Modernize Russia?" (2009) 76 *Social Research* 257, 276; Maria Popova, *Politicized Justice in Emerging Democracies: A Study of Courts in Russia and Ukraine* (CUP 2012), 139–145; and notes 16–19 below. See also discussion in Chapter 2, Section III.A.
[7] Daniela Piana, *Judicial Accountabilities in New Europe: From Rule of Law to Quality of Justice* (Ashgate 2010), 44 (table 1.8).
[8] At the same time, Piana overestimates the power of judicial boards and court managers that are in fact marginal players in the Czech Republic. They are either advisory bodies to court presidents (judicial boards) or their subordinates (court managers) and thus they are far less influential.
[9] Court presidents are limited only by the requirement to consult these issues with judicial boards.
[10] For a similar conclusion, see Zdeněk Kühn, "The Democratization and Modernization of Post-Communist Judiciaries" in Alberto Febbrajo and Wojciech Sadurski (eds.), *Central and Eastern Europe after Transition* (Ashgate 2010) 177, 190.

Perhaps even more surprisingly, the introduction of the judicial council model of court administration may strengthen this pattern and further empower court presidents. Virtually all materials of the European Union and the Council of Europe suggest that judicial councils empower judges. However, the judiciary is not an "it" but a "they,"[11] and one may plausibly argue that only certain segments of the judiciary will benefit from this institutional change. The analysis of mechanisms of judicial accountability in Slovakia after the introduction of the Judicial Council of the Slovak Republic clearly shows that after the initial setback in the first five years of the JCSR's functioning, Štefan Harabin – former President of the Supreme Court of Slovakia – won control over the JCSR and court presidents climbed back into power. Hence, it was court presidents and the President of the Supreme Court in particular who benefited from this judicial reform. The whole judicial reform thus went full circle. One may also object here that individuals matter, and had it not been for Štefan Harabin, this would have never happened in Slovakia. I have already addressed this objection in Chapter 7 and I will not repeat myself here. In short, Štefan Harabin could not achieve his "coup de JCSR" alone, and if he had not done it someone would have done it anyway.

Another important insight of this book is that what matters is who de facto holds judges to account and not who can do so de jure. While Czech and Slovak political actors de jure can hold judges to account by several means, de facto they use these measures rather sparingly, because the political costs of such actions against individual judges are very high. In contrast, court presidents do not have to explain their actions to voters. In addition, they benefit from the veils of apoliticism and professional legitimacy. Hence, court presidents use mechanisms of judicial accountability more often and with a higher success rate than political actors. In addition, many mechanisms of judicial accountability available in the Czech Republic and Slovakia operate differently from how they were originally envisaged. More specifically, Czech and Slovak court presidents took control of several judicial accountability mechanisms at the expense of other principals.

This claim that court presidents play a critical role in the CEE judiciaries is not novel. Daniela Piana in her book studying judicial governance in the Czech Republic, Hungary, Poland, Bulgaria, and Romania stressed that court presidents play a significant role in holding judges to account.[12]

---

[11] Adrian Vermeule, "The Judiciary Is A They, Not An It: Interpretive Theory and the Fallacy Of Division" (2009) 14 *Journal of Contemporary Legal Issues* 549.
[12] Piana 2010, above note 7, 43–44.

She also rightly pointed out that court presidents are "endowed with cognitive resources (information about the situation of the court, information about the local social system with which the courts interacts), but also with political resources (leadership within the court, prestige, eventually acknowledgement from the academy or the other legal actors)."[13] In other words, information asymmetry and political capital work in favor of court presidents.[14] Other authors writing on courts in the CEE concur.[15]

Peter Solomon observed a similar pattern in Russia. According to him, Russian court presidents "still control some discretionary perks (vacation packages, help in obtaining apartments, or getting children into schools or nurseries); chairs handle the evaluations of judges and interpret data in letters of reference for potential advancement; chairs decide when judges should be disciplined and whether to do this informally or proceed with formal proceedings at the Judicial Qualification Commissions, including about possible firing for cause."[16] Solomon concludes pointedly that "[t]he chair of the court in Russia is and remains a 'boss,' a super authority who manages his domain and represents the court in the outside world, including in informal dealings with local authorities, whose support still matters for the well-being of the court."[17] More recently, Schwartz and Sykiainen confirmed Solomon's conclusions and showed how the court presidents managed to exploit the gaps in the law and unofficially continue to play a leading role in selecting judges, their promotion, evaluation, and disciplining, and in case assignment.[18]

Lydia Müller observes similar practices in other post-Soviet republics – Ukraine, Moldova, Armenia, Azerbaijan, and Belarus – and concludes that "the comprehensive powers of court presidents are one of the

---

[13] Ibid., 44.
[14] Piana was thus right in general, but she was wrong regarding the role of court presidents in the Czech Republic, because she severely underestimated their de facto power.
[15] See, for example, Michal Bobek, "The Administration of Courts in the Czech Republic – In Search of a Constitutional Balance" (2010) 16 *European Public Law* 251, 253–254; or Piana 2010, above note 7, 43–44. For my own take on this issue, see David Kosař, "The Least Accountable Branch (Review Essay)" (2013) 11 *International Journal of Constitutional Law* 234, 249–250.
[16] Peter H. Solomon, "Authoritarian Legality and Informal Practices: Judges, Lawyers and the State in Russia and China" (2010) 43 *Communist and Post-Communist Studies* 351, 354.
[17] Ibid., 354. See also Peter H. Solomon, "The Accountability of Judges in Post Communist States: From Bureaucratic to Professional Accountability" in Anja Seibert-Fohr (ed.), *Judicial Independence in Transition* (Springer 2012) 909–935.
[18] Olga Schwartz and Elga Sykiainen, "Judicial Independence in the Russian Federation" in Anja Seibert-Fohr (ed.), *Judicial Independence in Transition* (Springer 2012) 971–1064, in particular at 995–996, 1003, 1008–1009, 1012, 1018–1027, and 1031–1034.

most pressing issues and constitute structural deficiency in the countries of Eastern Europe, the South Caucasus and Central Asia."[19] Her research shows that court presidents have played a key role in controlling the judiciary in virtually all countries under the Soviet sphere of influence. As the former Justice of the Slovak Constitutional Court put it, court presidents were "the most reliable cadres [who] not only implemented party resolutions, but, in practice, ruled over the judges and personified the dictatorship and the subordination of the system of justice."[20]

Therefore, the claim that court presidents are the key principals of judges in the CEE is not surprising to those who are well acquainted with court administration in that region. The most significant contribution of this book is that it, to my knowledge, for the first time provides robust empirical evidence for this argument. Furthermore, it demonstrates how court presidents can retain control over most mechanisms of judicial accountability both under the Ministry of Justice model and under the judicial council model of court administration, and explains how they did it.

In this context, it is illuminating to contrast the role of court presidents in CEE with the role of court presidents in the civil law jurisdictions in West Europe. Court presidents in Germany, Austria, France, and Italy were historically very powerful figures. When one visits the German Imperial Court of Justice in Leipzig,[21] he is stunned by the sheer splendor and the grandeur of the ballroom that spans almost the entire floor of this majestic building, which served as a part of living quarters of the first Imperial Court President Eduard von Simson. The Vice President of the French Council of State has been the highest paid civil servant in the

---

[19] See Lydia F. Müller, "Judicial Administration in Transitional Eastern Countries" in Anja Seibert-Fohr (ed.), *Judicial Independence in Transition* (Springer 2012) 937–969, at 965.

[20] Alexander Bröstl, "At the Crossroads on the Way to an Independent Slovak Judiciary" in Jiří Přibáň, Pauline Roberts, and James Young (eds.), *Systems of Justice in Transition: Central European Experiences since 1989* (Ashgate 2003) 141, 143. See also Stanislaw Frankowski, "The Independence of the Judiciary in Poland: Reflections on Andrzej Rzeplinski's Sadownictwo w Polsce Ludowej (The Judiciary in Peoples' Poland) (1989)" (1991) 8 *Arizona Journal of International and Comparative Law* 33, 40–47; Inga Markovits, "Children of a Lesser God: GDR Lawyers in Post-Socialist Germany" (1996) 94 *Michigan Law Review* 2270, 2292–2293; Otakar Motejl, "Soudnictví a jeho správa" in Michal Bobek, et al. (eds.), *Komunistické právo v Československu* (MUNI Press 2009) 813, 817–818; Zdeněk Kühn, "Socialistická justice" in ibid., 822, 825; or Eliška Wagnerová, "Position of Judges in the Czech Republic" in Jiří Přibáň, Pauline Roberts, and James Young (eds.), *Systems of Justice in Transition: Central European Experiences since 1989* (Ashgate 2003) 163, 167.

[21] Note that this building has been the seat of the German Federal Administrative Court (*Bundesverwaltungsgericht*) since 2002.

country and has occupied a beautiful office in the *Palais Royal* in Paris.[22] French, German, Austrian, and Italian court presidents also used to handle case assignment according to their own criteria, to evaluate rank and file judges, to discipline judges, and to have a major say in promotion of judges and other personnel matters.

However, this has gradually changed after World War II. German court presidents have undergone the most profound transformation of their role. Postwar German jurists have placed a strong emphasis on the independence of individual judges and set the strict limits on how court presidents may interact with rank and file judges. Cases are assigned strictly on random basis according to the criteria set in advance.[23] Even the general rules on the case assignment are not stipulated by court presidents, but by the Judicial Board (*Präsidium*) of each court. Though the court president is a member of this board, regular judges have a majority there.[24] Moreover, regular judges can challenge the assignment of a particular case before administrative courts if they believe that the rules of case assignment were breached.[25] The Judicial Service Courts have also forbade court presidents from making any remarks that might influence the future performance of judges, even on matters of case management and efficiency.[26] Similarly, any evaluation of judges must deal only with the outer order of judicial business, and not its core, or how the law is applied.[27] As a result of these changes, some commentators suggest that German court presidents "have lost the capacity to give instructions to rank and file judges on matters related to particular cases ... and ... come closer to the common law model of *primus inter pares* than the dominant figure (boss) normally associated with court heads in the civil law world."[28]

---

[22] Regarding the stature and role of the Vice President of the French Council of State, see, for example, Bruno Latour, *The Making of Law: An Ethnography of the Conseil d'État* (Polity 2010) 58–60 and 91.

[23] See Anja Seibert-Fohr, "Judicial Independence in Germany" in Anja Seibert-Fohr (ed.), *Judicial Independence in Transition* (Springer 2012) 447–519, at 481–483.

[24] See Art. 21a *Gerichtsverfassungsgesetz* (German Constitutional Law on Courts).

[25] See Judgment of the German Federal Administrative Court of November 28, 1975 (BVerGE 50, 11 = NJW 1976, 1224).

[26] Johannes Riedel, "Recruitment, Professional Evaluation and Career of Judges and Prosecutors in Germany" in Giuseppe Di Federico (ed.), *Recruitment, Professional Evaluation and Career of Judges and Prosecutors in Europe* (IRSIG-CNR 2005) 69–126, at 98–107.

[27] Anja Seibert-Fohr, "Constitutional Guarantees of Judicial Independence in Germany" in Eibe H. Riedel and Rüdiger Wolfrum (eds.), *Recent Trends in German and European Constitutional Law* (Springer 2006) 267–288, at 271.

[28] Peter H. Solomon, "The Accountability of Judges in Post Communist States: From Bureaucratic to Professional Accountability" in Anja Seibert-Fohr (ed.), *Judicial*

Other West European civil law countries did not go as far as Germany in curtailing the powers of court presidents, but they still changed the role of court presidents profoundly. In Italy, lower rank judges gradually took over the Italian judicial council, *Consiglio Superioere della Magustratura*, which decides on most matters regarding the career of individual judges.[29] Regular judges also succeeded in assuring that the regular evaluations of their performance in practice affect neither their rank nor their pay. As a result, judges are promoted almost always on the basis of their seniority,[30] and the court presidents can no longer use this carrot to please individual judges. Similarly, case assignment plans prepared by the court presidents are tightly controlled by the Italian judicial council, where lower rank judges have a majority, and individual judges may also object in writing to these plans.[31] In Austria, court presidents can no longer decide on case assignment by themselves. Similarly to Germany, rules of case assignment are determined by another body, the Personal Senates (*Personalsenate*), in which court presidents are in the minority.[32] Even the French court presidents, who are still relatively powerful as they decide on case assignment and other important matters, witnessed a reduction of their powers in evaluating and promoting regular judges.[33]

All in all, the role of hierarchical oversight within the judiciary has been reduced in Western civil law countries over the past fifty years.[34] The main culprits of this shift were court presidents, who have gradually become more like primus inter pares rather than bosses of their courts.[35] The only

---

Independence in Transition (Springer 2012) 909–935, at 918. For an important caveat to this view, see Stephen Ross Levitt, "The Life and Times of a Local Court Judge in Berlin" (2009) 10 *German Law Journal* 169, 197–198; and Anja Seibert-Fohr, "Judicial Independence in Germany" in Anja Seibert-Fohr (ed.), *Judicial Independence in Transition* (Springer 2012) 447–519, at 502 (these two authors suggest that judges who seek promotion may be tempted to adjust their decision making according to the views of their court presidents).

[29] Giuseppe Di Federico, "Judicial Independence in Italy" in Anja Seibert-Fohr (ed.), *Judicial Independence in Transition* (Springer 2012) 357–401, at 360.

[30] Ibid., 371–374.

[31] Ibid., 378–379.

[32] See Art. 36 of *Richter- und Staatsanwaltschaftsdienstgesetz* (Austrian Law on Judges and State Prosecutors).

[33] See Antoine Garapon and Harold Epineuse, "Judicial Independence in France" in Anja Seibert-Fohr (ed.), *Judicial Independence in Transition* (Springer 2012) 273–305, at 285–286; and Peter H. Solomon, "The Accountability of Judges in Post Communist States: From Bureaucratic to Professional Accountability" in Anja Seibert-Fohr (ed.), *Judicial Independence in Transition* (Springer 2012) 909–935, at 920–921.

[34] Anja Seibert-Fohr, "Judicial Independence – The Normativity of an Evolving Transnational Principle" in Anja Seibert-Fohr (ed.), *Judicial Independence in Transition* (Springer 2012) 1279–1360, at 1329.

[35] See note 28.

area where court presidents seem to have retained some of their former power over rank and file judges is promotion.[36] Two conclusions emerge from this short comparison. First, under the current constitutional, legal, and professional environment in the West European judiciaries, court presidents are far more benign actors than in the CEE, which has not yet undergone this development. Second, it is unwise to transplant the Italian model of a strong judicial council, which served as a major inspiration for the Judicial Council Euro-model,[37] to the CEE environment, which is very different from the Italian one.

II.   The Judicial Leadership Theory of Judicial Councils

The previous section showed that court presidents are the masters of the postcommunist judiciaries and contrasted their role with their counterparts in the West Europe. Yet, the analysis of the impact of the JCSR in Slovakia delivers more. As the JCSR meets all five criteria of the Judicial Council Euro-model, it allows me to theorize about the role of judicial leadership under this Pan-European model. The analysis of the effects of the JCSR in Slovakia reveals a clear pattern: the introduction of the Judicial Council Euro-model of court administration into a bureaucratic judiciary in the medium term empowers judicial leadership, namely court presidents, who, in turn, use their newly acquired powers to punish their critics and reward their allies within the judiciary in order to preserve their privileges and influence. If I take into account the differences between the Czech and Slovak judiciaries in "the-JCSR" period, I must also add that internal division and widespread corruption within the judiciary at the moment of the establishment of the Judicial Council Euro-model may hasten and intensify this process. I will refer to this theory as to the "judicial leadership theory" (JLT) of judicial councils.

However, in order to generalize about the consequences of the Judicial Council Euro-model beyond Slovakia, it is important to emphasize the critical components of the Slovak case study: the specifics of the Judicial Council Euro-model, the specifics of the postcommunist judiciary, the focus on medium-term effects, and the dual explanation of why court presidents fight back in the new system. These four components set the

---

[36] See note 28 (on Germany); and Antoine Garapon and Harold Epineuse, "Judicial Independence in France" in Anja Seibert-Fohr (ed.), *Judicial Independence in Transition* (Springer 2012) 273–305, at 285–286 (on France).

[37] See Chapter 3.

limits of my book and must be kept in mind when theorizing about the impact of the Judicial Council Euro-model on judicial accountability.

First, the JLT applies only to a peculiar model of judicial council which meets the five basic criteria, namely entrenching this body in the Constitution, ensuring that judges have at least parity in that body, vesting the real decision-making power in that body, transferring most "personal competences" regarding a career of individual judges to that body, and selecting the Chief Justice or his equivalent as the chairman of the Judicial Council.[38] I referred to that type of judicial council as the Judicial Council Euro-model. Therefore, the JLT does not tell us what the effects of other models of court administration – such as the Court Service model or hybrid models[39] – are in the postcommunist judiciary. Similarly, the JLT does not address what the likely impact of the introduction of a judicial council, which does *not* meet the five criteria of the Judicial Council Euro-model, is in the postcommunist environment. It may well be that the judicial council, which is not entrenched in the constitution and can be modified by regular legislation, where judges are in a minority, which has weak advisory rather than decision-making powers, which has limited competences regarding the careers of judges, or which cannot be chaired by a court president, may yield different results.[40]

Second, the JLT speaks only about the impact of the Judicial Council Euro-model in a bureaucratic judiciary in the CEE. By a bureaucratic judiciary I mean the judiciary that has the following features: (1) it is a civil law judiciary,[41] (2) which is faithful to a hierarchical organization of authority,[42] where (3) court presidents hold significant powers. The

---

[38] For a more detailed exposition of these requirements, see Section II of this chapter.

[39] These two models are sometimes considered "judicial councils" as well, because many authors use the term "judicial council" as a generic label to refer to any independent intermediary organization positioned between the judiciary and the politically responsible administrators in the executive or in the legislature. For repercussions of this vague definition of judicial council, see Chapter 3.

[40] Such cooperative models of court administration, where judicial councils share many powers with the Ministry of Justice exist in Poland and Estonia. See Adam Bodnar and Lukasz Bojarski, "Judicial Independence in Poland" in Anja Seibert-Fohr (ed.), *Judicial Independence in Transition* (Springer 2012) 667, 669–679; and Timo Ligi, "Judicial Independence in Estonia", in ibid., 741–755. For a general description of the "co-equal judiciary," see Cristina Parau, "The Drive for Judicial Supremacy," in ibid., 619, 627–634. See also Chapter 3.

[41] The differences between civil law and common law judiciaries are discussed in more detail in Chapter 2, Section IV.

[42] The differences between the coordinate and hierarchical ideals of authority are discussed in more detail in Chapter 2, Section IV.

typical examples of bureaucratic judiciaries are postcommunist countries in the CEE.[43] These countries have built their judicial systems on the hierarchical ideal, relying on the Austrian, German, or French interwar models. However, given the long rule of the communist regime they, in contrast to their Western European counterparts,[44] did not undergo a similar transformation toward a more coordinate ideal. Nevertheless, bureaucratic judiciaries do not exist in Europe only. We can find a strong bureaucratic culture also in South-East Asia[45] and Latin America and thus JLT may[46] be applicable to these countries as well.

On the other hand, it is necessary to emphasize an important limit of my theory. The JLT does not claim that the Judicial Council Euro-model would have the same effects in a common law judiciary, where judges are appointed in the later stage of their career and thus they are not socialized within the judiciary, in the judiciary that is closer to the coordinate ideal (horizontal accountability) rather than the hierarchical ideal of authority,[47] or where court presidents do not have significant powers beyond their representative and adjudicatory functions.[48] It is thus important to check first whether the judiciary under study really has the features of a bureaucratic judiciary, both de jure and de facto. This also means that even if we assume that Judicial Council Euro-model is the best solution for Italy, it could bring about the same results in the CEE only if the Italian and CEE

---

[43] See Peter H. Solomon, "The Accountability of Judges in Post Communist States: From Bureaucratic to Professional Accountability" in Anja Seibert-Fohr (ed.), *Judicial Independence in Transition* (Springer 2012) 909–935.

[44] See ibid., at 915–922 (who shows that German and French judiciaries moved from the bureaucratic model toward the "intra-organizational accountability").

[45] See, for example, Neil Chisholm, "The Faces of Judicial Independence: Democratic versus Bureaucratic Accountability in Judicial Selection, Training, and Promotion in South Korea and Taiwan", 62 *American Journal of Comparative Law* 893; Brent T. White, "Rotten to the Core: Project Capture and the Failure of Judicial Reform in Mongolia" (2009) 4 *East Asia Law Reform* 209; or David Law, "How to Rig the Federal Courts" (2011) 99 *Georgetown Law Journal* 779.

[46] Of course, the JLT is applicable to these countries only if its other conditions are met as well.

[47] See Chapter 2, Section IV.

[48] The role of court presidents can be eliminated or balanced in many ways. For instance, if judges are promoted strictly on the ground of seniority, court presidents cannot play any role in that process. Similarly, random case assignment and reassignment by software eliminates any external influence. Salary bonuses can be prohibited. Other mechanisms of judicial accountability, which are typically controlled by court presidents in the CEE, might be transferred to representative bodies of judges or reviewed by special bodies with a mixed composition. Finally, if court presidents serve short nonrenewable terms and are selected on a rotational basis, it is less likely that they will accrue significant power.

judiciaries are alike in terms of bureaucratic accountability. As was shown earlier,[49] this assumption was false.

Some CEE counties realized, often only after several years of the (mal-)functioning of the judicial council model, these hierarchical patterns within the postcommunist judiciaries, and attempted to reduce the influence of the court presidents. For instance, in Croatia court presidents cannot sit on the judicial council.[50] Similarly, Poland banned court presidents from membership of its National Council of the Judiciary in 2007.[51] The Slovak Parliament adopted the same incompatibility rule in 2011.[52] However, these attempts had only limited effects. The culture of bureaucratic accountability and mental path-dependence proved to be too strong. Court presidents still had a variety of ways how to control the judicial council indirectly. They can suggest their preferred nominees to the judicial council to other judges and push them through with their authority.[53] They can sometimes even install their marionettes to the leadership of the judicial council.[54] Their powers at the court level are also often left unaffected and they still decide on case assignment and reassignment of judges, conduct evaluation of judges, and have to consent to promotion of judges to their court.[55] This "judicial oligarchy"[56] is simply very difficult to dismantle.[57] Hence, the JLT puts forth the case that the leadership of the judiciary, namely court presidents, throughout the hierarchy, is

[49] See above notes 29–31.

[50] See Art. 125(7) of the Croatian Constitution.

[51] See Bodnar and Bojarski, above note 40, at 673.

[52] See Art. 33(2) *in fine* of the 2004 Law on Courts, as amended by Art. III.2 of Law No. 467/2011 Z.z.

[53] For instance, Štefan Harabin sent a letter to Slovak judges few days before the election of new judicial members to the JCSR in May 2012 in which he identified his preferred judges he would elect. See, for example, *Harabin sudcom napísal, koho bude voliť do Súdnej rady*, Pravda.sk, May 24, 2012, available at http://spravy.pravda.sk/domace/clanok/174535-harabin-sudcom-napisal-koho-bude-volit-do-sudnej-rady/; or *Harabin sudcom napísal, koho sa chystá voliť do súdnej rady*, Aktuality.sk, May 24, 2012, available at www.aktuality.sk/clanok/207237/harabin-sudcom-napisal-koho-sa-chysta-volit-do-sudnej-rady/.

[54] See Alan Uzelac, "Role and Status of Judges in Croatia" in Paul Oberhammer (ed.), *Richterbild und Rechtsreform in Mitteleuropa* (Manzsche Verlags 2001) 23–65, at 44.

[55] See, for example, Peter H. Solomon, "The Accountability of Judges in Post Communist States: From Bureaucratic to Professional Accountability" in Anja Seibert-Fohr (ed.), *Judicial Independence in Transition* (Springer 2012) 909–935, at 927–930.

[56] That is how both Alan Uzelac and Otakar Motejl referred to court presidents; see Uzelac, above note 54, at 43 (regarding Croatia); and Otakar Motejl, "Pohled ministrů spravedlnosti" in Jan Kysela (ed.) *Hledání optimálního modelu správy soudnictví pro Českou republiku* (Kancelář Senátu 2008) 13–16, at 14 (regarding the Czech Republic).

[57] See also Section IV of this chapter.

empowered by the introduction of a Judicial Council Euro-model, regardless of whether they sit on it by definition or not.

Third, the JLT explains the effects of the Judicial Council Euro-model in the medium term after its establishment. It builds on the chief insight from game theory – that power holders should be expected to change their behavior after a new reform is introduced. In other words, it focuses on what happens *after* the court presidents learned the ropes of the new game rather than on the immediate effects of the Judicial Council Euro-model *before* the court presidents adapted their behavior to the new model. In fact, the experiences with the JCSR in Slovakia during the first five years of its existence attests to the fact that the Judicial Council Euro-model may in the short-term limit the power of court presidents and unite the judiciary behind a common cause. However, I believe that what matters is what happens after the initial enthusiasm wanes and relevant actors eventually find out how to exploit the new system.

Here it is also important to add that the JLT does not explain why and under what circumstances the Judicial Council Euro-model is adopted. In this aspect, the JLT differs from Ginsburg's insurance thesis,[58] Hirschl's hegemony preservation thesis,[59] and Erdos' postmaterialist trigger thesis,[60] all of which focus on why and when questions. More specifically, the JLT does not make the claim that judicial leadership, namely court presidents, planned the "hijacking" of the Slovak judiciary and designed the JCSR accordingly. The Slovak case study in fact refutes this potentially promising argument. It shows that court presidents had little influence on the design of the JCSR and were not among the major supporters of the Judicial Council Euro-model. On the contrary, incumbent court presidents at the moment of the introduction of the JCSR felt threatened by the new model and vigorously opposed it. They had good reasons to do so. They were "bosses" of their courts under the Ministry of Justice model and they were afraid that their powers would be transferred to the judicial council, a fact which would inevitably result in the loss of their privileges and influence. However, once the Judicial Council Euro-model went through the Slovak Parliament, incumbent court presidents had no choice other than to learn the tricks of the new game

---

[58] Ran Hirschl, *Towards Juristocracy: the Origins and Consequences of the New Constitutionalism* (Harvard University Press 2004).

[59] Tom Ginsburg, *Judicial Review in New Democracies: Constitutional Courts in Asian Cases* (CUP 2003).

[60] David Erdos, *Delegating Rights Protection: The Rise of Bills of Rights in the Westminster World* (OUP 2010).

in order to preserve their traditionally dominant role. It took them five years – one term of the JCSR.

Fourth, for understanding the JLT it is important to keep in mind that there is a dual rationale of why judicial leadership and court presidents in particular fight back in the new system. The first motivation is obvious – to preserve their influence within the judiciary. However, it is not only about the power. While many court presidents long for power and enjoy their influence and media attention, not all of them would be willing to fight for these reasons alone. There is another motivation that may be even stronger. In Slovakia, as well as in most countries in CEE, the position of a court president comes with many material perks. Court presidents have a significantly higher salary than regular judges at the same level. They have the best offices and wide secretarial support. They have a reduced case load, if any at all.[61] They often define the rules of case assignment so that they are assigned only certain types of cases that they like or are good at. They usually have more law clerks. Presidents of top courts also have official cars with their own drivers. Sometimes even something petty such as the right to a special parking space in the Prague or Bratislava city center matters. Many court officials simply do not want to operate without these privileges. What is more, some long-serving court presidents are no longer able to function without these perks. They cannot imagine themselves having the normal case load (in terms of both quantity and composition) and fewer law clerks. They are no longer judges in the true sense. As a result, they did everything to preserve their status. It is their only means of survival within the judiciary. Not surprisingly, they employ all sticks and carrots at their disposal in order to achieve this aim.

These are the four core components of the JLT of judicial councils. I have still to address two more factors – which I identified as potential contributors to the effects of the Judicial Council Euro-model in Slovakia – but I could not determine their real impact since these two factors were not present in the Czech Republic. These two factors are a high level of division and widespread corruption within the judiciary. The only observation I can make is that, given the fact that factionalism and corruption did not permeate the Czech judiciary to the same degree, these two factors may have hastened and intensified the effects described by

---

[61] In the Czech Republic, court presidents usually have only one-fourth of the case load of a regular judge (vice presidents usually have half of the standard case load), but some presidents of large courts are reportedly so busy with administering their courts that they do not decide virtually any cases.

the JLT. In other words, if there are no significant factions among judges and the judiciary "receiving" the Judicial Council Euro-model is relatively homogenous, the effects of the Judicial Council Euro-model may be different. Similarly, if judges are the "crème de la crème" among jurists in a given country and meet the highest ethical standards, the Judicial Council Euro-model may also work differently. However, in order to test the importance of these two potentially "aggravating factors," I would need to find two countries, both of which adopted the Judicial Council Euro-model but differed regarding the level of factionalism and corruption within the judiciary before the introduction of the new model. The Czech Republic and Slovakia cannot be used for this purpose, because they have different models of court administration, and thus one must look for another pair of case studies.[62]

One may object here that the four components of the JLT set such strict assumptions that no state other than Slovakia can meet them. I do not think so. In the CEE, there are many countries that established judicial councils that meet the criteria of the Judicial Council Euro-model, and virtually all of these countries meet the three criteria of a typical bureaucratic judiciary. Therefore, there are plenty of opportunities to test the JLT in this region. More specifically, Bulgarian, Croatian, Hungarian,[63] Romanian, and Ukrainian judicial councils are ideal case studies to prove or disprove my theory. Other judicial councils in the region, such as the ones in Poland, Slovenia, and the Baltic States, may be employed to test the boundaries of the JLT, as these countries either did not adopt judicial councils that meet all the criteria of the Euro-model[64] or their judiciaries moved away from the bureaucratic accountability toward a coordinate model.[65] One may even go beyond the CEE and test the JLT in other parts of the world, where postauthoritarian countries decided to replace the Ministry of Justice model of court administration with the judicial council

---

[62] For instance, one could try to compare Slovakia with Hungary before Orbán's 2011 judicial reforms.

[63] Regarding Hungary, this claim applies only to the judicial council model at place before Orbán's 2011 judicial reforms.

[64] Poland and Slovenia fall into this group.

[65] For instance, Estonia is one of such countries in the CEE region. See, for example, Peter H. Solomon, "The Accountability of Judges in Post Communist States: From Bureaucratic to Professional Accountability" in Anja Seibert-Fohr (ed.), *Judicial Independence in Transition* (Springer 2012) 909–935, at 929–930; and Timo Ligi, "Judicial Independence in Estonia" in Anja Seibert-Fohr (ed.), *Judicial Independence in Transition* (Springer 2012) 739–791.

model. Latin American countries[66] and Mongolia[67] seem to be particularly promising case studies for testing the JLT beyond Europe.

Finally, the JLT has also a predictive value. It suggests that the introduction of a strong judicial council into a hierarchical civil law judiciary will likely in the medium term empower judicial leadership who will pursue their own interests and strive for preserving their privileges and influence. Put bluntly, had the Czech Republic adopted Motejl's High Council of the Judiciary in 2000, it would have very likely[68] caused the same effects as in Slovakia, because the Czech judiciary met all the four key components of the JLT. At the same time it is naïve to think, as many Czech judges do, that there were no Harabin-like characters in the Czech judiciary who would have seized the opportunity and rigged the Czech judicial council. It is rather a wishful thinking, which can easily be refuted by the so-called judicial mafia case that involved, among others, the then Vice President of the Supreme Court of the Czech Republic,[69] and by other controversies.[70] Therefore, judicial reformers in civil law countries should proceed with caution when introducing a strong judicial council and at least be aware of the potential pitfalls of this model.

[66] See, for example, Linn A. Hammergren, "Do Judicial Councils Further Judicial Reform? Lessons from Latin America," Carnegie Endowment Rule of Law Series' Working Paper No. 28.
[67] See, for example, Brent T. White, "Rotten to the Core: Project Capture and the Failure of Judicial Reform in Mongolia" (2009) 4 *East Asia Law Reform* 209. The JLT should also be taken into account in judicial reforms in Asia which are still under preparation. For instance, the United Nations Development Programme (UNDP) initiated a five-year project called "Strengthening access to justice and protection of rights in Vietnam," which supported a number of Vietnam's key priorities in legal and judicial reform from now until 2014 (see http://vccinews.com/news_detail.asp?news_id=18962).
[68] Note that, as mentioned earlier, the level of division and the level of corruption within the judiciary were arguably lower in the Czech Republic, which may affect the consequences of a strong judicial council model to some extent.
[69] In the "judicial mafia" case, the President of the Supreme Court of the Czech Republic initiated a disciplinary motion against her Vice President, Pavel Kučera, for his interference in the pending criminal investigation against the Vice Prime Minister, who was prosecuted on corruption charges. The High Court of Prague after protracted procedural disputes found Pavel Kučera guilty and dismissed him from judicial office. However, Pavel Kučera appealed to the Supreme Court, which eventually found in his favor and quashed the judgment of the High Court of Prague.
[70] For instance, in 2011 the Minister of Justice initiated a disciplinary motion against the president and vice president of the Regional Court of Brno for violating the case assignment rules in bankruptcy cases. Several other Czech judges faced disciplinary or criminal prosecution for issuing fake bankruptcy orders, for assigning lucrative ex officio cases to their friends among advocates or for falsifying documents.

III.   The Judicial Council Euro-model: Toward the System
of Dependent Judges within an Independent Judiciary?

In the previous section I argued that the Judicial Council Euro-model empowered court presidents and I proposed the JLT theory of judicial councils. However, the Slovak case study also provides an answer to the more general question, whether this Euro-model increases or decreases judicial accountability. For methodological clarity, I divided this question into two subquestions: (1) whether there is any change in how *often* are judges held to account after the introduction of the Judicial Council Euro-model?; and (2) whether there is any change in how *severely* are judges held to account after the introduction of the Judicial Council Euro-model.[71]

The Slovak case study showed that the Judicial Council Euro-model increased the accountability of individual judges, in both frequency and intensity. Regarding the former, the number of disciplinary motions against judges, reassignment of judges outside their previous specializations, and reassignment of cases increased significantly. Regarding the latter, the reassignment of judges, case assignment and reassignment techniques, and disciplinary motions entailed more severe consequences and salary bonuses skyrocketed. I understand that judicial councils in many CEE countries are still in their formative stages and it is not clear that they will increase the accountability of judges to the same degree and by the same means as in Slovakia. Nevertheless, I still believe that there is one more general lesson to be drawn for the entire region from the introduction of the Judicial Council Euro-model in Slovakia.

My argument is embarrassingly simple: the Judicial Council Euro-model increases the independence of the judiciary, but does not necessarily increase the independence of individual judges. On the contrary, self-government of judges, exemplified by the Euro-model, may have deleterious effects for judges who dare to criticize the work of the judicial council and its members. Similar negative examples that have been reported from Hungary,[72]

---

[71] See Introduction and Chapter 4.
[72] See, for example, Károly Bárd, "Judicial Independence in the Accession Countries of Central and Eastern Europe and the Baltics" in András Sajó and Lorri Rutt Bentch (eds.), *Judicial Integrity* (Martinus Nijhoff 2004) 265, at 287–288; Zoltán Fleck, "Judicial Independence and its Environment in Hungary" in J. Přibáň, P. Roberts, and J. Young (eds.), *Systems of Justice in Transition: Central European Experiences since 1989* (Ashgate 2003) 12; or Zoltán Fleck, "Judicial Independence in Hungary" in Anja Seibert-Fohr (ed.), *Judicial Independence in Transition* (Springer 2012) 793.

Romania,[73] Bulgaria,[74] Croatia,[75] and Ukraine[76] suggest that this pattern is widespread in the region and Slovakia is not unique in this respect. Yet further evidence can be found in other post-Soviet states with judicial councils.[77] To paraphrase John Ferejohn, who once referred to the U.S. judiciary as "[the] system of independent judges within a dependent judiciary,"[78] I refer to the Judicial Council Euro-model as "the system of dependent judges within an independent judiciary."

This finding has broad repercussions for judicial reforms. By repercussions I do not mean suggestions on how to improve the existing standards. This is not a normative project and so it stops short of offering prescriptive remedies, even though some of them are obvious.[79] What this book conveys is that we should rethink some of the current paradigms about

---

[73] See, for example, Parau 2012, above note 40, at 643–656; Ramona Coman and Cristina Dallara, "Judicial Independence in Romania" in ibid., 835; or Bogdan Iancu, "Constitutionalism in Perpetual Transition: The Case of Romania" in Bogdan Iancu (ed.), *The Law/Politics Distinction in Contemporary Public Law Adjudication* (Eleven International Publishing 2009) 187, 196–198.

[74] See, for example, Daniel Smilov, "EU Enlargement and the Constitutional Principle of Judicial Independence" in Adam Czarnota, Martin Krygier, and Wojciech Sadurski (eds.), *Spreading Democracy and the Rule of Law: The Impact of EU Enlargement on the Rule of Law, Democracy, and Constitutionalism in Post-Communist Legal Orders* (Springer 2006) 31; Diana Bozhilova, "Measuring Success and Failure of EU-Europeanization in the Eastern Enlargement: Judicial Reform in Bulgaria" (2007) 9 *European Journal of Law Reform* 285; Maria Popova, "Be Careful What You Wish For: A Cautionary Tale of Post-Communist Judicial Empowerment" (2010) 18 *Demokratizatsiya* 56; Thierry Delpeuch and Margarita Vassileva, "Lessons from the Bulgarian Judicial Reforms: Practical Ways to Exert Political Influence on a Formally Very Independent Judiciary" in Leny E. de Groot-van Leeuwen and Wannes Rombouts (eds.), *Separation of Powers in Theory and Practice: An International Perspective* (Wolf Legal Publishers 2010) 49; and Maria Popova, "Why the Bulgarian Judiciary Does Not Prosecute Corruption?" (2012) 59 *Problems of Post Communism* 35.

[75] See Uzelac, above note 54; and Alan Uzelac, "Amendments to the Law on Courts and Law on the State Judicial Council – Elements of the Reform of the Organizational Judicial Legislation" in Goranka Lalić (ed.), *Croation Judiciary: Lessons and Perspectives* (Netherlands Helsinki Committee 2002) 37–69, at 54–61.

[76] See Maria Popova, *Politicized Justice in Emerging Democracies: A Study of Courts in Russia and Ukraine* (CUP 2012) in particular at 139–145.

[77] See in particular the situation in Ukraine described in ECtHR, January 9, 2013, *Volkov v. Ukraine*, no. 21722/11; or in Angelika Nußberger, "Judicial Reforms in Post-Soviet Countries – Good Intentions with Flawed Results?" in Anja Seibert-Fohr (ed.), *Judicial Independence in Transition* (Springer 2012) 885. See also chapters on Armenia, Belarus, Kyrgyzstan and Kazakhstan, and Russia in ibid.

[78] John Ferejohn, "Independent Judges, Dependent Judiciary: Explaining Judicial Independence" (1999) 72 *Southern California Law Review* 353, 362.

[79] For instance, the corrosive effects of salary bonuses or the dual role of the JCSR in disciplining Slovak judges are clear.

judicial reforms, judicial independence, and the functioning of courts in general.

First of all, results from Slovakia as well from the Czech Republic suggest that we should approach with the same caution both external and internal accountability of judges.[80] While most recent documents on judicial independence and judicial councils acknowledge that improper pressure on a judge can stem from within the judiciary, it has been generally accepted that internal pressure is somehow less dangerous, perhaps for historical reasons. Recent scholarship also proceeds on the assumption that independence from politicians is at the heart of the normative importance of independent courts to the rule of law.[81] My findings challenge this view and show that internal pressure can be at least as dangerous as pressure from politicians. This means that if we want to have a holistic picture of judicial accountability we should keep a close eye on the powers within the judiciary and on court presidents in particular. This aspect was already addressed in the previous two sections where I discussed the powers of court presidents and proposed the JLT of judicial councils.

This brings me to the second repercussion. There has been too much emphasis on the independence of the judiciary recently, both in scholarly literature and in policy documents, whereas the independence of individual judges has been rather neglected. What is worse, sometimes the independence of the judiciary and the independence of individual judges merged into one thing. The results of my study suggest that it is high time to swing the pendulum back and refocus our attention on the independence of individual judges. That is what Germany did after World War II and this investment paid off.[82]

We should also accept that the independence of the judiciary and the independence of individual judges are two different things and that increasing the former does not automatically improve the latter.[83] In fact, the Slovak case study suggests that if one wants to reinstate the independence of individual judges in Slovakia, one must reduce the powers of the JCSR or reduce the number of its judicial members, which means that one

---

[80] On this distinction, see Part IV (External Controls) and Part V (Internal Controls) in Guy Canivet, Mads Andenas, and Duncan Fairgrieve (eds.), *Independence, Accountability and the Judiciary* (British Institute of International and Comparative Law, 2006).

[81] See, for example, Maria Popova, *Politicized Justice in Emerging Democracies: A Study of Courts in Russia and Ukraine* (CUP 2012).

[82] See above notes 23–28.

[83] See also Carlo Guarnieri, "Judicial Independence in Europe: Threat or Resource for Democracy?" (2013) 49 *Representation* 347, 353.

has to reduce the independence of the judiciary.[84] That former is exactly what the Slovak Minister of Justice Lucia Žitňanská did in 2011: she adopted several measures in order to protect the independence of judges against the actions of their colleagues who controlled the JCSR.[85] This picture – the Minister of Justice as a savior of judges' independence – must sound like science fiction to the European Commission and the Council of Europe.

The third insight is that judicial reforms in the CEE, advocated jointly by the European Union and the Council of Europe, have often been naïve.[86] The transplantation of the Judicial Council Euro-model into Slovakia is a typical example of this naïveté. The European Union and the Council of Europe as well as domestic actors simply believed that a bad model (the Ministry of Justice model) would be necessarily replaced by a good model (the Judicial Council Euro-model) and did not check whether the new model would work not only in sunshine, but also when it rains or snows.[87]

Unfortunately, this is a typical flaw of designing social mechanisms. As Binmore suggested, "[n]obody would ever propose constructing an aeroplane or a bridge without giving a great deal of thought to how the mechanism would stand up to the stresses and strains it will face when built, but the idea that one should give the same care and attention to the design of social mechanisms is typically greeted with scorn."[88] This sentence perfectly describes the drawbacks of the Judicial Council Euro-model. Put bluntly, the JCSR was born to be hijacked. It was only a matter of time before it happened.

Finally, my book swims against the tide in one more respect. It implicitly suggests a heretical idea – that the Ministry of Justice model may be

---

[84] This is precisely what the centrist government in Slovakia attempted to do in 2011, but met with a huge backlash, both from (not only pro-Harabin) Slovak judges and from various international organizations of judges. Most of the judicial reforms that this centrist government managed to pass were suspended, challenged before the Slovak Constitutional Court, or distorted by rulings of the Supreme Court of Slovakia.

[85] These measures included introducing a special two-month period for judges reassigned to panels dealing with issues outside their area of expertise so that the impugned judge can get acquainted with this new area of law, prohibiting discretionary reassignment of cases by court presidents, a tighter control of software used for random case assignment, increasing the powers of judicial boards vis-à-vis court presidents, and a requirement to publish statistics about the work of individual judges so that their performance can be checked by external actors. For further details, see Law No. 33/2011 Z. z.

[86] Not to mention that the European Union and the Council of Europe ignored the historical development of the judiciaries in this region and their specifics.

[87] Ken Binmore, *Game Theory: A Very Short Introduction* (OUP 2007) 104.

[88] Ibid., at 104.

superior to the Judicial Council Euro-model in some environments.[89] The Slovak case study in fact makes a strong case for the claim that the Ministry of Justice model, and not the Judicial Council Euro-model, is the better choice out of these two[90] models for some countries in the CEE. The Minister of Justice model may yield suboptimal results and generate tensions between judges' principals, but it retains a system of checks and balances, albeit imperfect, which prevents any principal from taking control of the majority of accountability mechanisms. It also unites judges and allows them to gel together, which minimizes infighting within the judiciary. Moreover, any Minister of Justice is held to account by voters every four years. As a result, the Minister of Justice model is more difficult to hijack. Last but not least, it is the proverbial "devil we know." In contrast, the Euro-model replaces the system of checks and balances with the concentration of powers and grants the group that controls the judicial council at any one moment almost unfettered power with no democratic accountability. The mandate of members of the Judicial Council Euro-model is usually longer and if its members buy the support of enough judges or other principals they are almost untouchable. In addition, given the novelty of the Judicial Council Euro-model, its problems and limits were not known in advance and thus they could not be taken into account.

Against this backdrop, it is ironic that the United Nations, the European Commission, the Council of Europe[91] and various international organizations of judges such as European Association of Judges (EAJ) and European Network of Councils for the Judiciary (ENCJ),[92] with their vocal advocacy for the Judicial Council Euro-model and contempt for democratically elected branches, to a great extent legitimized the actions of the JCSR and its chairman, Štefan Harabin. These international and supranational bodies provided Harabin with the necessary "veil of legitimacy," which he used skillfully. In his interviews with the media, Harabin likes to

---

[89] For a similar complementary argument, see Maria Popova, "Why the Bulgarian Judiciary Does Not Prosecute Corruption?" (2012) 59 *Problems of Post Communism* 35.

[90] But recall that there are models of court administration other than the Ministry of Justice model and the Judicial Council Euro-model (see Chapter 3). In fact, several CEE countries that introduced the judicial council model did not opt for the Euro-model. For instance, Poland never transferred virtually all powers regarding the career of judges to its National Council of the Judiciary (NCJ) and, moreover, in 2007 it banned court presidents from membership in the NCJ – see Bodnar and Bojarski, above note 40, at 669–679. Estonia also preferred the cooperative model of court administration, where judicial councils share many powers with the Ministry of Justice – see Ligi, above note 40, at 741–755.

[91] See Chapter 6.

[92] See notes 160–162 below.

emphasize that he did not create the JCSR, that the European Commission required it from Slovakia as a condition for joining the European Union and that virtually all international bodies recommend the Judicial Council Euro-model as the best model of administration of courts.[93] Unfortunately, he is right on this one.

IV. Mechanisms of Judicial Accountability in Transitional Societies

Each country and each transition is unique. I draw my conclusions here primarily from the experience of the CEE countries in transition from the communist regime to democracy. However, I believe that most of the specifics of holding the CEE judges to account after the fall of the communist rule are common to other transitional societies.

First of all, no transitional judiciary starts from scratch. There are always legacies from the past that must be taken into account. In the CEE, most countries came into being after the dissolution of the Austro-Hungarian Empire, suffered greatly during World War II and almost immediately after that war witnessed a communist coup d'état that brought about four decades of communist rule. While all these periods must be factored in,[94] the Communists ruled for the longest period and left the most important mark on CEE judiciaries.

The communist takeover of the Czechoslovak judiciary after 1948 is a particularly illustrative period since the Communist Party used almost every possible mechanism to tame judges. One can also see the perverse logic in its steps. It first packed the courts with lay judges in order to gain control over the judicial system and to outvote professional judges until it trained *its* own professional judges and staffed the courts with them.[95]

---

[93] See Chapter 3.

[94] Note that it would be misleading to claim that everything bad within the CEE judiciaries has its roots exclusively in the communist era. On the contrary, certain features had been prevalent in these judiciaries since their independence after World War I and they became anomalous only due to their obsoleteness or deformation. These features included, among other things, the creation of special courts, selective case assignment, strong powers of court presidents, and relaxing the criteria for judicial office. However, such historical analysis would require a separate book. For an examination of legacies extending back before World War II, see also Zdeněk Kühn, *The Judiciary in Central and Eastern Europe: Mechanical Jurisprudence in Transformation?* (Brill 2011) 9–14; and Martin Mendelski and Alexander Libman, "History Matters, but How? An Example of Ottoman and Habsburg Legacies and Judicial Performance in Romania," Frankfurt School Working Paper No. 175 (September 30, 2011), 1–4.

[95] See Kühn 2011, above note 94, at 34–36.

It simply could not rely on prerevolutionary professional judges applying prerevolutionary law with a prerevolutionary mindset. Single judges were replaced by panels for similar reasons.[96] At the same time communists abolished high courts, the conservative bastions of the interwar judiciary, and channeled political cases to the newly established State Court. The creation of the State Court, a truly revolutionary court, for an interim period was also inevitable since the ordinary courts could not be "trusted" at that time, as Communists openly admitted few years later. Finally, they granted vast powers to the General Prosecutor to overcome potential resistance from the bench. The most resistant judges were given long-term prison sentences in order to create an atmosphere of fear within the judiciary and tame professional judges educated in the interwar era.[97] The standard account was that there is no contradiction between the judiciary's independence and its obedience to the Party.[98]

Once the Communist Party consolidated its power within the judiciary, it created a structure that allowed for the relatively easy maintenance of its control over the judiciary. The communist regime abolished most special courts and centralized the control of the judiciary in the single institution – the Supreme Court. The Supreme Court could remove any case pending before a court of first or second instance and decide it itself, issue "interpretative guidelines"[99] – irrespective of any real-life pending case – to unify the divergent case law of the lower courts and decide on "extraordinary appeals," which could be initiated with no time limits against any decision of an ordinary or a special court in Czechoslovakia. The Communist Party also introduced short terms for judges and effective retention mechanisms. In the meantime, the Czechoslovak judiciary witnessed large-scale "jurisdiction stripping." The resolution of economic disputes was channeled into the state arbitration and the administrative courts were replaced by the oversight of the General Prosecutor.[100] The "sovietization" of the Czechoslovak judicial system in the early 1950s was

---

[96] Ibid., at 104–105.

[97] See Chapter 2, Section II.E.

[98] See Kühn 2011, above note 94, at 57–62 and 123; or Frankowski 1991, above note 20, at 34.

[99] For further details, see Zdeněk Kühn, "The Authoritarian Legal Culture at Work: The Passivity of Parties and the Interpretational Statements of Supreme Courts" (2006) 2 *Croatian Yearbook of European Law and Policy* 19; Kühn 2011, above note 94, at 128–129; or Frankowski 1991, above note 20, at 36–41.

[100] For a good overview of extrajudicial contentious procedures in the socialist countries, see René David and John Brierley, *Major Legal Systems in the World Today* (3rd ed., Stevens 1985) 251–261; or, more recently, Kühn 2011, above note 94, at 36–40.

completed with the reorganization of the public prosecution according the Soviet model of *prokuratura*.

The following three decades, from the 1960s until 1989, are no less interesting. This period teaches us two lessons. The first is that no one can control the judiciary without the help of people *within* the judiciary. The second, drawing on experience from the so-called normalization, the period between the crushing of the Prague Spring of 1968 and the Velvet Revolution of 1989, is that it is possible to control the judiciary with the help of relatively *few* "trusted" judges. Within the hierarchical model of "state administration of courts," based on the Austrian model, it was enough to control the positions of court presidents and to staff each court with a few reliable judges. Third, this time the Czechoslovak communist regime used subtler techniques to control the judiciary than after the coup d'état in the late 1940s and early 1950s. These techniques included assigning sensitive cases only to reliable judges, "small talks" of court presidents with defiant judges, regular retention elections, "interpretive guidelines" issued by the Supreme Court to ensure that lower court judges knew how to decide on the issues that the Communist Party cared about, the selective publication of case law that guaranteed that no judgment that steered too far from the Communist Party's line attracted attention, and the careful screening and socialization of new judges.

Poland underwent similar development. In the first phase, during the Stalinist era (1944–1955), "unreliable" prewar judges were gradually eliminated from the courts of general jurisdiction and replaced by a new breed of Party activists, who usually lacked a thorough legal training; military courts were strengthened; "interpretative guidelines" of the Supreme Court and "extraordinary appeals" were introduced; and "secret sections" were created at various levels of the military and the regular judiciary to handle the most politically sensitive cases.[101] In the second phase, the post-Stalinist era (1956–1989), "a variety of 'remote control' mechanisms replaced 'manual steering.'"[102] The 1962 Law on the Supreme Court provided that Supreme Court Justices would be appointed for only five years, which kept them on a short leash, authorized a justice's dismissal if he failed to guarantee proper fulfillment of his duties, subjugated the Supreme Court to the general supervision of the Council of State (a body absolutely dominated by the Party) and encouraged the Supreme Court

---

[101] Frankowski 1991, above note 20, at 36–40.
[102] Ibid., 41.

to use "interpretative guidelines" widely.[103] At lower courts, the "dirty job" was done by special panels of carefully selected "reliable" judges and by court presidents, who were, without exception, Communist Party members. We can thus see a similar pattern to that in Czechoslovakia – the Party exercised tight control over the selection of court presidents and the appointment of Supreme Court Justices and that was enough to control the entire Polish judiciary.[104] The only major difference from the Czechoslovak scenario was the Solidarity movement, which divided the Polish judiciary and led to widespread purges and resignations in the 1980s.[105] No such resistance by judges took place in Czechoslovakia.

The taming of other judiciaries in the CEE also went through these two-stages: crude and sweeping changes after the communist take-over and more subtle techniques in the later years of communist rule.[106] Unfortunately most judicial reforms after 1989 tackled only the crude measures from the first phase of communist rule and preferred a quick large-scale solution, such as the creation of a judicial council. Much less attention was paid to small-scale mechanisms that the Communist Party used to control the judiciary in the latter phases of its rule. It is clear that mechanisms of judicial accountability cannot work properly if these historical institutional legacies are not factored in.

In addition to the institutional legacies, there were also mental legacies of the past. During the communist era, lower court judges were not allowed to speak up against their superiors, be they appellate judges or court presidents. Court presidents carefully assigned cases among judges so as to achieve the desired results. Supreme Court judges selected the "correct" decisions to be published in centralized official collections of judgments. Senior judges who conducted judicial training sessions in the communist era often just summarized the "right" solutions to the existing problems. No dissent and no alternative reasoning were allowed. As a result, personal courage was heavily lacking among judges in the communist era.

This hierarchical culture of obedience was difficult to overcome. The judicial performance evaluations systems introduced in Slovakia and the

---

[103] Ibid., 41.

[104] Ibid., 42–46.

[105] According to Frankowski, in August 1980, when Solidarity was created, one thousand Polish judges (28 % of the judiciary) ultimately joined the ranks of Solidarity. After the suppression of that movement, several judges were dismissed and almost five hundred judges, one-eighth of the entire judiciary, resigned between 1983 and 1986 (Frankowski, "The Procuracy and the Regular Courts as the Palladium of Individual Rights and Liberties – the Case of Poland" (1987) 61 *Tulane Law Review* 1307, 1329).

[106] See Inga Markovits, *Justice in Lüritz* (Princeton University Press 2010).

Czech Republic in 2000, and 2002 respectively, attest to it. Both the Czech and Slovak systems contained the elements of the Soviet style of evaluation of judges. The very title of the Czech "judicial competence evaluation" made the focus of the evaluation clear. Court presidents were supposed to primarily test judges' knowledge of statutes and case law published in the Official Collection edited by the Supreme Court. The entire evaluation exercise could even result in a dismissal of an "incompetent" judge. The Slovak system fared no better. It focused primarily on correctness of judges' decisions, not their skills, and also buttressed the bureaucratic patterns within the Slovak judiciary, because the assessment was vested in the court presidents and appellate judges. Both systems implicitly discouraged plurality of opinions and free flow of ideas among judges and, instead, entrenched the communist-era mentality. These two ample examples thus show that any postcommunist judiciary had to undergo not only institutional, but also mental transition.[107]

Apart from the institutional and mental legacies from the past, all countries in transition to democracy face another transitional justice dilemma – to what extent they should purge the judiciary. As a rule, after the fall of authoritarian or totalitarian regimes, most countries are not in a position to dismiss a majority of the judges from the predemocratic era as there are not enough people to replace them. The only country in the CEE, where significant purges of communist judges took place was the former German Democratic Republic, but its position was highly specific due to the unification of Germany and the large pool of available lawyers in West Germany willing to take judicial office in East Germany.[108] As Kühn has observed, "[i]n contrast to East Germany, there was no West Czechoslovakia, West Poland or West Hungary which may have easily ... restaffed judicial posts virtually overnight."[109] Poland at least purged its Supreme Court,[110] but there was little pressure on lower court judges to leave the bench. The Czech

---

[107] See also Michal Bobek, "The Fortress of Judicial Independence and the Mental Transitions of the Central European Judiciaries" (2008) 14 *European Public Law* 99, 107–111 (who argues that mental transition of CEE judiciaries must focus on courage, morality, knowledge, and responsibility).

[108] See Erhard Blankenburg, "The Purge of Lawyers after the Breakdown of the East German Communist Regime" (1995) 20 *Law & Social Inquiry* 223, 235–242; Markovits 1996, above note 20, at 2271–2272; or Martina Künnecke, "The Accountability and Independence of Judges: German Perspectives", in Guy Canivet, Mads Andenas, and Duncan Fairgrieve (eds.), *Independence, Accountability, and the Judiciary* (British Institute of International and Comparative Law 2006) 217, 229.

[109] Kühn 2011, above note 94, at 163.

[110] On this aspect of judicial reforms in Poland, see, for example, Daniela Piana, "The Power Knocks at the Courts' Back Door – Two Waves of Postcommunist Judicial Reforms" (2009) 42 *Comparative Political Studies* 816, 820; or Wojciech Sadurski, *Rights before*

Republic, despite its sweeping lustration laws, left most judges in place. In other countries in the CEE the public demand for reckoning with the past was much less, and so the judiciary was to a large extent left intact.[111] This is the case with Slovakia, Hungary, Romania, and Bulgaria.

However, I must add one caveat here. I do not claim that the judges who remained in service from the communist period all lacked judicial independence and moral integrity. The main point is that such judges could have remained on the bench. However, a limited purge within the judiciary is not a feature peculiar to transitions in the CEE. David Dyzenhaus and Hakeem Yusuf showed that judges successfully resisted transitional justice mechanisms in South Africa and Nigeria as well.[112] In all countries, they managed to do so by invoking the spell of judicial independence.

This leads me to the third factor in every transition – overemphasis on judicial independence. This initial overemphasis on this aspect in judicial reforms in transitional societies is understandable. However, it comes at great long-term cost, because it cements personal continuity within the judiciary[113] and "virtually exclude[s] any debate on other values a judicial system should safeguard."[114] This may eventually result in several problems. The first is that little attention is paid to mechanisms of judicial accountability and especially to those that operate within the judiciary, often outside the media spotlight. The second is that once politicians and scholars realize that mechanisms of judicial accountability ought to be revamped or strengthened, they face an uphill struggle. Judges, supported by rule of law scholars and foreign advisors who often do not understand the specifics of transitional judiciaries, fight back and the chances to rebalance judicial accountability with judicial independence later on are rather slim. This is a fine example of the well-known paradox of the rule of law reforms – that early reforms can create obstacles to the future ones.[115] The third is that, having secured

---

Courts: A Study of Constitutional Courts in Postcommunist States of Central and Eastern Europe (Springer 2005) 43.

[111] For my own take on this issue, see Kosař 2013, above note 15.

[112] See, David Dyzenhaus, Judging the Judges, Judging Ourselves: Truth, Reconciliation and the Apartheid Legal Order (Hart Publishing 2003) (on South Africa); and Hakeem Yusuf, Transitional Justice, Judicial Accountability and the Rule of Law (Routledge 2010) (on Nigeria).

[113] In fact, judges in all transitional scenarios skillfully invoke the notion of judicial independence in order to prevent or alleviate purges within the judiciary. See ibid.

[114] Bobek 2008, above note 107, at 100.

[115] Mariana Mota Prado, "The Paradox of Rule of Law Reforms: How Early Reforms Can Create Obstacles to Future Ones" (2010) 60 University of Toronto Law Journal 555.

independence, the judges are at risk of becoming "a law unto themselves" that may lead to a distorted view of judicial independence.[116] I have shown that all three of these dangers materialized in Slovakia. Other scholars report that Romanian and Bulgarian scenarios are not much different.[117]

In addition to legacies from the past and overemphasis on judicial independence, all transitional countries must also address novel challenges that emerge in the new democratic regimes. In the CEE, two such challenges stand out – a temporary shortage of judges that allowed incompetent judges to join the bench and corruption.[118] The shortage of judges resulted from several factors. The most important ones were low salaries and huge case-loads in the early 1990s that led to the voluntary resignation of judges who preferred to seek the new opportunities available in the private sector and discouraged the best graduates from the law schools from joining the judiciary; the need for more judges due to increased litigation; a general shortage of lawyers inherited from the communist era; and purges within the judiciary. Due to these cumulative factors, even poorly prepared candidates could join the judiciary in the 1990s.[119] This is not to say that all or most new judges from this period are incompetent. My point is rather that there is a huge disparity among CEE judges in terms of quality.

The second challenge, corruption, was an even greater danger. During the communist era, the Party controlled the judiciary and the salaries of all workers were more or less the same, which left little room for judges to be corrupted by private parties. In contrast, the postcommunist regimes brought about huge disparities in income and its first millionaires, while judges' salaries initially remained very low. Moreover, external checks on the judiciary became somewhat looser. This set up created strong incentives for corruption, to which many judges in the CEE succumbed. Slovak, Bulgarian, and Romanian judges were particularly well known for their venality,[120] but this

---

[116] See Frank Emmert, "The Independence of Judges – A Concept Often Misunderstood in Central and Eastern Europe" (2001) 3 *European Journal of Law Reform* 405.

[117] See above notes 73–76. However, the problems of the Hungarian judicial council were overwhelmed by Orbán's judicial reforms (see Chapter 3, note 50).

[118] Parau also considers these two factors the key shortcomings of CEE judiciaries; see Parau 2012, above note 40, at 639–643 and 649–656.

[119] For more details on the replacement of judges after the collapse of communism, see Kühn 2011, above note 94, at 164–169; or Bobek 2008, above note 107, at 118–119.

[120] See sources in Chapter 6, Section IV.D (on Slovakia); Parau 2012, above note 40, at 639–643 and 649–656 (on Romania); and Maria Popova, "Why the Bulgarian Judiciary Does Not Prosecute Corruption?" (2012) 59 *Problems of Post Communism* 35 (on Bulgaria).

problem haunted all judiciaries in the region.[121] Other transitional judiciaries are not exempt either.[122] To sum up, both of these new challenges – a shortage of judges that allowed poorly prepared candidates to join the bench and corruption – should also have been taken into account when designing mechanisms of accountability.

Finally, there is one more factor that has serious repercussions on mechanisms of judicial accountability in most transitional societies – the limited transparency of their judiciaries. In the CEE, this opacity to a certain extent results from the very features of the typical civil law judiciary, where decisions are made predominantly by panels and not individual judges, separate opinions are prohibited, and which consists of thousands of judges. In addition, very little information is available about individual judges, the selection and promotion of judges usually takes place behind the scenes, and only a minority of judgments is published. The combination of these factors makes it very difficult for someone outside the judiciary to grasp where individual judges stand on particular issues. This institutional design may be intentional and is supposed to shield judges from individual accountability.[123] Nevertheless, the problem is that people within the judiciary, and court presidents in particular, know what individual judges think about this or that issue and how they vote. If these people are vested with the power to hold judges to account, they may easily use this information.

These specifics of judiciaries in transition, institutional legacies from the past such as strong powers of court presidents and Supreme Court justices, personal continuity within the judiciary, a temporary shortage of judges, overemphasis on judicial independence, increased incentives for corruption, and limited transparency, each on its own, affect the functioning of mechanisms of judicial accountability in those countries. Once more I have to emphasize that what matters is to whom, for what, via what mechanism, how often, and how much judges are actually held to account, and not what the law says about these mechanisms. The Czech and Slovak

---

[121] See Kathryn Hendley, "'Telephone Law' and the 'Rule of Law': The Russian Case" (2009) 1 *Hague Journal on the Rule of Law* 241, 252–253 (on Russia); Uzelac, above note 54 (on Croatia); or case studies on CEE countries in Transparency International, *Global Corruption Report: Corruption in Judicial Systems* (CUP 2007)).

[122] See also Yusuf, above note 112, at 174–175; or case studies on non-CEE countries in Transparency International, *Global Corruption Report: Corruption in Judicial Systems* (CUP 2007).

[123] See the discussion on the French "culture of judicial accountability" in Chapter 2, Section IV.

case studies show that many mechanisms of judicial accountability operated "in the shadow of the law" and that the gap between de jure and de facto judicial accountability was wide. This may be the case for other transitional societies too.

Mechanisms of judicial accountability in transitional societies are also particularly prone to misuse. Selective accountability that allows for bullying critics within the judiciary and shielding the allies from the reach of accountability mechanisms is the most dangerous of the accountability perversions. It may emanate from any principal of judges. A common wisdom suggests that politicians would be the main culprits in the rise of this phenomenon,[124] but the Slovak case study showed that selective accountability comes predominantly from within the judiciary – from court presidents. They bought the support of their allies with huge salary bonuses, increased the case loads of their critics and reassigned them to panels outside their area of expertise, ensured that only their allies were promoted, and initiated disciplinary motions against the most "recalcitrant" judges.[125] They also managed to achieve significant support among Slovak judges by portraying themselves as saviors of the judiciary who protect the interests of judges against politicians and the Minister of Justice's demands for better performance. Some instances of selective accountability in Slovakia may have resulted from unclear standards and incomplete information about the performance of all judges, but most of these actions were intentional and clearly driven by mala fide motivation.

Several recent cases before the European Court of Human Rights (ECtHR) suggest that selective accountability is a problem in many CEE countries. For instance, in *GazetaUkraina-Tsentr v. Ukraine* a local journalist criticized Mr Y, the Chairman of the Kirovograd Regional Council of Judges. Mr Y subsequently lodged a civil claim for defamation and won before the courts of Kirovograd Region. The ECtHR acknowledged the importance of internal independence of judges and eventually found a violation of the right to a fair trial, because the material submitted by the applicant company demonstrated the possible risk that all judges in

---

[124] For examples of such phenomenon in Eastern Europe, see ECtHR, July 11, 2006, *Gurov v. Moldova*, no. 36455/02, §§ 34–37.

[125] See Chapter 6; and in particular Jana Dubovcová, "Umožňuje súčasný stav súdnictva zneužívanie disciplinárneho konania voči sudcom, zneužívanie výberových konaní a dáva výkonnej moci oprávnenie zasiahnuť do súdnej moci?" in Transparency International Slovensko (ed.), *Výzvy slovenského súdnictva a možnosti zlepšenia existujúceho stavu* (Transparency International Slovensko 2010) 50, 54–56.

the Kirovograd region would be influenced by the threat of disciplinary proceedings or other career-related decisions by Mr Y.[126] In *Agrokompleks v. Ukraine*, the president of the Higher Arbitration Court had given direct instructions to his deputies to reconsider the earlier court's ruling. The ECtHR again found these acts of the court president contrary to the principle of internal judicial independence.[127]

Selective case assignment and reassignment seems also to have permeated other judiciaries in the region. Apart from *DMD GROUP, a.s. v. Slovakia*[128] discussed in the Slovak case study, Strasbourg judges tackled this issue in applications against Lithuania and Ukraine. In *Daktaras v. Lithuania*[129] the President of the Criminal Division of the Supreme Court of Lithuania lodged a petition with the judges of that division to quash the Court of Appeal's judgment and, subsequently, the same President appointed the judge rapporteur and constituted the Chamber which was to examine the case. The President's petition was eventually upheld by the Supreme Court. The ECtHR held that "when the President of the Criminal Division not only takes up the prosecution case but also, in addition to his organizational and managerial functions, constitutes the court, it cannot be said that, from an objective standpoint, there are sufficient guarantees to exclude any legitimate doubt as to the absence of inappropriate pressure."[130] A similar problem arose in *Bochan v. Ukraine*,[131] where the ECtHR opined "the applicant's fears that the judges of the Supreme Court ... had a prefixed idea concerning the outcome of the case and that the judges to whom the case had been transferred ... would have to consider the case in accordance with the Supreme Court's view could be held to be objectively justified."[132] Recent literature suggests that these cases are just the tip of the iceberg.[133]

The other three phenomena, judicial accountability avoidance, simulating judicial accountability, and output excesses of judicial accountability

---

[126] ECtHR, July 15, 2010, *Gazeta Ukraina-Tsentr v. Ukraine*, no. 16695/04, §§ 33–34.
[127] ECtHR, October 6, 2011, *Agrokompleks v. Ukraine*, no. 23465/03, §§ 137–139. For another suspicious example of holding Ukrainian judges to account, see ECtHR, January 9, 2013, *Volkov v. Ukraine*, no. 21722/11.
[128] ECtHR, October 5, 2010, *DMD GROUP, a.s. v. Slovakia*, no. 19334/03.
[129] ECtHR, October 10, 2000, *Daktaras v. Lithuania*, no. 42095/98, §§ 35–38.
[130] ECtHR, October 10, 2000, *Daktaras v. Lithuania*, no. 42095/98, §§ 35–38, § 36.
[131] ECtHR, May 3, 2007, *Bochan v. Ukraine*, no. 7577/02.
[132] ECtHR, May 3, 2007, *Bochan v. Ukraine*, no. 7577/02, § 74. For another example of abusing case reassignment, see ECtHR, October 9, 2008, *Moiseyev v. Russia*, no. 62936/00, §§ 182–184.
[133] See Solomon 2010, above note 16; Parau 2012, above note 40; Coman and Dallara, above note 73; and Smilov, above note 74.

are also pervasive in transitional societies. I have referred to several examples of these phenomena in the Czech Republic and Slovakia. In the Czech Republic, a Supreme Court judge who repeatedly plagiarized complete articles of other scholars was not removed or otherwise penalized.[134] In Slovakia, many judges escaped disciplinary sanction by invoking various procedural loopholes in the disciplinary code. Complaints were declawed in both countries and so was judicial performance evaluation in Slovakia. Hence these two mechanisms merely simulated judicial accountability. As to output excesses, in both countries splitting the cases into separate files became a favorite technique to boost judges' outputs artificially.[135] Some court presidents went even further and assigned easy cases to themselves to achieve the same aim.[136]

To be sure, these three phenomena are not unique to transitional societies. In established democracies, judges also sometimes avoid punishment by a disciplinary court by reason of a short time-limit or by successfully invoking various procedural loopholes; complaints by the parties or judicial performance evaluations may become toothless; and the "new public management" paradigm, now so popular in Western Europe,[137] may cause some judges to try to boost their performance by artificially multiplying the number of decided cases. However, professional and peer pressure are so strong that these instances are minimized and, if they occur, the exposed judge is either held to account or resigns voluntarily. In contrast, judges in new democracies often do not resign and instead fight for their office to the end, even if they have clearly violated their ethical or judicial duties, and sometimes they win.

Neither the specifics of transition to democracy nor the judicial accountability perversions were sufficiently taken into account by most judicial reforms in the CEE. Instead, these reforms focused primarily on implementing a uniform template entailing an insulated, autonomous,

---

[134] Decision of the Supreme Court of the Czech Republic of October 30, 2008, case no. 1 Skno 10/2008.

[135] For further details, see Chapter 5, Section III.E.

[136] See, for instance, a disciplinary motion against the President of the Municipal Court of Brno (Czech Republic) for assigning to herself easy cases in violation of the work schedule; see Judgment of the High Court of Olomouc of December 7, 2007 *Judge M. K. (no. 1)* and Judgment of the Czech Supreme Court of May 27, 2009 *Judge M. K. (no. 2)*. In Slovakia, such misuse of case assignment took place as well, but it has not been disciplinarily prosecuted.

[137] On the rise of "new public management" in court administration in Europe, see Elaine Mak, "The European Judicial Organisation in a New Paradigm: The Influence of Principles of 'New Public Management' on the Organisation of the European Courts" (2008) 14 *European Law Journal* 718.

and self-perpetuating judiciary.[138] This template rests on an assumption that peer pressure is sufficient to ensure the proper functioning of mechanisms of judicial accountability. While peer pressure may work well in Germany or France, where a strong esprit de corps exists among judges and where there is a general consensus on what a judge may and may not do,[139] or in common law countries, where the meritocratic system generates strong personalities who follow and protect their code d'honneur, it does not necessarily deliver in postcommunist countries. As Parau put it, "[i]t is doubtful that professional or peer accountability, for example, can work if the peers themselves are corrupt; or if a judge belittles what his peers think of him; or if there is an agreement among presiding judges not to hold certain of their colleagues accountable; or if they are pursuing ideological ends."[140] As I argued in the previous section, the Euro-model of court administration even entrenched some of the most fundamental problems that bedevil the CEE judiciaries.

To sum up, judicial accountability has to be understood predominantly as a response to particular problems, rather than an abstract notion. Common mechanisms of judicial accountability are effective in dealing with common problems. To the extent that problems are not common, then common solutions are not necessarily the right thing.[141] The previous paragraphs showed that the accountability problems transitional judiciaries face are quite different from those that trouble established democracies.

V.   Oversight of Judges: Why Fire Alarms Do Not Work?

In Slovakia, there were enough complaints as well as newspaper articles that pointed at abusive disciplinary motions and reassignment, excessive salary bonuses, and other accountability perversions.[142] There has also

---

[138] See also Cristina Parau, "The Dormancy of Parliaments: The Invisible Cause of Judiciary Empowerment in Central and Eastern Europe" (2013) 49 *Representation – Journal of Representative Democracy* 267; or Cristina Parau, "Explaining Judiciary Governance in Central and Eastern Europe: External Incentives, Transnational Elites and Parliament Inaction" (2015) 67 *Europe-Asia Studies* 409.

[139] On this aspect, see the next section.

[140] Cristina Parau, 'Piana, Daniela (2010) Judicial Accountabilities in New Europe: From Rule of Law to Quality of Justice (book review)" (2011) 45 *Law & Society Review* 791, 792.

[141] See, mutatis mutandis, John Bell, "Judicial Culture and Judicial Independence" (2001–2002) 4 *Cambridge Yearbook of European Legal Studies* 47 (contrasting judicial independence in Spain and Sweden).

[142] See references in Chapter 6.

been media coverage of the irregularities within the JCSR. This raises two questions: How is it possible that the fire-alarm oversight did not work in Slovakia? Why political leaders did not fix the problems caused by the JCSR?

To answer the first question, we must first get back at the conditions of a successful fire-alarm oversight. In this type of oversight, principals wait for signs that agencies are improperly executing policy: they use complaints from concerned groups to trigger concern that an agency is misbehaving.[143] However, fire alarms are only useful when they are credible.[144] To create credible fire alarms involves establishing appropriate procedures for managing the collection and dissemination of information about an agency's activities.[145] This requires that the agency must follow several requirements.[146] First, an agency cannot announce a new policy without warning, but must instead give "notice" that it will consider an issue. Second, agencies must solicit "comments" and allow all interested parties to communicate their views. Third, agencies must allow "participation" in the decision-making process. Fourth, agencies must deal explicitly with the evidence presented to them and provide a rationalizable link between the evidence and their decisions. Fifth, agencies must "make available" a record of the final vote of each member in every proceeding.

The JCSR met neither of these conditions. Under Harabin's leadership the JCSR did everything to avoid any external check. It was reluctant to publish the transcripts of its hearings. In order to avoid participation of other stakeholders, the JCSR held its meetings in awkward locations that dissuaded the public and journalists from attending them. When this practice did not dissuade NGOs and members of foreign embassies, the JCSR resorted to the so-called per rollam voting. This "voting by letter" is a voting without calling a meeting, which meant that nobody could attend the JCSR's meetings. Comments on the JCSR's policies were not welcomed and policies were announced without any notice. The evidence brought

---

[143] Matthew D. McCubbins, Roger G. Noll, and Barry R. Weingast, "Political Control of the Bureaucracy" in Peter Newman (ed.), *The New Palgrave Dictionary of Law and Economics* (Palgrave Macmillan 1998) 50, 53.

[144] Arthur Lupia and Matthew D. McCubbins. *The Democratic Dilemma: Can Citizens Learn What They Need to Know?* (Cambridge University Press 1997), 220.

[145] See Matthew D. McCubbins, Roger G. Noll, and Barry R. Weingast, "Administrative Procedures as Instruments of Political Control" (1987) 3 *Journal of Law, Economics, and Organization* 243; or Matthew D. McCubbins, Roger G. Noll, and Barry R. Weingast, "Structure and Process, Politics and Policy: Administrative Arrangements and the Political Control of Agencies" (1989) 75 *Virginia Law Review* 431.

[146] McCubbins, Noll, and Weingast 1998, above note 143, at 54.

by other stakeholders was often disregarded and voting in the JCSR was secret. Hence, for instance, when the JCSR voted for lodging a disciplinary motion against a Supreme Court judge, outsiders did not know who voted for the motion and who voted against.

The same logic explains why fire alarms failed not only vis-à-vis the JCSR, but also vis-à-vis the judiciary. The standard mechanism of fire-alarm oversight in the context of the judiciary is complaints against individual judges.[147] For a complaint mechanism to work properly, someone must collect and disseminate sufficient information of what courts are doing. This did not happen in Slovakia until 2011. Until then, very few judicial decisions were published in law journals or online, judges often prohibited recording of the court hearings, and very little information on the internal functioning of the judiciary was available to the public. The complaint proceedings themselves were rather secretive. Neither complaints themselves nor the replies to them (or at least abstracts of these replies) were publicized. The other problematic feature of the Slovak complaint mechanism was the fact that complaints were not processed by an external complaint agency, but by court presidents who had their own agenda. It was not in their interests to attract the attention to the court they presided over since it would question their competence and leadership. The secretiveness of the Slovak complaint mechanism, coupled with the fact that complaints were processed by court presidents thus made this important accountability mechanism dysfunctional. The same set of issues declawed the complaint mechanism also in the Czech Republic. As a result, third-party supervision of the judiciary was minimal in both countries.

To answer the second question, it is helpful to first enrich the debate on court administration to accommodate the existence of political "slack," which can protect the agency responsible for court administration (a judicial council or another body) while it either confers private benefits on organized interests.[148] "Slack," as defined by the economic theory of regulation, is the effect of information and monitoring costs that shield the actions of a regulator from observation by a rational electorate.[149] When

---

[147] For explanation why this mechanism of judicial accountability is a typical example of fire-alarm oversight, see Chapter 3.

[148] See, mutatis mutandis, Michael E. Levine, "Regulation, the Market, and Interest Group Cohesion: Why Airlines Were Not Reregulated", in Marc K. Landy, Martin A. Levin, and Martin Shapiro (eds.), Creating Competitive Markets: The Politics of Regulatory Reform (Brookings 2007) 217–220.

[149] The term "slack" was first introduced into the political economy literature by Joseph P. Kalt and Mark A. Zupan, "Capture and Ideology in the Economic Theory of Politics" (1984) 74 American Economic Review 279.

members of a polity find the information necessary to monitor public officials too expensive to be worth acquiring or organizing to act upon, they
create slack.[150] In the presence of slack, self-regarding regulators can "sell"
policies to special interests in return for career support (help in achieving
reelection, reappointment, or postregulatory employment).[151] Slack disap-
pears when the actions of the regulator become the subject of such intense
public scrutiny that the costs to stakeholders of becoming informed on the
matter drop to nearly zero. The politically salient issues that are so publicized become part of the "public agenda". As a result, they are so widely
discussed in the media and elsewhere that no member of the polity can
easily remain unaware of them.

The JCSR managed to accumulate and preserve a huge "slack" after its
creation in 2002. Apart from the battle over the position of the President
of the Supreme Court and chairmanship of the JCSR in 2003 that attracted
media attention,[152] everything played in its favor. In the context of the
judiciary, the expertise on judging is concentrated within the guild itself
and the information asymmetry is high under any circumstances.[153]
Slovak circumstances made the slack even bigger as none of the three categories of mechanisms that politicians can choose from to reduce agency
costs – (1) internalization and ideology; (2) hierarchy and second-party
supervision; and (3) third-party supervision[154] – worked properly.
Ideology became a swearword after forty years of the communist rule.
Indoctrination of judges could not be utilized as there was little consensus
on judicial virtues among Slovak politicians[155] and hence there were no
generally recognized substantive standards against which politicians could
judge JCSR's and judges' actions. Hierarchical supervision did not work
either as court presidents were no longer extended hands of the Minister
of Justice. On the contrary, the interests of the JCSR and court presidents
were often mutual.[156] In addition, whistle-blowers within the judiciary
were silenced by rewards as well as by sticks.[157] Finally, third-party supervision of the judiciary was minimal as the complaint mechanism was

---

[150] Anthony Downs, *An Economic Theory of Democracy* (Harper 1957).
[151] Levine, above note 148, at 248.
[152] For further details, see Chapter 6.
[153] See Chapter 1, Section II.
[154] Tom Ginsburg, "Comparative Administrative Procedure: Evidence from Northeast Asia"
(2002) 13 *Constitutional Political Economy* 247, 248–250.
[155] See Section V of this chapter.
[156] See Section I of this chapter.
[157] See Chapter 6, Section IV.D.

toothless.[158] In other words, Slovak politicians utterly failed to monitor their top bureaucrats.

Due to these circumstances, even Harabin's return to presidency of the Supreme Court in 2009 could not break this slack. Despite his controversial actions, the JCSR under his presidency benefited from bureaucratic slack until July 2010, when the centrist coalition led by Prime Minister Iveta Radičová, and in particular her Minister of Justice Lucia Žitňanská, started to openly question JCSR's policies and entered into media tussles with the Supreme Court President Štefan Harabin. The results were several sets of hearings and interpellations in the Slovak Parliament and an explosion of media coverage that placed the issue of court administration on the public agenda, thereby dramatically lowering information and organization costs to the consuming public. The issue eventually became politically salient, thus eliminating the veil of slack that protected the JCSR and Štefan Harabin from public scrutiny.

However, even once the slack was destroyed, the centrist coalition was not able to force Harabin and "his" JCSR to heed the will of the general electorate. It failed for two reasons. The pragmatic one is that the change of the large-scale structure of the JCSR requires an amendment of the Slovak Constitution, for which Radičová did not have enough votes. The other, in contrast to general wisdom, was judicial independence. Judicial independence became sloganized and any criticism of the JCSR or Harabin was immediately portrayed as a threat to judicial independence. Like in 2000,[159] Harabin and his allies had called for powerful international allies to help him to sustain the pressure exercised by Žitňanská and civil society. Harabin send a letter to Lord Thomas, the then president of the ENCJ, to comment on Žitňanská's judicial reforms.[160] The Association of Slovak Judges (*Združenie sudcov Slovenska*) asked for an opinion of EAJ. Both the ENCJ president[161] and EAJ[162] issued statements that rather supported Harabin's position. This again shows that judicial independence blocks a

---

[158] See Section IV of this chapter. For more details, see Chapter 6, Section IV.D.

[159] See Chapter 6, Section III.D.

[160] For instance, Harabin send a letter to Lord Thomas, the then president of the ENCJ, to comment on Žitňanská's judicial reforms; see "Bude ministerka Žitňanská rešpektovať názory Lorda Justice Thomasa?", Dimenzie, No. 10/2010, 28–29.

[161] Reply of John Thomas, President of the ENCJ, to Štefan Harabin, Brussels, September 17, 2010.

[162] EAJ, Resolution Concerning the conformity with international standards of Judicial Independence of the amendments / proposed amendments to the status of judges in the legislation of the Slovak Republic, Istanbul, September 4, 2011. Žitňanská's judicial reforms were also discussed at the previous meeting of EAJ held in Malta on May 6, 2011.

lot of thinking about judicial accountability and that transnational community of judges has its own agenda. Eventually, a stroke of luck saved Harabin from more troubles as Radičová's government lost a vote of confidence on October 11, 2011 after a dispute on Eurozone bailout.

To be sure, the slack existed in the Czech Republic too. Ideology did not fly high due to the aversion caused by the communist regime's overuse of this technique. Indoctrination was also difficult for the lack of consensus on judicial virtues. Court presidents emancipated from the Ministry of Justice, which in turn weakened hierarchical supervision, and the complaint mechanism was declawed by court presidents. The only difference from Slovakia was that whistle-blowers within the judiciary were not silenced in the Czech Republic. Interestingly, even in the Czech Republic there was a Minister of Justice who attempted to resurrect the balance between the Ministry of Justice and court presidents – Jiří Pospíšil (2006–2009 and 2010–2012). He also met with a strong opposition of court presidents and also finished in his function[163] before he could have passed his judicial reform in the Czech Parliament.

This brings me to the question how politicians can monitor judges. The Czech and Slovak examples show that, given the absence of internalization and ideology, they cannot let judges monitor themselves and cannot rely on court presidents anymore. They might still influence appointment of judges to apex courts, but hierarchical supervision has generally weakened throughout Europe.[164] The Ministry of Justice cannot conduct comprehensive "police-patrol" oversight by itself as it is impossible. There seem to be only three solutions left. First, politicians may rely on whistle-blowers within the judiciary, but whistle-blowers are rare. Second, politicians may improve third-party supervision. This means that they have to design the complaint mechanism properly and make sure that this fire alarm mechanism is credible. Therefore, they must provide sufficient information about the functioning of the judiciary to the users of courts and flag problematic behavior of judges they want to eradicate. They must also make sure that someone else than court presidents who have their own interests at stake will proceed the complaint and, after filtering out the frivolous complaints, responses[165] to the complaints must be published.

---

[163] He was dismissed by the Czech Prime Minister in June 2012 for issues that were not related to judicial reforms.

[164] See, for example, Carlo Guarnieri and Patrizia Pederzoli, *The Power of Judges: A Comparative Study of Courts and Democracy* (OUP 2002) 54–55; or Guarnieri 2013, above note 83, at 348 (discussing the situation in Italy).

[165] These results can be published initially in anonymous or even aggregate form.

Finally, politicians should not rule out occasional "police patrol prowls" as a complementary technique to third-party supervision. Police-patrol oversight is more comprehensive and effective than commonly believed[166] and certain irregularities cannot be tracked by litigants.[167] In the context of the judiciary occasional "police patrol prowls" mean that the Ministry of Justice or another organ will screen the random sample of closed case files for irregularities in selected courts each year. This is less effective than comprehensive police-patrol oversight, but if each judge knows that once in five years there will be inspection at her court, she will have significant incentive to avoid any irregularities. Of course, "police patrol prowls" must be exercised with caution as they will inevitably come under severe scrutiny by judges, NGOs, and media.

VI. Judicial Virtues Matter

At the end of Chapter 2 I suggested that the answers to the three questions – who is accountable, to whom, and for what – to a great extent determine how judges are held to account and may even lead to distinctive "cultures of judicial accountability."[168] Then I briefly described cultures of judicial accountability in two civil law (France and Japan) and two common law (the United Kingdom and the United States) jurisdictions.

The American, British, French, and Japanese judicial systems differ significantly from each other and set out different incentives for judges, but irrespective of a peculiar culture of judicial accountability, all of these countries have one thing in common. They have developed conceptions of accountability-as-a-virtue. More specifically, there is a well-developed sense among academics, lawyers, and judges themselves of how judges ought to behave, what it means to be a good judge, and the existence of relatively firm if not altogether clearly articulated expectations means that judges are judged on whether they meet them. That is what Lawrence Solum

---

[166] McCubbins, Noll, and Weingast 1998, above note 143, at 54.

[167] For instance, if a court president assigns easy cases to themselves in order to increase their leisure time and not in order to affect the outcome of the case, litigants will hardly blow the whistle. Similarly, when a judge does not inform the enjoined party to the case (or other potential participants to the dispute that must be de lege informed), the enjoined party will not know about the dispute and thus will not be able to lodge a complaint. Moreover, certain judicial proceedings are not adversarial and if a judge pleases the only party, there is no one to report this misconduct.

[168] See Chapter 2, Section IV.

discusses nicely in his writings on judicial virtues.[169] Richard Posner talks about similar things in his recent book on "How Judges Think."[170] Even when you talk to litigators in the United States or the United Kingdom, this comes up almost inevitably: "I was before so-and-so and he's a great/ sharp/demanding" or the contrary.

In France and Japan, it is different because an individual judge's performance is less visible and thus less susceptible to external evaluation, but there are well-developed internal expectations, and thus also a form of informal accountability. For instance, the French judiciary sets its own rules, the so-called *obligations déontologiques des magistrats*[171] that make these expectations clear. French scholars also have clear views on this issue, even though they debate it less openly than their common law colleagues.[172] In other words, interactions between key stakeholders in these four judiciaries gradually developed into what Barbara Romzek has called the "expectations context of accountability."[173] In other words, in these countries there is "a generally recognized standard" that sets the benchmark and any deviation from this benchmark has clear and foreseeable consequences.

By contrast, there is no such consensus in transitional societies. In transformed judiciaries, those informal expectations have not had the time to develop naturally. In the CEE, most states came into being after World War I and they had only twenty years of state building under democratic rule. World War II halted this process, and a few years after the end of that war all countries in the region witnessed a communist coup d'état. The communists ruled the region for four decades, until 1989. Put together, this means that democratic rule was suspended for fifty long

---

[169] Lawrence Solum, "Virtue Jurisprudence: A Virtue-Centred Theory of Judging" (2003) 34 *Metaphilosophy* 178; or Lawrence Solum, "A Tournament of Virtue" (2004) 32 *Florida State University Law Review* 1365.

[170] Richard A. Posner, *How Judges Think* (Harvard University Press 2008).

[171] See *Conseil Supérieur de la Magistrature: Recueil des obligations déontologiques des magistrats*. Édition 2010, Dalloz-Sirey, 2010; or Jean-Francois Weber, "Éthique, déontologiques et responsabilité des magistrats" in Thierry Renoux (ed.), *La Justice en France* (La documentation française 2013).

[172] But see Roger Errera, *Et ce sera justice: Le juge dans la cité* (Gallimard 2013); Antoine Garapon (ed.), *Les juges: un pouvoir irresponsible?* (Nicolas Philippe 2003); Antoine Garapon and Ioannis Papadopoulos, *Juger en Amérique et en France: Culture juridique francaise et common law* (Odile Jacob 2003); or chapters of French speaking authors in Canivet, Andenas, and Fairgrieve, above note 80.

[173] Barbara S. Romzek, "Enhancing Accountability" in James L. Perry (ed.), *Handbook of Public Administration*. (2nd ed. Jossey Bass 1996) 97, 98.

years. These five decades distorted the values shared by judges and the means of achieving them. This environment led to a conundrum. On the one hand, the new democratic regimes could not return to the pre-World-War II state of affairs altogether, because the view of judges and their role had meanwhile moved around the world. On the other hand, catching-up with Western countries was not a natural development either. These opposing tendencies led to fierce disagreements about what judges can and cannot do, both on and off the bench, what a persuasive judgment should look like and what it means to be a good judge. As a result, even the key judicial virtues are contested here and there is no "generally recognized standard" against which one can judge a judge's actions. This, in turn, allows the principals to substitute their own, often self-serving, views for the general standard.

This leads me to my final observation. In Chapter 1 I made a clear distinction between judicial accountability as a virtue and as a mechanism and decided to focus on the latter, because I think that we have to be clear about when an accountability relationship exists before we ask whether that relationship satisfies certain other principles or values, and that in keeping these questions distinct we retain a role for a descriptive theory that does not immediately become mired in normative controversies.[174] I still believe that a definition of judicial accountability that is free of strong normative elements provides major gains. However, I must admit that these two concepts of accountability are related more closely that I initially thought. As Bovens has argued, processes of account giving and account holding cannot operate without standards against which the conduct of actors can be assessed.[175] Mechanisms of judicial accountability, after all, are just means for achieving judicial accountability as a virtue and the choice of mechanisms must depend on the understanding of the virtue. They ensure that judges remain on the path of virtue.[176]

I argued above that societies where the rule of law and democracy are more established have more developed conceptions of accountability-as-a-virtue. Transitional societies lag behind in this respect and as long as they do not find at least a basic consensus on judicial virtues and create their own "expectations context of accountability," no reforms or

---

[174] Here, I concur with Philp; see Mark Philp, "Delimiting Democratic Accountability" (2009) 57 *Political Studies* 28, 48–49.

[175] See Mark Bovens, "Two Concepts of Accountability: Accountability as a Virtue and as a Mechanism" (2010) 33 *West European Politics* 946, 962.

[176] See ibid., 954.

institutions will do the job. One can transplant models of court administration or revise existing mechanisms of judicial accountability, but no one
can transplant judicial virtues. Notions of accountability as a virtue in new
democracies must be (re)produced, internalized, and, where necessary,
adjusted through processes of account giving, and this will take time.[177]
Only then may accountability perversions that mar the transitional judiciaries disappear.

---

[177] On the need to change the mentality of CEE judges, see Bobek 2008, above note 107.

Annex A

Court System of the Czech Republic

Number of Czech courts and their titles:

- The Constitutional Court (*Ústavní soud*)[1]
- The Supreme Court (*Nejvyšší soud*)
- The Supreme Administrative Court (*Nejvyšší správní soud*)[2]
- Two high courts (*vrchní soudy*)[3]
- Eight regional courts (*krajské soudy*)
- Eighty-six district courts (*okresní soudy*)
- Military courts (*vojenské soudy*)[4]

www.juradmin.eu/en/eurtour/eurtour_en.lasso?page=detail&countryid=25

---

[1] The Czech Constitutional Court is a Kelsenian type of constitutional court and deals only with constitutional review. Therefore, it is not considered a part of the ordinary judiciary.
[2] The Supreme Administrative Court of the Czech Republic was established only in 2003.
[3] The High Court of Olomouc was established only in 1996.
[4] Military courts were abolished in the Czech Republic in 1993.

Court System of the Czech Republic

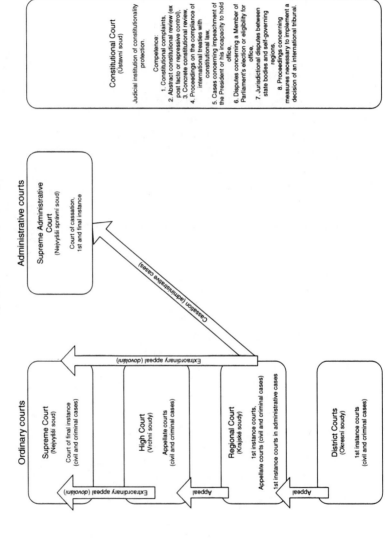

Ordinary courts

Supreme Court
(Nejvyšší soud)

Court of final instance
(civil and criminal cases)

High Court
(Vrchní soudy)

Appellate courts
(civil and criminal cases)

Regional Court
(Krajské soudy)

1st instance courts,
Appellate courts (civil and criminal cases)
1st instance courts in administrative cases

District Courts
(Okresní soudy)

1st instance courts
(civil and criminal cases)

Extraordinary appeal (dovolání)

Extraordinary appeal (dovolání)

Appeal

Appeal

Administrative courts

Supreme Administrative Court
(Nejvyšší správní soud)

Court of cassation,
1st and final instance

Cassation (administrative cases)

Constitutional Court
(Ústavní soud)

Judicial institution of constitutionality protection.

Competence:
1. Constitutional complaints,
2. Abstract constitutional review (ex post facto or repressive control),
3. Concrete constitutional review,
4. Proceedings on the compliance of international treaties with constitutional law,
5. Cases concerning impeachment of the President or his incapacity to hold office,
6. Disputes concerning a Member of Parliament's election or eligibility for office,
7. Jurisdictional disputes between state bodies and self-governing regions,
8. Proceedings concerning measures necessary to implement a decision of an international tribunal.

Annex B

Court System of Slovakia

Number of Slovak courts and their titles:

- The Constitutional Court (*Ústavný súd*)[1]
- The Supreme Court (*Najvyšší súd*)[2]
- Eight regional courts (*krajské súdy*)
- Fifty-four district courts (*okresné súdy*)
- Military courts (*vojenské súdy*)[3]
- The Special Court (*Špeciálny súd*)[4]
- The Specialized Criminal Court (*Špecializovaný trestný súd*)[5]

  www.juradmin.eu/en/eurtour/eurtour_en.lasso?page=detail&countryid=26

[1] The Slovak Constitutional Court is based on a Kelsenian model of constitutional adjudication and deals only with constitutional review. Therefore, it is not considered a part of the ordinary judiciary.

[2] As there is no Supreme Administrative Court in Slovakia, the Slovak Supreme Court is also a highest court in administrative law matters.

[3] Military courts were abolished in Slovakia in 2009, 16 years later than in the Czech Republic.

[4] The Special Court (2004–2009) was a special criminal court that had jurisdiction over certain public officials and over corruption, organized crime and other serious offences. Appeals against judgments and decisions of the Special Court were determined by (the Special Division of) the Supreme Court. The Special Court was found unconstitutional by the Slovak Constitutional Court in 2009.

[5] The Specialized Criminal Court was established in 2009 in order to replace the Special Court, which was struck down by the Slovak Constitutional Court (see the previous note).

Court System of the Republic of Slovakia

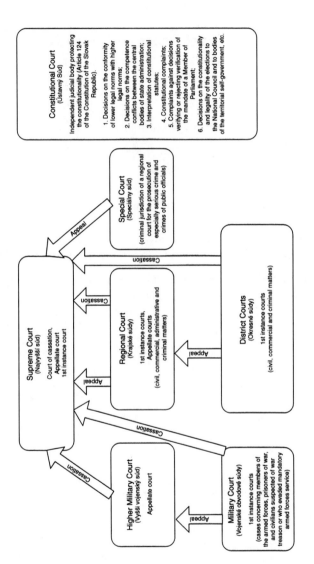

Constitutional Court
(Ústavný Súd)

Independent judicial body protecting the constitutionality (Article 124 of the Constitution of the Slovak Republic).

1. Decisions on the conformity of lower legal norms with higher legal norms;
2. Decisions on the competence conflicts between the central bodies of state administration;
3. Interpretation of constitutional statutes;
4. Constitutional complaints;
5. Complaints against decisions verifying or rejecting verification of the mandate of a Member of Parliament;
6. Decisions on the constitutionality and legality of the elections to the National Council and to bodies of the territorial self-government, etc.

Special Court
(Špeciálny súd)

(criminal jurisdiction of a regional court for the prosecution of especially serious crime and crimes of public officials)

Supreme Court
(Najvyšší súd)

Court of cassation, Appellate court 1st instance court

Regional Court
(Krajské súdy)

1st instance courts, Appellate courts (civil, commercial, administrative and criminal matters)

District Courts
(Okresné súdy)

1st instance courts (civil, commercial and criminal matters)

Higher Military Court
(Vyšší vojenský súd)

Appellate court

Military Court
(Vojenské obvodové súdy)

1st instance courts (cases concerning members of the armed forces, prisoners of war, and civilians suspected of war treason or who evaded mandatory armed forces service)

Appeal

Cassation

Cassation

Cassation

Cassation

Appeal

Appeal

Annex C

The Number of Judges in the Czech Republic and Slovakia (1993–2010)

Year	Number of Czech judges	Number of Slovak judges	Ratio [Czech judges vs. Slovak judges]
1993	2059	1038	2,0
1994	2178	1087	2,0
1995	2250	1116	2,0
1996	2308	1176	2,0
1997	2390	1180	2,0
1998	2481	1183	2,1
1999	2577	1225	2,1
2000	2660	1243	2,1
2001	2716	1222	2,2
2002	2814	1203	2,3
2003	2878	1233	2,3
2004	2920	1222	2,4
2005	2995	1255	2,4
2006	3019	1274	2,4
2007	3044	1292	2,4
2008	3029	1346	2,3
2009	3063	1338	2,3
2010	3048	1351	2,3

Note: All numbers reflect the state as of December 31 of a given year.

BIBLIOGRAPHY

Joel D. Aberbach, *Keeping a Watchful Eye: The Politics of Congressional Oversight* (The Brookings Institution Press, 1990).

Paloma Aguilar, 'Judiciary Involvement in Authoritarian Repression and Transitional Justice: The Spanish Case in Comparative Perspective' (2013) 7 *International Journal of Transitional Justice* 245

Philip Alston, 'Hobbling the Monitors: Should U.N. Human Rights Monitors be Accountable?' (2011) 53 *Harvard International Law Journal 561*.

Karen J. Alter, 'Agents or Trustees? International Courts in Their Political Context' (2008) 14 *European Journal of International Relations 33*.

Kora Andrieu, 'An Unfinished Business: Transitional Justice and Democratization in Post-Soviet Russia' (2011) 5 *International Journal of Transitional Justice* 198.

Peter Aucoin and Ralph Heintzman, 'The Dialectics of Accountability for Performance in Public Management Reform' (2000) 66 *International Review of Administrative Sciences* 45.

Violaine Autheman and Sandra Elena, *'Global Best Practices-Judicial Councils: Lessons Learned from Europe and Latin America'* (IFES, 2004).

Ian Ayres, *Carrots and Sticks: Unlock the Power of Incentives to Get Things Done* (Bantam, 2010). ISBN 0553807633.

Susan Bandes, 'Judging, Politics, and Accountability: A Reply to Charles Geyh' (2006) 56 *Case Western Reserve Law Review 947*.

Károly Bárd, 'Judicial Independence in the Accession Countries of Central and Eastern Europe and the Baltics' in András Sajó and Lorri Rutt Bentch (eds.), *Judicial Integrity* (Martinus Nijhoff 2004). ISBN 9789004140059.

Lawrence Baum, *The Puzzle of Judicial Behavior* (University of Michigan Press, 1997).

Olivier Beaud, 'Reframing a Debate among Americans: Contextualizing a Moral Philosophy of Law' (2009) 7 *International Journal of Constitutional Law 53*.

Paul Beaumont, 'The European Court of Justice. By Hjalte Rasmussen (short review)' (*European Law Books*) (available at: www.europeanlawbooks.org/reviews/detail.asp?id=103).

Ceran Belge, 'Friends of the Court: The Republican Alliance and Selective Activism of the Constitutional Court of Turkey' (2006) 40 *Law & Society Review 653*.

John Bell, 'Judicial Culture and Judicial Independence' (2001–2002) 4 *Cambridge Y.B. Eur. Legal Stud.* 47

Judiciaries within Europe: A Comparative Review (CUP, 2006).

'Reflections on Continental European Supreme Courts' in Guy Canivet, Mads Andenas, and Duncan Fairgrieve (eds.), *Independence, Accountability, and the Judiciary* (British Institute of International and Comparative Law 2006).

Richard Bellamy, 'The Democratic Qualities of Courts: A Critical Analysis of Three Arguments' (2013) 49 *Representation* 333.

Richard Bellamy and Cristina Parau, 'Introduction: Democracy, Courts and the Dilemmas of Representation' (2013) 49 *Representation* 255.

Jeremy Bentham, *An Introduction to the Principles of Morals and Legislation* (first published 1781, OUP, 1996).

Simone Benvenuti, 'The French and the Italian high councils for the judiciary: Observations drawn from the analysis of their staff and activity (1947–2011)' (2012 IPSA World Congress, Madrid, July 8–12, 2012).

Fernando Casal Bértoa, 'Parties, Regime and Cleavages: Explaining Party System Institutionalization in East Central Europe' (2012) 28 *East European Politics* 452.

'Post-Communist Politics: On the Divergence (and/or Convergence) of East and West Government and Opposition' (2013) 48 *Government and Opposition* 398.

'Party Systems and Cleavage Structures Revisited: A Sociological Explanation of Party System Institutionalization' (2014) 20 *Party Politics* 16.

Alexander Bickel, *The Least Dangerous Branch* (Bobs-Merrill, 1962).

Ken Binmore, *Game Theory: A Very Short Introduction* (OUP, 2007).

Muriel Blaive and Nicolas Maslowski, 'The World of the Two Václavs: European-Minded vs. National(ist) Intellectuals in Czechia' in Justine Lacroix and Kalypso Nicolaïdis (eds.), *European Stories: Intellectual Debates on Europe in National Contexts* (OUP 2010).

Erhard Blankenburg, 'The Purge of Lawyers after the Breakdown of the East German Communist Regime' (1995) 20 *Law & Social Inquiry* 223.

Michal Bobek, 'The Fortress of Judicial Independence and the Mental Transitions of the Central European Judiciaries' (2008) 14 *European Public Law* 99.

'Quantity or Quality? Re-Assessing the Role of Supreme Jurisdictions in Central Europe' (2009) 57 *American Journal of Comparative Law* 33.

Michal Bobek, 'The Administration of Courts in the Czech Republic – In Search of a Constitutional Balance' (2010) 16 *European Public Law* 251.

Michal Bobek and David Kosař, 'Global Solutions, Local Damages: A Critical Study in Judicial Councils in Central and Eastern Europe' (2014) 15 *German Law Journal* 1257.

Adam Bodnar and Lukasz Bojarski, 'Judicial Independence in Poland' in Anja Seibert-Fohr (ed.), *Judicial Independence in Transition* (Springer 2012).

Lukasz Bojarski and Werner Stemker Köster, *The Slovak Judiciary: Its Current State and Challenges* (Open Society Fund, 2011).

Mark Bovens, 'Analysing and Assessing Accountability: Conceptual Framework' (2007) 13 *European Law Journal* 447.

Two Concepts of Accountability: Accountability as a Virtue and as a Mechanism (2010) 33 *West European Politics* 946.

Mark Bovens and others, 'Does Public Accountability Work? An Assessment Tool' (2008) 86 *Public Administration* 225.

Sophie Boyron, 'The Independence of the Judiciary: A Question of Identity' in Guy Canivet, Mads Andenas, and Duncan Fairgrieve (eds.), *Independence, Accountability, and the Judiciary* (British Institute of International and Comparative Law 2006).

Diana Bozhilova, 'Measuring Success and Failure of EU-Europeanization in the Eastern Enlargement: Judicial Reform in Bulgaria' (2007) 9 *European Journal of Law Reform* 285.

David Brody, 'The Use of Judicial Performance Evaluation to Enhance Judicial Accountability, Judicial Independence, and Public Trust' (2008) 86 *Denver University Law Review* 115.

Alexander Bröstl, 'At the Crossroads on the Way to an Independent Slovak Judiciary' in Jiří Přibáň, Pauline Roberts, and James Young (eds.), *Systems of Justice in Transition: Central European Experiences since 1989* (Ashgate 2003).

Stephen B. Burbank and Barry Friedman (eds.), *Judicial Independence at the Crossroads: An Interdisciplinary Approach* (SAGE Publications, 2002).

Ladislav Cabada, Vít Hloušek, and Petr Jurek, *Party Systems in East Central Europe* (Lexington Books, 2014).

Brandice Canes-Wrone, Tom S. Clark, and Jee-Kwang Park, 'Judicial Independence and Retention Elections' (2012) 28 *Journal of Law, Economics, and Organization* 211.

Guy Canivet, 'The Responsibility of Judges in France' in Guy Canivet, Mads Andenas, and Duncan Fairgrieve (eds.), *Independence, Accountability, and the Judiciary* (British Institute of International and Comparative Law 2006).

Guy Canivet, Mads Andenas, and Duncan Fairgrieve (eds.), *Independence, Accountability, and the Judiciary* (British Institute of International and Comparative Law 2006).

Mauro Cappelletti, 'Who Watches the Watchmen? A Comparative Study of Judicial Responsibility' (1983) 31 *American Journal of Comparative Law* 1.

Zuzana Čaputová (ed.), *Zodpovednosť sudcu: Sudcovská etika a disciplinárna zodpovednosť* (VIA IURIS, 2011).

Jean Carbonnier, *Droit civil. Introduction* (21st ed., Presses Universitaires de France, 1992).

Rebecca Bill Chavez, 'The Appointment and Removal Process for Judges in Argentina: The Role of Judicial Councils and Impeachment Juries in Promoting Judicial Independence' (2005) 49 *Latin American Politics & Society* 33.

Neil Chisholm, 'The Faces of Judicial Independence: Democratic versus Bureaucratic Accountability in Judicial Selection, Training, and Promotion in South Korea and Taiwan', (2014) 62 *American Journal of Comparative Law* 893.

Stephen J. Choi and others, 'What Do Federal District Judges Want? An Analysis of Publications, Citations and Reversals' (2012) 28 *Journal of Law, Economics, and Organization* 518.

David S. Clark, 'The Organization of Lawyers and Judges' in Mauro Capelletti (ed.), *International Encyclopedia of Comparative Law, Volume XVI: Civil Procedure* (Mohr Siebeck 2002).

Tom S. Clark, *The Limits of Judicial Independence* (CUP, 2010).

Joe Cochrane, 'Top Indonesian Judge Held in Corruption Case' *The New York Times* (New York, October 3, 2013).

Stephen Colbran, 'The Limits of Judicial Accountability: the Role of Judicial Performance Evaluation' (2003) 6 *Legal Ethics* 55.

Ramona Coman and Cristina Dallara, 'Judicial Independence in Romania' in Anja Seibert-Fohr (ed.), *Judicial Independence in Transition* (Springer 2012).

Victor Ferreres Comella, *Constitutional Courts and Democratic Values: A European Perspective* (Yale University Press, 2009).

André Comte-Sponville, *Dictionnaire philosophique* (PUF 2001) 624 (quoted in Guy Canivet, 'The Responsibility of Judges in France' in Guy Canivet, Mads Andenas, and Duncan Fairgrieve (eds.), *Independence, Accountability, and the Judiciary* (British Institute of International and Comparative Law, 2006) 30.

Francesco Contini and Richard Mohr, 'Reconciling Independence and Accountability in Judicial Systems' (2007) 3 *Utrecht Law Review* 26.

Jean-Paul Costa, *Le Conseil d'État dans la societé contemporaine* [The Conseil d'État in Contemporary Society] (1993).

Javier Couso, 'Judicial Independence in Latin America: The Lessons of History in the Search for an Always Elusive Ideal' in Tom Ginsburg and Robert A. Kagan (eds.), *Institutions & Public Law: Comparative Approaches* (Peter Lang Publishing 2005).

Frank Cross, 'Judicial Independence' in Keith E. Whittington and others (eds.), *The Oxford Handbook of Law and Politics* (USA, OUP 2008).

John Cunliffe and Andrew Reeve, 'Dialogic Authority' (1999) 19 *Oxford Journal of Legal Studies* 453.

Mirjan R. Damaška, *The Faces of Justice and State Authority: A Comparative Approach to the Legal Process* (Yale University Press, 1986).

Jiří Dan, 'Psychologická vyšetření uchazečů o přijetí na pozice právních čekatelů a státních zástupců v letech 1998–2010' No. 10/2011 Státní zastupitelství.

Jozef Darski, 'Decommunization in Eastern Europe' (1993) 6 *Uncaptive Minds* 73.

René David and John Brierley, *Major Legal Systems in the World Today* (3rd ed., Stevens, 1985).

Roman David, *Lustration and Transitional Justice: Personnel Systems in the Czech Republic, Hungary, and Poland* (University of Pennsylvania Press, 2011).

Philip Dawson, *The Oracles of the Law* (University of Michigan Press, 1968).

Kevin Deegan-Krause, 'Uniting the Enemy: Politics and the Convergence of Nationalisms in Slovakia' (2004) 18 *East European Politics and Societies* 651.

Kevin Deegan-Krause and Tim Haughton, 'A Fragile Stability: The Institutional Roots of Low Party System Volatility in the Czech Republic, 1990–2009' (2010) 17 *Czech Journal of Political Science* 227.

Thierry Delpeuch and Margarita Vassileva, 'Lessons from the Bulgarian Judicial Reforms: Practical Ways to Exert Political Influence on a Formally Very Independent Judiciary' in Leny E. de Groot-van Leeuwen and Wannes Rombouts (eds.), *Separation of Powers in Theory and Practice: An International Perspective* (Wolf Legal Publishers 2010).

Giuseppe Di Federico, 'Independence and Accountability of the Judiciary in Italy: The Experience of a Former Transitional Country in a Comparative Perspective' in András Sajó (eds.), *Judicial Integrity* (Brill Academic Publishers 2004).

Giuseppe Di Federico (ed.), *Recruitment, Professional Evaluation and Career of Judges and Prosecutors in Europe* (IRSIG-CNR, 2005).

Adam Dodek and Lorne Sossin (eds.), *Judicial Independence in Context* (Irwin Law, 2010).

Anthony Downs, *An Economic Theory Of Democracy* (Harper, 1957).

Christopher Drahozal, 'Judicial Incentives and the Appeals Process' (1998) 51 *Southern Methodist University Law Review* 469.

Ján Drgonec, 'Disciplinárna zodpovednosť sudcov – Mechanizmus a podmienky jej uplatnenia: Prvá časť: Inštitucionálne zabezpečenie' (2006) 58 *Justičná revue* 413.

'Disciplinárna zodpovednosť sudcov – Mechanizmus a podmienky jej uplatnenia: Druhá časť: Uplatňovanie disciplinárnej zodpovednosti v praxi disciplinárneho súdu' (2006) 58 *Justičná revue* 601.

Jana Dubovcová, 'Sudnictvo a korupcia' in Emília Sičáková-Beblavá and Daniela Zemanovičová (eds.), *Protikorupčne nastroje* (TIS 2003).

'Umožňuje súčasný stav súdnictva zneužívanie disciplinárneho konania voči sudcom, zneužívanie výberových konaní a dáva výkonnej moci oprávnenie zasiahnuť do súdnej moci?' in Transparency International Slovensko (ed.), *Výzvy slovenského súdnictva a možnosti zlepšenia existujúceho stavu* (Transparency International Slovensko, 2010).

Patrick Dumont and Frédéric Varone, 'Delegation and Accountability in Parliamentary Democracies: Smallness, Proximity and Shortcuts' in Dietmar Braun and Fabrizio Gilardi (eds.), *Delegation in Contemporary Democracies* (Routledge 2006).

John Dunn, *Democracy: A History* (Atlantic Monthly Press, 2005).

David Dyzenhaus, *Judging the Judges, Judging Ourselves: Truth, Reconciliation and the Apartheid Legal Order* (Hart Publishing, 2003).

'Accountability and the Concept of (Global) Administrative Law' in *Global Administrative Law* (Acta Juridica, 2009) 3.

Frank Emmert, 'The Independence of Judges – A Concept Often Misunderstood in Central and Eastern Europe' (2001) 3 *European Journal of Law Reform* 405.

Zsolt Enyedi and Fernando Casal Bértoa, 'Party System Closure and Openness: Conceptualization, Operationalization and Validation' (2014) (available at: http://ppq.sagepub.com/content/early/2014/09/08/135406881 4549340.abstract).

Zsolt Enyedi and Fernando Casal Bértoa (2014), 'Elite and Mass Dynamics: The East Central European Example', paper presented at the OPPR Workshop on "Parties and Democracy in Post-communist Europe" at EUI on September 18–19, 2014 (available at: http://whogoverns.eu/elite-and-mass-dynamics-the-east-central-european-example/).

David Erdos, *Delegating Rights Protection: The Rise of Bills of Rights in the Westminster World* (OUP, 2010).

Roger Errera, *Et ce sera justice: Le juge dans la cité* (Gallimard, 2013).

William N. Eskridge, 'Overriding Supreme Court Statutory Interpretation Decisions' (1991) 101 *The Yale Law Journal* 331.

Gil Eyal, 'Anti-Politics and the Spirit of Capitalism: Dissidents, Monetarists, and the Czech Transition to Capitalism' (2000) 29 *Theory and Society* 49.

    The Origins of Postcommunist Elites: From the Prague Spring to the Breakup of Czechoslovakia (University of Minnesota Press, 2003).

James D. Fearon, 'Electoral Accountability and the Control of Politicians: Selecting Good Types versus Sanctioning Poor Performance' in Adam Przeworski and others (eds.), *Democracy, Accountability, and Representation* (CUP 1999).

Edwin L. Felter, 'Accountability in the Administrative Law Judiciary: The Right and the Wrong Kind' (2008) 86 *Denver University Law Review* 157.

John Ferejohn, 'Law, Legislation, and Positive Political Theory' in Jeffrey S. Banks and Eric Alan Hanushek (eds.), *Modern Political Economy: Old Topics, New Directions* (Cambridge University Press 1995).

    'Independent Judges, Dependent Judiciary: Explaining Judicial Independence' (1999) 72 *Southern California Law Review* 353.

    'Accountability in a Global Context' IILJ Working Paper 5/2007 (available at: www.iilj.org/publications/2007-5Ferejohn.asp).

John Ferejohn and Larry Kramer, 'Independent Judges, Dependent Judiciary: Institutionalizing Judicial Restraint' (2002) 77 *New York University Law Review* 962.

Owen Fiss, 'The Right Degree of Independence' in Irwin P. Stotzky (ed.), *Transition to Democracy in Latin America: The Role of the Judiciary* (Westview Press 1993).

Zoltán Fleck, 'Judicial Independence and its Environment in Hungary' in Jiří Přibáň, et al. (eds.), *Systems of Justice in Transition: Central European Experiences since 1989* (Ashgate Publishing 2003).

'Judicial Independence in Hungary' in Anja Seibert-Fohr (ed.), *Judicial Independence in Transition* (Springer 2012).

Stanislaw Frankowski, 'The Procuracy and the Regular Courts as the Palladium of Individual Rights and Liberties – the Case of Poland' (1987) 61 *Tulane Law Review* 1307.

'The Independence of the Judiciary in Poland: Reflections on Andrzej Rzeplinski's Sadownictwo w Polsce Ludowej (The Judiciary in Peoples' Poland) (1989)' (1991) 8 *Arizona Journal of International & Comparative Law* 33.

Barry Friedman, *The Will of the People: How Public Opinion Has Influenced the Supreme Court and Shaped the Meaning of the Constitution* (Farrar, Straus and Giroux, 2009).

Benjamin Frommer, *National Cleansing: Retribution against Nazi Collaborators in Postwar Czechoslovakia* (CUP, 2005).

Walter B. Gallie, 'Essentially Contested Concepts' in Max Black (ed.), *The Importance of Language* (Prentice-Hall 1962), 121–146.

Denis Galligan, 'Principal Institutions and Mechanisms of Judicial Accountability' in Rudolf V. Van Puymbroeck (ed.), *Comprehensive Legal and Judicial Development: Towards an Agenda for a Just and Equitable Society in the 21st Century* (World Bank Publications 2001).

Antoine Garapon (ed.), *Les juges: un pouvoir irresponsible?* (Nicolas Philippe, 2003).

Antoine Garapon, 'Une Justice 'Comptable' de ses Decisions?' in Guy Canivet, Mads Andenas, and Duncan Fairgrieve (eds.), *Independence, Accountability, and the Judiciary* (British Institute of International and Comparative Law 2006).

Antoine Garapon and Harold Epineuse, 'Judicial Independence in France' in Anja Seibert-Fohr (ed.), *Judicial Independence in Transition* (Springer 2012) 273–305.

Antoine Garapon and Ioannis Papadopoulos, *Juger en Amérique et en France: Culture juridique francaise et common law* (Odile Jacob 2003).

Charles Gardner Geyh, 'Informal Methods of Judicial Discipline' (1993–1994) 142 *University of Pennsylvania Law Review* 243.

'Rescuing Judicial Accountability from the Realm of Political Rhetoric' (2006) 56 *Case Western Reserve Law Review* 911.

John Gardner, 'Some Types of Law' in Douglas E. Edlin (ed.), *Common Law Theory* (CUP 2007).

Lech Garlicki, 'Politics and Political Independence of the Judiciary' in András Sajó and L. R. Bentch (eds.), *Judicial Integrity* (Brill Academic Publishers 2004).

Nuno Garoupa and Tom Ginsburg, 'Guarding the Guardians: Judicial Councils and Judicial Independence' (2009) 57 *American Journal of Comparative Law* 103.

'The Comparative Law and Economics of Judicial Councils' (2009) 27 *Berkeley Journal of International Law* 53.

'Hybrid Judicial Career Structures: Reputation Versus Legal Tradition' (2011) 3 *Journal of Legal Analysis* 411.

Nuno Garoupa and Maria Maldonado, 'The Judiciary in Political Transitions: The Critical Role of U.S. Constitutionalism in Latin America' (2011) 19 *Cardozo Journal of International and Comparative Law* 593.

Nicholas Georgakopoulos, 'Independence in the Career and Recognition Judiciary' (2000) 7 *University of Chicago Law School Roundtable* 205.

James Gibson, 'Judicial Institutions' in R. A. W. Rhodes and others (eds.), *The Oxford Handbook of Political Institutions* (USA, OUP 2006).

Ruth Bader Ginsburg, 'Remarks on Writing Separately' (1990) 65 *Washington Law Review* 133.

Tom Ginsburg, 'Comparative Administrative Procedure: Evidence from Northeast Asia' (2002) 13 *Constitutional Political Economy* 247.

Judicial Review in New Democracies: Constitutional Courts in Asian Cases (CUP, 2003).

'Pitfalls of Measuring the Rule of Law' (2011) 3 *Hague Journal on the Rule of Law* 269.

'Courts and New Democracies: Recent Works' (2012) 37 *Law & Social Inquiry* 720.

Siri Gloppen and others, *Courts and Power in Latin America and Africa* (Palgrave Macmillan, 2010).

Wendell L. Griffen, 'Judicial Accountability and Discipline' (1998) 61 *Law and Contemporary Problems* 75.

Carlo Guarnieri and Patrizia Pederzoli, *The Power of Judges: A Comparative Study of Courts and Democracy* (OUP, 2002).

Carlo Guarnieri, 'Appointment and Career of Judges in Continental Europe: The Rise of Judicial Self- Government' (2004) 24 *Legal Studies* 169.

Judicial Independence in Europe: Threat or Resource for Democracy? (2013) 49 *Representation* 347.

John O. Haley, 'The Japanese Judiciary: Maintaining Integrity, Autonomy, and the Public Trust in Law' in Daniel H. Foote (ed.), *Law in Japan: A Turning Point* (University of Washington Press 2008).

Linn A. Hammergren, 'Do Judicial Councils Further Judicial Reform? Lessons from Latin America Carnegie Endowment Rule of Law Series' Working Paper No. 28, 2002.

Sean Hanley, 'Dynamics of New Party Formation in the Czech Republic 1996–2010: Looking for the Origins of a "Political Earthquake" (2012) 28 *East European Politics* 119.

Tim Haughton, 'Exit Choice and Legacy: Explaining the Patterns of Party Politics in Post-communist Slovakia' (2014) 30 *East European Politics* 210.

John Hazard, *Communists and Their Law* (University of Chicago Press, 1969).

Xin He, 'Black Hole of Responsibility: The Adjudication Committee's Role in a Chinese Court' (2012) 46 *Law & Society Review* 681.

'Judicial Innovation and Local Politics: Judicialization of Administrative Governance in East China' (2013) 69 *China Journal* 1.

M. Todd Henderson, 'From Seriatim to Consensus and Back Again: A Theory of Dissent' (2007) *Supreme Court Review* 283.

Kathryn Hendley, '"Telephone Law" and the "Rule of Law": The Russian Case' (2009) 1 *Hague Journal on the Rule of Law* 241.

Richard S. Higgins and Paul H. Rubin, 'Judicial Discretion' (1980) 9 *Journal of Legal Studies* 129.

Lisa Hilbink, *Judges beyond Politics in Democracy and Dictatorship: Lessons from Chile* (CUP, 2007).

'Agents of Anti-Politics: Courts in Pinochet's Chile' in Tom Ginsburg and Tamir Moustafa (eds.), *Rule by Law: The Politics of Courts in Authoritarian Regimes* (CUP 2008).

Kathrin Hille, 'Putin tightens grip on legal systém' *Financial Times* (London, November 27, 2013).

Ran Hirschl, *Towards Juristocracy: The Origins and Consequences of the New Constitutionalism* (Harvard University Press, 2004).

'The Question of Case Selection in Comparative Constitutional Law' (2005) 53 *American Journal of Comparative Law* 125.

'The Judicialization of Mega-Politics and the Rise of Political Courts' (2008) 11 *Annual Review of Political Science* 93.

Stephen Holmes, 'Judicial Independence as Ambiguous Reality and Insidious Illusion' in Ronald Dworkin (ed.), *From Liberal Values to Democratic Transition: Essays in Honor of János Kis* (Central European University Press 2004).

Nadejda Hriptievschi and Sorin Hanganu, 'Judicial Independence in Moldova', in Anja Seibert-Fohr (ed.), *Judicial Independence in Transition* (Springer 2012), 1119–1196.

Luc Huybrechts, 'A Commentary Lasser's Analysis from the Belgian Court of Cassation's Perspective' in Nick Huls and others (eds.), *The Legitimacy of Highest Courts' Rulings: Judicial Deliberations and Beyond* (T.M.C. Asser Press 2009).

Bogdan Iancu, 'Constitutionalism in Perpetual Transition: The Case of Romania' in Bogdan Iancu (ed.), *The Law/Politics Distinction in Contemporary Public Law Adjudication* (Eleven International Publishing 2009).

Abby Innes, *Czechoslovakia: The Short Goodbye* (Yale University Press, 2001).

Vicki C. Jackson, 'Judicial Independence: Structure, Content, Attitude' in Anja Seibert-Fohr (ed.), *Judicial Independence in Transition* (Springer 2012) 19–86.

John A. Jolowicz (ed.), *Public Interest Parties and the Active Role of the Judge in Civil Litigation* (Milano, Giuffrè 1974).

Joseph P. Kalt and Mark A. Zupan, 'Capture and Ideology in the Economic Theory of Politics' (1984) 74 *American Economic Review* 279.

Pamela Karlan, 'Electing Judges, Judging Elections, and the Lessons of Caperton' (2009) 123 *Harvard Law Review* 80.

John P. Kelsh, 'The Opinion Practices of the United States Supreme Court 1790–1945' (1999) 77 *Washington University Law Quarterly* 137.

Herbert Kitschelt, Zdenka Mansfeldova, Radoslav Markowski, and Gabor Tóka, *Post-Communist Party Systems: Competition, Representation, and Inter-Party Cooperation* (CUP, 1999).

Ivan Klíma, *Judge on Trial* (Knopf, 1993).

Dimitry Kochenov, *EU Enlargement and the Failure of Conditionality* (Kluwer, 2008).

Jana Kolomazníková and Luděk Navara, 'Pravým důvodem odvolání soudců je zřejmě jejich minulost', IDnes.cz, March 17, 1999.

Jan Komárek, 'Judicial Lawmaking and Precedent in Supreme Courts: The European Court of Justice Compared to the US Supreme Court and the French Cour de Cassation' (2008–2009) 11 *Cambridge Yearbook of European Legal Studies* 399.

'Questioning Judicial Deliberations' (2009) 29 *Oxford Journal of Legal Studies* 805.

'When Umpires Strike Back: Some Distinctions between (Judicial) Lawmaking and Legislation' in LAWTE (eds.), *Liber Amicorum Tom Eijsbouts* (Asser Press 2011).

'Institutional Dimension of Constitutional Pluralism' in Matej Avbelj and Jan Komárek (eds.), *Constitutional Pluralism in the European Union and Beyond 231* (Hart Publishing 2012).

'Reasoning with Previous Decisions: Beyond the Doctrine of Precedent' (2013) 61 *American Journal of Comparative Law* 149.

Donald P. Kommers, *The Constitutional Jurisprudence of the Federal Republic of Germany* (2nd ed., Duke University Press, 1997).

'Autonomy versus Accountability: The German Judiciary' in Peter H. Russell and David M. O'Brien (eds.), *Judicial Independence in the Age of Democracy: Critical Perspectives from around the World* (University of Virginia Press 2001).

Lewis Kornhauser, 'Is Judicial Independence a Useful Concept?' in Stephen B. Burbank and Barry Friedman (eds.), *Judicial Independence at the Crossroads: An Interdisciplinary Approach* (SAGE Publications 2002).

David Kosař, 'Lustration and Lapse of Time: Dealing with the Past in the Czech Republic' (2008) 4 *European Constitutional Law Review* 460.

'Conflicts between Fundamental Rights in the Jurisprudence of the Czech Constitutional Court' in Eva Brems (ed.), *Conflicts Between Fundamental Rights* (Intersentia 2008).

'Transitional Justice and Judicial Accountability: Lessons from the Czech Republic and Slovakia' (2010) (unpublished manuscript, available at: http://ssrn.com/abstract=1689260).

'The Least Accountable Branch' (Review Essay) (2013) 11 *International Journal of Constitutional Law* 234.

'Rozvrh práce: opomíjený předpoklad soudcovské nezávislosti a klíčový nástroj pro boj s korupcí soudců' [Case Assignment: The Overlooked Precondition of Judicial Independence and the Tool Against Judicial Corruption], (2014) 153 *Právník* 1049.

Daniel Ryan Koslosky, 'Toward an Interpretive Model of Judicial Independence: A Case Study of Eastern Europe' (2009) 31 *University of Pennsylvania Journal of International Law* 203.

Ľuboš Kostelanský and Vanda Vavrová, *Harabinovi sudcovia zarobili viac ako premiér*, Pravda, August 12, 2010.

Eva Kovačechová and Peter Wilfling (eds.), *Presvedčivosť a transparentnosť rozhodovania súdov*, VIA IURIS, 2012.

Eva Kovačechová and Zuzana Čaputová (eds.), *Vybrané aspekty disciplinárního súdnictva*, VIA IURIS, 2012.

Alex Kozinski, 'The Many Faces of Judicial Independence' (1998) 14 *Georgia State University Law Review* 861.

Anthony T. Kronman, *Max Weber* (Stanford University Press, 1983).

Pavol Kubík, *Bez podateľne: Štefan Harabin sa už pre zákony netrápi*, TREND, March 10, 2010 (available at: www.etrend.sk/trend-archiv/rok-2010/cislo-10/bez-podatelne.html).

Keď losuje Štefan Harabin: Na Najvyššom súde majú rozhodnutia predsedu občas väčšiu váhu ako paragrafy, TREND, March 11, 2010 (available at: http://ekonomika.etrend.sk/ekonomika-slovensko/ked-losuje-stefan-harabin-2.html).

Najvyšší reaguje: Sedem trestných sudcov tvrdí, že spisy dostávajú "neexistujúce senáty", TREND, March 17, 2010 (available at: www.etrend.sk/trend-archiv/rok-2010/cislo-11/najvyssi-reaguje.html).

Pavol Kubík and František Múčka, Ako úraduje Štefan I. Čistič: Pôsobenie nového šéfa Najvyššieho súdu SR varuje pred rozširovaním jeho kompetencií, TREND, September 30, 2009 (available at: http://ekonomika.etrend.sk/ekonomika-slovensko/ako-uraduje-stefan-i-cistic-2.html).

Zdeněk Kühn, 'Worlds Apart: Western and Central European Judicial Culture at the Onset of the European Enlargement' (2004) 52 *American Journal of Comparative Law* 531.

'The Authoritarian Legal Culture at Work: The Passivity of Parties and the Interpretational Statements of Supreme Courts' (2006) 2 *Croatian Yearbook of European Law and Policy* 19.

'Historický a komparativní kontext domácí diskuse o postavení soudní moci' in Jan Kysela (ed.), *Hledání optimálního modelu správy soudnictví pro Českou republiku* (Kancelář Senátu 2008).

'The Democratization and Modernization of Post-Communist Judiciaries' in Alberto Febbrajo and Wojciech Sadurski (eds.), *Central and Eastern Europe After Transition* (Ashgate 2010).

The Judiciary in Central and Eastern Europe: Mechanical Jurisprudence in Transformation? (Brill, 2011).

'Judicial Administration Reforms in Central-Eastern Europe: Lessons to be Learned' in Anja Seibert-Fohr (ed.), *Judicial Independence in Transition* (Springer 2012).

Zdeněk Kühn and Hynek Baňouch, 'O publikaci a citaci judikatury aneb proč je někdy judikatura jako císařovy nové šaty' (2005) 13 *Právní rozhledy* 484.

Martina Künnecke, 'The Accountability and Independence of Judges: German Perspectives' in Guy Canivet, Mads Andenas, and Duncan Fairgrieve (eds.), *Independence, Accountability, and the Judiciary* (British Institute of International and Comparative Law 2006).

Tradition and Change in Administrative Law an Anglo-German Comparison (Springer, 2007).

Dimitrios Kyritsis, 'Representation and Waldron's Objection to Judicial Review' (2006) 26 *Oxford Journal of Legal Studies* 733.

Jan Kysela (ed.), *Hledání optimálního modelu správy soudnictví pro Českou republiku* (Kancelář Senátu 2008).

Mark Landler, 'German Judge Cites Koran, Stirring Up Cultural Storm' *New York Times* (New York, March 23, 2007).

Philip M. Langbroek and Marco Fabri, *The Right Judge for Each Case: A Study of Case Assignment and Impartiality in Six European Judiciaries* (Intersentia, 2007).

Vera Lange, 'Public Interest in Civil Law, Socialist Law, and Common Law Systems: The Role of the Public Prosecutor' (1988) 36 *American Journal of Comparative Law* 279.

Carl Larenz and Claus-Wilhelm Canaris, *Methodenlehre der Rechtswissenschaft* (3rd ed., Springer 1995).

Christopher M. Larkins, 'Judicial Independence and Democratization: A Theoretical and Conceptual Analysis' (1996) 44 *The American Journal of Comparative Law* 612.

Mitchel de S. O. L'E Lasser, *Judicial Deliberations: A Comparative Analysis of Judicial Transparency and Legitimacy* (OUP, 2004).

Bruno Latour, *The Making of Law: An Ethnography of the Conseil d'État* (Polity, 2010), available also in French (*La Fabrique de Droit: Une ethnographie du Conseil d'État* (2002)).

David Law, 'The Anatomy of a Conservative Court: Judicial Review in Japan' (2009) 87 *Texas Law Review* 1545.

'How to Rig the Federal Courts' (2011) 99 *Georgetown Law Journal* 779.

'Judicial Independence' in Bertrand Badie and others (eds.), *The International Encyclopedia of Political Science* Vol. 5 (SAGE 2011).

Andrew Le Sueur, 'Developing Mechanisms for Judicial Accountability' in Guy Canivet, Mads Andenas, and Duncan Fairgrieve (eds.), *Independence, Accountability, and the Judiciary* (British Institute of International and Comparative Law 2006).

Alena Ledeneva, 'From Russia with Blat: Can Informal Networks Help Modernize Russia?' (2009) 76 *Social Research* 257.

Philippe Lemaire, 'Le Contrôle Fonctionnel de Gestion (1)' in Guy Canivet, Mads Andenas, and Duncan Fairgrieve (eds.), *Independence, Accountability, and the Judiciary* (British Institute of International and Comparative Law 2006).

Michael E. Levine, 'Regulation, the Market, and Interest Group Cohesion: Why Airlines Were Not Reregulated' in Marc K. Landy, Martin A. Levin, and Martin Shapiro (eds.), *Creating Competitive Markets: The Politics of Regulatory Reform* (Brookings 2007).

Stephen Ross Levitt, 'The Life and Times of a Local Court Judge in Berlin' (2009) 10 *German Law Journal* 169.

Ling Li, 'The "Production" of Corruption in China's Courts: Judicial Politics and Decision Making in a One-Party State' (2012) 37 *Law & Social Inquiry* 848.

William Li and others, 'Using Algorithmic Attribution Techniques to Determine Authorship in Unsigned Judicial Opinions' (2013) 16 *Stanford Technology Law Review* 503.

Tomáš Lichovník, the President of the Judicial Union, expressed this opinion on a nationwide TV channel; see 'Ministerstvo vydalo seznam soudců z KSČ, čtyři jména poté vyškrtlo' (*Česká televize*, January 7, 2011) (available at: www.ceskatelevize.cz:8001/ct24/domaci/111953-ministerstvo-vydalo-seznam-soudcu-z-ksc-ctyri-jmena-pote-vyskrtlo/).

Timo Ligi, 'Judicial Independence in Estonia' in Anja Seibert-Fohr (ed.), *Judicial Independence in Transition* (Springer 2012) 739–791.

Milan Lipovský, 'Sťažnosť pre porušenie zákona a konanie o nej – niekoľko poznámok' (2004) 56 *Justičná revue* 671.

Marc A. Loth, 'Courts in Quest for Legitimacy: A Comparative Approach' in Marijke Malsch and Niels van Manen (eds.), *De begrijpelijkheid van de rechtspraak* (Boom Juridische Uitgevers 2007).

Arthur Lupia and Matthew D. McCubbins, *The Democratic Dilemma: Can Citizens Learn What They Need to Know?* (Cambridge University Press, 1997).

Jonathan Lynn, 'Czech Republic Called Potential Economic Tiger' *Journal of Commerce* (September 2, 1993).

Geert W. Mackenroth and H. Teetzmann, 'Selbstverwaltung der Justiz: Markenzeichen zukunftsfähiger Rechtsstaaten' (2002) *Zeitschrift für Rechtspolitik* 337.

Elaine Mak, 'The European Judicial Organisation in a New Paradigm: The Influence of Principles of "New Public Management" on the Organisation of the European Courts' (2008) 14 *European Law Journal* 718.

Philippe Malaurie and Patrick Morvan, *Droit civil: introduction générale* (2nd ed., Defrénois, 2005).

Kate Malleson and Peter H. Russell (eds.), *Appointing Judges in an Age of Judicial Power: Critical Perspectives from around the World* (University of Toronto Press, 2006).

Lord Mance, 'External Institutional Control over Judges' in Guy Canivet, Mads Andenas, and Duncan Fairgrieve (eds.), *Independence, Accountability, and the Judiciary* (British Institute of International and Comparative Law 2006).

James Markham, 'Against Individually Signed Judicial Opinions' (2006) 56 *Duke Law Journal* 923, 930 (quoting Letter from President Thomas Jefferson to Justice William Johnson (October 27, 1820)).

Inga Markovits, 'Children of a Lesser God: GDR Lawyers in Post-Socialist Germany' (1996) 94 *Michigan Law Review*.

Justice in Lüritz (Princeton University Press, 2010).

Jerry Mashaw, 'Accountability and Institutional Design: Some Thoughts on the Grammar of Governance' in Michael W. Dowdle (ed.), *Public Accountability: Designs, Dilemmas and Experiences* (CUP 2006).

Jean Massot and Thierry Girardot, Le Conseil d'État (1999).

A. James McAdams, 'Transitional Justice: The Issue that Won't Go Away' (2011) 5 *International Journal of Transitional Justice* 304.

Matthew D. McCubbins and Thomas Schwartz, 'Congressional Oversight Overlooked: Police Patrols Versus Fire Alarms' (1984) 28 *American Journal of Political Science* 165.

Matthew D. McCubbins, Roger G. Noll, and Barry R. Weingast, 'Administrative Procedures as Instruments of Political Control' (1987) 3 *Journal of Law, Economics, and Organization* 243.

'Structure and Process, Politics and Policy: Administrative Arrangements and the Political Control of Agencies' (1989) 75 *Virginia Law Review* 431.

Matthew D. McCubbins, Roger G. Noll, and Barry R. Weingast, 'Political Control of the Bureaucracy' in Peter Newman (ed.), *The New Palgrave Dictionary of Law and Economics* (Palgrave Macmillan 1998).

Martin Mendelski and Alexander Libman, History Matters, but How? An Example of Ottoman and Habsburg Legacies and Judicial Performance in Romania, Frankfurt School Working Paper No. 175 (September 30, 2011).

John Henry Merryman and Rogelio Perez-Perdomo. *The Civil Law Tradition? An Introduction to the Legal Systems of Europe and Latin America* (3rd ed., Stanford University Press, 2007).

Eva Mihočková, Šikanovanie v talári, Plus 7 dní, December 12, 2011 (available at: www.pluska.sk/plus7dni/vsimli-sme-si/sikanovanie-vtalari.html).

Raphael Minder, 'Spain's Chief Justice Quits over Claims of Misusing Public Money' *The New York Times* (New York, June 21, 2012).

Charles de Secondat Montesquieu, *The Spirit of the Laws*, Vol. 11 (first published 1748, CUP, 1989).

Glenn G. Morgan, *Soviet Administrative Legality: The Role of Attorney General's Office* (Stanford University Press, 1962).

Otakar Motejl, 'Soudnictví a jeho správa' in Michal Bobek, et al. (eds.), *Komunistické právo v Československu* (MUNI Press 2009).

Richard Mulgan, *Holding Power to Account: Accountability in Modern Democracies* (Palgrave Macmillan, 2003).

Lydia F. Müller, 'Judicial Independence as a Council of Europe Standard' (2009) 52 *German Yearbook of International Law* 461.

'Judicial Administration in Transitional Eastern Countries' in Anja Seibert-Fohr (ed.), *Judicial Independence in Transition* (Springer 2012) 937–969.

Nadya Nedelsky, 'The Wartime Slovak State: A Case Study in the Relationship between Ethnic Nationalism and Authoritarian Patterns of Governance' (2001) 7 *Nations and Nationalism* 215.

'Divergent Responses to a Common Past: Transitional Justice in the Czech Republic and Slovakia' (2004) 33 *Theory and Society* 65.

'Czechoslovakia, and the Czech and Slovak Republics' in Lavinia Stan (ed.), *Transitional Justice in Eastern Europe and the former Soviet Union: Reckoning with the communist past* (Routledge 2008)

Lorne Neudorf, 'Promoting Independent Justice in a Changing World' (2012) 12 *Human Rights Law Review* 107.

Gar Yein Ng, *Quality of Judicial Organisation and Checks and Balances* (Intersentia, 2007).

Philippe Nonet and Philip Selznick, *Law & Society in Transition: Toward Responsive Law* (Transaction Publishers, 2001).

Angelika Nußberger, 'Judicial Reforms in Post-Soviet Countries – Good Intentions with Flawed Results?' in Anja Seibert-Fohr (ed.), *Judicial Independence in Transition* (Springer 2012).

David M. O'Brien and Yasuo Ohkoshi, 'Stifling Judicial Independence from Within: The Japanese Judiciary' in Peter H. Russell and David M. O'Brien (eds.), *Judicial Independence in the Age of Democracy: Critical Perspectives from around the World* (University of Virginia Press 2001).

Morris S. Ogul and Bert A. Rockman, 'Overseeing Oversight: New Departures and Old Problems' (1990) 15 *Legislative Studies Quarterly* 5.

Christopher Osakwe, 'Gordon B. Smith, The Soviet Procuracy and the Supervision of Administration (Book Review)' (1980) 28 *American Journal of Comparative Law* 700.

Andrea Orzoff, *Battle for the Castle: The Myth of Czechoslovakia in Europe, 1914–1948* (OUP, 2009).

Hans-Jürgen Papier, 'Zur Selbstverwaltung der Dritten Gewalt' (2002) *Neue Juristische Wochenschrift* 2585.

Cristina Parau, 'Piana, Daniela (2010) Judicial Accountabilities in New Europe: From Rule of Law to Quality of Justice (Book Review)' (2011) 45 *Law & Society Review* 791.

'The Drive for Judicial Supremacy' in Anja Seibert-Fohr (ed.), *Judicial Independence in Transition* (Springer 2012).

'The Dormancy of Parliaments: The Invisible Cause of Judiciary Empowerment in Central and Eastern Europe' (2013) 49 *Representation – Journal of Representative Democracy* 267.

'Explaining judiciary governance in Central and Eastern Europe: External Incentives, Transnational Elites and Parliament Inaction' (2015) 67 *Europe-Asia Studies* 409.

William Partlett, 'Judicial Backsliding in Russia', JURIST – Academic Commentary, September 30, 2014 (available at: http://jurist.org/academic/2014/09/william-partlett-russia-reform).

Alan Paterson, 'The Scottish Judicial Appointments Board: New Wine in Old Bottles?' in Kate Malleson and Peter H. Russell (eds.), *Appointing Judges in an Age of Judicial Power: Critical Perspectives from around the World* (University of Toronto Press 2006).

Lawyers and the Public Good: Democracy in Action? (CUP, 2011).

Randall Peerenboom (ed.), *Judicial Independence in China: Lessons for Global Rule of Law Promotion* (CUP, 2009).

Rogelio Pérez-Perdomo, 'Independence and Accountability' in Rudolf V. Van Puymbroeck (ed.), *Comprehensive Legal and Judicial Development: Towards an Agenda for a Just and Equitable Society in the 21st Century* (World Bank Publications 2001).

Vlad Perju, 'Reason and Authority in the European Court of Justice' (2009) 49 *Virginia Journal of International Law* 307.

Mark Philp, 'Delimiting Democratic Accountability' (2009) 57 *Political Studies* 28.

Daniela Piana, 'The Power Knocks at the Courts' Back Door – Two Waves of Postcommunist Judicial Reforms' (2009) 42 *Comparative Political Studies* 816.

Judicial Accountabilities in New Europe: From Rule of Law to Quality of Justice (Ashgate, 2010).

Daniela Piana and Antoine Vauchez, *Il Consiglio superiore della magistratura* (Il Mulino 2012).

Nicola Picardi, 'La Ministère de la Justice et les autres modèles d'administration de la justice en Europe' in Giovanni E. Longo (ed.), *L'indipendenza della giustizia, oggi* (Judicial independence today: liber amicorum in onore di Giovanni E. Longo 1999).

Hanna Fenichel Pitkin, *The Concept of Representation* (University of California Press, 1967).

Zuzana Piussi, 'Nemoc tretej moci' [The Disease of the Third Branch], 2011, [Slovakia, 52 min.]

Béla Pokol, 'Judicial Power and Democratization in Eastern Europe' in Proceedings of the Conference Europeanisation and Democratisation: The Southern European Experience and the Perspective for the New Member States of the Enlarged Europe (2005).

Delia Popescu, *Political Action in Václav Havel's Thought: The Responsibility of Resistance* (Lexington Books, 2011).

Maria Popova, 'Political Competition as an Obstacle to Judicial Independence: Evidence from Russia and Ukraine' (2010) 43 *Comparative Political Studies* 1202.

'Be Careful What You Wish For: A Cautionary Tale of Post-Communist Judicial Empowerment' (2010) 18 *Demokratizatsiya* 56.

Politicized Justice in Emerging Democracies: A Study of Courts in Russia and Ukraine (CUP 2012).

'Why the Bulgarian Judiciary Does Not Prosecute Corruption?' (2012) 59 *Problems of Post Communism* 35.

Eric A. Posner, 'Agency Models in Law and Economics' in Eric A. Posner (ed.), *Chicago Lectures in Law and Economics* (Foundation Press 2000).

Richard A. Posner, 'What Do Judges and Justices Maximize? (The Same Thing Everybody Else Does)' (1993) 3 *Supreme Court Economic Review* 1.

The Federal Courts: Challenge and Reform (Harvard University Press, 1999).

How Judges Think (Harvard University Press, 2008).

Mariana Mota Prado, 'The Paradox of Rule of Law Reforms: How Early Reforms Can Create Obstacles to Future Ones' (2010) 60 *University of Toronto Law Journal* 555.

Mariana Prado and Michael Trebilcock, 'Path Dependence, Development, and the Dynamics of Institutional Reform' (2009) 47 *University of Toronto Law Journal* 341.

Radoslav Procházka, *Mission Accomplished: On Founding Constitutional Adjudication in Central Europe* (CEU Press, 2002).

Attila Rácz, *Courts and Tribunals: A Comparative Study* (Akadémia Kiadó, 1980).

J. Mark Ramseyer, 'The Puzzling (In)Dependence of Courts: A Comparative Approach' (1994) 23 *The Journal of Legal Studies* 721.

J. Mark Ramseyer and Frances McCall Rosenbluth, *Japan's Political Marketplace* (rev. ed., Harvard University Press, 1997).

J. Mark Ramseyer and Eric Rasmusen, *Measuring Judicial Independence: The Political Economy of Judging in Japan* (University of Chicago Press, 2003).

John Rawls, *Political Liberalism* (Columbia University Press, 1993).

Laura Krugman Ray, 'The Road to Bush v. Gore: The History of The Supreme Court's Use of the Per Curiam Opinion' (2000) 79 *Nebraska Law Review* 517.

Philippe Raynaud, 'La loi et la jurisprudence, des lumières à la révolution française' (1985) 30 Archives de philosophie du droit 61.

Robert Reed, 'Le contrôle informel: L'institution judiciaire, les juges et la societé (1)' [Informal Control: The Judiciary, Judges and Society (1)], in Guy Canivet, Mads Andenas, and Duncan Fairgrieve (eds.), *Independence, Accountability, and the Judiciary* (British Institute of International and Comparative Law 2006).

Thierry S. Renoux (ed.), *Les Conseils superieurs de la magistrature en Europe* (La documentation francaise 1999).

Thierry Renoux, 'Juges et magistrats' in Thierry Renoux (ed.), *La Justice en France* (La documentation française 2013).

Johannes Riedel, 'Recruitment, Professional Evaluation and Career of Judges and Prosecutors in Germany' in Giuseppe Di Federico (ed.), *Recruitment, Professional Evaluation and Career of Judges and Prosecutors in Europe* (IRSIG-CNR 2005) 69–126.

K. Roach, 'Dialogue or Defiance: Legislative Reversals of Supreme Court Decisions in Canada and the United States' (2006) 4 *International Journal of Constitutional Law* 347.

Ira P. Robbins, 'Hiding behind the Cloak of Invisibility: The Supreme Court and Per Curiam Opinions' (2012) 86 *Tulane Law Review* 1197.

Pavol Rohárik, 'The Judiciary and Its Transition in Slovakia after 1989', in Jiří Přibáň, Pauline Roberts, and James Young (eds.), *Systems of Justice in Transition: Central European Experiences since 1989* (Ashgate 2003).

Barbara S. Romzek, 'Enhancing Accountability' in James L. Perry (ed.), *Handbook of Public Administration*. (2nd ed., Jossey Bass 1996).

Peter H Russell and David O'Brien (eds.), *Judicial Independence in the Age of Democracy: Critical Perspectives from around the World* (University of Virginia Press, 2001).

Pavel Rychetský, 'Pohled ministrů spravedlnosti' in Jan Kysela (ed.) *Hledání optimálního modelu správy soudnictví pro Českou republiku* (Kancelář Senátu 2008) 20–24.

Wojciech Sadurski, *Rights before Courts: A Study of Constitutional Courts in Postcommunist States of Central and Eastern Europe* (Springer, 2005).

Charlie Savage, 'A Judge's View of Judging Is on the Record' *The New York Times* (New York, May 15, 2009).

Andreas Schedler, 'Conceptualizing Accountability' in Andreas Schedler and others (eds.), *The Self-Restraining State: Power and Accountability in New Democracies* (Lynne Rienner Publishers 1999) 13.

Andreas Schedler and others (eds.), *The Self-Restraining State: Power and Accountability in New Democracies* (Lynne Rienner Publishers, 1999).

Kim Lane Scheppele, 'Declarations of Independence: Judicial Responses to Political Pressure' in Stephen B. Burbank and Barry Friedman (eds.), *Judicial Independence at the Crossroads: An Interdisciplinary Approach* (SAGE Publications 2002).

Karel Schönfeld, 'Rex, Lex et Judex: Montesquieu and la bouche de la loi Revisited' (2008) 4 *European Constitutional Law Review* 274.

Herman Schwartz, *The Struggle for Constitutional Justice in Post-Communist Europe* (University of Chicago Press, 2000).

Olga Schwartz and Elga Sykiainen, 'Judicial Independence in the Russian Federation' in Anja Seibert-Fohr (ed.), *Judicial Independence in Transition* (Springer 2012) 971–1064.

Stephen Sedley in Foreword to Michael Addo (ed.), *Freedom of Expression and the Criticism of Judges: A Comparative Study of European Legal Standards* (Ashgate 2000).

Jeffrey A. Segal and Harold J. Spaeth, *The Supreme Court and the Attitudinal Model Revisited* (CUP 2002).

Anja Seibert-Fohr, 'Constitutional Guarantees of Judicial Independence in Germany' in Eibe H. Riedel and Rüdiger Wolfrum (eds.), *Recent Trends in German and European Constitutional Law* (Springer 2006) 267–288.

'Judicial Independence in European Union Accessions: The Emergence of a European Basic Principle' (2009) 52 *German Yearbook of International Law* 405.

'European Perspective on the Rule of Law and Independent Courts' (2012) 20 *Journal für Rechtspolitik* 337.

Anja Seibert-Fohr (ed.), *Judicial Independence in Transition* (Springer 2012).

Anja Seibert-Fohr, 'Judicial Independence in Germany' in Anja Seibert-Fohr (ed.), *Judicial Independence in Transition* (Springer 2012) 447–519.

'Judicial Independence – The Normativity of an Evolving Transnational Principle' in Anja Seibert-Fohr (ed.), *Judicial Independence in Transition* (Springer 2012) 1279–1360.

Martin Shapiro, *Courts: A Comparative and Political Analysis* (University of Chicago Press, 1981).

Shimon Shetreet, *Judicial Independence: The Contemporary Debate* (Springer, 1985).

Shimon Shetreet and Christopher Forsyth, *The Culture of Judicial Independence* (Brill, 2011).

Shimon Shetreet and Sophie Turenne, *Judges on Trial: Independence and Accountability of the English Judiciary* (2nd ed., CUP 2013).

M. P. Singh, 'Securing the Independence of the Judiciary: The Indian Experience' (2000) 10 *Indiana International and Comparative Law Review* 245.

Daniel Smilov, 'EU Enlargement and the Constitutional Principle of Judicial Independence' in Wojciech Sadurski, et al. (eds.), *Spreading Democracy and the Rule of Law?: The Impact of EU Enlargement on the Rule of Law, Democracy and Constitutionalism in Post-Communist Legal Orders* (Springer 2006).

Gordon B. Smith, *The Soviet Procuracy and the Supervision of Administration* (Sijthoff & Noordhoff, 1978).

Jonathan Soeharno, *The Integrity of the Judge: A Philosophical Inquiry* (Ashgate, 2009).

Peter H. Solomon, 'Authoritarian Legality and Informal Practices: Judges, Lawyers and the State in Russia and China' (2010) 43 *Communist and Post-Communist Studies* 351.

'The Accountability of Judges in Post Communist States: From Bureaucratic to Professional Accountability' in Anja Seibert-Fohr (ed.), *Judicial Independence in Transition* (Springer 2012) 909–935.

Lawrence Solum, 'Virtue Jurisprudence: A Virtue-Centred Theory of Judging' (2003) 34 *Metaphilosophy* 178.

'A Tournament of Virtue' (2004) 32 *Florida State University Law Review* 1365.

László Sólyom, 'The Separation of Powers Is Integral to the Fabric of Democracy' (2013) 7 *Journal of Parliamentary and Political Law* 159.

Katarína Staroňová, 'Projekt "Súdny manažment" ako protikorupčný nástroj' in Emília Sičáková-Beblavá and Miroslav Beblavý (eds.), *Jedenásť statočných: prípadové štúdie protikorupčných nástrojov na Slovensku* (Transparency International Slovensko 2008).

Vladimír Stibořík, 'Všechno jsem soudil podle svědomí' interview (*Mladá fronta DNES*, March 18, 2010) 2 (attached to Luděk Navara, 'Šéf vrchního soudu rozhodoval v 80. letech v politických procesech' in Vladimír Stibořík, 'Všechno jsem soudil podle svědomí' interview (*Mladá fronta DNES*, March 18, 2010)) (available at: http://zpravy.idnes.cz/ sef-vrchniho-soudu-rozhodoval-v-80-letech-v-politickych-procesech-phs-/ domaci.aspx?c=A100317_215456_domaci_abr).

Bernard Stirn, *Le Conseil d'État: Son rôle, sa jurisprudence* [The Conseil d'État: Its Role and Jurisprudence] (Hachette 1991).

Kaare Strom, 'Delegation and Accountability in Parliamentary Democracies' (2000) 37 *European Journal of Political Research* 261.

Zhu Suli, 'The Party and the Courts' in Randall Peerenboom (ed.), *Judicial Independence in China: Lessons for Global Rule of Law Promotion* (CUP 2009), 52–68.

Cass R. Sunstein, 'Incompletely Theorized Agreements' (1995) 108 *Harvard Law Review* 1733.

Cass R. Sunstein, 'If People Would Be Outraged by Their Rulings, Should Judges Care?' (2007) 60 *Stanford Law Review* 155.

Jeffrey Sutton, 'A Review of Richard A. Posner, How Judges Think (2008)' (2010) 108 *Michigan Law Review* 859.

Ján Svák, 'Slovenská skúsenosť s optimalizáciou modelu správy súdnictva' in Jan Kysela (ed.) *Hledání optimálního modelu správy soudnictví pro Českou republiku* (Kancelář Senátu 2008).

Alec Stone Sweet, *Governing with Judges: Constitutional Politics in Europe* (OUP, 2000).

'Constitutional Courts and Parliamentary Democracy' in Mark Thatcher and Alec Stone Sweet (eds.), *The Politics of Delegation* (Routledge 2003).

Brian Z. Tamanaha, *Beyond the Formalist-Realist Divide: The Role of Politics in Judging* (Princeton University Press, 2010).

G. Alan Tarr, *Without Fear or Favor: Judicial Independence and Judicial Accountability in the States* (Stanford University Press, 2012).

E. W. Thomas, *The Judicial Process: Realism, Pragmatism, Practical Reasoning and Principles* (CUP, 2005).

James Thomas, *Judicial Ethics in Australia* (3rd ed., Reed International Books, 2009).

José J. Toharia, 'Judicial Independence in an Authoritarian Regime: The Case of Contemporary Spain' (1975) 9 *Law & Society Review* 475.

Transparency International, *Global Corruption Report: Corruption in Judicial Systems* (CUP, 2007)

Alexei Trochev, *Judging Russia: Constitutional Court in Russian Politics, 1990–2006* (CUP, 2008).

'Meddling with Justice: Competitive Politics, Impunity, and Distrusted Courts in Post-Orange Ukraine' (2010) 18 *Democratizatsiya* 122.

Aviezer Tucker and others, 'From Republican Virtue to Technology of Political Power: Three Episodes of Czech Nonpolitical Politics' (2000) 115 *Political Science Quarterly* 421.

Otto Ulč, *The Judge in a Communist State. A View from Within* (Ohio University Press, 1972).

Roberto Unger, *What Should Legal Analysis Become* (Verso, 1998).

Frank K. Upham, 'Political Lackeys or Faithful Public Servants: Two Views of the Japanese Judiciary' (2005) 30 *Law & Social Inquiry* 421.

Raul A. Sanchez Urribarri, 'Courts between Democracy and Hybrid Authoritarianism: Evidence from the Venezuelan Supreme Court' (2011) 36 *Law & Social Inquiry* 854.

Hugo Uyterhoeven, *Richterliche Rechtsfindung und Rechtsvergleichung. Eine Vorstudie über die Rechtsvergleichung als Hilfsmittel der richterlichen Rechtsfindung im Privatrecht* (Verlag Stämpfli, 1959).

Alan Uzelac, 'Role and Status of Judges in Croatia' in Paul Oberhammer (ed.), *Richterbild und Rechtsreform in Mitteleuropa* (Manzsche Verlags 2001) 23–65.

'Amendments to the Law on Courts and Law on the State Judicial Council – Elements of the Reform of the Organizational Judicial Legislation' in Goranka Lalič (ed.), *Croation Judiciary: Lessons and Perspectives* (Netherlands Helsinki Committee 2002) 37–69.

'Survival of the Third Legal Tradition?' (2010) 49 *Supreme Cour Law Review* 377.

Georg Vanberg, *The Politics of Constitutional Review in Germany* (CUP 2005).

'Establishing and Maintaining Judicial Independence' in Keith E. Whittington, et al. (eds.), *The Oxford Handbook of Law and Politics* (OUP 2008).

Juan E. Vargas and Mauricio Duce, *Informe sobre independencia judicial en Chile* (Due Process of Law Foundation, 2000).

Alexander Vashkevich, 'Judicial Independence in the Republic of Belarus' in Anja Seibert-Fohr (ed.), *Judicial Independence in Transition* (Springer 2012).

Adrian Vermeule, *Judging under Uncertainty: An Institutional Theory of Legal Interpretation* (Harvard University Press, 2006).

Judicial Mechanisms of Democracy: Institutional Design Writ Small (OUP, 2007).

Adrian Vermeule, 'The Judiciary Is A They, Not An It: Interpretive Theory and the Fallacy Of Division' (2009) 14 *Journal of Contemporary Legal Issues* 549.

Wim Voermans and Pim Albers, '*Councils for the Judiciary in EU Countries*' (Council of Europe, European Commission for the Efficiency of Justice (CEPEJ), Strasbourg 2003).

Stefan Voigt, 'The economic effects of judicial accountability: cross-country evidence' (2008) 25 *European Journal of Law and Economics* 95.

Stefan Voigt and Lars Feld, 'Economic Growth and Judicial Independence: Cross Country Evidence Using a New Set of Indicators' (2003) 19 *European Journal of Political Economy* 497.

'Making Judges Independent – Some Proposals regarding the Judiciary' in Roger D. Congleton and Birgitta Swedenborg (eds.), *Democratic Constitutional Design and Public Policy – Analysis and Evidence* (The MIT Press 2006).

Mary L. Volcansek and others, *Judicial Misconduct: A Cross-National Comparison* (University Press of Florida, 1996).

Jean Voltaire, Adrien Quentin Beuchot, and Pierre Auguste Migerm *Œuvres de Voltaire*, Volume 48 (Paris: Lefèvre, 1832).

Jaroslav Vorel, *Alena Šimáková a kol. Československá justice v letech 1948–1953 v dokumentech. Díl I.* (Praha, Úřad dokumentace a vyšetřování zločinů komunismu 2003).

Eliška Wagnerová, 'Position of Judges in the Czech Republic' in Jiří Přibáň, Pauline Roberts, and James Young (eds.), *Systems of Justice in Transition: Central European Experiences since 1989* (Ashgate 2003).

Jeremy Waldron, 'Dirty Little Secret' (1998) 98 *Columbia Law Review* 510.

'Is the Rule of Law an Essentially Contested Concept?' (2002) 21 *Law and Philosophy* 137.

Clifford Wallace, 'Comparative Perspectives on the Office of Chief Justice' (2005) 38 *Cornell International Law Journal* 219.

Stephen L. Wasby and others, 'The Per Curiam Opinion: Its Nature and Functions' (1992) 76 *Judicature* 29.

Jean-Francois Weber, 'Conseil supérieur de la magistrature (CSM)' in Thierry Renoux (ed.), *La Justice en France* (La documentation française 2013).

'Éthique, déontologiques et responsabilité des magistrats' in Thierry Renoux (ed.), *La Justice en France* (La documentation française 2013).

Max Weber, *The Methodology of the Social Sciences* (Edward Shils and Henry A. Finch trs., Free Press 1949) 90.

Brent T. White, 'Rotten to the Core: Project Capture and the Failure of Judicial Reform in Mongolia' (2009) 4 *East Asia Law Reform* 209.

Keith Whittington, 'Legislative Sanctions and the Strategic Environment of Judicial Review' (2003) 1 *International Journal of Constitutional Law* 446.

Diana Woodhouse, 'Judicial Independence and Accountability within the United Kingdom's New Constitutional Settlement' in Guy Canivet, Mads Andenas, and Duncan Fairgrieve (eds.), *Independence, Accountability, and the Judiciary* (British Institute of International and Comparative Law 2006).

Günter Woratsch, *Zpráva o stavu slovenské justice – fenomén Štefan Harabin*, Pecs, April 23, 2011.

Hakeem Yusuf, *Transitional Justice, Judicial Accountability and the Rule of Law* (Routledge, 2010).

Pavel Žáček, ' "Sachergate": první lustrační aféra', *Pamět' a dějiny*, No. 01/2007.

Václav Žák, 'Economists or Lawyers: Institutional Foundations of Emerging Democracy: The Czechoslovak example' in Lene Bogh Sorensen and Leslie C. Eliason (eds.), *Fascism, Liberalism, and Social Democracy in Central Europe: Past and Present* (Aarhus University Press 2002).

Markus Zimmer, 'Judicial Independence in Central and East Europe: The Institutional Context' (2006) 14 *Tulsa Journal of Comparative and International Law* 53.

Miscellaneous sources

'Councils for the Judiciary: States without a High Council' *preliminary report* (CCJE 2007) 4, Strasbourg, March 19, 2007.

'In the Shadows: A Look into the Texas Supreme Court's Overuse of Anonymous Opinions' (*Texas Watch*, May 2008) (available at: www.texaswatch.org/wordpress/wp-content/uploads/2009/12/PerCuriamReportFinal.pdf) 1).

'Mezi soudci z KSČ se ocitli neprávem. Zvažují žaloby' (*Lidové noviny*, January 12, 2011).

1998 Accession Progress Report on the Czech Republic.

1999 Accession Progress Report on Slovakia.

2000 Accession Progress Report on Slovakia.

2002 Accession Progress Report on the Czech Republic.

Agenda 2000 – Commission Opinion on the Czech Republic's Application for Membership of the European Union, DOC/97/17 (Brussels, July 15, 1997).

Beschluss 'Selbstverwaltung' der Bundesvertreterversammlung des Deutschen Richterbundes [Motion for Self-Administration by the Assembly of Federal Representatives of the German Association of Judges], adopted on November 15, 2002 in Kiel (summary of the motion published in *Neue Juristiche Wochenschrift* 2002, Heft 42, XXVII–XXXIV).

'Bude ministerka Žitňanská rešpektovať názory Lorda Justice Thomasa?', Dimenzie, No. 10/2010.

CEPEJ, *European judicial systems, Edition 2010 (data 2008): Efficiency and quality of justice* (hereinafter "the 2010 CEPEJ Report").

CEPEJ, *European judicial systems, Edition 2012 (data 2010): Efficiency and quality of justice* (hereinafter "the 2012 CEPEJ Report").

Committee of Ministers, Recommendation No. R (94) 12, October 13, 1994 in: '37 Yearbook of the European Convention on Human Rights' (1994) 453.

Confirmation Hearing on the Nomination of John G. Roberts, Jr. to be Chief Justice of the United States Before the S. Comm. on the Judiciary, 109th Cong. 55 (2005) (statement of John G. Roberts, Jr., Nominee to be Chief Justice of the United States).

Conseil Supérieur de la Magistrature: Recueil des obligations déontologiques des magistrats. Édition 2010, Dalloz-Sirey, 2010

Consultative Council of European Judges (CCJE), Opinion no.10 (2007) to the attention of the Committee of Ministers of the Council of Europe on the Council for the Judiciary at the service of society (Strasbourg, November 21–23, 2007).

Alessia Di Pascale and Pier Luigi di Bari, 'Completed Questionnaire for the project Contention National Report – Italy' (2014) (available at: http://contention.eu/docs/country-reports/ItalyFinal.pdf).

Delenie spisov u Š. Harabina zákon neporušuje, konštatuje Súdna rada: Z kancelárie rady prišla po mesiaci odpoveď na otázky TRENDU, TREND, April 12, 2010 (available at: www.etrend.sk/ekonomika/delenie-spisov-u-harabina-zakon-neporusuje-konstatuje-sudna-rada.html) European Charter on the Statute for Judges [Strasbourg, July 8–10, 1998].

European Charter on the Statute for Judges [Strasbourg, July 8–10, 1998].

Government of Montenegro, *Action Plan: Chapter 23 Judiciary and Fundamental Rights*, June 23, 2013.

Harabin odvolal predsedov súdov, spustil kontroly. Sme.sk, October 4, 2006, (available at: www.sme.sk/c/2929137/harabin-odvolal-predsedov-sudov-spustil-kontroly.html).

Harabin odvolal ďalších sudcov, Topky.sk, October 5, 2006 (available at: www.topky.sk/cl/10/127310/Harabin-odvolal-dalsich-sudcov).

Harabin sudcom napísal, koho bude voliť do Súdnej rady, Pravda.sk, May 24, 2012 (available at: http://spravy.pravda.sk/domace/clanok/174535-harabin-sudcom-napisal-koho-bude-volit-do-sudnej-rady/).

Harabin sudcom napísal, koho sa chystá voliť do súdnej rady, Aktuality.sk, May 24, 2012 (available at: www.aktuality.sk/clanok/207237/harabin-sudcom-napisal-koho-sa-chysta-volit-do-sudnej-rady/).

Judges fired for mismanagement, The Slovak Spectator, August 23, 1999 (available at: http://spectator.sme.sk/articles/view/3914/1/).

Letter from Thomas Jefferson to William Johnson (October 27, 1822).

Lietajuce spisy, TREND, April 28, 2010 (available at: www.etrend.sk/trend-archiv/rok-2010/cislo-17/lietajuce-spisy.html).

Minister spravodlivosti J. Liščák označil sudcov za "smradov" a "frackov blbých ako tágo", Sme.sk, April 16, 1997 (available at: www.sme.sk/c/2071456/minister-spravodlivosti-j-liscak-oznacil-sudcov-za-smradov-a-frackov-blbych-ako-tago.html).

Minister Liščák zavádza a nemá dôveru sudcov, Sme.sk, May 5, 1997 (available at: www.sme.sk/c/2073444/minister-liscak-zavadza-a-nema-doveru-sudcov .html).

Ministerstvo chce opäť posilniť Najvyšší súd a Súdnu radu, *Sme,* May 19, 2010 (available at: www.sme.sk/c/5383676/ministerstvo-chce-opat-posilnit-najvyssi-sud-a-sudnu-radu.html).

Ministerstvo vydalo seznam soudců z KSČ, čtyři jména poté vyškrtlo' (*Česká televize,* January 7, 2011) (available at: www.ceskatelevize.cz:8001/ct24/domaci/ 111953-ministerstvo-vydalo-seznam-soudcu-z-ksc-ctyri-jmena-pote-vyskrtlo/).

Odmeny udelené sudcom Najvyššieho súdu v roku 2002, *Pravda,* December 20, 2002.

Recommendation CM/Rec (2010)12 of the Committee of Ministers to member states on judges: independence, efficiency and responsibilities, adopted by the Committee of Ministers on November 17, 2010.

Report on Civil Liability of Judges, International Association of Judges (IAJ-UIM), Study Commission II, 2003.

Resolution of The European Network of Councils for the Judiciary (ENCJ) on "Self Governance for the Judiciary: Balancing Independence and Accountability" (May 2008).

András Sajó, Courts as Representatives (lecture), November 18, 2012 (available at www.fljs.org).

Symposium Roundtable "An Exchange with Jeremy Waldron" published in *International Journal of Constitutional Law* (Volume 7, Issue 1, 2009).

The European Network of Councils for the Judiciary (ENCJ), Councils for the Judiciary Report 2010–2011.

The Federalist No. 78, 464 (Alexander Hamilton) (Clinton Rossiter ed., 2003).

Transparency International Slovensko (ed.), *Výzvy slovenského súdnictva a možnosti zlepšenia existujúceho stavu* (2010).

Transparency International Slovakia, *Kto je s kým rodina na našich súdoch,* Sme.sk (Bratislava, November 10, 2013).

U některých soudců pochybuji, jestli vůbec znají platné právo' (*Hospodářské noviny,* September 9, 2011.

Un Juez Ante La Justicia [A Judge Before the Court], El Pais (Spec. Issue) (Spain) (available at: www.elpais.com/especial/caso-garzon/).

Wikileaks, cable 08PRAGUE499, CZECH JUSTICE SYSTEM: INCOMPLETE REFORMS.

INDEX

abuse of mechanisms of judicial
    accountability, 76, 92, 95, 295
accession conditionality theory of
    judicial councils, 11
accountability
    behavioral, 39, 50
    broad, 33
    contingent circumstances of, 20, 382
    decisional, 39, 50
    definition, 32–36, 52
    institutional, 51, 52
    legal, 53, 54
    narrow, 34
    political, 51–54
    public, 30
accountability as a concept, 30
accountability as a mechanism, 19
accountability as a virtue, 19, 428–431
accountability gap, 29
accountability nesting problem, 49, 391
accountability perversions. *See* judicial
    accountability perversions
accounting agents. *See* principals
    of judges
accountability relationships
    among, 48
    overlap between, 49
Amendment to the Law on Courts
    and Judges adopted by the Czech
    Republic in 2008, 186, 187, 221,
    224, 231
Andorra, 37
anti-mečiarism, 246, 259
appeal, 103–106
appeals and quasi-appellate
    mechanisms, 103, 105, 193, 217,
    268, 300

appointment of judges
    to the grand chamber, 84–85, 196,
    209, 225, 230
    to the position of court president or
    vice-president, 195, 200, 209, 224,
    230, 277, 289, 311, 313, 322
Armenia, 394
Article III judges, 43
Association of Slovak Judges, 253, 426
Austria, 131, 395, 397
authority
    coordinate, 114, 115
    hierarchical, 114, 115
Azerbaijan, 394

Baxa, Josef, 173, 175
Belarus, 394
Belgium, 132, 134
Beneš, Edvard, 177
blind distribution of cases, 91
Brožová, Iva, 174
Bulgaria, 5, 123, 132, 393, 416, 417
bureaucratic judiciary, 399
Bureš, Jaroslav, 173–175, 185

Canada, 76
career judiciary, 113–116
career track to the judiciary, 189
case assignment, 44, 91, 195, 202, 203,
    210, 211, 226
    phases of, 281
China, 49, 99
Civic Democratic Party (ODS), 160, 161
civil law systems, 12, 13, 37, 47, 56, 69,
    74, 75, 80, 84–86, 104, 115, 116,
    173, 176, 200
    post-communist, 13

CPSIA information can be obtained
at www.ICGtesting.com
Printed in the USA
LVOW10s0023070917
547768LV00013B/220/P

9 781107 531048